CHURCH GROWTH BULLETIN

CHURCH GROWTH BULLETIN

SECOND CONSOLIDATED VOLUME

September 1969 to July 1975

edited by
Donald A. McGavran

William Carey Library

533 HERMOSA STREET • SOUTH PASADENA, CALIF. 91030

Library of Congress Catalog Card Number 77-5192
International Standard Book Number 0-87808-702-8
Price $7.95x

In accord with some of the most recent thinking in the academic press, the William Carey Library is pleased to present this scholarly book which has been prepared from an author-edited and author-prepared camera-ready manuscript.

Published by the William Carey Library
533 Hermosa Street
South Pasadena, Calif. 91030
Telephone 213-682-2047

PRINTED IN THE UNITED STATES OF AMERICA

IMPORTANT MESSAGE TO THE READER...

ADDRESS CHANGE: All subscription-related correspondence
should be sent to: Overseas Crusades, 3033 Scott Blvd.,
Santa Clara, California 95050, U.S.A. Please disregard
the former address printed in issues prior to July 1974.

MISSING PAGES: To avoid needless repetition, the Church
Growth Book Club inserts in each issue of the Church
Growth Bulletin have been deliberately omitted. The re-
sulting gaps in page numbers need trouble no one. There
is no missing text. Information on the Church Growth
Book Club can be found at the back of this volume.

HOW TO USE THE INDEX: The index prints proper names in
solid capitals, and concepts, such as church growth,
evangelism, and discipling, in lower case letters.
Where a concept occurs repeatedly in the same article,
usually it is indexed only once.

CHURCH GROWTH
BULLETIN

Address:
FULLER THEOLOGICAL
SEMINARY
135 N. Oakland
Pasadena, Calif. 91101

DONALD A. McGAVRAN, B.D., Ph.D
Director

SEPTEMBER 1969   Subscription $1 per year   Volume V.I, No. 1

The Components of Missionary Theory

by A.R. Tippett

The two basic components of missionary theory and action may be designated
as (1) <u>theological</u> and (2) <u>anthropological</u> - theological, because the message
is a word from God concerning His purpose for, and promise to man; anthropological because it has to be communicated within the structures and organization
of human societies. This message is theological because it concerns not only
the inner life of man, his spiritual experience, but also his eternal state.
It is anthropological because this takes place in an earthly environment on
which man depends for his physical life and where these spiritual experiences
have to be worked out in a series of human relationships that are culturally
conditioned. When Jesus spoke of the disciples as being <u>not of this world</u> and
yet in the same utterance as being also <u>in the world</u> he was demonstrating a
basic dichotomy in the Christian mission. Both in missionary policy-making
and in missionary action in the world these two components must be kept in
equilibrium.

While it is true that we cannot say the Church will certainly grow because
of this balance, for in the last analysis the growth is of God, nevertheless we
can safely affirm the opposite, namely, that growth will be obstructed when these
components are in a state of imbalance. This obstruction of church growth due to
human missionary policy and action that develops one component at the expense of
the other, may be called in biblical phrase, "limiting the Holy One of Israel"
or "quenching the Spirit." Both the Old and New Testament thus speak of human
attitudes that hinder the work of God. If we are to be engaged in carrying out
the Great Commission, the terminology of which suggests it is to be operative
until the end and is therefore applicable to us today, we ought to ask the question: Do our attitudes as reflected in either our missionary policy or action
help or hinder the purpose of God in the world and for the world?

We can also affirm that if we are to create, as far as is humanly possible,
a 'climate' which is propitious for church planting and church growth we should
pay attention to the balance of these two components in our missionary policy

SEND correspondence, news, and articles to the Editor, Dr. Donald McGavran, at the
Institute of Church Growth, Fuller Theological Seminary. Published bi-monthly, send
subscriptions and changes of address to the Business Manager, Norman L. Cummings,
Overseas Crusades, Inc., 265 Lytton Avenue, Palo Alto, California 94301, U.S.A.
Second-class postage paid at Palo Alto, California.

and action. In both my reading of church history from the dynamic position and in church growth research I observe some undefined but nevertheless definite relationship between balanced policy and action on the one hand and the manifest blessing of God in the form of quantitative or qualitative growth on the other.

When I speak of the theological component in missionary theory and action I am not thinking in denominational terms. Church growth cross-denominational studies show clearly that this can be discounted as a factor in growth. Those critics who imagine church growth is denominational church extension have not read much about church growth. The theological component concerns the nature and content of the message. The idea of mission, if not the word, is scriptural. If this is to be our norm we have a message to proclaim, an experience to share through witness, a goal of bringing men to Christ and then into a fellowship of believers, and thence into the world again to participate in service and witness. The whole we call the ministry of the Church. That part which communicates the good news in one way or another we call the mission. Both this salvation theme and the idea of its communication to men run through the Scriptures. Whether you accept my semantics or not you must accept this basic theological component - that is, if you accept the Bible on its own terms.

When mission policy and/or action is theologically defective in its basic concept of mission we frequently find one or two effects - either the subsequent growth is warped in some way, or the church that was planted has become static. The New Testament struggles with syncretism show that warped growth was a real problem from the start. I have seen some tragic cases of syncretism in supposedly Christian churches that can be traced back to defective theological nurture in the planting days. Sometimes a church is planted by means of a service project but the theological dimension is not developed. It is planted in a time of some crisis and gains some initial growth. Then it is static for a century. The problem of Christian/pagan co-existence, especially where a church comprises half a tribe and has resigned itself to a co-existence without a missionary sense of responsibility to the other half, is another example of a defective theological component. It may have been defective advocacy or defective follow-up - but it is theological.

The anthropological component of missionary theory and action reminds us that "our conversation is in the world." We deal with human beings in human situations, with felt needs that have to be met, and personal relationships that have to be preserved. They live in formal or customary structures and communicate in the language that suits their condition. In many diverse cultural situations the Church at large is represented by a local fellowship which must be relevant. An enclosed or sealed off church, a church which contributes to social projects but never participates, which has no concern for social justice, is defective in the anthropological component of its mission. It also tends to become static.

Faith and function have to be kept in equilibrium, belief and action, the theological and the anthropological, the hope beyond and the situation in the world. My categories are abstractions for purpose of analysis. In reality they integrate into each other, but it was our Lord who made the distinction in the first place. Although we have to aspire to things not of this world, we must

witness in the world and win the world for Christ. To be faithful in this and
to pay attention to it in our theory and practice so that neither dimension is
neglected seems to me to be, at least, a serious attempt to bring our programs
into line with what Jesus revealed of His will in mission. One is therefore
not surprised that research does suggest a frequent relationship between such
a policy and effective church growth. Although the harvest is of God He certainly allows the farmer's part to count for something in the harvesting.

As ethnography is the basis of anthropological theory, so research into
the planting and growth of churches provides the data and repetitive patterns,
the missiological ethnography, on which a theory of mission can be based. This
research is in harmony with the experiences of both the New Testament Church and
the history of the expansion of Christianity, and time after time we find ourselves saying that the Bible still speaks to us today. Despite the changing
environment due to technological advance and acculturation the basic issues the
Church has to face in mission are not new. The theoretical principles of church
planting and cultivation are abiding. Of course the environment, the cultural
forms and historical factors will differ from field to field and from generation
to generation, but the basic principles remain. Thus there are two components -
one theological, biblical, abiding; and the other anthropological, which applies
and relates that which is abiding to each precise situation where men need to be
won for Christ.

THE LORD CASTS OUT DEMONS TODAY by Keith Bentsen, SWM-ICG '68

I have been surprised to discover the element of animism that is to be
found among Latin Americans today. Had I been a missionary to China or Africa I
would have readily recognized it and dealt with it as such. But I have been
working in Argentina among civilized, westernized Latin Americans who are well
educated and live in well ordered towns and sophisticated cities.

I was first jolted into this awareness when a missionary friend commented
that he had had more contact with demonism in northern Argentina than in Borneo,
where he had previously served a missionary term. This sounded strange to me,
as I had traveled in many parts of Argentina, well before he was in the country,
and never had I been conscious of any demonic activity. But soon, in the providence of God, and in the very city where I myself was residing, several cases of
severe demon oppression were brought to me that I might minister to them. My
inadequate faith to deal successfully with them stimulated me to study both the
Scriptures and the real spiritual needs of many people of my adopted land.

Soon the light came to me. The original Indian civilizations in the New
World had been, of course, thoroughly animistic. So also were the millions of
Negro slaves brought over from Africa. And, strange as it may seem, in a large
measure so were the white Europeans that discovered the New World. Even Roman
priests practiced black magic and procured contact with spirit powers. And
these three peoples, brown, black and white, were amalgamated into one "Church"
under the cloak of an impure, non-enlightened Romanism. Mass conversions to

the new faith did not at all rid the people of their former animistic tendencies. Without doubt, the faulty, non-biblical shepherding of Roman Christians in the New World paved the way for the present phenomenal growth of spiritism, which is probably the most ascendant religion in Latin America.

Diverse forms of spiritism can be found on all rungs of the social ladder. From the humble peasant, through the artisans and professionals of the middle classes, to the sophisticated in intellectual circles - there is a type of spiritism which appeals to each. Spiritism is found combined with simple folk-Catholicism, with classical Catholicism, and with everything in between. It can be found in non-religious circles as well.

Becoming aware of these animistic elements in Latin American culture has caused me to adapt my presentation of the Gospel, making it, I trust, more relevant to my listeners. It has also enlarged my own vision of Christ as the Lord over all principalities and powers. It has caused me to stand in awe of the power of the Holy Spirit as He faithfully delivers men and women from the grip of Satanic powers.

MISSIONARIES AND "CIRCUMCISION"   by Gernot Fugmann

A valuable idea in church growth theory and theology arises from the basic difference between the tribal and the supra-tribal structures. Tribal structures could also be defined as homogeneous units. There are the given segments in a society into which a missionary can go. This fundamental experience has been discovered by church growth theory. What is its importance?

Quite often when working on the mission field the missionary expects people to cross their own tribal barriers in order to become Christians. They must fulfill certain conditions before they as pagans can be accepted. They are not received freely and unconditionally when showing their intention to become Christians. But rather, they are - probably unintentionally - made to cross barriers. In order to hear the Gospel they often are expected to cross the language barrier. In order to understand the Gospel they are expected to cross the educational barrier, having to adapt themselves to alien pattern of thoughts. In order to obey Christ they must go through a whole rigmarole and procedure of examination, endurance and learning. This can be compared to a hurdle race. The difference among many missions being the number of hurdles they are expected to jump, instead of the reverse taking place, namely that the missionaries cross the barrier into the homogeneous units.

"Missionaries crossing barriers into homogeneous units" is the evangelical approach, the equivalent of Christ's incarnation into the world. He crossed all the barriers thought to be between man and God. In fact, he showed that there were none. This was the basic difference between His Gospel and His relation to God and the Jewish religion and their approach to God. For in the opinion of Christ's contemporaries, in order to become a Jew, thereby having claim on salvation, the people of other nations had to cross the barrier of circumcision and the mosaic law. Jesus brushed away all such conditions for anyone to be saved.

The same problem was also a major issue in early Christianity - between Paul and the Jewish-Christians, who wanted pagans to become Jews first with circumcision and the acceptance of the mosaic laws as condition to be acceptable as Christians. Christianity repeatedly fell back into this position. The 'circumcision' or barriers demanded varied. In the pre-Reformation Church "circumcision" was "good works" and bought merit. Many a missionary makes civilization and education into a hurdle or a barrier. We should take the imitatio of Christ's incarnation seriously. If we did, we missionaries would become fully incarnate in the world of the tribal homogeneous unit. Such unconditional approach is the only theologically correct evangelical approach. Therefore, it is a vital question to all missionaries what 'circumcision' barrier or hurdle we perhaps unintentionally erect which prevents the free incarnation of Jesus Christ.

SOME VIEWS OF CHURCH GROWTH WRITERS IN RECENT BOOKS

How the Church Grew in Southern Mexico:

The history of the Evangelical Church in Tabasco demonstrates the power and potential of the individual believer, however humble and unlettered, when the Holy Spirit is allowed freedom to work in his life. It demonstrates too the contagious quality of the Gospel message when it is communicated on a person-to-person, family-to-family basis, within a familiar context of language and mores. Without a doubt, these were the most important factors contributing to the rapid-growth period of the Tabasco Church.

Bennett: Tinder in Tabasco

Avoid a Time Gap After Conversion:

The surest way to have an active evangelistic church is to avoid a time gap between the initial enthusiasm of conversion and the effective evangelistic witness of the converts. The first days of a new church are of particular importance....

Neil Braun In Experiments in Church Growth in Japan
by Braun, Boschman and Yamada

Theology of Expectance Wanted:

When the missionary theory is based on data from Islamic, Buddhist and Hindu areas we tend to find an emphasis on just 'being there' and 'being obedient' all of which is quite true, but the note of 'expectance' is weak, the cross is clear but the victory is indistinct. (The writer goes on to show that a theology of mission is needed from a theologian out of a people-movement situation to make up for this theological deficiency.)

A.R. Tippett: Verdict Theology in Missionary Experience

Growth in Latin America:

If the current rate of growth does not decrease, Evangelical Churches in Latin America will have more than doubled in communicant membership in the ten-year period between 1960 and 1970. There is every reason to expect this to happen again in the decade between 1970 and 1980. If the Church continues to grow at the present rate, there will be over thirteen million communicant members by 1980. This will give the Evangelical community more than twenty-seven million members, or 8 per cent of the population.

Read, Monterroso and Johnson: Latin American Church Growth

FEED-BACK ON POLOGAMY

The recent number of the Church Growth Bulletin on Polygamy (Vol. 5, No. 4, March 1969) continues to attract attention and commendation. We wish we had space to publish all the correspondence in full. We refer our readers back to the original series of articles. We have had response from many field missionaries belonging to a wide range of different denominations, showing that polygamy is a common problem to all kinds of mission. Some, like T.C. Cunningham, a Council Director, with the Assemblies of God, have expressed their appreciation of the attempt to relate the problem to scriptural teaching.

We know that we have not all the answers to polygamy but having identified many of the problems, we do not think the Church at large really appreciates the cross-cultural issues involved, or that Christian scholarship has adequately investigated the way in which the early Church faced them. Our main purpose, therefore, was to stimulate discussion regarding both the social functions of polygamy and the attitude of the Church (especially the foreign missionaries) to it. Turning to the Scriptures we pointed out that our traditional position is more western and ethical than scriptural. None of the writers of our original series of articles went as far as he might have gone, as we were trying to be provocative rather than polemical.

Gilbert Olson of Sierra Leone has taken us to task for not going far enough. He resists the idea of excommunication of Christians taking other wives after baptism in a society which is polygamist and has no civil laws against the custom. In place of this he calls for the correction of the problem by a better program of Christian education after baptism in the following terms:

We are affirming that polygamists once baptized be taught the values of a truly Christian home and be encouraged not to take further wives, and that sons and daughters of Christians likewise be taught the value of a truly Christian home and be encouraged by their parents and the Christian community to have monogamous marriages.

Further interesting correspondence comes from Richard Addington Hall of the College of the Ascension, Birmingham, England, who has recently written a university thesis on "Marriage Law in the Ghanian Churches: The Christian Approach to Polygamists." As an example of the type of interest the original articles stimulated, and the critical depth at which they are being read, we cite three points from his reply to our number.

(1) Ralph Winter (p.64) notes "the simple fact that when one man has two
wives another man has none." This is of course true, but it should
not be taken to imply that every polygamist is condemning another man
to permanent celibacy. On the contrary in Ghana, where there are approximately 135 wives to every hundred husbands, only about 3% of the
men are permanently single. The reserve of wives is provided by the
custom of women marrying much younger than men and thus having longer
in the married state (changing husbands when they are widowed). The
1960 Ghana Population Census (Special Report E, Selection 4.5) suggests
that if the present customs as to age of marriage continue polygamy
will increase to 150 wives per hundred husbands in ten years. Monogamy would force young women to remain unmarried (and therefore vulner-
able) at an age when society expected them to be married - unless it
was made economically possible for men to marry younger.

(2) The interpretation of the verses in the Pastoral Epistles which advise
that church officers should have only one wife is exactly paralleled
by I Timothy 5:9 which advises that a widow should have been the wife
of one husband (English translations tend to obscure the parallel.) I
do not believe that polygamy was known in the New Testament world. It
is my hypothesis that the practice can only flourish in certain conditions incompatible with an urban cash economy such as existed in the
Roman Empire.

(3) My conclusions are more radical than yours. I would allow Christians
to marry polygamously if they believed that to be the right course in
their particular circumstances. In some traditional societies customary obligations, which cannot properly be unilaterally discarded, will
require some Christians to take a second wife, notably when the first
wife is barren, when the Christian is obliged to 'inherit' a widow and
perhaps in the case of certain chiefs.

To this Dr. McGavran raised the following question:

Your assumption is that "in some traditional societies, customary obligations which cannot be unilaterally discarded will require some Christians
to take a second wife, notably when the first wife is barren, when the
Christian is obliged to inherit a widow and perhaps in the case of certain
chiefs." In other words, that when it is right for the Christian would
depend on what is legal in that society. In England, what is right for
the Christian would depend on English law as well as the Christian religion. In America the same. Now, suppose that with the coming of a post-
Christian majority, (the 'pill', coitus strictly for pleasure and to
stimulate pleasant and meaningful interpersonal relationships,) the law
in England and America were to allow extra marital sexual intercourse, or
second wives, or homosexual relations, would you still hold that what is
right for the Christian depends on what is legal in his culture?
    In your letter you may want to leave this question unanswered, but
all perceptive readers will raise it.

The reply came:

>You ask me to write to a query arising from my earlier letter. I think there is an important distinction between what is legally allowed in a society and what is legally or morally required of people. Ghanaian custom, if not the traditional law, requires certain individuals to be polygamous. They are failing in their duty to the society, and perhaps more important, to specific individuals in the society, if they refuse to take as a second wife a woman who is an obligation on them. Western law may allow various forms of sexual immorality but is unlikely to require them of Christians. I would not reject the theoretical possibility that love might demand extra marital sexual intercourse of a Western Christian and would approve it if such circumstances were proved, but I can't think of such a situation and would be very suspicious of anybody who argued they were so compelled by Christian love.

The question of the missionary attitude to polygamy has been discussed by several church growth writers, especially those from Africa (Wold, 1968:71, 92, 118, 138, 175-183; Grimley & Robinson, 1966:177-187, 278), and frequently as an obstruction to church planting. It certainly militates against the winning of communal units whole.

We publish some of this correspondence, not because we believe the answers are necessarily here, but because we believe the answers must be found - and found quickly. These questions come especially from West and East Africa, where large social groups are currently open for decision-making.

We have frequently pointed out the urgency of winning these responsive communal units while they are winnable. Christianity is not the only option before them. In ten years they may be Moslem or Communist or may have adapted their Neopagan syncretism to a secular co-existence. We do not argue merely to win numerical growth, but for the biblical reason that when God brings a field to ripeness He expects the laborers to be sent into harvest ingathering. Yet time after time our research reveals that the missionary attitude to polygamy hinders the ingathering, in spite of what appear to be quite genuine conversions to Christ. We now must distinguish between the cultural institution of polygamy and the missionary attitude to polygamy. We must start asking such questions as: Is the foreign missionary reading his western ethical thinking into the Scripture he cites? Is he ignorant of the fact that polygamy performs some basic social functions in a society, and these cannot be removed without providing adequate substitutes? Missionary, fraternal worker, and national pastor must all answer to the Lord of the Harvest if they heed not the Great Commission when the harvests are ripe, or if they allow their attitudes to obstruct the ingathering by denying baptism to sincerely repentant and believing converts.

It is time the Church began more critical thinking about such questions. A Mission Board which really wishes to demonstrate its sincerity might establish a fund for this kind of research, send a top-flight missionary to SWM-ICG for nine months to study polygamy and missionary attitude to it, and then support him while he travels in Africa for comparative research with a specific set of vital questions, and returns to Pasadena to write up his findings for publication. If feedback shows anything at all, it shows an urgency of feeling among field missionaries, that something be done right now about our attitudes to polygamy. Will any Board spare a good academic man and support him for such a project?

> Six decades ago P.T. Forsyth wrote these words:
>
> "Theological differences come out in a new light when the practical
> test of missions is applied. Some of them sink out of sight, but
> some become sharper than ever. One source of the decay of mission-
> ary interest is the decay in theological perception and conviction."
>
> The context of those words was a discussion of the lack of any real idea of
> mission in Unitarianism. Today, perhaps he would have Universalism in mind.

RESEARCH AND THE PRESENT CHALLENGE - A.R. Tippett

After five years of writing articles and paragraphs for the Church Growth
Bulletin, this is the first time I have shared a 'gripe'. One of my recent
M.A. advisees wrote to another church on his field for certain statistics for
his thesis. It was a reasonable request. The man's Board had given him the
year for study. He had some superb material but there were gaps: hence his
request. The reply came as follows:
> While being interested in your M.A. thesis and sympathetic to your request
> it is a practical impossibility to provide the facts and figures. I would
> imagine that researching these facts and figures is the crucial part of
> your thesis and to have any accuracy would require at least six month's
> full time work for one person. We certainly have no staff member available
> to do this research....

Now as these were basic facts and figures about the state of the work of God
in that church and area I should have thought they would have been readily available. Surely a shepherd should know whether he has 99 or 100 sheep in his flock!
The above paragraph must mean either that this particular church does not keep
statistics, or, if it does, it has no confidence in their accuracy.
> The letter went on:
> We are very sympathetic to research into the work of the Church in _____,
> but feel that such research is secondary when we are considering the steward-
> ship of time when faced with the present challenge.

What a horrible piece of rationalization and self-justification! How do
these good folk think they are to face the "present challenge" if they are ignorant of its precise nature? How can you deal with stewardship if you are unaware of who and where your people are, and whether or not they are mobile? And
how can you know where the opportunities for evangelism and service are, without
some kind of a physical picture of human distribution? How could a church secretary be so blind as to fail to see that the researcher was hoping to be able
to indicate something of the precise nature of that "present challenge?"

Time has gone by and the thesis is finished. Fortunately my advisee's own
fellow missionaries responded well. He had to redefine the limits of his field of
research, and he recognizes the gaps in it. However, as far as it goes it is a
first class study. It brings to light a great many important facts about the

"present challenge" and the opportunities which might well have been overlooked. I imagine his Church as a whole will thank him for his work.

The tragedy is the other Church might have both contributed to it and shared from its results. By setting itself aside and denegrating research - for this is what it has done if it hopes to handle present challenges without prior research - it classifies itself as a hit-or-miss mission. Would men go to the moon without prior research? Would men establish a business concern, or build a reservoir or highway without prior research? If I was appointing a man as steward for a great project (stewardship was the word used by the church secretary) I would expect him to know all about it, and to be diligent in filling the gaps in his knowledge, so that he would be better able to meet the challenge of his task.

Fortunately this is not a typical case. We have a great deal of useful information sent in from time to time and we appreciate it. When a missionary gives up his furlough to do research here it may be he has to write back to his field for certain facts and figures. It makes all the difference in the world to him when one fellow missionary goes to a little trouble to help him fill his gaps.

In this day of terrific social change when dangers to the Church and opportunities are alike tremendous the more we can know about the situations we face the better stewards we should be. But the collection of information is a cooperative business. Much of it is in libraries and archives, much is on the field. Field and research center must keep in touch and learn to expect to give to, and receive from each other. This is true Christian symbiosis.

The church is herself the strongest proof that the Gospel also belongs to the heathen. Consequently we must do mission work, not because we possess the Gospel, but rather we have the Gospel only because it is intended for the heathen. Otherwise we would make ourselves Lords of the Gospel and abuse the ministry of reconciliation. But because God wants missions to the heathen, we are the church.

Georg F. Vicedom: The Mission of God

CONFERENCE ON EVANGELISM, BOGOTA, COLOMBIA

The First Latin American Conference on Evangelism has been scheduled for Bogota, Colombia, November 21-30. Preliminary notice leads us to look forward to it with anticipation, and we have much pleasure in inserting this brief notice in our Bulletin in the hope that missions will send along delegates.

Rev. Efrain Santiago, Secretary of Social Services in the Cabinet of Governor Luis Ferré of Puerto Rico will present the keynote address. Santiago is a gifted evangelist and was for several years Coordinator of the Billy Graham Evangelistic Association for Latin America and Spain. He will be supported at Bogota by Rev. Miguel Suazo of the Latin America Mission. Planners anticipate the attendance of some eight hundred delegates.

SONS OF TIV: A STUDY OF THE RISE OF THE CHURCH AMONG THE TIV OF CENTRAL
NIGERIA   by E. Rubingh.
            Review by David B. Barrett, Columbia University

This is a comprehensive case study in depth of what may very probably be
the fastest growing church in the whole of Africa today - The Tiv Church of
Christ, a body of 180,000 Sunday attenders in a tribe of one million, increasing by over 20,000 each year.

The book begins with a lengthy theological and historical introduction to
the subject of mission in Nigeria. The immensely complex traditional society and
religion of the Tiv are then described, based on the author's own research. Next
follows a historical account of the evangelization of the Tiv from 1911 onwards
by the Dutch Reformed Church mission from South Africa. The second half of the
book deals with the multitudinous problems of present-day Tiv Christianity.

As a case study in the disciplines of anthropology, history of mission, and
missiology, this is an excellent piece of work packed with a mass of valuable
detail. The remarks which follow are not intended as a criticism, but rather are
some reflections, arising out of the book, concerning the communication of church
growth data to the growing circle of readership who (a) know nothing of the area
such a study describes, and (b) are not yet convinced of the value of such studies.

My first point is that studies like this ought in the future to include very
considerable apparatus (maps, tables, diagrams, appendixes, indexes), if their
highly complex argument is to convince critical readers. Sons Of Tiv, for example, has no detailed maps indicating the location of all places mentioned in
the text; no historical maps illustrating the spread of such important phenomena
as the Bible School movement; no charts or diagrams elucidating the meteoric rise
of the Tiv Church itself; no photographs of the personalities involved, etcetera.
There is an index of names, but such an index is of little use to the large number
of readers who do not read every book right through, but who want certain information only. Such persons require a detailed subject index, where they can immediately find key subjects like conversion, conversion rate, population growth,
baptism rate, preaching worship, medicine, schism, revival and the like. Apparatus
such as I am suggesting is, of course, expensive and increases the price of the
book, but without it, such studies will not convince the critics.

The second point is that church statistics in Africa are often much more detailed and accurate than secular statistics (such as tribal populations); hence
they should at the very least be given in full in appendixes, even if the author
does not analyse them himself. As I discovered myself in 1965, the growth of the
Tiv Church has massive statistical documentation, which when plotted in graph form
(a simple way to spot mistakes, bad guesses, etc.) furnishes illuminating insights.
Despite the extraordinary picture of growth revealed by the Tiv figures, Mr.
Rubingh gives only one short table (p.169). I would like, therefore, to illustrate
the possibilities of even elementary analysis of such situations, based on some of
the meager numerical data given in the book.

First, let us assume that the present population of the Tiv is one million,
and that their annual rate of increase is similar to that of the present population explosion in Nigeria, namely 3.0 per cent per year. This means an increase

(births minus deaths) of 30,000 Tiv every year, divided among Protestants, Catholics and animists as shown in the 'natural increase' column below. Second, Tiv Protestants (180,000) are increasing by 10,000 a year, of which 14,600 are by conversion from animistic society. The figures for Tiv Catholics are roughly half of this, as shown below.

TABLE: ANNUAL RELIGIOUS CHANGE AMONG THE TIV, 1969

Adherents	Present size	Natural increase	Conversion increase	Total increase
Protestants	180,000	5,400	14,600	20,000
Catholics	90,000	2,700	7,300	10,000
Animists	730,000	21,900	- 21,900	- 0
Total Population	1,000,000	30,000		30,000

One can make some startling deductions from this kind of table. One such is that the massive annual increase of 30,000 a year for the two churches fails to decrease the total number of animists at all. And even with the enormous growth of the Tiv Church, Protestant converts each year are still much less than the natural increase among animists. And so on.

If one presents comparative data in this way, and then discusses all the possible implications and explanations of the trends thus revealed, it adds a new and vivid dimension to church growth analysis which will be important in getting readers to take this emerging discipline seriously.

THE CHURCH GROWS

"In spite of the turmoil in southern Nigeria with the Civil War, the expansion of the Church continues in the North. Last summer, two of the Nigerian evangelists (newly ordained) went to a village just 8 miles across the river beyond the station of Uba where we lived most of the last 10 years, and baptized on one day and at one place 108. Sixty-two others made their first public confession of Christ and would from that point prepare for Christian baptism. This sort of response is very common in our area. One of our largest "churches" spread over more than 11 villages with a membership of over 1,000 has a pastor who will not allow his assistant pastor to be assigned to an area in "new villages." He says, "If he goes, who will help me baptize?! I can't possibly keep up alone!" The response in most of our areas is so great that even the 25 new evangelists being produced each year by our Bible School cannot keep up to the growing demand for evangelism AND nurture."

(Excerpt from a letter of John Grimley to Allen Finley, Nov. 1967)

CHURCH GROWTH
B U L L E T I N

from the
INSTITUTE OF
CHURCH GROWTH

Address:
FULLER THEOLOGICAL
SEMINARY
135 N. Oakland
Pasadena, Calif. 91101

DONALD A. McGAVRAN, B.D., Ph.D.
Director

NOVEMBER 1969   Subscription $1 per year   Volume VI, No. 2

Beyond Ecumenism Part I

by Ralph D. Winter

In a recent article in <u>Christianity Today</u> (Sept. 12), Dr. John A. Mackay takes current ecumenical leaders to task for losing missionary vision as they pursue global Christianity. He feels that the original ecumenical movement stressed <u>both</u> mission and unity but that "now unity is not for mission. Unity is for unity. This obsession with unity for its own sake, this movement towards sentiment in structure with no clear understanding of or commitment to the task of a united church locally or in the world, is what I call <u>ecumenicalism</u>." It is his opinion, that "the ecumenical movement tends to be less and less motion outwards and onwards towards frontiers. It becomes instead increasingly motion towards the realization of an ordered, ecclesiastical structure. In a subtle manner, dedication to mission becomes merely the pursuit of harmony."

Let us go on to quote four of his points to see how this concentration on unity has veered from the objectives of mission outreach and church growth:
"One: In view of the religious nominalism that marks the lives of the majority of the men and women who have been baptized and confirmed in churches of the Protestant tradition, should not priority be given to a united movement toward spiritual awakening in these churches rather than to a top-level, ecclesiastical effort to merge church denominations and confessions in a single organizational structure?"

"Two: When Christian unity is equated with institutional oneness and episcopal control and when both of these are regarded as indispensible for real unity, let this not be forgotten - the most unified ecclesiastical structure in Christian history was the Hispanix Catholic Church, which was also the most spiritually sterile and the most disastrously fanatical."

"Three: Would it not be wise to consider the fact that in the Roman Catholic Church there are more than 600 orders that do not function under the jurisdiction of the Vatican or of a local bishop, and many of which have had a history of dynamic and creative activity?"

"Four: Dare the phenomenon be ignored that many of the most dynamic, creative, and cooperative Christian enterprises of our time are being carried on in this

SEND correspondence, news, and articles to the Editor, Dr. Donald McGavran, at the Institute of Church Growth, Fuller Theological Seminary. Published bi-monthly, send subscriptions and changes of address to the Business Manager, Norman L. Cummings, Overseas Crusades, Inc., 265 Lytton Avenue, Palo Alto, California 94301, U.S.A. Second-class postage paid at Palo Alto, California.

nation and around the world by men and women who, while loyal to their own denomination, work in a truly ecumenical spirit with Christians of other denominations to achieve important Christian objectives?"

Clearly, something beyond mere ecumenism is needed lest vital energies
dead-end in the institutionalism of ecumenicalism. Mackay's vision is more ample
than that of many ecumenical leaders of today in his awareness of the legitimacy
of wholesome "enterprises" that are not part of what may be called the municipal
structure of Christianity. A Roman order is as different a structure from the
Bishop's diocese as General Motors is different from the State of Michigan. Yet
neither the World Council of Churches nor the National Council of Churches recognizes as readily as Mackay that there exist vital "Protestant orders" like the
Latin America Mission, Inter-Varsity, the Overseas Missionary Fellowship, etc.
The typical perspective of conciliar leaders would seem to be a sort of ecclesiastical socialism since they are so chary of non-official Christian enterprises.
But Mackay's intuition is sound, since the oikoumene included more than the
governmental structure of empire. It included not only all the people but all
of the structures, both "public" and "private." But if the now common phrase,
the ecumenical church is a phrase whose true meaning is now lost, let us coin
another. Let us speak of going "beyond ecumenism" to "the oikoumenical church."
Let us begin again by defining the oikoumenical church as including both
"diocesan" (parish, denominational, conciliar) structures and "order" structures
(the Christian societies, such as the Bible societies, the missionary societies,
etc.,) whether inter- or intra-denominational.

Thus properly to foster the structural growth of the Christian church requires a truly oikoumenical concept. It is not enough to champion either the
diocese or the order, either the denominational structure or the society structure. We must recognize the warp and woof -- the critical need of each for
the other. The Billy Graham Evangelistic Association must be seen as just as
much a part of the oikoumenical church as is the Free Methodist denomination.
If we can just get beyond ecumenism we may be able to believe this.

Several brief observations are possible. This view is "beyond" the view of
the stereotyped ecumenical leader we have mentioned. It is also "beyond" the
hyper-denominational mentality of certain tight-knit evangelical churches. It
is also beyond the thinking of many missionaries who have fled the deadness of
older Protestant denominations in the U.S. and are setting up new denominations
overseas, assuming that these new denominations can somehow stay healthy over
he generations without the help of the other kind of structures. That is, the
overseas national church must be more than a mere denomination. Its full mission
can only be realized if its members are able to participate in a variety of
optional "societies." Furthermore, the overseas national churches cannot solve
this problem merely by getting together as denominations, not even by forming
inter-church agencies that are controlled and limited by denominational budgets.
Why? Note, in the next article, what happened to the SVM.

This problem is sometimes complicated by artificial theological models
representing ideal unity. But the trouble is that our sociology is not as good
as our theology. The "City of God" takes a lot of designing. One thing we do
know, however, (call it the Winter Principle if you like) is that the resources
for any basically optional program will decrease as its appeal increasingly ap-
proximates the concerns of the (non-existent) average man. This illuminates the
fate of the mission agency whose income is raised as part of a larger denominational budget which discourages designated giving. How long would a super-
market last that only sold packages that contained a cross-section of all its
goods? (To be continued)

THE RISE AND FALL OF THE STUDENT VOLUNTEER MOVEMENT by David M. Howard

In the history of modern missions, probably no single factor has wielded a greater influence in the world-wide outreach of the Church than the Student Volunteer Movement. The names of its great leaders - men of the stature of John R. Mott, Robert G. Wilder, Robert E. Speer, to name a few - stand high in the annals of the foreign missionary movement. Its watchword, "The evangelization of the world in this generation" was so profoundly influential in motivating students for overseas service that John R. Mott could write, "I can truthfully answer that next to the decision to take Christ as the leader and Lord of my life, the watchword has had more influence than all other ideals and objectives combined to widen my horizon and enlarge my conception of the Kingdom of God."

The SVM had its distant roots in the famous Haystack Prayer Meeting held at Williams College in 1806. Out of that meeting grew two very influential developments. First was the Society of Brethren at Andover Theological Seminary. Second was the American Board of Commissioners for Foreign Missions, the first North American foreign mission agency. One of the members of the Society of Brethren in later years was Royal Wilder, who sailed for India under the ABCFM in 1846. Returning to the U.S. for health reasons in 1877, he settled in Princeton, N.J., where his son, Robert, soon formed the Princeton Foreign Missionary Society at Princeton University. The members of this Society declared themselves "willing and desirous, God permitting, to go to the unevangelized portions of the world." Their prayers and activities bore fruit in the summer of 1886.

At the invitation of D.L. Moody, 251 students gathered at Mt. Hermon, Mass., for a month-long Bible conference in July, 1886. A great burden for world evangelization was gripping some of these students. A memorable address given by one of the Bible teachers, Dr. A.T. Pierson, contained the seed form of the SVM watchword, and he is generally credited with having originated it. As a result of Pierson's challenge, plus other motivations, including "The Meeting of the Ten Nations" and lengthy prayer meetings, 100 students volunteered for overseas service during the conference.

The foundations of the SVM were laid that summer, and the movement was formally organized in 1888. During the school year of 1886-7 Robert G. Wilder and John Forman, both of Princeton, travelled to 167 different schools to share the vision they had received of world evangelization. During that year they saw 2,106 students volunteer for missionary work. Among these were Samuel Zwemer, Robert E. Speer, whose influence in missions during the next decades is almost incalculable.

The SVM was formally organized in 1888 with John R. Mott as its chairman. The growth during the next thirty years was phenomenal. In 1920 (the peak year statistically) 2,783 students signed the SVM decision card, 6,890 attended the quadrennial convention at Des Moines, and in 1921, 637 Volunteers sailed for the field, this being the highest number in any single year. The motivations were genuine, the grounding in biblical principles was solid, and the leadership had a burning vision for world evangelism.

But in 1920 an ominous change began to take place. "The Missionary Review of the World" (a journal founded by Royal Wilder in 1877) analyzed the SVM convention at Des Moines as follows:

"The Des Moines Volunteer Convention... was marked by a revolt against the leadership of the 'elder statesman'. That convention was large in number but the delegates were lacking in missionary vision and purpose and were only convinced that a change of ideals and of leadership was needed. They rightly believed that selfishness and foolishness had involved the world in terrible war and bloodshed and they expressed their intention to take control of Church and State in an effort to bring about better conditions. The problems of international peace, social justice, racial equality and economic betterment obscured the Christian foundations and ideals of spiritual service."

William Beahm, in a doctoral dissertation on the history of SVM, analyzed that convention as follows:

"Their emphasis shifted away from Bible study, evangelism, life work decision, and foreign mission obligation, on which the SVM had originally built. Instead they now emphasized new issues, such as race relations, economic injustice, and imperialism... And the rise of the social gospel blotted out the sharp distinction between Christian America and the 'unevangelized portions of the world.'"

This desire by the youth to turn their attention to social issues (which were amazingly similar to the issues of 1969!) and away from the needs overseas was accompanied by a second significant development. The movement had begun as a student activity and had maintained a touch with the grass roots on the campuses without a bureaucratic overhead. Now, however, it was felt that a more extensive administrative structure was needed, so the executive committee was expanded from six to thirty members at one stroke. The plague of "committee-itis" began to set in. It became top-heavy in organization and weaker on the direct outreach to students.

By the 1924 convention attention was turning rapidly from world evangelism to the solution of social and economic problems. "The Missionary Review" stated that in 1924 "They failed to make much impression or to reach any practical conclusions. The SVM seemed doomed."

The watchword soon became conspicious by its absence. The all-time high of 2,783 who signed decision cards in 1920 stands in stark contrast to the 25 who signed in 1938. Attendance at Des Moines of 6,850 in 1920 dwarfs the Toronto convention of 1940 with 465 in attendance.

It would be a gross over-simplification to claim that the factors mentioned above were the only ones in the decline of the SVM. The immensely complicated world of post-World War 1, with its materialism, secularism, isolationism, affluence, and all that made up the "Roaring Twenties", was not the most conducive to a program of Bible study and world evangelism. However, the fact remains that the SVM shift in emphasis from world evangelism to social and economic problems, and its sudden growth in bureaucracy, coincide precisely with its rapid decline. In 1941 William Beahm claimed that "... it has almost ceased to be a decisive factor in the promotion of the missionary program of the churches."

In 1959 the SVM, which had been practically dormant since the 1940's merged with several other movements to form the National Student Christian Federation. This in turn merged in 1966 into the University Christian Movement, which in 1969 voted itself out of existence. Thus the final vestige of a once gallant and world-shaking movement were quietly laid to rest.

RADIO AND CHURCH GROWTH   by Donald McGavran

"On the grassy Tanzanian plain a stately Masai herdsman strides behind his scrawny cattle, a lion killing spear in one hand a country-music-blaring Japanese transistor radio in the other. Transistors sway from the long necks of plodding camels deep in the Saudi desert, and from the horns of oxen ploughing furrows in Costa Rica. Radios are replacing equipment in the tea stalls of Pakistan.... For Peru's 12 million inhabitants there are more than 600 radio stations, and radio reaches the ears of virtually every man, woman and child in the country. In Guatemala, six times as many people listen to radios as read newspapers. Black Africa which had fewer than 400,000 radios in 1955 has at least 6,000,000 today. ... It is left on from morning to night, pouring out fuel for hopes and dreams. The possibilities that exist in this force are enormous." (International Christian Broadcasters Bulletin, January 1968)

Yes, the possibilities are enormous. One thanks God for what has been done and longs for radio which issues in church growth.

Effectiveness in use of radio lies in ever increasing connection between broadcast and formation of new churches on new ground. The connection must be two way from where churches are being established to the radio station and from the radio station to the church planting evangelists.

Radio at present is enamoured of broadcasts which reach large numbers of people. Broadcasts which reach ten million are considered much better than those which reach ten thousand. Consequently, broadcasts in standard languages - Hindi, Swahili, Hausa, Spanish, Mandarin - are considered better than those in local dialects such as Mangyan, Kui, or Higi. But such considerations are mistaken. Suppose, for example, that among the 50 thousand Kui speaking persons a strong people movement to Christian faith is going on, a thousand a year are being baptized, and practically every one of the 50,000 knows about the Christian faith and considers becoming Christian a real option. Under these circumstances, it might be much more important for the radio station at Addis Ababa to broadcast carefully prepared messages in Kui to that small spot in Zambia than to broadcast in Swahili to 60,000,000 in East Africa. To be sure, it should be possible to do both; but the Kui broadcast has much greater importance for the discipling of the Kuinga tribe of 50,000 souls than the East Africa wide broadcast. All East Africa will not be won. Most of the 60,000,000 will not listen, and if they did listen, have no intention of becoming Christian. None of their relatives has become a Christian. Becoming a Christian is not a real option - even if they listen. But among the Kuinga, becoming a Christian is a real option.

Suppose, therefore, that together with preaching the Gospel to sixty million, the radio beamed a series of messages from Christian Kuingas to the Kuinga nation. Some of the messages might be from the Bible, some would intone passages to be committed to memory, some would be Kuinga hymns and some like the following might be from specific persons to specific persons. Thus, "To my uncle Mangala, land owner in Kebratola, son of Bishram, son-in-law of the wise man of Thandapani: greetings from Thakurdas. After studying the Gospel for a year, and carefully considering all things, we have become Christians as a body in this village. We have built a church and worship there every evening. We have banned liquor at our feasts. We no longer fear the evil spirits. Jesus Christ our Lord gives us peace and quiet. We recommend the Christian faith to you. Come and see us. Worship God with us. This voice comes to you from your nephew who awaits your coming."

Then suppose further, that, prior to this series of messages: a) transistor radios had been sold very widely among the Kuingas; b) a system for making tapes and sending them to Ethiopia quickly had been perfected; c) two thoroughly trained Kui speaking Christians were in charge of the radio program in Kui and lived in Zambia; d) the two men were closely in touch with the progress of the Kuinga churches; e) the existing Kuinga Church of 5,000 communicants, were geared to care for ten thousand converts a year, should that number come to Christ as a result of the radio-cum-face-to-face-inter-twined-program.

Given this kind of "radio", our present expectations of men dribbling into the Church a few at a time, could be radically revised.

The time has come to pass from panegyrics about the power of radio. What we need now is campaigns of evangelism among people pre-disposed to accept Christ (see the tremendous ingatherings in Indonesia, Nigeria, Brazil, and many other places). These campaigns should combine radio intelligently together with church planting evangelists to win for Christ whole segments of society. All who wish to place their faith intelligently on Jesus Christ, and to be organized into churches, can be discipled and baptized.

Let us now create teams of radio specialists and church planting evangelists, conduct campaigns in specially receptive societies (whether these be urban or rural, of this nation or that, is of secondary importance), and bring the Gospel effectively to whole units of mankind. In the great commission, the Lord charges Christians to disciple ta ethne - those are the exact Greek words. Ta ethne mean precisely the tribes, the clans, the discrete, separate societies of mankind. The combination of radio with personal visitation and visible presence carefully timed, in close sequence, with full provision made for winning, instructing, baptizing, and organizing into churches, is urgently demanded. Nothing stands in its way.

An article in the January 1968, of International Christian Broadcasters, is entitled, "The Vital Link Between M/R and EID" - Missionary Radio and Evangelism in Depth. This illustrates an early stage of what we have in mind. Evangelism in Depth, according to its own program and timetable, is carried on where there are many existing churches. It is usually carried on where great mission resources are available. Missionary radio has been and will be of great use under such circumstances. The campaign uses radio and radio uses the campaign. The population touched by the campaign is particularly likely to make decisions for Christ. Similarly, in the populations in which small or large people movements are going on, thousands of persons are likely to make decisions for Christ. Radio must be concentrated on these in connection with face to face proclamation and service.

Truly, the possibilities that exist in radio are enormous - but much more by way of coordinating it with "church planters on the spot" will have to be done before they are realized. Radio must measure its effectiveness not only by the millions of listeners but even more, by the numbers of new congregations and units of shalom (Christian cells-churches) established.

FOLK ART SPARKS "PEOPLE MOVEMENT" by Ralph Toliver

> "Ang sabi ni San Pablo
> Doon sa Unang Corinto,
> Kapitulo kinse, bersikulo uno..."

The scene is a country village in southern Luzon, Philippines. The occasion is a wedding - an all-day affair in these parts. The singer of the impromptu verse is a Tagalog farmer, gray of temple and gnarled of hand. The mode is the traditional guitar-plus-solo style of old Filipino culture. But the content - what is he singing about? Though this is a wedding, when you would expect the singing of love songs, the old farmer is singing of the death and resurrection of Christ as the basis of salvation. He begins:

> "Saint Paul says
> In First Corinthians
> Chapter fifteen, verse one..."

But then his opponent stands to his feet, guitar ready, to give a rebuttal. A rebuttal? Yes, for this is a stylized debate. Now it is time for this other side to sing its piece:

> "Let's hear the advice of James,
> In chapter two, verse fourteen,
> That a man has no salvation
> If his works cannot be seen..."

Counterrebuttal follows rebuttal all through the long day, with respite now and then for food and drink. This refreshment, incidentally, is the debaters' only pay. Guests are pleased no end with the display of sudden sallies and off-the-cuff replies, for this is singing and strumming in the old, old style, with the added zest of clash of wits, turn of phrase, and the challenge to endure to the end of the day.

But how does the Bible come to be used for such a contest? Herein hangs an intriguing tale, for in one case it precipitated a minor "people movement," turning scores to Christ, and the end product was the planting of a local church.

The story begins, strangely enough, when a group of Jehovah's Witnesses came some years ago to Barrio Natunuan, a farming village sprawled on the slopes of an extinct volcano overlooking Batangas Bay. At first the sect found quite a hearing. "But," says Abdon Rosales, one of the singing debaters, "we learned that they do not pray in the name of Jesus, and how can you approach God apart from Jesus?"

The Jehovah's Witnesses, however, had brought innovation to this nominally Roman Catholic barrio. Suddenly the singers of the village - Abdon Rosales, Nicolas Castillo, and Cirilo and Domingo Areta - had new source material for their folk singing. From the Bibles the Witnesses sold them they memorized lengthy passages to use in their folk art for wakes, weddings, fiestas, birthdays. They memorized the genealogies of Genesis, the exodus from Egypt, and much of the New Testament. And they challenged other teams of debaters from distant towns and villages.

In November 1966 a one-week open-air campaign was held in front of the house of Jose Castillo, with Bible study in the mornings led by missionary Roger Snyder and evangelistic preaching in the evenings by Mauro Brion, recently come as pastor of the church in Bauan. There were eighty commitments to Christ that week, fifty-four on Saturday night alone. In January 1967 the Natunuan Evangelical Church was organized, with leaders appointed by Pastor Brion.

Go to Natunuan on a Sunday morning and watch the people worship. You will find the same singers, the same flow of Tagalog language, the same plunking of guitars used before in the stylized debates. But there is a difference. Listen to them over there under the great mango tree in front of a neighbor's house, overlooking the blue bay in the distance, as they sing:

"I will tell you now of Jesus my Lord,
Who has spoken to me through His Holy Word.
He came to me when I was lost in sin,
I opened the door and asked Him in..."

We don't debate anymore," someone will explain. "We give our testimonies now, or sing sections of the Bible, maybe John seventeen or one of the Psalms. Or we may give a short sermon in song." Sounds as if the folk art has been converted as well as the people!

People involved in church planting do well to look closely at what has encouraged growth in a church such as the one in Natunuan, and ponder the following points:

1. The village of Natunuan was a homogenous unit of society. The people were barrio-mates, many of them related by blood or marriage. They were ready to move together.

2. They were prepared people. Not only had the monolithic image of the Roman Catholic Church begun to fade, but they were prepared for the acceptance of the truth through the memorization of long portions of Scripture.

3. The Bauan church was near enough and cared enough to help bring the barrio people to meaningful decision and to aid in the nurturing and shepherding of the new Christians.

4. The town church was prepared for a people movement - a multi-individual commitment to Christ. They were not taken aback when the barrio people came to accept Christ by families and groups, the normal procedure in Malayo-Polynesian culture, of which the Filipino people are a part.

5. The leaders of the town church saw the Spirit of God at work and did not stumble at incidentals. For instance, the barrio folk did not know evangelical terminology, but used some of their own terms to describe spiritual experience.

6. By folk ingenuity, a new content came to an old art form, with unforseen spiritual results. Then the content was again changed, and this folk art became a dynamic means of witnessing to Christian faith.

7. Christian radio impinged on the hearts of the Natunuan people because (1) the message was in their own dialect and idiom. (2) it met an immediate need, explaining the meaning of what they already knew by rote, and (3) the voice became a person when the radio pastor came to the barrio - very important in a face-to-face, family-oriented society.

8. The Bauan pastor, missionaries, and local believers brought faith, concern, and steadfastness to the task of shepherding the new believers. In church planting nothing can take the place of post-decisional nurture and encouragement.

I have no objection to putting things into a new language to suit our day, or of putting our worship and witness into new forms suited to our day. Indeed this seems essential. My concern is that it should be the same eternal message which we transmit within these new forms of dialogue, experiment and worship.

A. R. Tippett   Verdict Theology in Missionary Theory

MISSION EXECUTIVES AND STRATEGY PLANNING by C. Peter Wagner

Mission executives would do well to ask themselves honestly if the time spent in the missionary field conferences is being used to the best advantage. I have recently become convinced that many items on our traditional agendas, not the least of which is "station reports," could be substituted by realistic and creative strategy planning sessions.

One of the most obvious shortcomings has been the failure to set realistic goals. Whereas not having specific goals may be a very comfortable situation (since failure then becomes virtually impossible), this must not continue. We must measure exactly how effective our missionary work really is, but obviously no measurement can be taken without definite goals. Granted, setting goals is risky. Without goals almost any kind of work can be made to look like success. Planting two new churches in a year may make some of us content. But if our goal had been ten, the same two would have produced frustration.

No commercial enterprise could long expect to hold the confidence of the general public if it persisted in using the shoddy methods of evaluating success or failure that have characterized much missionary work. Prayer letters and missionary magazines have developed great skill in projecting an image of busyness and blessing while skirting such important issues as whether the writers have been fulfilling the Great Commission or not. I have seen missionaries move to a station where the church has 35 members, report great blessing for five years, and leave the church with 35 members. It would be unfair to classify this as deceit since it reflects more or less the way the rules of our missionary game have developed. The only reason the general public does not demand the same hard-headed accounting from the missionaries they support as they do in their businesses is that they have been conditioned over two or three generations to believe that such accounting is both impossible and carnal.

This is far from the truth. It sounds like a Screwtape letter. It will assure us only of participation in a retarded work.

If we agree to set goals, what kind of goals should we set? Since the primary objective of missionary work is presumably to fulfill the Great Commission, perhaps we can take our clue from that.

The commission of Mt. 28:19-20 is more complete, more detailed, and less susceptible to textual problems than the one in Mark 16:15. Of its four key verbs, three in the Greek are participles ("go ye," "baptizing," and "teaching", and only one imperative ("make disciples"). Making disciples, then, is what the Great Commission is all about. Going, preaching, baptizing, teaching, and scores of other good missionary activities are all subservient and means toward the end of making disciples.

This is extremely important in setting missionary goals. Disciples can be counted by missionaries as readily as profit can be counted by businessmen, votes by politicians, or successful operations by surgeons. Each human profession has its own means of gauging success in the number of men and women who become faithful followers of Christ as a result of the particular type of missionary work they do.

Some will reject this criterion of missionary success as being too pragmatic, too objective, too simplistic, too carnal. But if they do, they risk disharmony with the angels in heaven. The Bible tells us that the angels of God rejoice over even one sinner that repents. If one causes joy, two causes a double measure, and immediately we're dealing with numbers. The primary goal of missionary work is to make multitudes of disciples for our Lord.

That is not to say that other good work that missionaries do is all wood, hay and stubble. But we must shift our thinking to ultimates. The ultimate question does not involve asking how many missionaries we have, how many meetings are held, how many seminary diplomas are awarded, how many penicillin injections are applied, how many radio programs are transmitted, how many tracts are distributed, or how many exotic languages are translated -- good as all these works are. All the worthy, secondary activities must be evaluated in terms of the primary goal of all missionary enterprise -- the fulfillment of the Great Commission.

If we could look at our churches with the same cool and calculating eye that a physician uses to diagnose his patients, strategy planning would be enhanced immeasurably. Unfortunately, the training programs which prepared most of us for missionary work did not teach us how to do this, and as a result some do not even think it is possible to distinguish a sick from a healthy church. Be assured that it is. Lacking scientific expertise in our own field of church development, we have lamentably contented ourselves with witch doctor techniques.

Healthy churches are growing churches. Missionaries interested in good strategy planning should know how their churches are growing in comparison to other churches of the area. Statistics are as necessary for the diagnosis of church health as a thermometer is for diagnosing physical health. Missionaries to Brazil should know, for example, that the churches there are growing at an average rate of 11% per year. They should not evaluate their growth rate against Nicaragua where churches are growing at only 3% per year. But Nicaragua might ask why it is so far behind neighboring Honduras where churches grow at 8.5% per year.

Once the goals are set and the research done, how is strategy planned? It might be well to review the method that the Apostle Paul used to plan his strategy. His second missionary journey is the most illuminating, since by then he was a "veteran missionary" and he had taken one furlough during which he undoubtedly diagnosed the health of the churches he had planted.

Although the Roman Empire was united politically in the first century, it nevertheless was an ethnic patchwork of cultures and sub-cultures, just as virtually every country in the world is today. During his second term, Paul directed his missionary efforts and resources almost exclusively toward only one patch in the ethnic quilt -- the synagogue community. The cultures of Galatia, Asia Minor, Achaia, and Macedonia differed from one another in details which any anthropologist could describe, but the sub-culture of the synagogue community was predictably uniform no matter in which one of the major cultures of the day it was found.

Before beginning his second term, Paul, guided by the Holy Spirit, held a "strategy planning session," and saw ahead of him a series of ripened harvest fields. He set his face like flint toward the synagogue communities, and there he planted Christian churches. Where there was no synagogue, such as in Amphipolis and Apollonia, he did not even stop to preach. Where he followed the Spirit-given strategy of planting the seed of the Gospel in the synagogue community he had good success, but where he departed from it, such as in Athens, the results were far less than satisfactory.

Paul had access to no resources in the first century that we cannot tap in our twentieth century. In fact, we have many more physical and material resources with the same Holy Spirit who gives power to use them. Unhappily, we have not always been in the position to allow the Holy Spirit to show us how best to use our resources. The computer, for example, could be used to good advantage in strategy planning, but few have considered it. I have even heard the possibility debunked as unspiritual.

We must ask the Holy Spirit to guide our thinking and planning these days in order that we might know where the soil is fertile for sowing and the field ripe for harvesting. Let us put aside sowing in stony ground or attempting to reap green fields when the harvest in the next valley is ripe and fruit falling to the ground and rotting. No farmer holds his harvesters responsible for reaping where the grain is not yet ripe, but he does hold them responsible for losing ripe grain. Can we expect less from God? Let us look to Him, not for static or unproductive programs, but for sound strategy that will produce fruit - thirty, sixty, and one hundred-fold.

> The whole idea of the Christian mission depends on the idea of the Church. Here we have the fellowship of the people of God, called out of darkness into light, and sent out again to introduce others to that light.... We have here the basic processes of church growth - incorporation of persons converted from the world, growth in grace within the fellowship, outreach into the world to share the new experience.... The Church and the Christian mission are involved together in the world situation. By divine charter the Church is a missionary body and cannot be otherwise without denying its essential nature.
> A. R. Tippett   Verdict Theology in Missionary Theory

BOOKS

Dr. Allen Tippett's new book: VERDICT THEOLOGY IN MISSIONARY THEORY

This weighty little book is the nearest thing to an indispensable Biblical, theological, and practical handbook for the man who would respond to the Christian mission today.

Part I is the Biblical section which in four marvellously concise chapters offers, respectively, the distinctive contributions to mission theory of the prophet, the psalmist, our Lord, and the Apostle Paul.

Part II draws in contemporary thought and presents in four quotation-studded chapters the points of current tension in mission theory:

    Dialogue and Presenting the Gospel
    Christian Presence and Witness-bearing
    The Call of God: To Proclaim and To Serve
    Universalism or Power Encounter

Part III unfolds in four more chapters a gold mine of practical wisdom, sparkling with anthropological insights:

    The Relationship of Social and Religious Change and the Missionary/
    Christian Mission Meeting Social Change   Role in It
    Indigenous Principles in Mission Today
    Continuity of Faith: Flexibility of Form

This eminently readable little book comes from a tough-minded scholar who is at the same time deeply spiritual and extensively experienced in the front line of the Christian mission. See the order blank if you would like to get a copy.

Announcing <u>William Carey Library</u> publications:

With over 40 career missionaries coming each year for advanced studies at the Fuller School of World Mission, it is inevitable that a wealth of knowledge and insight would be written up <u>each</u> <u>year</u>: over a dozen theses (averaging well over 250 pages), many lengthy research documents, and literally hundreds of scholarly papers--the product of over 40,000 hours of work of experienced missionaries.

No conventional publisher could handle this load. No conventional publisher operates in such a way as to be able to market a book of special interest to only 300 key people, for example. (Yet documents of this kind are often immeasurably more important to the people involved than books of general interest.) No conventional publisher knows its way around the unique foreign labyrinth of the missionary world.

Thus was born the William Carey Library, which is sort of an unofficial shadow of the School of World Mission at Fuller. A careful study has been made of available printing prices and specific firms who can produce quality books in short runs. As for distribution, World Vision's MARC (Missions Advanced Research and Communication Center) has established a documentation center, called MARC/DOC, which will begin in January to publish quarterly abstracts of all missions documents, short and long, that are available either through MARC/DOC or elsewhere. This center will immeasurably facilitate the flow of documents strategic to the Christian Mission, including William Carey Library publications.

Three strategic books have already appeared (in October) under the William Carey Library label. (Three others are in progress):
    1. CHURCH GROWTH THROUGH EVANGELISM-IN-DEPTH is an exciting, readable evaluation of "saturation evangelism" campaigns, specifically the Latin America Mission's famous Evangelism-in-Depth. Chapter Two, for example, condenses Dr. McGavran's church growth theory into 24 pages! The next chapter does the same for EID. Other chapters present variations of the Latin American scheme in Nigeria, Congo, etc., and critiques by Rosales, Wagner, and Peters. The final chapter offers church-growth guidelines for all such programs of evangelism.
    2. THEOLOGICAL EDUCATION BY EXTENSION is the second to appear, combining three books under one cover (and 648 pages!). The first book tells the amazing story of the extension seminary movement in Latin America that has gone from one school to 60 other schools in six years. The second book under the same cover condenses a three-day EFMA-IFMA Seminary Extension Workshop held at Wheaton last December. The third book tells how you can analyze your own situation and implement this new approach. The idea is simple: <u>extension</u> means the institution fits into the student's schedule rather than vice versa, and this twist, amazingly, enables countless keen men in local congregations suddenly to be available for serious theological study and ordination. One by-product of this movement in Latin America is a massive program of collaboration in writing special textbooks for ministerial training by extension. Dr. Ted Ward of Michigan State University calls this program "the largest single non-governmental educational development project in the world today."
    3. The third book needs no introduction to readers of this bulletin: the first five (not four) years are reprinted, with a new index and a single series of page numbers, in one volume of 408 pages for only $4.45. See the order blank for all the William Carey Library books mentioned here.

MORE CHURCH GROWTH THEORY AND THEOLOGY

SELF-CENTEREDNESS AND THE CHOKE LAW Donald McGavran on Hillman and Sapsezian

The last fifteen years have seen a great increase of parochialism among the traditional denominations, including the largest of all, the Roman Catholic Church. They interpret the missionary task in terms of improving the milieu of which the Christian is a part. Limited missionary resources are absorbed in fields where the good seed has been sown and a limited harvest reaped. Extending the Gospel to new fields and bringing the liberating rule of Christ to more and more people is stigmatized as "triumphalism." Membership growth is not regarded as a trustworthy evidence of an authentic proclamation of the Gospel. Missionaries are exhorted to devote themselves to the pastoral care of the converted and the increase of justice and brotherhood in "Christianized" peoples. All this increased parochialism means that the Church introverts itself, becoming concerned not with the evangelization of the world but with the improvement of the already triply blessed populations which have large Christian minorities.

This parochialism, isolationism, and self-centeredness defends itself, of course, against the charge. On the one hand, as illustrated by the following quotation from Aharon Sapsezian, Geneva's "Monthly Letter About Evangelism," maintains that world evangelization is motivated by self-aggrandisement and is therefore self-centeredness!! The Communists accustomed us to hearing that black is white and totalitarianism is liberty, but it is surprising to find this upside-down usage in a Monthly Letter About Evangelism put out by the Division of World Mission and Evangelism. On the other hand, as Father Hillman points out in the following passage, certain Roman Catholic writers (by the simple expedient of using the words 'mission' and 'missionary' to describe whatever particular problem happens to appear most urgent to them) make these grand words parochial i.e., concerned with the already Christian.

Father Hillman's remarks come from The Church as Mission, Herder and Herder, 1965, and are used with permission, though the underlining is mine. Aharon Sapsezian's paragraphs come from A Monthly Letter About Evangelism put out by DWME (Oct.- Dec. 1968). Dr. Sapsezian is arguing that current theological education is selfish. All over the world it is preparing men to minister exclusively to the already Christian or bring men into existing churches. Theological education is not working - as he thinks it should - for the benefit of mankind, the increase of justice and mercy, regardless of what people believe. He advocates that the Church through its ministers and trained laymen go out into the world, but insists that any extension of the Gospel, any multiplication of churches on new ground is triumphalism and less than really Christian. To be really Christian - one judges - each church should be concerned that its own society (local or national) become better. It is this exclusive concern with one's own which is so similar to that which Father Hillman depicts and deplores.

Now let us turn to the quotations themselves. Father Hillman says:

"So nowadays, when people speak about the "renewal of the Pentecostal spirit" and the "essentially missionary nature of the Church," we must be circumspect; and when we are told, in the words of Cardinal Feltin, that "the whole Church must set itself in a state of missionary activity," we must be cautious. What these writers are primarily thinking about, more often than not, are the serious social and pastoral problems of the Church in parts of Europe and the Americas. And when one hears the new theology of the missions being expounded, if he listens carefully, he will recognize that these theories are concerned almost exclusively with what most Anglo-Saxons still call "pastoral theology." By using the words "mission" and "missionary" in relation to whatever particular problem happens to appear most urgent to them, Catholic writers have engendered some considerable confusion; and invariably, they have lost sight of the precise aims of missionary activity as formulated in the official documents of the Church. By confusing the "de-Christianized" social milieux of Europe and the Americas with the non-evangelized gentes of the rest of the world, it should become possible, in this new orientation of the Church's missionary function, to intensify "missionary zeal" while at the same time demanding no more sacrifices than are presently being made for the extension of the Church among the peoples of the non-Western world. The result is that, in good conscience, the Church may remain primarily an affair of Europe and the Americas. The proper care of the existing flock is surely capable of absorbing more and more of those missionary resources which even now amount to little more than a parsimonious token.

With all of this very earnest and often profound concern over the mission of the Church in the modern Western world, there sometimes seems to be almost a tacit assumption that the Church is already known and accessible throughout the rest of the world. And therefore, it is concluded, all that remains is to intensify our zeal in watching over the existing flock; and, while gathering in as many as possible of the lost sheep, to prepare for the attacks of the Antichrist (usually Communism), as we await the conversion of the Jews and the return of the Lord. In this conception, the Church's pastoral functions, home missions, social action, university students, workers, poor peasants, blind intellectuals, old folks, orphans, etc., may all be regarded as the proper objects of "missionary activity."

Even in the missions of Asia and Africa, there is this strong tendency to permit the present limited missionary resources to be absorbed almost exclusively in fields where the good seed has already been sown once. Among missionaries in India, this has come to be known as the "choke-law." The successful evangelization of large numbers of people in one or another region, especially when this achievement is coupled with a chronic shortage of personnel, is apt to result in the total stagnation of missionary expansion among the remaining non-evangelized peoples. So many missionaries are taken up with the pastoral care of the converted that further expansion is "choked." This problem was dealt with in a special instruction from Rome to the Bishops of India, "not just exhorting . . . but positively enjoining" that new mission stations be established among those not yet evangelized, and that each bishop should make available exclusively for this work at least two missionaries, with the names of these missionaries being sent to Rome within six months after the reception of the instruction. This was in 1893. In his report on the work of evangelization in India, submitted to the Episcopal Conference of India in 1951, Bishop William Bouter had once again to bring up the old question of "stagnation and absorption in parochial duties to the exclusion of work 'ad paganos' (the "choke-law") . . . owing to insufficiency of personnel." Thus the failure to understand the urgent nature and the specific goals of missionary activity is not confined to Europe and the Americas only.

Dr. Sapsezian is arguing that theological education needs radical recasting. One major reason for this, which he advances, is that the seminary trains men to serve the Church and should be training them to serve the world. He says:

traditional convictions which have supported the theological education are being shaken. Yesterday's presuppositions are under tremendous pressure; their validity ... is doubted ... (We have today) an informed intuition concerning the inadequacy of the Church's witness and mission in today's world. ... the institutional machinery of the Church, set up for missionary productivity ... is beginning to reveal defects of operation and adaptation to a situation which is sociologically different ... the dissemination of religion and membership growth are not the most trustworthy evidences of an authentic proclamation of the Gospel of Jesus Christ ... the renunciation of triumphalism ... (is) strengthened by a certain theological enrichment that issues from a deeper study of the Word of God, where one can arrive at a clearer insight into the Church and its presence in the world ... The contemporary vision of the universal Church with a universal mission makes it obvious that church-centeredness is a false security; the Church and its ministry gain their authenticity when they exist for others, in turning toward the world ((but not, be it marked, for reconciling the world to God in Christ. That is supposed to be part of the self-centeredness. DM)) ... A perversion of theological education is to consider it an investment of the institutional church from which she can garner advantages for herself (her perpetuation, her numerical growth, her influence, etc,) ... Theological education does not exist for the protection of the Church but for her reproval, for her judgment in the light of God's Word ((but not, be it marked, of the Great Commission! DM)) in order to spur her on to the path of greater faithfulness ((in every good work except discipling the nations. DM)) ...
    It became extremely difficult to identify the insertion of the Church in the missio Dei with the inevitably church-centered activity of the men whom we designate as "ordained ministers" ...
    If theological education is subordinate to mission - we repeat: mission in terms of our engraftment as people in the missio Dei ((from which bringing the peoples of earth to faith in Jesus Christ consistently is excluded as selfish self-aggrandisement. DM)) the anomalous nature of its orientation toward the "ordained" is patent and toward the laity is avowedly negligent.

Much of what Dr. Sapsezian says about the need to enlist the laymen in the work of God is good sense. Truly the Church exists as God's instrument in the world and truly God loves the world and longs for its salvation.

But Dr. Sapsezian's sharp dichotomy, to which I have called attention by the bracketed inserts, is false. It is not to the interest of the Church to win men for Christ and scatter congregations across a district or a country. It adds enormously to her burden. Furthermore, the Church can help the world most, precisely by winning as many out of the world to ardent "separated but solid" Christian life as possible. It would be fatuous to think that what the

Church <u>does</u> is more important than what the Church <u>is</u>. The presence in the United States of millions of both black and white men and women living in conscious discipleship to Jesus Christ is what gives hope that the tensions of today may be lessened and the injustices eradicated. Of course, these ardent Christians must <u>do justice</u>; but before they can, they must <u>be Christian</u>.

Dr. Sapsezian would benefit the cause of theological education if he would cease attempting to smear the propagation of the Gospel with the taint of self-interest, and press his legitimate point that theological education should take in <u>both</u> clergy <u>and</u> laity, and go on to say that both should be trained to redeem <u>both</u> souls <u>and</u> societies. We need not "less caring for the people of God" but more - only the saved can help save others. We need not less propagation of the faith but more - only the seeding of Africa south of the Sahara with a hundred thousand Christian congregations will meet the physical, social, economic, and political needs of that continent.

At this point Father Hillman's plea deserves hearing. The "choke-law" alas, does operate. When a section of some society (tribe, caste, city, or plateau) becomes Christian, the tendency is for the present limited missionary resources to be used almost exclusively <u>there</u>. Too much attention is paid to those partially Christian populations while the solidly non-Christian populations languish without a chance to hear of the Saviour or to find courage and light for social reform through discipleship to Him.

A longer version of the article in the May <u>Bulletin</u>, "The Evangelization of Africa in the Twentieth Century," will appear in the January, 1970 issue of <u>International Review of Missions</u>, under the title "AD 2000: 350 Million Christians in Africa." Readers interested in the extension of these studies to other parts of the world, and who would like to contribute to this research themselves, are invited to write for a copy of the longer article from the author: Rev. D. B. Barrett, c/o School of World Mission, Fuller Theological Seminary, 135 N. Oakland Avenue, Pasadena, California 91101.

THOUSANDS OF MISSIONARIES FROM TRIBES TO TRIBES by Vernon Tank SWM-ICG 1968

About 1945 a strong people movement to Christ broke out in the Ami tribe of the Highlanders of Taiwan - a Malayan tribe living in the eastern mountain fastnesses of the island. By 1960 over half of the Ami had become Christian and many ministers had been trained in the Bible School near Hwalien Kang on the east coast.

In November 1968 four of these Highlander ministers and their families were sent to northern Borneo (East Malaysia) as missionaries to the Iban Tribe which numbers about 300,000 souls. Several strong people movements have been underway in that tribe and its affiliates since the 1950s. Whole valleys have turned to Christ. At least twenty Ibans have been ordained. Missionaries from converted tribes to tribes who have yet to believe are the order of the day.

Taiwanese Highlander missionaries are helping these movements. Highlander missionaries do not need the extensive anthropological training Eurican missionaries need. They do not have to overcome Eurican cultural overhang. Since they were head hunters only a few years ago, they can tell a vivid story of Christ's redemption. <u>And they are not Western or white</u>. Perhaps the next great advance in missions is for the wealthy denominations of Eurican to help send thousands of missionaries <u>from the tribes to the tribes</u>, from Asians to Asians.

THE BEGINNINGS OF A PEOPLE MOVEMENT? by Manuel Gaxiola SWM-ICG 1969

Adolfo Cruz is a pure-blooded Mixtec Indian who 23 years ago left his hometown, San Pedro Tida in the state of Oaxaca, Mexico. He drifted to Mexico City, and finally migrated to the United States. He heard and believed the Gospel and is now the pastor of the Apostolic Church in Escondido, California. This spring Pastor Cruz returned home for the first time, but had been preceded by the Bible and the Holy Spirit.

About five years ago an airplane dropped New Testaments on the outskirts of San Pedro. These were eagerly picked up and read by the Indians. Since the Catholic priest comes once a month to say mass, they thought he would explain the things they were reading. However, when he arrived, he told them that those who dropped the New Testaments were condemned and also wanted the people in San Pedro to be condemned.

He ordered all the books brought to him. After piling them in the village plaza, he burned them. Fortunately, some people kept their New Testaments and read them at home. As a result, several of these men believed Christ and as a symbol of the new life quit drinking and smoking.

When Pastor Cruz arrived in San Pedro Tida he went to see his friend, the school principal, who called a special assembly and introduced Adolfo as "our eminent fellow-townsman who has gone to the United States." When Adolfo talked to the children in the Mixtec language they applauded for fifteen minutes.

Next Pastor Cruz met with the local power structure. The <u>Presidente Municipal</u> and all the councilmen, together with most of the people, gathered together at the town hall and heard Adolfo preach several times. After the first sermon or address, rain fell for the first time in nine months. The townspeople took this as a good omen. After the last sermon, they said, "We will accept the Gospel and build a big chapel even if the Catholic priest does not agree."

Pastor Cruz left San Pedro after promising to return soon. The Mixtecs promised to wait for him. Their cordiality was to a fellow Indian. They are very fanatical and cruel to outsiders. At the same time Adolfo was among them, in another town they tied a Baptist preacher to a chair for fifteen days, giving him neither water nor food.

Pastor Cruz went to Oaxaca, the state capital, and there found many relatives. Seven of them were baptized on May 5th by Pastor Fragozo of the Apostolic Church. They are planning to visit San Pedro and share the Good News with their kith and kin.

Pastor Cruz is now back in California and in two or three months will return to San Pedro. He plans to remain there four or five months at a time (in order to retain his immigrant status in the U.S.A. he must spend at least one day here every six months). The Church in California has promised to support him and he is confident that the Lord will give him a great harvest of souls not only in San Pedro but in many villages around.

He believes all his preaching must be done in the Mixtec language. I have advised him not to preach in Spanish (though he uses that language in California) and to encourage the Christians to compose Mixtec songs and do the many things that express in their mother tongue what they will be receiving from the Lord.

We are praying Pastor Cruz will lead a people movement to Christ among his people. Do join us in intercession.

(Rev. M. Gaxiola is Executive Secretary of the Iglesia Apostolica de la Fe of Mexico - a vigorous indigenous Church of about 10,000 communicants.)

AMERICAN CHURCH GROWTH EXPLORED by Dr. Medford Jones

The first annual Church Growth Colloquium - to consider church growth and evangelization in North America - was held at Emmanuel School of Religion, Milligan College, Tennessee, June 16-20, 1969.

Present were 120 people from twenty church bodies, including twenty-three regional and national executives, educators from eight colleges and seminaries, and three editors.

The attendance, wide denominational involvement, new ideas and insights, high morale and optimistic courage at this unusual meeting were astounding. The "Unity of the Spirit" was most apparent. Many said that the means of renewal and world evangelization were evident. Delegates returned home determined to do what they could in their own places.

The fresh emphasis upon the divine-human phenomenon which is the Church was inspiring. Church growth was defined as the extensive qualitative and quantitative increase of the living Body of Christ. The healthy church was seen to be characterized by rapid growth and reproduction. The Church, endowed with the means and ability to grow, is God's instrument for world evangelization. The world is evangelized and God's will carried out as myriads of rapidly multiplying churches are spread around the world.

Methodologically speaking, the healthy Body of Christ functioning naturally and unimpeded was the basic means of growth stressed. The Body, headed by Christ, nurtured by the Word, empowered by the Holy Spirit and mobilized by the priesthood of believers, exists to serve God and man. It is God's will for the Church to grow. The Church grows as it serves people. People are served through dynamic Christian fellowship. While there are many facets of fellowship, the growth of the Church depends on the multiplication of fellowship units within each church, which minister the Word and love of God. The Colloquium insisted that all churches must expound the ministry of believers, multiply fellowship units, make teaching and proclamation Biblical, intensify the fellowship and become involved with people. Such churches can grow rapidly and start additional churches.

The subjects dealt with during the four days were:
    The Biblical Basis of Church Growth.
    The Scientifically Measurable Factors of Church Growth.
    Environmental Influence Factors. Effects of Aging.
    Why Churches Stop Growing. How to Activate "Stopped" Churches.
    How to Diagnose the Problem and Project the Remedy. How to Motivate.
    How to Enlarge the Sunday School. How to Recruit Enough Workers.
    How to Develop the Congregation Through Face-to-Face Groups.
    Lay Evangelism. Home Bible Study Groups. Visitation Evangelism.
    Crucial Factors in Starting New Churches. Stewardship and Finance.

The Second Annual Church Growth Colloquium is tentatively projected for August 31-September 3, 1970, on the Emmanuel School of Religion campus, Milligan College, Tennessee 37682.

((We congratulate Dr. Jones on this exploration of American church growth. Millions in North America have not yet accepted Christ. Such colloquiums should be held in many places. Editor))

UNBAPTIZABLE BELIEVERS IN LATIN AMERICA
((Letters from several parts of Latin America have come in recently on this crucial problem. Here are excerpts. Editor))

"In Latin America, literally hundreds of thousands of unmarried couples live together and rear their families. Each of the two persons concerned was properly married in church, or by civil rite years ago. Then that marriage broke up. Each partner later settled down with some other man or woman and has had several children."
Then the Gospel arrives and one or the other of the partners is converted. Sometimes both are. Up to this point all are happy, both the converted persons and the local church. Converts live faithfully with their partners. But then the problems begin. First, the church will not baptize these new believers. Second, the church will not give them the Lord's Supper. Third, neither husband or wife can be officially active in the affairs of the church. They are third class Christians. They are unbaptizable believers.
Were divorce laws in existence, the churches would probably accept a divorced and remarried man or woman; but in most of these Catholic coun- tries either there are no divorce laws, or the divorce costs far more than the masses can afford. A man, whose marriage broke up when he was a young fellow of eighteen, even if he has lived faithfully with his second woman for twenty years and reared five to twelve children, and is now a believer and committed to faithful living, cannot be baptized. Even though truly converted, he is not really accepted by the church. As far as I know, no traditional Protestant Churches or 'faith-mission' Churches accept such converts. In not accepting them, do we do right? What Scriptural warrant do we have for refusing to baptize them? Is our action pleasing to God? (Keith Bentson SWM-ICG 1968)

Page 32

Another veteran missionary writes:

The fact that here virtually all people of the masses are living in common-law marriage keeps missions and Churches from practicing Scriptural baptism. Because of poverty, government red tape, and transportation difficulties, marriage of such persons required months - or years - of waiting. And who would ever think of baptizing such persons before they were married! Have you or anyone else made a study of the practice of baptizing new converts living in common-law marriage and then, through church discipline weeding out those who are unfaithful afterwards? Are there statistics as to how such a policy turns out?

A third letter says:

You will recall I wrote about the problem of Evangelical churches in this country refusing to baptize persons living in common-law marriage - (here this means everyone but the rich). I wondered if it would be right to baptize sincere believers living in common-law marriage, and pointed out that there is no biblical prohibition of such baptism. You replied, advising me to give it a try.

I followed your advice. First, appealing to Scripture, I obtained approval from our mission board. Second, when a Christian cannot marry legally, for reasons beyond his control, I encouraged our pastors to baptize him. Scripture recognizes only repentance and faith as requirements for baptism. I soon learned that baptizing such believers was an earth-shaking precedent for any mission. Have we ever rocked the boat! Word got around quickly! Many are astounded, erroneously concluding that we have "lowered the standards." Some of my best friends have called me "liberal" and "universalist."

The effect of this policy on church growth has been tremendous! The Spirit of God has put His seal on our simple obedience to His commandment to baptize! Churches are multiplying like never before - but only in those areas where our workers have accepted the new policy.

It is not simply because we now baptize all truly repentant believers. It is rather, if I have judged correctly, that we - like Peter - give a positive invitation: "Repent and be baptized every one of you ..." Yesterday, for example, eight new believers sat as a group in a small village learning that they should now be baptized. We could treat them as a group. We didn't have to call them aside and say to each one, "Now tell me brother, are you legally married?" I don't know anything about their marriage relationship; we will straighten that out afterwards. But at least, we didn't have to divide (and thus discourage) them into the "acceptables and the unacceptables" - purely human grounds which have nothing to do with faith or regeneration!

The Editor of <u>Church Growth Bulletin</u> replied as follows:

I am pleased to know that you are following biblical precepts in regard to the baptism of penitent believers.

I am not surprised that this new policy has opened the doors of the Christian life to many. Since almost all there (but the rich) are living in common-law marriage, and since you no longer allow common-law marriage to be an insurmountable barrier to baptism, you may confidently expect continued acceptance of Christ. However, let me voice two words of caution. Make sure that they are penitent, and believers. Let your instruction before baptism emphasize that the Christian life means both Christ's power and continual growth in grace.

Make clear that faithfulness in marriage relationships is one of the outcomes of life in Christ (I Cor. 6:18, Col. 3:1-17) and, whatever the past has been, from now on they will remain faithful to their spouses.

With the increased number of believers, you will have a chance to lead people to accept Christ in family groups. It should be quite normal for a man and wife, his sons and their wives, his daughters and their husbands, his brothers and their families, and the children who have reached the age of discrimination - all having been instructed and all having affirmed their faith in Christ - to be baptized on the same day.

The new churches will, of course, need a well planned, biblical, and yet simple, system of instruction. I suggest you get from the Assemblies in El Salvador, the little pamphlet, "Reglamento Locale," adapt it to your denominational polity and theology, and print it. Make it the simple guide for all your churches, and insist that lay leaders know it thoroughly.

Hold frequent and short leadership training institutes. In them teach your Reglamento Locale. Unless you do a tremendous job of teaching and leadership training, your numerous converts and new churches will become nominal Christians.

Please let me know from time to time of the way God is blessing your labors. The whole church growth readership - of more than 4,000 - is interested in your bold experiment.

WHAT DOES MR. DYCK MEAN? by Donald McGavran

"Surely the incarnation was not a tactical maneuver to win men to God. Christ gave Himself unreservedly so that others might live, regardless of men's response ... People want to be accepted as they are, to be confirmed in their own beings. Each in his own idiom is crying for identity, longing for fulfillment and true selfhood. Jesus fully recognized and satisfied this basic need. Nor did He ever take advantage of their helplessness. Service that recognizes the worth and dignity of a person will never stoop to exploit another - least of all for the sake of winning him to Christ. It is simply another case of ends not justifying means!' Peter Dyck, Mennonite Central Committee, in (<u>Service News</u>, October 1968, Elkhart, Indiana).

We have the greatest respect for the Mennonites. They are doing very Christian tasks all around the world. But we must ask, "What does Mr. Dyck mean?"

If he means that it is wrong to say to a mother whose baby is dying for lack of powdered milk, "We will give you milk if you become a Christian," then we agree.

If he means that while giving the powdered milk, it is wrong to say, "My sister, this is very temporary help. I am glad to give it to you, but would you not let me give you also the permanent help, the everlasting life, available through belief on Jesus Christ, for you and your baby?" then we disagree.

As Mr. Dyck says, Christ did give Himself unreservedly that "others might live." But in the Bible, it is clear that "to live" is to be "in Christ," to "believe on Him," to be "a member of His Household." He constantly emphasized that He Himself was the bread of life, without eating which (no matter how much powdered milk they ate) men would die. "I am the bread of life ... He who eats this bread will live forever." He said on another occasion, "What shall it profit a man if he gain the whole world and lose his own soul." "No one knows who the Father is, except the Son and anyone to whom the Son chooses to reveal Him." Any Christian who gives things to men, no matter how helpful, while concealing from them the Bread of Life and the Water of Life, is, in Lesslie Newbigin's words, "guilty of the folly of turning from the Spirit to the flesh."

We agree with what we think Mr. Dyck was trying to say, i.e., that aid should not be used as a bribe or a cudgel to 'bring men to Christ.' That is, of course, true, simply because no one can come to Christ except along the pathway of his own individual act of faith. But Mr. Dyck overstated his case. We doubt if he would himself defend his position.

We are particularly troubled by that word "exploit." Is it possible to "exploit" a person by introducing him to the Saviour? Does Mr. Dyck buy what God's enemies affirm, "that coming to Christ is mere euphemism intended to cover up sheep stealing"? Mr. Dyck probably does not mean it this way, but his sentence sounds very much as if he believed that "winning a man to Christ" was the equivalent of aggrandizing one denomination at the expense of some other.

In discussing essential matters such as conversion, winning men to Christ, adding them to the Lord, leading them to decide for Christ or to receive Christ, we must use clear and exact language. We must be biblically sound and theologically correct. Church Growth Bulletin believes this issue is important. If anyone believes that winning men to Christ imperils their "worth and dignity" we will print a 1200 word article by him - and comment on it. Let Christians of different convictions at least communicate with each other.

CHURCH PLANTING IN EUROPE   by Donald McGavran

One of the most encouraging reports to come to my desk this year is the Reporter, the magazine of the Greater European Mission. The Spring issue tells about church planting in various parts of Europe. In addition to preaching the Word, and teaching the Bible this mission is finding that the best way to conserve men and women who have accepted Christ is to form local churches.

The Spring issue is devoted to incidents such as the following taken from "Church Planting in the Saar" by Rachel Kliewer.

"Can you imagine what it would be like to live in a town of ten thousand people who have only two state-owned churches in which a personal relationship with Christ is never preached? This is the condition of most of the villages and towns here in Germany's Saar region ..."

"But our work resulted in saved people, and saved people need follow-up, they need fellowship with other believers, they need to be taught in the Word of God. The answer was to start Bible studies for adults and children. Now three years later a group of believers has been established. The new converts meet in a hall of a local cafe."

"... Another group "found" a workshop on the edge of town that could be renovated quite easily into a chapel. This is a step of faith but more a step of unity in that they will be working together toward the goal of church organization ... In another town "Evangelist John Unrau stayed on with the new believers and a meeting hall was found shortly after the tent was taken down ..."

"Meeting places, a program of meetings and Bible studies, crowds of people, and even a national pastor do not necessarily add up to church planting if the individuals in the group are not growing spiritually into full maturity in Christ. So we always seek to help men and women day by day grow in Christ. Tom was known as the town drunk before. Not only has his life changed, but he is gaining a knowledge of the Scriptures. His own testimony is that the brightest spot in his week is when he can worship together with the other believers ... We are looking to the future, expecting great things from our GREAT GOD!!"

Where everybody is baptized in infancy, and each person, at least nominally, belongs to the Church, is it legitimate when he has experienced the new birth in Christ, to induct him into a separate congregation? This is the universal practice in the United States of America, where practically all people won in evangelistic campaigns have a nominal connection, back in childhood maybe, to some Church. This is also the universal practice in Protestant mission in Latin America.

If what is being written about post-Christian Europe is only half true, abundant opportunity exists there for the establishment of thousands of living congregations of personally converted men and women. Nothing could be better for the State Churches than for hundreds of thousands of their members to become renewed Christians in Churches (denominations) dedicated to new life in Christ.

We wish the Greater European Mission God's rich blessing in its important work!

COMITY, MONOPOLY AND MISSION   by J. C. Wold

The disadvantage of the denominations for church growth comes not where they are in competition but where they are not. Denominations are the only form of the Church with which we are familiar. This form functions well in an area where each benefits from the competition of others, but it inhibits the spread of the Gospel when one denomination is alone in an area. Unfortunately - because of comity arrangements, isolation, and lack of workers - there are many regions in Liberia where one denomination has total responsibility for preaching the Gospel. In some instances a Church with a monopoly has ignored whole villages for decades, making no attempt whatever to.establish churches there until threatened by the spread of a competing Church. Comity agreements were devised in the first place to make sure that the denominations would spread out so as to give as many people as possible the chance of hearing the Gospel. They were never meant to limit the spread of the Church or to reserve certain territory for one denomination in a proprietary sense. When comity agreements are used to stake out territory, they are being misused.

American Protestant missionaries habitually think of their own congregation as having responsibility for only a small part of the community. In their own hometown their church was just one of several, sharing the ministry to the spiritual needs of the whole community. In the isolated sections of Liberia they find themselves, and should see themselves, in a VOLKSKIRCHE situation, with the responsibility of being the only Church in the entire area. Their doctrine of the Church does not do justice to the situation. They are used to thinking of it as a small, called-out group. Back home the congregation had perhaps fifty faithful members, and when they get fifty members in Liberia they are inclined to be content and to suppose that they are adequately ministering to the area. What they forget is that at home there were ten other churches in town, each with fifty members or more. In Liberia their congregation is the sole minister of Christ. The result is that the community remains under-churched.

The question is, can one denomination be catholic (i.e., all-inclusive) when it is the only denomination in a village? Where this is so, it must not be content with one church building. Why should there be just one? A single church cannot minister to the needs of the whole community. The one denomination could readily multiply its churches, build several chapels, have several ministers, and serve the community far better. But, outside of Monrovia, I do not know of any place in Liberia where this has been done. Missionaries and pastors usually have a small-denomination mentality. In the monopoly situation, unless the Church resolves to grow and multiply, God, impatient for the tribes' liberation, will probably bring other denominations into their area. This will break comity agreements; but unless the Churches themselves can break out of their small thinking for the sake of souls to be saved, those agreements should be sacrificed.

(Pastor Wold has one of the fresher minds of today. He puts the truth interestingly. He talks good sense. His recent book, God's Impatience in Liberia, from which the above gem on theory and method of mission is taken, is fascinating reading. Much of it applies to missions in Asia and Latin America. All of it applies to other lands in Africa. It should be widely read. Your bookstore or missionary society will get it for you from Eerdmans Publishing Company. $2.95. The Editor)

CHURCH GROWTH
BULLETIN

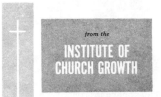

Address:
FULLER THEOLOGICAL
SEMINARY
135 N. Oakland
Pasadena, Calif. 91101

DONALD A. McGAVRAN, B.D., Ph.D.
Director

JANUARY 1970   Subscription $1 per year   Volume VI, No. 3

Urban Church Planting

No question which faces missions today is of greater importance than urban church planting. How to multiply churches in cities is a crucial question.

The Early Church grew to power in the great cities of the Roman Empire - Jerusalem, Antioch, Alexandria, Ephesus, Corinth, Rome, Carthage. But the Eurican pattern of church with its large, beautiful, and expensive building, has proved difficult to reproduce in the towns and cities of the Africasian world.

The problem is not to reach the city. Missionaries and national ministers and laymen have long since "reached" the cities. That is where large numbers of them live. Many missionaries never get off paved streets. They have reached the city; but they have not multiplied congregations there - and that is the task. Only as that is done, only as thousands of churches are established in urban areas, will it become possible to influence individuals and societies in such a fashion that a just, merciful and peaceful society becomes somewhat more possible.

One way out of the impasse is to find cases where men have found ways to multiply churches in cities. Taking the whole world into account, and parti- cularly centering our attention on Asia, Africa, and Latin America, instances can be found of effective propagation of the Gospel. As Christians attend to these, learn from them, adapt them, "go, and do likewise," the cities will become again what they were in the early days of the Church, seedbeds of Christianity.

The lead article in this issue is a beautiful description of one successful planting. It has much to say to everyone engaged in reconciling urban man to God in Christ.

Melvin Hodges, in his fine article, speaks realistically and influentially to urban church planters. No executive of mission has more firsthand experience in this field. Let the clarity and simplicity of his contribution deceive no one. His inspired common sense is a fitting addition to Mr. Greenway's argument.

SEND correspondence, news, and articles to the Editor, Dr. Donald McGavran, at the Institute of Church Growth, Fuller Theological Seminary. Published bi-monthly, send subscriptions and changes of address to the Business Manager, Norman L. Cummings, Overseas Crusades, Inc., 265 Lytton Avenue, Palo Alto, California 94301, U.S.A. Second-class postage paid at Palo Alto, California.

Ernest Poulson, Principal of the Singapore Bible College, writes out of experience. One congregation of Chinese converts in <u>one</u> highrise apartment has recently been contributing 1000 Singapore dollars a month ($333 US dollars) to the further propagation of the Gospel. When once the Christian religion starts to flow through the wage and salary earners among the urbanites, Christian mission will come into its own.

From two Congresses on Evangelism, we garner emphases which urban church planters need to incorporate in all their efforts. And, let it always be remembered that urban church planting is an essential ingredient <u>in urban justice</u>. The Church is more than social action; but even if we limit ourselves for the moment, the Church-as-social-action should vigorously plant churches so as to get at least some Christians to engage in works of justice and mercy!   The Editor.

TRAINING URBAN CHURCH PLANTERS IN LATIN AMERICA   by Roger S. Greenway

The decisive battles for the soul of Latin America will be fought in the cities. Latin America will be predominantly urban by 1970. Whether or not the city masses will turn in great numbers to biblical Christianity depends on whether the Protestant Churches learn how to evangelize the cities effectively.

Cities today have a far greater potential for church growth than most Protestant leaders realize. Within the next decade thousands of new churches can be planted in urban Latin America. The receptivity of the masses, particularly the new immigrants to the city, comes as a great surprise to church workers long accustomed to thinking that urbanites are the hardest people in the world to evangelize. If church leaders will throw aside this customary attitude of defeat and frustration and make some effort to reach the masses along the lines that we will suggest, they will find to their amazement that "the harvest indeed is plenteous." All that is needed, besides the power of the Holy Spirit, are trained workers with a vision for church planting.

We must admit, unfortunately, that trained workers with a vision for planting churches are not found just anywhere. Sometimes the Lord raises them up "from nowhere," but more often, as with the twelve disciples, they have to be enrolled in a training program where they learn from others how to do the job. That is precisely what we are doing at the Mexican Christian Institute in Mexico City, to which I shall refer as "The Institute." Our thesis is that, given the situation as it is today in Latin America, the only relevant way to train church leaders and workers is to combine theological competence with a passion for the multiplication of churches. We believe that this can best be accomplished when the theological school itself acts as a church planting institution, and faculty and students together are engaged in establishing churches. From the viewpoint of The Institute, any graduate who still does not know how to plant new churches is a failure, no matter how good his grades may have been in school.

The Plan In Action

The Institute has planted a dozen new churches in metropolitan Mexico City in the past two years. Our method is one of the oldest and simplest, and also the least expensive. It consists of intensive house-to-house visiting in certain areas of the city where there is no Gospel witness, the sale of Bibles along with a personal, verbal testimony in the home, the invitation to a neighborhood Bible class, and the subsequent establishment of iglesias hogarenas, churches-in-the-house.

To show how this works let us take the example of Mr. Sergio Morales and the Colonia Pedregal Carrasco. Sergio enrolled in the Institute in September, 1968, at the age of nineteen. He came from the State of Guerrero and was recommended to us by a Wycliffe Bible translator who had been instrumental in his conversion. Indian was his first and Spanish his second language. He spoke in a somewhat halting way and it was obvious that he was sometimes groping for the right Spanish word.

During his first semester at the Institute, Sergio received the usual Bible school instruction, plus a heavy dose of evangelism. He learned how to use the Bible in personal work and how to conduct home visitation. His initial fear and self-consciousness disappeared as he got involved in the practical work. Then in February, 1969, Sergio was among the group of students that I took with me to plant a church in the Colonia Pedregal Carrasco. Sergio, as well as the others, knew what our goal was, and knew also the steps that would lead toward it. We would not leave this colonia until a church had been planted.

The Colonia Pedregal Carrasco is what some people would call a shanty area on the south side of Mexico City. The residents are newcomers to the city, most of them having arrived within the last five years. They do not have much more than "squatters rights" to the land on which they have built their houses. We covered most of the colonia each Sunday for a month and found many people who were sincerely interested in the Bible. Within three weeks we had Bible classes started in three different houses. One of these houses, overrun with children, had to be abandoned when we found that it was a home of prostitutes and the respectable families from the neighborhood would not come near it. Unfortunately, the other families would not allow these women and children to come to their houses for Bible study either. That group just had to be dropped for the time being.

The first formal service was conducted on April 17. Because Sergio had shown particular enthusiasm for this colonia, I made an exception to my usual policy of placing only second or third year students in charge of new churches and I gave him the responsibility for the development of this one. Most of the people with whom he had to deal were old enough to be his parents or grandparents, but his pleasant smile and humble ways were enough to win their friendship and respect. If they felt "lost" in the big city, so did he. They both were camposinos at heart, and they understood one another. His love for the Lord was warm and contagious. He visited tirelessly, inviting new people to the services, reading the Scriptures in the homes, and praying for the sick.

The big test came last summer. I was away for three months and Serfio was left to carry on the work with his team of students, all of them just finishing their first year at the Institute. Upon my return in September, Sergio showed me the simple, stone chapel which he and the others had built. The roof is made of tar paper; the floor is of dirt. But it is filled with people twice each Sunday, and that is what is important. Money-wise, the only outside help has been the gift of ten crude church pews, a pulpit, and a chalk board. The offerings which were begun with the very first service have paid for the rest.

Sergio told me that he wore out two pairs of shoes while visiting the families of the colonia during the summer months. The results are obvious!

An Atmosphere of Perennial Evangelism

For a long time I had doubts as to whether the traditional type of training being given in Bible institutes and seminaries was really geared to the needs of our day. After all, most of our students in Latin America would not be called to serve well-established churches, yet that is what we seemed to be equipping them for. Our graduates would be expected to carve out their own congregations through evangelism, yet this was one area in which they would have very little experience upon graduation. Added to this problem was the fact that while on the one hand the urbanization of Mexico, like most parts of Latin America, was increasing at a rapid pace, we seemed to be concentrating our major efforts in the rural areas and small towns, and our impact in the metropolitan area of Mexico City was negligible.

About the time I was struggling with these questions, a powerful little book came into my hands. It was entitled, Church Growth Through Theological Education, written by A. Clark Scanlon and published in Guatemala in 1962. The following three quotations summarize the most important points which the author makes:

It is not enough to teach evangelism. The lateness of the hour demands that theological institutions evangelize. Institutes and seminaries cannot and must no usurp the place of the local church in evangelism, but there are many types of aggressive evangelism that students can spearhead to the benefit of all the churches (p. 35).

Evangelistic campaigns are not the only way in which an institute or seminary can encourage church growth. A second important way is personal evangelism by both faculty and student body. There is no substitute for a teacher whose life is dedicated to personal soul winning. No amount of instruction in evangelism equals it (p. 38).

To grow to their full stature as soul-winners, students must be taking courses and reading books and at the same time be at work in search for the lost. During vacation months students can help in or even lead evangelistic campaigns. They can work in rural churches, or in city campaigns.
    Then too, throughout the year, students should be kept in an atmosphere of a perennial evangelism. Winning the lost and seeking widespread church establishment must be a constant experience. The seminary should teach students harvest methods and people movements in local situations. The seminary or institute itself can become a useful instrument of evangelism (p. 60).

I would carry Scanlon's arguments just one step further, and say that to properly prepare church workers the theological or Bible institute or seminary must train them to plant churches, and in view of the rate of urbanization in Latin America, the planting of urban churches must receive primary attention.

Training and Trusting

The preparation of successful urban church planters involves two basic elements: training them in the Scriptures and the basic techniques of evangelism and church growth, and trusting that God will use their simple, yet sincere witness to the Gospel to bring men to believe in Christ. At the beginning, when I looked at my students with their rural background, their limited knowledge of Christian doctrine, and their inexperience as far as city life was concerned, I doubted whether they could become effective church planters in the urban setting. But experience has shown that it can be done, and what we have learned in Mexico City should be applicable throughout the Latin American world. Here are some of the things we have learned, most of them "the hard way."

First of all, you must set your sights directly on the planting of churches, and not just on "carrying on evangelism" in general. This comes as a surprise to many of the new students, especially those from the older churches. They have all distributed tracts, and most of them have had some experience in personal evangelism. But to look at a map of the city and say, "By God's grace we will plant a church in that unevangelized colonia," and then go do it, is an entirely new experience for them.

Secondly, it must be recognized that certain areas of the city are more receptive than others. We have experimented in just about every type of colonia, including the huge apartment houses. In general we have found that the most receptive colonias are those whose residents are new immigrants to the city (within the first ten years of their arrival) and they are also the areas having the greatest density of population. Middle class apartment dwellers are perhaps the hardest to reach. The desire for anonymity seems to attract them to the apartment complexes, and apartment life in turn fosters this same spirit among the residents. Students must be trained to look for receptive areas. In our experience, ground level, upper-lower and lower-middle class homes open up the most readily to the door-to-door evangelist. The question to ask when considering a new area to evangelize is: Who comes to the door? If they are wealthier homes with maids, you might as well forget it. The maid will keep you from ever reaching the man or lady of the house. In the apartment houses, the physical barriers are difficult to get around, such as buzzer-speakers at the entrance, guards, and "peek holes" in the doors. In the sprawling new colonias, however, the one-story, three room houses are easily approachable, and the man or lady of the house greets you at the door. These are the people you want to reach.

Third, the students must know how to articulate the Gospel. It is discouraging to find how few evangelicals know how to express the essence of their faith to an unbeliever. This is the primary task of the first semester course in Evangelism at the Institute. Students have to learn to proclaim not just their "experience," but the biblical message of reconciliation with God through faith in the atoning work of Jesus Christ. This is especially important in a program such as ours in which students do most of the preaching in the young churches. For this reason our Thursday chapel services at the Institute are dedicated to the study of the Scripture passage which will be used in all the missions the following Sunday. It is our conviction and experience that churches grow through the faithful preaching of the Word, and this requires that those who are in charge of the preaching receive as much help as possible in the preparation of their messages.

Fourth, <u>students who have learned to plant urban churches can do the same thing in rural areas</u>. I emphasize this because many of our students have been sent to the Institute by Wycliffe Bible Translators who are eager to see them return to the tribes after they graduate. While they sympathize with our urban church planting program, they are a bit fearful that the young people will not be able to apply the things they have learned in the city to the rural or tribal situation later on. I do not believe that they have anything to fear. To substantiate the claim that successful city church planters can, with a little thought and effort, adjust themselves back again to the rural situation, I would cite the example once again of Mr. Sergio Morales. During a recent vacation period, Sergio went back to his own village where various individuals had been studying the Scriptures in isolation from one another for some time. No one as yet had been baptized. Within a matter of a few weeks Sergio had these people meeting together for Sunday worship, whole families instead of merely individual persons were studying the Bible, and just before Christmas a letter arrived from this group requesting that a pastor be sent out to baptize the whole congregation. Plans are now being made to conduct a four-week Extension School in Sergio's village next summer. The main teacher will be Sergio himself, and he will use materials which he has learned at the Institute. If this is any indication of what we can expect in other areas, then we can be confident that successful city church planters will be equally effective elsewhere.

The Role of Established Churches

Old, established city churches ought to do far more than they are now doing to plant daughter churches in the heavily populated new colonias of Latin American cities. A recent study of the twelve churches we have established in the past two years shows that roughly one-third of those in attendance are sympathizers or new converts, one-third are persons who first believed the Gospel in their home village before coming to Mexico City but found no church home until our students came to their doors, and another third consider themselves members of some other city church but, having moved to a new colonia, live at too great a distance for regular attendance. <u>There is no reason, except inertia, why the established churches are not following up on their members who have moved to the new colonias and planting new churches in their homes</u>.

The name of Dr. Moises Lopez should be mentioned in this connection as one Mexican pastor who has seized the opportunity and has done outstanding work in and around Mexico City. Dr. Lopez is a medical doctor and a Presbyterian minister. Without much help from others, he has sought out the families of one of the downtown churches who have moved to the suburbs, and he has planted more than twenty new churches in this way. Dr. Lopez is a man of boundless energy and missionary passion, but more than anything else he has the vision of a great city dotted everywhere with Christian churches. Would that there were more pastors like him!

Training urban church planters is a program that should challenge everyone engaged in theological education. We at the Institute have learned a few things,

but there is need for much more study and experimentation. Some mission board
or national Church ought to consider establishing an Urban Church Growth Institute
somewhere in Latin America, where students and pastors from all the denominations
could be trained in the most successful church planting techniques.

?? SINFUL TO NUMBER ??

During a period of plateau in the growth of a Church in Central
America, the Annual Report to the Board of Missions contains a
statement reflecting a common judgment concerning the value of
numbering.

After hazarding a guess that the number of believers is "about
2500," the report continues, "It is not always best to number
Israel."

A page or two later, the same report continues, "On the mission
farm there are 201 chickens, 17 mules, 2 burros, and 8 steers,
heifers and calves."

(P. Enyart, SWM-ICG 1970)

SURMOUNTING SEVEN OBSTACLES TO CHURCH GROWTH   by Melvin L. Hodges

Churches finding themselves in a low production cycle should engage in an
analysis of the "soil" to see how the situation might be improved. Here are some
areas of difficulty that deserve watching:

I

A church fails to grow when its leaders become victims of defeatism. When
a fatalistic attitude of unbelief prevails, faith for revival and growth dies,
and in discouragement pastor and people say, "It can't be done!" Some find
support for this attitude in their interpretation of Scripture portions - "There
shall be a falling away"; "The love of many shall wax cold." To them church
growth is impossible because the times are against it!

Some say America has had her chance and now can only expect judgment. But
what about the whole new generation of young Americans, many of whom have never
seen revival? They need a chance!

While some prophecies foretell the great apostasy, others proclaim a last-
day outpouring of God's Spirit. Both events are going to take place and perhaps
they will occur side by side. While we are in the earth, God is glorified in our
producing much fruit. A positive stand of faith is essential for church growth.

II

Some churches fail to grow because they have lost their mobility and have
become prisoners of their buildings. They have reduced their activities to those
things they do within the four walls of the sanctuary.

Many churches have withdrawn from areas where new contacts are made; they no longer hold street meetings, cottage prayer meetings, jail services, or visitation campaigns so their groups are isolated from the world they should be reaching. In some instances almost the only effort to reach the outside world is in the evangelistic campaign with a guest speaker. If the people come, fine! But if not, what more can they do?

The Early Church carried on without any particular emphasis on church buildings. The early disciples preached in the temple, on the streets, in the houses, in schools, and wherever opportunity afforded. So also in the early days of the Pentecostal outpouring. Services were held in homes, in storefront buildings, in vacant church buildings, in schools - anywhere an opening could be obtained. More recently we have sometimes allowed our church buildings to seal us off from the world we must reach! For the church to grow, it must regain its mobility.

III

A third situation which hinders church growth might be called a "family-clan" mentality. This was illustrated to me in one Central American church made up entirely of Indian people. The society in that area was built around the family-clan principle. The church grew rapidly for a while, then growth leveled off and there were no new converts. Upon inquiry, I learned that all the converts were members of one family clan. When membership reached the limits of the clan, growth stopped. In fact, it is possible that the members would not have welcomed additions from other families as it would have disturbed the security of those in control.

The same thing has happened to a lesser degree in other places where the church membership is made up of three or rour families. These families may become sealed off from the rest of the community. Then there are no more "bridges of God," as Dr. Donald McGavran would say.

A church needs new material. Revival, like a fire, burns low if it has no new material to feed upon. God expects us to find ways to move out of our isolation and into contact with the world. We are the salt of the earth. God is not calling us to isolation but to contagion. We must expose the world to the Gospel.

IV

A fourth hindrance to church growth is the "pastor-do-it-all" mentality. As a young pastor, I made the common mistake of thinking the all-important aspect of the ministry was the sermon. Later, I came to realize that one of the pastor's most important tasks is to put his church to work.

Ephesians 4:11, 12 bears this out. We are told God has placed in the church apostles, prophets, evangelists, pastors, and teachers "for the perfecting of the saints, for the work of the ministry, and for the edifying of the body of Christ."

I originally thought this referred to three parallel purposes. Later I learned this verse should be read without commas. There is only one thing in focus: the edifying of the body of Christ. To this end pastors, evangelists, and teachers are to prepare the saints for the work of their ministry - for this

is not just a pastor's ministry but the ministry of the entire body of Christ.
As the pastor understands that an important part of his ministry is to help the
members fulfill their own divine calling as members of the body of Christ, he
will surely have a growing church.

V

The church fails to grow when it is self-centered. A certain tension has
always existed between evangelism, which is reaching the world for Christ, and
the perfecting of the saints in Christian graces. Spiritually inclined people
face a very real temptation to withdraw from the rugged task of winning the world
and retreat into the enjoyment of spiritual gifts and graces for their own sakes.
Some are so concerned about deepening their own spiritual lives and enjoying the
exercise of spiritual gifts that they have lost their practical usefulness to the
kingdom of God.

God wants the two poles of evangelism and Christian perfection to be kept in
proper tension. We must never lose sight of the fact that the ministry of the
Holy Spirit is not only in us, but also through us, as witnesses to a lost world.

VI

Some churches fail to grow because of a weak spiritual incentive. The
spiritual dynamics of prayer, intercession, and waiting on God have been lost.
The tendency then is to substitute the natural for the spiritual and to carry on
the work of God on a natural plane. Some engage in a round of activities
throughout the year with one program after another until there is no time left,
and perhaps no real desire, to seek God for revival and advance. We cannot have
true church growth if we settle for second best.

VII

We may be in bondage to traditions and religious habits. Somewhere along
the line we may lose our sense of expectancy that God will break in upon us in a
fresh way and reveal Himself to us. We begin to follow a routine of spiritual
exercises. Our worship and spiritual activity lose their freshness. Where is
the old-fashioned "burden for souls"? Where is the weeping and wrestling with
God in fervent prayer? Does the desire for God's work to prosper take priority
over our own interests and comfort?

God can break through in any church again. Faith can be revived and the
church loosed from its indifference and formality. God intends for the church
to grow. Let us ask Him to renew our faith so we can approach our task with
courage and vision.   (By kind permission of Advance)

EVERY THIRTEEN STORY BUILDING A PARISH   by E. N. Poulson of the Singapore
     Bible College.

Faced with a housing problem common to most newly emerging nations, the
government of the Republic of Singapore established an industrious program of
construction. To date, more than 600,000 people (out of a population of just
over 2 million) have been resettled, not always by their own choice. Slum
dwellings, squatters' shacks and thatched villages have been demolished in favor
of multi-story flats. Subsidized by a popularly elected government, these new

dwellings are clean, virtually fireproof and cheap.

As commendable as the program is it is not without serious complications. Formerly the people lived in homogeneous units. Flats create "neighborhoods" that are multi-racial, multi-lingual and multi-religious. In time, the experiment may produce an object lesson in national solidarity. For the present it is confusing and upsetting to the masses. Surrounded by strangers, many flat-dwellers are lonely.

Such a climate would be welcomed by the Church in Singapore were she not overcome by cultural inertia. Traditionally believers have assembled in western style buildings, complete with steeple. A secular government makes no allocation of land for churches, and most denominations cannot afford to buy land and erect new buildings near each housing development area. Rather than alter their image, most churches have "bowed to the inevitable" and are content to draw a few inhabitants across town to the old sanctuaries. Even those churches that have been built (either by foreign subsidy or by going into great debt) are so "foreign" in appearance and approach that there has not been effective penetration of the community.

Yet the fact remains that these socially unsettled thousands of people are winnable. The Gospel and the Church can meet the very needs these urbanites feel most keenly.

Some Christians, including the faculty and students of the interdenominational Singapore Bible College, have a plan for church planting which has already borne some fruit. Each highrise building has about 1,200 occupants. We believe a church (congregation) can be planted right in the building where the people live.

More than half a dozen such churches have emerged as a result of intensive door-to-door evangelism within each building. In some instances services have been held in the flat of a believer. At least three worshipping groups are housed in a ground-floor shop. During the week the "church" is used as a kindergarten, the fees of which pay the rent. Other congregations have been helped in the initial stages, by an older sponsoring church or by a group of concerned individuals.

The interior decorations and arrangements of the shops or flats have been kept simple, in keeping with the other shops and flats in the same building. There are no traditional religious symbols except, perhaps, for a simple cross. No invited person is expected to walk any farther than he would have to in order to buy a kati of rice. Nor would he dress differently than to enter the flat of a neighbor. Nor would he enter a place so strange that he felt uncomfortable.

With determination and faith an indigenous church can be planted in every building with minimum expense and maximum contact with the population. We believe a mighty multiplication of such churches - very like New Testament churches - is both feasible and the will of God.

URBAN CHURCH PLANTING AND EVANGELICAL THEOLOGY

The Bogota Latin American Congress on Evangelism (November 21-30, 1969) in its incisive declaration affirmed:

> Our theology of evangelism determines our evangelistic efforts, or lack of them. The simplicity of the Gospel is never in conflict with the theological dimensions. The essence of the Gospel is the self revelation of God in Jesus Christ. We reaffirm the historicity of Christ according to Scripture: His incarnation, His crucifixion, and His resurrection. We reaffirm the unique quality of his mediatory work, as a result of which the sinner finds pardon for his sins and justification by faith alone, without repeating that sacrifice. We also reaffirm that Christ is the Lord and Head of the Church, and that the final manifestation of His Lordship over the world will be made evident in His second coming, the hope of the redeemed. This is the good news which, when proclaimed and accepted, radically transforms man.

This sound theology must be applied in the rapidly growing cities. In them recent incomers are searching for community. They are much more winnable than they have been. If the Gospel is preached to them - not to city dwellers in general - they will believe and be baptized. That definitive volume which every missionary should own, Latin American Church Growth, says,

> The man who heard the Gospel before he migrated to the city, but felt unable to accept it because of family pressures, finds in the city a social anonymity and economic independence which enable him now to accept the Gospel .... urbanization provides opportunity for church growth based on personal conviction. The old structured family life, gives way to a more open stance, which in turn necessitates new values of discipline, education, family relationships, a-d social contacts....
> The fast growing indigenous Churches, with their urban bases and lay orientation, have particular appeal to the new urban dweller. In them he finds an opportunity to belong to a church whose activism fits his newfound sense of personal power. The positive Evangelical message helps answer his questions concerning the new society in which he finds himself. He sees that his peers enjoy responsibility, authority, and status and he is encouraged to enhance his own.... New leaders emerge. Former nonentities find or are given new opportunities in which to develop latent capacities (p.237ff).

Without sound theology, Christians will live in a responsive, urban population and literally not see it. They will carry on splendid mission work but plant no new centers of the divine life. With sound biblical theology, however, Christians see the receptive multitudes in the great cities and, with a feasible methodology, are able to become multipliers of societies of the redeemed, which are also the most potent ingredient of the just society - churches.

HARD BOLD PLANS FOR CHURCH MULTIPLICATION   by James Montgomery SWM-ICG 1963.

In the Philippine Islands, Overseas Crusades and others have developed a strategy of evangelism which is based in considerable measure on what Overseas men learned at the Institute of Church Growth. This was especially useful when about sixty leaders of the Church came back from the Singapore Congress on

Evangelism asking: What can we do? The plan for evangelism which we set forth was eagerly taken and developed still further.

Now about eighty-five denominations, including the large UCCP of 145,000 communicants, the many small missions, and the indigenous Churches, are collaborating in an All-Philippine Congress on Evangelism to be held May 15-23, 1970. Eighty percent of its budget is being raised in the Philippines, where receptivity toward the Evangel is much greater than it has ever been and where, I believe, we stand on the threshold of a mighty awakening. We are planning an evangelism which will result in nationwide rapid and sound church growth in cities and barrios. (James Montgomery is Field Director of Overseas Crusades.)

A PERSONAL WORD FROM DONALD MCGAVRAN

William Carey Library has brought out, in one easily read, well-indexed volume, five years of Church Growth Bulletin. It costs only $4.75. I urge you to order it at once, while the supply lasts. A check to William Carey Library, 535 Hermosa Street, South Pasadena, California 91030, U.S.A. gets you the book.

Libraries will be pleased to know that a clothbound edition at $6.95 is available.

A compendium of missionary knowledge. Many experienced missionaries, mission executives and professors of mission write on church growth. Rural church growth, urban church growth, prayer and growth, radio and communication of the Gospel, evangelism, mission policies, people movements, church growth from Islam, the biblical basis of church growth, objections to church growth, these answered, and hundreds of other subjects are treated.

A book you cannot afford to be without. Rich in ideas to share with national colleagues. A great aid in becoming a more effective and faithful missionary.

CHURCH GROWTH
BULLETIN

from the
INSTITUTE OF CHURCH GROWTH

Address:
FULLER THEOLOGICAL
SEMINARY
135 N. Oakland
Pasadena, Calif. 91101

DONALD A. McGAVRAN, B.D., Ph.D.
Director

MARCH 1970   Subscription $1 per year   Volume VI, No. 4

1970 Retrospect and Prospect

by A. R. Tippett

In 1960 the main items in the church growth library were McGavran's Bridges of God, and How Churches Grow, Church Growth and Group Conversion (which he edited) and Pickett's Mass Movements in India. It was from that limited but potent collection that modern church growth studies began. I say "modern," meaning the phase which has been guided by Donald McGavran. We all admit that further back is a foundation body of other writings. William Carey's Enquiry was a church growth document in our sense of the term. Nevius, Venn, Allen and Clark struggled with our problems: why churches do or do not grow, what kind of churches should be planted and how, and so forth. The pre-war World Dominion research studies were often our starting point.

McGavran started his Institute of Church Growth at Eugene, Oregon with the aid of a program of research scholarships. Some of the researches of these early and formative days were published in India. The church growth lectureship was established with the first lecturer Bishop J. Wascom Pickett. Eventually those lectures appeared as The Dynamics of Church Growth. The following year the lectureship was given to a panel - Nida, Guy, Hodges and McGavran - and this encounter led to the publication of Church Growth and Christian Mission, probably one of the most influential books we have published in the sixties. The lecture-ship has continued at Pasadena and two of these appear in recent publishers' lists.

One of McGavran's great ideas has been "Get the facts and make them available." The hope has been that when made available others will build on the work and make corrections. This is the scientific way and some of our critics forget it. McGavran had done research in Africa, the Philippines, Mexico and other places and developed a series of useful case studies. In 1963 he brought out Church Growth in Mexico. It became a model for the standard type of church growth case study. During the last decade similar studies have appeared on Brazil, Korea, Nigeria, Liberia, Tabasco (Mexico) and a smaller book on Japan, not directed from the Institute. These all have a similar structure and approach because they follow a model. As literary productions, they are not of equal

SEND correspondence, news, and articles to the Editor, Dr. Donald McGavran, at the Institute of Church Growth, Fuller Theological Seminary. Published bi-monthly, send subscriptions and changes of address to the Business Manager, Norman L. Cummings, Overseas Crusades, Inc., 265 Lytton Avenue, Palo Alto, California 94301, U.S.A. Second-class postage paid at Palo Alto, California.

quality, but as a total collection they present an amazing assembly of data and each adds to the general weight of church growth methods and theory. Furthermore they have drawn from missionary sources which otherwise would not have been tapped at all.

Sometimes church growth has been criticised for the sameness of these works but this is to misunderstand their scientific function. Using the same testing tools, in the same way, under the same set of rules, in a number of different one-country situations, should demonstrate whether or not the findings represent universal principles. This was McGavran's idea from the beginning, and the very sameness, which is sometimes criticised, has won widespread acceptance for the basic principles involved.

Read's New Patterns of Church Growth in Brazil opened up the whole area of Pentecostal church growth for our consideration - a new dimension which turned out to be highly significant. Shearer's Wildfire: Church Growth in Korea was a superb demonstration of some of McGavran's important theories which were hard to challenge against these statistics. Shearer also showed what could be done with missionary archives and set the direction for future research methods. Both the techniques of data collection and the dimension of ethnohistory were improved. Wold's God's Impatience in Liberia moved into the area of dynamics.

The years of experiment showed us the need for expanding our faculty and our course electives. A new type of experiment came with Solomon Islands Christianity for which a faculty member was released and lived in the island villages in a leaf house like the people. This was sponsored by the CWME but the orientation was that of church growth. It restated a number of theoretical aspects of the church growth viewpoint to meet some of the critical misinterpretations and was accepted by some who had been critical. It developed a number of theoretical points which church growth had accepted but not stressed. It introduced new dimensions of economics, social structure, culture change and primitive religion and was the first church growth study to attempt to reconstruct "the stuff of life" where the grass-roots church has to be planted, as its reviewers have pointed out.

A major research project, CGRILA, with good funding by the Lilly Endowment, was undertaken by Read, Monterroso and Johnson. A great deal of material has been assembled at Fuller for future research. A report has been published in a nice binding, Latin American Church Growth. This surveys the Spanish and Portuguese world of Central and South America. It was the first attempt at a comprehensive picture of this kind, and is given to the public with the idea that they will feed into us corrections and further data. As a research body, of course, we claim neither perfection nor completeness: we are concerned with the continual and relentless pursuit of accurate data and are thankful when people put us right. Feedback is important. Church growth research is a process of correction. We know much today that we had no idea of in 1960.

The CGRILA project applied the standard McGavran model in a regional area (instead of one country) - an area, we now admit, too wide for the time and resources we had available. Nevertheless, the success of the project is that it demonstrates the potential for large-scale church growth reconstruction - that the national can be extended to the regional. It gives us a preview of at least one aspect of research we might expect in the seventies. Where it failed it was at points where churches and missionary bodies could not (or would not) cooperate or provide accurate statistical data. It is a criticism of missionary record-keeping, not church growth research.

A battle of some kind has always been raging about missionary theory. Theory is important because it affects the allocation of funds and personnel, the precise points of thrust and kinds of program on the mission field. Theory might be methodological or theological and it may be conducive or obstructive to growth. For the whole decade, church growth theory has been very much in the 'firing line.' Our critics have included several types of people: mission board members and supporters who feel church growth threatens their vested interests, faithful missionaries whose long service in resistant fields has reacted against McGavran's harvest theology, missionaries who have had no church growth because of paternalism and bad missionary methods and are self-defensive about it, ethno-centric missionaries whose methods were western and individualistic and had a predisposition against group decision-making, and critics on and off the field who refused to accept our frame of reference with respect to the use of Scripture. Many of our critics were perfectly sincere, others were angry, some were in honest intellectual disagreement, but mostly they were intensely self-defensive. When I terminated my twenty years on the field and joined McGavran at the end of 1961, having joined him because his Bridges of God "rang a bell" with me, and feeling that I had something to add to it, I was astonished at the heat of theoretical and self-defensive opposition to the church growth idea, and the number of people who seemed to think it was "just a passing idea." The WCC con-sultation on church growth, which McGavran, Pickett and I myself attended, and which produced a very important Statement, I think was the turning of the tide in this respect. Thereafter we had a new right to speak, as it were.

Now it is 1970. The Institute has moved to Fuller Theological Seminary, with better financial undergirding, better academic standing and a specific degree program for those who desire to organize their study and research, and we are still in the theoretical 'firing line'; but we are entrenched on a hill-top instead of being 'peppered' in a valley. McGavran now has a team of supporters and these include possibly more anthropological credentials than in any other missionary school in the country. Alumni are scattered all over the world. An ever-increasing array of masters' degree research theses cover several exploratory aspects of our discipline that have not yet appeared in print: probably one of the most important current missionary collections in the world. That every year forty or more experienced missionaries should consider it worth their while giving up their furlough time to come to the School of World Mission shows a new acceptance of the idea of church growth in 1970 that is a far step from the 1960 position.

Today the critics who remain have shifted their position. Through the sixties they have 'shot at' church growth under the regular theological jargon of the period - dialogue, Christian presence, the Spirit in other religions, the whole man, the new humanity, obedience, denominational extension and so forth. Quietly, without ever saying so in public, the operating missionary world (or at least that part interested in bringing the pagan world to personal commitment to Christ) has accepted the general idea of the church growth viewpoint. Over the decade two or three times a year, long seminars have been held for missionaries. Many of these have had 100-150 persons register. Perhaps we have dealt with some two thousand or more missionaries over the decade. Sometimes we have visited foreign countries for similar seminars - Guatemala, Japan, Ethiopia and so forth. As individuals our faculty is in continual demand as consultants for mission boards and for missionary consultations - New York, Chicago, Montreat, Philadelphia, Phoenix, for instance. These have been Episcopalian, Presbyterian, Disciples of Christ, Baptist, Covenant, Mennonite and many others. At least it seems that we enter the seventies with a hearing which we did not have a decade ago. The missionary world has perhaps overcome much of its self-defensiveness and is prepared to let us make investigations and recommendations.

In the last ten years I have been engaged for specific field situation research in Melanesia, Africa, Mexico and North America (Indian). I have seen missionaries at work and I have been more and more impressed with the way our alumni tackle their problems. If they do not have all the answers they have at least come to grips with the real issues. Often, when others are frustrated, our men are getting through. They have a plan. They understand the issues involved. And some of them are planting churches where they did not do so before.

During the last decade we have reached out in our courses in new directions: the ant'ropological basis of leadership, culture and personality and theological extension training. Dr. Winter's symposium, Theological Education by Extension, is a major work, which filled a felt need and sold out its first edition in less than three months. Another approach to theory was Bradshaw's Church Growth Through Evangelism-in-Depth which has also sold out. Dr. McGavran's own re-analysis of church growth principles and procedures, that is, the theory that lies behind his case study model, has just come off the press under the title, Understanding Church Growth. The theory and the case study have to stand or fall together - a point which some of his remaining critics still overlook.

In the area of theology our production has been less impressive. This does not mean that we have no theological undergirding. We had rather hoped that the theologians would produce a theology of mission - a much-needed work. Some of the theological and biblical issues on which we stand have been dealt with in Verdict Theology in Missionary Theory, the first conservative book on the idea of mission as it works out in present-day missionary debate. Another small book, Church Growth and the Word of God, will be on sale about the time this Bulletin appears. Both of these are meant for conservative Christians. Does this mean that the seventies will see us moving out into the area we have hitherto left to the theologians? It may well be so. It suggests, however, that if we are drawn out into philosophical or theological dialogue, church growth is not likely to depart from biblical presuppositions or from the rooting of theology in the missionary field situation. Our gospel, like the cross itself, is embedded in solid earth.

Over the years we have been helped by a number of splendid scholars as part-time and visiting professors. They have contributed to teaching, research and writing and by participation in our seminars.

I think the seventies will also see a deepening of the anthropological dimensions of church growth research: cultural dynamics, acceptance and rejection, the conversion experience in group movements, and the process from animism to Christianity.

The increasing use of the computer has not escaped us. One or two of our projects have made use of it. We have the facilities available at MARC, an organization with which we have a close affiliation in numerous ways. Some of our current plans already for this year are experiments aiming at the preparation of a model for feeding data into the MARC data bank. This is all in line with our purpose of collecting facts and making them available. I have no doubt that the computer and its new developments will be a regular part of our program in the seventies. We hope that soon all missionary boards and supporting churches will be devoting 5 percent or more of their budgets to precise research in church planting and church growth. Now, if we do become so dependent on the computer (and I expect that this will be a common trend of life in the world), we shall certainly need to safeguard the spiritual dimensions. Improved research equipment requires also the sharpening of spiritual tools. I do not believe the threat of the seventies lies in the intensification of secularity as much as the weakening of spirituality. The effect may be the same but the dynamics are different. For me the most important issue as we go forward into the seventies can be put in the form of two questions:

What do we really mean by the Christian mission today?
Is the present theological mood tenable without rejecting
the authority of the Word of God?

Retrospect and prospect. We thank God for bringing us safely through the exciting sixties and we trust Him for guidance as we look forward into the unknown before us - the seventies.

Statistical Footnote:

From my own records, which are reasonably accurate but may not be quite complete, I have noted something of the scale of resource-sharing during the decade. The missionaries who have come have belonged to seventy-three different denominational or missionary structures, and have done their service in fifty-four different countries. The critics who think and write of church growth as merely denominational extension have to make their evaluations against this backdrop of ecumenicity. These men have both drawn from and added to our resources. A.R.T.

DR. GEORGE PETERS SETS DOWN SOME PRELIMINARY CONCLUSIONS OF HIS RESEARCH ON EVANGELISM ACROSS THE WORLD.

My studies have been most enriching and have led me to the following preliminary conclusions:

First, a new age of evangelism has broken in upon the evangelical wing of the Church of Jesus Christ. Evangelism is becoming a primary and determining concern in the minds of many Christian leaders, and a dynamic force in many individuals, churches and organizations. I can only attribute this to a new visitation from above. God is graciously raising up His servants to challenge

His people and to channel His forces into world evangelism. This is evident from the serious, penetrating and practical thinking which God has stimulated on the various continents and in several countries. While He is operating sovereignly, He is also operating mysteriously and generously. He is not limiting Himself to one man or one society. He is present in Latin America, Africa and Asia. We pray that He may also revisit North America and Europe in a new wave of evangelism.

Second, this is an age of great campaigns, and evangelicals ought to capitalize on the present psychological and sociological mood. Great campaigns are evident in many places. They are sponsored by numerous organizations, each following his pattern and each claiming unique success. No impartial observer will deny that much good is resulting. God is at work in these campaigns in a marvelous way. They are a tremendous factor in advancing the cause of God. However, to compare and evaluate them is a sensitive and difficult matter. Each believes in his own sanctity and knows himself divinely guided, scripturally oriented and practically efficient and effective. This is the way it ought to be. He, who is not sold on and enthusiastic about his cause will not succeed. Yet, critical and objective evaluations are most essential. It is evident that no one possesses the sole nor the whole key to success. While each one is a teacher, each one must also remain a learner. Continuous changes in time and culture demand continuous modification.

Third, the present-day national, interdenominational and united campaigns are making a tremendous and wholesome impact upon the community and should not be underrated. They play a vital part in Christianity and are of great benefit to the churches. They are, however, not the most effective answer to evangelism and church building. With the exception of New Life for All, they are not making the contribution to church growth which is generally expected. Somehow smaller and denominationally sponsored programs seem to be more effective in bringing converts into the churches. This seemingly negative aspect need not be the fault of the evangelism agency as such. It may only point to some weakness in the program which could be remedied or it may indicate the failure of the churches in the follow-up work. It could be a combination of both factors. Here is a subject for diligent and objective research.

Fourth, in general the churches in the mission fields are insufficiently prepared for great harvests and plenteous reaping. With few exceptions, neither pastors nor congregations are ready to absorb and care for a large influx of new converts. Thus the losses are tremendous; the casualty rates are out of propor- tion. Here is a most crucial area and needs prompt attention and wise action.

Fifth, a more radical return to the New Testament and fuller cultural, sociological and psychological adaptations are demanded than any of the present great movements are manifesting if genuine, lasting and impressive results are to be achieved and if justice is to be done to the present overwhelming possibilities.

Two demands are upon us:

One: In keeping with the book of Acts, we must aim at household and com- munity evangelism that will lead to household and community conversions. In all my studies of saturation evangelism, I have failed to discover anything like household and community movements. What I missed even more sadly was the fact

that neither vision nor understanding for such movements were present. The
cultural overhang of American individualism dominates all efforts. Household
and community movements were not expected, neither were they in the plans and,
therefore, they did not occur. In fact, they are feared by many because people
fail to distinguish between personal (a psychological concept) and individual
(a sociological concept). Group decisions and group experience may be just as
personal and genuine as individual experience is. Such movements are deeply
rooted in the book of Acts. They were frequent and were welcomed by the apostles.
They were the results of saturation evangelism in Jerusalem, Lydda, Antioch, and
Ephesus. Paul mentions numerous households which experienced salvation. They
are in the will and plan of God. Saturation evangelism movements ought to study
this phase more diligently, bring their work more in line with its principles,
prepare workers for it, and earnestly pray and strive for such movements.

Two: The vitality and success of any movement depends upon several dynamic
factors. First, the degree it achieves in accommodation by a process of adaptations in methodology, patterns of operation and communication; next, the degree
of mobilization it is able to inspire and enlist. Third, the relevance of the
message it proclaims and lives. This is a sadly neglected factor in most growth
and movement studies. It needs more emphasis. Finally, much depends on the
depth of harmony, smoothness and soundness in relationships, and degree of
adaptation in organization which it is able to attain. Each one of these four
factors seems of equal significance and each one can be demonstrated in the
dynamic movements of today. What we need is a merging of these factors into one
mighty stream and embody them in a movement that will be dynamic, functional,
flexible, continuous, and contagious.

In all of this we want to acknowledge the Holy Spirit, convinced that without
His blessed presence in power and salvation all our labors are in vain. Knowing,
however, that He works through human channels and in keeping with cultural
patterns and social relationships, we want to dedicate ourselves, our knowledge,
and our tools to Him for the glory of God and the salvation of countless people.

(Dr. George Peters is Professor of Missions at Dallas Theological Seminary,
Dallas, Texas.)

Missions Advanced Research & Communication Center
(MARC) is a ministry of World Vision International.
The Center is seeking basically to act as an
information clearing house about the work of
Missions and the Church. It presently has a staff
of fourteen men and women and is engaged in a
number of worldwide survey projects. MARC publishes a bi-monthly Newsletter, which is available
free of charge to those interested in missions.
If you would like to have more information, or
receive a copy of the Newsletter, write to MARC,
919 West Huntington Drive, Monrovia, California
91016.

EVANGELISM CRUSADES AND CHURCH GROWTH   by Edward Murphy
(The providential and urgent current emphasis on evangelism has much to
learn from church growth principles and procedures. We publish Edward Murphy's
important analysis with pleasure. It is a splendid example of the kind of
thinking needed. Mr. Murphy is Field Director for Overseas Crusades in Colombia.)

The Setting
From 1964 to 1967 "Large Scale Mobilization Crusades" was our main activity.
Overseas Crusades, with the help of Rev. Santiago Garabaya and Rev. Luis Palau,
helped many Churches and missions in Colombia carry on purposeful, well-planned
campaigns of evangelism.

Each crusade was preceded by nine months training in the spiritual life.
The whole church was mobilized in open-air evangelism, visitation evangelism and
person-to-person evangelism. Each member of the church was taught the principles
and practice of commending Christ to his relatives and friends. Each church was
also trained in the follow-through ministry, especially in the "Brother's Keeper"
program.

Spectacular growth was granted in many churches. Some showed 100 percent
or more increase in membership after the crusade. Many had 200 to 300 percent
increase in attendance. God gave to Overseas Crusades (our mission) the privilege
of setting forth new concepts of evangelism and carrying on new aggressive ways
of evangelism which missionaries and national leaders had thought impossible in
Colombia. The public began to see the solidity and spirituality of the message
of the Evangelical Churches. The first bold open-air meetings in the history of
Colombia since the times of "The Violence" were held. The first banquets sponsored
by the Evangelical Churches were enjoyed. Thousands upon thousands became
inquirers. In 1966 alone, 8,000 inquirers who had signed decision cards were
counselled. Membership in Evangelical Churches in Colombia grew from 30,156 in
1960 to 63,810 in 1966 and then to 84,487 in 1969.

The following four are typical outcomes:
The Mennonite Brethren Church in Barrio Villa, Colombia, Cali, grew from 11 members
to 50 and has continued to grow.

St. Marks Presbyterian Church in Barrio Popular, Cali, grew from 25 members to 70.

The Cumberland Presbyterian Church in Barrio La Floresta, Cali, grew from an attendance of 40 to 120. Converts from the crusade were being continually baptized.

The United Crusade in the city of Ibague, Tolima, with five Evangelical churches
and five preaching points had spectacular increase. Two thousand inquirers signed
cards. Membership more than doubled.

The Evaluation.
When the criterion used is "continuing membership in the church," we can
begin to see the relationship between the evangelistic campaigns and the real
growth of the Church. Propositions such as the following are clear.

1. With only two exceptions, the greatest growth resulted from single congregation crusades, not city-wide, united crusades.

2. The most blessed local church crusades were held in working-class, barrio churches, while the least blessed were held in downtown or upper middle class congregations.

3. Our first local crusades were all in downtown "city churches." Great numbers of inquirers came forward. The permanent results were small. Both we and the churches were dissatisfied. We blamed them for failing in the follow-up program. They blamed us for not helping them more. We later came to understand that the main failure was in trying to build U.S. style, downtown churches where the responsive don't live, instead of in the working-class barrios where the responsive do live.

4. Neither the churches nor ourselves were prepared for the overwhelming response in number of inquirers. Most "decisions for Christ" were never followed through by the churches. Thus in Ibague where 2,000 decided for Christ, most were not brought into the fellowship of the church. The churches simply did not know how to shepherd this number.

5. In most churches where real growth took place, something approaching real revival had taken place during the pre-crusade period.

6. Most converts who remained in the church already enjoyed some type of living relationship with that church. Some were members of families who were a part of the church, or had been invited by friends. The most successful local church crusades were held in working-class barrios of the great cities. This is the growing edge of the Church in Colombia, and in most of Latin America.

7. The crusades that showed less "fruit that remains" were held in the downtown churches. As our first crusades held in Cali were held in these larger, downtown churches, they were the most disappointing. This was true of our crusade in The Christian and Missionary Alliance, which was the first one we ever held in Cali, and in the Mennonite Brethren which we held in Cali. Though in all of these crusades we had a high number of inquirers contacted, in all of them we had a small result. We have since some to realize that crusades held in these downtown churches must be considered as large scale, seed-sowing, evangelistic approaches. They pick up people off the streets who live all over the city, and even in other parts of Colombia. Thus a great percentage of these people could not possibly ever become members of those churches.

8. Downtown churches are basically inaccessible to the responsive populations of these cities, the working-class people who live out in the lower-class barrios. To attend church, they would have to spend precious money on bus rides every week. This the majority are in no condition to do. Many of them will find their way into local churches in the barrios. But if there are no barrio churches, they will be lost as far as any follow-up program is concerned, no matter how good it may be.

The only exception to this rule has been the crusade held in the Central Presbyterian Church in Cali. Out of about 150 professions of faith there, 45 were baptized three months later; but this was a special church. Central Presbyterian is a middle-class church, consisting of strong family units. Most of the converts were members of the extended families or close friends

of these people. Furthermore, the pastor has been most faithful in putting
into operation the Brother's Keeper program. Since his members were of the
middle class, and since they were working with middle-class converts, an
immediate rapport was established. During the baptismal service, three months
later when 45 new converts were baptized, the pastor asked the "Brother's
Keepers" to come and stand behind these spiritual babes that they had
nourished up to this moment of baptism. Some 35 or 40 church members took
their places behind the converts. It was one of the most emotional baptismal
services that I have ever attended.

9. A good combination of spiritual dynamic and sound church growth principles
    (appropriate strategy in the light of the sociological, economic, and poli-
    tical realities) is required for real church growth. We are therefore giving
    renewed emphasis to the spiritual lives of believers and helping them discover
    their gifts and function in the Body.

We are also emphasizing strategy by holding strategy conferences with pastors
and leaders of the many Evangelical denominations throughout the nation.

BIGGER THAN CONVERTING AN INDIVIDUAL   A note on P. T. Forsyth.

    Sixty years ago P. T. Forsyth preached a sermon on "The National Aspect of
Missions." It was on the occasion of the centenary of Rev. William Knibb, who
apparently was a missionary to the West Indies. This is not important. Forsyth
was saying important things, however. He was struggling with an idea of something
bigger than individual conversion: the winning of large social groups, of nations.
This is a church growth dimension, even though he says it in a different way from
us.

> There is something still higher than conversion either to our creed
> or empire. The sole object of missions is not conversions. Of course
> it seeks conversions, but not that alone ... There is a grander word
> than even "conversion": it is "redemption" .... Knibb, at the call
> of God, had to leave the work of conversion, and take his glorious
> part in the wider work of redemption. He left the converting of indi-
> viduals for the mission of redeeming the whole class. The one
> necessitated the other. He had to become the champion of his converts.
> First he gave the blacks a freedom which made them unfit to be slaves,
> then he had to take from the whites a freedom which made them unfit
> to be masters. Redemption was effected by Christ for the whole race.

    Forsyth pre-dates our discussion on people movements, but he speaks of the
"races within the race" as church growth speaks of "homogeneous units." He saw
that "there is a Christ of nations as well as a Christ of souls."

A.R.T.

DR. FULLER'S DREAM: Dr. Charles Fuller long dreamed of a School
of World Mission at his Seminary. It became a reality in his
lifetime when the I.C.G. transferred from Eugene to Pasadena.
The improvements which came with the transfer are reflected in
the growth of the institution, its enlarged faculty and research
output. After five graduations at Eugene, the next is the fifth
at Fuller. It marks our first academic decade.

CHURCH GROWTH CALCULATIONS: FACTS AND FALLACIES, NO. 1   by Ralph D. Winter

The Church Growth Bulletin focuses on the physical, quantitative, numerical growth of the Christian community. This is not because this is the most easily measured dimension of church growth. Often a static church is failing to grow numerically because of some deficiency in its ministry that can be remedied, and the comparison of its growth rate to that of another church is the most direct and concrete basis on which to mount a search for the solution. Numerical growth may not, in itself be important, but like the number of degrees of temperature a person has, it may point to something else. This use of a numerical growth rate may be termed diagnostic.

Closely related to diagnosis is the need for appraisal and planning. Sao Paulo is building a church auditorium to seat 25,000 worshippers. This project is based on a shrewd analysis of the momentum of a specific movement. With 3,000 new church congregations being formed per year, much planning is involved - not only in regard to buildings, but in respect to leadership training, the development of Sunday School literature, the need for total reorientation of millions of people becoming Christians. But the use of church growth rates for planning is different from the use of growth figures. Diagnosis may employ the measurement of (and comparison between) the growth rates of various denominations or sub-groups within a denomination. Planning requires one to guess about future growth rates and to calculate the potential results.

A wise man is cautious in the measurement of past growth or the prediction of the future growth. Many factors make up growth. Three churches may each begin the year with 100 members and end with 110 members, and thus each have an average net annual growth of 10 percent. But they may have gone through utterly different experiences.

Careful calculation of "growth rate" tells very little about the situation. This does not mean that it is of no use to look at the overall, net growth rate, but it means that a little knowledge is a dangerous thing and other quantitative factors may enter into the picture.

An even more serious trap lies in lumping together statistics from fast and slow growing areas. Slow growth in a single congregation can be disguised by good growth generally in the area. Or, slow growth in a subordinate linguistic unit can be disguised by good growth in other areas where another language is spoken and has become the language of the church. Some Spanish-speaking denominations in Latin America have a minority whose native language is, say, Quechua. By lumping together the growth of both Spanish and Quechua congregations, the specific results in each group disappear. Note that the "average" rate of growth for two disparate communities may be no more useful than, say, the average height of all fence posts and telephone poles in the State of Ohio. The latter figure might come out to be ten feet, yet no single fence post or telephone pole is anywhere near that figure.

Lumping disparate rates of growth together is deceptive in diagnosing the past, and misleading in predicting the future. But that must remain for another time.

COMMUNICATING THE GOSPEL BY DRAMA.   News item by Clyde Cook

These past two summers a group of students from Biola College has presented the Gospel in a vivid way through a play which deals with life after death. Almost 6,000 commitments for Christ have been made after the performances and thousands of others have been brought face to face with the reality of life after death and the importance of their eternal destiny.

We live in a day when many are exposed to the communication media of radio and television, and find preaching either uninteresting or something with which they cannot identify. The effective use of drama to bring preaching into focus in life situations has been proven.

In the play "Revolt at the Portals," six characters arrive at the office of Mr. Peters to determine their final destinations. A busy executive, a hypochondriac, a woman trusting in good works, a sky diver, a hippie and a young college student arrive to discuss their philosophies of life and to hear the verdict regarding their eternal destiny. The portals to the after life - one gold and one black - are evident on the stage. In the first part of the drama the audience is amused by the comedy. As it proceeds it becomes more serious until finally the announcement is made that there is only one true believer among the six. The others argue with Mr. Peters, try to bribe him, declare it was not fair and that they did not know the rules. Peters shows that the way to Heaven had been clearly explained and he restates the Gospel clearly and takes the one through the gold door. Now the others try praying but they are forced to open the black door through which they face eternity without God in a dramatic conclusion.

This play has been presented in many countries in Southeast Asia and India and here are some of the reports:

"The King's Players on the King's Business" reads the headline on the Youth for Christ in India report. It goes on to say, "If statistics could speak, here they are: after some 36 performances in four countries, nearly 1700 out of 14,000 that attended have made commitments for Christ. But statistics are not all for one who has seen the King's Players in action, performing in Calcutta, Madras, Vellore and Bangalore during their brief halt in India - this team of young people from Biola College, U.S.A., has made a deep impact on many more lives."

A missionary writes from the Philippines:

Their ministry is effective. They have more invitations to schools and churches than they can meet. The response is tremendous . . .

One of the purposes of the King's Players is to show missionaries and nationals that drama is an effective mode of evangelism and encourage them to use it in their own ministries. This is more than seed-sowing if given the proper follow-up. The Church grows as nominal Christians and non-Christians alike are confronted with some specific aspect of the Gospel, as we have seen in this case.

CHURCH GROWTH
B U L E T I N

from the
INSTITUTE OF CHURCH GROWTH

Address:
FULLER THEOLOGICAL
SEMINARY
135 N. Oakland
Pasadena, Calif. 91101

DONALD A. McGAVRAN, B.D., Ph.D.
Director

MAY 1970   Subscription $1 per year   Volume VI, No. 5

Jesuits Yes, Presbyterians No!

by Ralph D. Winter

It may seem strange that the Church Growth Bulletin would in the same issue applaud the words of a Jesuit who wrote 200 years ago, and deplore the work of a Presbyterian who wrote only four months ago. Perhaps history is repeating itself. Two centuries ago Protestant theologians had their ponderous reasons for not attempting literally to fulfill the Great Commission--and Father Baegert shot them to pieces in the ringing critique which we include in this issue. (Further remarks below will introduce his material.)

However, shortly after Baegert wrote in 1771, William Carey wrote his famous Inquiry. This was perhaps the first time anyone in history summarized not only all mission efforts up to his time (1792) but also the countries and continents of the entire globe, giving a breakdown of estimates on population and the percentage of Christians. He asked the same question that Baegert raised--why can't Protestants send missionaries? But also, he displayed an unparalleled quantitative grasp of the task yet unfulfilled. This concrete, quantitative emphasis was a solid part of the reason his Inquiry, more than any other document, set off a quarter of a century of extensive structural proliferation in the development of the Protestant missionary tradition, a tradition which in an important sense could really be said to have begun with his efforts.

But today that Protestant effort is staggering and losing its momentum. This reverse development might be forestalled if the March 4, 1970 Frankfurt Declaration were taken seriously. (We hope it will be, and are printing it in full in the July issue of Church Growth Bulletin.) But the slow-down in the older American mission agencies seems inevitable so long as the thinking of their leadership is to any significant degree represented by Dr. James E. Goff. For that reason we must in this issue disagree with a Presbyterian.

We do not comment on Dr. Goff's review of Latin American Church Growth with anything like the pleasure with which we present, further on, the Jesuit article with which we find considerable agreement. Indeed, we count Dr. Goff a friend of the Institute of Church Growth, and the writer has held him in esteem as a personal

SEND correspondence, news, and articles to the Editor, Dr. Donald McGavran, at the Institute of Church Growth, Fuller Theological Seminary. Published bi-monthly, send subscriptions and changes of address to the Business Manager, Norman L. Cummings, Overseas Crusades, Inc., 265 Lytton Avenue, Palo Alto, California 94301, U.S.A. Second-class postage paid at Palo Alto, California.

friend for many years. Nevertheless, the seriousness of his charges compel us
to defend not merely the book but the facts of the case. We thus present the
highlights of his review along with a brief explanation of why we feel it gives
a very unfair--however well-intentioned--and highly distorted picture of a valuable
book which clearly stands in Carey's tradition.

We Disagree With a Presbyterian

Carey achieved many firsts: his Bible translation efforts are among the
most outstanding, and have, since the time of his unique burst of energies, been
imitated by immense programs in many organizations. But his quantitative studies
have been followed by efforts comparatively few and feeble. Last year, however,
there appeared the most extensive quantitative study of the Protestant movement in
any continent outside of Europe: Latin American Church Growth, by Read, Monterroso
and Johnson. It is the result of the collaboration of many people, as well as the
generosity of two mission societies (Presbyterian and Pentecostal--in lending Read
and Johnson), but was substantially made possible by a grant from Lilly Endowment
Incorporated.

Highly important in evaluating Goff's review of this book is an honest recognition of the real purpose of the book. The book is very extensive in its coverage (including seventeen countries) and is more exact despite its wealth of data
than anything else on the subject (religious statistics are notoriously faulty and
fallible). It is vastly more detailed and precise, of course, than was Carey's
Inquiry. But its purposes do not vary one whit from those of Carey.

The comprehensive but highly flimsy facts in Carey's Inquiry eminently served
their purpose. Neither Goff nor anyone else can find statistical flaws in either
Carey's Inquiry or in Latin American Church Growth that allow us to disregard their
theses. The theses cannot be invalidated by a list of minor errors. However, to
our deep chagrin and embarrassment, Dr. Goff's review of the more recent work finds
far more than minor errors and, in fact, claims that as a result the book is "invalidated." Now, we appreciate the immense investment of time which his review has
entailed, and much of it will be of some real help at the time of a second edition
of the book. Meanwhile, however, with genuine reticence and after a good deal of
delay, we have decided both that it will be necessary to warn readers of Goff's
review, and that the substance of our comments will be of interest to all who are
following our various studies of both the physical and spiritual dimensions of
church growth.

Goff's Threatening Arithmetic. On the face of it, Goff's review is admittedly
devastating! His attack utilizes both theology and arithmetic. Let us take the
arithmetic first. The review itself gives three pages to what Goff calls "errors,
contradictions, and inconsistencies on a grand scale," but he has a supplementary
list that runs fourteen pages longer. We must do somewhat the same: the general
readership of the Church Growth Bulletin would not want to take the time to read
through a point-by-point consideration of all his paragraphs. That kind of an
analysis we will be glad to make available to those who write for it. What can we
say here briefly in general?

First of all, we do not deny that there are some internal inconsistencies in
the book. They are not the result of carelessness so much as proof of the fact
that 1) it really is a multi-authored book, (Right up to press time each chapter
indicated which of the three authors had written it.) and, 2) that it was written

over a two and a half year period of time during which many different sources as
well as figures from different dates were collected. In this respect the book
presents something parallel to the Synoptic problem. The differences prove independence of endeavor; the close correspondences strikingly confirm the overall
picture.

On the other hand, the dreadful fact--which it is most painful to point out--
is that in his lengthy review Goff himself makes several monstruous mistakes which
desperately mislead the reader and invalidate a very great part of all that he
says. Basic to his review is his extensive treatment of Chapter Two (which is a
"statistical overview" of the seventeen countries studied) in which are found what
he correctly understands to be "the basic charts in the book." He takes page after
page to scatter these charts to the winds. He boldly claims all of them are wrong
and must be redrawn. But, tragically, practically everything he says is invalidated
by a single error of his own: He apparently did not stop to think that the <u>current</u>
annual growth rate (of either the general population or the evangelical church) cannot and must not be derived by computing an <u>average growth rate over a seven-year</u>
<u>period</u>. On pages 49 and 55 the authors give for the seventeen countries their best
estimates of <u>the current evangelical growth rate</u>, that is, the rate of growth <u>in</u>
<u>1967</u>. On both these pages appear the same column of figures. But when Goff attempts
to check this column, he uses data for 1960, wherever he can find it (in the book or
out of it) and proceeds to calculate <u>the average growth rate between 1960 and 1967</u>.
Then when he finds that only one of the seventeen <u>averages</u> he derives is the same as
<u>the current rate for the year 1967</u> estimated by the authors, he is naturally conster-
nated, and with a sort of holy indignation, uses his own figures to invalidate all
the other charts in the chapter and to cast a shadow on the whole book. He tears to
shreds an accurate map of Chicago because it does not look like St. Louis! This is
so tragic a mistake that a bit of clarification is necessary.

First of all, it is perfectly possible for the evangelical growth rate during
a seven-year period to remain constant (as it did in one of the seventeen countries)
so that <u>the average rate of growth over the whole period</u> (calculated by Goff) could
in fact be the same as <u>the rate of growth at the end of the period</u> (presented by
the book). This is the same as to say that the <u>average</u> speed of a car <u>over a seven</u>
<u>mile trip</u> might, in a given case, be the same as <u>the speed of a car at the very end</u>
of the trip. But it is clearly a great error to suppose that this would necessarily,
or even usually, be true. Proof of this is very simply the fact that fourteen out
of fifteen of Goff's <u>average</u> figures clearly differ from the <u>current</u> figures the
authors give for 1967.

In Dr. Goff's slight favor is the fact that in one of the two instances this
column of figures is given--the first time it is presented (on page 49)--the column
is indeed unfortunately mislabled in a way implying "average" figures. We must be
frank to admit this error and to admit that this erratum might well head the list
for the errata of the book. Moreover, one can well imagine that the unsophisticated
reader of the book might be confused to find the same column of numbers labeled
"current" on page 55. What is very hard to understand, however, is that a highly
sophisticated researcher like Dr. Goff--especially after he himself calculated the
average figures and found them almost all different--would fail to realize that the
second rather than the first column designation was correct. He went to considerable difficulty to round up the 1960 membership figures that are necessary for the
<u>averages</u> which he calculates, but he did not realize that the 1960 figures for any
population of any kind are of no value whatsoever for determining the 1967 <u>current</u>
growth rate. When, for example, in making up his new column he cannot locate 1960

figures for two of the countries, he explains that "the Evangelical Churches in Chile and Venezuela are omitted from this table [his new table] because the Book does not give their 1960 communicant membership. The reader is thus unable to calculate their current Evangelical growth rates." [p.4, Italics mine]

This misunderstanding bedevils almost his entire Review. Thus even when he comes to the end of the book he disputes the 10% growth rate estimated for all of Latin America and does so again by weighing against the 10% figure of the book his own 1960-1967 average calculations, which are simply not relevant. The fact is that the velocity of growth in 1967 was greater than the average for 1960-1967. It is the book, not the Review, that is correct. In fact, in nine out of the fifteen calculations in his new column, he errs in at least the third digit. Almost equally imprecise is he in his later recalculation of "total percentage growth," where four out of fifteen of his numbers are wrong.

It is certainly not our purpose to suggest that the book needs no correction. The alarming tendency in Goff's arithmetic is to make small matters big, or unfairly to interpret the book against itself. For example, the book speaks of a 6.5% growth rate for Chilean Evangelicals as being "conservative." He then calls it an error when the book elsewhere suggests a more realistic 8.5%. But this tendency to exaggerate what errors there are and actually to strain to create still others where they are not is unfortunately not confined to his treatment of the arithmetic in the book.

Goff's Threatening Theology. What is truly amazing about the review is that it offers not the slightest word of appreciation for the wealth of quantitative data that, for the first time, make the outline of the Protestant movement in Latin America stand out in bold relief. But if it seems that the only reason Goff gives attention to the statistics in the book is the opportunity they afford for attempting to undermine the book, this tendency is even more apparent in his handling of the non-statistical statements in the book.

For example, the authors of the book suggest that, in regard to "economic and political disunity" in the Andean republics, "the building of roads..air transportation and radio communication are increasing unification." Goff exaggerates their meaning: "for the authors, simple solutions such as roadbuilding will solve all problems." The authors present a map locating iron and steel industries. Goff makes them say "iron and steel deposits" and then loftily observes: "steel is manufactured, not mined" But their map says nothing about deposits. The last line of their text ahead of this map speaks of "steel production," which is what the map locates. In the midst of many pages written appreciatively of the new developments in Roman Catholicism, the authors say that "one of the positive lessons that Evangelical missions can learn is..." He amplifies their statement to say "Protestants can learn primarily!"

This will sufficiently caution the reader in accepting the review's interpretations at face value. In a certain sense we do not mind the tendency to distort the meaning of the book in order to hold it up to ridicule, since those are false issues. The real issues in Goff's theological approach to the book are those places where he does not need to distort the book in order to disagree with it:

> The church can grow, in other words, if it finds people in trouble..people who are hurting..people in their time of deepest need..(but) what does biblical theology have to say of the practice of taking hold of people where they are not free, of making use of economic, psychological, or sociological pressures for conversion

need..(but) what does biblical theology have to say of the practice
of taking hold of people where they are not free, of making use of
economic, psychological, or sociological pressures for conversion
in order to increase church membership?
This line of objection displays profound ignorance of both the Bible and the
Christian doctrine of God's providence. It was Jesus himself who sought out
those in sorrow and trouble: "Come unto me all ye who labor and are heavy
laden." When the academic churchmen of his day complained that he dealt with
the poor, those in need, Jesus retorted, "I did not come to call the righteous
but sinners to repentance." It is thus no accident that of 13 million Christians in India, 98% have come from the outcaste stratum of population. This is
surely in part simply because man's extremity is God's opportunity.

Perhaps Dr. Goff's personal mission is to express his concern for the poor
through withdrawal into a career of writing about themes of social justice, far
from the raging heartache in the slums of Latin America. But is it appropriate
for him to belittle the Pentecostals who--far more than Presbyterian mission-
aries--are out in those slums demonstrating first-century Christian individual
concern for the confused newcomers to the megalopolis?

We Agree with a Jesuit!

((From 1751 to 1768 the German, Johann Baegert, S.J., was a missionary
among the Indians of Lower California. Two hundred years ago he wrote and in
January 1771 published his famous Observations in Lower California, a translation of which was brought out in 1952 by the University of California Press at
Berkeley.

In Chapter Nine of his Observations Father Baegert, remembering no doubt
his arduous years among extremely primitive people, takes Protestants to task
about their lack of zeal in missions. This he could quite legitimately do, for
the beginning of significant Protestant missions did not occur till some years
later. His pointed questions arise straight out of the Bible. We commend them
to readers of Church Growth Bulletin, urging that they forward this copy to
supporters and friends. Baegert's questions are germane today.

Of course Father Baegert is really arguing that Protestant schismatics
constitute no true Church--as proved by their lack of missionary zeal! With
this, few today--Protestants or Roman Catholics--would agree. The last hundred
and fifty years have seen a tremendous outpouring of converting and gospel-
proclaiming effort on the part of almost all Protestant Churches. They awoke
to missions at different times. (A great American denomination--The Churches
of Christ, two and a half million baptized believers--is only just now beginning
to take the great commission seriously.) But they awoke.

With the kind permission of the University of California Press, we reproduce below Father Baegert's Chapter Nine on its two hundredth anniversary,
because though his main argument no longer applies, it nevertheless constitutes
a timely plea for a costly faithfulness to the mission of God. World evangelization is a difficult, dangerous task which unites all true Churches in the
fellowship of the cross. Many are turning from this blood-marked track and
rationalizing their turning by all sorts of psychological and theological arguments. History for all such is coming full circle.

Some Christian leaders today (both Protestant and Roman Catholic) are
denigrating conversion and preaching that the era of church planting is over.

In certain circles "indifference and tolerance for all religions . . . are increasing from day to day." Leading men to accept the Saviour, accept baptism, and become responsible members of the Church--in some quarters--is accounted disreputable proselytization. Should any part of the Church turn from the glorious task of world evangelization, it would be faced by Father Baegert's embarrassing questions.

Carrying out the great commission is, as Karl Barth has said, one of the marks of the Church. The true Church is always proclaiming Christ and persuading men to become His disciples. The true Church is always seeking the lost and bringing them back to the fold. The true Church believes in conversion--in conversion to Christ who is the Way, the Truth and the Life, the Light of the World, the Bread of Life, the Living Water, and the Resurrection. Father Baegert believed all this--and we believe it too. This is where any valid theology of missions begins.   Ralph Winter, Professor of the History of Missions SWM-ICG))

CHAPTER NINE: SOME QUESTIONS DIRECTED TO PROTESTANTS AND PARTICULARLY TO PROTESTANT MINISTERS   by Johann Jakob Baegert S.J.

Although I am writing a report and not a controversy, I may be permitted to interrupt my narrative and address myself to the gentlemen of the Protestant faith (it may happen that this small volume will get into their hands). In connection with the two California martyrs whose fate was described in the preceding chapter, I should like to ask some questions of the Protestants, and particularly of their ministers, concerning the lack of zeal these gentlemen show in converting heathen. Such conversions are, however, characteristic of the True Church of the New Testament, which does not say: "In viam gentium ne abieritis" (Do not set your feet into idolatrous provinces and lands), but on the contrary: "Go into the world and preach the word of God to all men." The Holy Scripture frequently and emphatically demands of Christian preachers to seek converts. This work of conversion must be carried on in order to conform with the many prophecies . . . .

The Protestants have the best opportunity of carrying out the work of converting nonbelievers in both the West and the East Indies, for there, as everyone knows, their trade and power is very great. It would be much easier for them and they would be more successful than the Catholics, for they have nothing else to preach to the pagans but their doctrine of faith . . . . Nevertheless, I have not heard or read anything up to now about Protestant missions or missionaries in the East or West Indies.

For a long time Catholic circles have been waiting for the first volume of edifying letters from Protestant missionaries, or for a martyrology of Lutheran and Calvinistic preachers who became martyrs in India. However, so far no one knows or can guess when one or the other volume will go to the press or see the light of day. Yet, on the Catholic side, more than thirty volumes of edifying letters have already been published by the Jesuits alone, although this collection was not started until toward the beginning of this century and contains less than a third of the total letters. In their book of martyrs, almost a thousand blood-witnesses can be counted. Yet this order is not so old as Protestantism, and there are perhaps a hundred Protestant preachers to one Jesuit priest . . . .

Therefore, with their permission, I ask these Protestant gentlemen:

First: If the Apostles had remained in their fatherland, sitting at home behind the stove, where would the world and especially our Germany be today? And since the Apostles could neither live forever nor go to every part of the world, they alone could not convert all the heathen, and the growth of the Christian church was thereby limited. But under the guidance and foresight of God, who watches over His Church, the Apostles left successors who would always follow in their footsteps and carry on their work of conversion in accordance with Psalm XLIV: "Pro patribus tuis nati sunt tibi filii." Now where in the Protestant church are such apostolic twigs, such successors of the first Fathers of the Church, who, like the Apostles, would zealously dedicate themselves to the conversion of idolaters and to the growth of the kingdom of Christ? When will one be able to say of the theologians of Wittenberg and Geneva: Their call went out into the world and they have been heard in all the corners of the earth preaching the Gospel to the pagans. (Psalm XVIII.) Daily preachers are born to take the place of Luther and Calvin, but none to convert the heathen; Luther and Calvin were not missionaries either.

Second: I ask, does the definite command of Christ, "Go ye into all the world and preach the Gospel to every creature" (Mark XVI), include the Protestant preachers, or does it not? If it does, why do they not obey, and why do they wish to remain idle spectators of the Catholics, resembling those who buried their talent of silver or those found by the Father to be idling in the market place? On the other hand, if Christ's command has no meaning for them, then they cannot be counted among successors of the Apostles, but only as followers and partisans of Luther and Calvin. That the aforementioned command of Christ does not really concern them seems to be proved, partly by their behavior and their own secret admission, partly by the fact that Christ would endow them with spirit and courage to fulfill this command as he did His Apostles and others. In more than two hundred years, as experience has shown, this has not come to pass; for whatever task God chooses a man, He will give him the means, talents, and strength needed to accomplish it.

Third: I shall not speak of the hundred other prophecies concerning the conversion of heathens. (They would all have to be false if it depended upon Protestants . . . But, may I ask, what of the particular prophecy of Christ in Matthew XXIV that, before the end of the world arrives, the Gospel shall be preached everywhere and to all nations? It is certain that if, on the one hand, the Protestants have the only true Gospel and religion in their possession, and on the other hand, their preachers will not do better in the future than they have done in the past two and a half centuries in preaching the Gospel among the heathen, then the Judgment Day will never dawn. They want no part in the work of converting heathen and, to all appearances, will do even less of it in the future. Among them, indifference and tolerance for all religions and superstitions, including theism and atheism, are increasing from day to day. These deformities, which originated among the Protestants, are nothing but "mali corvi malum ovum," that is, evil fruit from an evil tree. Of course these gentlemen know quite well how to scatter their seed on the already plowed and seeded field of the Catholic Church . . . They catch the fish which are near to the shore . . . yet eagerly avoid sailing on the high, raging sea of idolatry . . . in Canada, China, Japan, Malabaria (India), or in the land of the Caffres.

For such work they have neither courage nor imagination.*

Fourth: I am asking you what do you think of Christ's saying in Luke XI:
"Qui non est mecum, contra me est, et qui non colligit mecum, dispergit," that
is: he who is not with Christ is against Him, and he who does not help Him to
gather, scatters and destroys? The Protestant gentlemen, their clergy as well
as their worldly authorities, truly do not help Christ to bring all the pagans
into the fold of the Church. They let the good shepherd sweat and run, but they
themselves do not lift a foot to lead the erring sheep on the right path and to
unite them under the shepherd's staff of Christ. Their pilots and seamen have
been trying to find a northern route to the Orient for almost two hundred years,
so that their merchant ships may reach Japan and China in less time; but their
preachers do not search for any ways to penetrate into Abyssinia, Tibet, the
Great and Lesser Tartary, there to enlighten age-old heretics or to baptize
idolaters or other unbelievers. What conclusion may be drawn from that? As
was said before, and as Christ Himself has said, the Protestants are not for
Christ; therefore they are against Him. In no way do they help to gather the
heathen into His Church . . . .

Fifth: Good merchandise can be sent into every part of the world; it will
find buyers everywhere. The old philosophic-theological proverb says: "Bonum
est communicativum sui." Why then, if their religion is so evangelical and
good, do the Protestants not seek to introduce it into all parts of the world
and bring the light of Faith to so many nations who live in darkness and in the
shadow of death? Why do the Dutch not only omit preaching the Heidelberg cate-
chism or the canons of their Dordrecht synod in Japan, where they monopolize all
trade, but eagerly conceal their Calvinistic religion before the Japanese? They
deny their religion; they do not wish to be known as Christians, but solely as
Dutchmen. The image of Him, whom they consider their God and Saviour, they even
trample underfoot. How shameful! Never has any greed and avarice brought any
Roman Catholic nation to this! Before the rise of the two new evangelists of
Wittenberg and Geneva, no one would ever have believed it possible that a Christian nation could go so far. This brings no honor to the Calvinistic (or as
they wish to call it, Reformed) religion or its adherents, but should rather
cause them to doubt the quality and truth of this sect which leads the subjects
of a great state to commit such a fantastic, un-Christian, and blasphemous deed.
The English and the Dutch (in particular the latter) trade in all things in all
the corners of the globe, and they will do anything for profit.** Should even
Satan himself have a shipment to any of the four continents, he surely would
find much courtesy in Amsterdam and soon have a ship ready to sail at his
service. The one thing they do not wish to export and bring to the market,
however, is their religion . . . It is certain that all the preachers in Holland
have as little desire as Satan himself to convert one single pagan . . . or to
lead him to Heaven.

---

*The occupation of non-Catholics is not to convert heathen, but to pervert
Christians, said Tertullian more than fifteen hundred years ago (De praescript.
adv. haer. cap. 4).

**The captain of the Dutch ship which took me from Cadiz to Ostend plucked
the chickens and scummed the soup himself.

Sixth: If Protestant preachers fear misfortune and death, and perhaps for this reason lack courage and do not dare to venture among foreign nations and barbarians, why then do they not show any concern for the eternal salvation of their colonial slaves in America and the Negro slaves from Guinea and elsewhere? Surely from them they have nothing to fear. Why do they let them perish like dogs?

There is not one inhabitant (in these colonies) who does not have a slave; some own as many as thirty or more. Up to now little effort has been made to convert these heathen; only a few are baptized; and yet, with small effort, a wonderful community could be assembled from those people, considering that many of the slaves have already a good deal of understanding (of the Christian religion) after so many years of contact (with their masters). Some even have the desire to become Christians, as I have heard from them. But their masters do not permit it, for baptized slaves cannot be resold. Thus writes the Danish Lutheran pastor Boeving in his description of the Dutch colony near the promontory of Bonaespei.

If those preachers of the Augsburg and Geneva Confession are kept at home by their wives and children, if family and house prevent these gentlemen from a voyage to the pagan kingdoms in the East or West, why do they grumble about the Catholic Church and curse her so mightily because she demands celibacy of all those who voluntarily enter her priesthood? Why does their church not wish to remember St. Paul's saying (I Corinthians VII): "I have no command from the Lord as to chastity, but I do advise it"; nor Christ's utterance (Matthew XIX): "Whosoever forsakes his house or field in my name . . ."? Both celibacy and voluntary poverty, though not indispensable, are of service in promoting the conversion of pagans in far distant lands according to the will and command of the Lord. Two big obstacles are thereby removed. The Protestant preacher, however, speaks, as in Luke XIV: "I took a wife, or wish to take one, I have a house, etc., and it is full of children; therefore I cannot . . ."

Hence among the Roman Catholic clergy Christ has His helpers and the Apostles have their faithful successors, in the persons of the missionaries, dedicated to the conversion of heathen. To teach and baptize the unbelievers, the missionaries travel throughout the world, penetrating into regions where no profit-hungry merchant nor daring pioneer has ever been before. They work and sweat with Christ for the salvation of souls; they want to see their Faith spread into all the corners of the world and make Christians of all men, no matter who they might be. Some they instruct and baptize, others they prepare for Heaven; they preach the kingdom of God to those who are nothing to them, from whom they get nothing, and from whom they can expect nothing but death and martyrdom. For the sake of this work, they leave their homeland and, with it, everything, to sail over the seas. Like St. Paul, they fear no dangers, but suffer shipwreck, hunger, and thirst, and dwell in deserts, exposed to ugly vermin. They live among wild beasts and such human beings as are only distinguishable from beasts by their bodies. They risk their lives a hundred times, and spill their blood in a hundred different ways. Meanwhile, the Protestant lip servant puts his hands in his pockets and watches indifferently the horrors of idolatry in so many lands. He lets millions of black and white pagans perish . . . not in the least bothering or thinking of coming to their aid, in spite of God's explicit command to help them and save them from eternal damnation.

Now I beseech the modest and truth-loving Protestant reader to lay aside
all prejudices and, in honor of God, draw his own conclusions and tell me in
all sincerity: Where and on which side is the love of neighbor, the true mark
of the disciple of Christ? On which side, pray, the Catholic or the Protestant,
is the spirit of the True Church? . . . .

THE LAST WORD ON POLYGAMY   by The Archbishop of East Africa

((A year ago Church Growth Bulletin discussed polygamy and church growth,
defending the position that a man with more than one wife, coming to Christian
faith from a society and religion which sanctioned polygamy, should not be
denied baptism simply because of his several wives. We held that there is no
biblical sanction for denying baptism to a polygamous penitent believer.

The Polygamy Issue has excited wide discussion all around the world. Many
have written applauding our understanding of the Bible. No one has written
controverting this position. Some have written to advocate that we did not go
far enough. The Churches, these think, should permit polygamy. Some have
written defending monogamy as the only right system for today. We have printed
some of the feedback; but after this issue we must close these columns for
further comment.

The Archbishop of East Africa has sent in the following comment. We print
it because of the opening sentence of his last paragraph. Truly, the Church
has to work out its teaching against the real situation--and this is no longer
exclusively the old rural tribal setting to which so many speak and which still
prevails for over a hundred million Africans. The Church must take "the new
polygamy" into its reckoning. The distinction between 'the new polygamy,' age-
old adultery, and new-fashioned promiscuity grows less and less.

Church Growth Bulletin, however, has not been talking about the Church's
position on the nature of marriage among Christians. We have confined ourselves
strictly to the one issue: is the possession of several wives, honorably taken
in accordance with law, custom, and prior religion, biblical reason to deny
baptism to a penitent believer? We answer, "NO." We believe the Churches

should at once remove the rules which deny baptism on these grounds to penitent believers. This roadblock to the growth of the Church is not required by the Bible. Once the roadblock has been removed, we are inclined to agree with the Archbishop--the Church should work out its teaching about the nature of marriage against the real situation--in the light of revealed truth, we would add. The Editor.))

THE NEW POLYGAMY

The Church Growth Bulletin for March 1969 (Volume V, No. 4) is largely devoted to the subject of polygamy. The present writer would call attention to some other factors that appear to exercise considerable influence in the changing pattern of marital relations, which are not confined to what has been described as the "missionary societies' preferred package deal for the ending of polygamy," and which are not referred to in the Bulletin.

No reference appears to have been made to some of the basic factors which brought about a polygamous society, that is to say the sociological principles which made polygamy possible and, indeed, inevitable. Among many of the tribes in Eastern Africa it was strongly held that girls at puberty should be accounted nubile and so were married. Men, on the other hand, although accorded certain sexual privileges, were not allowed to marry until after their tribal responsibilities in warfare and defence had been completed. This inevitably meant that the number of marriageable females very considerably exceeded the number of males allowed to be married.

The movement away from polygamy may have been, and in many cases indeed was, brought about as a result of Christian teaching. But it must also be recognised that changing structures within African society itself have influenced the situation. Disparity of age between husband and wife is very much less likely to be significant to the same degree as was the case in old tribal conditions. Economic factors of a different nature now operate; men cannot afford to be polygamous. And furthermore, with the development of education at all levels available to girls, a girl is predisposed to reject an invitation to become a second or third wife to a man already married. Moreover, there are women who prefer to follow a career rather than become a member of a polygamous household, indeed rather than marrying at all.

But side by side with this there is coming into being what may be described, from an African point of view, as "the new polygamy," differing almost entirely from the old.

The first signs of this were seen in the growth of towns and the development of the dual economy. Men came to towns to work for wages, leaving the wife and children to till the family holding. Periodical visits took place, exchanging the money needed by the wife to clothe and educate the children, in exchange for food for the man at work in the town. Protracted separation rarely meant that the woman took another husband, but frequently meant that a man in his loneliness took another, though often temporary, wife, by whom he had children; only to discard, in many cases, both temporary wife and her children when he returned to his rural home.

In more sophisticated circles, the western pattern is being followed. Some professional men are doing what some professional men in Europe and America have been doing for some time. A pretty girl is taken on as a companion after work, often retiring to a bar or club together, then going on to a dance hall. After remaining a "steady" for a time, the girl may be discarded for another; but sometimes they may settle down together without any form of marriage, after a complete rift with the former wife and family has taken place.

It is therefore against the background of the new social patterns in African society that the Church's teaching about the nature of marriage has to be worked out and propagated. And it must be added that women's organisations in Kenya, not directly connected with the Church save only through the membership in the Christian Church of a number of their members, are pressing strongly for monogamy and the stability of family life, as being essential to the future well-being of the children of today, who are the country's citizens of tomorrow.

Leonard, The Archbishop of East Africa.

Latest William Carey Book

The Twenty-Five Unbelievable Years is a concise heartening summary of what has happened in world missions since the close of the Second World War. Many, even missionaries, do not realize how unbelievably optimistic the picture of world Christianity has become during these years. Just what the people back home need, too, since it restores optimism by means of hard facts.

"...it is perhaps unintentionally a brief, readable course in modern world geography and political history...puts the Pope, Billy Graham, the World Council of Churches, the world pentecostal movement, the population explosion, Mao Tze Tung and Biafra into a single picture, and tells us with hard statistics what has happened to Christianity and the World Christian Mission...illuminates crucial issues no one else is even thinking about...a brilliant piece of work." -C. Peter Wagner

120 pages, softbound, $1.95, $2.25 postpaid to any address. Write to William Carey Library.

MUCH NEEDED INFORMATION SERVICE LAUNCHED

Under the capable leadership of Dr. Vergil Gerber, Executive Director, a valuable missions information service is now available to missions executives, missionaries, and professors of missions.

Enclosed is a folder describing how you may avail yourself of the services of the EVANGELICAL MISSIONS INFORMATION SERVICE.

CHURCH GROWTH
BULLETIN

Address:
FULLER THEOLOGICAL
SEMINARY
135 N. Oakland
Pasadena, Calif. 91101

DONALD A. McGAVRAN, B.D., Ph.D.
Director

JULY 1970   Subscription $1 per year   Volume VI, No. 6

MISSION IN SIX CONTINENTS

CHURCH GROWTH IN EUROPE AND AMERICA   by   Donald McGavran

The coming flowering of the Church of Jesus Christ in Europe and America
waits on a clear recognition of the fact that <u>enormous numbers here are living
their lives out of Christ</u>. In a vague metaphysical sense, it may be that, since
God is omnipresent and all men are made in His image, everyone is already 'in
Christ'. But in the vital moral sense and as far as conscious purpose is concerned, it is clear that multitudes are utterly indifferent to God and other multitudes actually hate Him. They neither worship Him nor read His Word. They do
not know His power in their lives. They live in the flesh, knowing nothing of
the Spirit. They do their best to live without Christ. That <u>'enormous numbers
in Eurica are living out of Christ'</u> is, therefore, literally true. Sophisticates
who airily dismiss the fact from their calculations deceive themselves by loose
language.

Till this widespread alienation is recognized, and normal Christians, congregations, and denominations actively seek these lost persons, and woo and pray
them into a conscious redemptive relationship to Jesus Christ, the Church will
limp. Renewal, so greatly talked about, does not consist in nominal Christians
getting a social conscience or in committed Christians joining unbelievers in
good works. Renewal consists in fervent faith in Christ, in intentional union
with the Vine. "Apart from me," said our Lord, "you can do nothing." Apart
from Him - no matter how many your good works - your branches wither, and are
gathered, thrown into the fire, and burned.

Any renewal which does not result in intense effort to win men to personal
faith in Christ and responsible membership in His Church is either truncated or
fraudulent. The first sign of renewal is multitudes of converts, new Christians
and revived old Christians regularly gathering together and devoting themselves
"to the apostles' teaching, and fellowship, to the breaking of bread, and the
prayers." <u>Where</u> they do these things makes little difference. It may be in magnificent church buildings or humble homes, in vacant dance halls, rented rooms,
or in caves! But responsible cells will be formed and will multiply. Church
Growth is an ineradicable concomitant of any renewal worth the name.

SEND correspondence, news, and articles to the Editor, Dr. Donald McGavran, at the
Institute of Church Growth, Fuller Theological Seminary. Published bi-monthly, send
subscriptions and changes of address to the Business Manager, Norman.L. Cummings,
Overseas Crusades, Inc., 265 Lytton Avenue, Palo Alto, California 94301, U.S.A.
Second-class postage paid at Palo Alto, California.

This is why the following article by Donald Gill, describing a determined effort to win New England back to Christ is so important. New England - the home of the pilgrim fathers and the birth place of so much of American Christianity - is full of men and women, boys and girls living without Christ. Any real Church in New England will measure the effectiveness of its new life both by the number of its new members and new Christian cells and by the ardency of their life in Him. The New England Evangelistic Association is spending $100,000 in 1970 and expects to spend $400,000 to this end in 1975. These sums are mere external indications of the blood, sweat, toil, and tears, the days of prayer and yieldedness of will being marshalled in this significant enterprise.

Church Growth is an intensely spiritual and biblical way of looking at life. Church Growth is not a numbers game at all. Rather, it is Christians living under the discipline of theologically sound doctrines. The theological foundations described in the preceding paragraphs and in the article which follow are not unusual among Christians. But they are currently being decried and denied today by very vocal parts of the Church and so it becomes necessary to lift them up and affirm them afresh.

EVANGELISM AND CHURCH GROWTH IN NEW ENGLAND   by
Donald H. Gill, Executive Director, Evangelistic Association of New England.

The primary objective of my first six months in New England was simply to "soak in the situation." There were things we needed to know. Among the points we were primarily interested in were: the climate of the area in regard to evangelism; indications of the relative potential for church growth in urban, suburban and rural areas; resources of the Christian community throughout the six-state area; the history and previous accomplishments of our Association; indications from ministers, our directors, and other Christian leaders as to the role our Association should play in the New England situation.

Those six months led us to the following conclusions:
1) Evangelism and church growth belong together. They compliment each other as separate parts of the total process by which people learn the good news and then join in the fellowship of faith in Jesus Christ. We could see that our strategy for New England would need both. Bradshaw's Church Growth and Evangelism-in-Depth influenced our thinking. As one means of developing a strategy, we entered on a five year consulti relationship with the Office of Worldwide Evangelism-in-Depth. We also began a church growth research and planning function, to be manned by a staff of its own.
2) Personnel resources are crucial. Wherever churches seemed to be growing rapidly we found able, intuitive, well-trained ministers and lay leaders. We noticed these leaders knew where they were headed. They firmly believed that good growth would accompany their efforts and seemed able to plant this conviction in others around them. We began to realize that widescale growth among the churches of New England would depend upon training and developing many more leaders of this sort.
3) Potential for turnaround situations is unlimited. Many churches in New England have been sagging in attendance and in spirit. In some cases this seemed related to sociological problems, in other cases to spiritual disinterest, and in some cases to the parched theological desert in which the congregation was struggling to stay alive. Yet many churches in the last category seemed to be searching the horizon for an oasis, and some were finding it in a solid ministry of the Word. One thing sorely neede is a means of sharing information about churches with a high potential for turnaround, and those already experiencing solutions to specific problems.
4) Minimum essentials for growth. While many factors may affect church growth we identified four without which a congregation would be unlikely to grow. These were:

a. The Evangel -- without the message of God's good news in Christ at the center of the life of a church, growth seemed unlikely. Growing churches tended to be evangelical in conviction.

b. Concern -- growth depends heavily upon a caring fellowship at the heart of church life, in which a substantial proportion of the congregation must be involved.

c. Unity of Purpose -- without a common sense of mission in the community, growth is unlikely. Unless there is a determination to reach out and win new people to Christ, the congregation will live to itself.

d. A Plan -- it seemed possible to have the above three elements and still not grow. Growth required a well-thought-out plan through which the congregation could relate to the community.

While the above conclusions are subject to further testing, we are sufficiently convinced of their validity to begin a program aimed at making effective evangelistic outreach and healthy church growth an observable pattern of Christian life throughout New England. Thus we proceeded to draw up the following program within which specific objectives could be pursued.

Objectives

The ultimate objective of the Evangelistic Association of New England must be to evangelize New England. The command of Jesus Christ to communicate the Gospel to all men allows for no lesser goal. Even our name suggests we take this urgent task seriously.

The proximate objectives may be stated more specifically as follows:
"1. Constantly to challenge the Church to the primary task of evangelism as stated in the Great Commission of the Lord of the Church.

2. To help the Church discover real renewal so that evangelism can naturally and spontaneously follow.

3. By channeling new ideas and fresh methodology to Churches, to encourage and aid them to evangelize vigorously.

4. To be a 'scouting party' for the evangelizing Church, through imaginative experimentation, exploring ways to communicate the Gospel to present, unbelieving society."

Strategic considerations suggest that high priority be given:
"To establishing suburban churches as an evangelical voice proclaiming the Gospel to the present unbelieving society," and

"To supporting the Evangelistic Association as a research and action agency." The following programs seem best suited to achieving these objectives.

Program 1.   Church Growth Research And Planning

Objective:
To assist the Church establish a strategy for effective evangelism and church growth.

Target Market: All New England:
1,500 Churches, 30 Denominations and Area Councils,
Independent Associations (IVCF, Campus Crusade, Young Life, etc.)
Christian Educational Institutions (day schools, high schools, colleges, seminaries and training institutes).

Method:
>   Make studies and analyze congregations and neighborhoods.
>   Encourage congregations to implement them.
>   Plan development of each.
>   Apply the best church growth techniques to each.

Performance Evaluation:
>   The development and adoption by the clientale of the New England market of plans and programs of church growth aimed at this objective and arising out of the use of these and other methods.

Program II.   Personnel Resources Development

Objective:
>   To assist the Church in identifying, improving, and utilizing its personnel resources to accomplish evangelism and church growth.

Target Market:
>   Ministers and Lay Leaders.
>   Youth Workers, Teachers, and Congregations.

Method:
>   Seminars, Retreats, and Conferences such as Congress on Evangelism.
>   Personnel Counselling and Classes such as VBS, Bible Classes, clubs.

Performance Evaluation:
>   Participating in the above.

THE THEOLOGICAL BEDROCK OF MODERN MISSIONS - THE FRANKFURT DECLARATION

March 4th, 1970 is the historic date on which the Frankfurt Declaration was signed by eminent German Theologians and Missiologists. In years to come, it may well be recognized as a turning point in modern missions. The Declaration immediately created a great stir in Germany. Signers - singly and in groups - sent in their names to Dr. Peter Beyerhaus and signed declarations to their missionary societies and church headquarters. Some did not sign but violently opposed the Declaration, charging that the Declaration imported into Germany the fundamentalist-liberal quarrel splitting American Churches. But more favored the Frankfurt Declaration than opposed it.

This magnificent statement of missionary purpose was then translated into English and printed in the June issue of Christianity Today. What had happened in Germany started happening in the United States. Individuals, missionary societies, congregations, and schools of missions. began studying the Frankfurt Declaration, and going on record as believing that it well described essential biblical missions. Denominations printed it in their national magazines.

The Frankfurt Declaration fights today's battles. It speaks to today's deviations and confusions. It is based on the Bible. It states clearly in contemporary terms what biblical principles mean for the Christian Mission to the world. It describes the "insidious falsification of motives and goals" of Churches and missionary societies. It is deeply concerned because of "the inner decay" of Christian faith and action. It sets forth seven Indispensable Basic Elements of Mission and in regard to each declares certain truths and opposes certain errors.

Church Growth Bulletin prints the Frankfurt Declaration in full in this issue. We believe that congregations and mission stations, older denominations and younger denominations, ministerial associations and missionary gatherings will want to study this document. They will duplicate and send it to all mission stations and all congregations. They need not write Church Growth Bulletin for permission to quote it in part or in the whole. The more it is quoted, the better it will serve its purpose.

How to Use The Frankfurt Declaration is the central question. The following ways present themselves.

1. Sign and send to the missionary society of your denomination. This should be done by thousands of individuals. Everyone reading Church Growth Bulletin or Christianity Today should get off a letter at once saying, "I have read the Frankfurt Declaration and heartily desire my Church to carry out this kind of mission." This should be done also by congregations. Missionary societies are sensitive to what congregations want. Any congregation which studies the Frankfurt Declaration, assembles 100 or 500 signatures, and sends them to denominational headquarters and to missionary society headquarters saying, "We have studied the Frankfurt Declaration carefully. It describes the kind of missions we will support. We hope you carry out this kind of missions." will mightily influence church and mission policy.

2. Study the Frankfurt Declaration as an exact description of the fundamental crisis now shaking the Christian world mission and resolve to engage in and pray for the kind of biblical missions described. Let those studying, sign the document and covenant with each other to let these principles of mission guide their future activities. A large part of today's crisis lies in just this fact - that many Christians do not know that some well-known missionary societies have swung over recently to the kinds of activity which the Frankfurt Declaration finds necessary to expose and oppose. The days to give blindly are past. The time has come to give discriminatingly - knowing what the issues are. The Frankfurt Declaration is a concise and well balanced statement of the contemporary issues in mission. Let missionary societies, ministers, and missionary-minded men and women study this profound statement drawn up by ardently Christian and ardently missionary scholars.

3. Teach the Frankfurt Declaration in Bible Colleges and Seminaries as essential to understanding the current world of mission. The Indispensable Basic Elements of Mission are an excellently condensed theology of Christian mission. Each of the seven elements could occupy two weeks, thus providing a semester's course in Theology of Mission.

4. Missionaries in their prayer letters should quote pertinent sections of the Frankfurt Declaration, gradually in the course of a year or two covering the seven basic elements. They would thus educate their supporters in biblical missions. No one is more concerned than the missionaries that mission continue on a sound, biblical base. That which the Frankfurt Declaration denounces and opposes will, if permitted to multiply, gradually diminish sendings of missionaries and proclaiming the Gospel and converting those outside of Christ. The danger is real. Some major boards are already sending fewer and fewer missionaries, engaging in a vast redefinition of mission, and diverting to "many good works" funds given for the evangelization of the world.

5. National leaders and their missionary assistants should translate the Frankfurt Declaration into the leading languages of earth - hundreds of them. It is already in Portuguese and Spanish. It should be taught in Asian, African and Latin American seminaries and theological training schools. Younger Churches should carry out their own missions on these principles. This Declaration should be studied by the Churches of Asia, Africa and Latin America and made the subject of addresses and resolutions at annual conventions and synod meetings.

<u>DR. PETER BEYERHAUS TO VISIT ASIA</u>

Missionaries of the Neuendettelsau Mission in New Guinea and the General Secretary of the International Fellowship of Evangelical Students have invited Dr. Beyerhaus to give lectures in New Guinea and Japan. Dr. Beyerhaus is taking his sabbatical from the University of Tubingen to speak in New Guinea in March and April and in Japan in April and May. He will then return to Germany via Korea, China, Taiwan and Indonesia, reaching Germany in mid-August.

In view of the leading role he has played in framing and circulating the Frankfurt Declaration which so clears the air in regard to the world mission of the Church, many will want to invite him to deliver some lectures in the above countries or others along the way. No one is better qualified to speak on the great theological issues which confront the Church and the missionary cause. Nationals and missionaries concerned about the tendency in many quarters today to "dissociate evangelism and conversion altogether from mission and to assume that mission has nothing at all to do with winning converts or planting churches" (I am quoting Canon Douglas Webster, the Anglican missiologist) might very well invite Dr. Beyerhaus to deliver some lectures on the theological crisis in modern missions and then assemble suitable gatherings to consider the matter.

His address is: Institut fur Missionswissenschaft
Der Universitat Tubingen
74 Rubingen, Den
Hausserstrasse 45, Fernsprecher 71/2592
Germany

BOOKS   BOOKS   BOOKS

William Carey Library Inc., is a Pasadena house specializing in publishing scientific studies of the communication of the Gospel, the multiplication of churches, and the liberation of multitudes into the freedom of Christ. Factual information about what is actually happening in the spread of the Christian Faith is essential knowledge for Churches and missionaries. WCL believes this knowledge must be made available FAST. Publication becomes possible when any congregation, missionary society, or individual puts up money enough to run off 500 to 1000 copies of some sound study. The society or person paying the bill assumes the chief responsibility for distributing or selling the books. In addition to those disseminated in this way, a certain number will be sold through notices such as the following in Church Growth Bulletin and other magazines.

CGB readers should scan these book notices and order several books a year. Nothing opens the eyes to the possibility of church growth, like reading about what God has done and is doing to expand His Church around the world. Every missionary and every minister should read several books a year about communicating the Gospel and multiplying Christian cells in populations other than their own.

Dr. Ralph Winter, Professor of the History of Missions at Fuller's School of World Mission (SWM-ICG), has rendered the cause a notable service in working out a financially feasible way to disseminate scientific studies of the growth of the Churches quickly.

You may order by using the last four digits of the ISBN numbers, e.f. 401-0 in the first book in the list. Five or more books receive a 20% discount, ten or more

are 40% off. But please add 30 cents per book on all orders to cover postage
and handling. (Bookstores are not charged for handling and are billed for the
exact amount of postage. Same discount rate.) California residents must add
5% sales tax. Send order to Wm. Carey Library, 533 Hermosa St., South Pasadena,
California 91030. Join the Church Growth Book Club - get 40% off - see back page.

CHURCH GROWTH THROUGH EVANGELISM-IN-DEPTH, by Malcolm R. Bradshaw.
"Examines the history of Evangelism-in-Depth and other total mobilization approaches to evangelism. Also presents concisely the 'Church Growth' approach to
mission and proposes wedding the two...a great blessing to the church at work in
the world." World Vision Magazine. 1969: 152 pp. $2.45. ISBN 0-87808-401-0

THE PROTESTANT MOVEMENT IN BOLIVIA, by C. Peter Wagner.
An excitingly-told account of the gradual build-up and present vitality of Protestantism. A cogent analysis of the various sub-cultures and the organizations
working most effectively, including a striking evaluation of Bolivia's momentous
Evangelism-in-Depth year and the possibility of Evangelism-in-Depth for other
parts of the world. 1970: 265 pp. $3.95. ISBN 0-87808-402-9

THE CHURCH GROWTH BULLETIN, Vol. I-V, edited by Donald A. McGavran.
The first five years - thirty issues - of this now-famous Bulletin which probes
past foibles and present opportunities facing the 100,000 Protestant and Catholic
missionaries in the world today. No periodical edited for this audience has a
larger readership, or speaks to more current concerns.
    1969: 408 pp. Library Buckram $6.95, Kivar $4.45. ISBN 0-87808-701-X

THEOLOGICAL EDUCATION BY EXTENSION, edited by Ralph D. Winter.
A husky handbook on a new approach to the education of pastoral leadership of the
Church. Gives both theory and practice and the exciting historical development
of the "largest non-governmental voluntary educational development project in the
world today." Ted Ward, Prof. of Education, Michigan State University.
    1969: 648 pp. Library Buckram $7.96, Kivar $4.95. ISBN 0-87808-101-1

THE TWENTY-FIVE UNBELIEVABLE YEARS, 1945-1969, by Ralph D. Winter.
A terse, exciting analysis of the most significant transition in human history in
this millenium and its impact upon the Christian movement. "Packed with insight
and otherwise unobtainable statistical data...a brilliant piece of work."
    C. Peter Wagner. 1970: 100 pp. $1.95. ISBN 0-87808-102-X

PEOPLES OF SOUTHWEST ETHIOPIA, by Alan R. Tippett.
A recent, penetrating evaluation by a professional anthropologist of the cultural
complexities faced by Peace Corps workers and missionaries in a typical rapidly
changing African State.
    1970: 304 pp. $3.95. ISBN 0-87808-103-8

NEW PATTERNS FOR DISCIPLING HINDUS: THE NEXT STEP IN ANDHRA, INDIA by
        B.V. Subbamma.
Proposes the development of a Christian movement that is as well-adapted cultur-
ally to the Hindu traditions as the present movement is to the Harijan tradition.
Nothing could be more crucial for the future of 400 million Hindus in India today.
    1970: 192 pp. $3.45. ISBN 0-87808-306-5

THE CHALLENGE FOR EVANGELICAL MISSIONS TO EUROPE: A SCANDINAVIAN CASE STUDY
        by Hilkka Malaska.
Graphically presents the state of Christianity in Scandinavia with an evaluation
of the pros and cons and possible contributions that existing or additional Evangelical missions can make in Europe today.
    1970: 156 pp. $2.45. ISBN 0-87808-308-1

THE PROTESTANT MOVEMENT IN ITALY: ITS PROGRESS, PROBLEMS, AND PROSPECTS,
    by Roger E. Hedlund.
A careful summary of preliminary data; perceptively develops issues faced by Evangelical Protestants in all Roman Catholic areas of Europe. Excellent graphs. Must
reading for all missionaries to Europe.
    1970: 266 pp. $3.95. ISBN 0-87808-307-3

TAIWAN: MAINLINE VERSUS INDEPENDENT CHURCH GROWTH, by Allen J. Swanson.
A provocative comparison between the older, historical Protestant churches in Taiwan
and the new indigenous Chinese churches. Staggering implications for missions everywhere that intend to promote the development of truly indigenous expressions of
Christianity.
    1970: 216 pp. $2.95. ISBN 0-87808-404-5

GOD'S MIRACLES: INDONESIAN CHURCH GROWTH, by Ebbie C. Smith.
A fascinating, factual account of the expansion of Christianity in the Indonesian
archipelago. Intensely interesting reading. Anthropological context and advance of
the Christian Movement highlighted.
    1970: 216 pp. $3.45. ISBN 0-87808-302-2

LA SERPIENTE Y LA PALOMA, by Manuel Gaxiola. (In Spanish)
The impressive inside story of the Apostolic Church of Mexico, an indigenous denomination (which never had the help of any foreign missionary) as told by a professional
scholar, now Director of Research for that Church.
    1970: 200 pp. $2.95. ISBN 0-87808-802-4

NOTES ON CHRISTIAN OUTREACH IN A PHILIPPINE COMMUNITY, by Marvin K. Mayers.
The fresh observations of an anthropologist coming from the outside provide a valuable, however preliminary, check list of social and historical factors in the context of missionary endeavors in a Tagalog province.
    1970: 71 pp. $8\frac{1}{2}$ x 11, $1.45 ISBN 0-87808-104-6

THE FRANKFURT DECLARATION

on the Fundamental Crisis in Christian Mission

"Woe to me if I do not preach the Gospel!" (I Corinthians 9:16 RSV)
    The Church of Jesus Christ has the sacred privilege and irrevocable obligation
to participate in the mission of the triune God, a mission which must extend into all
the world. Through the Church's outreach, His name shall be glorified among all people
mankind shall be saved from His future wrath and led to a new life, and the lordship of
His Son Jesus Christ shall be established in the expectation of His second coming.

    This is the way that Christianity has always understood the Great Commission of
Christ, though, we must confess, not always with the same degree of fidelity and clarity. The recognition of the task and the total missionary obligation of the Church
led to the endeavor to integrate missions into the German Protestant churches and the
World Council of Churches, whose Commission and Division of World Mission and Evangelism was established in 1961. It is the goal of this division, by the terms of its
constitution, to insure "the proclamation to the whole world of the Gospel of Jesus
Christ, to the end that all men may believe in Him and be saved." It is our conviction that this definition reflects the basic apostolic concern of the New Testament
and restores the understanding of mission held by the fathers of the Protestant missionary movement.

    Today, however, organized Christian world missions is shaken by a fundamental
crisis. Outer opposition and the weakening spiritual power of our churches and missionary societies are not solely to blame. More dangerous is the displacement of their
primary tasks by means of an insidious falsification of their motives and goals.

Deeply concerned because of this inner decay, we feel called upon to make the following declaration.

We address ourselves to all Christians who know themselves through the belief in salvation through Jesus Christ to be responsible for the continuation of His saving work among non-christian people. We address ourselves further to the leaders of churches and congregations, to whom the worldwide perspective of their spiritual commission has been revealed. We address ourselves finally to all missionary societies and their coordinating agencies, which are especially called, according to their spiritual tradition, to oversee the true goals of missionary activity.

We urgently and sincerely request you to test the following theses on the basis of their biblical foundations, and to determine the accuracy of this description of the current situation with respect to the errors and modes of operation which are increasingly evident in churches, missions, and the ecumenical movement. In the event of your concurrence, we request that you declare this by your signature and join with us in your own sphere of influence, both repentant and resolved to insist upon these guiding principles.

Seven Indispensable Basic Elements of Mission

1. "Full authority in heaven and on earth has been committed to me. Go forth therefore and make all nations my disciples; baptize men everywhere in the name of the Father and the Son and the Holy Spirit, and teach them to observe all that I have commanded you. And be assured, I am with you always, to the end of time.
(Matthew 28: 18-20)

We recognize and declare:

Christian mission discovers its foundation, goals, tasks, and the content of its proclamation solely in the commission of the resurrected Lord Jesus Christ and His saving act as they are reported by the witness of the Apostles and early Christianity in the New Testament. Mission is grounded in the nature of the Gospel.

We therefore oppose the current tendency to determine the nature and task of mission by socio-political analyses of our time and from the demands of the non-christian world. We deny that what the gospel has to say to people today at the deepest level is not evident before its encounter with them. Rather, according to the apostolic witness, the gospel is normative and given once for all. The situation of encounter contributes only new aspects in the application of the gospel. The surrender of the Bible as our primary frame of reference leads to a shapelessness of mission and a confusion of the task of mission with a general idea of responsibility for the world.

2. "Thus will I prove myself great and holy and make myself known to many nations; they shall know that I am the Lord." (Ezekiel 38: 23) "Therefore, Lord, I will praise thee among the nations and sing psalms to thy name." (Psalms 18: 49 and Romans 15: 9)

We recognize and declare:

The first and supreme goal of mission is the glorification of the name of the one God throughout the entire world and the proclamation of the lordship of Jesus Christ, His Son.

We therefore oppose the assertion that mission today is no longer so concerned with the disclosure of God as with the manifestation of a new man and the extension of a new humanity into all social realms. Humanization is not the primary goal of mission. It is rather a product of our new birth through God's saving activity in Christ within us, or an indirect result of the Christian proclamation in its power to perform a leavening activity in the course of world history.

A one-sided outreach of missionary interest toward man and his society leads to atheism.

3. "There is no salvation in anyone else at all, for there is no other name under heaven granted to men, by which we may receive salvation."
(Acts 4: 12)

We recognize and declare:

Jesus Christ our Saviour, true God and true man, as the Bible proclaims Him in His personal mystery and His saving work, is the basis, content, and authority of our mission. It is the goal of this mission to make known to all people in all walks of life the gift of His salvation.

We therefore challenge all nonchristians, who belong to God on the basis of creation, to believe in Him and to be baptized in His name, for in Him alone is eternal salvation promised to them.

We therefore oppose the false teaching (which is circulated in the ecumenical movement since the Third General Assembly of the World Council of Churches in New Delhi) that Christ Himself is anonymously so evident in world religions, historical changes, and revolutions that man can encounter Him and find salvation in Him without the direct news of the gospel.

We likewise reject the unbiblical limitation of the person and work of Jesus to His humanity and ethical example. In such an idea the uniqueness of Christ and the gospel is abandoned in favor of a humanitarian principle which others might also find in other religions and ideologies.

4. "God so loved the world so much that he gave his only Son, that everyone who has faith in him may not die but have eternal life." (John 3: 16)
"In Christ's name, we implore you, be reconciled to God!" (2 Cor. 5: 20)

We recognize and declare:

Mission is the witness and presentation of eternal salvation performed in the name of Jesus Christ by His Church and fully authorized messengers by means of preaching, the sacraments, and service. This salvation is due to the sacrifical crucifixion of Jesus Christ, which occurred once for all and for all mankind.

The appropriation of this salvation to individuals takes place first, however, through proclamation which calls for decision and through baptism which places the believer in the service of love. Just as belief leads through repentance and baptism to eternal life, so unbelief leads through its rejection of the offer of salvation to damnation.

We therefore oppose the universalistic idea that in the crucifixion and resurrection of Jesus Christ all men of all times are already born again and already have peace with Him, irrespective of their knowledge of the historical saving activity of God or belief in it. Through such a misconception the evangelizing commission loses both its full, authoritative power and its urgency. Unconverted men are thereby lulled into a fateful sense of security about their eternal destiny.

5. "But you are a chosen race, a royal priesthood, a dedicated nation, and a people claimed by God for his own, to proclaim the triumphs of him who has called you out of darkness into his marvellous light." (I Peter 2: 9)
"Adapt yourselves no longer to the pattern of this present world."
(Romans 12: 2)

We recognize and declare:

The primary visible task of mission is to call out the <u>messianic, saved community</u> from among all people.

Missionary proclamation should lead everywhere to the establishment of the Church of Jesus Christ, which exhibits a new, defined reality as salt and light in its social environment.

Through the gospel and the sacraments, the Holy Spirit gives the members of the congregation a new life and an eternal, spiritual fellowship with each other and with God, who is real and present with them. It is the task of the congregation through its witness to move the lost - especially those who live outside its community - to a saving membership in the body of Christ. Only by being this new kind of fellowship does the Church present the gospel convincingly.

<u>We therefore oppose</u> the view that the Church, as the fellowship of Jesus, is simply a part of the world. The contrast between the Church and the world is not merely a distinction in function and in knowledge of salvation; rather, it is an essential difference in nature. We deny that the Church has no advantage over the world except the knowledge of the alleged future salvation of all men.

We further oppose the one-sided emphasis on salvation which stresses only this world, according to which the Church and the world together share in a future, purely social, reconciliation of all mankind. That would lead to the self-dissolution of the Church.

6. "Remember then your former condition:...you were at that time separate from Christ, strangers to the community of Israel, outside God's covenants and the promise that goes with them. Your world was a world without hope and without God." (Ephesians 2: 11-12)

We recognize and declare:

The offer of salvation in Christ is directed without exception to all men who are not yet bound to Him in conscious faith. The adherents to the nonchristian religions and the world views can receive this salvation only through participation in faith. They must let themselves be freed from their former ties and false hopes in order to be admitted by belief and baptism into the body of Christ. Israel, too, will find salvation in turning to Jesus Christ.

<u>We therefore reject</u> the false teaching that the nonchristian religions and world views are also ways of salvation similar to belief in Christ.

We refute the idea that "Christian presence" among the adherents to the world religions and a give-and-take dialogue with them are substitutes for a proclamation of the gospel which aims at conversion. Such dialogues simply establish good points of contact for a missionary communication.

We also refute the claim that the borrowing of Christian ideas, hopes and social procedures - even if they are separated from their exclusive relationship to the person of Jesus - can make the world religions and ideologies substitutes for the Church of Jesus Christ. In reality they give them a syncretistic and therefore antichristian direction.

7. "And this gospel of the Kingdom will be proclaimed throughout the earth as a testimony to all nations; and then the end will come." (Matthew 24: 14)

We recognize and declare:

The Christian world mission is the decisive, continuous saving activity of God among men between the time of the resurrection and second coming of Jesus

Christ. Through the proclamation of the gospel, new nations and people will progressively be called to decision for or against Christ. When all people have heard the witness about Him and have given their answer to it, the conflict between the Church of Jesus and the world, led by the Antichrist, will reach its climax. Then Christ Himself will return and break into time, disarming the demonic power of Satan and establishing His own visible, boundless messianic kingdom.

We refute the unfounded idea that the eschatological expectation of the New Testament has been falsified by Christ's delay in returning and is therefore to be given up.

We refute at the same time the enthusiastic and utopian ideology that either under the influence of the gospel or by the anonymous working of Christ in history, all of mankind is already moving toward a position of general peace and justice and will finally - before the return of Christ - be united under Him in a great world fellowship.

We refute the identification of messianic salvation with progress, development, and social change. The fatal consequence of this is that efforts to aid development and revolutionary involvement in the places of tension in society are seen as the contemporary forms of Christian mission. But such an identification would be a self-deliverance to the utopian movement of our time in the direction of their ultimate destination.

We do, however, affirm the determined advocacy of justice and peace by all churches, and we affirm that "assistance in development" is a timely realization of the divine demand for mercy and justice as well as of the command of Jesus: "Love thy neighbor."

We see therein an important accompaniment and verification of mission. We also affirm the humanizing results of conversion as signs of the coming messianic peace.

We stress, however, that unlike the eternally valid reconciliation with God through faith in the gospel, all of our social achievements and partial successes in politics are bound by the eschatological "not yet" of the coming Kingdom and the not yet annihilated power of sin, death, and the devil, who still is the "prince of this world."

This establishes the priorities of our missionary service and causes us to extend ourselves in the expectation of Him, who promises, "Behold! I make all things new." (Revelation 21: 5 RSV)

Unless otherwise indicated, biblical quotations are taken from the New English Bible.

This declaration was unanimously accepted by the "Theological Convention," a regular meeting of theologians who want to be faithful to scripture and confession, at their session on March 4, 1970, in Frankfurt, West Germany.

Among the first signers are the following:

Prof. P. Beyerhaus, Th.D., Tubingen   Prof. O. Michel, Th.D., Tubingen
Prof. W. Bold, Th.D., Saarbrucken   Prof. W. Mundle, Th.D., Marburg
Prof. H. Engelland, Th.D., Kiel   Prof. H. Rohrback, Ph.D., Mainz
Prof. H. Frey, Th.M., Bethel   Prof. G. Stahlin, Th.D., Mainz
Prof. J. Heubach, Th.D., Lauenburg   Prof. U. Wickert, Th.D., Tubingen
Herr Dr. A. Kimme, Th.D., Leipzig   Prof. J. W. Winterhager, Th.D., Berlin
            Prof. W. Kunneth, Th.D., Ph.D., D.D., Erlangen
            Prof. G. Vicedom, Th.D., D.D., Neuendettelsau

CHURCH GROWTH
BULLETIN

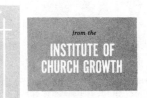

from the
INSTITUTE OF
CHURCH GROWTH

Address:
FULLER THEOLOGICAL
SEMINARY
135 N. Oakland
Pasadena, Calif. 91101

DONALD A. McGAVRAN, B.D., Ph.D.
Director

SEPTEMBER 1970   Subscription $1 per year   Volume VII, No. 1

Notable Church Multiplication in Colombia

by Charles Bennett
SWM-ICG '66
Director of Research, Missionary Aviation Fellowship

Three years ago the mainly urban-centered Presbyterian Church of Colombia*
decided to look at its long-neglected, rural congregations· in the northwest.
It gathered detailed information on the area, its people and fifteen existing
congregations, then invited three outside consultants to help them evaluate
the data.

Most of these congregations had suffered greatly during the civil war of
the 1950's and were discouraged and thoroughly convinced that they could do
nothing until missionaries or educated ministers returned to pastor them.
The believers in three lowland congregations, however, showed signs of vitality
and optimism. Their new life was due in large part to contacts with the
nearby, spontaneous Cauca River Movement (related to the Latin America Mission)
which, on a thoroughly indigenous basis, has started eighty-two congregations
in a little more than a decade.

The study commission decided to concentrate available resources on the
three lowland congregations and to have all highly trained personnel--two

---

*In 1968, the Presbyterian Church of Colombia, with a total communicant
membership of 1,882, in 46 small congregations (average 32 per congregation)
was a sick, younger Church. Since it reported 1,500 communicants in 1952, it
was growing at only 17 percent per decade, which means that it was not
conserving all its own children. It is thus typical of many sick, little
denominations in Latin America and other continents. Mr. Bennett's account
of 'notable growth' is newsworthy because it shows one way in which such
Churches, afflicted with the disease of slow growth, can, at least to some
degree, recover their health. Everything the Presbyterians did, any Church
could do. The account is rich with insight.   Donald McGavran

SEND correspondence, news, and articles to the Editor, Dr. Donald McGavran, at the
Institute of Church Growth, Fuller Theological Seminary. Published bi-monthly, send
subscriptions and changes of address to the Business Manager, Norman L. Cummings,
Overseas Crusades, Inc., 265 Lytton Avenue, Palo Alto, California 94301, U.S.A.
Second-class postage paid at Palo Alto, California.

missionaries and one Colombian pastor--act as resource people to aid the local lay leaders, rather than assume direct leadership themselves.

They emphasized church planting, agricultural improvement, and education. The goal was effectively to evangelize the region, help the people solve urgent social problems, establish a self-sustaining presbytery, and withdraw outside personnel and funds at the end of eight years. These goals and the eighteen basic presuppositions of the project were defined clearly and distributed to all involved. Perhaps the most crucial presupposition was that mature local believers, rather than highly educated Colombians and Americans (outsiders) were to set priorities for the churches.

In less than three years since the project began the number of Presbyterian congregations in the northwest has jumped from fifteen to thirty-six. Baptized adult members have increased from 295 to only 390, but the Presbyterian community has much more than doubled and now numbers at least 2,200. Many will be ready for baptism soon, including 57 couples trying to meet the complicated Colombian requirements for civil marriage. Most of the growth, predictably, has been sparked by the wide-awake, lowland congregations and may be considered an extension of the Cauca River Movement led by Victor Landero; but the formerly introverted, highland churches are learning by example and have started a few congregations of their own.

The new congregations do not act like traditional Presbyterians. Some are more like Pentecostals. They go in for guitars, hand-clapping, faith-healing and occasional instances of "tongues." Enthusiastic lay workers, paid and unpaid, are constantly on the move. One man leaves clothes to be washed in three different places so he will not be delayed. None of the churches have resident ordained pastors; but one church with no resident pastor of its own insists on paying a full salary to one of its lay leaders so he can visit the new congregations the church has started.

The traditionally educated ministers of the national synod have been quick to accept the validity of the new emphasis and have authorized the elders of three rural churches to administer the Lord's Supper without the presence of a minister. An experimental lay presbytery for the northwest is under study and will be launched probably next year, four years ahead of schedule. An extension leadership training program geared to the local situation to prepare rural churchmen for ordination, is already under way and has full approval of the synod. All this is good church growth procedure and is to be found in some form in most rapidly growing Christward movements around the world of which the research director of the Missionary Aviation Fellowship sees many.

Missionary Aviation Fellowship soon will locate plane and pilot in the midst of the churches to extend the ministries of the local leaders of both the Presbyterian and the Latin America Mission-related congregations as they press on, preaching Christ and persuading men and women to become His disciples and responsible members of His Church, engaged in "doing good to all men."

The dynamic for the rapid expansion of the Presbyterian churches has not come from the formal eight-year program designed to serve the whole man. On the contrary, contacts with the Cauca River Movement have provided most of the impetus for church-planting evangelism and charismatic manifestations. The eight-year program, however, has given freedom and encouragement to the lay leaders, helped them in their attempts to improve local social conditions, and is beginning to train some for the ministry and others to meet the challenges of the future. The thirty-six present congregations are only the beginning. Bright hope exists for the future, provided that the older

Presbyterian leaders and the new can center their affections on the trend of church pattern which, on spiritual resources available to soundly converted country people living in Christ, is indefinitely reproduceable.

OF WHAT BRANCH OF THE CHURCH IS THIS WRITTEN?*

"Only very marginal efforts have been made hitherto to relate the studies in most missionary [training schools] to the specific work missionaries are meant to be preparing for . . . . The serious study of ethnology is almost entirely ignored. It still seems to be felt that a missionary society is doing well if it sends a few of its brightest members to obtain (advanced) degrees, whereas perhaps 50 percent of its members need a first degree and the abler ones need a Ph.D. What is urgently necessary is to have men who can a) bring the most developed modern sciences, particularly ethnology and sociology, to the service of the Church and the shaping of her work: and b) to secure appointments in the new universities of Africa and so exercise apostolate in that milieu . . . c) train Africans in our seminaries in a similar way to share confidently in the leadership of the new graduate society . . . . At present such men hardly exist--not because there is insufficient ability within these missionary societies, but because neither missionary [administrators] nor church [executives] have yet come to realize the academic level which a fair number of missionaries now need to attain." (Adrian Hastings, Church and Mission in Modern Africa, p. 48)

*Answer in third box in this issue.

WHY DO SOME CHURCHES GROW WHILE OTHERS DO NOT?   Taylor Pendley, SWM-ICG '70 Secretary of Church Building and Pioneer Missions of the Baptist General Convention of Texas.

((Mr. Pendley administers a church-planting program in Texas and Minnesota-Wisconsin. He led in planting 54 churches in Dallas County, Texas in the 1950's. Intrigued by the School of World Missions' dedication to propagating the Gospel overseas, he came here for two quarters of graduate study and research. We encouraged him to interview growing churches in California. One part of what he found forms the article which follows. It has meaning for missionaries and ministers of all lands. Most of the factors he names as influential in church growth would apply, in somewhat different forms, to be sure, in most cultures.   The editor))

California, the land of smoggy sunshine, crowded freeways, and wall-to-wall people, has churches of many varieties. Some are experiencing rapid growth while others are static. What makes one church grow while another does not?

Answers might lie in location of building, availability of parking, or income sufficient to provide staff and program. Doubtless these do help a church to add new members, but some churches with all these ingredients do not grow. Why?

To obtain an answer to this question, during my two terms at SWM-ICG, I asked pastors and laymen in greatly growing churches a series of questions. I was given a close look at the whole operation by most gracious pastors and their assistants.

Growing churches varied in size from 100 to 8,700 members. One had an attendance of 15,600 at four morning worship services on Easter Sunday, 1970. The smallest had its beginning two years ago in a multiracial community where another church had failed in the same building. Over 100 converts have been baptized in the two years, while only 10 have been received from other churches. The oldest, now-growing church had its beginning seventy-five years ago. All these churches classify themselves as "conservative-evangelical."

One of the questions was, "When did your church begin to grow in a noticeable manner?"

Some of the answers were:
"When we found out where people hurt and ways to help them."
"When we quit begging people to come to us and instead, went to them." (Layman)
"When we realized that the people in the community didn't care whether we lived or died [in fact, one church had died and no one even noticed], we decided it was time for the church to see what could be done to help people find new life through belief in Jesus Christ."
"We discovered that 50 percent of the people in our community didn't claim any religious affiliation. We sought to get acquainted with these people and to minister to their needs. Most did not know that God or anybody cared for them. We have tried to help them be what God wants them to be."
"We found that busy businessmen in our area didn't know the first principles of Christian love. We have helped these people overcome biblical illiteracy and through small groups, have sought to teach them how to know the warmth of genuine Christian love and fellowship. It works; we have our building full at each of three services every Sunday morning. Rather than go deeper in debt, we are planning two week-night sermons that will duplicate the Sunday morning service."

Another question asked was, "What unusual things do you do that cause your church to grow?"

I visited a "Walk-In, Drive-In Church." It has accommodations for 1,700 people inside the sanctuary and 1,000 on the lawn. Seven hundred cars can park in the terraced lot. People can worship, listening to the sermon on their radios as they view the minister through a 25-foot opening in the glass wall. This church is receiving an average of 900 people per year into the membership. Sixty-five percent of these either have no church affiliation or have been out of church more than ten years. Hundreds of the 7,000 worshipers are not members, but attend regularly.

Another growing church uses a bus to bring people to church. After two months of operation, Sunday School and worship attendance increased by 80 people. Plans are being made to purchase additional buses. A "bus captain" visits the communities and arranges the time when the bus will come to the door for the riders. Several churches I visited provide transportation of some type.

One church has been using a "Code-A-Phone" ministry for eleven years. It has found this the best source for prospects. People who have problems call the "Strength for Today" number and hear a recorded message. All members are encouraged to pass the telephone number on to people with whom they come in contact. Recently the pastor, in his recorded minute-and-a-half sermonette, invited the caller to pray with him and accept Christ. Forty-one people prayed into the phone. Each prayer was recorded and laymen went to see the forty-one. Those with the most difficult problems were referred to the pastor.

Two churches operate a 24-hour telephone service to help people who are lonely, have suicidal tendencies, are "hooked on dope," and are troubled about a multitude of other things. Men and women operate the service on four-hour shifts. Each gives four hours one day each week. All have been trained by licensed counselors. One church receives an average of 180 calls each week.

One growing church asks each new convert to have a seven-week Bible study in his home, with a lay person from the church as teacher. The new convert is requested to invite all his old friends to him home to share in the study. This has helped new converts to keep their friends and introduce them to Christ. This church also provides cassettes of the pastor's sermons. Volunteers have purchased these tapes and recorders which they take to interested friends so they can listen to the sermons in the privacy of their homes. Many conversions have resulted from this ministry.

Churches which are growing are making good use of Bible studies, meeting at times convenient to the people; using laymen and women to witness; preaching simple sermons; and are trying new ways of getting into touch with people. Pastors of growing churches move ahead with "possibility thinking." Negative thinking does not seem to be a part of them. Could some of these things make your church grow, too?

JUST BEFORE CHRISTMAS

May we tender a suggestion to American readers? Your friends in Brazil, Ethiopia, Indonesia, or elsewhere, would value a year's subscription to Church Growth Bulletin. Highly relevant reading! Geared to the central drive of all missionary labor! Whether a missionary is a nurse, educator, literature expert, bishop! doctor!! or mother superior!!!, he or she is vitally concerned about the communication of the Good News. And that is what Church Growth Bulletin is all about. Issue after wonderful issue sets forth examples of church multiplication, roadblocks to effective missionizing, and how to remove them, principles of communication involved in evangelism, and how to help evangelism, medicine and education result in men and women, boys and girls becoming responsible members of Christ's Church. That's the goal!

And, by the way, Christmas is coming. Why not drop Norman Cummings a line at 265 Lytton Ave., Palo Alto, California 94301, give him the addresses of a couple of your missionary friends, and ask him to send them a sub-scription--starting with this September issue? It will reach them just before Christmas.

Oh, yes, please enclose the check: one dollar for each address!!

MISSION EXECUTIVES ATTENTION PLEASE

In recounting eight things missionary societies must do to survive in the seventies, Dr. Davis emphasizes point 6 as follows:

"6. Recognize that the product is the important thing, not the machine. The spread of the Gospel, the establish-ment of the Church, is the reason for our being, the reason people join our organization, give us their money, and pray for our success." (Raymond J. Davis, General Director Sudan Interior Mission, Evangelical Missions Quarterly, Summer 1970, p. 225)

PACIFIC PANORAMA   by Alan R. Tippett

((Dr. Tippett has been engaged in a four-month research concerning the impact of Christianity on the islands of the South Pacific. So much nonsense has been written about the missionary movement in that area, that a factual study seemed overdue. In the following article, Dr. Tippett tells in a very brief, preliminary way, how the islands have become solidly Christian, missions have changed into Churches, and Christians are playing an essential part in the changing world.   The editor))

My project was a diachronic study of Pacific missions through history, not a synchronic analysis of the Pacific today after 150 years of missionary enterprise. I was concerned with documents in libraries and archives rather than current operations. Nevertheless, I did observe national Churches at work in Hawaii, Fiji and Tahiti.

I

A Waikiki tourist newspaper gave its front page to the Sesquicentennial celebrations of the arrival of the first missionaries in Hawaii. The article began: "Visitors to Hawaii right now have a once-in-a-lifetime opportunity to step into Hawaii's non-Michener past . . ."--a neat implication, articu-lating what Hawaii in general thinks about the misrepresentations of the novel and film Hawaii.

I worshipped in the beautiful Kawaiahoa Church, whose architect was Hiram Bingham. It is currently under the ministry of Dr. Abraham Akaka, a highly respected Hawaiian public leader, himself the fruit of the early mission. The church and its worship service, though bearing some marks of acculturation, nevertheless preserve many Hawaiian cultural values and are run by Hawaiians.

I also attended the dedication (re-opening) of the Mission Houses Museum. To pass through these buildings is to have their history reconstructed through the various focal points of material culture. The missionaries who lived there and used these things become alive and assume their authentic places in history. One sees how they lived, studied, translated and maintained their devotional lives. One discovers what they really did for the Hawaiians through education, printing, literature and religious teaching aids. One shares their suffering and excitement because the guides who escort you know the history and have read the missionary journals.

By way of a specific missionary presentation, the Sesquicentennial Committee organized a re-enactment of the landing of the first missionaries, the party entering the bay in a brig similar to the Thaddeus. The presentation was based on the journal of the voyage. A 24-page booklet of entries selected from that journal was distributed to the large crowd on the shore. The mission party, complete in 1819 costumes, came ashore to narrate their experiences to modern radio and T.V. interviewers. Dr. Akaka, speaking on "Why I'm glad they came!" pointed out that the destruction of the pre-Christian religious system before the missionaries arrived deprived the people of the normal mechanisms of decision-making and for judging right from wrong. He said they were on their death-bed, unless they could find a new way. The message the missionaries brought met an urgent need.

The Church in Hawaii today has bilateral outreach. In Honolulu, a modern American city, it maintains a delicate balance between the modern world and Hawaiian values, offering a way of Christian expression to urban Hawaiians. The other dimension is nearer the folk-way, expressing an enthusiastic faith in traditional rhythms under itinerant preaching. More than a century ago the Church became autonomous and carried on its own missions in the undiscipled populations of Polynesia and Micronesia.

Only ten thousand pure Hawaiians survive today plus a hundred thousand part-Hawaiians. The Caucasians treble that and the Japanese double it, not to mention Filipinos and Chinese. These migrants have brought more than denominations; they have brought the religions of Asia. One informant said, "Hawaii is still a mission field."

ii

Fiji has a quarter of a million pure Fijians, of whom about 90 percent belong to one Christian Church. I confine my observations to that one denomination. It is strongly organized with a well-distributed ministry and a highly developed congregational participation at all levels. It cultivated indigenous elements from the beginning, and if its progress has been retarded at any point it has been due to traditionalism rather than foreign paternalism. The social and church structures bear strong resemblances. As in Hawaii, one finds more

acculturation and innovation in the urban centers and tradition is stronger
in the rural areas. The Church is quite autonomous and affiliated with the
original overseas sending Church with equal conference status. Any Australian
appointed to Fiji today is a member of the Fiji Conference and subject to its
authority and discipline.

Social involvement in the community is also well-developed and an active
program of youth work extends to the furthermost island. The concepts of
responsible stewardship at home and missionary outreach beyond are both strong.

Of course, the Fijian Church has her share of problems, but if she fails
to handle them wisely it is not for the want of institutional apparatus, which
is geared for religious and social action, through indigenous leadership at
all levels. Her current problems stem from rapid social change, urbanization
and race relations. As in Hawaii, the last century ended and this began with
massive indenture of plantation labor, upsetting the social and ethnic balance
and creating problems of population distribution and land tenure.

Two hundred and fifty thousand Indians, Hindus and Moslems live in Fiji.
About 4,000 of them belong to the Church I am describing and have independence
in regional congregations and a central synod, which permits them to handle
business in terms of their own cultural values. In conference they meet with
the Fijian Church and together they have a burden for the evangelization of
the Hindus.

In the Fijian villages one finds a truly ongoing Church without missionary
supervision. I found people using devotional aids I had written myself more
than a decade earlier. However, new material was coming out, prepared by
Fijians, and I knew the need for mine was nearly finished. Here is Henry
Venn's principle of euthenasia: the mission dies that a Church may be born;
the missionary vanishes that local ministries may emerge. I visited the old
seminary where once I taught. Several of my students were now in key positions.
They opened the door for their old teacher to speak to them, but I knew I was
no longer their teacher. They were the men with their hands on the controls.

One thing I fought for but never saw in my day was a central theological
seminary for the South Pacific, for select men from each field to train
together in the Pacific context rather than America and Australia. With this
I envisaged a university and occasionally was quoted in the press for saying
so. Both these institutions are realities today. One of our SWM-ICG men
(Lopeti Taufa) is on the faculty of the former. He has his men reading about
church growth and has introduced new dimensions of field research into his
courses.

III

The story of the Church in Tahiti is difficult to narrate. I know it
best through the documents. With that background Tahiti came to me as a
shock, because the original church planting was done by English Congregation-
alists and the first thing that strikes you when you arrive is the French-ness
of everything. This is the land of Cook and Wallis and Bligh. The early
mission records, the narrative of the conversion of the people from paganism,
and the cultural descriptions are all English. Then suddenly across the pages
of history a shadow falls, which some historians call "French aggression."

The L.M.S. missionaries found it impossible to operate as British Protestants under what they called "the bishop and the gunboat" and thus in the course of time their work was passed over to a French Protestant mission. This eliminated the British-French issue and left the Roman Catholics and Protestants face to face under French rule, language and orientation. Today everything is thoroughly French. Bougainville has replaced Cook; the British Consul, Pritchard, is the villain; characters noted for duplicity in the British-French struggle have streets named after them and the missionary who accepted French rule and stayed on is better remembered than men who did far more for the growth of the Church. Catholicism grew with the political impetus and Protestantism first declined--and then recovered--but as a French Church.

Consequently Catholicism and Protestantism co-exist today in reasonable balance (the latter a little stronger) recognizing each other with some ecumenicity in relationships and promotional material.

I was in Tahiti on my second visit for Bastille Day (the 'Day' lasts for ten!). Papeete harbor was filled with French warships and the waterfront with gambling booths. One realizes how, under the French, so much old Polynesian permissiveness remains. It is here the French Church confronts the world. My <u>official</u> program of the Fete announced:

"Papeete's Fete is a blast. It's more inebriated than the most endless fraternity party. It's more hip-swinging than the hippiest twist . . . [These superlatives apply, of course, only to those with the prior credentials of baptism into what makes Polynesia an endlessly interesting and pleasing experience.]
"The Fete in the outer islands is based on the same inclination to revelry--song and uninterrupted fun. Its deadset purpose is the same unhindered dash to fertile abandon . . . thrust into life's loose pleasures . . . the partying of the world's freest people . . ."

The Tahitian Christians have to witness in a permissive world which smiles on sex, gambling and drunkenness. These are their social problems. The Church reacts with counter functions--the annual collection, the watch-night, the blue cross (pledging) and competitive performances--by which, "the way of the church people" is marked off from that of "the outside people. The Bastille Day sideshows cater openly and almost entirely for drinking and gambling. The Church says that excess (drunkenness and gambling that affects others) should be pledged against. It is the old Polynesian value of <u>taboo</u>.

Unsolemnized 'marriage' is common and an old Tahiti pattern. Sometimes a parish has so many unmarried couples with families that a communal ceremonial 'clean-up' is organized to legalize the existing situation. This is not to justify the practice but to give these families real entity. Feasting follows. This is a real attempt to deal with the tragic problem that 50 percent of the Tahitian couples are not legally married. The Tahitians set a high value on their Church, are devoted in their care of the buildings and do draw on its pastoral and congregational resources in facing their problems.

IV

In Hawaii, Fiji and Tahiti there is an active Church in the community. These three environments and their problems differ. Each Church is unique in its confrontation with the world. They differ because of historical conditioning--international rivalry, internal politics and theological emphasis. Scars of the XIXth century are still manifest, but the missionary effort has always planted a Church in the human situation.

Each of these localities has been drastically modified since the first missionary parties arrived, due to western commerce and migrations from Asia. Currently in each place the main emerging acculturative factor is tourism with its new complex of problems and its new forms of western ethnocentricism.

Yet the Christian mission is still relevant. The mission stations have gone, replaced by indigenous Churches which arose some generations back, by people-movements, usually on a basis of villages, large extended families, or even whole tribes. The new evangelism of the Pacific will still need to deal with groups, but often they will be smaller units because migrant family structures go back only a generation or two, and caste among the Indian immigrants has vanished in Fiji. But, because no generation can live on the experience of its fathers, because the Asian migrants were largely the animistic levels of the Asian religions and because of the rapidity and continuity of culture change, although the Pacific is very different today from that discovered by the first missionaries, nevertheless it is still a mission field. In parts of Melanesia, the New Guinea Highlands, North Australia and Indonesia, the Pacific Churches have their overseas missions today as well as those mission fields at their own doors. And some of these fields are certainly ripe to harvest. Indeed, the documents show that there never has been a time since missionary enterprise first entered the Pacific when there was not some field ripe and calling for harvesting.

WHY TRAINING NATIONALS AS PASTORS AND MINISTERS HAS LAGGED

"The second reason [why training a national ministry has been delayed] is that the training for priests imposed by the Council of Trent was far too hard for new Churches. It just was not possible to establish Tridentine standards of seminary formation . . . in many mission lands. A few priests might be trained in this way, but by and large it was not possible. Mechanisms suitable for adult Churches, and indeed for adult Churches of a particular character and culture, were being imposed under quite different conditions. The human character of the ministry and ways of training for it must vary and do vary according to the society and the condition of the Church in which it has to function, and norms which could apply fruitfully to the old Christian countries of Europe simply stifled growth when applied in mission lands." (Adrian Hastings, Church and Mission in Modern Africa, p. 23. Fordham University Press, 1967 $5.50) ((This same reason stifles much Protestant growth, too.
The editor))

LIVINGSTONE: INNOVATOR OF INDIGENOUS IDEAS   by Richard Hostetter

David Livingstone, in the 1840's and 50's, recommended economy of men
and money and the need of trusting young Churches to assume responsibility
and Christian maturity. During most of his missionary life, Livingstone
labored under the shadow of debt and deprivation. He was committed to making
the most of limited resources, concerned that missionaries be proportionately
distributed according to need and response, and emphatic about the responsibility of people who had accepted the Gospel. If people would not respond
to the message, he strongly advocated moving on to those not yet reached.

Donald McGavran, in a recent Church Growth Bulletin, writes,

"The successful evangelization of large numbers of people in one or
another region, especially when this achievement is coupled with a chronic
shortage of personnel, is apt to result in the total stagnation of
missionary expansion among the remaining non-evangelized peoples. So many
missionaries are taken up with the pastoral care of the converted that
further expansion is 'choked.'"[1]

With McGavran, Livingstone understood the "choke law" well over one
hundred years ago. Livingstone recommended a committee decide how much money
should be spent upon areas or stations:

"A Committee is often necessary to prevent wasteful expenditure of money,
as individual missionaries are not generally capable of judging how much
ought to be expended on their stations and whether their stations in the
changing circumstances of the country ought to be continued as such . . .
for each person loves his own station and wishes it to be advanced by every
means, and when it is almost useless to the general cause his local attachments prevent his discerning this."[2]

Concerning the distribution of missionaries, Livingstone was unselfish
and realistic:

"The population in this country is very thin indeed, and they [the wars]
are making it still thinner. I don't know what the new missionaries will
think of it when they come. My opinion is they would have been more
usefully employed somewhere else. There are now fewer than 12 missionaries to about 40,000 Bechuanas [in what is now South Africa], while in
India one missionary may have six hundred thousands . . . I am fully convinced to send more missionaries here, while the wants of India, China,
etc., are so great, is nothing less than misplaced benevolence."[3]

---

[1]Donald McGavran, "More Church Growth Theory and Theology" in Church
Growth Bulletin, November 1969, Fuller Theological Seminary.

[2]Schapera, David Livingstone Family Letters (London, Chatto and Windus
1959) Vol. I, p. 95.

[3]Ibid., p. 66.

In fact, Livingstone actually believed that too many missionaries in one area retarded progress:

"The Colonial market is literally glutted with missionaries. I do not believe that equal advantages are enjoyed by any town or village in the United Kingdom as those which are pressed on Algoa Bay, Uitenhuge, Graaf Reinet, and Colesburg. With such an overflowing supply from Europe, will the Hottentots ever watch out for themselves . . . I fear, never.
"I am more and more convinced that in order to effect the permanent settlement of the gospel in any part the natives must be taught to relinquish their reliance on Europe."[4]

Should an area ever be abandoned? Livingstone believed money spent on the Bakhatla and Wanketse tribes had been wasted due to their deaf ears. "Give them up," he said.

"The Bakhatla have a deaf ear to all God's invitations of mercy and though they had some excuse in an unfortunate missionary, yet their conduct has been outrageous to him and the gospel . . . Upwards of £1,000 have been spent on this small and insignificant tribe. It is high time they were given up, for we cannot but look on money spent on those who deliberately reject the gospel as so much abstracted from the Heathen beyond and given to those who deserve it not. . ."[5]

What was Livingstone's conviction concerning the length of attention given to a people who had responded to the Gospel? Did he believe in a permanent work of preaching to such peoples on the part of missionaries? Absolutely not. "People must be made aware of their responsibilities. They must be made to feel that a missionary is a privilege not to be enjoyed forever for nothing. Other doors ought to be opened . . ."[6]

Concerning the Hottentots who were slow to assume their Christian responsibilities, Livingstone wrote, "Mr. Freeman said if our Society abandoned the Hottentots they would sink again into their former state . . . But are our stations to be kept up forever . . . Perpetual tutelage and everlasting leading strings would enfeeble angels. But who cares for the millions beyond."[7]

Livingstone was most doubtful concerning the philosophy that a concentration of many missionaries in an area would, in turn, cause many converts. He stated:

". . . i.e., if you increase missionaries so that they bear a proportion of more than one to 3,000 . . . in ten years the . . . communicants will

---

[4]Schapera, op. cit., p. 108.

[5]Ibid., p. 90-91.

[6]Ibid., Vol. 2, p. 86.

[7]Schapera, Livingstone's Missionary Correspondence (London, Chatto and Windus, 1962).

be very much less per man employed than if the proportion had been one
to 20,000 . . . .
"Time is more essential than concentration. Let the seed be sown.
There is no more doubt of its vitality and germination, than there is of
general spring and harvest in the course of nature."[8]

Many took offense at Livingstone's suggestion that some mission fields
had had ample opportunity. In a letter to his parents, he confided:

". . . I have given mortal offense to a portion of the brethren by
writing that all the Hottentot churches should be made independent at
once; they have been supplied with the gospel for half a century, and
are now better able to support their pastors than you are . . . . To
those who have been accustomed to look upon small Hottentot villages,
the inhabitants of which are nearly all converted, as fields involving
the most excruciating responsibility, my depreciation of their fields
and magnification of the heathen world beyond seem twofold heresy."[9]

Whether we agree with Livingstone's beliefs and ideas or not, an investigation of his journals, diaries, and correspondence easily convinces us that
he deserves to be recognized as a pioneer in advocacy of indigenous ideas.
In the present dialogue involving indigenous missionary method, David
Livingstone must be given due credit for his early observation and sensitivity.
The real pity is that his missionary contemporaries and descendents were and
have been slow or indifferent in paying heed to him.

Livingstone was a man ahead of his time in believing that the real
answer to African evangelism lay not in the number of missionaries, but in
the witnessing to non-Christian Africans by those of their countrymen who had
become Christians. He magnified the multitudes who had not yet heard as the
basic task of the missionary.

---

[8]Schapera, Livingstone's Missionary Correspondence, pp. 299-300.

[9]Schapera, Livingstone Family Letters, Vol. II.

((Mr. Hostetter's article is reproduced from the Summer Issue of "Christian
Mission Today" by kind permission of the editor, Mr. Hammond.))

COCHABAMBA, BOLIVIA.

Meeting in a joint field conference, over 100 missionaries representing
the Andes Evangelical Mission and the Evangelical Union of South America,
voted to support the group of German missiologists who issued the "Frankfurt
Declaration" last March. Among those who agreed to back the declaration were
seven German missionaries serving in Bolivia under the AEM.

"Declarations of one kind or another are commonplace in Germany," said
missionary Jürgen Ehrich. "But this one, written by respected theologians of
the Lutheran Church, is an unusual and courageous effort to counterbalance

the liberal, humanistic theology that has dominated the scene in Germany for all too long. I would add my voice to the appeal that evangelical Christians all over the world indicate their support of what this document represents."

Since 1959 the AEM and the EUSA have been working together in Bolivia with the same national Church, the Unión Cristiana Evangélica, and have enjoyed close cooperation in many areas of the work. This was the first time they had met together in a joint field conference. General Directors Joseph S. McCullough (AEM) and Hubert Cook (EUSA) had travelled from the USA to be present.

((Comment: This kind of action should be taken by Churches and missions all over the world. Copies should be sent to supporters so they know the kind of missions they are praying for and giving to.   The editor))

Today's Expert on Church Growth

By Dwight P. Baker   (Taken by permission from *ETERNITY*)

Donald Anderson McGavran is the dean of spokesmen for the church growth viewpoint in Christian missions today as well as being dean of the School of World Mission at Fuller Theological Seminary. The church growth thesis is a double one: (1) that the basic business of Christian missions is to win men to Christ, to extend the Church; and (2) that in most societies the most proper way for people to become Christians is in groups. These points lead to two charges: (1) Most mission societies—some consciously, some without realizing it—are doing the wrong thing. They are doing many good works whether or not the good deeds lead to conversion and church growth, instead of consciously subordinating all their activities to the primary goal of winning men and peoples to Christ. (2) When they do seek to win converts, most missionaries go about it in the wrong way. They insensitively force a western social pattern, individualistic conversion, on societies whose normal way is to make religious and other decisions in concert as family or larger groups.

Everyone, missionary to layman, knows that Islamic fields are hard to work. A convert may be won here, one there, but no great ingathering is to be expected. The labor is protracted and tedious, and the results are meager. When 50,000 Moslems in Indonesia came to Christ within the space of three years and did so as whole communities, McGavran might well have said: That is what I have been talking about all along. For Moslems, for Hindus,

for others "the greats obstacles to conversion are social, not theological." In fact, in his latest book, *Understanding Church Growth* (Eerdmans, 382 pages, $7.95), he does say it, several times.

He began saying this or something very much like it back in the 1930's. Then, in *Church Growth and Group Conversion* (Luckow [India] Publishing House, 116 pages, $1.75), he, with J. W. Pickett and G. H. Singh, stated that if mission effort in India was to become productive, it must beware of generalized do-goodism and cease diffusive evangelism. To obtain fruit, missionaries must concentrate on responsive peoples and bend every effort to arouse a people movement to Christ among them. A people is any tribe, lineage, clan, or caste which marries only within itself, has distinctive customs, and possibly speaks a separate language or dialect. Locating a people that is responsive to the gospel is done by looking around and seeing from which groups individuals and more particularly families are being won to Christ. A people movement is comprised of a series of group conversions that ideally continue until the whole of a tribe or caste acknowledges Jesus as its God, the church as its house of worship, and the Bible as its Scriptures.

In their study of mission work in east India, McGavran and his collaborators found it was always one or two out of the multitude of castes in any one area that were responsive to the gospel. Yet invariably the missionaries of the region were unaware that the bulk of their converts were coming from one single

caste and were spreading their labors indiscriminately among all the castes. Or, worse, some were deliberately slighting the responsive segment, for usually it was the unprestigious untouchables who were open to the gospel.

Set down in the short compass of this little book are the main principles which inform all of McGavran's later work. Later editions of the book added a chapter by A. L. Warnshuis showing that though the studies had been conducted among the castes of India, the principles obtained are universally valid. In *The Bridges of God* (Friendship Press, 158 pages, paper, $2.50 which came two decades later, McGavran elaborated his distinctions between discipling the peoples (bringing an ethnic unit to acknowledge the Lordship of Christ) and perfecting (training up the disciples new and old in the faith). In it appears his devastating argument against a static, mission station-centered approach and for a flexible, people-movement strategy in missions. If there are any in recent missions literature, this book is a classic.

In *Understanding Church Growth* McGavran comprehensively examines the methodological how's, the sociological why's, and the theological ought's of church growth. The book is a virtuoso performance. Those who have read his *How Churches Grow* (Friendship Press, 188 pages, paper, $2.50), and the essays in *Church Growth and Christian Mission* (Harper & Row, 252 pages, $5.00) which he edited, and his earlier books will meet again points they have seen before, enriched with much new

material. The breadth of McGavran's discussion and the wealth of materials he draws upon are formidable. A lifetime of study on the diverse ways churches in different cultural, economic, historical, and geographical milieus have grown is brought into play. McGavran ranges from anthropology to history to sociology to linguistics; he interacts with writers on indigenous church principles; and he replies to current theories of mission.

Understanding Church Growth intertwines two themes: the almost limitless complexity of the factors which go into the planting and growth of any particular church, and the steadfast faithfulness God calls us to in our labor for the extension of the church, the fellowship of the redeemed.

In stressing church growth, McGavran is writing about what the chief objective of the Christian world mission should be and how mission endeavor should be carried out. At no point is he trying to set up a how-to manual to fit some local situation. He is seeking to make explicit, and reform, the largely unarticulated set of priorities that churchmen abide by when they make decisions for or against any piece of church work, whether it be church planting, shepherding existing congregations, or doing service to the world. Whether speaking against the leaden traditionalism of past mission policies or the heavy pessimism of current theories of mission, his voice is a salutary corrective that needs to be heard—and heeded—today.

(All books mentioned are available at a discount from the CHURCH GROWTH BOOK CLUB)

CHURCH GROWTH
BULLETIN

from the
INSTITUTE OF
CHURCH GROWTH

Address:
FULLER THEOLOGICAL
SEMINARY
135 N. Oakland
Pasadena, Calif. 91101

DONALD A. McGAVRAN, B.D., Ph.D.
Director

NOVEMBER 1970   Subscription $1 per year   Volume VII, No. 2

A Mission Executive Speaks Out

by

C. Peter Wagner

((At the August 1970 Field Conference of the Andes Evangelical Mission (AEM)
Rev. C. Peter Wagner, Associate General Director, in his annual report, made
the following points about mission today and in the coming decade. He, not
unnaturally, also spoke to his colleagues about other aspects of the Andes
Mission. Since, however, we are giving only those parts of the address which
will be of interest to readers of the Church Growth Bulletin, we have omitted
everything of merely local import.

The notable forward steps being taken by this great mission are significant to all committed to great commission missions. This is the kind of
thinking and mission planning which is occurring in board after board, Church
after Church, and country after country.   The Editor))

Futurology

Now that we are into the decade of the seventies, what can we discern as
indications of God's will for the AEM? Admitting that any prediction of the
future needs constant reevaluation as the years go on, I would like to set
forth four areas in which I hope definite progress will be made during the
next ten years.

1. Our knowledge of the dynamics of church growth in Bolivia in general and
   of the peasants of the Andes (so largely Indian by race) in particular
   will soon increase to the point where we can intelligently place workers
   where their ministry will reap much more fruit than has been possible in
   the past.

SEND correspondence, news, and articles to the Editor, Dr. Donald McGavran, at the
Institute of Church Growth, Fuller Theological Seminary. Published bi-monthly, send
subscriptions and changes of address to the Business Manager, Norman L. Cummings,
Overseas Crusades, Inc., 265 Lytton Avenue, Palo Alto, California 94301, U.S.A.
Second-class postage paid at Palo Alto, California.

2. Instead of five or six AEM men, who are fluent in Quechua and Aymara (Indian languages) as most others are in Spanish, we should have between twenty and thirty by 1980. Most of them will have a dual ministry of church planting and leadership training. One or two will specialize in Quechua literature. Quechua and Aymara language study will be available for all who desire it.

3. We will be working with a greatly enlarged Church if the growth rate for the decade of 1960-70 of the Unión Cristiana Evangélica is maintained for ten more years. While we suffer (with many other Churches) from a dearth of reliable statistics, we hope the Lord will so bless evangelistic efforts in Bolivia in general and the UCE in particular that by 1980 we will have the joy of seeing some 75,000 believers in fellowship with perhaps 1500 UCE churches. If this happens, the government of the UCE will have to be modified to handle the new situation efficiently. The subdirectives will likely be the real power centers, with the central government acting merely as a coordinating agency for the denomination.

4. In theological education, the residence programs will continue while extension education becomes, numerically speaking, the principal method of leadership training. Enrollment in the George Allan Seminary should have passed the 500 mark.

By looking forward in this manner, we do not mean to give the impression that we are in the least usurping the place of God, who holds the future in His hands, but we do believe that God expects us to discern the signs of the times and set long-term goals based on careful, forward thinking as well as immediate goals based on our present situation. We have spoken of the long term; now let us focus on some of the more immediate developments and plans.

Missiology

A major movement in the thinking of missions worldwide is under way. While strong opposition to what is now known as "church growth theology" is expected to continue among those who hold the humanistic point of view articulated at the Uppsala Assembly of the WCC, and while pockets of resistance among evangelicals (especially from those who minister in highly resistant sectors of population) still exist, the phenomenon of the rapid spread of the church growth theory of missions is a major factor in almost every country which has a Christian church.

As a result of the publication of Latin American Church Growth, the IFMA and EFMA jointly will sponsor a consultation of 50 top executives of missions working in Latin America in Elburn, Illinois, next September. The purpose is to implement the findings of the book. In January of this year, Dr. J. B. A. Kessler read a paper entitled "The Principles of Church Growth," as the basis of discussion for the Evangelical Fellowship for Missionary Studies in London. Perhaps the most significant development of all was the Frankfurt Declaration on the Fundamental Crisis in Christian Mission drawn up by a group of Lutheran theologians in Germany led by Peter Beyerhaus in the month of April. The signers, who have taken a public stand against humanization as a sufficient end of mission (advocated by their own denomination and the WCC) have appealed for signatures of evangelicals in other parts of the world who will support them in their stand. ((The AEM did sign the Declaration. Editor))

Theological Stratification in Latin America

The ferment aroused by the Frankfurt Declaration is being reflected in Latin America. The Bogotá Congress on Evangelization has now become a milestone for evangelicals of the continent. The Latin America Mission doubled the size of the current En Marcha Internacional and dedicated the entire issue to it. Some of the messages there, some of the books which were published and distributed, and the personal exchange of ideas among the delegates, have sparked an unprecedented theological ferment among Latin American evangelical leaders. With the publication of Latin American Church Growth in English, Portuguese and Spanish, the church growth point of view will play a significant role in theological development in Latin America. The George Allan Seminary and other seminaries now teach courses in church growth. The first official intertext to be published by the Latin American Committee for Theological Texts (CLATT) is on church growth. A paper on the biblical and theological basis of church growth will be presented in the first meeting of the Fraternidad de Teológos Lationamericanos to be held here in Carachipampa in December 1970.

The Roman Catholic Church

The internal problems of the Catholic Church in Bolivia are extremely acute. Never has the Catholic Church been so rent by disagreements and divisions. When the bishops met in Tarija for their annual assembly in April, a group of 100 priests jointly signed a 2000-word document which was published in most of the newspapers of the country, entitled "Points of Reflection on the Ministry of Priests in Bolivia." It seems particularly significant in three areas: (1) Theological. "The younger priests," it says, "energetically reject the traditional forms of structures and of sacramentalization." Rarely has the sacramental structure of the Catholic Church been called into question by its own leaders in public. The priests suggest that the Church "rediscover its vocation of service in the liberation of man, and of conversion to faith, not to sacramentalism." (2) Cultural. The frank recognition that "there is no such thing as a single Bolivian culture, but rather a series of sub-cultures," and that the church must gear her programs to this reality, comes as a belated, but realistic, observation which could have far-reaching consequences. (3) Ministerial. The priests admit that "we have no ministers who come from certain ethnic groups such as Quechuas and Aymaras." What must they have thought when they saw scores of Quechua and Aymara pastors gathered at the World Vision conference? "It is the duty of foreign missionaries and Bolivians to raise up a clergy completely indigenous, geared to the heterogeneity of the sub-cultures."

In an article called "The Crisis in Bolivia's Seminaries," written (but not signed) by Dominican Jordan Bishop, and published in Herder Correspondence in May, the true condition of the Bolivian clergy and theological education is painted in bold strokes. Jordan Bishop writes:

A crisis over the nature of seminary education in Bolivia which has been simmering for several years reached the point in February where the country's one major seminary has been closed for the current academic year--which in Bolivia runs from February to November. The crisis is all the more intense in view of the shocking imbalance between Bolivian and foreign-born clergy. At present 78 percent of the clergy--716 out of the 913 priests working in Bolivia--are foreign born. In addition, the average age of Bolivian priests is considerably greater than that of their foreign-born colleagues. Moreover, the position has been getting steadily worse over the last century or so. In 1888, for example, the archdiocese of La Paz had 138 indigenous diocesan clergy but in 1968 only 29: the number has been dropping at a rate of almost 1 percent a year--while of course the population of the archdiocese has increased considerably. During the past ten years only sixteen Bolivians have been ordained to the priesthood in the whole country.

The crisis came to a head when the conservative bishop of Cochabamba, Mons. Gutierrez, succeeded not only in closing the Seminary which had been run since 1965 by the liberal order of Spanish priests, OCHSA, but also in forcing the priests, who had subsequently moved to minister in Villa Bush, out of the diocese. Soon after, when Mons. Gutierrez was away in Tarija, a group of enraged laymen took over the bishop's palace by force for some days.

Emphasis on Aymara and Quechua Ministry

Recently Ray Morris and Bruce Anderson have gone through the Quechua and Aymara courses in the Maryknoll language school with much profit. This is only a small start in implementing the decision of our last field conference to increase our emphasis on the Quechua and Aymara ministries. The Spanish Language School has started a Quechua department . . . Since it is evident that most Bolivian church growth in the future will take place among those whose mother tongues are Quechua and Aymara, it is only proper that the AEM should give top priority to developing this evangelistic and church-planting ministry.

Goals for the Immediate Future

1. Sponsor an international church growth seminar for Quechua and Aymara evangelism. Pinpoint areas of particular responsiveness, and multiply churches in those areas. Develop Quechua language study facilities.
2. Expand the extension seminary program to keep pace with church growth, and move steadily into a B.D. program.
3. Strengthen the regional boards of directors of our national Church (UCE) and impart a vision for evangelism and church planting in each of them.
4. Set up and begin operation of the radio recording studio, and gear radio ministry so it will be an aid to church growth in responsive areas.
5. Update statistics of all the work as a basis for competent evaluation of the past and analysis for future planning.

((Five other goals of less interest to the readers of CGB were set forth.
Editor))

Conclusion

As opportunities for AEM ministry continue to increase, we not only thank the Lord for His blessings and promises, but we also recognize that Satan is not going to let the work progress unchallenged. Our weapons are spiritual, not carnal, but the promise of Christ, "lo I am with you always even to the end of the age" is as valid now as it was in the first century. Defeat will come only if we do not take advantage of the power of the Holy Spirit in our individual and collective lives. May we as a team move forward in this power, never doubting, and pushing on from victory to victory. "Thanks be to God, who giveth us the victory through our Lord Jesus Christ."

PLAIN VANILLA AND CHURCH GROWTH   by Wendell W. Broom, SWM-ICG '70
Professor of Missions at Abilene Christian College

PLAIN VANILLA MISSIONS	CHURCH GROWTH MISSIONS
Plan mission strategy out of experience and background of sending church.	Plan strategy on the evidence of receptivity of people.
Establish base in permanent "mission stations." Missionaries serve the institutions.	Establish bases in multiplying congregations. Missionaries follow the churches.
Open to the option of paternally guiding the churches.	Restricted to a fraternal relationship.
Plant churches with a permanent minority-consciousness set for a holding action.	Plant churches which intend to liberate entire tribes in Christ and move on to liberate others.
Geared to subjective fulfillment of missionaries' or home church's dreams and goals.	Geared to an objective attainment: countable Christians and countable churches.
Plant churches with terminal life (like hybrid corn or mules).	Plant churches with generational life (like rabbits and bermuda grass).
Continue strategy once set as official policy, whatever changes occur in the field situation.	Review strategy constantly by evaluating growth and receptivity relative to known opportunities.
View the one world as one place filled with one people.	View the one world as a mosaic of varying cultures and distinctive homogeneous units.
Count chiefly on the human forces operating in the mission field through poverty, production, mechanization, famine relief, education, and the like.	Count chiefly on God's movements or purposes among the nations in revolutions, famines, prosperity, migrations, revivals, people movements, and the like.

TO SERVE OR TO PROCLAIM   by Canon John V. Taylor, C.M.S.*

To serve or to proclaim--is this really a valid choice? Or is the call
to serve _and_ proclaim?

I find it significant that the subject I have been given to speak on
contains neither of these opposed words. Instead it uses a phrase with a
sober seventeenth-century ring: "The Propagation of the Gospel." It reminds
one of the creation of the Congregatio de Propaganda Fide and the founding
of the "Society for the Propagation of the Gospel in Foreign Parts" in 1701.
And the meaning of the word "propagate" according to the Oxford English
Dictionary, is "to multiply, reproduce, extend; to spread from person to
person or from place to place a statement, belief, practice, etc."

The phrase, therefore, does not specify the means and methods by which
the knowledge of Christ is to be multiplied or reproduced, nor does it define
the speed of its extension. But it affirms that the primary aim of mission
and the primary task of any missionary Church is to spread from person to
person and from place to place a _statement_ of what Jesus Christ is, a _belief_
in His saving power and relevance today, and a _practice_ of His way of life
in the corporate fellowship He created. Whether in any given situation this
"spreading from person to person" can best be advanced by spoken proclamation,
or by the silent example of a few Christians living in deeply honest and
loving community, or by compassionate service of men in different varieties
of need, or by undogmatic discourse and friendship with men of other faiths,
or by participation in the struggle for a more just and human society, is an
entirely secondary question.

To it, the answer I believe is that all these things are necessary, as
facets or ingredients of the whole, and that the Holy Spirit provides the
Christian community with a diversity of these gifts for the sake of the one
Mission. The Christian engaged in inter-faith dialogue must never think that
he can entirely eliminate proclamation from his programme or say to the
preacher, "I have no need of thee," though he may sometimes ask him to be
more discreet and opportune. Neither must the Bible translator or radio
evangelist say to the Christian social worker, "I have no need of thee."
But, and this is the crux of what I have to say, if it is true, as I believe
it is, that mission must be defined as the propagation of the Gospel, then
there is no facet of its many-sided activity which is not consciously and
deliberately communicating a message.

---

*Canon John V. Taylor is General Secretary of the famed Church
Missionary Society of the Anglican Church, the author of The Primal Vision
and other books, and an influential member of the World Council of Churches
and the Division of World Mission and Evangelism.
In the spring of 1970, he delivered a series of lectures on missions
and missiology at Fuller Seminary's School of Missions and Institute of
Church Growth. The excerpt just quoted is one of his significant contributions. Church Growth Bulletin is happy to share his sound thinking with our
readers and sharpen one crucial point.

Comment

At SWM-ICG, the foregoing sentiments expressed by Canon Taylor meet with cordial approval. They are, indeed, what the church growth school of thought has always held and taught. We too believe that "mission must be defined as the propagation of the Gospel." We too believe that whether in any given situation "spreading from person to person can be best advanced" by this means or that is "an entirely secondary question." We hold that this clear distinction between ends and means is of vital importance to Churches and missionary societies.

At one place, however, we would like to change one word. In making this change we are not engaged in a pedantic exercise, but rather are emphasizing a sine qua non of progress in mission. We hope Canon Taylor will agree and rejoice, perhaps, that by giving opportunity for the change, he has helped emphasize the great need for checking all means and methods against the degree of accomplishment of the ends sought.

In the last sentence of the excerpt, we would change "is not" to "should not be." The words "is not" convey the meaning that "every facet of its many-sided activity" actually is "consciously and deliberately communicating a message," and furthermore communicating it as much as it should.

The facts, unfortunately, are that the various "ingredients of the whole" (activities of individual Christians, churches, or missions) contribute to the propagation of the Gospel in very varying degrees. Some may contribute tremendously in one decade and very little in another. Some may actually hinder the propagation of the Gospel. Missionary action which was acceptable to Africans in 1920 is entirely unacceptable in 1970. The hospital, so greatly needed when the government maintained none, is much less needed when medical schools turn out multitudes of national doctors.

Furthermore, it is quite possible for a national Christian or a foreign missionary to help people (educate them, medicate them, lead them to the barricades, or work with them in field or factory) in such a way that the Gospel is obscured. It is possible to let our light shine in such a way that men glorify not our Father in Heaven but ourselves.

The position that church or mission activities are good simply because Christians carry them out (they are parts of a mission program, the Church has done them for the last fifty years, or other reason) is untenable. No better way could be found to canonize the status quo. The fact of the matter is that every facet is not communicating a message.

But it should be. The present distribution of good activities can be so reviewed, measured, adjusted, and renewed that all of them (or at least most of them) do communicate the message of life, do help to propagate the Gospel.

This is one focus of church growth theory. Evidence from Church after Church and land after land (Eurican Churches as well as Afericasian Churches) forces us to believe that Christian Churches and missions can be very much more effective than they are. Slow growth of the Church is not natural. In many places it is a disease and should be cured. In the torrent of social change, practices effective a few years ago are now outmoded and should be revised or jettisoned.

Church growth thinking rejoices in the many means and methods used for the propagation of the Gospel. We are not against dialogue, presence, social action, or charity. We are for them. We hold that they have value in themselves; but also (a) that in addition they have value as means to spreading the news of the Savior from person to person and culture to culture; and (b) that they ought to be constantly reviewed to see how effective they are in communicating the Good News. Proclamation of the Gospel, of course, should also submit to this same review.

Canon Taylor's great predecessor, Canon Max Warren, on reading How Churches Grow, marked out for special approbation the chapter titled "Checking Methods Against Actual Growth." He realized that methods can so easily be defended on subjective grounds of all sorts. It is salutory to evaluate them against an objective measure of accomplishment. Membership increase, of course, is not the only measure; but it is one rather good measure and it can readily be applied.

Everyone believes that the activity in which he engages is absolutely necessary for the propagation of the Gospel. The exponents of every new idea in missions fervently believe it will help spread the Gospel from person to person. They are sure it "ought to work." Good stewards of God's grace, however, must resolutely ask, not "ought it work?" but "has it worked?" Has it, in fact, helped in the propagation of the Gospel? How much? How little?

In short, Christians engaged in mission, agreeing entirely that the propagation of the Gospel is a very complex enterprise employing many means, need to remember that "every facet of its many-sided activity should be consciously communicating the message of Christ." That is sound missiological theory.

AFRICAN INDEPENDENT CHURCHES AND SEMINARIES   by Fred H. Burke
Witbank, S. Africa

Members of African Independent Churches (AIC) number about three million in South Africa. The zeal of many in these churches is commendable. The great majority of their ministers, however, lack training and Bible knowledge. This has opened the door to many tragic errors in doctrine and practice.

Can these thousands of ministers be given help in understanding the Scriptures? Can their efforts be channelled into effective evangelism? If so, what an impact this could make in Africa!

The All Africa School of Theology (AAST) exists to do just this. We train hundreds of AIC ministers. This was also the objective of a conference of evangelism held in Mamelodi, and sponsored by AAST.

Classes in Sunday School evangelism, youth evangelism, literature evangelism, and evangelism through personal witness were taught. Missionaries and African ministers who specialize in these fields gave their time freely.

A remarkable spirit of unity and Christian love pervaded the conference. Those present responded enthusiastically to the ministry of the Word. The entire conference accepted a plan for a coordinated project of Total Evangelism. In a Sunday morning meeting, high ranking government officials, including the prime minister of the two million Tswana people, testified of what Christ means to them. The climax of the conference was the graduation service for AAST students. A challenging message given in the anointing of the Holy Spirit gripped the hearts of the hundreds present. About a hundred ministers, in their clerical attire, flocked to the altar either to receive Christ in a personal experience or to dedicate themselves to Him more fully. The forty students-- leaders of the Independent Churches--who received their diplomas also dedicated themselves to God's service.

God's Word says, "Not by might, nor by power, but by my Spirit." The key to unlock closed doors and closed hearts is God's Spirit poured out upon His people, a forgetting of all denominational barriers, the unstinted flow of Christian love, and a desire to help, not rule, God's heritage.

Is the Sick Man Healed?

"The mission field has deepened. There is universal realization of the need to take up into Jesus Christ all that is good in the non-Christian cultures and even in the non-Christian religions, so that Christianity in its turn can play its part as "leaven" within them. This policy of respectful approach gave birth, with the Pope's blessing, to the Secretariat for non-Christian Religions and the Secretariat for non-Believers. It is this type of penetration rather than numerical increase which is seen (by some) as the end of missions."
S. Masson S. J., World Christian Handbook, 1968, p. 9.

Comment. Father Masson is presenting a certain strain of missionary thought in the Roman Catholic Church and in some Protestant communions also. But this obscure language does not really present the issue. Most Christians, I suppose, seek to employ a 'respectful approach' to other cultures and religions; but would deny that in so doing they were "taking up into Jesus Christ all that is good in . . . . non-Christian religions . . . so that Christianity can play its part as leaven within them." They would reject these phrases on the ground that they were full of double meanings. Clarity is needed.

The church growth school of thought shares the thirst for clarity. For example, we would maintain that the degree of respect shown to ideologies, the amount of sensitivity to other cultures and religions, the Christian's choice of proclamation, presence, good deeds, literature, or radio, and the degree to which the Christian religion should clothe itself in cultures should always be subordinate to the supreme question as to whether the man is healed. They are all means, not ends. Granting that stainless steel surgical instruments are superior to copper, it is better to perform a surgical operation which cures with copper instruments, than not to cure with stainless steel. If the "type of penetration" described by Father Masson is really of God, it will add to the number of those liberated into the marvelous freedom of His sons. If sooner or later it does not add to their number, it is of little value as mission.   D.M.

Page 108

ONE LONE RIFLEMAN
by R. Arthur Mathews

"On August 6, 1944, exactly two months after the invasion of Normandy, the entire reinforcement pool for infantry forces in Europe consisted of

One Lone Rifleman."

So says S. L. A. Marshall in his book, Men Against Fire. To avert disaster, the high command had to switch air force trainees to the infantry.

What had happened? War planners at the top, carried away with excitement over the wonderful capabilities of mechanization for winning a war, pressed all available personnel into mechanized units. They reasoned that the infantry belonged to the oxcart era and had little to do with winning modern wars. Little did they realize that their action created a critical imbalance in the fighting force and seriously prejudiced the chances of success. A by-product of this situation was the slump in the morale of the foot sloggers. The exaggerated claims of top brass caused the infantry to have a very inferior opinion of their place in this business of fighting and winning wars. On top of this, the mechanized units were frustrated because of their inability to clinch the victory on the ground without the infantry.

The point has an obvious application to "the wars of the Lord" against Satan's hosts. There are the same strategy planners: "We are producing the most educated, articulate, and brilliant sidewalk superintendents the world has ever seen," says John Gardner in No Easy Victories. There are the same overstatements on the exalted role of the specialist and the declining usefulness of the church-planter--and the same need to transfer to the less spectacular ranks of those whose chief business is to proclaim Christ and persuade men to become His disciples and responsible members of His Church. Most missions face this danger and this need.

The main lessons we must learn are (1) that balance must be safeguarded. We cannot allow experimentation by men at the top to prejudice the cause at the front. (2) that the priority force is the force that does the church planting. It is not the part of missionary wisdom to strengthen the specialist services at the expense of the men in contact with those who seek Jesus.

The minds of young people have been turned toward specialist functions. Counselors at universities and Bible colleges have encouraged students to seek appointments where their "valuable training" would not be "wasted." Mission leaders under pressure have gone along with the trend.

What will now happen? Unless missions, conservative as well as liberal, act soon, the answer to this question could by 1980 read: "Christian Mission's entire reinforcement pool of church planters consists of

One Lone Church Planter."

((Used in slightly adapted form by kind permission of East Asia Millions and R. Arthur Mathews.))

THE NORMAL BODY OF CHRIST   by Merton Alexander, M.D., Kibuye, Burundi

Being of a scientific frame of mind through medicine, and knowing man through his corporate structure, the normal structure (as anatomy), function (as physiology) and the abnormal (as pathology), I draw analogies from our physical bodies concerning the Body of Christ, and meditate on them as I practice medicine here in the highlands of Burundi.

What catalyzed the Renaissance, was the climate of thought permitted by the ecclesiastical authorities. The Renaissance held that one could, without violating the sanctum sancorum or intruding into divinely forbidden areas, delve into natural phenomena, seeking natural causes for natural effects. Modern medicine rests on the assumption that it is permissible and necessary to "behold" the human body, even if it is the temple of the Living God.

Similarly, the philosophical basis of the church growth point of view, is that it is permissible, and even necessary, to "behold" the Body of Christ, the Church.

What is catalyzing present thought as to church growth is the conviction that one can investigate spiritual phenomena without doing dishonor to God as Spirit, or invading the sacred, or preempting the divine prerogative. Church growth men have maintained both unquestionable devotion in worship and perceptive intellectual inquiry. They have enhanced the grandeur of the Church without diminishing reverence for it.

When I consider the Church to be veritable Body, with conceptual dimension, form and function, I feel the power and person of God the Son, and God the Spirit. I permit myself to seek normality as well as abnormality. I recognize a Church, grotesque because of a perpetrated mal-development, as Church. I see a structure, mal-functioning to its own maiming as well as its inability to perform its designated task, as nevertheless a church structure. It is possible to say, "the part of the Church with which I am involved or have helped to develop is off God's norm, not only in the intellectual but the pragmatic realm." I can no longer use "The Church" as a validating rubber stamp for whatever church has happened to grow up. Nor, what is a worse tragedy, use the Holy Spirit as a rubber stamp for the imperfect, arrested, and malformed churches we see about us.

When I consider the Church to be veritable Body, with conceptual dimensions, form and function, I am filled with longing that it be normal Body, perfect Body. I desire its imperfections to be cured. Christ can certainly command His Body to be whole. The perfect Life which once walked the Judean hills and the perfect Spirit which now indwells the Body encourage me to dream of the day when all segments of the Body, every homogeneous unit as we say in church growth theory, will be filled with the rosy hue of perfect good health. I am encouraged to devise steps toward that end and to use "surgery" and "medicines" given us by God to bring Churches suffering from mal-development, maiming, or other abnormality back to their godly dimensions. For after all, the Church is the Normal Body of Christ.

URBAN CHURCH PLANTING   by Donald McGavran

Nairobi, Kenya is expected to become a city of 1,500,000 by 1975. New
roads, new water mains, new developments reach out in all directions.

A representative committee of the main-line Churches has proposed that
a goal of one church to ten thousand citizens be set and has allocated such
and such a number of congregations to the Anglicans, the Friends, the
Presbyterians, the Africa Inland Church, and other denominations. This goal,
when achieved, would mean 150 congregations in 1975. <u>Is this adequate planning?</u>

Since there may be 500,000 Indians, Muslims, and Marxists, and these to
date seldom become Christians, the plan really calls for one church for each
6,000 Africans from tribes in which large numbers have already become
Christian. Is this adequate planning?

If each of the 150 churches has 2,000 communicants and is composed of,
say, 100 chapels or house churches each of which has about 20 communicants,
then Nairobi will have 300,000 communicants, or 600,000 Christian community
and the plan approaches adequacy. But if each of the 150 congregations has
perhaps 300 full members, (and few if any chapels or house churches) then the
city will have only 45,000 communicants (90,000 community) and the plan will
leave Nairobi woefully underchurched.

If the mainline denominations church only 90,000 the other 900,000 will
be won by the African Independent Churches, the Muslims, the Marxists, or the
Animistic Materialists.

Plans for the cities in Africa must not assume that the slow church
growth of the past thirty years, heavily subsidized from abroad, will mark
the next thirty. <u>Plans should assume that most of the million can be churched</u>
and <u>that this church expansion will pay for itself.</u> We must perfect plans
which proceed on the reasonable premise that churches which include 300,000
communicants in a modern African city can support an adequate ministry and
build adequate buildings.

The one thing needful is not enough foreign money to evangelize Nairobi.
The one thing needed is obedience, intellect, and courage enough to disciple
a winnable city of 1,500,000 souls.

((Mr. Van Tate, a Churches of Christ missionary working in Nairobi, and a
graduate of SWM-ICG in 1970, contributed the data on which this article is
based.))

CHURCH GROWTH
B U L E T I N

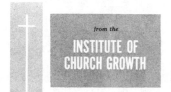

from the

INSTITUTE OF CHURCH GROWTH

Address:
FULLER THEOLOGICAL
SEMINARY
135 N. Oakland
Pasadena, Calif. 91101

DONALD A. McGAVRAN, B.D., Ph.D.
Director

JANUARY 1971   Subscription $1 per year   Volume VII, No. 3

Theology: With or Without the Bible

by A. F. Glasser

This past fall, students at the School of World Mission were deeply involved in studying the Old Testament treatment of Israel's mission to the nations. This broadened understanding of the relation between the cultural and evangelistic mandates and sharpened the issue of syncretism (false and true). How God would have his people engage in religious encounter. Why His call to the Servant role is so crucial to the mission of the Church. The themes are many and important. One of the books assigned for collateral reading was The Kingdom of God by Dr. John Bright of Union Theological Seminary, Richmond. All were impressed with Dr. Bright's concern that the Church profit from the tragic record of Israel's rejection of the Servant role and the failure of Judaism to become a missionary religion. Every so often he turns from exegetical problems to give impassioned appeals that the Church be the Church.

"We must be a more missionary Church! We are engaged today in an ideological struggle; dynamic ideas do battle for the minds of men. We cannot stand aside from that battle--and to participate in it is mission. The Christian gospel may be never so redemptive, but it will redeem no one who has never heard its summons. And millions have not! Scarcely one of us but meets dozens of such each day as he goes about his daily employment. It is not enough that we support missions; were we to support ten times as much, it would not be enough . . . The Church that will not contend for the spirits of men is no true Servant; it will not even survive, nor does it deserve to. The Church must reach out into the community (of the nations) and bring new people into its fellowship. That is what it is for, and we criticize it if it does not . . . As a Church and as individuals we must learn at once, that the vigorous propagation of the faith is the Church's life blood." (pp. 254, 266)

Appeals of this sort are most congenial to the Church Growth Movement. Indeed, we commend Dr. Bright's responsible handling of Scripture to all who contemptuously regard this movement as the "Last Hurrah of Edinburgh 1910." We implore its critics to emulate the nobility of the Bereans who examined the Scriptures to see whether these things were so (Acts 17:11). In a very real sense, it is a very small thing if this movement be judged of man (I Cor. 4:1-5). "If this undertaking is of men, it will fail; but if it is of God, . . . [its

SEND correspondence, news, and articles to the Editor, Dr. Donald McGavran, at the Institute of Church Growth, Fuller Theological Seminary. Published bi-monthly, send subscriptions and changes of address to the Business Manager, Norman L. Cummings, Overseas Crusades, Inc., 265 Lytton Avenue, Palo Alto, California 94301, U.S.A. Second-class postage paid at Palo Alto, California.

critics] might even be found opposing God" (Acts 5:39). Our continuing concern
is that the leaders of the Church throughout the world not lead the people of God
astray by denigrating the task of evangelism with its concomitants of gospel
proclamation, membership training, and the multiplication of organized congregations. According to Dr. Bright evangelism is a chief and irreplaceable mark of
vital Christianity.

Down the hall from Dr. Bright at Union, Richmond, is the office of Dr. D.
Donald G. Dawe, the new Professor of Theology. Recently, Dr. Dawe contributed a
widely heralded "think piece" to his fellow Southern Presbyterians ("For
Assessing Missions: A New Criterion," Presbyterian Survey, September 21, 1970).
One could wish that Dr. Dawe and Dr. Bright had had a chat together over an open
Bible before he had written his paper. Today's theologians can profit greatly
from listening to biblical scholars. Theology is in disarray in Protestantism
in our day because of the penchant too many theologians appear to have for
failing to come to grips with Scripture.

Dr. Dawe begins with a comparison between America's growing isolationism in
foreign policy and the growing disenchantment of some mainline Churches with
their missionary programs. He admits that traditionally understood, the "intended outcome for missions was the conversion of non-Christians to faith in
Jesus Christ as Saviour and Lord." He amplifies this: "The universality of
Christianity was to be actualized by bringing men of every nation into the
discipleship of Christ through a personal decision." So far so good, although
we would modify the emphasis on individualism to conform to the present-day
reality that throughout the world two-thirds of all Christians are the result of
"people movements" akin to what took place among the Jewish people of Palestine
during the first years of the Christian Church (Acts 2-8), No slow, one-by-one
ingathering that disrupted the social relationships of people.

When Dr. Dawe seeks to link missions in the past with the situation facing
the Church in the world today, he reveals that he is not too aware of what is
actually taking place. With no attempt at documentation he affirms that the
outcome of missions, as with America's foreign aid programs, has been "frustration and failure." As for the Church in Asia, Africa and Latin America--he
dolefully concludes that "future prospects are not promising." We will forgive
a professor of theology for not having had the time to read Dr. Winter's The
Twenty-Five Unbelievable Years (1945-1969), written to bring up to date Dr.
Kenneth S. Latourett s seven-volume History of the Expansion of Christianity.*
Furthermore, we will commend Dr. Dawe for his contention that when a Church
turns aside from its mission overseas to preoccupy itself with homeside concerns
it is guilty of "failure of faith." But when Dawe defines his "new criterion"
for evaluating mission in our day, we must protest. Nothing remotely resembling
Dr. Bright's clarion call to advance. Rather, a summary rejection of God's
command to all men everywhere to repent (Acts 17:31). Attention is to be
focussed on "the impact of Christian witness on human communities, even religious
communities." Not rejoicing over people coming under the Lordship of Christ, but
"discerning God's work in the humanizing of cultures and religions without
necessarily destroying or replacing them." Dr. Dawe argues,

---

*The bargain of the century: you can now get these books, second only to
the Bible in importance, at an inconceivably low price! See the last page of
this bulletin!

"The humanizing and renewal of religion in India (under the challenge of Christianity) to give rise to new forms of Hindu religion and social life may seem to us the hidden work of God. But is it not the redemptive work of God? . . . To view the Christian mission in the world in terms of its relation to human religious communities and their changes allows us to confess in a new way the Lordship of Jesus Christ. Our mission is not to make his Lordship universal."

Dr. Dawe's new criterion was succinctly grasped by the editor of Survey. He published the final section of the article under the sub-heading, "Not Universal Lordship."

It is not our purpose to engage Dr. Dawe in debate. We have not sought to reproduce the dominant emphases of his thesis to expose the theological confusion of our day. In our judgment, his presentation abounds with affirmations that simply are not true.

Why, then, have we set this theologian over against his colleague? Because of the place of Scripture in their approaches to the mission of the Church. Dr. Dawe makes no appeal to Scripture, apart from a use of Isaiah 55:11 in a context that would doubtless surprise Dr. Bright! But Christians are called of God by the example and instruction of Christ to live in accordance with his will revealed in Scripture. There is a scandal to the Canon as there is a scandal to the Cross. The latter tells us that apart from the consequences of that redemptive event men are without hope and without God. The former warns us against adding to or taking away from what it says about God's redemptive purpose for mankind (Revelation 22:18, 19). The scandal is that the Christian is shut up to what God has revealed. Dr. Dawe affirms so easily: "The Christian affirmation is that the mystery of God and his love for mankind, hidden in each of the great religions, was manifested in the life, death, and resurrection of Jesus Christ." But where does he find this novel idea in Scripture?

Recently, Dr. Robert J. Marshall, the President of the Lutheran Church in America, was invited to speak to the leadership of a sister body, the American Lutheran Church. He used the occasion to reply to those who were critical of Lutheran missions. His remarks were published in The Lutheran (December 2, 1970), and are worthy of sober reflection. Dr. Marshall formerly was the Professor of Old Testament at the Chicago Lutheran Theological Seminary and his address is biblically oriented. He analyzed the manner in which the Jerusalem Council reviewed the missionary work and practice of the Apostle Paul (Acts 15). He particularly stressed the manner in which Paul's missionary outreach grew rather than diminished in the months and years following this ecclesiastical investigation. In application Dr. Marshall exposed the fallacious reasoning of the critics of the Church's overseas work whose only recommendation is that it be closed down once and for all. This vigorous leader unconditionally pledged his own devotion to the Church's irreplaceable task of preaching the Gospel and planting new congregations in those places where the Church does not yet exist. His final appeal:

"We will work for the Church to fulfill its primary function to proclaim the Gospel, administer the Sacraments and provide pastoral ministry . . . And we will reach out through the immediately available channels of our organized churches to obey the apostolic injunction to remember the poor . . . The most rapidly growing churches are in Africa and the South Pacific. It would appear as if God's Spirit has plans for these places, and the people there are calling, 'Come over and help us.'"

We like this. The trumpet is giving no uncertain sound (I Cor. 14:8) and many Lutherans will respond. We are bold to believe that God will bless his Church in the days ahead through the bold and biblical missionary leadership of Dr. Marshall. And in conclusion, we confidently affirm that the more central the Scriptures are in the thinking of God's people, the more concerned they will be to carry out Christ's mandate to disciple the nations. Our missionary obedience today is related to the consummation of his worldwide purpose tomorrow. And this means the glorious consummation of the extension of his Universal Lordship.

SEQUENCE OF HARVESTS

When the missionary has general supervision of an area and is responsible for directing village pastors, he needs to stress continually that village congregations have to be won and rewon for Christ with each generation. The imagery of "fields white unto harvest" not only means harvesting today, but also a sequence of harvests. No generation can live on the experience of its predecessor. Many of our second-generation problems arise from this erroneous assumption. The congregational outreach into paganism, the spiritual growth within the fellowship, and the organic growth of the structure and leadership of the young church all depend on this winning of each generation. What farmer would buy a field with the intention of harvesting only a single crop? A. R. Tippett, "Church Growth or Else?" World Vision Magazine

---

JERICHO IN ETHIOPIA
((This formal statement was prepared by a team of missionaries serving in Ethiopia, to inform their Board in America that a new Macedonian Call has come which demands that they "lengthen cords and strengthen stakes." Read it carefully. Perhaps, with the eye of faith you also can see the beginnings of a "new day" in the area where you are working.))

Something wonderful and awesome is happening in this part of Ethiopia. The walls of resistance to the Good News that we have felt over the years are crumbling before our eyes. Various sociological, psychological and economic factors have played a part in this sudden reversal, and we praise God for bringing these various factors to bear upon the situation all at one time. A completely new climate for the Gospel has been created which now affords impetus and expression to deep spiritual hunger that has been subdued for centuries.

To witness such an awakening is a rare opportunity. There is a mass mood which enables the casting off of traditional values and taboos, and the acceptance of something new--almost anything new. This kind of people's movement has occurred before in various parts of the world.

. . . .

The control of Satan is being challenged throughout this area. Many people are beginning to recognize the trickery and deceit of the witch doctors and are seeking freedom from their terrors. Some, still driven by fear, venture to leave the side of Satan only because they have heard that this Someone called Christ is more powerful and can keep them from Satanic retaliation. Others follow the Christward movement in selfishness, seeing that the new Christians do not have to spend time and money on sacrifices to the spirits. For many, the phenomenon of deliverance from demon-possession, experienced by friend or relative, is a convincing inducement to profess Christianity.

These hundreds, soon thousands, are deserting Satan's numbers because they seek something better. Whatever the motivation, they have momentarily slipped out of Satan's grip into a cultural vacuum. But the people cannot tolerate such a vacuum for long. They must, and will fill it as best they can. Already we have seen evidence of this. In one area, illiterate people for a time clamored to buy Bibles, thinking that evil spirits would be warded off by placing a Bible under the pillow at night. Those people gave up old fetishes only to substitute a new one. The challenge--the enormous responsibility--is to fill the vacuum quickly with the truth and light of God's complete message before it becomes just a more sophisticated extension of Satan's kingdom, filled with materialism, cultism, or, perhaps more tragic, another syncretistic form of Christianity.

The prospect is overwhelming! For years we chipped away at the walls of resistance with the achievement of only a few chinks here and there for reward. Now the trumpet has blown, the walls have suddenly fallen flat, and the evangelist here has to cope with a landslide. No evangelist here has ever faced anything like this before. The day of arduously seeking contacts for personal encounter is over. Now the evangelist is sought, even sorely pressed, to make some provision for teaching, for counsel, for encouragement, for enablement. The number of seekers is great, the needs many. The exhausting task is to spread time and resources as thinly and widely as possible. How much can be expected from one evangelist? How much lasting value can derive from a starvation diet of spiritual crumbs so widely scattered? To leave a Bible or printed literature in villages where no one can read will not solve the problem. Until enough Ethiopian evangelists are trained, the only means we now have for multiplying the number of Gospel voices is to use tape-recorded messages. Even this is inadequate at best. A tape recording cannot answer questions and deal with problems.

The burden of burgeoning opportunity is not only the evangelist's. Continually increasing work loads at the hospital provide more listeners for a Gospel witness in the waiting area, in the clinic and the ward. But it also overtaxes the staff. Adding to the burden is the knowledge of a new manifestation of medico-spiritual need as more people come to Christ. Since they have believed, they cannot return to the witch doctor for customary "help" in time of illness and distress. So they are turning to us. Their needs are legitimate and often urgent. But to respond means the extension of our rural medical commitment. How shall we staff a mobile medical unit or support additional village dresser clinics? We cannot say, "We are glad you have believed, Brothers; but don't come to us with your problems!"

We should have had the faith and foresight to anticipate this breakthrough and been prepared to meet the challenge. May God forgive our failure and help us now to give all we have to redeem this precious moment of history. The disturbing uncertainty of imminent political change may mean a sudden end to the

propagation of the Gospel by missions here. May God help us while there is yet
time to turn this anti-Satan move into a genuine and total Christward move.
This new life stirring within the people must be brought to birth before it
miscarries into some grotesque form of half-truth. We ask for your fervent
prayers, your understanding and your support. This phenomenon may never again
occur here. This time WE dare not fail!   END

ACHTUNG! What if this appeal came to you--assuming you were a member of the
American Board to whom it was addressed? WHAT WOULD YOU DO? Or, what if you
were one of the missionaries that drafted this appeal. WHAT WOULD YOU DO?

THINKING ABOUT JERICHO IN ETHIOPIA--WHAT WOULD YOU DO?   by Arthur F. Glasser

   Actually, one of those who drafted this appeal wrote to Dr. McGavran,
seeking his counsel. In part, this is what he received by way of reply:

   "Your task now is obviously that of organizing dozens, scores of churches
   where new Christians will meet for worship, instruction, and mutual
   encouragement; of training men from each congregation to lead these new
   believers. Most people movements have been led by workers, pastors,
   catechists, evangelists and teacher-preachers (the name varies) of very
   small educational attainments. You must begin where you are. You must
   not trust the mission station congregation to do the itineration, the
   supervision, the direction, the discipling, the baptizing, training of
   workers-in-service, the laying down of courses of instruction which is
   required. Do not let indigenous church theory force you to starve the new
   converts. You need a big, strong system of instruction, supervision,
   direction and leadership training--and God has put you there to be that
   system . . ."

   God's impatience in Ethiopia! Currently, at the School of World Mission
we have several missionaries from Ethiopia studying with us. Gunnar Kjaerland
of the Norwegian Lutheran Mission is researching the problem of planting the
Church among the nomadic people in the South. Other studies by Kermit D. Hultgren
of COEMAR (United Presbyterian U.S.A.), Rev R. Jones of the Christian Missionary
Fellowship, and Joseph Wold of the Board of World Missions of the Lutheran Church
in America all confirm the exciting reality of unprecedented opportunities for
service and harvest in Ethiopia today. In their judgment the best days of
missionary service may lie in the days ahead.

   And yet, there are those who do not believe this. In today's mail we
received a letter from a missionary who has experienced much agony of spirit
over the decision of his Board to terminate his service in Ethiopia. After
eighteen years out there he has been recalled because of the Board's desire to
"Ethiopanize" its program. He is deeply conscious that "God is moving" (his
words) in Ethiopia today. And one reads between the lines that it would be a
great privilege for him to have a part in reaping the vast harvest God is granting
the Church at this time. But no, he has been assigned the role of a "promoter"
back home in the American Church.

   The Church Growth movement is deeply committed to the indigenization of
the churches. But it has never endorsed the automatic reduction of western
personnel for theoretical reasons, especially from a country at a time when
people have never been so winnable and when doors have never been so open to

their contribution. Actually, insofar as Ethiopia is concerned, the probability is that despite the rapid growth of the Church there in recent years, there are more unsaved Ethiopians today than when missionaries first entered. Furthermore, church growth research has long since demonstrated conclusively that the departure of missionaries does not automatically contribute to the growth of national churches. On occasion, just the opposite has taken place. Students of church growth are wary of arm-chair theorizing. And they wojld wonder why the Board in question does not redeploy its missionaries within Ethiopia. If it wants them out of the way of the existing Church, some valid reason may warrant such a decision. But if the Board has an overriding concern for the evangelization of all the peoples of Ethiopia, it should either open new areas or second its personnel to other missions. For there are some societies which are posting "Help Wanted" notices. These signs of faith augur well for the future, and for the people of Ethiopia.

Because biblically the salvation of souls is the highest priority, the primary concern of the Church is the communication of the Gospel. Effective communication results in church growth. This primary concern is often forgotten in the pursuit of sound but secondary objectives and interests. Churches cease thinking in terms of essential strategy. All too often vested interests and a preoccupation with a variety of good projects determine both their convictions as to strategy and the disposition of their resources.   Donald A. McGavran, April 18, 1970

STRAWS IN THE WIND

Following World War II there was a rapid proliferation of "service" agencies committed to assisting in the task of worldwide evangelization. They provided expertise in a variety of fields--aviation, radio, literature, graphic arts, audio-visual communication, linguistic analysis, Bible translation, etc. They were content to be servants of missions, and in the years that followed gained the approbation and gratitude of the older bodies.

In recent months, however, one discerns changes in the offing. Not only have these organizations grown in size, experience and discernment, but they are beginning to feel their years! And their oats! Gone is the charismatic founder with his ardor and conviction. A new generation has come to the higher levels of administrative authority. This has inevitably meant a measure of internal crisis.

Under new leadership some organizations have tended to solidify procedures through preoccupation with the methods God blessed in the past. Others, sensing peril in this incipient traditionalism, have reached out for renewal. They have become dissatisfied with what Gardner calls "the outer husks of things." Fortunately, many already effective agencies are choosing this way.

So far, so good. No one objects when an outwardly successful organization expresses the desire to be quickened in its life and vision. And yet, missions can underestimate what is meant by the phrase "renewal in vision."

Missionary aviation is a case in point. Everyone knows about the Missionary Aviation Fellowship with its 160 adults, serving more than 40 missions with 35 planes and hundreds of radios from 27 bases in 14 countries. Many have thanked God and the MAF times without number for its valuable service, cheerfully rendered for more than twenty-five years. No organization has added such luster to the concept of "servant of missions."

And yet, MAF's new leadership has done a good deal of reflecting on the role of their organization in the overall task of discipling the nations. They have seen the impact (both helpful and harmful) of their technological presence on isolated, primitive cultures. They have observed missionary methodology at its best, and at its worst. Although always loyal to the missions they serve, they have at times had deep searchings of heart over their participation in programs they could not heartily endorse. Hence the endless debates behind closed doors. They have sought the renewal of their strength through waiting on the Lord. Some of their key administrators have also begun to study in depth such disciplines as anthropology, sociology, and church growth.

All this has resulted in renewal of vision. We now find that MAF is assuming a new stance as it seeks to fill its role in the missionary movement of our day.

Recently, we received a copy of MAF's revised statement of policy. It should be read and pondered by all mission administrators. It reflects the new vision. It is sober, for its implications are far-reaching. What are the new emphases? They follow:

1) The focus of service is the emerging national church, not the missionary society. Ponder what this will mean to the mission whose outlook is traditional and parochial.

2) The dominant concern is that this church grow and "give every person a valid opportunity to accept or reject Jesus Christ . . . in terms of his own culture and value system."

3) In essence, new meaning is poured into the old IMC Whitby Slogan (1947) --"Partners in Obedience." Obedience first, then partnership. MAF senses that it has an obedience to render to God along the line of its vision and calling. From now on it expects its field personnel "to take and active interest in the total ministry of the persons and organizations whom they serve." Here is the recognition of an achieved mutuality between itself, the missions and the churches. Although prepared to understand and cooperate in all possible ways with mission agencies and national churches, MAF "cannot always be limited" in its service by their "organizational customs and traditions."

What this will mean for the future is anyone's guess at this point. But of one thing we can be sure. MAF's revised policies indicate that service agencies are no longer content to have minority or peripheral status in the evangelization of the world. Although they shall continue to serve along the lines of their competence, they will increasingly be concerned about priorities, productivity, and church growth. How incumbent it is on missions to respond creatively to this new stirring of heart and mind. May the "infection" spread! May all Christians everywhere, regardless of their organization relationships, increasingly ask one another before launching out into any new (or old!) programs:

"Will this contribute to the growth of the Church?"
"If not, why should we move forward? Probably the
Lord of the Harvest has something better for us to do!"

Mutually Interdependent Decisions

Once upon a time a learned gentleman heard about a "people movement." "Oh, just like Constantine baptizing unbelievers," he said. When told it was not like that at all but rather, "A multi-individual, mutually interdependent decision to believe on the Lord Jesus Christ," he was puzzled. He said, "I understand what multi-individual and conversion are but what is mutually interdependent?" The answer given was that "each takes the step in light of what the other is going to do." "Oh," he said, "That is not biblical. Decision must be individual to be valid. I wish I could discuss it further with you but I really must leave as I am getting married tomorrow."

And off he went to be involved in a multi-individual, mutually interdependent decision that would affect his whole life.

...Contributed by Professor Clyde Cook, Missions Department,
Biola College.

CHURCH GROWTH CALCULATIONS, NO. 2 — Ralph D. Winter

On an earlier occasion (Vol. VI, No. 4, March 1970) we introduced the subject of growth calculations. We distinguished between their diagnostic and their predictive uses, and in particular we showed how misleading it is to lump together the statistics from fast and slow-growing populations when making a diagnosis of the past.

Now we must go on to show that predictive calculations are also consistently misleading when based on the average rate of growth of two disparate populations. The table below shows for Africa and Asia separately what happens when you project to the year 2000 the average annual growth rates for 1900-1965.

	1900		1965		2000
African Christians	4	+4.62 %/yr=	75	+4.62 %/yr=	365*
Asian Christians	9	+3.015%/yr=	62	+3.015%/yr=	175
African plus Asian Christians	13	+3.70 %/yr=	137	+4.00 %/yr=	540
			However, 137	+3.70 %/yr=	488
			so the discrepancy is		52

*All numbers in millions

These figures make clear that if we had predicted the total for the year 2000 by using the average rate of growth for the two areas lumped together (e.g. 3.7%) we would guess 52 million less. In other words the rate for the two together goes from 3.7% up to 4.0% in order to arrive at the total of 540 million derived from handling the two areas separately. That the combined rate would grow larger is reasonable when you consider the face that the faster growing area, precisely because it is growing faster, becomes steadily a larger proportion of the total base. This leads us to the generalization that: When two populations are growing at different but constant rates, the average rate of growth of the two together will not remain constant but will gradually increase to approach the faster of the two rates.

This phenomenon, incidentally, is one of the enigmas in the population explosion: predictions based on present world rates of growth always seem too small as time goes on. Why? Because the present rate is an average of both fast and slow-growing countries. Similarly, we might expect even the average growth rates here observed for Africa and Asia to be pessimistic as a basis for prediction since they are also averages of both fast and slow-growing Christian subcommunities in each region. As a matter of fact, David Barrett,* in his very thorough consideration of the African situation, actually did treat the subpopulations separately just as has been suggested here. The reason his projection (350 million) does not rise above the projection for Africa indicated here is not because the projection of sub-populations violates our rule but because, as he clearly stated, he introduced cautionary reductions--he based his estimate on half the present conversion rate (in addition to natural increase). Also, despite his conservative reductions his projection reduces the pagan reservoir to 12% by 2000 A.D. The Asian projection above is much more likely to be pessimistic.

One thing we have not mentioned is the fascinating technique for calculating the fact, for example, that a growth from 4 million to 75 million in 65 years is equivalent to an average annual increase of 4.62%. That will have to come up later.   END

WITHIN THE POSSIBLE

Warren Berggren, M.D., speaking at the Fifth International Convention of Missionary Medicine, told of babies dying of malnutrition from homes on the mountain from which other babies had come with malnutrition. "We had shown the mothers what to do," he went on, "how to deal with the situation with milk and meat; but back on the mountain, they had no milk-producing animals and no meat. We had taught them to do something they could not do."

Do missionaries and ministers serving in Asia, Africa and Latin America do the same thing in evangelism? Are the decisions for Christ we press people to make really impossible or almost impossible? Should we be working for decisions which are possible in their situation? Should we be advocating ways of deciding for Christ which so fit the circumstances that they become possible, and are in fact done?

Dr. Berggren went on, "We found in one population that 75 percent of them had resources enough so that they could use the means we advocated--which we discovered after learning that our 'milk and meat' formula would not work. That left 25 percent of the population which could not use the formula. We decided for the time being to by-pass the 25 percent and concentrated on the 75 percent, while we sought to devise a new way to meet the unique problem of the minority."

---

*David B. Barrett, "A.D. 2000: 350 Million Christians in Africa," International Review of Missions, Vol. 59, No. 233, January 1970, pp. 39-54.

There is no need to detail what Dr. Berggren's formula was. The point is that he was operating within the possible. That is where we all have to operate. The good is not the ideal good, but "the most ideal good under the circumstances." Good that cannot be done, ceases to be good.

Great advance awaits the Church as she learns to present the timeless, changeless Gospel in habiliments which make its acceptance possible. Just one illustration will etch in a small part of the picture. The Gospel as presented to Indians in North and South America has frequently been wrapped in Spanish or English language and culture. No matter how passionately presented in that vesture, its acceptance was an impossibility to an Indian who intended to remain within his own culture and language. Again and again, when the Gospel has been presented to Indians in their own heart language, and within their own culture and residential patterns, they have found its acceptance possible. Similar examples from Asia and Africa could easily be multiplied. Non-biblical barriers have frequently been erected--sometimes by missionaries and more often by national churches. The first culture group to become Christian takes to itself an "in" status and finds it very convenient and natural to insist that others join them, in their society, fight in their armor, and marry their youth. Christianity becomes almost a caste movement and the Gospel increasingly is proclaimed in ways in which it is impossible for other culture groups to hear it.

The Gospel should be advocated within the possible.

THE DAM HAS BROKEN!

In a fourteen-month period the William Carey Library has brought into print 26,000 books and 22,000 smaller publications on mission strategy. Then, the newly formed Church Growth Book Club, in only its first four months of operation, has processed 708 orders asking for 2,100 titles from among 50 different books from six different publishers (Eerdmans, Zondervan, Friendship Press, Moody Press, Fortress Press, as well as the William Carey Library). The vast majority of these books were sold at 40% to 50% off. How has this come about? Will it last? Why this new emphasis? We have been asked to give a brief account.

Let's start with the Church Growth Bulletin. What readers get in this bulletin is only a tiny glimpse of the immense amount of excitement that week by week rolls into written form at the School of World Mission and Institute of Church Growth. It comes from the kind of experienced, cross-cultural ambassadors you see on the colored photograph clipped to the front of this issue.

In the past five years, however, over 80 book-length investigations have been produced. These are not so easily distributed. Even in the abbreviated air-weight edition of our missions curriculum, there are 27 advanced courses plus 13 new, doctoral-level courses. These classes stir up and stimulate insights that work like yeast in the raw dough of the data brought back from dozens of fields. The results are not student exercises in library research, but vital contributions to urgent, immediate matters of field strategy.

However, until a bit over a year ago there was no way for this vital thinking to be economically reproduced. Our faculty constantly gets letters --perhaps 2,000 a year--asking profound questions about specific situations. Until recently backbreaking correspondence has been the only channel of communication beyond the literal physical return to the field of some 300 men and women who have gone back after studying with us. But what are 300 among 30,000 missionaries at work? Somehow it seemed essential to offer more than "graduates by the dozens" and "letters by the hundreds." We lacked serious books by the thousands.

Dr. McGavran's Bridges of God had long been in orbit, and other Institute of Church Growth publications had begun to make their way, some informally in humbly bound books printed in India, others stylishly produced by traditional publishers. But these were only a trickle. It was still rarely possible to help a person writing in specific questions even if the insights he sought were contained between the covers of a library copy of a manuscript sitting right on a shelf in Pasadena.

But now we hope we have broken the dam. Between 1967 and 1969 we made a study of the "care and feeding" of conventional publishers. It turned out that leading religious book publishers were not the least bit refractory or uninterested in highly specific missions books; their smoothly oiled machinery was simply geared up for a broad, popular U. S. market.

It was not possible for them to plunge into a big, new, expanded program of publishing specialized missions books when almost each one had its own unique market. You are pounding on the wrong door if you ask a taxi to take you to a distant city. Publishers may pass by outstanding books by accident. It is much more often that outstanding books are passed by because a specific publisher has correctly appraised the discrepancy between the kind of people who know his label and the proper audience of the book in question.

But the same automobile that is commonly used as a taxi can also be used for other purpose: we were delighted to discover that the book-producing process can be harnessed for "instant printing" or specialized works for micro-markets, and that even the book club mechanism, with a bit of thinking could be made to serve the far-flung corners of the earth. How?

Typesetting can be replaced by modern, high-quality carbon-ribbon, Selectric typewriting. A non-justified (irregular) right-hand margin is more and more common and--of all things--is, we are told, more readable! After reducing composition costs, modern lithographic firms can then produce books that can be conventionally priced even if only 1,000 copies are printed.

Distribution must usually be tailor-made for each book, and well planned in advance. In the case of thirteen books thus far, mission agencies have shouldered specific responsibility. If you don't want to "make money" on books you had better not lose money either, or you'll run out of fuel. A book club gives people who cannot get to bookstores a real price break, even on regular publishers' books, since the club arrangements require at least three books to be purchased (or two including the new selection) and enables us to just barely meet costs, we hope. We are especially grateful for the unusual arrangement which we have been able to make with Zondervan for the marketing of the Latourette series on the Expansion of Christianity.

CHURCH GROWTH
BULLETIN

from the
INSTITUTE OF
CHURCH GROWTH

Address:
FULLER THEOLOGICAL
SEMINARY
135 N. Oakland
Pasadena, Calif. 91101

DONALD A. McGAVRAN, B.D., Ph.D.
Director

MARCH 1971   Subscription $1 per year   Volume VII, No. 4

Hindus Move to Christ

by

The Rt. Rev. Anand Rao Samuel, Church of South India

Andhra State in India has a population of more than fifty million people. Its language is Telegu. Its peoples are of various social standings and economic positions. About thirty-five percent of the population is literate.

The Gospel was brought to the state nearly a hundred and fifty years ago by outstanding missionaries. It prospered chiefly among the lower castes and the landless people. A numerous Church was formed by 1900, chiefly among the Baptists, Anglicans, Lutherans and Methodists. A notable expansion took place before World War II under the leadership of the late Bishop Azariah and others -Indians and missionaries.

Today a great movement toward the Lord Jesus Christ is on among caste Hindus in Andhra State. This is the result of decades of preaching the Gospel, establishing schools and colleges, running hospitals, and carrying on other services in the name of Christ. Hundreds of thousands of Hindus have been profoundly influenced by the life and teaching of Jesus Christ. Their influence, too, has been remarkable. Two outstanding examples are Mahatma Gandhi and Pandit Jawaharlal Nehru.

Throughout India, but especially in Andhra, the impact of the Gospel directly and indirectly has produced a revolution in the thinking of the people. Because of certain age-old religious beliefs, the people have had no desire to change their lot even when that was unbearable. They thought their efforts would be futile.

Into this climate of life and thought came the Gospel of Jesus Christ. According to it, all are equal in the sight of God. Every man has value. God so loved the world that He was born as a man, Jesus, who lived, died and rose that all men may be saved. Any one who accepts Him as Lord and Savior becomes a new creature, has victory over sin, loves and serves his fellowmen. These straightforward truths of the Gospel have had a great impact upon the people.

SEND correspondence, news, and articles to the Editor, Dr. Donald McGavran, at the Institute of Church Growth, Fuller Theological Seminary. Published bi-monthly, send subscriptions and changes of address to the Business Manager, Norman L. Cummings, Overseas Crusades, Inc., 265 Lytton Avenue, Palo Alto, California 94301, U.S.A. Second-class postage paid at Palo Alto, California.

India's sadhus and rishis forsake material possessions to pursue salvation. Inner thirst drives them to try to know God and live in fellowship with Him. The Hindu religion puts the emphasis on man's pursuit. Man has to attain illumination by works (karma), devotion (bhakti) or knowledge (gyana).

In Christ Jesus this order is reversed. It is not we who find God, but God who finds us. The Son of Man came to seek and to save that which is lost. It is not by our good works or merit that we gain new life, but by accepting what God has done in Christ. The Gospel - for those who believe it - puts an end to frustrating and frantic efforts to know God.

This new life, which Hindus have been desiring, is now evident among poor Indians of low origin who call themselves Christians. What is the secret? Ask highly placed Hindus. Christians in whom the change has come about usually fulfill humble roles as laborers and workers in the fields of these rich Hindus. The laborers have been talking to their employers in regard to new life, joy, and peace in Christ. The employers see that the Christians are faithful in the work entrusted to them. They are honest. They do not work on Sundays, which looks very strange to Hindus. Why? they ask. Because it is a Holy Day - the Day on which Jesus Christ rose from the dead, giving life and victory to all who believe in Him. Thus for Hindus in Andhra State Jesus Christ is taking on a new importance and the Gospel a new significance. As the Greeks once said, many Hindus now say, 'We would see Jesus'.

Some Hindus attend Sunday worship services. Great numbers attend festival services. They come to revival meetings thinking maybe Jesus gives new life, maybe He is the living God. Often when a member of a Hindu family is sick, the father or mother invites the Christian pastor, teacher or layman to the house and asks for prayer. If no one is available, Hindus themselves will pray in the Name of Christ. God often honors their simple faith and heals the sick.

A Hindu girl of 14 years of age had a Christian friend from whom she learned a Christian song. That song led her to accept Jesus Christ as her Lord and Saviour. Her father was not at all happy about her singing Christian songs, praying in Christ's Name and joining in Christian worship. He forbade her to have anything to do with the Christian religion. Shortly after this her father woke up in acute pain. Nothing gave him relief until the daughter quietly came to him and prayed in the Name of Jesus. After a short while, the father slept peacefully for the rest of the night. The next morning he remembered what had happened. He called his daughter to his side and gave her permission to do all he had forbidden before his illness. He became friendly and open to the Gospel.

The rest of the family have been baptized and, although the father continues as a Hindu, they all live together as a family. The girl is being used of God to preach the Gospel in all the villages round about. When she visits her relatives she talks to them quietly of Jesus and His love and tells them what joy He brought into her life. She invites the pastor and other evangelists to these villages to speak to her relatives about the Gospel. She also conducts worship services and renders a healing ministry.

Many Hindu women have become literate in the past one hundred years. Through Christian schools they have come into contact with Christians. Some of the glow of Jesus Christ shows in their lives. The women are well to do, so they need not go out to work. They have much leisure and often read the Bible. They breathe the new air of freedom, fellowship, love and peace. They begin to practice certain things they have learned. The Word of the Bible comes to life in them in crises like sickness, death, grief and calamity. They turn to Jesus Christ in prayer. Their prayers are answered. God honors their simple faith. They yield their lives to the Lord Jesus Christ. He becomes the living God in their lives.

Women who have had a deep spiritual experience sometimes ask us for baptism. If their husbands or parents are willing, we give the necessary instruction and baptize them by immersion because it is more meaningful to an adult. We take them along with other Christians of the village in procession to a nearby tank or river. Often Hindu friends out of curiosity come to see what is happening. After baptism there is a brief service of thanksgiving and exhortation.

If husbands or parents are against their being baptised, we ask them to go back to live the changed life and pray for the other members of their family. Quite often the family recognizes the change that has taken place. They are better wives or daughters, more loving and considerate, honest and hard working. Husbands and sons are influenced, and often ask to be baptized.

The Andhra movement may be called a family movement. The family stays together and provides that fellowship and solidarity so essential for the new believer. If on the other hand, against the wishes of family, a person is baptized he is estranged. The family then looks upon Christianity as a religion that takes dear ones away, and upon Jesus Christ as one who divides the family. Great discretion and wise handling is called for in these cases.

This movement may also be called a lay movement. God is raising laymen and laywomen to spearhead this movement - laborers, leather workers, rickshaw pullers and carpenters. They are not paid employees of the Church, but they are the Church in the World. They are effective witnesses to the Lord Jesus Christ. One such part-time worker has been instrumental in bringing many Hindu men and women to Christ. Through him a crippled woman believed. She cannot use her legs. She has to drag herself around. She had no joy or hope in life before she heard of Jesus Christ and accepted Him. She is now a radiant witness. She is bringing many to know Jesus Christ. She, too, is a volunteer worker. Preaching is her wage. Leading people to the Lord is the breath of life to her. Jesus is still the only one who transforms people. He is the only one who gives them new life and hope.

India desperately needs Jesus Christ who is still on the fringe of its life. He must be at the center of India's life and culture. Men build many plans and schemes for the development of this great nation; but unless the spirit of Christ is infused into our millions, all these will fail.

The challenge comes to the Church in India. Rise up and follow the Master to the point of complete obedience, to death if necessary, so that the people of India may come to know Jesus as their Lord and Saviour.

LIFE STYLE

...a heavy responsibility is laid on us to help the Church recover a life style in which evangelism is the key.

Donald Gill, Executive Secretary,
Evangelistic Association of New England

Do You Believe the Sixteen-Year-Old Document Below?

Africa Committee, DFM   A 744
156 Fifth Avenue   (Confidential)
New York 10, N. Y.
January 6, 1955

The Discipling of Africa in This Generation

Dr. D. A. McGavran

Conditions in animistic Africa encourage the belief that all Africa south of the Sahara may be discipled in this generation. Despite many problems and difficulties, whose reality and seriousness cannot be gainsaid, the supremely important fact in regard to Africa is that, barring its Moslem population, practically all the rest of its people are able within this present century to be won to Christian faith.

Seven great reasons make this likely. 1. A younger church of twenty millions has been established largely within the last fifty years. 2. A vast animistic exodus is going on which will deliver scores of millions of animists to other faiths in the next thirty years. 3. The rising economic potential of Africa makes it relatively easy for the pastorate to be self-supporting from the beginning and for church income to rise with the rising income of the membership. 4. The strong sense of community, the tribalism which is the life of all Africans, makes group accessions available to speed sound church growth. 5. Present relatively quiet political conditions are favourable to church growth. 6. Many governments in Africa are friendly to the idea of the discipling of Africa. 7. It has now been universally recognized that, despite their present primitiveness in many places, Africans are potentially as able a race as any and hence their discipling is as desirable as any. These and other favourable conditions mean that vast numbers of growing multiplying churches can now be established and that the conversion to Christian faith of Africa south of the Sahara is now possible in the foreseeable future.

This situation is vitally important to the Christian Churches. Africa offers incomparably great opportunities for church growth. Fifty million persons may be won for Christ in the next thirty years. No such open door has ever faced Christendom. Here is a continent which may be brought into the kingdom of Christ in this generation. We cannot say that the African opportunity is merely somewhat more favourable than that in other countries. The difference in degree has become so great that it amounts to a difference in kind. In Africa there is a new dimension in missions. Elsewhere "missions" means world friendship, sowing the seed, doing good in the name of Christ, winning one or two per cent of the country for Christ, cooperating with a national church which thirty years from now will comprise a very small minority of the total population. But in Africa south of the Sahara, "missions" means reaping the harvest, winning ninety per cent of the population to Christian faith and cooperating with a national church which thirty years from now will comprise a huge majority of the total population. The unparalleled and momentous nature of the Africa opening, to the visitor from India, towers up above the horizon like Mount Everest.

Yet curiously and tragically the tremendous and unique call of an entire continent in process of turning to Christ is seldom clearly heard. The older churches and their missions seem unaware of the one continent which can be--not merely evangelized but--<u>discipled</u> in this generation. Consequently in many places open doors are left unentered, boys are sent to do men's jobs, individuals instead of tribes are claimed for Christ, the denominations of Protestantism, from Anglicans to Pentacostalists, work as separate uncoordinated churches and priceless opportunities are permanently lost. There are several reasons for this 'ordinary approach to an extraordinary situation.'

First, is the equalitarian doctine which underlies so much of modern missions. Equalitarianism asserts that missions must be carried out everywhere--'to all the world'--and therefore all missions must be considered equally valuable. According to this doctrine a mission board would correctly nourish work in Africa in proportion as it was able to nourish its other missions elsewhere; and mission boards would correctly be only relatively interested in Africa--as in one responsibility among many. The custom of treating Africa as just one more mission field to take its turn at missionary funds and staff along with many other fields where a growing conquering church has not yet been established and probably cannot be for the next thirty years is very widespread. As a result, the magnitude of the Christian harvest in Africa is not seen, and, if it is seen, it is not acted upon.

Second, is the fact that our times have seen a great development in the auxiliary services of Christian Missions. The true end of missions is obscured by the multiplicity of good things done by missions. The centrality of baptizing the peoples is hidden by a plethora of services rendered to the unbaptized peoples. Thus when the sudden opportunity to induct animistic Africa into the Christian Church in this generation presents itself, the eyes of Christian leaders are blinded by the many good works now being carried on by missions--good works which are expected to result in no discipling at all.

Third, is the fact that the central task of missions is obscured by some of the problems which make up part of that task. There are unquestionably grave problems in connection with missions in Africa. To lead discipled tribes into such a deep and real knowledge of God that each member becomes a 'born again' Christian; to combat race price amongst white people which is such a real stumbling block to Africans and such a real denial of the gospel; to lift a hundred million people into literacy; to secure social justice for the economically exploited; to develop African leadership and turn over to it the management of church and mission; while using the magnificent educational opportunities of today for the benefit of the African, to prepare for the years ahead when states will not do all their education through churches;--all these and many others are urgent tasks. Yet they are not the main task and must not take its place--<u>that</u> is discipling the peoples. These accompanying tasks can be undertaken with the greatest chance of success if the actual induction of the peoples into the Christian Church proceeds at the greatest rate of speed. None of the tasks can be successfully accomplished if half of the animists--or all of them--become Moslems or Communists! It is poor mission strategy to forget that the baptizing of unbaptized peoples in this generation when they want to be baptized is the central task. Only if it is accomplished will these other problems find their satisfactory solution. Yet Satan always suggests that it would be better strategy to stop discipling for a while to pay attention to some accompanying problem. Naturally Satan suggests the course which obscures the call of God to bring His people out of bondage NOW.

Fourth, amongst some the opportunity is not seen because of the preoccupation with individualistic processes, concepts and habits of evangelism and church

growth, in a day when whole peoples (tribes) are being called by God to leave
Egypt for Canaan. Hendrik Kraemer gives much credit for the rapid discipling
of sections of Indonesia to the fact that some of the earlier missionaries
"claimed whole tribes for Christ" rather than attempting to convert a few
persons out of the tribes to Christian faith. Acquaintance with group conversion, so urged by Dr. Warnshuis and Bishop Pickett, would enable Christians to
recognize the magnitude of the African opportunity.

Fifth, the opportunity is sometimes not seen because with the more
advanced African churches, whose independence of action is rightly respected by
missions, great opportunities fail to be recognized or grasped while mission and
church are engaged in respecting each other's rights. Thus for example, there
are tremendous opportunities in the Northern Territories of the Gold Coast, but
utterly inadequate efforts to meet these are being talked about by the strong
national churches of southern and central Gold Coast and the missions close
their eyes to the open door because it is in the churches' field.

Sixth, the concept of a planned discipling of a ready continent is something novel to those accustomed to thinking of missions as cautious advance
among resistant non-Christians. That a ready continent really exists can hardly
be conceived. Though for many years we have been praying for His kingdom to
come, it is difficult to believe that all of Africa south of the Sahara can now
be turned to Christ. The day of large scale coordination of missionary effort
to serve a tremendous exodus of men, women and children from their lands of
bondage has arrived, and is so unexpected that we scarcely know what to do with
it. The sociological and theological understandings of such movements or whole
peoples is largely lacking. We are trying to shepherd peoples with the tools
used for a one-by-one process of conversion. All this demands (a) that the
attention of the churches of the world be focused on the overwhelming opportunity for the discipling of Africa; and (b) that a strategy of massive
ingathering be initiated and given an absolute priority in men and resources.

How long the favourable conditions described in the beginning of this
statement will last no one knows. Many signs indicate that they will not last
long. They are here today. They will probably not be here thirty years from
now. The extremely favourable situation strikes anyone coming into Africa
from Asia. But equally certainly any visitor from Asia is quite sure that the
revolutionary tide which has engulfed Asia will engulf Africa. The time is
short. Among the factors which urge haste are the following.

At present an inactive Islam lies all across the northern edge of animistic Africa and deeply infiltrates all of East Africa. Even in its relatively
inactive state many of the tribes of West Africa are adopting it as the easiest
world religion into which to emerge. Should Islam become active with many
Moslem nations coming to self consciousness, its rate of advance would be
greatly accelerated.

The uneasy political condition throughout the world threatens multiplication of disturbances such as Mau Mau and of major changes in control such as
those anticipated in Nigeria. As such changes occur, the work of discipling
may become much more difficult. Now is the accepted time....

1971 Comment by Donald McGavran

"The Discipling of Africa in This Generation" was written in October
1954. I had gathered the evidence on which it was based in April, May and

June 1954 during a trip across Africa from Mombasa to Accra by train, car, bus, truck, paddled canoe and airplane.

Church Growth Bulletin seldom prints sixteen year-old observations; but is doing so this time for three cogent reasons.

a) This good news was so unexpected that it was not believed, and today it must be. When, in October 1954, the report was read out to a New York gathering of mission executives convened by the chairman of the Africa Committee, it was met with amused scepticism. When, in January 1955, it was circulated as the mimeographed document reproduced above, it elicited no resolve to multiply resources in Africa, no determination to learn how better to disciple those who wanted to be followers of the Lord, no survey to see whether these extraordinary affirmations were really true, and indeed no interest at all. Such scepticism and unbelief should now end.

b) "The Discipling of Africa in This Generation" is now supported by much additional data which makes action even more desirable and urgent. Dr. Barrett's considered forecast that Christians in Africa will by the year A.D. 2000 number 357,000,000 was first published in the Church Growth Bulletin for May 1969. The enlarged form, in the January 1970 issue. This scientific forecast - widely quoted since by Time and other national news magazines - abundantly supports the 1955 article, which can no longer be shrugged off. The mighty discipling is going on and will continue for the next few decades. Nothing can stop it, though large scale withdrawing of missions can slow it down and reduce its Christian color. Whole highly winnable tribes can turn to Marxism, Materialism, or Islam.

c) Grave danger exists that what happened in 1955 will happen again in 1971. Barrett's forecasts and other similar reports of receptive peoples may again be read with 'amused scepticism'. It is still possible for open doors to be left unentered, to send boys to do the work of men, for individuals to be claimed for Christ instead of tribes, and for priceless opportunities to be permanently lost. What the day demands is sacrificial action. Missionary societies, supporting laymen and ministers, missionaries, and African church leaders of note should so center prayer, giving, evangelism, discipling and perfecting on Africa that the great turning now in process continues a deeply Christian process and leads tens of millions to an intimate knowledge of the Saviour and His Word, making possible marked ethical and cultural advance.

This 1955 article is being reprinted with the prayer that the massive pessimism with which great commission missions are regarded in many quarters will be replaced with a sober understanding of the new day which God gives the Churches and a firm resolve to respond to these unprecedented opportunities as Christians should. The next thirty years must see

The Discipling of Africa South of the Sahara.

THE INESCAPABLE PRIORITIES

".....The Christian knows from the outset that the salvation of a single soul is more important than the production or preservation of all the epics and tragedies (and other great literature) in the world."

C. S. Lewis in Christian Reflections (Eerdmans)

The Elburn Consultation

by C. Peter Wagner

Through an oversight, Church Growth Bulletin has not yet informed its readers of one of the most significant missionary gatherings of recent months, the Elburn Consultation on Latin America. This meeting of fifty invited delegates, executives of missions ministering in Latin America and some professors of missions, was convened last September by the Evangelical Missions Information Service under the leadership of Dr. Vergil Gerber.

IFMA-EFMA mission leaders had become disturbed because of the findings of Latin American Church Growth which has recently been published in English, Spanish and Portugese, written by William Read, Victor Monterroso and Harmon Johnson. As the final published document relates, "Disturbed by the evident failures of some IFMA/EFMA missions in producing vigorous church growth as disclosed by the book, the delegates examined their programs related to the evangelization of Latin America, and made a series of recommendations." The following are excerpts from the Elburn findings:

1) Recognizing the need for standardizing procedures for the gathering of statistical data on the Protestant Church in Latin America, we suggest that the Evangelical Committee on Latin America establish a committee to develop a standard format in the hope that these procedures would be adopted by all IFMA/EFMA missions.

2) We recognize the goal of biblical evangelism to be the bringing of men into a living relationship with Christ and His Church and not just an attempt to communicate the facts of the Gospel to the minds of our listeners.

3) We would encourage missions and national churches constantly to review their field activities in order to assign high priority to responsive areas, maintaining the missionary force at such a level of mobility that these areas will be effectively occupied.

4) The evangelistic task in Latin America is far from completed. The work of evangelical and evangelistic missions needs to be continued in cooperation with the expanding national churches. Multitudes of Latin Americans, especially in the cities and among the lower classes are responsive, and if the Gospel is proclaimed to them in a relevant manner, large numbers can be expected to yield their lives to Christ and become faithful members of His church.

5) High priority in missionary recruitment and deployment should be given to the evangelist and church planter. Many national leaders feel that more missionaries ought to be setting the example on the growing edge of the church rather than becoming involved in the internal development of churches already firmly planted and organized.

6) When other missionaries such as teachers, social workers, technical specialists, etc., are deployed, their respective roles be evaluated according to their contribution to evangelism and church planting.

7) Recognizing that at times an overly-rigid application of indigenous church principles has resulted in our failure to share responsibility and resources in a way that might have enhanced optimum church growth, we would recommend a restudy of our policies in this area.

The Church Growth Bulletin commends our brethren who met at Elburn, and would hope that hundreds of other leaders in church and mission in Latin America, both missionaries and Latin Americans, gather in similar study sessions throughout the continent. Latin American Church Growth is a veritable gold mine of solidly biblical and soundly pragmatic insights as to causes of growth and nongrowth in the churches to the south.

The report of the Elburn Consultation is available from Evangelical Missions Information Service, Box 794, Wheaton, Illinois 60187.

DISTORTION OF MISSION

Father Eugene Hillman in his stimulating book, The Church as Mission goes to considerable length to point out that "confusion on the meaning of the Church's missionary function is bound to lead to disastrous conclusions, even if such are not intended." He quotes a missiologist (R. Hoffman) who made a special study of the various connotations of the words "mission" and "missionary" used by the Church to focus attention on its needs in France, and the resultant loss of interest of its youth in the foreign mission apostolate--"and this in a country which was a leader in Europe in promoting foreign missions."

"We might think of this tendency in an admittedly far-fetched analogy. If all of the most articulate writers in the medical field were members of a certain school of thought in the United States, and were profoundly influenced by their experience with one presumably great modern American medical problem, the rest of us--reading their works for ten or twenty years--might eventually come to believe that the major threat to world health today is obesity. At least, we might find it difficult to believe that, in fact, the major threat is just the opposite-- in the much larger world outside of America. Has something like this happened to our thinking about the mission of the Church in the modern world?"

The Church as Mission, Herder & Herder, p. 31

News

RHODESIA ACTS FOR CHURCH GROWTH   by Tilman Houser, SWM-ICG '69

I have just returned to Lundi from Salisbury, Rhodesia, after attending and lecturing at a Church Growth Seminar sponsored by the Evangelical Fellowship of Rhodesia. Dr. Don Smith of Daystar, a promising new missionary society, conducted the seminar. Africans and missionaries (about equal numbers of each) from Swaziland, Zambia, Malawi and Rhodesia registered at the University College of Rhodesia for the five-day seminar January 11 to 15, 1971. A carload of Nazarenes drove nearly a thousand miles from Swaziland to be there. Other groups represented were Baptists, Wesleyans, Brethren in Christ, Salvation Army, Dutch Reformed, Team, and Free Methodists. All told, eleven denominations attended.

A great deal of interest was shown in my study of the growth of the Free Methodist Church in Rhodesia. Both missionaries and Africans saw parallels in their own situations. Keen interest was shown in church growth concepts. The discussions from the floor were a smashing experience to some of the people involved in traditional missionary work and led to deep thinking and re-evaluation of their programs.

Since returning to Rhodesia, I feel God is readying His people for an exciting time of church growth in Africa.

YAMADA ON CHURCH GROWTH IN JAPAN

One of the new cheering developments is Africasians writing on church growth. Rev. Takashi Yamada of Kobayashi, Japan, reads all he can find on church growth. He knows Japanese society from the inside out. He tries out promising principles concerning the communication of the Gospel and observes how they work. He writes in Japanese for Japanese his convictions and findings about how congregations multiply.

Recently published is his Church Growth Pamphlet Series: Number 3 (448-3 Hosono, Kobayashi City, Miyazaki Ken, Japan). Its meaning would be sealed off from the English speaking world, except that Mr. Yamada's fellow worker, Mennonite Paul Boschman, has translated it into English and published it in mimeographed form, thus making it possible for hundreds, who do not have the privilege of knowing Japanese, to profit from Mr. Yamada's insights.

Hundreds of thousands of Africasians are busy propagating the Gospel. The wealth of knowledge and experience these workers and pastors have ought to issue in much writing. Missionaries can help in several ways.

a) Circulate church growth writings, now available in the great languages like Japanese, Spanish, Portugese, Hindi, and Mandarin.

b) Encourage ministers and others experienced in successful propagation of the Gospel to write up their own convictions. (See lead article by Bishop Anand Rao in this issue).

c) Translate significant church growth writings into English and publish them as pamphlets, books, magazine articles, mimeographed booklets, and cassettes.

Christian Mission should hear from hundreds of Yamadas.

ENNS BECOMES MISSION EXECUTIVE

Rev. Arno Enns, Conservative Baptist Missionary who has spent many years in western Argentina, has just been appointed Executive Secretary for Latin

America for the C.B.F.M.S. Mr. Enns has a B.D. (1952) from Fuller Theological Seminary and an M.A. in Missiology (1967) from the School of World Mission and Institute of Church Growth there.

Conservative Baptist missions in Latin America will be led by a veteran missionary with advanced training in missions.

His book on the growth of Evangelical Churches in Argentina is an accurate, readable account of the major Protestant denominations and will be off Eerdmans press soon. It is entitled MAN, MILIEU and MISSION IN ARGENTINA, and is a notable contribution to missiology.

GROUP CONVERSION IN COLOMBIA by Norman Piersman

Jose was saved a year ago in Blas De Lezo and was baptized with his wife and three oldest children on Palm Sunday 1970. At four months old in the Lord, he made a long trip back to his home village. There he gave his testimony to his many relatives and left a Bible. In November 1970, the Lord in a dream showed him his people coming up out of the river after being baptized. This spurred him on to plan another trip.

On Saturday, January 2, 1971, he and I reached this village and presented the plan of salvation, intimating that the next day would be the "day of decision". Sunday morning Jose preached and I asked for decisions. Nineteen received Christ. At the evening gathering, thirty more responded to the invitation. After further biblical teaching we asked people to gather for the special orientation classes to be held the next day. Wednesday many villagers were present to see their first Protestant baptismal service. We gathered at the banks of the Sinu River. Twenty-four of Jose's relatives - his mother, brothers, sisters, cousins, brothers-in-law, nephews and nieces - testified to their new faith in Christ and obeyed the Word in baptism.

That same day we met with those whom we had chosen to lead the new church. We asked Jose's brother to teach the Bible to new believers, the local school teacher to give the main Sunday School lesson, and another man to prepare a children's talk each Sunday. Another brother was named as Bible salesman. The new church elected a lady who could read well to manage the small library. All five were given materials and a brief how-to-do-it session.

Jose stayed on for some days to teach Christians how to use their new Bibles, share with them some more hymns, teach them more about prayer and lead them into an experience of family devotions. How true the Word is - "believe on the Lord Jesus Christ and you shall be saved, you and your household".

TEAM MINES RICH VEIN

"TEAM's Venezuela field had a men's retreat in May 1970 to study papers on Church Planting and Missionary-National Relationships. A number of recommendations were made which the Field Council later approved. One was that Ken Larson and Norman Chugg be sent to El Salvador to find out how the Assembly of God Bible Institute trains its students to start new churches.

"In our eighteen day trip we met with leaders of the Foursquare Mission in Panama; the Gospel Missionary Union in Panama; the Christian Reformed Mission in Mexico; the Central American Mission in Guatemala, El Salvador, Honduras, and Costa Rica; the Presbyterians in Guatemala; the Latin America Mission in Costa Rica; the International Baptists in El Salvador; and the Assemblies of God in El Salvador. We felt fortunate in having been able to meet with many of the major leaders. We must have interviewed some 50 people as we carried out the purposes of our trip."

Norman Chugg   Kenneth Larson

January 1970   Apartado 355, San Cristobal, Venezuela

Comment This mimeographed report of 19 pages is well worth getting from Mssrs. Chugg and Larson. They saw a great deal and have described it with care.

Many should launch similar expeditions. A great deal of church planting is going on. Those who do it have valuabel testimony to share. In each kind of population, a different kind of planting occurs. The testimony of those who have begun strong churches is, of course, weightier than that of those whose plantings have been sparse and weak.

Any mission or Church which sends a learning expedition should ask those sent to read that notable book, Latin American Church Growth before going. It is available in Spanish, Portugese and English. The more the team knows about the processes of church growth before it sallies out to learn, the more it will benefit from the trip.

Take national leaders on such scouting expeditions. And, of course, include them in the study of Latin American Church Growth. They have much to contribute and much to learn.

The "Church Growth Book Club" offers another valuable resource to national leaders and missionaries. The long lack of literature describing the establishment and nurture of congregations is coming to an end. Thanks to the Book Club prices are reasonable. A portion of every mission and church budget should be spent for books which describe how better to do effective evangelism - evangelism which, like Paul's, leaves behind it a trail of new churches.

In 1966 the great Wheaton Congress on Evangelism regretting former "complacency with small results long after a larger response could have been the norm" and "failure to take full advantage of the response of receptive peoples" urged "that research be carried out by nationals and missionaries in all parts of the world to learn why churches are not growing...to evaluate church growth opportunities now overlooked, and to review the role, methods and expenditures of our agencies in the light of their significance to evangelism and church growth". TEAM's safari to Central America is part of the research which Wheaton urged. One of the very hopeful signs of our day is the mounting desire to discover those populations which God has prepared to leave Egypt and those methods of missionizing which God is currently blessing to the spread of the Gospel.

CHURCH GROWTH
BULLETIN

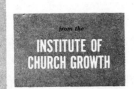

from the
INSTITUTE OF
CHURCH GROWTH

Address:
FULLER THEOLOGICAL
SEMINARY
135 N. Oakland
Pasadena, Calif. 91101

DONALD A. McGAVRAN, B.D., Ph.D.
Director

MAY 1971   Subscription $1 per year   Volume VII, No. 5

CONTENTS

WITHOUT CROSSING BARRIERS

"Men like to become Christians without crossing linguistic, racial or class barriers"

This vitally important principle of church growth explains in part why some congregations grow and others do not.

In March 1971 career missionaries, studying at Fuller's School of Missions and Institute of Church Growth, contributed from their experience in many lands illustrations of this principle. The Rev. Walther Olsen, missionary to France, selected the following, believing they would help nationals and missionaries be more effective communicators of the Gospel.

Biblical hurdles to accepting Christ must, of course, be left in place. But non-biblical hurdles should be removed. Men must repent of their sins and believe on Jesus Christ, for that is a biblical hurdle. Since nothing in the Bible requires a man (in becoming a Christian) to study the Bible or worship God in a foreign language, it is poor policy to require that to become a baptized believer, the convert must cross linguistic lines. That non-biblical hurdle should be removed.

SEND correspondence, news, and articles to the Editor, Dr. Donald McGavran, at the Institute of Church Growth, Fuller Theological Seminary. Published bi-monthly, send subscriptions and changes of address to the Business Manager, Norman L. Cummings, Overseas Crusades, Inc., 265 Lytton Avenue, Palo Alto, California 94301, U.S.A. Second-class postage paid at Palo Alto, California.

Churches tend to grow when men becoming Christians join others of their own race - tribe, sub-tribe, caste, or clan. When becoming Christian means joining a different 'breed' of men, church growth is always slowed down. Sometimes it is stopped. Conglomerate churches grow slowly.

The following incidents show how in many lands observing the principle speeds up and disregarding it slows down the propagation of the Gospel.

Without Crossing Linguistic Barriers:
Vietnam: In 1954, about 10,000 Thai people from North Vietnam came to the South and settled in Tung-Nghie, about 20 miles from Dalat. Several hundred of these turned to the Lord by the influence of a Thai Christian who worked for the government and by the relief program of the Vietnamese Church. A church was built and a Vietnamese preacher was sent there to shepherd them. The Gospel has been preached in Vietnamese and the services have been in Vietnamese. During the last 16 years, five Vietnamese preachers were assigned one after another to that church and that people. The church "plateaued" for many years, after which it declined. The linguistic barrier prevents the church from growing. The Thai people have their own language. Their men speak Vietnamese but their women do not. They use their own language in their own homes. The Vietnamese preacher does not speak Thai, the Bible is not translated in Thai. If the Thai could become Christian without crossing the linguistic barrier, thousands will come to the Lord.
.....Truong-van-Tot.
Brazil: When the Janz team, a Canadian evangelistic team working in Germany, conducted a campaign in Curitiba, Brazil, about two years ago, the German message was competently translated into Portuguese. However, the whole campaign had a German overtone. As a result, it did not really penetrate the Portuguese community although it produced good results among those who still speak German.
.....John Klassen.
California: Out of approximately 650 Taiwanese speaking students in Los Angeles, about 50 were attending different Chinese or American churches and only a handful were participating occasionally in other church activities. When a Taiwanese speaking church was formed in Los Angeles, the total attendance tripled in three months, Many are actively at work. .....Samuel Kau.

Without Crossing Class and Race Barriers:
India: In my study of congregations in the city of Madras, I found that churches grew best in one ethnic unit. Churches established in a peta (ward) of one caste, grew faster and better than conglomerate churches containing all castes. Both Emmanuel Baptist and Bethel Baptist began to grow when their members (Mala by background) after separation from two conglomerate mother churches evangelized their own caste.
More remarkable was the following case. There was practically no growth from Malas while the Mala Christians were mixed in with the predominantly Madiga community of the St. Thomas Mount Baptist Church. Then the Malas separated and formed the Bethel Church. Immediately a web movement started among the non-Christian Malas. One family after another came for baptism. The movement is still going on. .....Gollapalli Cornelius.
The Bahamas: The poorer people (few possessions, no formal education, living in drunkenness and fornication, unable to obtain or hold a good paying job) do not come to our church even though I have been able to enter into intimate friendships with them. This is probably because the national Christians are better dressed and better educated. They aren't aware of this class distinction but the poor people are. .....Dick Kay.

France: A French pastor warned our missionaries against working with both low and middle classes simultaneously. He affirmed that to do so would alienate both. We gave him slight credence, but soon found that these two groups do not mix. Middle class parents withdrew their children from a C.E.F. "club" when they learned of the presence of lower class children.   .....Walther Olsen.
Japan: Burakumin (descendents of the outcast feudal group) of Japan live in segregated communities outside metropolitan areas. Meetings in the home of a Christian woman in such a community were well attended. But to come the half mile into town to meet with Christians at regular or special meetings was an insurmountable barrier.   .....Mildred Morehouse.
Nigeria: The Tiv Church is one of the fastest growing Churches in Nigeria. The Tiv number more than a million and have their own language. Though some know Hausa, they speak their own language. Partly because the Reformed Mission has used the Tiv language for worship and Christian instruction, and Tiv converts poured into Tiv speaking congregations, growth has been large and now more than 150,000 souls attend church every Sunday.

However, a large clan in the western reaches of Tivland has been very cold to the Gospel. Many evangelists from other Tiv clans have been sent in there with very little results. The people apparently think that to become Christian means renouncing their own clan. The Church is now waiting for one of the few converts from this clan to finish his Bible training and is praying this resistant clan will see they can become Christians without crossing clan barriers.   .....Abe Vreeke.

OUR APOLOGIES

In the March 1971 issue, on page 129, our typist dropped out one line and our proof reader (fifteen demerits) failed to catch it. The correct version reads: "The Discipling of Africa In This Generation" is now supported by much additional data which makes action even more desirable and urgent. Dr. Barrett's considered forecast that Christians in Africa will by the year A.D. 2000 number 357,000,000 was first published in the Church Growth Bulletin for May 1969. The International Review of Missions picked it up and printed it in a slightly enlarged form in the January issue.

Laity Mobilized: by Neil Braun. Impressive evidence that church growth occurs when unpaid laymen teach, preach and evangelize. A clergy-centered church life blocks growth.   Eerdmans 1971 - $3.95

WHAT CAN CHRISTIANS DO ABOUT IT?

In September 1969, at Abidjian in Ivory Coast, West Africa, the World Council of Churches called an All Africa Conference of Churches. Eugene Carson Blake spoke there. Professor Jacques Blocher, Director of the Nogent Bible Institute of France, was present throughout.

In a recent issue of PULSE he states that he was saddened by the fact that throughout the conference a new and non-biblical direction in mission was pressed on the delegates and finally adopted. The whole thing was organized so that the African Churches would line up behind mission as humanitarian action. He writes, "To evangelize " today is to act so that the war in Vietnam, the apartheid in South Africa, the horrors of exploiting capitalism, cease.   'To preach the Gospel' is to fight behind Che Guevara. During the conference I heard hardly anything said about the sin of man or repentance. Sin, if we spoke of it at all, is the present situation of society and repentance is the revolution."

In short, humane action is emphasized and propagating the Gospel is down graded if not entirely omitted. This is simply another illustration of an increasingly common situation. Christians must ask themselves whether this is right. Is it God's will for today?

If the answer Christians give is 'no', what can they do about it? They can of course speak in their assemblies and synods, in their conferences and debates. They can write about it. And they can vote with their dollars. They can support the kind of missions and the kind of mission organizations which intend to preach the Gospel. They can withhold dollars from those organizations which disguise their real intent by subtly redefining terms till 'to preach the Gospel' is "to fight behind Che Guevara."

The Editor

COMMON-LAW MARRIAGE AND THE PROPAGATION OF THE GOSPEL by George Patterson

((Previous issues of Church Growth Bulletin have carried several articles discussing the correct attitude toward men and women living in common-law marriage who become believers in Christ and seek baptism in His Church. Usually these, as young people of eighteen years of age, or thereabouts, were married in the Roman Catholic Church. When the marriages broke up, each then with the passage of the years took on another partner (or several other partners in succession). Finally each "settled down" with some one and children were born of the union. At this stage they heard the Gospel and were converted.

Now what should be done? Some Churches and missions in Latin America hold that such persons are "unbaptizable believers". They may come to church, give to the church, but may not be baptized. Since practically speaking divorce is impossible and to go back to the first partner is equally out of the question, they must remain in limbo - believers in Christ, but out of His Church.

George Patterson of Honduras, a Baptist missionary, about three years ago decided that a more Christian procedure was to baptize any sincere believer living faithfully with his partner. His reasons have been detailed in this Bulletin.

In 1970, we asked Mr. Patterson how his experiment had turned out and placed seven questions before him. He has very kindly answered these and we pass them on to our readers, confident that hundreds will be vitally interested in his reply.

The Editor))

Olanchito, Honduras
24th August, 1970

Dear Dr. McGavran:

I am happy to pass on information about our "unbaptizable believers".

A. Increase in Christians and Congregations.

Our mission began work in the Aguan Valley of northern Honduras about 16 years ago, with one missionary family on the field. In about the sixth year another missionary family came and a resident Bible Institute was begun. About four years ago this resident BI was closed and the two families relocated in other fields. I began my work then and am the only missionary in the field. At that time there were two congregations established as churches, with baptized members totaling about 70.

At present we have 22 congregations totaling approximately 490 baptized members. All these are churches with their own ministry; that is, they carry on without any outside help other than our in-service training program to prepare new lay elders or pastors.

It would be misleading to attribute this growth simply to the new policy of baptizing repentant believers in common-law marriage. Only about 25 to 30 couples in all these congregations are in that category. But I would say definitely that nine of these congregations would never have been born had we not initiated the policy. Their leaders, or our first valuable contacts, were persons who could not get legally married.

I attribute the growth primarily to our change to an extension Bible Institute , and to the fact that our Bible Institute is geared to plant churches as well as train their leadership. We do not separate evangelism and education at all. We do not have "students" as such, but only workers; the Institute exists only to help them step by step to carry out Christ's commands. We have kept it simple, gearing our lessons to the semi-literate (in comic book format), and have not prepared men for a vague future but for the immediate local work.

Nevertheless, I praise God for the baptism problem, because it put us all through a cleansing fire and changed our attitude toward God's grace. It must be granted (even symbolically by baptism) to the most degraded sinner, no matter how legally tangled his marriage prospects. No more paralyzing suspicions! No more doing the impossible (like turning stones to bread) to prove he is a child of God! Our attitude toward baptism has changed; it is no longer seen as something to be earned but something for the sinner: the worse he is the more he needs it! (John baptized the worst of sinners in the moment they confessed; but the "good guys" he sent off with their tails between their legs.)

So the increased church growth really came about more because of our controversy and the resulting stubbornness in following the Apostles, than simply because we could now baptize certain couples.

Not one of the pastors or workers who has opposed our policy has enjoyed any significant part in the new church growth. They now gain their members mostly by proselyting from our loyal people, convincing them that we are "modernists".

B.   Breakdown in morals in the Church?

I have seen no indication of moral breakdown. We have had numerous cases of immorality, as any churches in Latin America have with their new Christians. Our churches have disciplined them and I think have come out the stronger for it.

In the last three years our new churches with the policy of baptizing people in common-law marriages have averaged about one case of gross immorality apiece. Our other churches have averaged more than two apiece, all among duly "proven" members. In some cases they have not applied discipline.

I observe that the spiritual tone of a church is not so much how separatistic its doctrine is, but how loving and evangelistic it is. The new churches are growing; they are excited and happy. None of the legalistic churches are growing;

they are not starting any new works; they have no vision; their young people are dis-
illusioned with the slowness of it all. These are the circumstances which breed sin,
not simply recognizing a common-law marriage as binding!

C. Increments of the lay leaders.

Only about four of our "leaders" are not legally married; we have tried to avoid
the scandal of using such brethren in places of public leadership. But some of them
have simply risen up with gifts of the Holy Spirit which we cannot deny nor quench.
They have caused us embarrassment because of the false charges that our opposition
has made, that we are "ordaining fornicators". As I see it now, we have no more right
to deny them a place of leadership than we do baptism, if they have done everything
possible to legalize their marriage; we consider them married in the sight of God.

D. Increased effectiveness in evangelism.

Let me add to the above that our new policy has allowed us to take Christ's
Great Commission literally and seriously. He said to teach them to observe all His
commands. As I see it, these can be summarized in seven broad commands for a church:
Repent, Baptize, Love, Celebrate the Lord's Supper, Pray, Give, Teach or Witness.

We teach all our new churches' leaders to do these seven things, NOTHING MORE,
NOTHING LESS. If we keep it that simple it is that easy. Preaching formal sermons
is not necessary, nor public invitations and a host of other traditions which have
muddled our work in the past.

This orientation toward obedience, rather toward teaching the Word as an end in
itself compelled us to adapt our present baptism policy. To compromise God's grace
and Christ's commands on this point now would ruin our whole thrust; it would deny
the very basis of our church multiplication program. It would halt our attempt to
find that seed which will fall into Honduran soil, grow and reproduce endlessly by
itself; because we would have destroyed our one most valuable motivating force, which
is simple, direct obedience to those commands of Christ, nothing more, and nothing
less.

If we were to reverse our policy on baptism now, it would virtually halt our
growth--not because of the numbers who live in common-law marriage, but because it
would throw us into legalism, and we could not feel free any longer to offer God's
grace as recklessly as the Apostles did.

E. Opposition to our proposals.

Dr. McGavran, I am afraid had I foreseen the opposition I would not have had
the courage to pay the price. Warn your students that if they try to open the
doors of God's grace in this respect, they are going to suffer.

Our opposition has polarized and gone to seed; they do nothing now but criticize us. We have a few pastors here who are absolutely dedicated to thwart me and
our "modernism." They have told lies of the basest sort; they have circulated
petitions; one petition was sent to our mission demanding my removal; they sit
around in their meetings plotting and scheming. It has aged me and it has hurt.
Most of these men were my best friends. I find it hard to forgive them; God must
give me grace!! I have gone weeks at a time with a sour stomach and have lost
weight and have paid and paid again for our new policy. Many times I have been

tempted to throw in the sponge. These men go to our new congregations and tell our new lay workers that they are not fit to preach; they have no diploma, etc., and they tell the new converts that fornicators will not enter the kingdom, etc. They have destroyed two new churches, discouraging and sowing suspicion and doubt. They have caused us to make endless trips to many others to pick up the pieces and start again. We have sweat, wept and worried because of their relentless attacks until we felt dizzy every time we heard that they had hit another village.

Do not encourage any student to pioneer this policy unless he's got guts, and knows the Word of God inside and out as it relates to the doctrines of grace, baptism and marriage. In other missions and denominations the opposition will be worse because they are more established. The issue gets to the deepest roots of men's convictions.

In my field, the Aguan Valley, there are only three churches which are opposing me, but their pastors travel incessantly to our other works and in a few minutes they can do damage which it takes us months to repair; their arguments sound very biblical to these uneducated peasants.

F.   Others who have copied the Baptist Program.

I know of none who have done it openly. The reformed churches invited me for conferences to help them start churches among the less educated people in their area; they copied some of our ideas and I got some ideas of theirs. They wrote saying that there were several baptisms as a result; I had encouraged them to baptize all truly repentant believers. We discussed the marriage problem but they considered it only as an academic question. I believe some of them are thinking seriously; they will have problems.

G.   My present judgment about requiring marriage before baptism.

God has blessed us in direct proportion to our confidence in His free and accessible grace. We are not thwarting His grace by requiring marriage where it is known to be possible and convenient, but it is not biblical to require it before baptism. In the Bible baptism always came first, and such problems were dealt with afterwards, as in the case of the Corinthians (comparing Acts with the letters). So I personally prefer only asking them to promise to get married if they can. We see to it that they do; there is no problem.

In my own judgment, to deny baptism to a man who tries to get legally married and cannot is pure idiocy, unless we are prepared to advise him to separate from his common-law wife. If it is a true case of fornication Scripture leaves us no choice. He must "flee from fornication". I Cor. 5 and 6 tells us to kick out fornicators from the services! So my own judgment is:

1.   The church must determine if it is a case of fornication or if they are actually married in the sight of God.

2.   If it is fornication they must be excluded from all fellowship (Paul said it, not me) unless they separate.

3.   If they are married in the sight of God, then let's stop all this fuming about sex and fornication and tell them to keep living together as God commanded, and grant them all privileges of any other truly repentant believer.

Pardon my preaching!   In His service, George Patterson
                                                 Conservative Baptist Foreign Mission

THE REVOLUTIONARY MASSES AND CHURCH GROWTH

"Jesus did not come as a social reformer. He refused to deal with political and politico-economic or social questions. The interpretation
of His mission or of the development of early Christianity as the product of a class struggle has no basis in fact. On the other hand and in
actual fact, however, a new type of life, of a different and original
quality, had come into the world in Christ, which did exercise and will
forever exercise a very profound transforming influence and will venture on the most searching interference with the social order.....it
will succeed in destroying and breaking down evil institutions and in
inaugurating new ones.....Beyond all national and other forms of unity,
it will push forward toward an ideal religious unity which will be spiritual, inward and living."

(Robert E. Speer, The Finality of Jesus Christ, Eerdmans 1968, p.225)

THE NAME OF THE GAME by Daniel P. Fuller, Dean of Divinity Faculty, Fuller Theological Seminary

In all serious endeavors in which people are engaged, they are greatly helped
in reminding themselves of the fundamental objective they are trying to attain. A
Christian real estate broker in Southern California recently said that he believed
the reason for the outstanding success of his company was that he kept reminding
himself and his salesmen that their basic objective was to service people--"to sell
people's houses to people"--as he put it. Every football team knows that the name
of its game is to get a higher score on the scoreboard than the opponent. Recently
I saw a football game in which the team I was rooting for gained twice as much
yardage both in passing and pushing as the other team, and yet because of costly
turnovers, my team left the field in the despondency of defeat. In football, the
"name of the game" is WIN! Just as my team's school says in one of its cheers,
"Who are we? Blair High School! What do we do? WIN!"

We who have been called to impart God's Word to others can truly help ourselves
by keeping in mind the name of our game. The apostle Paul knew his objective as a
minister of God's Word so well that it keeps popping up in his writings in many different contexts. When discussing whether he would prefer to depart and be with
Christ or stay on to minister for awhile, Paul told the Philippians that he would
surely choose to live, so that their faith might increase (Phil. 1:25). He also
spoke of dying as a martyr as something occurring in the course of upbuilding the
Philippians' faith (Phil. 2:16).

After founding a new church in Thessalonica, Paul went southward to Athens and
Corinth. But hearing that the new believers back in Thessalonica were undergoing
severe persecution, he was so distressed that he wrote to this new church to say he
was sending Timothy back "to establish you in your faith" (I Thes. 3:2). Then he
continued, "When I could bear it no longer, I sent (Timothy) that I might know your
faith, for fear that somehow the tempter had tempted you and that our labor would
be in vain" (3:5). Here Paul makes it clear that all his efforts for the Thessa-
lonian church--his journeys over land and sea, his "moonlighting" by making tents,
his concentrated preaching and exhorting, his godly conduct (cf. I Thes. 2:1-12)--

all would become totally useless if the faith of the church were to vanish. Paul's whole objective, then, in preaching at Thessalonica had been to instill faith in the new Christians by persuading them to trust no longer in vain idols but in the living and true God. And after the church was founded, his objective was to do everything possible to maintain and strengthen their faith.

We conclude that "the name of the game" - the supreme objective - for a minister of the Word is to persuade unbelievers to put their trust in God and to work to strengthen the faith of those who already believe. As far as Paul was concerned, all his labors were meaningful only if they resulted in gaining new believers or in strengthening the faith of those who had already professed Christ. Since we are a comparatively small number of laborers who have the immense task of bringing the Gospel to the world, we do well to remember the name of our game, and to conserve our time and energy for the supreme objective. When we pray, preach, teach, or write, it will help us to remember that our objective is either to inculcate or strengthen faith. And the way to evaluate the priority of the many other tasks concomitant with preaching God's Word is to ask how essential they are for supporting a ministry which understands well the name of its game.

CENSUS DATA AND ESTIMATING CHURCH GROWTH by Julian C. Bridges

Decennial national censuses of population are fruitful sources of information for the study of the growth of Churches in many countries.

The 1956 edition of the Demographic Yearbook of the United Nations lists 17 countries from North and South America alone which include information on religious preference in their general censuses. Many nations in other parts of the world, which likewise follow this practice, are also listed.

In the Americas the data on religion distinguishes between Protestants and Catholics, and in countries which form a part of the British Commonwealth, information is provided according to each leading Protestant or Evangelical group.

Reliability and Validity of Census Data. The degree of reliability of information on religious preference found in the national censuses usually varies with the experience of the particular country obtaining the information. Any nation which has been recording religious data over at least one or two decades is probably publishing quite reliable information. Some countries, such as Mexico, for example, have obtained the religious preference of its inhabitants since as early as 1900. Since 1940 the number of Evangelicals in Mexico has been published not only according to the country's 32 major federal entities (mostly states) but also on the level of the nation's 2,377 civil subdivisions, similar to counties in the United States. Most nations of the world which ask the religion of their citizens also now publish the data of the local level.

As for the validity of the data, it can only be assumed that a question concerning the religious creed of a respondent, and included among other items of a census schedule, would be answered with a fair degree of honesty and openness. Of course, also one must have confidence in the census enumerators. As for published data, most nations now submit raw data to be programmed into computers, and the results are often published directly from computerized forms rather than having the information recopied, thus reducing human error considerably. At any rate, this information is the most reliable, valid, and complete data on its population which a particular country provides to the world.

The Use of Population Census Data in Estimating Church Growth

Strengths and Limitations of Census Data. One distinct advantage national censuses possess over data gathered by religious groups themselves is that the latter usually have great difficulty in securing complete and accurate information. Protestant denominations, for example, if they can obtain information at all, encounter such problems as locating non-resident members of churches. This becomes more magnified, even in developing countires, as increased geographical mobility of inhabitants takes place. Rural-urban migration, for example, complicates considerably the problem of obtaining accurate statistics on church members.

Most denominational data is published only on a state or provincial basis, whereas population census information is now obtainable on the local or even community level. Government data on religion also usually includes the preference according to sex; thus, it is possible to make comparisons between these two variables. Social and economic characteristics about a local area may also be learned, and inferences can often be drawn as to some reasons for church growth, or the lack of it, in the particular area.

A final advantage in the use of census data is that comparisons may be made as to the growth pattern of specific areas, from one census to the next. For example, information on the number of Protestants in an area or locality reveals a marked change in comparison with total population change, therefore such a locality may be singled out for special study. Also, Protestant denominations can compare their own growth statistics for a particular locality with those of the census to determine their degree of growth in relation to the total Protestant community.

There are four obvious limitations to governmental censuses; (1) it often enumerates only the total membership of the Protestant or Christian community, not the actual number of full members (communicants), churches, ministers, or other detailed information; (2) it seldom provides the particular denomination preference of the respondent; (3) it is usually taken only once every ten years; and (4) it pays no attention to homogeneous units.

Thus, the data on religious preference in the census are no substitute for church statistics, even in the year the census is taken. They are, however, a valuable supplement to such statistics. They provide the single most complete and accurate source of religious data on a nation's inhabitants anywhere obtainable.

CHURCHING URBANITES

"Tremendous amounts of missionary treasure and life have been poured out in "city work" in Afericasia. But city work is not the task. The assignment is not to "reach the cities". The Church has already done that. The task is to bring the urban multitudes to faith and obedience. The goal to be constantly held in mind is so to preach and live the Gospel that baptized believers in increasing numbers flow into existing congregations, and form themselves into new congregations, which ramify and branch out through the wards, barrios, colonias, mohullas, and other sections of urbania, soon to be occupied by 1,500,000,000 human beings.
                    Donald McGavran (Understanding Church Growth: 281)

BISHOP STEPHEN NEILL ON CONVERSION.

No question is more central to church growth than this: Does natural man, fallen man, pre-Christian man need to be converted? Does every man need to repent of his sins, believe on the Lord Jesus Christ, and become His openly confessed disciple in His Church?

The Church Growth Bulletin answers these questions affirmatively. We believe that children of Christian parents need to be converted, to turn to Christ, and in His Body become new creatures. We believe that conversion is a universal need of all men. Jews need to be converted. Moslems need to be converted. Buddhists and Marxists need to be converted.

Nothing we have read recently puts the matter as succinctly as five paragraphs by Bishop Stephen Neill which were printed in the "Church of England Newspaper" for November 13th, 1970 and are being reproduced by permission.

"It is constantly said that old ideas of mission must be completely replaced by those that are new and relevant. This is a statement that needs elucidation, and much useful discussion can arise out of it. But I wonder whether the heart has not gone out of the missionary enterprise in all the mainline Churches for another and deeper reason.

"If we put the plain question, "Do we want people to be converted?" From many of our contemporary ecumenical theologians the answer will be a resounding "No". If we are evangelicals, must not the answer be a resounding "Yes"?

"For years I have been looking for a word which will take the place of the now very unpopular word "conversion", and have not found it. I am well aware of all the possible objections to the word. But I have an uneasy feeling that those who hesitate to use the word are also rejecting the thing.

"Those of us who have come to Christ, even from a profoundly Christian background, have known what it means to be "without hope and without God in the world" (Eph. 2:12). Are we prepared to use Paul's language, however unpopular it may be? We desire all men to say Yes to Christ. But there are countless ways of saying Yes to Christ which fall short of the surrender that leads to salvation. Do we know what we are really talking about?

"It seems to me that the time has come when we ought to be done with circumlocutions and not be ashamed to say exactly what we mean."

THE SOILS: A CHURCH GROWTH PARABLE by Ralph D. Winter

It so happened that my "senior sermon" at seminary in 1956 was devoted to an analysis of the Parable of the Four Soils, commonly called the Parable of the Sower. Thus it was that I had occasion to go into some depth as to its meaning. I found that it is one of only three parables that occur in all three of the synoptic gospels, and that it is the only one of those three which has in each case the same structural function of introducing that stage in the ministry of Jesus during which the "training of the twelve" took place.

The Parable is thus a pivotal one which both sums up the public ministry of Christ and also lays the basis for His private ministry to the twelve disciples. Unfortunately, most people take it to be merely a summing up of his public ministry without any further purpose in view. Thus, a good deal of discussion has gone on as to which of the four kinds of soils represent people who are truly converted. For example, what about the third soil in which the seed takes root and grows up, but does not produce fruit? Is this a case of truly converted people or not? If not, God pity today's church. If it is, how do we understand John 15 where the branches that do not bear fruit are cast out and burned? And so on.

Rather than to attack these traditional questions directly it would be better to ask a more basic question, "How does this Parable set the stage for what Jesus did next, namely, focus his efforts on a specific and small group of people.

As soon as this new question is posed, the whole thing becomes very simple. Quite obviously Jesus got different kinds of responses from different people whom he handily grouped into four categories. And equally obviously he continued to preach the Word to only one of those groups, namely, the disciples. These were those in whose hearts were the qualities that the Parable of the Soils defines as good soil. That is to say, these are the men to whom the seed of the Gospel could be safely committed knowing that in return that Gospel seed would be multiplied in the subsequent ministry of those men, some forty, some sixty, some hundred-fold. The fruit appears in the form of further seed-sowing of the Gospel.

Thus looking back on the other three soils, we do not ask whether they represented truly converted people or not. We see that the parable has a very simple object, namely that of helping a gospel propagator decide, not who is truly converted, but with whom he may concentrate his ministry, so as to multiply his time, and not merely spend it.

When in seminary I applied this parable to the parish minister who (if he did not concentrate on a few disciples whose hearts could be described as "the good ground") would be running around spreading himself thin and never getting the work done. Whereas, were he to give most of his attention to reproducers and multipliers of the seed, then, the limited seed he had available in terms of time and energy would be multipliable by this strategy, rather than simply spent in relative futility.

After going to Guatemala my feelings about this parable were unexpectedly confirmed by sharing my thoughts with the American Indians of Mayan extraction with whom I lived for some years. These agricultural people understood at once the significance of the parable. To them there is an annual period of near-starvation when the greatest possible temptation of a family is to eat up those final few handfulls of corn which have been reserved since harvest time for seed corn at the time of planting when the next season rolls around. People who have to choose between near-starvation at one moment and the complete hopelessness of eating up their seed corn will, I can assure you, make very clear distinctions between the kind of ground which will reproduce and the kind that will not. You may be sure that they do not sow their precious few grains of corn on the beaten foot-paths between their field and the next. They do not squander those very few grains of corn on the rocky ground, or on the ground where the corn will grow up but not bear much fruit. To them, the significance of the parable is quite obvious. It is a lesson in how best to sow seed.

Thus, the ultimate missionary significance of this parable emerges with crystal clarity: this parable is the stoutest biblical basis for seeking receptive peoples and for investing our time with those who will reproduce.

As an epilogue to these observations about the Parable of the Soils, let us refer to the specific instruction which Jesus gave to the disciples. I wondered for many years just why he told them not to take any money with them, and not to stay in more than one home in a town, and why he wanted to make sure that they did not accept the hospitality of a home which was unwilling to let them stay for more than one night. The answer to these questions is all very simple - he wanted them to make sure that they found truly receptive people. He did not want them to carry money with them, lest they be able simply to pay for their night's lodging, and thus stay in a town which did not really want them. He wanted them to go, go, go until they found truly receptive hearts, knowing that if they did they would not have difficulty about hospitality and lodging. If they did not receive hospitality, the Lord did not wish them to disguise their failure by means of funds they took with them.

Here again, then, we find the same basic principle that we are to seek those whose hearts respond and to spend our time with them. Mission lies in seeking that kind of person, that kind of group. Only in this way will the very precious hours we have be spent with maximum effectiveness in the multiplication of the seed, which is the Word of God, and the multiplication of those vital fellowships which are the core of His Church.

HOW IMPORTANT IS CULTURE?

"On the whole, the New Testament seems, if not hostile, yet unmistakably cold to culture. I think we can still believe culture to be innocent after we have read the New Testament; I cannot see that we are encouraged to think it important."

C.L. Lewis in Christian Reflections (Eerdmans)

BRING IN THE VACUUM CLEANER: THE RIGHT WAY TO SAY IT. by Donald McGavran

1. Statements like the following are common in missionary speeches and writings today. All of us have heard and read hundreds.

   The Church in Hong Kong (substitute Tokyo, Bombay, Santiago, Kinshasa) is not recognized as indigenous. Dynamic, dedicated and talented local leadership is in short supply. After 100 years of Christian work the Christians number only 6 per cent of the total population.

   The greatest weakness is that the missionaries are too foreign and have not sufficiently adapted to the national culture. The Churches they have founded - only 2 per cent of the total population - seem like foreign enclaves.

   We are coming to the end of an era. Missionaries must step out of the role of leadership. Control by the missions must cease. Small and weak as the national Churches are they must take charge and sink or swim.

2. These statements are at best quarter truths. They are perhaps better de-
    scribed as cowardly betrayals of the faith. They focus on the negative.
    They are enslaved to the past. They evince no knowledge of the probable
    future. Their authors apparently disbelieve in the promises of Christ. They
    do not march under the banner of Him on whose robe is written King of Kings
    and Lord of Lords.

    The modicum of truth contained in them should be expressed - if at all - in a
    Christian frame work.

3. What a different outlook is at once secured when Christians speak conscious of
    their Faith. Let us take each of the above and - knowing ourselves to be His
    whom every tongue shall confess - voice it so that our faith shines clear.

    After 100 years of Christian work, Christians in Hong Kong (or any other
    city) number 6 per cent of the population - a wonderful 260,000 souls. In
    the next thirty years as these churches become increasingly indigenous -
    thoroughly Chinese in culture and leadership - the great satisfactions of
    the Christian life and the tremendous liberation which life in Christ
    brings is certain to lead multitudes to commit their lives to the Great
    Shepherd.

    In missions today and tomorrow, both nationals and missionaries as never be-
    fore understand cultures and are presenting Christ in almost all of the rich
    cultures of the world. Starting from two per cent of the total population -
    this new nationally acceptable Christianity has a brilliant future before it.
    With the ending of European Empires the Christian Faith is free of the
    handicap of appearing to be "the religion of our foreign rulers", the reli-
    gion of the West. It will fit every culture. It will swim in every culture
    like the fish swims in the sea. We stand in the sunrise of the missionary
    enterprise.

    In missions we are coming to the end of the difficult hesitant exploratory
    era. Hundreds of thousands of nationals lead the enterprise and call
    loudly for missionary comrades to work along side them. The task is tre-
    mendous. Two billion have yet to hear of the Saviour. The day is far spent
    and there are more winnable people on earth than there ever have been before

4. The pessimism of many who love to cudgel the existing Churches and missions is
    not merely stupid, it is sinful. It betrays the Church. It denies the Lord.
    We suspect it does not really represent the convictions of those who have
    fallen into the habit of using the trite, traitorous phrases. Bring in the
    vacuum cleaner. Make the house clean for the Bridegroom.

CHURCH GROWTH
BULLETIN

from the
INSTITUTE OF
CHURCH GROWTH

Address:
FULLER THEOLOGICAL
SEMINARY
135 N. Oakland
Pasadena, Calif. 91101

DONALD A. McGAVRAN, B.D., Ph.D.
Director

JULY 1971   Subscription $1 per year   Volume VII, No. 6

Will Green Lake Betray the Two Billion?

Contents

WILL GREEN LAKE BETRAY THE TWO BILLION?

By 'Green Lake' I mean, of course, the great gathering of evangelical
mission leaders - perhaps 600 of them - September 27th to October 1st, 1971 - at
the famous conference grounds in Wisconsin. Over a hundred missionary societies-
both denominational and interdenominational will be represented.

The meeting is convened to consider Church-Mission Relationships and to
hammer out policies regarding those which are theologically sound, practically
possible, and edifying to Churches and Missionary Societies. The fire under the
meeting is the increasingly difficult and complex matter of right relationships
between Missions and Churches which they found.

What is right in relationships varies enormously. When a mission first
arrives, there is no church and hence no relationship. As congregations multiply, relationships arise. The stronger and larger the Church, the more natural
it is for the Mission to fade out of the picture. What needs to be done in
each situation is different. Some Missions have nothing to turn over to and
ought therefore to continue in charge. Some ought to turn over today. Some
ought to have turned over years ago. Some Churches have taken full charge - and
stopped evangelizing. Some Churches are in charge and multiply congregations in
New Testament fashion.

SEND correspondence, news, and articles to the Editor, Dr. Donald McGavran, at the
Institute of Church Growth, Fuller Theological Seminary. Published bi-monthly, send
subscriptions and changes of address to the Business Manager, Norman L. Cummings,
Overseas Crusades, Inc., 265 Lytton Avenue, Palo Alto, California 94301, U.S.A.
Second-class postage paid at Palo Alto, California.

A missionary in Latin America writes in May 1971, "Too many Missions here control everything - finances, program, form of worship, and hymnology. The Church is firmly under the Mission. Paternalism and religious imperialism run rampant."

As a result of all this, many Missions are being diverted from their main task to frustrating and endless discussions with the leaders of the new denominations. Many Africasian Churches turn from their God-given duties and turn on their founders in a 'struggle for independence'. Is there some way out of this morass? This question underlies Green Lake '71.

By 'the two billion' I mean those multitudes of men and women who do not know Jesus Christ as Lord and Saviour. They are found in all six continents, but by far the largest numbers are in Asia, Africa and Latin America. In these lands, blocks of humanity are found (numbering tens of thousands and sometimes millions in each block) in the midst of which can be found no church, no Bible, and no Christian. In the whole world, only about one billion call themselves 'Christians'. Two billion have never heard His name effectively.

True, the two billion exist in the neighborhood of the Africasian Churches - but this fact must be understood with exactitude. In most places in Asia one finds a few Christian congregations - with a small combined membership, often less than five hundred - surrounded by hundreds of thousands of non-Christians most of whom have never heard the name of Jesus. One often finds a whole denomination, whose total membership is less than 5,000, as the sole Christian witness in the midst of a million people.

In some lands a large younger Church (with membership of several hundred thousand, let us say) has come into being by the union of smaller Churches. But the fact remains that in its neighborhood large blocks of humanity exist whose members have no real chance to accept Jesus Christ. To see this clearly let us observe Japan.

Japan, with a population of about 100,000,000 has in it the United Church of Christ (the Kyodan) with a membership in 1968 of 193,455 (total community). Despite this large denomination, with many ordained ministers, church buildings, seminaries, and colleges, one would not have to travel far to find a block of a million in which were only a few small, weak Kyodan congregations - each averaging, let us say, 35 in attendance at Sunday worship. To imagine that this "great national Church", is proclaiming the Gospel to all the people of Japan - let alone proclaiming it effectively would be naive.

The largest of the "united Churches" are only one or two per cent of the total population in their lands and leave great blocks of humanity unevangelized.

In most lands, the Church has grown from the underprivileged, the masses, and the victims of the social order. It is not only small, but also weak. Furthermore, it has often grown in one segment of society only, so is cut off by geographic, ethnic, and linguistic barriers from the rest of the people in its own land. Thus in Burma, the strong Baptist Church (membership 222,000) is largely tribal (Karen, Chin, Kachin) and is not evangelistically potent among the twenty million Buddhist Burmese. The great Church of South India has arisen very largely from the Scheduled Castes (the former Untouchables). Consequently though it has some educated members, it finds it difficult to evangelize the middle and upper castes. The conclusion of the whole matter is that as far as reconciling the two billion is concerned, it would be the height of irresponsible optimism to count on the Afericasian Churches alone to do the job. They will play an important part; but so must "specially sent ones" - missionaries. The evangelization of the world will continue to require the combined resources of Eurican and Africasian Churches. Whitby said a true word about 'partnership in obedience.'

By 'betray' I mean that it is possible for Churches and missionary societies to act in such a way that those to whom God sends them remain with no knowledge of the Saviour. In 1968, Church Growth Bulletin asked the Fourth Assembly of the World Council of Churches: Will Uppsala Betray the Two Billion? I wrote, "By 'betray' I mean any course of action which substitutes ashes for bread, fixes the attention of Christians on temporary palliatives instead of eternal remedies, and deceives God's children with the flesh when they long for the spirit. By 'betray' I mean planning courses of action whose sure outcome will be that the two billion will remain in their sins and in their darkness, chained by false and inadequate ideas of God and men."

Because of the pressure of church-mission relationships, today in many mission circles, it has become fashionable to withdraw missionaries. The half-truth that missionaries work themselves out of a job is popular today. Some executives talk as if, when they withdraw missionaries, they have done well. The erroneous belief spreads that when we turn over to some weak small Church - of 25,000, it may be - and diminish the number of missionaries, we please God. This noxious miasma affects all missionary societies and deafens youth to the cries of the perishing. To be sure, withdrawing missionaries from limited territories in which a vigorous Church is adequately discipling men and ethne is good. And withdrawing missionaries, when expelled by the State, is unavoidable. But these are exceptions to the rule. Unless the Church sees them as exceptions, she will sleep instead of march. Unless Green Lake trumpets abroad the need for more missionary resources, she will leave most of mankind worshipping the Baals not Jehovah.

Of course, Green Lake will not deliberately turn from the discipling of the nations. Yet long range goals are often forgotten in fierce opinions concerning short range objectives. It is abundantly possible to work for "splendid church-mission relationships whether the Gospel is communicated or not."

Is the over-riding goal cordial church-mission relationships? If Green Lake answers 'Yes' and piles argument on argument, failing to emphasize the compelling purpose which demands the vast outpouring of life which is mission, then the two billion will be betrayed. If principles governing cordial relation-ships are stated regardless as to whether they guarantee an ever more effective evangelization, the two billion will be betrayed. If those formulating findings, do not constantly advocate relationships which drive Churches and Mission out into ceaseless sacrificial "reconciliation of men to God in the Church of Jesus Christ", their findings are likely to betray the two billion. If church leaders, reading the findings, are not led to multiply missionizing, then - no matter what else happens - Green Lake will have betrayed the two billion.

A famous meeting of Asian leaders took place a few years ago in Thailand. For three days they considered Asian Mission to Asia. They discussed a burning question - the relation of their missionaries to the churches!! "Our mission-aries must be members of the churches where they work," they said. They said little about bringing the ethne of Asia "to the obedience of the faith" (Rom. 1:5).

The relation of missionaries to churches is important, but mainly as it enables effective discipling to take place. It has little importance in itself. If Churches and Missions enjoy cordial relationships, if ministers of any land and missionaries from abroad work harmoniously together - while millions starve for lack of the Bread of Heaven - what profit?

On the verge of Green Lake '71, it must be said: Church-Mission relationships have little importance in themselves. They are important chiefly if they enable effective discipling of men and ethne to take place.

Church Growth Bulletin hopes that Green Lake will recognize that there are many church-mission relationships, each correct in a given situation. Time should not be wasted trying to name the one solution which is theologically or theoretically correct. Delegates hold many theologies of 'church' and 'mission' Endless discussions can take place as to which are correct. We believe all are correct which enable the passion of our Saviour for the salvation of men to be fulfilled. None is 'correct' which looks on contentedly while Macedonia - and Philistia - languish for the Gospel.

Returning to the comment of the Latin American missionary, we dare say that the enemy is neither 'paternalism', nor 'religious imperialism'. These would be forgiven by both national leaders and missionary theorists, provided multitudes were being 'added to the Lord'. And, if multitudes were being added, religious imperialism would disappear like the morning mist. Paternalism is particularly onerous in static little denominations. Growing Churches bear it easily and outgrow it rapidly. To a considerable degree, the basic problem is not faulty relationship, but lack of growth. When Churches get stuck at a few hundred or a few thousand members, they and their Missions haggle about church-mission relationships. What many Missions and Churches need is Spirit-filled growth. As this happens, better relationships will come about more easily.

A most effective contemporary block to evangelization is the silly assumption that when a new denomination has been established in a land, the founding mission should either withdraw from that whole land, or work as an agent of that denomination. For example, one large American Church has a daughter of 4,220 communicants in one of the Philippine Islands. The American Church is now turning authority over to that tiny denomination and withdrawing from the Philippines! The new denomination and the old, both think that this is correct procedure. Were the founding mission to go into an adjacent island and vigorously plant churches, its daughter would feel aggrieved. "If you work anywhere in the Philippines," it says, "you must work under us." This little denomination cannot keep the Roman Catholics out of "its territory." It cannot prohibit the Adventists, the Methodists or Brethren from planting churches within a hundred yards of its congregations, but it bravely prohibits its own father from evangelizing the neighboring island!

This strange error is everywhere observable. It has become a new orthodoxy. Green Lake should rectify it. Correct church-mission relationships must disavow 'dog in the manger comity'. Each Africasian Church should be sole authority in all that territory where it is actively evangelizing. There the Mission should either keep out or assist the Church to evangelize. But all territory where the Church is not evangelizing should be open. Any Mission should be able there independently to proclaim the Gospel.

The fathering Mission advancing on new ground may ask ministers of the national Church to advise it. Under episcopal church government, the Mission will no doubt operate under a national bishop. But the desideratum is not suitable relationships. The desideratum is effective advancement of the Gospel. In places, the Mission evangelizing on new ground will work entirely independently - exactly as would an incoming Roman Catholic Mission. In places it will act under close supervision of its daughter Church already established on old ground. In both places it will multiply sound congregations and turn them over to the national Church.

God grant that Green Lake '71 terminates the costly, frustrating and interminable discussions between Church and Mission concerning jurisdiction, so that both can turn to their real business. Mission is neither inter-church aid nor right relationship. Mission is bringing men and ethne to a saving knowledge of Christ in His Church. The time has come to take off the winding sheets which tie Missions and Churches into introverted, non-growing ecclesiastical organizations. Unbind him, the Lord commands, and let him go. I have work for him to do

Better, sweeter church-mission relationships are essential. God has, I am persuaded, guided those who are convening this gathering. In all the urgent problems facing His servants there, let them, however, work out solutions which establish "church-mission relations which encourage churches to multiply." Then history will record that, far from betraying the two billion, Green Lake strode forward to redeem them.

SINCE WE ARE ALL GROWING OLDER, LET'S GROW BOLDER!   by Arthur Glasser

Many of us have been around a long time. This means we have largely come to terms with our calling. We know something of our limitations but have enjoyed the touch of God's grace, enabling us to do that which we could never have done by ourselves. It is in the area of missionary methodology, however, that we are particularly prone to settle into a routine that reflects the wisdom of our seniors and is congenial to ourselves. But GL '71 is upon us, calling all missionaries to bestir themselves, "rekindle the gift of God" (II Tim. 1:6) and grow bolder. Why so? Because no missionary or society or national church is as yet living up to capacity, and we all know it! If such were not the case there would be no need to hammer at the theme of the "two billion".

The William Carey Library multibook Crossroads in Mission specially prepared for GL '71, is a good tonic for those who are growing older and need to grow bolder. Listen to its five authors: Blauw contends against the heresy of developing a "theology of missions" that transforms the missionary task into one of the activities of the Church rather than "the criterion for all its activities." Scherer contends that "under the traditional politico-geographical definition (of mission), the task could be considered nearly over; but under the new interpretation (the reintegration of the total human family under the Lordship of Jesus Christ), it has just begun." Beyerhaus wants us to get beyond bowing to the immaturity of those who argue that we should encourage the younger churches to seek the sort of self-sufficiency that will make them not only independent of any other Church but isolate them from the total stream of God's life in the world. We must get beyond the tension between local church autonomy and the unity and catholicity of the whole Church, and seek responsible participation in the greater task of proclaiming the Lordship of Jesus Christ, directed towards every nation and to every aspect of the nation's life. Street calls for younger churches "coveting the higher gifts" and thereby extending the apostolate until the whole Christian corpus participates in the work of Mission. <u>Beaver</u> calls for the rejection of Willingen's (1952) exaggerated declaration that "Every Christian is a Missionary." There is an apostolate of God. He also presses us to examine critically all our old methods. "New forms, new ways and new means for world mission must be devised." Only by far more vigorous service and more effective ministry will the missionary movement "become recognized as representative of a supranational universal community of believers in which peoples of East, West, and the Third World unite and point the way to their brethren!"

All in all, the issue is clear. We are growing older; let's become bolder. Many of us have spent happy years serving Christ overseas. We have been exposed to the inevitable: that all human organizations tend to deteriorate with the passage of time. But we have also some experience with the ways in which God seeks to deliver missions from "the deadly drift" that they might be more effective in pushing forward His missionary enterprise. My own society, the <u>Overseas Missionary Fellowship</u>, has enjoyed many such "times of refreshing." On one occasion we had a GL '71 all on our own! It was the occasion when we sought to prepare ourselves for our 100th birthday. What actually took place?

Well, the debate among our leaders was never so vigorous. We knew that as a Caucasian-dominated mission we were doomed to extinction. More, we also knew that in the Asia of the future, the missionary presence was needed to keep before the churches the vision of the "two billion," at their very doorstep and in distant lands. We were also convicted over our failure to impart widely the vision of the apostolate to these younger churches, and were dull in perceiving that in spite of ourselves God had been doing this very work within certain of them. But He needed something from us that we were slow to understand. He wanted us to be willing to cut loose from our Western moorings, reject our Caucasian dominance, and open our doors to all He was calling to embrace the missionary calling. He wanted qualified Asians at all administrative levels so that virtually a new society might be born: multiracial, supranational, living demonstration of the abiding validity of the missionary calling and the oneness of the Lord's people. He wanted more than the Church. He wanted Mission too, a Mission that would move with the times.

Years have passed since those agonizing deliberations in Singapore, 1964. But they have witnessed an Asian apostolate emerging from Japan to Indonesia that is serving in ways that are a joy to behold. But are Western missionaries no longer needed? You should read EAST ASIA MILLIONS! They are needed as never before!

What shall we say in conclusion? The general Director of our OMF, Michael C. Griffiths, reports that the very evident leading of God within the Fellowship argues against the theorist with his predictions of a "constantly dwindling Western missionary force of steadily increasing specialization and sophistication, so that soon the only international contributions to national churches are theological professors, mass communication experts, and purveyors of new gimmickry on world tours." Griffiths likes (and so do we!) the affirmations of a Tamil leader, Theodore Williams of India:

> There is no place for national isolation in the Christian
> church ... the mission of the church is not the job of any one
> national church ... the Christian church, whether in Asia or
> elsewhere, cannot give up its character as a body transcending

> racial and national barriers. It is supranational and should
> never be bound by narrow nationalism.... There is also the
> need for a healthy exchange of Christian insights gained in
> different national and cultural contexts.... There is no
> place for feeling that the foreign missionary should be here
> as long as he is needed and then pull out when he has performed
> his task. In the supranational fellowship of the church, which
> has a worldwide mission, the foreign missionary need not be a
> temporary factor.

As we all grow older, let's believe that this viewpoint represents the wave of the future. But if we are to act upon its implications we'll have to grow bolder!

AN ANTHROPOLOGIST LOOKS AT MISSION-CHURCH TRANSITION by Alan Tippett

At a recent 'round table exchange' between American Indians and professional anthropologists, one Indian anthropologist asked, "Is anthropology dead?" and went on to answer, "If you only want to use us as a research laboratory, yes. If you want to work side by side with us for the betterment of our ethnic development, no. But then you will have to follow our directives."

At a Fijian church synod during the war a young missionary was appointed to replace an old one. The senior Fijian pastor, in welcoming him, said, "It is not your job to tell us what we need, but to show us how to get what we want." The young Chairman 'got the message'. His period of office was one of rich experiment in new patterns of mission, with new relationships between nationals and expatriates. Out of this new partnership came many innovations, which neither nationals nor expatriates could have achieved alone.

Had the old pastor said, "Missionary, go home!" the Church would have been looser. As it was, new concepts of mission emerged by the inter-relationship. For example, the Fijians saw their responsibility not only in the internal workings of the Church, but also in the evangelization of the 200,000 Fiji Indians. Not long before this another Fijian pastor said to me, "You people brought the Indians to this land, you evangelize them." I lived to hear him speak for the motion when the Fijian-controlled synod appointed a Fijian to the task of Indian evangelism. Scores are, of course, needed.

I see now that the on-going mission of the Church was saved by the change in missionary-national relationships, not by withdrawing missionaries altogether. The success of the Mission-Church transition in Fiji was due to the pattern of planned phasing-out and phasing-in over twenty years. Had the political development been faster than that of the Church, we might not have had twenty years. Now I look back on them - years of real organic church growth, as I worked first over, then beside, and eventually under Fijian colleagues. I saw Henry Venn's dream of euthanasia enacted. A Mission died and a Church was born.

A New Autonomous Entity. There are good spiritual reasons why you do not achieve an indigenous Church by sending all the missionaries home at one point of time. I have found a recurring comment in scores of mission records, "We work towards an indigenous Church - but the time is not yet." Before missionaries leave they must demonstrate their sincerity about these words. They ought to show the nationals that they believe the time has come, that they rejoice because of it, and that, if required, they will work as subordinates under it. They have to demonstrate the role of colleague instead of master, indeed, even of servant. A mission which departs without that demonstration has presented a defective gospel. The indigenous Church needs a period of sharing in which the old missionary-national roles are reversed.

Anthropologically this period of transition, when the yount Church is feeling its new responsibilities, but while the expatriate is still present, is a dynamic process. Malinowski used a phrase "a new autonomous entity" for what I am describing - a state wherein expatriate and national experience new, inter-acting, inter-penetrating relationships.

In such a Church something of the old ethnic values and forms will tarry, something of the contact-institution will be incorporated, the undesirable and obsolete elements of tradition will be purged as also the foreignness and for-malism of the contact-institution. But the inter-penetration of the pure gospel with purified tradition should lead the participants, not into syncretism, but a new kind of indigenous entity, a unique complex of interactions - a process of church maturation. Here we have a formula:

> Sanctified tarriance and gospel incorporation, interpenetrating
> in the sharing process, should lead to indigenous church maturation.

Without some such process I do not see how either (1) the foreignized mis-sion churches can survive (let alone grow), or (2) the reactionary indigenous churches can adequately confront the current dynamic world situation. The formula is not a theory or hypothesis for testing, but an interpretation of observed facts in cross-cultural mission, which I have witnessed and participated in. My own faith, biblical understanding and theology have been enriched by this experience of new-level interaction with Fijian and Indian fellow Christians.

Other Situations - Other Patterns. The pattern of phasing-in and phasing-out is not the only viable way of demonstrating the experience. We must allow for the multiplicity of variant situations where the Mission-Church transition must be effected.

Another possibility is the policy of Mission-Church Co-existence. The mission continues to operate as a contact-institution, forming new fellowship groups by conversions from the world, organizing them into churches and estab-lishing them as autonomous entities as they come to spiritual and organizational maturity. With each new church-unit established the mission moves on further, evangelizing beyond its present frontier, maybe using the same language, maybe learning a new one, until the whole population is won. Here interaction is between two organizations - Mission and Church - rather than missionary and national within one organization. This offers scope for Mission-Church co-operating in evangelistic thrust. The policy is discussed and evaluated in Read's New Patterns of Church Growth in Brazil, where it is called The Brazil Plan.

Another possibility for speeding up indigenity, at least on the level of leadership and self-support, is the pilot project. An unusually large degree of autonomy is extended to one spiritually innovative village congregation in, say, a large valley of villages. If the efforts of this primary village lead to effective self-sufficiency, the case is bound to become a model for other villages to emulate. I am sure there are many other patterns, but their common point is that they are all <u>processes through time</u>. They do not permit total missionary withdrawal <u>at a point of time</u>.

   <u>Obstructions to Indigenity</u>. The movement towards indigenity is obstructed by methodological factors in the policy of the parent mission, and are therefore correctable - but only <u>through time</u>. Sudden home decision to force indigenity on a young Church shows up thus:

1. A failure to develop an adequate evangel in the young Church, so that the removal of the missionary terminates missionary outreach.

2. A failure to develop an adequate operating leadership structure that will survive after missionary withdrawal, so that internal affairs drift and the community impact is innocuous.

3. A failure to develop stewardship dimensions adequate for local Christian action within and without the Church.

These weaknesses can only be avoided by a period of planned education (instruction and participation) <u>on the level of village congregations</u>. No Church can realize its self-hood without a sense of mission, leadership, stewardship and community responsibility. These are "learned by doing". The virility of some folk churches demonstrates there is no lack of capacity. These "marks of the Church" are prerequisites of autonomy and should be <u>explored in partnership</u> by nationals and expatriates in the period of phasing-in and phasing-out.

   A period of mission paternalism terminated suddenly by withdrawing funds and personnel brings a familiar cry, "The Mission no longer loves us." Education for autonomy brings a new set of experiences to both parties. If the expatriate is still a foreigner he is at least "<u>our</u> foreigner". He is "one of us". Society receives him and creates a new role for him. He is part of the new autonomous entity.

   Except where the axe has already fallen to the root of the tree, hope surely lies in this direction. But this new kind of expatriate-national relationship does not come by putting on a pig-tail or wearing a national garment. It comes only when the expatriate treats the national as a mature adult person, respects his cultural values, speaks his language, shares his biases and, indeed, is ready to laugh or shed a tear with him.

   Across the world, the most urgent need in typical missions is not that the missionary should "go home", but rather that he should look critically at the situation he faces and ask himself if he <u>dare</u> go home without responsibly terminating his work and finding another Macedonia. If he has completed plowing and can honestly take his hand from the plow, then he will find another field in the valley beyond. In any case the old missionary role has to be modified - not with respect to the gospel message, but certainly with respect to the manner of communicating it, and the personal relationships involved in the process. In each forward movement of mission to unevangelized sections of cities and countrysides, we can be educating for indigeneity by experiment with excitement.

   As this is written with the Green Lake Conference coming up, I hope its emphasis will fall on improving missionary approaches so that the Church may grow quantitively, qualitatively and organically, rather than exploring ways of withdrawing from responsibility.

CHURCHES INSTEAD OF MISSIONS?   by Ralph Winter

During the past 25 years as the major denominations have become increasingly caught up in the Ecumenical Movement they have been challenged and enthralled by the "great new fact" of the emergence of the younger churches around the world. With a good deal of the same basic perspective, Evangelical missions in the same period re-emphasized "the indigenous church", measuring all success by the one yardstick of the health and life of a national church. Valuable and sound though these insights may have been, we are now in more ways than one entering upon a post-ecumenical era. As we look back upon the earlier period, we readily notice two grievous errors that somehow became intertwined with the valuable insights. Curiously, the same two errors are found in both ecumenical and evangelical thinking.

The first error puts so much emphasis upon the wonder and joy and rightful selfhood of the new national church that it seems to argue for the demise of the mission agency that was instrumental in its creation. Thus we have the ensuing discussion about "church-mission relations" which is so often characterized by such a preoccupation with the national church and its newly found autonomy that the mission field itself is lost sight of. At various times I have called this an unbiblical syndrome of "focusing on the one sheep that is found rather than on the ninety-nine that are still lost". R. Pierce Beaver laid the blame partially upon the leaders of the new national churches when he observed recently, that,

> At this moment each church in each land considers itself to be sovereign there, and few welcome the coming of new missionaries into the country no matter how inadequate present evangelism may be in relation to the territorial size and population of the country and the extent of available resources there. Effective mission throughout the world in the future demands the giving up of false pride and the baseless assertion of full sufficiency. There is no church large or small, ancient or very young, in any country today which appears thoroughly adequate to its responsibilities in evangelism and ministry.

He goes on to say that even the U.S. needs special gifts that only Asian and African missionaries can offer. It is true that the younger churches do not forever need pioneer missionaries around their necks. It is also true that the exchanging of fraternal personnel between sister churches is a new need in a new day. Nevertheless, sheer honesty about the unfinished task requires the admission that the need for "sending missions" is as great today as it has ever been. Two billion untouched people must be considered an equally "great new fact of our time"; the immensity of this fact must not be overlooked. The younger churches need not be counted out in this remaining task, but neither can the evangelization of the world be summarily dumped on their shoulders while mission societies in the world's wealthiest national pull back and are dismantled.

The second error intertwined in the thinking of the era just past is far more subtle than the existence of the two billion non-Christians. The first error wars against the Western-based missionary society and says it isn't needed. The second error is the strange assumption that not even the younger churches need missionary societies. Illogically it is assumed that once an overseas national church is well planted, it will just naturally grow and reach out and finish the job.

Even faith missions tend to make this error. Their missionaries may derive from older denominations that do not seem to be "on fire for the Lord," yet they have the idea that they are able to plant a national church that will

forever truly preach the word and be evangelistic and missionary in all the
proper ways. That is, the denominations at home may have grown cold, (and thus
justified the emergence of the "faith missions") but this is surely not going
to happen in the case of the denomination they themselves have labored to create
on the foreign field! They are determined to plant a true "New Testament church"
which will automatically reach out. Subconsciously, they feel that the formation
of a truly indigenous church precludes the necessity of a truly indigenous
mission!

Don't they realize that the New Testament merely shows us that in a fairly
limited and somewhat unenthusiastic fashion a brand new movement may indeed send
out one or two missionaries without effectively supporting them, and for only a
short time? Furthermore, the New Testament does not cover the case of a second
or third generation Christian movement--unless this is the list of seven churches
in Revelation, which as a group were by no means active in missions! Don't
these missionaries realize that even the Reformation churches did practically
nothing in foreign missions for something like 300 years, and that when missions
finally began it was due to the appearance of "societies of the warm hearted"
who took the lead and the initiative, and that to this day, considering the entire Protestant movement, the vast majority of mission work has been instigated
not by church structures but by specifically mission structures?

The "second error" in the case of the older denominational missions is a
bit more complicated. Their daughter churches have in many cases, late in the
game, been encouraged to establish their own denominational boards of home and
foreign missions. This seems to be the logical thing, but in most cases it has
been too late and too little. Furthermore, it has involved a structural assumption: that a centralized, denominational board is the only proper kind of
mission agency. Quite likely the fullest expression of Christian faith and
obedience in the lands of the younger churches will require the development of
semi-autonomous national mission societies, not just national churches, nor even
national churches with centralized mission boards. Someone should make a
study of the mission boards of the younger churches--this is John Sinclair's
suggestion--because their record thus far is mixed at best and in any case
crucially inadequate to the task of reaching the two billion. For twenty-five
years we learned that missions cannot take the place of churches. Now we must
understand that the opposite is also true.

YOUNGER CHURCHES - MISSIONARIES AND INDIGENEITY by Charles Kraft

In a day when the essence of the many fine treatises on the indigenous
Church has often been reduced to a mechanical imposition upon a missionary-
dominated Church of the "three-selfs" concept, we need to hear correctives
like the following:

> It may be very easy to have a self-governing Church which is
> not indigenous.... All that is necessary to do is to indoctri-
> nate a few leaders in Western patterns of church government,
> and let them take over. The result will be a Church governed
> in a slavishly foreign manner. This is going on in scores of
> mission fields today under the misguided assumption that an
> "indigenous" Church is being founded (W. A. Smalley, "Cultural
> Implications of an Indigenous Church" in Practical Anthropology
> 5:51-65, reprinted in Readings in Missionary Anthropology,
> W. A. Smalley, ed.).

We must remember that it is not until

> ...the indigenous people of a community think of the Lord as their
> own, not a foreign Christ; when they do things as unto the Lord,
> meeting the cultural needs around them, worshipping in patterns
> they understand; when their congregations function in participation
> in a body, which is structurally indigenous; (that) you have an
> indigenous Church (A. R. Tippett, Verdict Theology in Missionary
> Theory. Lincoln Christian College Press, 1969, pp. 133 & 136).

The most important criterion of indigeneity is the Church's self-image.
Is it a dominated Church, firmly controlled by both the representatives and
the concepts of a foreign culture? Paternalistic missionary work, has often
produced this type of domination and given the impression that, in spite of
the biblical demonstration of God's willingness to employ any culture as a
vehicle of his interaction with men, in these latter days He has required all
men to convert to Western religious, organizational, educational, and medical
patterns in order to operate His Church properly.

Such Churches (and schools and hospitals) have often, however, been
turned over to the direction of carefully indoctrinated nationals who have,
not a dominated, but a very dependent self-image. Such indigenized Churches
typically see themselves as foreign enclaves in their own nations, pitting a
foreign "Christian" system against the surrounding culture as if Christianity
were intended to be a competing culture rather than a redeeming leaven designed
to operate within any culture. To such Churches the models for their activity
lie outside of their own culture in the culture (and, often, the denominational
subculture) of the now departed missionary.

But there is a third kind of self-image among certain of the younger
Churches today. And this is the independent self-image of the truly indigenous
Churches. For these Churches, Christianity's battleground is within their culture rather than against it and the models to be employed in the development
and extension of Christianity in this context are those of their own culture
rather than those of another culture. For these Churches the qualifications for
leadership, for example, are built, as Paul's were (see I Timothy 3, Titus 1,
etc.), upon ideals already present in the society - including, when appropriate,
age, experience and/or social class - rather than upon such things as literacy
and schooling which, though appropriate in Western culture, may be irrelevant
and/or counter-productive in the indigenous culture, especially when combined
with youthfulness.

Over five thousand of such indigenous Churches (denominations) have sprung
up in Africa alone during the past century. Unfortunately, most of these have
been able to gain indigeneity only by separating themselves from missionary influence. Far preferable to this is the situation among many Pentecostal Churches
in Latin America where the number and influence of the missionaries is such that
the opportunities for foreign domination are kept to a minimum and Churches,
therefore, are indigenous from the start.

There is still great need for spiritually-mature and culturally-sensitive
missionaries who will follow Paul's example and train indigenous leaders to do
the same. Such missionaries (from Asia, Africa and Latin America, as well as
Europe and North America) will proclaim the Gospel, baptize converts, appoint,
train and work with natural leaders, and then get out of the way of the newly

planted cluster of congregations, occupying themselves with multiplying other clusters a few miles further on - or in a neighboring ethnic unit which the new Church is not likely to evangelize.

Missions must turn over authority and stay on. They must turn over to each cluster of congregations and go on to a new unit of the unreached myriads. Church-mission relationships must not be made an excuse for any mission pulling out of a large unevangelized population - or of turning evangelization over to a small, poor, slightly educated denomination of perhaps ten thousand communicants. Each succeeding cluster of congregations can be made more indigenous.

The missionaries of the next thirty years can learn from the church plantings of their predecessors and can establish new congregations in new fields increasingly congenial to the ancient cultures. Repeated new starts should achieve better and better cultural congruence.

In the many Churches still characterized by dependence or domination there is, likewise, continuing great need for foreign missionaries who, while not belittling the dedication of previous missionaries and nationals, will assist existing Churches toward true indigeneity and independence. The missionaries of the next thirty years - Eurican and Africasian - must be culturally and spiritually perceptive persons whose single aim is to stimulate the multiplication of truly indigenous and truly independent congregations and clusters of congregations, i.e. of Churches which are culturally so one with the people that they no longer seem in the least foreign.

"OCCUPY TILL I COME" by Edward Murphy, SWM-ICG 1971, Latin America
Director for Overseas Crusades

For several years articles have appeared claiming that, due to rampant nationalism and anti-western sentiment, the day of the missionary has passed. Other articles claim that since the Church has been planted all over the world, the missionary is an unnecessary figure - Churches can evangelize their own countries, are tired of missionary paternalism, and want to be left alone. Are these claims true?

We must be clear on several points. First, a paternalistic attitude of mission or missionary is clearly wrong and national leaders must direct the destinies of their own denominations large or small; but obviously, this does not imply that missionaries have no more work to do.

Furthermore, it is not true that the national Churches "want to be left alone." They do want to be considered "Churches" and not "missions" or even "younger Churches." They do resent the "big daddy" mentality of some foreign missionaries. But they do not want to be separated from the rest of the Body of Christ. I have yet to hear a national pastor declare "These missionaries should stop planting churches in our country. That's our job. We are perfectly capable of evangelizing all the unsaved in this land by ourselves. We resent their interference in our business." On the other hand, I have heard national leaders complain, "Our missionaries are busy at everything but direct evangelism and church planting. I wish they were more like the Apostle Paul, who knew when to let the new congregation alone so that he might move into a nearby area to begin the church planting cycle all over again."

The king commanded his servant to "occupy till I come" (Luke 19:13). Missionaries will be needed "till the Lord comes". That we do not need missionaries whom national Churches resent, all are agreed. That the Church will always need missionaries who have the apostolic gift and vision to plant churches or the teaching gift to help God's people walk in obedience to His will, all must emphasize. The missionary who sees "the Body" and is willing to serve it anywhere, humbling himself before God and His Church, will be welcome in any land.

Mission societies also will be needed "till the Lord returns". They will not call all their missionaries home to pastor churches in the sending country, fold up, and send their records to the archives of the Library of Congress! Until every nation has been evangelized, both missionary and the missionary society - the best structure yet devised to evangelize the world - will continue.

Paul, the great missionary, believed his missionary gifts were needed as long as there were pockets of population without Christ. He moved on and on. He did not return home to Antioch feeling that, since he had fathered a good many national churches in Asia, his job was finished and it was theirs to evangelize the whole land. He simply went to the next town - and the next - and began all over again. As long as there were nearby cities without the Gospel, Paul the missionary felt compelled to continue his God-given ministry. His genius as a missionary is seen in that he always took key leaders of the "national churches" with him. He taught both by his own example and by on-the-job training (Acts 14-20). Thus arose a corps of evangelists and church planters that multiplied his ministry many fold.

So engraved on his soul was responsibility to continue multiplying churches in Asia, in spite of the strong indigenous congregations already there, that God had to intervene in an unusual manner to get him to cross into Europe (Acts 16:6-7). When he did leave Asia for Europe, he continued his ministry in both areas until the long awaited occasion came to go to Rome and, perhaps, to Spain.

As long as Churches representing only a tiny proportion of the population exist in the midst of uncounted multitudes who "have not the knowledge of God" (I Corinthians 15:34) missionaries will be needed. That tremendous spiritual hunger stalks all over the world where national Churches already exist cannot be denied. That two billion have yet to believe is crystal clear. Therefore, I believe, the church planting missionary will be needed and will be welcomed by the Churches of all six continents, till the Lord comes.

DAVID LIVINGSTONE spoke to our problem long ago. Writing in 1860, he said -

... I have given mortal offense to a portion of the brethren by writing that all the Hottentot churches should be made independent at once; they have been supplied with the gospel for half a century, and are now better able to support their pastors than you are.... To those who have been accustomed to look upon small Hottentot villages, the inhabitants of which are nearly all converted, as fields involving the most excruciating responsibility, my depreciation of their fields and magnification of the heathen world beyond seem twofold heresy.

CHURCH GROWTH
BULLETIN

Address:
FULLER THEOLOGICAL
SEMINARY
135 N. Oakland
Pasadena, Calif. 91101

DONALD A. McGAVRAN, B.D., Ph.D.
Director

SEPTEMBER 1971   Subscription $1 per year   Volume VIII, No. 1

Important Light on
Missionary Attitudes

by Dr. E. C. Smith, SWM ICG '70
Kediri, Indonesia

The final chapter in <u>Schism and Renewal in Africa</u> not only constitutes a splendid summary of Barrett's entire thought, but also speaks powerfully to church mission relationships. The chapter is arranged under four main headings.

<u>The first heading is "Background"</u>. The theory begins by noticing that the foundations of African society center on home, family and community. Polygamy in many tribes provides security and status to family life. The coming of missionaries aroused widespread hopes and there was extraordinary response. Being overwhelmed by the response, mission had little time to understand African culture. In early years, missions were co-partners with European administrations in opposing evil practices such as human sacrifice, tribal warfare and slavery. After the Berlin Conference in 1885, missions seemed to extend on religious ground an attack on the traditional African society. The Africans felt that the missionaries were pressing an attack on their culture. While accepting the new religion, there was subconscious alarm at this assault on their society.

The alarm gave way to bitterness in that the hopes aroused by earlier Christian missions were not felt to be materializing. The societies of Africa were not being fulfilled but demolished. Such feelings produced religious tension. This religious tension created a tribal zeitgeist or atmosphere of pressure. This tension or pressure was the product of the gradual accumulation and interaction of the eighteen socio-religious factors which form a measure of cultural clash in a given tribe.

The tension reached a breaking point, usually, after the publication of the scriptures in the tribal language. With the coming of the Bible, the Africans began to feel they could discern a serious discrepancy between missions and biblical religion in relation to the traditional institutions under attack. The grievances became articulated in certain biblical themes, most often related to the Spirit and Love.

SEND correspondence, news, and articles to the Editor, Dr. Donald McGavran, at the Institute of Church Growth, Fuller Theological Seminary. Published bi-monthly, send subscriptions and changes of address to the Business Manager, Norman L. Cummings, Overseas Crusades, Inc., 265 Lytton Avenue, Palo Alto, California 94301, U.S.A. Second-class postage paid at Palo Alto, California.

Page 164

The biblical theme of love came to the forefront. While missions had exemplary records in most facets of love, they had failed in one point--that is at the point of love as listening, sharing, sympathizing and sensitive understanding in depth between equals. The root cause of independency then came to be seen as this failure in love, involving as it did the failure to understand, appreciate and adjust church life to Africanism. African women and charismatic leaders came into prominence as the guiding lights in independent movements.

The second heading is "Reaction to Mission". Various reactions began as tension increased. With the growth of the Christian community came numerous renewal and revival movements within the mission churches. Many movements remained in the churches and never came to separation. Many incipient movements were defused by sympathetic handling; others collapsed; still others separated and lived on successfully.

The onset of separation occurs after the zeitgeist increases to certain definite levels. The immediate cause of the actual succession (the flashpoint) is often trivial and of relatively small importance. After the tension reaches a certain level, almost any incident can become the last rain drop that begins the flood.

The third heading is "An Indigenous Christianity". Independent movements are characterized by an acceptance (often under new and original African forms) of the centrality of the historical Jesus as Lord. They are marked by a complex of new religious forms, and a new type of religious community. The "Church" is brought into conformity with the needs of the society. After they have established themselves, the movements begin to seek recognition. There is usually a gradual evolution toward a cross tribal character. Meanwhile, the movement usually enjoys rapid growth and tends to travel from tribe to tribe as it spreads along chains of tribes. In Africa now, the independent movement consists of one enormous single grouping of two hundred and ninety tribes stretching from Sierra Leone to Kenya and South Africa.

The last heading is "Reformation in Africa". The movement as a whole can be commended for its biblical character and has been characterized as an African Reformation. Independency remains an organic complex of six thousand religious movements both inside and outside the historical Churches. Of the future of independency, Barrett points out that the background causal factors of independency are largely unchanged. Although the mission Churches are now mostly independent of the missions, they are heir to the old missionary attitudes. As a result of insufficient dialogue between the historical Churches and the independent movements further schism and renewal will occur. Independency can be expected to show steady expansion. Dr. Barrett predicts that by the year 2000, independency will have spread from 290 tribes to around 470 and will have doubled its present numerical strength (thereby reaching a membership of fourteen million). Barrett concluces:

> Seen as the more dynamic and creative part of the entire complex
> of six thousand religious movements composing an incipient reforma-
> tion, independency is clearly playing an increasingly vital part in
> the rooting of the Christian faith in the soil of Africa (page 278).

WHAT IS THIS BOOK AND INDEPENDENCY SAYING TO US?

Schism and Renewal in Africa is an interesting book, from the standpoints of the tremendously important movement and the clever analysis made of it. Still, this is not its greatest value to missions. The germane question is, "What is this book saying to us?" I suggest several things the independency movement and Barrett's analysis of it are saying to missionaries in every land. It is far more than a book for church leaders in Africa. The same tensions exist in other climes and for much the same reasons.

1. The Exigency of Genuine Identification

African independency evolved largely from the missionary failure to attain a proper identification either with Africans or with African culture. Effective evangelism and church growth demand a new degree of identification between Christians of differing cultures. Identification as partnership between equals stands as one of the imperatives for mission.

Identification means living together with, working together with, understanding, respecting and serving. It is of necessity personal. True identification demands a giving of self. It is a summons to expose self, to be known. It involves a willingness to be rejected and to reoffer. Identification means to become like others in order to serve them. It includes accepting others as equals.

Jesus has given us the ultimate example of the meaning of identification. Paul indicates that although equal with God, Christ Jesus felt such equality not a matter to be grasped and held to at any cost, but voluntarily suspended the use of many of His divine attributes and came to earth, "...as a man and as servant, even dying the death of the cross (Phil. 2:5-11). Here is identification. No greater example could be given.

Many missions and missionaries stand judged before the example of Christ. Of Christ, John could write, "The Word became flesh and dwelt among us, and we beheld his glory...". Of many missionaries it might be said, "The missionary came and lived apart from us, and we beheld his prosperity". Identification on a deeper, more meaningful and personal level can open avenues of communication that would allow the dissipation of tension and leave church and mission free to continue serving in partnership in every land.

2. The Imperative of the Open Ear

Love is listening. Barrett found as the root cause of independency in Africa the failure to listen, sympathize and interrelate as equals. Some missionaries have been too busy and too proud to listen to what their co-workers have been saying. Our willingness to listen is an indication of the strength of our respect. To listen effectively, we must understand something of what we hear Listening requires a knowledge of the culture and the ways of communication within the culture. We must know enough of culture to listen attentively and perceptively.

3. The Full Implications of the Indigenous Church

The term, "indigenous Church" is on the lips of almost every missionary and is the avowed goal of most mission activity. However, we often fail to go beyond the ideas of the "three selfs", that is, self-support, self-government and self-propagation. There are fuller implications of indegeneity. The deeper and fuller implications, though often overlooked, are actually the more vital.

African independency sprang from a conglomerate of tensions that was born largely due to the failure and refusal of mission and Church to seek out Christia answers to the typically African problems and to pattern the type of Christianity and Church to meet the social and cultural situation in each of the tribes in Africa.

An indigenous Church seeks and finds throughly Christian expressions to meet the felt needs of the culture. It is thus, a Church patterned exclusively for one culture--for what would be indigenous for one culture would not necessarily be so for another. An indigenous Church seeks to "Christianize" rather than pulverize the culture. Rather than mounting an attack on existing culture and institutions, the indigenous Church seeks the values in existing culture and finds ways of expressing traditional needs and practices in ways that are at once throughly Christian and completely satisfying to the indigenous culture.

Christianization of the culture is of imperative importance. However, in this matter the missionary can be only a catalyst. His greatest service is in standing aside and allowing it to happen. More than this, the indigenization of any Christian movement should have the full support of and active cooperation from missionaries. Still, the missionary can advise but cannot institute cultural change. Cultural change, like happiness, comes from within. Missionaries can be advocates of change but never innovators. When missionaries are willing to work together with nationals to realize the full implications of the indigenous Church, the tensions and irritations can be defused, leaving room for full creative efforts to cooperative attainment of the Great Commission.

4.   The Creativity of Tension

Tension can be as creative as it is inevitable. Tension, when handled creatively, can give birth to a stronger and more vital movement. Tension when ignored, often leads to ruptured fellowship and schism. Responding to the existing tension, which both groups are willing to admit, missionaries and nationals can find new and more valid forms of church life and practice. In working through tensions and irritations the fuller implications of indigenity can be reached.

Two other matters connected with tension are, first, tension and schism are not always to be decried. Many independent movements have become strong, evangelistic expressions of Christianity. Many schismatic movements have been in the nature of renewal and revival (even one that began formally in 1517).

Secondly, missionaries should seek to understand the psychology of tension. When tension reaches a level sufficiently intense, almost any incident or cause will trigger the reaction. Missionaries are often startled by the small, insignificant item selected by nationals as a point of contention. The missionary must remember that the item that seems to him insignificant may be of extreme importance to one immersed in the culture. More likely, however, the incident that generates the explosion or reaction (flashpoint) is the final element in long-standing, continuous irritation caused by multiple factors. The reaction has likely been dormant for a long period before breaking surface.

Tension and reaction there will be! May there be as well creative response and true cooperative effort to work through the problems. In this way, out of a dangerous and explosive situation can come the creative answers that will eventuate in a Church more able to realize its divinely appointed mission.

5.   The Best of Both Culture and Christianity

In the midst of tension, missionaries and nationals must together seek to claim the best of both culture and Christianity, and coalesce the two so as to

realize the best of both. There is strength in cross-cultural communication.
Here is one of the frontiers of mission in the future--the attainment of valid
cross-cultural influence and fellowship, which will leave Christianity stronger
in both regions.

Furthermore, recognizing the presence of tension, missionaries and nationals
must seek to attain the best of both in regard to Independent Churches and continued fellowship with the Historic Churches. By creative work before the "flashpoint" is reached, we can realize the strengths that come from both independency
and conformity.

CONCLUSION

Schism and Renewal in Africa (Oxford University Press) is important for
two reasons. a) Its analysis of the independency movement in Africa is enlightening. b) Concerning the presence and nature of tension between missions and
younger Churches, it sets forth principles which every missionary ought to know
and by which he ought to guide his labors toward the extension of the Gospel and
the discipling of the nations. Church growth men will want to master this book
and meditate on the lessons which it holds for them as the work in every land.

MILLIONS OF UNOCCUPIED FIELDS

Rev. Walter Frank in a paper presented to the Annual IFMA Board
Retreat makes a striking affirmation, tremendously germane to
Church Mission Relationships. As the first suggestion for Ameri-
cans considering a ministry of evangelism and church planting in
Europe he says:

> Prayerfully study the religious situation of the country
> and choose an area where little or no Gospel witness
> exists. There are thousands of such areas in Europe.

Mr. Frank is correct. Despite the strong European churches there
are thousands of such areas in Europe--and millions in Africasia.

Church mission relationships must be so stated, mission theory and
theology must be so formulated that overseas missionary presence
and program be continually extended into all such areas. Unchurched
populations must be churched--baptized, discipled, incorporated in
the Body.

Sending missionaries--so essential to keep the Churches in all
six continents from lapsing back into concern for self--is one
of the marks of the true Church.

THE MISSIONARY STAGE   by Bernard Quinn D.Ms.

Missionary activity is that process by which, with the help of the whole
Church, the Church's full ministry of the Word and Sacrament, nurture and outreach, evangelism and social redemption, becomes effectively localized for
salvific service within human communities where it is not yet to be found, or to
be found only in weakness.

It is not possible to determine with mathematical precision just when the Church has achieved full maturity and thus has emerged from the missionary stage. It is to be remembered that the work of planting the Church in a given community reaches a kind of milestone when the congregation of the faithful, already rooted in social life and the local culture, enjoys a certain stability and firmness. The congregation is equipped with its own supply of local priests, churches, Christian families, seminaries, lay leaders, well respected Christian customs. It is endowed with those ministries and institutions which are necessary if the People of God are to live and develop. This description is applicable to a community described as a 'socio-cultural area', a nation, a tribe, a class, or a group of nations sharing the same culture.

Yet even where the Church's ministry can be said to be generally present in a given area, there can be vast geographical areas--plains, plateaus, forests, sections of cities, pockets, wards--within which neither the Church nor the Church's ministries are present. The same may be said when the Church's ministry is entirely isolated from a distinct social class which forms a closed world within an area where the ministry is already present and available to the rest of the population. In such areas, missionary activity is needed.

(Slightly edited...sense unchanged...Resonance, Winter '68, No. 5, p. 99).

THE HEART OF THE CHURCH MISSION BUSINESS

The task of missions is "to plant Christianity as a living power in each non-Christian land, develop there a Church which will have a life of its own and assume responsibility for the evangelization of its own nation. For a time longer or shorter, the missionary enterprise must remain to cooperate with the Church, and will then pass on into regions beyond, while further aid will be given, if needed, and under expedient arrangements, by the Churches of Christ, as by equal to equal in a common task."

(Robert Speer, Christianity and the Nations, 1910, p. 76)

SEMINARY PROGRAM IN CONGO VILLAGES   by Charles Ross, SWM ICG '67

The present emphasis in the Presbyterian Church in the Congo (60,000 communicants) is the establishment of "particular" churches, that is, self-dependent, autonomous cells which, though under local presbyteries and the General Assembly, are financiall viable. On a national scale there is a program of mass evangelism called "Christ for All". In its third and final year, it seems to be a success, because enthusiastic, if not always factual, reports continue to emerge and encourage the churches. For example, 918 people were converted or returned to the Church during one meeting in Luluabourg in November, 1967.

Both of these interests concern the Christian Kingdom in the Congo, yet strangely, our Church has had no program for continued organic growth, which is basic to the multiplication of self-governing local churches.

The Presbyterian Preachers' School at Luebo, in the Democratic Republic of the Congo, has evolved a simple program for church growth, and this is applied on week-ends in churched and unchurched villages. There are four parts to the program:

a) Three teams, composed of two students each, visit each house in the village. The evangelist joins one of these teams. If the people visited are Christian, we try to discover how each one became Christian; if they are non-Christian, we try to find out what their beliefs are; what has hindered them from becoming Christian; which of their families are Christian; and if they have been influenced by clan members to believe or refuse Christ.

b) Later, the students call the people to a place in the village (not always the church building), where a brief worship service is held. The sermon, previously prepared in class, contains elements of the local religious beliefs and their results in the life of the people; appropriate Bible verses are applied to these beliefs, with the results accruing from a new and different life in Christ. The student preacher asks if anyone would like to empty himself of his beliefs based on fear, and sustained by fear, and believe in the courageous Christ. Usually several--up to 30 people--respond.

c) Responders are separated into two groups: those returning to the Church after having abandoned it, voluntarily or otherwise, and those who are new Christians. The students, now in two teams, call each person individually and spend up to two hours discussing that person's beliefs, what he wants now to do with Christ, and how the new life in Christ is to be lived. We then call in the family of each person--if possible--and talk with them. Are they agreed that a member of their clan, or family, leave the ancestral cult for the Christian faith? How will this conversion affect them? Will their customary beliefs change? If some of the family are already Christian, how have they explained the Christian faith to other members of the family, clan or village? If they have been "silent Christians" we explain the necessity of the loyalty of the entire family and clan being centered in Christ. We discuss all objections openly and seriously.

d) The evangelist has been present with the students while talking with the converts. By late afternoon, when the discussions have usually terminated, the evangelist and students eat. During the meal they talk of methods of church growth and the need to concentrate on the family and clan rather than uniquely on the individual. Where there is no pastor, we invite several Christians to join us and inform them of church growth through family evangelism.

This part of the program is most difficult, because evangelists have been trained to preach to individuals. Furthermore, because (though reared in their clans) they are now living away from their own ancestral groups, evangelists tend to shun working through a family structure and stress single conversions. When they became Christians, they left their families and easily believe that others must do likewise.

A few months later we return to these villages. The results we find in the church are positive or negative, depending on the evangelist's follow-up with the converts <u>and their families</u>. In some villages there has been such strong growth that autonomous churches have resulted.

What is needed now is a program to explain to the Church the potential for church growth in family and clan evangelism. Experience has already shown this to be a valid method in village evangelism, and can be useful in cities as well. It now remains for the Church--in its General Assembly--to appraise the method and its results, accept it and implement it throughout the area where the Church is established.

I might add that the African Independent Churches--"Apostles"--have been evangelizing through families and clans for some years, and have had phenomenal growth.

SECRET OF REMARKABLE GROWTH   by Gerald Bates

Rwanda and Burundi Conferences of the Free Methodist Church showed a combined gain of 2,201 members in one year, attaining a combined membership of almost 12,000. If this continues, the Burundi Conference will double in less than three years and the Rwanda Conferences in less than five. In Burundi the gain was accompanied by 70% gain in overall giving.

<u>What is the underlying secret of this kind of growth at this time?</u> Familiar answers come to mind--dense population, a receptive animistic culture, and others. There is no denying their importance but they are not the decisive factors because other Christian Churches in the same general milieu are not experiencing this kind of growth.

The significant factors are the following: (i) These Churches are <u>evangelistically oriented</u>. They are geared for harvest. This is no passing fad; this is their basic understanding of what the Church is. The whole organizational structure of the Church reflects this passion. (ii) For some inexplicable reason the disparate parts of an adolescent Church have found a new and effective harmony. (iii) Missionaries have been maintained in purely church and evangelistic work after many other missions have retreated to the periphery and placed most or all their missionaries at the technician level.

TAKE HEART, BROTHER KOERNER: THE LORD REIGNS.   by Donald McGavran

Pastor Niels Koerner of the Evangelical Lutheran Church in Valdiva, Chile, is part of the Lutheran denomination there which, in the 1968 World Christian Handbook, is listed as having 8,000 communicants and 25,000 community. The denomination is ethnically German.

Mr. Koerner says, "Since 1900 the population of the country has increased three-fold, whereas our church membership has remained static or even decreased." He feels that evangelizing the Latin people of Chile and persuading them to become responsible members of the Lutheran Church is extremely difficult. The <u>German Lutherans</u> would not like it. In short, Lutherans in Chile constitute a small ethnic enclave and are acting normally. Hundreds of other denominations in the world are ethnic enclaves. What does an ethnic enclave do? What options are open to the Lutheran Church in Chile?

One, it can remain an enclave, gradually withering away as its membership is eroded by marriage and worldliness. Survival in this option depends on becoming a really closed caste, rewarding marriage within and punishing marriage without the Church.

Two, it can vigorously establish Lutheran congregations of Latins (normal Chilean citizens) in areas distant from its existing congregations. Thus the question of intermarriage will not arise. The Latin congregations will be given full autonomy and, if in the coming generations integration and intermarriage do take place, who are we to try to control the next century! German congregations would decline: Latin congregations would increase. Through them the Lutheran witness would be not only preserved but enhanced and, by becoming indigenous, would be more and more accepted by non-Lutherans. More importantly, by establishing Latin congregations, the Lutheran Church would become faithful to God's purpose for all Churches. This is a church growth option.

Three, it can put its ethnic pride in its pocket and deliberately integrate, i.e. become a Chilean denomination. American Lutherans are a far cry from German Lutherans, Chilean Lutherans would be a somewhat farther cry, but the transplantation would be complete. This Church of 25,000 (total community) would deliberately loose its Germanic coloration and cultivate a beautiful Chilean complexion. Such integration, so far steadily resisted by the diminishing denomination, is obviously the most constructive of the various options. "Three" is the better of the two church growth options, but is more difficult.

Pastor Koerner believes that only option one is possible. He supports his choice theologically in the following curious way. For his consolation, let me assure him that defeated church leaders commonly exegete the Bible in a similar fashion. Indeed, his exegesis may be merely a reflection of a prevalent pessemistic and erroneous understanding of God's will. Koerner says:

"Does the missionary task...really mean that Lutheranism should leave its mark all over the world from South India via South Africa to South America? Is it not possible to recognize that we do not possess the Word for South America? Others may have it, perhaps the Pentecostal Christians? Mission is not a form of church-strategy, marking the victorious route of the Gospel with little red flags.... The Church is sent into the world; but the full phrase reads, "As Thou has sent me into the world, I have sent them into the world" (John 17:19). Through being sent into the world, Jesus had to face death...His Church also may have been sent here in order to die. It may be a long and gradual death--not a heroic defeat." (IRM April 1971, page 275)

I hope the lay and clerical leaders of the Lutheran Church in Chile will feel better about it in the morning. And will exegete the Bible with a Lutheran scrupulosity for the clear revelation of why God sent His Son into the world. Without resolute subordination of our whims, and feelings, and prides, and limitations to the Word of God, all of us at times find biblical justification for our discouragements and cowardices. I know, Brother Koerner. I have been there. I too need forgiveness.

Take heart, fellow soldier, and pay whatever it costs to burst out of your ecclesiastical and ethnic ghetto and among the lost in Chile multiply true churches of Jesus Christ (of the Lutheran persuasion, of course--you can plant no other). Your goal for 1980 might be a <u>Latin</u> membership of 8,000 communicants. If you will send four of your best pastors to the School of Missions at Fuller Seminary in Pasadena, we shall happily share with you promising solutions of your problem worked out by Christian leaders from all over the world who face the same ethnic barriers your Church does.

Your disease is serious, my friend, but, properly treated, not fatal. I find it difficult to believe that the Lord has sent your Church to Chile to die. While not ruling out the possibility that the Sovereign Lord wills the death rather than the repentance of apostate Churches, your church is not apostate and it seems much more in harmony with biblical revelation and His compassionate nature to believe that He has sent your Church to Chile to proclaim the Gospel to the poor and multiply true churches of Jesus Christ in a thousand communities in that great nation. I trust this will seem reasonable to you.

DAVID HOWARD SAYS:

One of the most significant developments in the mission of the church in the past decade has been the emphasis on church growth. As one reads the rapidly growing volume of literature on this topic (both books and articles) the question often comes to mind, "What are the real biblical principles underlying this emphasis?" With a few notable exceptions, most of the writings have centered around the sociological, anthropological, and ecclesiastical aspects of church growth. They have emphasized the "what" and the "how". This has all been most stimulating and helpful, but the question of "why" keeps cropping up.

Now Dr. Alan Tippett, veteran missionary of the Fiji Islands and professor in the School of World Mission and Institute of Church Growth at Fuller Seminary, has undertaken the task of giving us a firm biblical basis for the "why" of church growth. Although brief, his book <u>Church Growth and the Word of God</u> (Eerdmans) is packed with valuable exegetical material. The broad scope of church growth as a biblical concept is covered in chapter one. The biblical ideas of diffusion, growth (with a plethora of imagery in the Scriptures), numbering, obedience and responsibility, conversion and mission, and continuity are all treated in this one chapter. While it is not the author's intent to give a detailed exegesis of every passage he cites, he has certainly provided an abundance of material. For those who wish to pursue this topic more deeply he has dropped enough seed thoughts to keep an exegete busy for a long time to come.

In subsequent chapters the author treats the dynamics of church growth, problems of non-growth, the current situation, and the Christian hope as related to church growth.

The concept of multi-individual decisions, which underlies the whole idea of a "people movement," is shown to be prominent in both Old and New Testaments. This section alone (in chapter two) is worth the price of the book, as it deals with such a fundamental concept. For those who criticize an emphasis on results, Dr. Tippett shows the New Testament ideas of ingathering as depicted in such images as the steward, the farmer, the husbandman, and the fisherman.

The emphasis in some contemporary theology on a "churchless ministry" (the adequacy of merely being a Christian in the world without relating to an institution which is often attacked as dying) is met head on with Scripture. The New Testament teaching on the centrality of the church in the work of Jesus Christ on earth is clearly developed. It is also demonstrated that there is no place for a local church without outreach. "The congregation and its outreach stand or fall together" (p. 67).

Finally, the Christian hope as related to the church and its outreach is admirably expounded. The Old Testament hope was fulfilled in Christ. The New Testament hope is shown as moving, under the leadership of the Holy Spirit in his church, towards the final consummation in Christ. Again it is the church that becomes the center of God's activity on earth. Therefore, the growth of that church must be part of God's total plan and must become central in the concern of his people.

For any who have read the church growth literature and perhaps been disturbed at times with the question of "why," this refreshing and careful analysis of the biblical principles underlying the entire movement is a welcome addition. It is one of the most significant books yet to be published on this topic and should be studied carefully by all missionaries and mission leaders.

(Mr. Howard is missionary director of Inter-Varsity Christian Fellowship, Madison, Wisconsin. His review first appeared in the Evangelical Missions Quarterly).

SEMINARY STARTS CHURCH GROWTH DEPARTMENT

Seminaries traditionally have well defined departments, hallowed by centuries and validated by need--Biblical Studies including Hermeneutics, Old and New Testament; Church History; Theology including Philosophy and Dogmatics; and Christian Ministries including Homiletics, Counselling, and Christian Education. It was this curriculum, devoted exclusively to preparing men to serve existing churches, which Bishop Newbigin had in mind when he wrote:

> For a thousand years, when Christendom was sealed off by Islam from effective contact with the rest of the world and was contracting not expanding, it lived in almost total isolation from non-Christian cultures.
>
> In this situation the illusion that the age of missions is over became almost an integral part of Christianity. The perpetuation of that illusion is revealed in our normal church life, in the forms of congregations and parishes, in our conception of the ministry, and in the ordinary consciousness of churchmen.
>
> Our theological curricula bear eloquent testimony to this illusion.
>
> (Peter Ainslie Memorial Lecture, Rhodes University, South Africa).

Today alert seminaries sense two heart-rending human needs--that of segments of 'Christian' populations which by virtue of moving or of growing up in highly secularized urban society have lapsed to Christian-tinged materialism, and that of "brining to faith and obedience" (Romans 1:5) thousands upon thousands of segments of non-Christian society in Asia, Africa and Latin America. Driven by these needs, seminaries are adding Departments of Church Growth to teach ministers in training all that can be known about God's great program of the discipling of the nations. Churches must infiltrate every family of man as fishes swim in the sea.

The official catalog for 1971-72 of Lincoln College and Seminary--a young and creative institution--has just come to hand. It devotes 8 pages and 69 courses to the Biblical Field, 6 pages and 45 courses to the Doctrinal and Philosophical Field, 4 pages and 20 courses to the Historical Field, and 13 pages and 85 courses to the Christian Ministries Field. In this last field is placed "The Department of Church Growth" with 6 pages, 38 courses, and three professors. This seminary is taking seriously the churching of the 150 mile long city growing up in Western Illinois between Chicago and St. Louis as well as of dozens of other urban connurbations growing furiously all over America. The seminary is preparing men who will start hundreds of new churches in America. It is also taking seriously the preparation of hundreds of missionaries on whose hearts the Lord has placed the discipling of the two billion. It is going to teach church growth at home and abroad.

Seminary leaders all over the world will do well to write to The Registrar, Lincoln Seminary, Lincoln, Illinois 62656, U.S.A. and get the catalog. It describes theological education which has shaken itself free of the great illusion which Lesslie Newbigin describes.

A FITTING NEW TERM

Spain is to be the West Indies Mission's next field, according to J. Allen Thompson, the general director. He said,

> We are convinced, after years of research and investigation that God would have us use in Spain the expertise acquired through 40 years in Cuba. Repeated calls from Spaniards to assist them in _evangelism and church planting_ was an important factor in our decision.
>
> Missionary News Service, July 15, 1971

Comment:
'Evangelism' has become an ambiguous word. We commend the West Indies Mission in saying forthrightly 'evangelism and church planting'! When propagating the Gospel is meant, when the goal is to multiply churches of Jesus Christ, each one a center of life and light, then we should all speak about 'evangelism and church planting'.

CHURCH GROWTH
BULLETIN

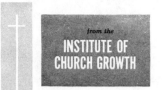

from the
INSTITUTE OF
CHURCH GROWTH

Address:
FULLER THEOLOGICAL
SEMINARY
135 N. Oakland
Pasadena, Calif. 91101

DONALD A. McGAVRAN, B.D., Ph.D.
Director

NOVEMBER 1971   Subscription $1 per year   Volume VIII, No. 2

A DEFINITIVE STATEMENT ON
CHURCH-MISSION RELATIONSHIPS

CHURCH-MISSION RELATIONSHIPS OVERSEAS   by Dr. Louis L. King**

Since the start of the modern missionary era, various forms of church-mission relationship have been practiced, ostensibly to make

---

**Among the many significant addresses delivered at GREEN LAKE '71--the great conference assembled in early October 1971 to consider church-mission relationships--the one started above and continued on the succeeding pages describes the situation most accurately and lays down biblical and practical guidelines for both Churches and Missions. It is so important that we are increasing our usual 12 pages to 16. Even so, we can print only the most significant three-fourths of the address. This luminous statement should be translated into many languages and printed as news, as a pamphlet on church-mission relationships, as material for conventions of churches and assemblies of missions to study and discuss, and as advanced thinking on missions.

Many forms of church-mission relationships achieve amicable relationships, but at the same time diminish mission. They quench the spirit of evangelism. They produce churches growing by biological increase only. What Dr. King proposes achieves harmonious relationships <u>and</u> heightens zeal to propagate the Gospel.

Dr. King is the Foreign Secretary of the Christian and Missionary Alliance, whose mission arm has 842 missionaries, an overseas budget of nearly five million, and has fathered Churches in 29 nations. We are confident his article will whet the appetite of readers and lead them to order:

1. *Missions in Creative Tension: The Green Lake '71 Compendium*, being the addresses and papers given there. (William Carey Library, $2.77 including postage)

2. A Symposium of Views on Church-Mission relations, written by noted leaders after the Green Lake experience. (Editor Peter Wagner, Moody Press)

SEND correspondence, news, and articles to the Editor, Dr. Donald McGavran, at the Institute of Church Growth, Fuller Theological Seminary. Published bi-monthly, send subscriptions and changes of address to the Business Manager, Norman L. Cummings, Overseas Crusades, Inc., 265 Lytton Avenue, Palo Alto, California 94301, U.S.A. Second-class postage paid at Palo Alto, California.

it possible for both the sending church and the receiving church to
be all that the New Testament intended each of them to be. Generally
eight forms are indicated, as follows:

> Mission dominance, or paternalism
> No mission, only the church
> Modified mission dominance
> Dichotomy, cooperation of autonomous equals
> Modified dichotomy
> Full fusion (or integration)
> Modified fusion (or functional integration)
> Partnership of equality and mutuality

Except for mission service agencies, all mission-church relations are comprehended in this list. For most 20th century evangelicals, however, full or modified fusion and full or modified dichotomy
have dominated men's attention. To these four, therefore, discussion
will be directed.

A. FUSION

Presently the organizational structure gaining favor for
accomplishing the New Testament ideal for the church is one in
which the mission is required to lose its identity by merging
itself into the church's organization. We want, therefore, to
examine some of the reasons argued in favor of amalgamating
mission with church. Of necessity the list will be suggestive,
not exhaustive. Each point, we know, has many ramifications
that would need to be more thoroughly explored; but direction
rather than a detailed road map is intended. Along the way we
shall briefly examine those reasons either in relation to their
scriptural undergirding or practical outworking in experience
to learn whether or not fusion helps or hinders achieving a
New Testament kind of church.

Here are some of the reasons offered in favor of fusion:

1. Oneness of the Church

The merging of the mission into the church is considered essential in order to achieve the "oneness" of the
Church. This emphasis came alive at the 1928 Jerusalem
Conference. Tambaram 1938 was the conference where for
the first time the younger churches were unconditionally
recognized as equal with the older churches. Whitby 1947
went further and disregarded the difference between older
and younger churches and called all churches everywhere
to "expectant and worldwide evangelism in the spirit of
partnership in obedience."[1] Since then the swing toward
unification of mission and church has been strongly marked.
At this point almost all ecumenically oriented missions
and churches have been unified.

The strongest impetus in all this has been the enormous
attention given to being "one" as set forth in John 17:21

and Ephesians 4:1-6. Arguing from these two passages, it is
asserted that organizational relatedness is essential to the
nature of the Church; therefore, the mission must not maintain a separate or distinct identity from the structured
church. Since the Church is indivisible, the church and the
mission must be joined. The mission must be so integrated
that the mission's property, money, and personnel become the
responsibility of the church. Anything less than this misses
the biblical requirement. The younger churches have adopted
the "oneness" concept with alacrity and lay it before mission
leaders with forcefulness.

Another argument closely allied with the "oneness" doctrine
maintains "that the principle of dichotomy [separate administration of mission and church] is not sound biblically....
Biblically, it cannot be sustained. Dichotomy is not known
in the Bible. It does not fit into the body structure of the
church."[2] "Equality in partnership seems the only logical
deduction from the Bible."[3]

The discerning student of the Word knows that these arguments are not based entirely on what the Bible itself teaches
but upon what it is thought to teach. The proponents for the
integration of church and mission have "eisegeted" (read into)
rather than "exegeted" (read out of) the Scriptures. There
is indeed teaching on the Church as "one" and as the "body,"
but not in the sense of organizational relatedness. They
have taken these grand concepts of the Church and gone outside Scriptures to make some logical deductions. The validity of the position taken must be understood in this light.
It is an assumed concept of the church.

The only certain position to take is that no specific
structure or pattern of church organization or of mission-
church relationship is prescribed in the New Testament. The
Bible gives only ideals of relationships. Particularly the
New Testament concerns itself with the life of the "body,"
the Church, and the relationship of its members to their
Head and to one another as persons. If we are to "deduce"
anything from the New Testament, it is that the "body"
structure should be such that the life-giving channels from
the Head are unrestricted and that nothing is permitted to
paralyze the obedient response of members to their Head.
When full response is inhibited, the "body" is not healthy.
The nature of mission-church relations then should be such
that best allows the church as Church to express and exercise
maturely its life in Christ. The type of structure for
relationship should be based on a functional relatedness to
this principle rather than on a noncontextual interpretation
that "oneness" and "body" necessitates organizational
relatedness.

2. <u>The Church IS Mission</u>.

The "Church IS Mission" idea is also used to support the
assertion that church and mission must be united. In this
context, ecumenists and many evangelicals are saying: the
church should be central in all missionary endeavor; missionaries must be a part of the church and amenable to the
official leadership or else the nature of the Church is
damaged; missionary work should be done <u>with</u> and <u>through</u>
the existing church; the central administration of the
national organization ought to decide and control when and
where and how missionaries work. The contemporary view is
that a church in a given country, or even in a region of a
country, has "homestead rights" and no one may enter except
to work under the direction of that church.[4]

But some of us have questions. Does the official leadership by itself constitute the church? Is the central administration of a denomination the church? Are missions
legitimate only if carried forward through the structured
church? If the answer is affirmative, then what should we
say concerning CMS, and OFM, and TEAM, and a host of other
missions which are not under any official church administration? Should we disallow them? or put "theology of the
church" aside and admit that they are the Church--the "Church
in action" or an "expression of the Church"? In any event,
on what scriptural basis has the Church defined as denomination become an adequate definition?

Again, has denominational administration been the best
vehicle for achieving a worldwide witness of the gospel?
Has the structured church leadership demonstrated necessary
sympathy for missions, and do they have a record of achieving
mobility?

The answer of western church history is not favorable. It
shows that official leadership of the church can be out of
sympathy with the missionary enterprise. Look at the dis-
approval and downright opposition that Justinian Welz[5] and
William Carey and others since them received from church
officers. Examine the various Reformation Churches in
Europe and the Church of England also. Many of them do not
conduct foreign missionary work from within the framework
of the church organization. It is structurally and officially absent. They have not knit missionary work with the
rest of the church's program. It is only the independent
association of people within these churches that sustains
missions through mission societies. Their money is not
raised centrally. These voluntary agencies are not in any
way controlled by the official administrative machinery of
the church.[6]

It is primarily in North America that denominations have
foreign missions within their organizational structure. But

these came into being only after many mission societies had
been established. With the passage of time, though, denominations have accumulated so many institutional and self-
serving interests that missionary work does not receive the
good will and concentration it deserves. Viewed historically
and currently, missions has not received adequate, sympathetic,
and financial consideration within the structure of the church:
church governments greet this matter with great reluctance.

With this knowledge, does it not seem strange to suppose
that the younger churches will give more favorable attention
to missions than European and North American denominations?
Are the mission-land churches less concerned with their
ecclesiastical and social self than the western churches? Is
their specific missionary intent such that they are more willing or ready or eager for world evangelization? Are they so
proclamation-centered that they do not neglect the non-
Christian frontier? Or are they institution-minded, given to
improving their resources, trying to get their membership to
rise in the social structure, devoting themselves to the main-
tenance of church for nourishing their members spiritually?
May not the national church's central organ of control be in
the same danger of debunking missions as the Reformation
Church--although it may be for other reasons, such as
finances? And have they not required that missionaries and
an increasingly larger proportion of our resources be devoted
to work among Christian people, for Christian people, and in
Christian institutions? Does not a large proportion of our
finances to the church simply become inter-church aid to
support its organizational and institutional life without any
missionary purpose? Do not the younger churches taking the
aid, more often than not sink into the unexciting business of
routine without growth or without evangelistic or missionary
outreach? In fusion of church and mission, can our determination to be missionary be preserved and nutured and structured?
In the fusion structure, are missionaries so organized that
they can resist the inveterate tendency of the church to self-
centeredness? If they do resist the younger church, what will
happen?

Already, where churches and missions have been joined, the
younger churches' pathological over-anxiety about their prerogatives in controlling the missions indicates what we can
expect.

Here is Dr. Herbert C. Jackson's indictment of the younger
churches. It was given in his inaugural address as Adjunct
Professor on the Senior Faculty of Union Theological Seminary
in New York City:

> Quite unintentionally a tyranny has arisen which
> stifles apostolate and militates very greatly against
> any real fulfillment of the Great Commission and
> against the freedom of the Holy Spirit to move where

He will.... This has produced a retraction in the
missionary witness that is worse than tragic, and at
a time when there are still vast areas that have not
heard the gospel and when the 'population explosion,'
the resurgence of non-Christian religions and numerous sociological factors are causing a steady decline
in the ratio of Christians to non-Christians in the
world.... This has also provided us with the situation that has given rise to the appalling frustration
that exists today among missionaries.[8]

By way of contrast, church history reveals it was the
mission societies, standing independent of the churches and
branded as "nontheological factors" by opposing church administrators, that pioneered with consumate courage and aggres-
siveness the world-wide advance of the gospel. The point is
that mission administration separate from the church's control is valid and very often necessary for missionary
endeavor.

3. A "Proper" Church.

Some younger church leaders have stated that the mission
must lose its identity by integrating with them in order for
them to be a "proper" church. Being "proper" also includes
recognition and contact with established denominations,
highly trained leadership, more respectable church buildings,
wearing the clerical collar (since this is "proper" among the
historic denominations), operating educational and medical
institutions as appurtenances of respectability and influence,
and belonging to a worldwide organization.

The mission joined to the church is viewed not only the
"proper" structure but the logical agency through which these
benefits can be achieved. The major issue here is not their
desire to be "proper" but the possible exploitation of the
mission. This occurs when the mission's resources are expended in supporting the church's ministry, establishing
central offices, providing pension funds, and raising the
salaries of officials--when the mission is not permitted to
focus on the world but on the church. The United Presbyterian
Church has spoken thus on this issue:

> It needs to be reasserted continually, without
> pomposity or irritation, that the Commission is more
> than a servicing agency for indigenous churches. It
> is an instrumental expression of the United Presby-
> terian Church's fulfillment of its mission to the
> world, and to assume that the ecumenical era demands
> a total subordination in program and the use of per-
> sonnel to the individual determination of indigenous
> churches would be a restrictive error.[9]

To the exploitation of the mission we add the calamity
wrought by the economic and political power that the fusion

of church and mission affords. Concerning this, a recent
correspondent wrote:

> Where fusion of church and mission has taken the
> form of an effort to fuse the mission structures with
> the structures of an autonomous church, the experience
> has been disastrous.... In the case of the Disciples'
> Church in Madhya Pradesh, India, the structural fusion
> of the church and mission saddled a small and poverty
> stricken church with a whole series of institutional
> structures for education and medical ministry which
> represents a tremendous reservoir of economic and
> political power. Struggle over these sources of secur-
> ity and power has very nearly wrecked the church.[10]

Examples abound of spiritual apathy, wrong relationships,
quarrelsomeness over finances, litigations over property, dis-
trust of church leaders, electioneering for office, and keeping missionaries home on account of the power and benefits
accruing to the church bureaucracy through fusion. Making the
mission's structure and strategy fit what is prescribed in the
minds of Africans and Asians to make them "proper" certainly
has helped neither the church nor the mission to accomplish
their God-appointed roles more successfully.

The idea is scripturally inadequate. The "proper" church
sends missionaries. Converts are won, new churches formed,
which in turn evangelize and send until the whole world has
heard. Churches were never meant to be ends in themselves
but means for enlarging and extending the spread of the
gospel. Nor do young churches exhaust their responsibility
in local evangelism. They, too, are to send. This activity
is natural to their essential nature and is required for
their maturity.

4. Financial Assistance a "Right."

Since the fusion of mission with church gives the younger
church equality with the older church, it is alleged that
financial assistance is a "right." This concept comes to the
fore because of "the new patterns observed in neighboring
ecumenical churches, the service rendered by Inter-Church Aid
and Refugee Service, the example of the World Health Organization and the operations of the United Nations. In all these
relationships the poorer groups may pay a small contribution
or none at all, but receive great benefits. They find that
this does not impair the sense of equality, involve sacrifice
of proper pride or the sense of dignity and independence.
They believe the international team of helpers or the financial assistance is received as a present from themselves to
themselves since they also are members of that international
body through which the gift came."[11] As applied to the church,
it is stated: "Financial resources in one part of the church
can be used in another part...the issue is never whether a

church has a right to spend that money."[12] "Any gift that a church has belongs to the whole body of Christ."[13]

Our response to such specious reasoning is that such a "right" is not right. Indeed, much of the failure in maintaining successful fellowship between missionaries and national Christians comes from financial relations. Far down below almost every other problem of mission-church relationship the fundamental thing is money. It is this dependence upon foreign money that creates an abnormal and truly dangerous situation for the church. Therefore, if and when aid is given, it should be recognized by both parties as exceptional and not unattended with danger to (1) the faith and (2) the activity of Christians and (3) their relations with the missionaries.

Full maturity in finances and propagation and government is a necessary Christian virtue, and has proved to be essential to church growth. In Korea, Burma, the South Pacific, and Uganda where there has been dramatic church growth, less foreign money has been spent in proportion to membership than in other mission fields of the world. There are sufficient church growth studies to show that when a church can take care of itself financially it is more relevant to its world, more evangelistic and missionary. The practice of biblical stewardship helps make this possible and therefore should be given priority and be everywhere applicable. Indeed, the Scriptures point out that liberal giving or the lack of it is an indication of one's spirituality (II Cor. 8 and 9).

By promoting a structure of relationship which assumes that a Christian community, by "right," can continually receive and yet not give or give so little as to not really matter, we are cutting a main artery which leads to the very "heart" of the church.

Dr. John R. Crawford, Professor at the School of Theology of Congo's Free Universtiy, recently concluded a research on the most important causes of money problems in the struggling Congo churches. He lists these three[14] at the top of some 29 given causes:

1. Christians don't take giving seriously enough.
2. Bad or doubtful handling of church funds.
3. Christians expect help from the outside.

What an open but tragic witness that their heart is not in the Lord's work! (Matt. 6:21). And doubly tragic if the continual infusion of finances keeps it that way. J. Merle Davis, in commenting about the national church's economic life, said: "It is self-evident that if a tree is to live it must draw its nourishment through its own roots and leaves."

In addition to creating a spiritual problem, foreign financial aid cripples initiative. Take India as an example. In

1967 India received 10 billion dollars in foreign assistance.
The bulk of this was provided as gifts or as loans on conces-
sional terms. It was estimated that one of every five U.S.
farms worked to feed India. But the foreign aid did not
relieve India of hunger and starvation; in fact, it compounded
them, for the availability of American food grains induced the
Indian government into extravagant industrial undertakings to
the neglect of agriculture. Also, the government sold the
foreign aid grain at a subsidized price considerably below the
open market price. The result of all this was that Indian
farmers withheld grain from delivery or produced only for their
own need. The eminent economic consultant, Walter Groseclose,
summed it up as follows in his article, "Foreign Aid Fizzle":

> The fact recognized by many in India, is that as long
> as U.S. agricultural aid is available, neither the
> government nor the people have incentive to improve
> domestic food sources.[15]

Illustrations abound to show that, even as for India, the
continuous flow of foreign finances dulls the younger churches'
incentive to give to sustain the Lord's work committed to them.
It does not train them in giving. Necessity is not laid upon
them. They become disobedient to the plain requirements of
the Bible. Seldom do they catch the vision of their service
to others. They will be strengthened only as they become instruments of Christ in sustaining His great mission through
their own money gifts.

Also, the flow of the mission's more abundant financial
resources into the young church divorces it from local financial and social realities. The structures the money supports
are not related to the actualities of the church's own financial setting. There is little attempt to assess the programs
in terms of the church's own obedience in stewardship.
Furthermore, being beneficiaries of the system, they do not
want to drop the comfortable status quo. They become myopic
and think primarily of self-interests. The system enables
them to live unrelated to financial actualities. It goes
contrary to scriptural instruction regarding stewardship and
actually trains them to be dependent.

5. Independence.

Some leaders of evangelical younger churches believe that
an amalgamation of mission with church will give them independence. They are saying:

> Western missions continue to reflect, more or less,
>   the colonial administrative pattern;

> The church is held in some subsidiary and subordinate
>   relation to an organization outside its country; and

> This undermines their integrity and selfhood.

They therefore want an end to their uncertain and ambiguous status. They desire to rid themselves of every vestige of ingrained characteristics of the colonial era as epitomized in the missionary's attitude and in present mission-church structures. They seek the goal of possessing authoritative final control in every department of their church's life and ministry. This, they insist, calls for a new structure of relationship. They believe the union of mission with church is that which will accomplish independence.

But, will it? What do we learn from the many missions and younger churches associated with the ecumenical movement who in the 1950s revamped their relationship structure in the manner evangelical younger churches are requesting today? Has the specter of colonialism been obliterated and the ex-hilarating spirit of independence truly prevailed? The answer is NO.

a. Neo-colonialism.

We learn that after two decades the new relationship is being branded as neo-colonialism.[16] Younger church leaders are saying the new structure was designed to maintain a special relationship with them, to retain influence and power in just those areas which had been under the mission's subjugation, and to insure a con-tinued projection of the mission's interests. Further-more, they testify, western Christians (fraternal workers, servants, technicians) have not functioned in a manner to promote the goal of self-reliance, of modern-ization, and of economic progress. Missionaries have not been sufficiently aware of the nationals' aspirations or accepted their goals of development and conscientiously subscribed to them. Rather, missionaries are playing the old colonial game in a new form. The new partnership rejects colonialism in principle but continues it in practice. After several years of a fused relationship, traces of patronage, paternalism, and condescension remain. There is still no true equality, no real partner-ship.

b. International cooperation.

In ecumenical circles the complaint is voiced that the younger church often judges a missionary "by the funds... which he brings with him, together with the funds his presence attracts for projects he designs, and which are usually not available for the church if he withdraws or resigns."[17] Financial considerations all too often force church leaders to fulfill the wishes of the missionaries against their own judgment. "This makes it difficult for a church to use its freedom of decision...."[18] And some ecumenists believe "...the present ways in which they try to manifest the universality of the Church by sharing

personnel are distorted forms."[19] For this reason, the
Uppsala Assembly of the WCC officially requested that
"new forms and relationships" be structured. They are
asking for "new relationships of genuine equality, new
respect for one another's identity and calling and new
ways of supporting one another in the task which God has
given to each one, within the fellowship of the universal
Church."[20] In particular they want a new structure that
provides for "international cooperation" in which missionary activity will be internationally supported, controlled, and directed.

Furthermore, much of the data from evangelical and
ecumenical sources discloses that the integration of
mission with church has proved to be thorny for both
sides. And although some see the fusion of the two
bodies as not only desirable but also inevitable,[21]
others do not consider it an altogether sufficient or
final solution. Some consider it a temporary arrangement pending a better way. Through it the kind and
extent of independence and equality the younger churches
seek has not yet been achieved; it still evades them.
Responsible men continue to question whether the pattern
and the conception behind it is the right expression of
the obedience God wants.[22] Since foreign personnel and
money are still there, fusion has not produced--and cannot produce or guarantee--the "freedom" the younger
churches seem to want. This is so because interpersonal
and interorganizational relationships are still there--
because people are involved. Being evangelical or ecumenical makes no appreciable difference in this context.

6. Conclusion About Fusion

The relationship structure that fuses the church and the
mission overclouds certain basic scriptural requirements. As
popularized and practiced, it perpetuates weakness in the
younger church in the very areas where maturity is needed.
Fusion causes the younger churches to delay or ignore the
implementation of biblical faith and mission. And in the
sending churches it has produced a discouraging situation:
they have degenerated into giving inter-church aid, of being
"supply depots." Although it is not the sole reason, it has
helped to produce a profound loss of initiative and money and
personnel for world evangelization. Admittedly these draw-
backs could be corrected, but the effort required would be
enormous.

Fusion in its unmodified form, then, does not foster either
in the sending church or in the receiving church the kind of
church the New Testament portrays. Daniel T. Niles correctly
said, "When a missionary church is reduced to the bare function of a recruiting agent of personnel and finances to support
another church, then the heart of the missionary conviction
has been betrayed."[23]

B. <u>MODIFIED FUSION</u>.

A modified fusion pattern has been proposed by Climenhaga and[24] Jacques[24] and more recently improved upon by Dr. George Peters[25] who calls it "Partnership of Equality and Mutuality." Peters takes into account the three major problem areas of (1) administration of the missionary and the mission expansion program, (2) integration of the missionary into the full life of the church, and (3) finances from overseas. He then lists seven advantages of a total partnership of church and mission with all matters of the mission's activity including policy, finances, administrations, and personnel being <u>church based</u>.

Proponents of modified fusion rightly and scripturally, with Peters, insist that "Christian missions must be focused on the world, not on the church with its organization and program. Missionaries as such are not sent for police action or church programming, but in order that the attack forces of the churches may be bolstered and that churches might be multiplied. The energies of the sending church must not be spent in perfecting church structures, drafting constitutions, exercising church discipline and superintending institutions. The goal of missions is not the structural and institutional life of the church community, but the proclamation of the gospel to those who do not confess Jesus Christ as Lord and Savior."[26]

"Missions must also be the mission <u>of</u> the new church, not only <u>for</u> the church." "The missionary's ministry must be rendered through the church, but not mainly to the church. Principally, he works neither in the church nor for the church but with the church. His service is mainly to the unevangelized world."[27] "This assignment is his by divine calling and mutual agreement, between him, his mission, and the national church...he has become a part of a conference to serve as a missionary with the church to unevangelized areas that must be reached with the gospel."[28]

Modified fusion is purposely designed to keep the evangelistic and missionary function of both the sending church and the younger church truly inviolate in accordance with the New Testament requirements for the Church. In this, it is commendable. Nothing, however, is spelled out about the extent of the church's independence and its obligations in stewardship. It is possible that the old and irksome paternalistic control will be reimposed once again through the injection of foreign personnel and finances into the younger church. It could thus be tied to western power centers more securely than ever before, and that as a permanently weaker partner.

Unfortunately the plan is so relatively recent we do not have enough details of its application or an illustration of its success. We await these with deepest and sympathetic interest.

C. DICHOTOMY.

We turn now to the consideration of dichotomy. This is the cooperation of autonomous equals. It allows the mission and the church to maintain their own organizations. But does it help or hinder attaining the New Testament ideal for the Church? Let us examine it as we did the fusion pattern. And since it has been so fairly represented by Dr. George W. Peters,[29] an opponent of the plan, we present his analysis:

> This pattern is based on the principle of organizational dichotomy in the field. The ideal is functional co-operation rather than separation or integration. According to this pattern, the mission and the church form two autono-mous bodies with separate legislative and administrative authorities though they operate in fraternal relationships and functional unity.
>
> The mission and the church are distinct, separate, and independent organizational bodies, parallel movements with distinct assignments. The missionary labors independently of the jurisdiction of the national church and under the direction of his board of missions. The degree of func-tional and spiritual interrelation of the two bodies, is either taken for granted or carefully delineated. Usually it is understood that the mission does not set up its own churches, but rather relates such to the national body and then becomes a functional serving agency to the ecclesias-tical structure.
>
> This is basically the pattern of numerous faith missions whose supreme goal is the evangelization of the world and the establishing of local congregations as lighthouses in many communities, and who are less concerned for larger structural units in the various lands. However, it is also well exemplified by the Presbyterian 'Brazil Plan' of 1916, hailed as a unique success as recently as 1968 by the Reverend C. Darby Fulton.[30]
>
> This program functions best according to the following principles: (a) The mission practices intensive work rather than extensive evangelization. It practices geo-graphical concentration rather than general dissemination of the gospel. To a certain degree, it follows the example of Paul who abode in one place for a considerable time, at least sufficient time for a church to be born. (b) Evan-gelism of a locality is undertaken for the purpose of establishing a functioning assembly or church. (c) After a church has come into being, it is led into fellowship with churches of similar persuasion and organization and thus linked to a larger national body. (d) The missionary officially dissociates himself from here on from the church and technically has neither right nor authority over this body of believers. He returns only upon invitation to assist and to minister as requested.

The arguments for this pattern of operation must not be
minimized. Based both on logic and sentiment, and in part
on experience, they seem sound, convincing, and beneficial.
In general they are somewhat as follows: (1) It best protects the autonomy and selfhood of the emerging national
church. No missionary sits in the church courts to exert
undue influence and to project his image into the image-
forming and legislative body. Spiritual self-reliance and
self-help become primary exercises from the beginning. It
is hoped that thereby not only tensions will be eliminated
and the western image of the church minimized, but also the
selfhood of the church will evolve more fully, its national
character will become apparent, and, above all, the church
will from the very beginning learn to depend upon its own
resources and particularly upon the superintendent of the
church, the indwelling Holy Spirit. All of this is basic
and crucial for a church if it is to function properly and
to fulfill the design of God for it in the community and the
world. Also, should an emergency demand the withdrawal of
all missionaries, the church would continue its function
without serious vibrations and interruptions.

(2) It best protects the missionary in his primary calling
and in his freedom and initiative as a 'sent one' for a particular task. It permits him to labor as a pioneer in the
'regions beyond' without becoming absorbed in a church-
centered program and wrapped up in the organizational and
institutional structure and life of the national church.

This aspect must not be minimized. While mission and church
belong organizationally together, the mission of the church is
larger than missions, the total function of the church is
larger than the sending forth of evangelists into the world of
unbelief and gospel destitution, beyond its own area of operation and influence. At the same time, it remains a New Testament fact that a church ceases to be New Testament in spirit
and design if it ceases to be missions as well as mission. No
church sent into the world (mission) can afford not to send
forth some of its members beyond its own region (missions).
Most of these 'sent-forth-ones' are evangelists, not to other
churches, but to the world in unbelief and without the gospel.
To envelop them in another church program, no matter where
this may be geographically, is doing injustice to their very
calling and assignment. They are missionaries, sent-ones,
beyond the borders of the church. This high calling must be
clearly grasped, emphatically taught, and zealously guarded.

It should be noted, however, that this evangelist-missionary
concept may not exhaust the interchurch ministries between the
older and younger churches and that there may be a place for
fraternal workers.

(3) It best protects the image of a board of missions as
being an agent of a unique task and particular assignment.

It is not a church board or a board that has legislative
authority over churches. It does not represent the church
in its total function. Neither is it merely a recruiting
agency. It is a board of a particular design and mission,
a board to send forth men and women of a particular calling
into a particular situation--the world of unbelief, destitute
of the gospel--for a singular purpose, the purpose of gospel
proclamation by every legitimate means and effective method,
and the establishing of functioning churches who will assume
their New Testament responsibility and calling and develop
their own selfhood and national character. This board is
not a mere service agency or 'supply depot.' It has not
received its authority and assignment from a national body,
nor is its sending forth subject to invitations and requests.
Its task is not completed with the rise of a national church.
It stands before its risen Lord, is subject to His unique
world, and boldly expresses the promptings of the spirit of
missions. Only then can the true image of a board of missions
be presented. This, too, must be zealously guarded and
energetically pursued.

Although Dr. Peters has so ably and fairly delineated the dichotomy pattern, he does not think it proves "functionally most effective, filially most satisfactory, scientifically most helpful" or
expresses "the highest Biblical idealism."[31] And except for a
brief paragraph in which he states he cannot fit it "into the body
structure of the Church,"[32] he does not elaborate further on his
opposing views.

Conclusion About Dichotomy

As for me, I hold that the pattern of mission-church relationship
ought not to have as its final criterion simply a compatible
relationship. Rather, I look at the dichotomy pattern as I do that
of fusion. I look to see if it allows both the older church and
the younger church to be New Testament kind of churches. Does it
meet the scriptural requirements regarding a church's function?
Most essentially, does it foster or stifle a passion for evangelism
and missions in both? That, it seems to me, is the test of all
tests. And dichotomy passes it quite well. The record of evangelism and missionary activity in both the older and younger
churches that have operated under this system is well known to us
and speaks for itself.

Problems there have been and are, but these have become acute
only when an exaggerated emphasis on developing the new church has
supplanted evangelism; when service jobs have displaced persuasion
evangelism (the kind that wins the lost and establishes them in
visible churches); when both church and mission have concentrated
their attention on the church rather than the unredeemed multitudes.

D. MODIFIED DICHOTOMY.

Those who practice modified dichotomy believe the existence of
the new churches has without doubt added a new dimension to missionary work--that younger churches do need assistance in certain
specialized areas. They therefore propose the mission's resources
in personnel and finances be divided. One segment would be (1) for
maintaining liaison and vital support with the national church, the
other (2) for pioneering and planting by the mission.

1. Maintaining Liaison and Vital Support.

In this the mission turns over to the church the development portion of its resources, usually without strings
attached. The authority and maturity of the younger church
is recognized, allowing it to use some funds and some missionaries as it sees fit. These missionaries are such as are
willing and able to participate fully in the life of the
church. The amount of money, the number of missionaries, and
the length of time involved are determined by a negotiated
agreement. At the end of the stipulated period, the agreement
is mutually examined with a view to renewing or modifying it.
The aim is for the church to work toward assuming full responsibility just as soon as possible. In this way the founding
mission maintains a good relationship with the church, and
gives help if it is needed.

2. Pioneering and Planting.

Since God is still calling, equipping, and sending pioneering,
church-planting missionaries, the framework is provided for
them to work unhampered by fragile considerations of church
jurisdiction. Their full energies are directed to planting
new churches, not merely servicing the existing ones. Their
work, however, is not merely in terms of geography. This
gives an unparalleled opportunity as well as responsibility
for the missionary to advance the gospel. The new ground for
missionary fresh starts is agreed upon, however--if at all
possible--between the church and the mission. Generally, all
populations not being effectively evangelized by existing
churches'are open to the mission to evangelize. The church is
asked to participate by sending personnel. There are clear
plans to incorporate the missionary-planted churches into the
existing ecclesiastical structure.

This pattern of relationship is in its beginning stages and still
too new to assess from experience. Like modified fusion, it seeks
to recognize fairly some responsibility to the national church and
at the same time to maintain its obligation to continually spread
the gospel in an everwidening area. It is a pragmatic and functional approach to mission-church relationship.

Authorities cited, for lack of space, have not been given here; but wil'
be found in Dr. King's address in *Missions in Creative Tension* (see p. 1
bottom).

CHURCH GROWTH
BULLETIN

from the

INSTITUTE OF CHURCH GROWTH

Address:
FULLER THEOLOGICAL
SEMINARY
135 N. Oakland
Pasadena, Calif. 91101

DONALD A. McGAVRAN, B.D., Ph.D.
Director

JANUARY 1972   Subscription $1 per year   Volume VIII, No. 3

Our First Priority

Joseph S. McCullough

FIRST THINGS FIRST.   It takes more than the average dose of
courage and determination to change
the course of an entire mission. Paul did just that when
the Lord showed him that his attempt to go into Bithynia was
misguided at that particular time (Acts 16:7). Now Joseph S.
McCullough, General Director of the Andes Evangelical Mission,
takes a similar step and brings church-planting evangelism
back to the heart and soul of the great organization he leads.
CHURCH GROWTH BULLETIN proudly reprints this editorial from
the Fall, 1971, issue of The Andean Outlook, with the hope
that it is representative of a widespread and growing restate-
ment of the first priority of missions.

Evangelism, once again, will be the primary thrust of the Andes
Evangelical Mission.

Reaching the unreached has always been our objective as a pioneer
mission. But somehow with the growth of a strong national church, we
began to think that the responsibility for evangelizing belonged to
this church. Our task would be to carry on the training program of
Bible Schools, seminaries, and other church supporting ministries such
as literature, radio, youth centers, camping, Bible conferences and so
forth. All of these are excellent and greatly needed and must continue.

In a new way, however, we believe the Lord would have us focus our
attention and efforts to direct evangelistic opportunities. As missionaries we need to set the example and pace for the national churches and
pastors. Our responsibility is to keep moving out to the cutting edge
of the work. As new churches are planted, we will continue to break new
ground rather than limit our efforts to organizing and training.

SEND correspondence, news, and articles to the Editor, Dr. Donald McGavran, at the Institute
of Church Growth, Fuller Theological Seminary. Published bi-monthly, send subscriptions
and changes of address to the Business Manager, Norman L. Cummings, Overseas Crusades,
Inc., 265 Lytton Avenue, Palo Alto, California 94301, U.S.A. Second-class postage paid at
Palo Alto, California.

Missionaries must be kept fresh and vital in their testimony and experience. We know of no better way to do this than through witnessing and soul-winning. The national believer must see the reality of this in the missionary in order that he might follow his example.

Somehow a missionary vision and thrust in the local church produces spiritual vitality, joy, zeal, enthusiasm and fellowship that is thrilling. Wherever this is lacking, whether in the church, the mission, or the missionary, the work becomes difficult, unexciting, and it gradually declines into a stagnant condition. When folks become occupied with only themselves they lose the joy of salvation and problems, misunderstandings and divisions are likely to arise.

Through the blessing of God we have seen the national church organization become autonomous. The nearly 250 churches, congregations and groups comprising some 13,000 adherents is cause for abundant thanksgiving. As we look at the unfinished task before us, however, we realize that what has been done isn't good enough. We must yet do better.

God's call to us as a mission is to complete the great Commission in our areas. This calls for every worker to be a witness. Only as the Gospel passes from one person to another can this great task be accomplished. Therefore, our first priority is and will be evangelism, utilizing every method and means to accomplish the task.

CHRISTIAN PRESENCE AND SIT-INS

Donald McGavran

In July, 1964, Student World published an editorial which said:

> The Federation has always been concerned with making Jesus Christ known in the academic world. Evangelization, witness and mission have long been the words used to describe this task. But the words have now become problems for many students.... They are too big and definite. They suggest a certainty of faith and purpose...which create difficulty for many people.... When we try to find words... to witness to our belief that in Jesus Christ God has reconciled the world to himself...we use the word 'presence' for that reality.

Father Jordan Bishop, former professor of church history in the Cochabamba Roman Catholic Seminary in Bolivia, says:

> The evangelizer who appears identified with human power of one kind or another runs the risk of betraying the gospel to a new kind of idolatry...the problem (runs) much deeper and in its context one can see the value or necessity of an approach such as that of Charles de Faucauld. (CDF said that a missionary was simply a Christian being there with a presence willed and determined as a witness to the love of God).

Many others could be quoted who, in regard to _evangelism_, admire and advocate "presence" as the ideal method. No pressure, no persuasion, no manipulating of persons. Just a Christian _being there_. In regard to _evangelism_, of course.

All this was passing through my mind when a question occurred to me. Why is it that no one is advocating "presence" as a mode of changing the social structure? Why not use "presence" to smash the unjust framework of society? No one suggests that Martin Luther King was too aggressive or too certain of his purpose. No one even hints that it would have been more Christian for him, in his battle for justice for his people, to have simply "been there with a presence willed and determined as a witness to the love of God." He should perhaps have said meekly to the Alabama whites, "I want to learn from you. How do race relations look to you? Please do not think that I have all the answers. Let us sit down and talk reasonably about it. For that is true Christian mission." No one criticizes Dr. King's marches, sit-ins, and pray-ins as self seeking, manipulating persons, and working for the advantage of his own race.

As I think about this puzzle, I am constrained to believe that in regard to ends which we believe are unqualifiedly good, men of good will do not hesitate to employ all their powers to bring these about. If my conclusion is correct, then the puzzle may be solved. Could it be that those who advocate "presence" as the sole correct way to evangelize have ceased to believe that becoming a Christian is an unqualified good?

When advocated as only one of many forms of evangelism, which is sometimes rightly used in the face of hostility, the case is otherwise. Under those circumstances, "presence" may be not only a good form, but the only possible form of evangelism. Charles de Foucauld used it in North Africa when Frenchmen were capturing nations and Moslem Algerians could well suppose that evangelism was merely the camouflage of an advancing imperialism. Under those circumstances "presence" was probably right; but this is no reason to suppose it right for today's student world in particular or for missions in general. We must learn to be discriminating in our choice of missionary methods.

MISSIONS' TWIN DANGERS

Roman Catholic Archbishop Lourdasamy, Associate Secretary of the Sacred Congregation for Evangelism of Peoples, has recently said that there is a danger that mission activity may become confused with two other activities:

1. _With economic and social development._ "We should not invest our resources primarily in the economic and cultural development of secular society (with the risk of falling into a sort of clerical paternalization tinged with colonialism), but rather strive to give to mankind, as it gropes for happiness, the imperishable light of the Gospel, which respects the culture of each country and the personality of each man."

2. **With pastoral and ecumenical activity.** "Often we find the word 'missionary' used wrongly, as to empty it of its own proper meaning.... Certainly there are many non-Christians and unbelievers in the western world who need to be evangelized. There are socio-cultural milieus that are foreign to the Gospel and in which genuine missionary activity would be necessary. These 'internal' missions in western countries will be profitable also to the 'external' missions, provided their authentically missionary character is preserved--as distinct from ecumenical activity or bringing back lapsed Catholics to the sacraments."

Many Protestants will agree with Archbishop Lourdasamy, and sound the warning note against confusing missions with other good activities of the Christian church.

CHALLENGE FOR A MILLION

Dr. Ebbie Smith, SWM '70

Led as never before by the Holy Spirit, the Indonesian Baptist Mission meeting in July, 1971, became a genuine revival. Prayer meetings scheduled for one hour lasted far into the night. A large part of one morning was taken up as missionaries went from person to person just to tell the other they loved him or her.

In this atmosphere of spiritual leadership, the Mission made some of the most revolutionary decisions that any mission ever attempted. First and foremost, the mission accepted the challenge to win one million souls in the next ten years. To do this, the mission voted to place priority on the planting of house churches among the millions of Indonesia. These house churches will be led by lay leaders and will require no building or other equipment. They will be free to observe the ordinances as they are led by the Holy Spirit. The Mission decided to build no more church buildings and to move completely away from the idea of subsidy (in fact, all churches and pastors will be self-supporting by July 31, 1973, and no new work will begin with subsidy from foreign funds).

The mission voted to discontinue the present program of seminary education and use the campus for conference grounds. The seminary staff will be reassigned as field evangelists to pioneer a new type of leadership training.

The Mission structure will be completely re-worked. Recognizing that missionary housing and standard of living have been hindrances to evangelism, the mission has taken action to bring housing and living standards more in line with the over-all policy of outreach and simpler living. Some of our residences that are too large and pretentious will be sold and replaced with more suitable buildings.

In keeping with this new pattern of work, the Mission found over $94,000 on the books that will be returned to the Foreign Mission Board as money we will not need under the new pattern.

The events of this momentous mission meeting were connected with the survey that our mission had planned for this summer. Two years ago, the mission asked Donna and me to study at Fuller Theological Seminary with Dr. Donald McGavran to make preparation for this survey. Arriving back in Indonesia last July, we brought with us the book that resulted from our study at Fuller Seminary. This book, God's Miracles: Indonesian Church Growth was the thesis we prepared. The entire idea of the study was background material for the survey. During this year several questionnaires were circulated to all missionaries, pastors, churches and members. The findings of these questionnaires were available to our missionaries and pastors as we began the survey. In addition several articles were shared with our missionaries as preparatory reading. Finally, we provided a series of books that some of our people read as additional preparation for the survey and strategy conference.

> YOU SHOULD READ EBBIE SMITH'S BOOK. The book mentioned in the above article, God's Miracles: Indonesian Church Growth, is available at the discounted price of $2.07 (plus postage and handling) to members of the Church Growth Book Club, 533 Hermosa Street, South Pasadena, California 91030.

THE DOSHISHA AND HOLINESS CHURCH REVIVALS

Tetsunao Yamamori*

A comparative study of the Doshisha and Holiness Church revivals in prewar Japan illumines the relationship of revival to church growth relevant to the Christian World Mission today.

Frequent entries are made in the annals of Japanese church history that a series of revivals followed the missionary and national Christian conventions of 1883 and that many Christians were revived and through them others came to accept the faith. Uncritical reading of historical documents about the revivals of the 1880's might incline the reader to reach an erroneous conclusion that the great growth of the 1880's enjoyed by some major Protestant denominations was singularly caused by the revivals. One gets such an impression by going over the narratives and accounts of some individual cases. It is true that in the period between 1882 and 1889, Congregational and Presbyterian Churches made extremely rapid gains--the Congregational Church from 1,000 to 9,000, and the Presbyterian Church from 2,000 to slightly less than 9,000. The former multiplied by nine--increased over 900 per cent and the latter by 4.5--450 per cent--in less than ten years. The Methodist Church which was in equal footing with the Congregational Church in 1882 advanced in this period, but not as greatly.

*Tetsunao Yamamori (Ph.D., Duke University) is Assistant Professor of Religion and Sociology at McMurry College, Abilene, Texas.

More careful reading of the documents, however, helps us correct this error. The facts are as follows. The "fires of spiritual 'revival'" began to burn among the foreign community in Yokohama in 1883.[1] They spread first to some of the firls' schools in the city and then to the Methodist-related Aoyama Cakuin in Tokyo. The flames of spiritual fires spilled over other places such as Kyoto, Sendai, Nagoya, Nagasaki, and Oita in Kyushu.[2] In each place, a small group of young Christians became spiritually vivified and those influenced by them professed their faith. "One of the most marked of these," wrote Cary, "was in the Doshisha."[3] It is reported[4] that several Christian students met in a daily meeting about the first of March, 1884. By March 16, the whole school, as the story goes, was influenced by this spiritual surge. But school authorities, especially the missionaries, tried to prevent the students from becoming extravagant in their behavior by urging

> as strongly as they knew how, that the regularity of
> school life be maintained as regards studies, meals,
> exercise, and sleep; that the prayer-meetings be held
> early in the evening and be rigidly restricted to one
> hour; and that special pains be taken to secure quiet
> during the evening.[5]

So the result was that, after some two hundred students were baptized,[6] things returned to normal.

UNIFORMITY CAN HINDER

"Enforcing a uniform policy in very diverse situations, thus failing to cultivate each homogeneous unit in the best way suited to it, is a major cause of slow church growth in Korea."

Captain Paul Rader, Salvation Army
D.Miss. Candidate, School of World
Mission

In other words, the Doshisha revival and the revivals of the 1880's in general took place in schools at different times each lasting for a short duration and did not develop into a spiritual combustion sweeping the entire nation in one big blaze. "Revival" meant in those days a gracious blessing of God's spirit, sweeping churches and schools and leading many in both communities to deeper dedication and also to new and more open commitment to Christ. Revival did trigger some conversions--among sodalities of students, but was confined to the schools. It was therefore unable to spread to families for students, residing in dormitories, were not in living contact with their families.

Holiness Revivals

The Holiness Church, an indigenous Christian movement founded in Japan by Jyuji Nakada in 1905, experienced the revivals of a different kind in the 1930's--those that actually resulted in great ingathering.

The people believing in the "pure gospel" preached revival, expected revival, and put their faith in revival. The revival for which these people were waiting finally began to take place at Yodobashi Holiness Church in Tokyo toward the end of November, 1919. Though it spread to various churches in the city, this revival was confined to the vivification of the pastors and members without the conversions of non-Christians into the faith and thus without greater growth in the membership. Commenting on the results of the revival of 1919-20, Nakada listed the following four items: (1) the qualitative development of the membership; (2) an increase in giving; (3) the spiritual unity with men of other denominations (mostly pastors) who shared in the revival meetings; (4) an increase in the spirit of evangelism.[7]

On May 19, 1930 there occurred another revival,[8] this time, at the Tokyo Bible Seminary where students had been earnestly praying for revival. When suddenly the prayer meeting turned into one of intensity and excitement, some students recognized this to be the revival and rushed to the homes of their professors with the news. They too joined the meeting and prayed shoulder to shoulder in loud voices. There were some who even began dancing.

They continued to pray. When Nakada returned to Tokyo from his trip to Korea and Manchuria, he encouraged the Holiness churches in Tokyo to hold prayer meetings from May 30 through June 7. And on June 8, a Pentecostal meeting was held at the seminary. For the next two and a half years, various revival meetings of both large and small scale were held in many different cities in Japan. The leaders of the Holiness Church traveled extensively, preached often, and prayed intensely.

Thus, by the end of 1930, the Holiness Church had an accession of 4,311 reaching the total membership of 12,046. At the end of the following year, there were 3,487 conversions. The growth continued 'till 1932 when the membership numbered 19,523.

A Comparison

In both cases, revival meant revitalization of existing Christians--those whose allegiance was already in Christ but lacked vitality. This was accomplished by incessant Bible study, intense prayer, and descent of the Holy Spirit. The outcome was vital Christian living and unequivocal desire to share the good news.

What made the difference between the two cases was that one took place among the Christians who were not in living contact with their families and relatives whose allegiance was not yet in Christ and the other occurred among those who were.

Furthermore, the way the revival was 'handled' made the difference. In the Doshisha revival, school authorities, especially the missionaries brought up in the tradition of the Eurican Church, resisted the unleashing of spiritual energy through cautious measures. In the 1919 Holiness revival, leaders while having prayed for revival earnestly and patiently, were unable to nurture it when it came. The story of the 1930 revival is told differently, however. The experience of the earlier revival and Nakada's leadership helped fan the spiritual fires beyond the walls of Tokyo across the entire country holding meetings in various Holiness churches. These revival meetings of both large and small scale deepened the spiritual life of the whole Holiness constituency and heightened its evangelistic zeal. And the members, in living contact with a non-Christian population, brought men and women into the faith.

NOTES

1. Charles W. Iglehart, A Century of Protestant Christianity in Japan (Rutland, Vermont: Charles E. Tuttle Company, 1959), p. 72.
2. Ibid., p. 73.
3. Otis Cary, A History of Christianity in Japan, Vol. 2 (New York: Fleming H. Revell Company, 1909), p. 171. Doshisha, located in Kyoto, is a school originally related to the Congregational Church founded in 1875.
4. Ibid.
5. Ibid., p. 172.
6. Iglehart, A Century of Protestant Christianity, p. 73.
7. Isamu Yoneda, Nakada Jyuji Den (Tokyo: Nakada Jyuji Den Kanko Kai, 1959), p. 303. The Title may be translated into English as "Biography of Juyji Nakada."
8. Ibid., pp. 418-429.

Comment on GL '71

RELEASING ENERGIES FOR CHURCH MULTIPLICATION

The Missionary News Service for October 15, 1971, says "The overriding thrust of Green Lake '71 was the realization that a great task of evangelization awaits the total church. A deep longing was manifest to have the best relationships with the churches which have been established around the world, the purpose being to release energies for reaching the unevangelized."

CHURCH GROWTH BULLETIN holds that Green Lake '71 was a most significant conference. It directed attention toward the continuing and urgent task of mission--bringing "ta ethne" to faith in Jesus Christ and obedience to Him, in His Church. Far from betraying the two billion, it richly served them at the point of their greatest need.

School of World Mission student body and faculty 1971-1972 (Dr. Winter
on sabbatical)

PROGRESS REPORT - SCHOOL OF WORLD MISSION

The missionaries and nationals engaged in study and/or research
at the School of World Mission and Institute of Church Growth this Fall
have numbered 81 persons, coming from 41 different countries and representing about 460 man-years of missionary service. These people come
from over 40 different denominations or missionary organizations. The
range is wide, from Assemblies of God, to Salvation Army, to Syrian
Orthodox, from Friends to Presbyterian, to Seventh Day Adventists. We
bring together various kinds of Baptists and various kinds of Lutherans. By race Americans rub shoulders with men and women of varied
origin--German, Canadian, English, Mexican, Peruvian, Liberian, Indonesian, Filipino, Chinese, Japanese, Korean, Taiwanese, Indian and
Norwegian. As every man has come to us of his own volition we may well
ask if there is anywhere in the world such an ecumenical community; and
as we share together in the devotional life of the school we have all
met Evangelicals from outside our own denomination.

The theses from last year's graduates include a number of interesting researches, Riddle's study of Kinshasa (Congo), Kjaerland's
work on illiterate Borana nomads (Ethiopia), Jones' strategy for his
denomination in Ethiopia, Daniel's "Indian Church Growth Dynamics",
Sauder's analysis of planning church growth (Honduras), Cornelius on
urban church growth in South India, Reed's relating of strategy and
receptivity in the missions of his denomination, and Voelkel's work
on Evangelical ministry among Latin American students. Our first
D.Miss. dissertation came from Alan Gates--a study of Chinese and
Taiwanese religion. Several other M.A. theses have been defended
since June.

We all benefited last year by having a national leader and a missionary from the same field and denomination. They came from Viet Nam. This year it is repeated from Indonesia. This kind of interaction is proving to be very profitable. Another valuable innovation in our program is the small group seminar. This has helped to deal with the greatly increased number of people studying here. We have had small group seminars, from five to ten persons, dealing with Japan, Oceania, urban situations, people movements and such topics of special interest to limited numbers. The unexpectedly large enrollment also led us to divide the group in Principles and Procedures, providing a speeded up one-term course for folk who could only spend one term in Pasadena. Thus we have met the large influx of people in an experimental manner, which we hope will be productive of many good things to come.

The doctoral program seems to be promising. We have a good number of men including several professors of missions from sister institutions scattered along the course at different stages. Their influence is felt in their good participation in the group seminars and other ways. This is a symbiotic experience, with the teacher often acting only as a catalyst for stimulating group interaction.

Alan R. Tippett

WHERE HAVE ALL THE "GENERALS" GONE?

The IFMA (Interdenominational Foreign Mission Association), which now represents 6,000 overseas missionaries, publishes once a year a section entitled "Opportunities" in its news bulletin. During the decade of 1961-1971, a dramatic shift in terminology has occured, reflecting without doubt some deep-seated changes in the articulating of missionary objectives. Back in 1961, only two missions (Japan Evangelical Mission and The Evangelical Alliance Mission) said they had opportunities for "church planters." In 1971, twenty of the IFMA missions are calling for church planters.

A survey of the opportunities for the categories of evangelists, general missionaries and church planters (there are many other categories that were not counted) shows that the old concept of "doing general missionary work" is now being replaced by the crisply-defined and measurable job description of "planting churches." In a day when some are questionning the validity of conversion-centered evangelism, this is a heartening sign for the missionary cause.

Where have all the generals gone? They are church planters, every one . . .

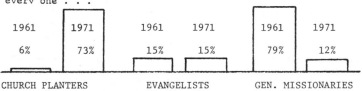

1961	1971	1961	1971	1961	1971
6%	73%	15%	15%	79%	12%
CHURCH PLANTERS		EVANGELISTS		GEN. MISSIONARIES	

Percentages of mission "opportunities"
--C. Peter Wagner

PAKISTAN: FEAR IN THE CROSS-FIRE

Bishop Chandu Ray

> War, that supreme scourge of a fallen mankind, often is
> used by God to prepare peoples' hearts for the Christian
> message, and great harvest has frequently been the result,
> like a silver lining in the dark cloud of human strife.
> But war also can divert the attention of Christian people
> and Christian churches from their passion to gather in the
> harvest before it passes. Bishop Chandu Ray, in the
> November Newsletter from his Coordinating Office for Asian
> Evangelism in Singapore, touches on these twin phenomena
> in his report on Pakistan.

Parts of East Pakistan look very much like the Nazi occupation
during the war; the army bark their orders, and the soldiers parade the
streets, towns and villages with finger on the trigger of their rifles.
The worst is that they have enrolled an army of volunterrs who are the
scum of society--the jail birds, the criminals, the ruffians. They
have been given uniforms, arms and authority and they are terrorising
the populace. Thus there is a sense of insecurity, fear and suspicion.
The army of occupation are trying to subject a proud people and as
someone said there is "martial lawlessness". Pitched battles are
being fought in many areas. Subversion is the order of the day.

In this cross fire, Christian churches, compounds and schools have
become a haven. Many flock to join Sunday Services. Most of these are
Hindus and animists. No large scale movement is visible among Muslims,
although here and there a few drift in. Many of these are begging for
baptism so that they may "belong". My impression is that the churches
are too fearful and too involved in questioning the "motive" of the new-
comer to accept the opportunity. They are too unsure of their own
vitality to accept a new and numerous influx. They do not think that
they have the personnel to instruct these people in the Faith. For
years they have failed to understand that orthodox Islam is no longer
holding the people--a proven fact when the socialist party was voted in
by an overwhelming majority of 98% against the Muslim league. And now
when the Lord is offering another opportunity, the church's answer is
"this is not the time". They are afraid that at such a time of fighting and bitterness, the Christians may become scapegoats.

THE QUANTITATIVE CASE FOR CONTINUING MISSIONS TODAY

Ralph D. Winter

Any responsible assessment of God's will for the world today must
be made in the light of the demographic facts. The Gospel is concerned
with real people, people you can count--their needs, their destinies,
their potential, in a word, their salvation. If a My Lai tragedy is
greater than a single murder, then, certainly as a general statement, a
village won to Christ is better than a single soul.

Of course there are needs for both reconciliation with God through
Jesus Christ the Savior and for just, peaceful and loving relations with
other men. Yet, it is uniquely true that there is no more potent ingredient in bringing about ethical relationships than the multiplication
throughout any given population of churches of Jesus Christ--units of
God's peace and righteousness. They are never as holy as God intends
for them to be, but they are always more holy than they would have been
without submitting themselves to His will. Sitting at the feet of
their Lord and feeding on His Word, ministering to each other and reaching out into the world, they are much more likely part of the solution
of the world's ill than part of the problem.

Granting that the churches in the shaded sections of the diagram
should renew and revive their members and lead them out into service
and witness, the reader should focus his attention on the white areas
of the diagram which represent people among whom there are either no
churches at all or a very thin sprinkling. The most urgent task in
the world today must continue to be the proclamation of the Gospel in
these areas and the brining of their peoples to faith in and obedience
to Jesus Christ. In terms of the obvious proportions--as well as many
other factors--there is clearly great need for continuing mission today.

(Westerners)	400 Million European Christians	200 Million North-American Christians	220 Million Latin American Christians	Non-Christian Westerners	10 Year Increase of Non-Christians
		50 M Russ Chr.			
	100 Million African Chr.	250 Million Non-Christian Africans			75 Million Increase
(Non-Westerners)	70 Million Asian Christians				
	2,150 Million Non-Christian Asians				650 Million Increase

CHURCH GROWTH
BULLETIN

Address:
FULLER THEOLOGICAL
SEMINARY
135 N. Oakland
Pasadena, Calif. 91101

DONALD A. McGAVRAN, B.D., Ph.D.
Director

MARCH 1972   Subscription $1 per year   Volume VIII, No. 4

The Great Debate

Since the publication of Donald McGavran's book, Bridges
of God, in 1955, the term "church growth" has been indel-
ibly incorporated into contemporary missionary jargon.
Because some of McGavran's ideas are threatening to the
missionary establishment, a reaction against them set
in almost immediately and critics began to assail the
"church growth movement." The ensuing "great debate"
has been considered healthy by all involved, and McGavran
has done the world of missions a considerable service by
collecting the pertinent documents in one volume, called
Eye of the Storm, and just published by Word Books of
Waco, Texas. Following are excerpts from McGavran's
introductory comments:

These eight doctrines (concerning the Church, conversion, culture, Christ, the Holy Spirit, universalism, discipling of the
nations, and practice of the faith) are intertwined with each other.
Many other doctrines also, such as the authority of the Bible, the
nature of revelation, the nature of God and man, sin and salvation,
free will and election, are inevitably involved. The opinions of any
man concerning what church growth is, the part it ought to play in
mission policy, and the share of attention--and budget--it should
receive, depend on his convictions concerning these doctrines....

Controversy is common about organizational matters. All of the
topics mentioned in this section have been storm centers. Strong
opinions are held about each of them pro and con. To a limited
degree, each has a bearing upon the communication of the gospel.
Indeed, there is no stronger evidence that the propagation of the
Christian faith is central to the life of the Church than that those
in favor of church union plead it desirable because a united Church
will be a more credible and effective advocate of the faith. They
quote our Lord's high priestly prayer, "that they may all be one...
that the world may believe." Occasionally a united church does grow

SEND correspondence, news, and articles to the Editor, Dr. Donald McGavran, at the Institute
of Church Growth, Fuller Theological Seminary. Published bi-monthly, send subscriptions
and changes of address to the Business Manager, Norman L. Cummings, Overseas Crusades,
Inc., 265 Lytton Avenue, Palo Alto, California 94301, U.S.A. Second-class postage paid at
Palo Alto, California.

better than separated churches; but often merged denominations grow
less and care less about growing. Church union has only a limited
bearing on credibility. Similarly those advocating transfer of
authority to nationals (a very necessary step) commonly appeal to
the dubious argument that nationals make the church grow better than
missionaries can. Occasionally they do, but usually where churches
were growing before transfer, they have continued to grow. Where
they were static before transfer, they have remained static....

   The debate proceeds before the Church and the verdict will be
rendered by its members. At stake is the whole future course of
Christian mission. Since the annual treasury of mission, out of
North America alone, is well in excess of two hundred million dollars
($200,000,000) per year, supporters of mission owe it to their Lord
to study carefully the major trends, listen to the arguments on both
sides, and vote with their dollars....

GAMES MISSIONARIES PLAY -- Fill in the missing name

"Give top priority to message of salvation" says _____
_____ to missionaries in January 21 discourse. "All other activity--whether social, ecumenical
or helping human progress--must flow from the preaching
of the Gospel.... Everything must be seen in relation
to evangelization, which can never be reduced to mere
sociological or cultural activity without failing in the
real and essential purpose of missionary activity."

Who said it? -- Answer on page 215

   Part of the confusion is doctrinal--on which no compromise is
possible--but part of it is caused by our sudden immersion in "one
world." Differences in the second part are negotiable. For example,
the phrase "mission in all six continents"--though not occurring in
the Bible--has suddenly become a new orthodoxy. It seeks to define
mission so that it is the same in every country. The pressure to
formulate this definition arose from Africasian churchmen who re-
sented their countries being so often the object of mission. It was
as if the "righteous West" was always evangelizing the "sinful East"!
Or rich Eurica was always giving largesse to poor Africasia! This
one worldwide definition of mission has obvious advantages; but its
fatal weakness is that mission cannot be the same everywhere, even
in one continent. What mission is depends partly on God's will and
partly on the population to which He sends His emissaries. When He
sends them in Berlin to wealthy, baptized youth, now alienated from
the state church, the program He ordains will be radically different
from that in Sumatra, where He sends them to pagan Karo Batak peasants longing for the gospel and eagerly accepting baptism and incorporation into Christian congregations. In short, mission in the six
continents is bewilderingly different, not the same....

GREEN LAKE AND THE TWO BILLION

One of the truly significant missionary meetings of 1971 was
the IFMA/EFMA-sponsored Green Lake '71 Conference on Mission-
Church Relations. In anticipation of the meeting, Church
Growth Bulletin published an article entitled "Will Green
Lake Betray the Two Billion?" in July, 1971. As a part of
the literary follow-up of this conference, we published Louis
L. King's incisive address in the November issue, and here we
are able to bring to our readers some of the post-GL'71 development. The first contribution is by one of the overseas
nationals present, Rev. Hector Espinoza of Mexico. He boldly
points out some of the weaknesses of Gl'71.

Now, attempting to meet some of the areas of weakness
Espinoza mentions, thirteen delegates to GL'71 have contributed to a new book called Church/Mission Tensions Today, to
be published by Moody Press later this year. As a preview
of the good things to come, we are proud to present brief
excerpts from five of the authors.

GRIM FACTS ABOUT GREEN LAKE '71   Hector Espinoza, Director
                                   Instituto Evangelístico de Mexico

When a conference is convened under the theme of "Missions in
Creative Tension," and the general intended purpose is squarely to
confront the thorny problems created by the relations between the
mission boards and the emerging national church, you can hardly expect anything but an exciting meeting.

Add to this the fact that there were to meet missionary executives representing hundreds of years of combined experience, together
with at least fifteen nationals from every continent in the world,
and you have the perfect setting for a lively interchange and surely
an unusual type of encounter.

Many of us, however, were not quite ready for the disappointing
outcome. Amid the ever-inspiring opportunity of healthy interchange
with dedicated men and brilliant missionary minds from all over the
world, there was the frustrating vacuum of not getting down to dialogue over the basic issues. I for one attended the conference with
the challenging question read only a few weeks before: "Will Green
Lake Betray the Two Billion"? pounding my brains. I held a high
expectancy regarding what we as nationals and mission executives
could do to reduce that haunting figure of TWO BILLION.

From the beginning it was not hard to observe a vast diversity
of personal attitudes and concepts regarding the national church.
Happily enough, the champions of giving the nationals a chance were
present. Also, those who openly advocated that the time had come
to give less time to administrative detail and more to evangelistic

efforts were there. At various times we heard from others who insisted that the missionary should move ever onward to new fields, pioneering in new areas, and doing the front line soldier's work. But there were many, unfortunately, still very many, who exposed the old mentality of allowing the national church some degree of freedom, but always maintaining a CIA type of control over the general situation of things.

It is to be regretted that instead of so much time being given to organizational structures, there could no more time be given to viable solutions to the individual missionaries who are the cause of tensions with the national church. Or perhaps part of the time could have been profitably used in presenting suggestions geared to inducing mission boards to accelerate the creation of national mission boards, or about the very delicate issue of tensions between the mission boards out on the field.

In our opinion, there was very little time and attention given to practical suggestions regarding the way to reach more people, more effectively, in less time with the Gospel of Christ. Should it not perhaps be wise to leave the matter of organizational structures in the hands of the national church, since it will be in her country where the adjustments will have to be made, and rather concentrate more on what internal modifications could be made in the sending churches of the home land, in order to provide the world with better missionaries?

To many of us nationals it was clearly evident that those "storm clouds in the horizons of the mission fields" are far more threatening and manifest in the skies of the sending church. Not that national churches face no threats or dangers. Most do, but it is also good to remember that many of those churches are young and daring and, like all "green horns," are enthusiastic and visionary and face the future with audacity and optimism.

By the end of the conference it was easy to discover at least one of the causes of tension: out of fifteen national "consultants," only six received the opportunity of addressing the conference in a general session, and then strictly only three minutes each. By then, it was obvious to some mission executives and nationals, that unfortunately there still widely prevails the old mentality of having the missionary do all the talking and let the national do all the hearing.

Over against the dissapointment of the near neglect of the "Two Billion," mention should be made of the timely and well written paper of Jack F. Shepherd. The uplifting and inspiring world-wide prayer meeting of Thursday night, and the forceful presentation of the morning devotional lectures by Dr. Edmund Clowney. As we heard Dr. Clowney speak, our souls felt refreshed, and our spirits energized.

And a new hope flooded our hearts as we prayed that God somehow—would move over the beloved sending church of the United States to provide the world with many more missionaries, but of the kind who

are undaunted in their vision, strong in their faith and sober and
wise in the midst of problems and tensions. The national church is
anxious to work alongside men and women who labor every day with a
high degree of expectancy of what the Holy Spirit is doing in them
and through them. We desire the beloved missionaries in our countries to be constantly encouraged and spiritually led by mature sending churches and the faith giants and prayer warriors of the home
land headquarter's office.

> MISSIONS IN CREATIVE TENSION, the Compendium of Gl'71,
> edited by Vergil Gerber, is now ready for distribution.
> This book contains all the previous study papers as well
> as the addresses of the conference itself. Get your copy
> now from the Church Growth Book Club (see insert). The
> Church Growth Book Club will also handle the new book,
> Church/Mission: Tensions Today, edited by C. Peter Wagner,
> when it is published later this year.

THE PRIMACY OF THE MISSIONARY FUNCTION   J. F. Shepherd, Education
                                              Secretary, C. & M.A.

An attempt was certainly made at Green Lake to set mission in
the context of the many-faceted comprehensive ministry of the church.
This is set out most strikingly in Ephesians 4. It does seem that
much of the ecumenical/evangelical tension over the tendency to polarize social action over against mission comes from the notion that
these two are the same thing and can be substituted the one for the
other. Peter Beyerhaus adds a new and respected voice to this whole
controversey, and his recent statement underscores the fact that
social action is not only a secondary aspect of mission, as he describes it, but actually resultant from the effect of the primary
saving mission. When there is proper perspective, he insists that
the two points of view can be balanced and brought together. His
statement is a beautiful example of the intimate relation of the
nature and function of the church:

> Mission occurs when--and only when--it is directed toward
> putting man's existence, through a conscious decision of
> faith, under Christ's Lordship and His effective spiritual
> power. In this way, man experiences lasting salvation, a
> salvation in which his non-Christian environment may tempor-
> arily participate. But salvation in the full sense of the
> word is not found primarily in these indirect effects.
> Rather, salvation is the new communion of the Holy Spirit
> through the bond of peace. For this reason, the center of
> the missionary commission always remains its call into com-
> munion with Christ. This communion finds its visible repre-
> sentation and sacramental realization through responsible
> incorporation into the Church. The planting and growth of
> the Church as the Body of Christ in the world remains the
> primary goal of mission within history. The transformation
> of the structures of this world is the result of a member-
> ship which is prepared to serve. This theological

association of the primary Christocentric being and the world-oriented function arising from it could in principle make possible a synthesis between the evangelical and the "ecumenical" understanding of mission.[1]

To apply the truth of this statement to the GL'71 issue is to insist that mission should have a place, even a first place, in the life of every church. It was clear at Green Lake that there had not been sufficient persevering faithfulness to guide the so-called "younger churches" into participation in mission.

An allusion needs to be made in passing to the fact that mission, as a particular function of the church, needs to be distinguished from other essential but different functions. The serious warning of Stephen Neill cannot be repeated too many times, "If everything is mission, pretty soon nothing is mission."[2] There is need to coordinate our mission terminology, but I want to urge that mission be defined specifically as "multiplication of churches." Such a definition could helpfully distinguish mission from evangelism or prophetic, pastoral, or didactic ministry. It would distinguish it as well from worship, fellowship and whatever other things properly belong to the doxological activity and service of the church.

One more observation can be added to the insistence that every church has, as a primary function distinguishable from all else it does, a responsible, organized missionary involvement; that is, there is to be an unending, dynamic continuity in the outreach in mission of every church "old or young." In other words, mission obligation is not fulfilled and exhausted when a new church is planted. Instead, mission is then to be reshaped and extended. Is this not the clear meaning of the Pauline concept of the apostolate as he described it to the young church at Corinth, "...our hope is that as your faith increases, our field among you may be greatly enlarged so that we may preach the Gospel in lands beyond you" (II Cor. 10:15b-16a)? Green Lake revealed that we had not taken seriously enough the need to keep mission going right on into the regions beyond the churches that were brought into being in the first phases of outreach. Too often we have lapsed into what Peter Wagner calls "the church development syndrome."[3] We have gotten a fixation on the churches with whom we are in "modified dichotomy" or "fused parallelism" and fail to keep going after that which is lost as the parable has it.

---

[1] Peter Beyerhaus, Missions: Which Way?, Grand Rapids, Zondervan, 1971, p. 68.

[2] Stephen Neill, Creative Tensions, London Edinburgh House, 1959, p. 80

[3] C. Peter Wagner, "The Church Development Syndrome," World Vision Magazine, October, 1972. See also Donald F. Durnbaugh, The Believers' Church, New York, Macmillan, 1968; James L. Garrett, Jr., The Concept of the Believers' Church, Scottdale, Herald Press, 1969; Francis A. Schaffer, The Church Before the Watching World, Downers Grove, Inter Varsity Press, 1971.

THE EVANGELISTIC MISSION OF THE CHURCH   J. Robertson McQuilkin, President, Columbia Bible College

The evangelistic mission of the church includes three elements: proclamation, persuasion, and establishing congregations of God's people.

Our mission is to go into all the world and proclaim the good news to every person (Mark 16:15); to be a witness to the very ends of the earth (Acts 1:8); to proclaim repentance and remission of sins to all nations (Luke 24:37). Of course, a proclamation of the gospel, even when "proclamation" is taken to mean effective communication, does not exhaust the responsibility of the church in its evangelistic mission.

The church is responsible not only to inform people but to win them. Only when men are won will God be satisfied. The Great Commissioner defined the mission as "discipling the peoples" (Matt. 28:19).

Finally, not only are the people of God responsible to win men to faith in Christ, but they are responsible to bring them into the visible congregation or family of God's children. If there is no such congregation it must be established. "I will build my church" (Matt. 16:18) states in advance what Christ intended to do and the book of Acts shows how the great commission was understood by those who heard it. They set about establishing churches. Birth is an individual matter but in God's plan it is birth into the family.

Once a congregation has been formed, there is the immediate need for all the functions of the church. If the evangelist has the capability or gift of providing for these other functions, his role may begin to change. Normally, however, the congregation itself as it begins to mature, should provide for these various ministries. Certainly if the evangelist continues to "evangelize" the Christians, there will be little maturing. And if he alone provides for all the pastoral and teaching ministry, the church may be stunted in its growth. The ideal would be for the church to mature rapidly, assume its responsibility for ministry to its own, and join the evangelist in winning those yet outside.

These three, then, are the components of the church's evangelistic responsibility: proclamation, persuasion, and establishing congregations of believers.

The official stand of the United Presbyterian Church emphasizes these three elements:

> The supreme and controlling aim of the Christian mission to the world is to make the Lord Jesus Christ known to all men as their divine and only Savior and to persuade them to become his disciples and responsible members of his church in which Christians of all lands share in evangelizing the world and permeating all of life with the Spirit and Trust of Christ.[1]

---

[1] *Missionary Research Bulletin*, Vol. XI, No. 8.

The International Missionary Council meeting in Madras in 1938
put it this way:

> Evangelism...must so present Christ Jesus in the power of
> the Holy Spirit, that men shall come to put their trust in
> God through Him as their Savior and serve Him as their Lord
> in the fellowship of His church.[2]

This is the evangelistic responsiblity of the church. What will
the world look like when it has been fully discharged?

When may the evangelistic mission of the church be judged complete? Since this question is eschatological, it may not be possible
to answer it with dogmatic precision. But we can judge to some extent.
The church's responsibility can hardly be assumed discharged until
every person has had opportunity to hear with understanding the good
news of the way to life in Christ.

Of course, saturation proclamation alone does not discharge
fully the church's responsibility. Its responsibility will not have
been discharged until all whom God is calling have responded to the
call, accepting Christ as Lord and Savior, and have been brought into
the fellowship of his people. God alone may judge when this has been
accomplished. And yet, so long as the Lord himself does not proclaim
a consummation by his own appearance, the church must assume that it
is her responsibility to do what he said to do.

Without trying to probe the part of God's purpose he has not seen
fit to reveal, what does the present state of obedience to His command
seem to be? Has the evangelistic mission been accomplished? Actually
the need is greater today than it every has been. There are more
people outside of Christ in the one land of Indonesia than there were
in the entire Roman Empire when the great commission was given. According to the conclusions of some demographers, if our Lord should return
today there would be more people in hell from this generation than
from all preceding generations combined....

It may be argued that the responsibility for a given area passes
from the foreign sending church to the local church once it has been
established. This may be a legitimate delegation of responsibility
just as the original sending congregation may have delegated its
evangelistic responsibility for those at a distance to the specially
called evangelistic missionary at an earlier stage of evangelistic
outreach.

But if there is a church that either cannot or will not reach
the lost nearby, those churches outside that range of direct responsibility cannot delegate their evangelistic responsibility to it any
more than they could to a non-functioning evangelist. The church
universal has an obligation to all people outside of Christ and may
not attempt to discharge this responsibility by delegating it to representatives who are not fulfilling it. God alone may judge whether
they cannot or simply will not, but the church at large must judge

---

[2] _Christianity Today_, November 11, 1966, Vol. XI, No. 3, pp. 4-5.

whether a local congregation or group of congregations is in fact
fulfilling the responsibility....

Of course there are areas in which the local church is discharging effectively the responsibility for evangelization and little, if
any, outside help is needed. A mission that has served in such an
area will need to refocus its aims and perhaps reallocate its resources, keeping in mind the primary mission.

But instead of concentrating on our primary reason for existence
as missions and missionaries, namely to develop new relationships and
innovative programs to forward this evangelistic task, we tend to resist change--for extraneous reasons....

Does the answer lie in such either/or solutions? Why do we lump
all "missionary" activity into a single rigid structural relationship?
Why do we not distinguish the roles of those we send overseas? Certainly when <u>ministry</u> to the <u>church</u> is the task, a move toward the
servant role is long overdue in many places. But when our <u>mission</u> to
the <u>world</u> is the task, we must maintain enough structural flexibility
to assure its completion.

THE END OF THE CHRISTIAN MISSION   Warren Webster, General Director
                                          C.B.F.M.S.

It seems fairly certain, as far as we can interpret history, that
the Western orientation of the world is rapidly coming to an end. This
need not in itself, however, pose a threat to the Christian world
mission.

One of the striking characteristics of the Christian faith has
been its repeated ability to survive the passing of an era and an
order of which it once seemed to be an inseparable part....

In the twentiety century, for the first time in history, it can
be truly said that the sun never sets on the church of Jesus Christ.
With the possible exception of the Mongolian People's Republic, there
does not appear to be another independent nation on earth in which the
church of Jesus Christ is not represented....

The great missionary fact of the present day is that "<u>the Church
is there</u>..., the Body of Christ in every land, the great miracle of
history, in which the living God himself through his Holy Spirit is
pleased to dwell.[1]

It is estimated that in the last 180 years more people have become Christians and more churches have been planted than in the previous 1800 years of church history. In the last 60 years Protestants
are said to have multiplied 18 times in the non-Western world.[2] Due

---

[1]Stephen Neill, <u>A History of Christian Missions</u>, Baltimore, Penguin
Book, Inc., 1966, p. 576.

[2]R. Pierce Beaver, <u>From Missions to Mission</u>, New York, Friendship
Press, 1964, p. 63.

in part to the population explosion, the number of professing Christians is greater than it ever has been before.

We frequently hear, however, that church growth is not keeping up with biological growth so that while the number of Christians in the world continues to increase, the Christian percentage of world population has been steadily declining from about one-third in 1940 to less than 30% today, with an expectation that it may not be more than 16% by the year 2000. Since many began to question these pessimistic prognostications, a group of former engineers and systems analysts in the missionary enterprise went to work to check out the figures and concluded they are largely based on false premises and poor arithmetic. In this connection Stephen Neill recently observed:

> For the first time an attempt has been made to arrive at a scientific estimate, based on population figures supplied by the United Nations and on the best available statistics from Christian sources.... It appears that in the past the Christian percentage has been overestimated, since the population of China, almost entirely non-Christian, is now held to be larger than was earlier supposed. When the necessary corrections have been made, the conclusion is reached that the percentage has been slowly increasing and will continue to increase; so that, if present trends continue, it will in the year 2000 stand higher than ever before in the history of the world. What is a little startling is that at that date less than half the Christians will belong to the white races.[3]

While the Lord of history is sovereign, and no man can say what must happen tomorrow, we know from Scripture that the God of the whole earth is at work in this age calling out a people for his name which ultimately will embrace some "from every tribe and tongue and people and nation" (Rev. 5:9)....

When our Lord commissioned his disciples to go "to the ends of the earth" (the spacial dimension) he promised to be with them "to the end of the age" (the temporal dimension). He also declared that the gospel of "repentance and forgiveness of sins should be preached in his name...throughout the whole world, as a testimony to all nations; and then the end will come" (Luke 24:47, Matt. 24:14).

This is the divine program for church and mission in time and space. The historical culmination awaits the geographical fulfillment. The end of the age awaits the completed proclamation to the ends of the earth. The indications are that the "Omega point" of history is nearer than it has ever been before.

THE DEMOGRAPHIC IMPERATIVE   Ralph D. Winter, Professor, School of World Mission, Fuller Seminary

In a recent article I found myself presenting a chart which indicated the existence of 2,150,000,000 non-Christian Asians. While

---

[3]Stephen Neill, Call to Mission, Philadelphia, Fortress Press, 1970, p. 79.

Christians constitute a higher percentage of the Asian population
than ever before, a far larger number of Asians do not know Christ
than when William Carey first headed for India. We must be deeply
grateful to God and to earlier pioneers that there are over ten million Christians in India, for example, but the perplexing fact is
that there are at least 500 subcultures in India alone as distinct
from each other socially as the blacks and whites in Birmingham, Alabama, and that in at least 480 of these entire subcultures there are
no Christians at all. Very bluntly, normal evangelistic outreach from
existing Christian churches in India is utterly inadequate to face this
challenge.

Note that I am not making a case here for the need of U.S. missionaries (although in many of these subcultures Western missionaries
might be just as acceptable, or more so, than any Indian or Asian).
What I am saying is that not even the Indian Christians can do this
job unless (1) they understand it to be a task of full-blown missionary complexity, and (2) they set up the proper mission machinery to
do the job. That is to say, what is most needed in India today is
the development of liberating fellowships of Christian faith among
the hundreds of millions of Indian people who live in the hundreds of
unreached subcultures. But the point is that these essential, crucial new fellowships in the unreached subcultures will not be planted
by existing churches as much as by mission structures that can effectively express the true Christian obedience of the existing churches.

We hear that there are already 100 such mission agencies in India,
either for evangelism within the pockets of population where there are
already Christians, or for real cross-cultural mission into pockets
that are as yet unreached. But who cares? No one even has a list of
these organizations. No one thinks it is important enough to make
such a list. The new, immeasurably improved, World Christian Handbook
for 1973 is projected for publication without such a list. There have
long been directories of missions originating in the Western world; no
one has yet begun a directory of the missions originating in the non-
Western world.

This is not a bizarre, off-beat curiosity. It is impressively
clear that the two thousand million non-Christian Asians will not be
reached unless it can become fashionable for the younger churches to
establish younger missions.

THE GOAL IS THE FOURTH WORLD   C. Peter Wagner, Professor, School
                                 of World Mission, Fuller Seminary

Some missions have stated that their goal has been to plant
churches, indigenous churches if you will, in the Third World. We
must grant that one of the noble, and indeed necessary, results of a
successful mission in the world is a church. But if the missionary
task is considered accomplished because a church now exists, the
original missionary vision has been lost. Note that the final element in the formula is the world. Disciples are made, not in the
church, but in the world.

At this point, the term "fourth world" may be helpful. The "fourth world" embraces all those peoples who, regardless of where they may be located geographically, have yet to come to Christ. In that sense, the fourth world is the top-priority objective of missions.

This pushes the statement of the goal of missions one notch further than the indigenous church. The indigenous church may become a great and dynamic instrument for the continued push toward the fourth world. But it is an unfortunate fact that in some cases it has instead become a hindrance to the discipling of the fourth world.

Therefore, the proper objective of a mission is not merely the establishment of a church, but ideally of a _missionary_ church which is in turn moving into the fourth world. If the mission has somehow been unsuccessful in transmitting its own missionary vision to the new church, it has not lived up to its best potential and highest calling.

Much more conscious effort needs to be dedicated to clarifying today's missionary objectives than missionary strategists have been willing to invest in the past. To consider the church as an end in itself rather than an instrument for "making disciples" in the fourth world, is to adopt a stunted objective. Stunted objectives will sooner or later stunt the fulfillment of the great commission.

The primary objective of missions needs to be distinguished from secondary or intermediate objectives. What are some of these inter-mediate objectives? As we list them, let us state clearly that just because they are intermediate, they are neither bad, inferior nor superfluous. If you live in New York City and want to drive to Pennsylvania, for example, you have to go through New Jersey. While you are moving through New Jersey you are glad to be there, but you are not satisfied with staying there if your goal is Pennsylvania. New Jersey is only an intermediate objective.

Some intermediate missionary objectives include a larger number of workers, an increased budget, more activity in sending and receiving churches, excellence in ministerial training, spiritual revival, culturally-relevant liturgy and music, translation of the Scriptures, distribution of certain quantities of Christian literature, wide dissemination of the gospel message through the mass media, the manifestation of social concern, and so on. As _intermediate_ objectives, all the above and many more good things that missionaries and churchmen do can be very useful in accomplishing the _ultimate_ objective of making disciples. If this distinction is kept clear, possibilities of continual, healthy church growth will increase.

A mature church is often another helpful instrument toward making disciples. Certainly, once disciples are made they must gather together in congregations (whether inside or outside of the institutional or more traditional churches is not relevant here) in order to share the _koinonia_ or Christian fellowship so necessary for Christian nurture and qualitative growth. But while the church _should_ be a help toward the task of reaching into the fourth world and making disciples there, it often is not. In this sense the church can be thought of as the automobile that takes you from New York City to Pennsylvania. If it is in good mechanical condition, it is a great help, but if the carburetor plugs in Jersey City and the transmission goes out in Newark, the car turns out to be a hindrance, and you realize you would have accomplished your objective of reaching Pennsylvania better if you had taken the train.

As everyone knows, some churches have plugged carburetors, so to speak. They are ineffectual in reaching the fourth world, and need to be bypassed. One does not have to go to the Third World to find examples, although they abound there as well. Right here at home we have an abundant supply of churches which have become introverted and centripetal. They give little thought and energy to the task of reaching the fourth world. In the 1960's, for example, a large segment of the fourth world gathered together on the West Coast of the USA in the hippie movement. Most of the "national churches" (the U.S. "establishment" in this case) were either hostile, indifferent, or incapable of reaching this curious fourth world group in an effective way. They didn't know what to make of the psychedelic drugs, the free sex and the Eastern mystical religions.

Because the "national church" could not or would not make disciples among these street people does not mean that the Spirit of God allowed them to be forfeited. He raised up agencies outside the established church (call them "missions" in our context) such as the World Christian Liberation Front in Berkeley and the Jesus People Movement in Los Angeles. These new "missions" did not worry about protocol, comity, or the agenda of the established church. They moved ahead with such evangelistic methods as coffee houses, street meetings, Hollywood Free Papers, baptisms in the ocean, and Christian communes, which predictably were little understood by the establishment. They wore beads, let their hair grow out, played guitars and went barefoot. As a result, many of the "national churches" did not even want these "missionaries" to attend their services. They said, in effect, "missionary, go home"! Here, right at home, we witnessed "creative tensions" between the mission and the church.

Although many U.S. churches still have not accepted this freewheeling new missionary movement, the trend, at least on the West Coast, is toward reduced tensions and more mature recognition of the all-important fact that the supreme task of both establishment and counter-culture is winning the fourth world. Therefore, a mutual appreciation is developing, based on the recognition that God can use each of the groups to make disciples in different segments of the fourth world. And, happily, some of the churches have now begun to listen to the "missionaries." As a result, many are experiencing revival themselves!

"We now have a national church," some missionaries say, "let the natives do the evangelism. We will now teach the Bible to the Christians, help them raise better crops, improve their hygiene, train

ANSWER TO "Games Missionaries Play" (page 208)
-- Pope Paul VI! --

their pastors, and teach them modern evangelistic methods. Since they speak the language better than we do, since they know the culture, since they are the right color, they now become responsible for the fourth world. We have done our job." In other writings I have called this sever fallacy in missionary strategy the "syndrome of church development." I would not keep stressing it if my experience had not confirmed that it is such a widespread and devastating error in the thinking of both contemporary missions and national churches.

Missionaries who fall into the syndrome of church development are often very gifted people. They can do almost everything better than national Christians. They can preach better sermons, they can organize more active church programs, they can lead choirs and play instruments better, they can teach Sunday School classes better, they can build better buildings, write better tracts, teach better seminary classes, they can start youth camps and youth centers, they can write constitutions and administer denominational offices with supreme efficiency. On top of all this, they are free--the church doesn't have to pay a cent for all this service. Sometimes, in fact, the missionaries are able to obtain sums of outside money that enlarge the church treasury rather than take from it.

But missionaries, somehow, can't _evangelize_ better than nationals!

The above may border on a caricature, but it is close enough to much current missionary mentality to raise a warning flag for discerning missionaries and churchmen. All the different activities involved in the syndrome of church development are good in themselves, and at one time or another a missionary may help the church by participating in them. But they are only temporary. A mature church can handle all of them. As men like Roland Allen and Henry Venn saw years ago, the less the mission gets involved in these internal affairs of the church, and the quicker the church itself assumes responsibility for these things under the Holy Spirit rather than under the missionary, the better for both mission and church. But even when the ideal is reached and the new church fully and effectively handles all its own internal affairs, neither the church nor the mission is relieved of its responsibility toward the fourth world.

NEEDED: CHURCH STARTERS   Michael Griffiths, General Director, O.M.F.

All over the world the greatest need is for "church-starters." The growth of population is such that an apparent growth rate of (say) 10% in the church may represent only a biological increase in Christian families and none being won from "paganism."

Nobody wants useless missionaries--mere ecumenical symbols, ciphers acting as liaison officers, and sources of foreign money. But there is one kind of missionary that everyone wants. That is the person who will identify himself closely with the people to whom he goes.... Missionaries who are soul-winners and church-starters are never likely to be outdated. They are welcome in any country, welcome in our own, welcome everywhere.

(_Give up Your Small Ambitions_, Chicago, Moody Press, 1971)

THE MISSIONARY VISION OF THE KOREAN CHURCH   Won Yong Koh, Pastor,
Korean Missionary Center
Church, Los Angeles

Many know the Korean Church as a successful mission field, and
a well-growing church, but very few know about the missionary movement
of the Korean church and its great vision for the world. Someone may
say, Korea is a small nation, how can she send many missionaries into
the world? But in the history of the church God has raised some
great nations like Britain and the United States, and He has also
raised very small groups like the Moravian Brothers. I believe that
the Korean church should contribute to the missionary movement in the
world during the next several decades, even though there is no freedom in North Korea yet and the South Korean church is only beginning
to act.

There is an unbelievable history of the missionary movement in
the early Korean church. The first church was organized in 1907 as
the Korean Presbyterian church. In that year they sent a missionary,
Rev. Kee Pung Lee, to Jeju Island. He was one of seven pastors ordained in Korea and even though Korea needed many pastors for the
national churches, they wanted to share the gospel with lost souls on
this Island which had a very different culture and language. This
took place just 23 years after the first Presbyterian missionary, an
American, Dr. Horace N. Allen, arrived in Korea.

In 1909 Rev. Kwan-Hul Chai was sent by the Presbyterian churches
to the eastern part of Russia, and Rev. Suk Jin Jan was sent to Tokyo,
Japan. There were also approximately ten Korean pastors serving in
Manchuria.

When the Korean Presbyterian church's General Assembly was
organized in 1912, they voted to send three missionaries to China.
The next year they sent Rev. Tae Ro Park, Rev. Bung Sun Sa, and Rev.
Young Hung Kim to San Dong Sung, China. They were the first missionaries to China from Korea. The Korean Presbyterian church continued
to send missionaries to China, including Evangelists and medical
missionaries until the end of the Second World War.

In 1919 the Japanese government began to persecute the Korean
church but the church continued its missionary movement in Northeast
Asia, until the Communists closed the door to missionaries in Russia,
China, and Manchuria. Most of the missionaries came back from the
Communist fields, but two of them, Rev. Dae Yung Lee and Rev. Jee II
Bang, did not return—they wanted to be persecuted with the Chinese
Brothers in Red-China—but the Red China government deported them in
1957. They returned to Korea with their families.

In these early years our forefathers had to struggle with many
problems and were persecuted by pagans and Japanese. They had to extend the Home-Mission-Plans, but sent and supported many missionaries
by themselves, even though they were poor materially. By the end of
the Second World War there were approximately 100 Korean missionaries
serving in Northeast Asian mission fields.

We were filled with sorrow when we lost our mission field in Northeast Asia and we wanted to know God's will for us. We began to consider Southeast Asia as our new mission field. Therefore, the Korean church began to send missionaries to Southeast Asia in 1955. At present our missionaries are working in Thailand, Hong Kong, Taiwan, Japan, Okinawa, Viet Nam, and Indonesia. Since 1966 our mission fields have been extended to Mexico, Brazil, Paraguay, Argentina, Bolivia, America, Canada, Ethiopia, Pakistan, and Sarawak Malaysia.

At present there are three denominational mission boards-- the Presbyterian, Methodist and O.M.S. churches--and seven interdenominational mission boards serving in South Korea.

We have two types of missionaries--one which reaches Koreans overseas and the other which reaches foreigners overseas. We call the missionary who is serving Koreans M-1 missionaries and the ones serving foreigners M-2 missionaries. Most of our M-1 missionaries are working in Japan, Canada and America, and the M-2 missionaries are working in the other nations. M-1 missionaries must be self-supported, but M-2 missionaries are supported by the Korean church. M-1 missionaries must extend their field to foreign people by the supporting of his church. This is the special method of the Korean mission today, because we are still a poor nation and cannot support all the missionaries overseas. About 200 Korean missionaries are working overseas at present.

It is thrilling to have so many wonderful missionary candidates in the Korean church today, but it raises a serious problem. Often I cannot sleep for thinking and praying about our needs. God is raising so many young people who are tasting revival and going out to be missionaries, but our two major problems of sending them overseas are finances and training.

Why are so many young people in Korea today desiring to be missionaries? Because of the great revival in 1957. Dr. Bob Pearce laid the foundtion for this revival at the pastor's conference in Seoul, Korea in 1955. Since that year pastors prayed for a great revival like the one in 1907. As a result of their prayers, the great revival broke out in the Korea N.A.E. Pastor's Prayer Conference in Sam Kak-Mountain Prayer Garden in 1957. It was the greatest revival in the history of our church, about 400 pastors were filled with the Holy Spirit and this soon spread to all the churches. Since 1957 many young people have been dedicating themselves to full-time Christian service. It is not difficult to find several young men praying in the church buildings even at midnight in Korea today. Many of them want to be missionaries.

The Korean church has a great spiritual vitality today. There are many candidates who are well educated, even above college level, who want to share Christ with lost souls overseas. Most Orientals have a similar cultural background, so we don't have the cultural overhang problem.... Korean missionaries should be good workers in Southeast Asia because of this similar cultural background--if we can solve the two above mentioned problems.

CHURCH GROWTH
BULLETIN

from the
INSTITUTE OF
CHURCH GROWTH

Address:
FULLER THEOLOGICAL
SEMINARY
135 N. Oakland
Pasadena, Calif. 91101

DONALD A. McGAVRAN, B.D., Ph.D.
Director

May 1972   Subscription $1 per year   Volume VIII No. 5

CHURCH GROWTH BURGEONING
AROUND THE WORLD –a personal report by Donald McGavran

Between last November 11th and March 15th, I had a splendid chance
to observe the rising interest in church growth in many lands. Fuller
Seminary gave me a sabbatical quarter. Union Biblical Seminary in India
asked me to teach there for six weeks. And hearing that I was going
out, church growth men in 12 lands asked me to help them conduct church
growth seminars. This I was delighted to do. It afforded me great opportunity to see first hand church growth potentials and responsive populations in many lands. I visited Taiwan, Hong Kong, the Philippines,
Thailand South, Indonesia, Singapore, Thailand North, South India,
Central India, West Pakistan, Ethiopia and England. In each of two
lands, two seminars were held. A total of 14 seminars were held. More
than 1500 ministers and missionaries attended. The journey also allowed
me to visit Prof. Peter Beyerhaus, the architect of the Frankfurt Declaration, in Tubingen, Germany where he is Professor of Mission in the
University. He is a prophet of God sent for our times.

I was cheered by what I saw in these four months and my findings
will interest readers of the Bulletin.

1.   All of the lands I visited had some men in them who were looking at
      church and mission work with church growth eyes. They compared
      traditional ways of mission with those which in fact communicate
      the Gospel and multiply congregations. These men had gotten
      together to discuss church growth, get out church growth sheets,
      share church growth books, send the Church Growth Bulletin to their
      friends, and in many other ways evangelize effectively. All along
      the way I found a welcome for the idea that the current seminar
      would be known as The First Annual Church Growth Seminar and that
      each succeeding year a church growth workshop in the national lan-
      guage would be convened - and manned by local churchmen and mis-
      sionaries. In Pakistan three previous church growth seminars had
      already been held, largely at the initiative of Fred Stock of the
      Presbyterian Mission.

2.   Church growth was being built into evangelistic campaigns and other
      Christian work. For example, in the Philippines, the seminar

SEND correspondence, news, and articles to the Editor, Dr. Donald McGavran, at the Institute
of Church Growth, Fuller Theological Seminary. Published bi-monthly, send subscriptions
and changes of address to the Business Manager, Norman L. Cummings, Overseas Crusades,
Inc., 265 Lytton Avenue, Palo Alto, California 94301, U.S.A. Second-class postage paid at
Palo Alto, California.

formed an integral part of "Christ The Only Way" campaign being led by Nene Ramientos and Jim Montgomery of Overseas Crusades. One of the Philippine objectives was to establish 10,000 (yes, ten thousand) Lay Evangelistic Group Bible Studies. Since these were led by laymen and each group (to warrant the name "evangelistic") had to include a large number of those who did not know Christ, it was expected that many groups would develop into new churches. If the campaign should start 1000 new churches - and that is quite possible - it will mark a new day in evangelistic campaigns.

3. Seminaries were finding that church growth was a part of their job. Seminaries sponsored and housed four of the seminars. The principals of two seminaries (which had been doing no church planting before) expressed determination to make church planting a part of their program. And why not? Ministers in training in Africasia, where only a tiny per cent of the population knows Christ, ought to be taught how to lead laymen to multiply congregations. Church growth through theological education!! Dr. Paul Gupta of Hindustan Bible Institute, which is going to start a B.D. program in 1973, thought his seminary could plant 100 churches in Madras City alone. At Union Seminary at Chiangmai, Principal John Hamlin and Professor Allan Eubanks showed themselves to be enthusiastic church growth men.

4. A new technique in communication was discovered in the Hong Kong Church Growth Seminar. All the lectures in English were translate into beautiful Cantonese by Wilson Chan of the Bible Society and taped by Bill Kinkade who duplicated and sold them. The tapes immediately made church growth thinking available to Christians who speak only Cantonese. Marvelous! Taping oral translations should be widely used to multiply effective communication of the Gospel across language barriers. On hearing of tapes available in Cantonese, Professor Tippett in Pasadena said, "Cantonese is what the Chinese in Fiji speak. Chinese ministers there ought to get copies of the Wilson Chan tapes."

5. In the Seminar held in London at All Nations Missionary College, under the leadership of Ron Davies and E. W. Oliver, a large number of church growth books were sold and an English Branch of the Church Growth Book Club opened. Soon CGB will print the London address from which sterling area people can order church growth books. It also appears likely that a British version of the Church Growth Bulletin will be published. Every two months, the British editor will get an air mail manuscript of this World Bulletin. He will then discard up to half of it, add 'made in the Commonwealth' news and articles, and mail out to his mailing list. This decentralization will benefit effective gospel propagation in any country where a church growth man is willing to gather and edit germane news and articles, keep his mailing list up to date, and mail out

the Area CGB. It will take several days every two months, but will
make the Bulletin more helpful. It will fit the culture better!
Any church growth men volunteering to be regional editors?

6. Many men, who had never set foot in the United States, shared in
holding great commission convictions and looking at the spread of
the faith with realism and accuracy. This is gratifying. The
School of Missions at Fuller Seminary has no monopoly on church
growth knowledge. We rejoice in the large number of men and women
devoting their lives to effective evangelism and to learning increasingly more about it. I rejoiced to meet notable church growth
men like Alex Smith of the OMF in Thailand and Peter Coterell of
the SIM in Ethiopia.

During the coming great increase of the Church, the cause needs
tens of thousands of nationals and missionaries who spread the
Good Tidings effectively. These men will teach in church growth
workshops, write church growth bulletins and do research in what
makes churches grow and not grow. In the power of the Holy Spirit
they will proclaim Christ far and wide, baptize millions, and
plant multitudes of congregations. Harnessing radio to people movements to Christ remains yet to be done. Speeding up sound discipling through skillful use of literature and tape recorders offers
exciting possibilities in the liberation of receptive populations.
Recorders, for example, are being used imaginatively to multiply
baptized believers among the Karens in North Thailand.

7. Clearing houses for national and foreign apostles are beginning to
develop. In a small way this is what each church growth seminar
is. Apostles exchange information about what methods God is blessing to the effective communication of Christ. The exchange takes
place across denominational, cultural, racial, and linguistic
lines. Those devoted to carrying out the Great Commission come
together and share what they know. And what we all together know
about obedient and joyful harvesting is very considerable!

8. Blessedly, the tired old problems were not often heard at these
seminars. In some quarters mission meetings have, alas - in the
dark days which have followed World War II - been marked by much
pessimism. The debris of old defeats (cliches about tensions,
missionary stupidity, renaissance of the great religions, weaknesses of nationals, the early expected demise of the missionary movement, ten good reasons why the Church is going down hill, glorification of littleness, and the like) have formed the substance of
addresses given by some national leaders and missionaries. In contrast, the seminars were marked by a healthy critical optimism.
Speakers told of triumphs of the Gospel, opportunities for advance,
and new churches which have been established. Problems were rec-

ognized as opportunities to work at solutions. The remarkable openness of so many populations in so many lands gladdened our hearts. Church growth people are proud to be part of the apostalate.

9. Urban church growth seemed increasingly possible. For example, Mr. Ezra, a Tamilian minister, told the seminar held in South India of planting 23 new urban churches - a remarkable story of how two missionaries of the Oriental Missionary Society came to Madras City fifteen years ago and, starting from scratch, with absolutely no church, have now 23 congregations, 1523 communicant members and a community of about 3000. If this has been accomplished by two foreign missionaries and their helpers, how much more could have been accomplished by those denominations in Madras City who fifteen years ago had 2000, 20,000, or 50,000 communicants and a battalion or two of able Indian laymen and ministers! Mr. Ezra's story was typical. Great numbers of people wait to be liberated into the glorious liberty of Christ - and those nationals and missionaries who have hard and bold plans for discipling and work forward in the power of the Holy Spirit, find their labors blessed by God.

10. The conciliar Churches and missions (which alas in some lands stayed aloof from the Church Growth Seminars) in Indonesia, North Thailand, West Pakistan not only attended but took vigorous part. In Indonesia, Mr. Maitimoe, the Executive Secretary of the Council's Committee on Evangelism, drew up a splendid set of findings which called for a series of regional church growth seminars, to help the churches meet the great opportunities for propagating the Gospel. I rejoiced at such action of conciliar groups. The tragedy of the Uppsala emphasis on social action in place of evangelism is that it comes at just the time when church-multiplying evangelism is the need of the hour. It is so welcomed by multitudes of Non-Christians. One hopes that in many lands the conciliar forces will return to vigorous proclamation of the Gospel, baptizing of penitent believers, and establishing tens of thousands of new churches. We should be much in prayer for this to happen.

GIVE AFRICANS A CHANCE TO LOVE JESUS CHRIST

THE. CLIMATE OF CHANGE IN AFRICA WILL DRASTICALLY AFFECT OUR PRESENT MISSIONARY PROGRAM...BUT FAR FROM ITS COMING TO AN END, I FIRMLY BELIEVE WE ARE STANDING AT THE THRESHOLD OF OUR GREATEST OPPORTUNITY...AS LONG AS MILLIONS REMAIN WITHOUT CHRIST, OF WHOM MULTITUDES ARE RECEPTIVE TO THE GOSPEL, WE NEED MORE, NOT FEWER, MISSIONARIES. IN WEST CAMEROONS, FOR EXAMPLE, MISSIONARIES WILL NEVER FIND THEMSELVES OUT OF A JOB UNTIL ONE AND ONE-HALF MILLION WESTCAMEROONIANS LOVE JESUS CHRIST AND ARE FAITHFUL MEMBERS OF HIS CHURCH. WITH THE IMMENSITY OF THE TASK OUR CALL TO MISSIONS IS PERRENNIAL.

Dr. Lloyd Kwast, Baptist Herald, April 1972

ASIA'S PULSE BEATS WITH MISSIONS   C. Peter Wagner

As current research in the School of World Mission is proving, the
missionary force which has arisen from the indigenous churches of the
Third World is greater than many had imagined. The team, consisting of
Peter Larson, James Wong and Edward Pentecost which is gathering and
analyzing all the data possible on the new younger missionary forces, has
compiled a list of almost 200 sending agencies outside of the Western
world. A complete directory of these will be published later this year
by James Wong in Singapore.

Meanwhile, new information is turning up. The April 1972 issue of
Asia Pulse (published by Evangelical Missions Information Service, Box
794, Wheaton, Illinois 60187) in a ten-page edition, reports five missionary movements in the Third World. Here are some of the items:

  * Hong Kong Churches Send Missionary to Peru -- Carpus Yip, a graduate of the Alliance Bible Seminary, left Hong Kong on January 22
for Lima, Peru. He is the seventh missionary of the Chinese Churches
Union of the Christian and Missionary Alliance. Others are now serving in Viet Nam and Indonesia.

  * Overseas Missionary Association Formed -- Eleven small Japanese
foreign missionary sending organizations met in Tokyo in July and
organized the Japan Overseas Missionary Association. Chairman of
the new group is Dr. Akira Hatori. The purpose of this new organization is to work more efficiently in the promotion of foreign
missions among evangelical churches in Japan. Most of the missionaries sent out thus far from Japan by local committees, are serving
under established missionary societies in the countries to which they
have gone. It is hoped that an executive secretary may in the future
handle finances and other problems from a central office.

  * Korean Missionary Agency Opens Office in Wheaton, Illinois --
The group formerly known as Korea Evangelical Inter-Mission Alliance,
and now called Korea International Mission (KIM) of Seoul, Korea, has
opened a branch office in Wheaton, Illinois. This is a Korean missionary agency which sends Korean missionaries to other lands. Rev.
Robert C. Morgan, formerly with Compassion, Inc. is serving as the
Executive Director of the United States branch.

  * First Pan-Malaysian Church Missions Conference -- Many Chinese
Christians from West Malaysia met at the end of November for the
first Chinese missions conference. Evangelical leaders from several
denominations sponsored the gathering. Rev. Tseng Ling-fong, Principal of the Overseas Bible Institute in Hong Kong was the featured
speaker. East Asia Missions commented on this gathering: "The OMF

considers the growing interest in missionary outreach among Asian
Christians as one of the most significant and exciting trends in
the church today."

* <u>Chinese Church Raises Huge Missionary Offering</u> -- The Grace Gospel Church of Manila, raised a total of over 200,000 pesos for their
missionary outreach at its recent missionary conference. This no
doubt marks the highest missionary budget of any single church in
Asia. The pastor, Rev. Cheng Kor is a refugee from mainland China.

If the two billion are going to be reached, the churches of the Third
World will have to move out with an effective missionary program along
with the Western churches. The harvest is great, but the laborers still
are all too few.

A WORD TO NATIONAL AND MISSIONARY SPEAKERS

Peter Wagner's article above brings into sharp focus the fact that
much anti-missions sentiment today is not really anti-missionary at all,
but rather anti-Eurican. All speakers must keep these two things separate. We must be pro-missionary. Because missionaries are of every
nation and color and tongue - and we need thousands more of them - we
must be careful not to use the word 'missionary' as a synonyn for 'Eurican'. Rather we must hold up the missionary vocation as a glorious call
ing open to Christians everywhere.

I recently heard a notable leader affirm that the missionary life
was no longer glamorous, but rather one of very humble service. He did
not intend, I am sure, to downgrade the propagation of the Gospel. He
intended to say that missionaries no longer had the 'glamorous task of
ordering nationals around', i.e. of administration. It is rather unfortunate to equate administration with bossing people around. If it ever
does that, it is poor administration. Good administration - by Aferi-
casians and Euricans - avoids pushing people around and is sensitive to
them as persons. But administration per se is not the apostolic calling.

The glamour of the missionary calling lies in "spreading the frag-
rance of the knowledge of Christ" not in exercising occasional administrative responsibilities. It lies in preaching the Gospel where it has
not been heard, pioneering movements of liberation, suffering for Christ,
and when evening falls marching in through the golden gates while trumpets blare and cymbals clash and the King welcomes the missionary home.

Let us sedulously avoid de-bunking the apostolic vocation. Let us
not picture the missionary life as drab. The task today is to multiply
missionaries of every Church, every tongue, every continent and nation.
And before men will become missionaries they need, with Missionary Paul,

to believe that in the call God has conferred on them the favor of a commission (Romans 1:5) to bring the ethne (the kindreds, families, clans, classes and castes) to the obedience of the faith.

Peter Wagner helps us glimpse the glory of the missionary calling by pointing out that hundreds of Africasian missionary societies are now sending missionaries to cultures and languages other than their own. The Lord will create many more. His arm is not shortened. The hundreds of millions who have yet to believe and who, filled with the Holy Spirit, have yet to surge forward into a life of righteousness, brotherhood and peace, await the coming of missionaries. When they have all heard the Gospel, we and they will rejoice in the Lord's return. Maranatha. Donald McGavran

A HISTORIC MEETING IN VIETNAM   Reginald Reimer

Good news coming out of Vietnam these days is rare indeed. Reports concern bomb tonnage, casualty figures and political strife. Little is known about the large Protestant missionary efforts and the many Christian churches there.

Among the church planting missions are the Christian and Missionary Alliance, the Southern Baptists, the Seventh Day Adventists, and the Mennonites. Of these the oldest and largest is the C & MA out of whose 60 year effort has grown the 106,000 member (community) Evangelical Church of Vietnam. About two-thirds of this church is made up of ethnic Vietnamese - who live on the plains - and the remaining third of tribesmen who live in the mountains - the Montagnards.

As early as the 1930's Vietnamese missionaries began cooperating with the American, Canadian and European missionaries of the C & MA In evangelizing the mountain tribes. At present 10 Vietnamese missionary families and 3 single men work among the tribes.

During 1970-71, the C & MA Mission in Vietnam tried the experiment of sending to the School of World Mission and Institute of Church Growth at Fuller Seminary a national-missionary team - Rev. Truong van Tot is a Vietnamese missionary evangelizing the Koho tribe and I am a Canadian missionary at work in the plains of Vietnam since 1966. We studied effective communication of the Gospel, i.e. church growth. Both of us completed 36 hours of tough graduate-level mission courses.

When we returned to Vietnam in the summer of 1971, he and I held the first Church Growth Seminar ever held in Vietnam. At Mr. Tot's suggestion, it was arranged by the missions committee of the Evangelical Church of Vietnam. Twenty Vietnamese missionaries - thirteen men and seven missionary wives - were present at this historic meet-

ing, the first meeting called especially for Vietnamese missionaries
in thirty-five years!!

Mr. Tot and I gave eight lectures on church growth principles.
After building a strong biblical base we explained the aid church
growth could get by harnessing the social sciences. People movements
were stressed as was the relationship of revivals to the growth of
the church. Many of the ideas were new to the Vietnamese missionaries
who have had little specialized training in cross cultural missions.
Mr. Tot, who had sat so quietly through nine months at the School of
Missions, suddenly - speaking his mother tongue fluently - reversed
roles and became a most vocal and effective teacher of church growth
principles. The faculty at Pasadena would have been proud of him.

It became obvious that Vietnamese missionaries need specialized
training for the cross cultural missionary task. While they do not
go out of Vietnam, thus crossing no national boundaries, they do
cross the pronounced cultural barriers within Vietnam. They go into
mountain cultures which for centuries have been at odds with their
own. They have to learn a new language and a new way of life. They
have to learn to respect the Montagnard culture.

We discussed the indigenous - tribal - expression of the Gospel
and indigenous forms of worship and of church. Mr. Tot appeared in
traditional Vietnamese dress, something I had not seen a Vietnamese
pastor do in recent years. It helped to make a point. The 20 Asian
missionaries welcomed the idea of indigenous tribal churches with a
feeling of great relief. It made sense to them.

People movements were a third major item of interest. They are
particularly important in light of the social structure of the tribes.
The best way for the tribes to become Christian is through people
movements. The Asian missionaries wanted additional information on
people movements. A Vietnamese version of Principles of Church
Growth by McGavran and Weld will be underway soon.

A final and very significant topic discussed was the formation
of an autonomous missionary society. These Asian missionaries expressed dissatisfaction with the token support they often get from the
Vietnamese Church. Their mission committee was only one of many
committees. The Church often by-passed opportunities for propagating
the Gospel among the Montagnards in order to do something closer at
hand. The Asian missionaries felt that Christians would give more
if they were approached directly. I predict the formation of a full-
fledged Vietnamese missionary society in the near future. It will be
much more effective in mobilizing Vietnamese Christians to disciple
the remaining tribes in South Vietnam's highlands than the present
regularly out-voted committee can be.

Mr. Tot and I have been asked to hold more seminars for various groups throughout the country. In seminars a missionary and a national working together is a very effective combination. Other missions working with Afericasian Churches ought seriously to consider sending missionary-national teams to the School of Missions. The C & MA is following up its first experiment by sending both mission chairman Nanfelt and National Church president Kamasi from their Indonesia field to SWM-ICG during 1971-72.

SEEING THE CHURCH IN THE PHILIPPINES   A. L. Tuggy & R. Toliver

One of the notable events in the Third World has been the completion of a three year study of the Churches in the Philippines. The book called Seeing the Church in the Philippines which was released at the Church Growth Seminar in Manila in early December 1971 and eagerly snapped up by the 400 and more delegates, sparkles with human interest. It is available from the Church Growth Book Club ($1.50 to members) and should be read by Christian leaders all over the world. This heartening book you must get and read. Some of its many merits are the following.

It describes many typical Third World church and mission situations. Small struggling congregations and denominations which cannot seem to get off the ground. Small clusters of congregations which are bursting with life. Denominations in which missionaries play a large part and those in which they play a small part. One which is growing steadily at the rate of eight per cent a year and doubling every ten years, and another which has not doubled in thirty years and apparently has no desire to do so.

This study - set in motion at the Winona Lake Church Growth Seminar about 1966 - was authorized and funded by three missions in the Philippines with help from their boards in America. They sent the men doing the study to the School of Missions at Fuller for a year's study of modern missions and church growth. Churches and missions in the islands welcomed the research and cooperated with it. They found It stimulated great commission missions. It generated in the congregations visited a continuing concern for evangelism. It began to deliver rewards while it was still in the data gathering stage.

It presents dozens of factors which, in the sovereignty of God, have worked for effective communication of the Gospel in dozens of different situations. Readers in Africa or South America will find many valuable ideas as to forms of evangelism which bring men to Christian decision, baptism, and responsible church membership. CGB recommends SEEING THE CHURCH IN THE PHILIPPINES for wide reading.

MORE MISSIONARIES NEEDED

The Coordinating Office for Asian Evangelism
(COFAE) is drawing up plans for the establishment of a
Pan Asian Missionary Service. Missionaries are needed
in many parts of Asia, since more than 97% of Asia
still does not confess Christ as Lord and Saviour.
Many churches in Japan, Korea, Indonesia, India, Malaysia and other countries are eager for missionary
involvement but lack information and contacts for the
use of their powers. For example, as I talked with
Japanese leaders about Japan's role in the freedom and
independence of Asian countries, and about Japan's
sending of economic missions to Asia, we felt that God
is calling Japanese Christians to lead in the coordination of many Asians who wish to go out as missionaries.
Dr. Chandu Ray, 8 Mount Sophia, Singapore 9

WHY NOT LEAVE THEM AS THEY ARE?   A. R. Tippett

With the mood of our day to let everyone "do his own thing"
in his own way, the missionary is often asked "Why not leave them
alone?" I have four answers.

1. On the level of social change, about 200 million people are
    in the process of changing their religion. They are seek-
    ing, considering, testing and deciding all promoted ideologies.
    It is common sense that Christianity should be one of those
    options.

2. On the level of Christian responsibility we have the old ques-
    tion of the "haves and have nots". Do we not have the re-
    sponsibility of sharing our physical and spiritual blessings?

3. On the level of the Scriptures, these teach that "the people
    of God" are responsible for the saving of the nations. The
    Church does the work of Christ in the world, and the Lord's
    "great commission" is "to all nations" and applies "to the end
    of the age" (Matt. 28:18-20).

4. On the level of human salvation, we have been given the word
    of God's purpose to save man from his sin. We are committed
    to bring men face to face with the claim of Christ (Rom.
    10:13-5). The word of reconciliation in Christ is committed
    to us (2 Cor. 5:14-19).

Why not leave them as they are? How can we if the Scriptures
are our "rule for faith and practice"? Christian mission is not up
for rationalization. Is the criterion to be in every man's own
mind? I, for one, do not believe that. The Church, the Bible, the
Christian mission, and my commitment: they hold together as a
totality.

A FRESH BREEZE BLOWING?   Donald McGavran

Church Growth Bulletin, by way of exchange, has for several years
received a Monthly Letter About Evangelism from the Division of World
Mission and Evangelism of the World Council of Churches at Geneva.
Issue after issue it discussed (not evangelism, but) renewal of existing Christians, social action, or kindly service. The following passage has not been taken from the Monthly Letter, but sounds like it.

> "Ernesto (Che) Guevara used to insist that 'the new revolu-
> tionary man' was conceived in love, self surrender and freedom.
> Is not this the heart of evangelism?"

The Monthly Letter About Evangelism was dedicated to reinterpreting 'evangelism' to mean everything but. It was part of Geneva's
massive effort to "enlarge" the great words of Christian mission so
that they move on the strictly human level. 'Mission' was not proclaiming Christ and multiplying churches but carrying out a program
of humanization. 'Evangelism' was social action. 'Conversion' did
not take place at all unless it promoted inter-racial brotherhood.
Its meaning began and ended in ethical relationships among men. Once
these had been established, reconciliation with 'God' had taken
place, no matter what god one worshipped. The coming Bangkok consultation on 'Salvation Today' (as set forth in the International
Review of Missions for the fall and winter of 1971-72) seems intent
on defining salvation as largely if not exclusively "this worldly."

What a surprise and what a joy it is therefore to receive the
March 1972 issue of Geneva's Monthly Letter on Evangelism. Aside
from a brief announcement of the resignation of Walter Hollenweger,
the founder and editor of the Monthly Letter, it consists entirely
of a report by Alan Walker, the noted evangelist who is Superintendent of the Central Methodist Mission, Sydney, New South Wales,
Australia. He tells of a campaign which is straight biblical evangelism. It ran under "God's direction," made nightly appeals for
"open commitment to Christ," and had as its primary purpose "to
reach people beyond the Church."

True, since Dr. Walker is part of the ecumenical movement, he
talks about 'social redemption'. In the campaign, he writes,

"controversial issues of society" were raised. The campaign "sought and won endorsement and cooperation from all Churches, Protestant and Roman Catholic." Yet most of these things are done by evangelical evangelists. What has been disastrous in conciliar 'evangelism' has been that these emphases have been <u>substituted</u> for seeking a trans-cendent and eternal change of status effected by faith in Christ lived out in obedient membership in His Church. Dr. Walker avoids this disastrous deviation. He writes:

> "So the challenge was heard again as the Church set out to pro-claim the Gospel in modern days to all people."
> "I challenged fifty young men to step forward this year and join the Christian ministry."
> "A motor bike gang arrived with the intention...to disrupt the meeting...A highlight of the campaign will forever be for me the night when 'Satan's Slaves' became 'Christ's Men'."
> "Lives were transformed."
> "An attack was launched on a serious current social problem, teenage drinking."
> "Evangelism is soon blighted by humanist-style belief which questions the fact of the supernatural."
> "By Sunday night, joy and excitement were running through the Valley. When the Christian climax was offered, many made Christian commitments at the counselling tent."
> "A husband and wife, separated, coming forward from different parts of the building, accepted Christ. Their marriage was subsequently restored."

Does this March 1972 issue of the <u>Letter About Evangelism</u> mark a real turning on the part of the Division of World Mission and Evangelism? Or will the new editor it appoints go back to the Hollen-weger emphases? It is too early to tell. One swallow does not make a summer. And the Geneva Line which came through so distinctly in <u>Renewal in Mission</u> at Uppsala is not merely an alternate way of missionizing and evangelizing. It rises from different theological roots. It is based on a new pluralistic hermeneutic which interprets the Bible in a way the Church has never understood it, and thereby denies its unity, authority and sufficiency.

Yet we congratulate the Division of World Mission and Evangel-ism on the March issue. We hope Geneva will move away from its leftist vanguard and toward the center. We hope the Division will turn to emphasizing vertical reconciliation, belief on Jesus Christ, and responsible membership in His Church. Without that, no amount of ethical action has any lasting root. Ethical action is not faith in Christ. It is a fruit of life in Christ. It is neither a root of the Gospel nor the Gospel itself. The Triune God, Father, Son

and Holy Spirit, intensely personal, is objective Reality. When no
man walks the face of the earth, He will still live and love and
rule. He has revealed Himself authoritatively and infallibility in
the Bible and in Jesus Christ as described in the Scriptures. The
supreme question for evangelism (and for all men) is whether men are
reconciled to Him through faith in Jesus Christ. We look forward
to future issues of <u>The Monthly Letter About Evangelism</u>.

500,000 IN PARIS   Doan Van Si

"Please send us a pastor," pled Mr. Despeisse, a Vietnamese
Christian on a visit to Vietnam from his home in Paris. On Easter
1970 a former Christian and Missionary Alliance missionary to Vietnam,
Rev. Daniel Bordreul, had gotten together a group of Vietnamese
Christians in Paris. Now the church with 50 adult members was strong
enough to call and support a Vietnamese minister.

The Evangelical Church of Vietnam, founded by the C & MA over
60 years ago, has lost a number of Christians who have fled Vietnam
in order to live outside the war zone. Some of these now living in
France compose this church.

"As Mr. Bordreul is busy with services on Sunday in many churches
in Paris," Mr. Despeisse said, "we have prayer meetings led by a
layman every Sunday that Bordreul is away. We have regular Sunday
School, too".

Asked about the spiritual life of Vietnamese Christians in
Paris, Despeisse replied, "They are all very zealous in the Lord's
service. Most have good jobs and lead a very convenient life".

President Mieng, head of the Evangelical Church of Vietnam,
declared "The time has come to send a Vietnamese missionary to Paris
to help strengthen the spiritual life of Vietnamese Christians there.
He will be the first Vietnamese missionary to be sent to France,
where in Paris alone live half a million Vietnamese.

((Comment: What a significant situation! We congratulate
President Mieng and hope he will instruct his "missionaries to
Paris" that, since they are <u>missionaries</u>, their major task - different from strengthening the spiritual life of existing Christians - is communicating the Gospel to multitudes of Vietnamese in
Paris who do not know the Lord. Multiplying Parisian churches made
up of obedient disciples of Christ is the basic task of missionaries
to Paris.   D. McGavran))

MALCOLM MUGGERIDGE ON CHURCH GROWTH

"Without a doubt, as a conventional wisdom, or consensus, becomes more explicitly a Christian, if not deliberately hostile,
there is a corresponding counter movement toward Christian commitment...In terms of actual converts in, for instance, Indonesia and
Africa, record numbers are turning to Christianity; while the Pentecostals are sweeping over Latin America, attracting Roman Catholics.
Curiously enough -- or perhaps not so curiously -- this upsurge of
Christian zeal is matched by a falling away in support for all
existing churches, and a loss of nerve on the part of their accredited leaders.

Consider a recent book: No Middle Ground by Roger Huber ("A
Celebration of the Liberation from Religion"). Huber following
the, as I consider, misconceived Bonhoeffer proposition about
religionless Christianity, calls upon his flock to abandon the terms
and practice of the Christian faith as hitherto understood and to
take advantage of the new freedom the 20th Century offers. No longer
do we merely search for new laws of nature; it is we who determine
the future of the evolutionary drama, and who decide "the shape of
this planet and of self consciousness itself." We alone are responsible; God has died, and has left us to fend for ourselves. This
portentous declaration is taken from the publication IMAGE, organ
of the Ecumenical Institute. Following it, Huber recommends the
takeover of churches - including his own (Central Presbyterian
Church, Montclair, New Jersey) by the congregation, and the abolition
of the role of priest or minister. We must all be in the world
together!! If ever God was needed by His creatures, it is surely
now. When the most energetic and vociferous of his particular
spokesmen are inclined, like Huber, to insist that He has died.

No doubt the other response - the revival of Christian enthusiasm - reflects an instinctive corrective in the flock to the doubts
and hesitations which have afflicted the shepherds, from the Vatican
downward." ESQUIRE, April 1972, page 39.

THE ASIAN MODEL OF THE CHURCH

The Christian Church was born in an Asian City. Shortly thereafter it entered Europe where it multiplied exceedingly, while in
Asia for many reasons, it did not spread. Consequently the model of
the Church now visible to Asians is a Western model.

This model has been greatly used of God to establish the Church
firmly in almost all Asian countries; but because it is a western
model it has not multiplied exceedingly. The time has now come for

Asians Christians to turn back to the Asian model and duplicate that.

The New Testament sets forth clearly what the Church intentionally, constitutionally and essentially is. The writers were all Asians. The members were all Asians. The congregations were all Asians. Western organizational complexities had not slanted the model in a European direction. These early churches, described exactly in the New Testament, must now become the standard for the multiplying congregations of the Asian missionary movement.

THE UNRESPONSIVE by David Liao, Eerdmans, 1971 is reviewed by Donald McGavran, Fuller Theological Seminary.

As the Church carries out the mandate of her Lord to disciple the nations, she continually meets unresponsive peoples. As missionaries carry the good news to the two billion who have yet to believe, they often encounter indifferent or resistant populations.

Sometimes unresponsiveness is due to hardness of heart, pride, or aloofness; but more often than we like to think, it is due to neglect. The gospel has been presented to an "unresponsive" ethnic unit in the trade language, not its mother tongue. The only church its members could join was made up of people of a different culture. The only pastors its congregations could have were those from another ethnic unit or subculture. For example, until recently the only option open to seemingly resistant Quechua Indians in Ecuador was to hear the gospel in Spanish, join Spanish-speaking congregations of mestizos, and sit under pastors of the ruling people of Ecuador.

It is the great merit of David Liao's book, THE UNRESPONSIVE, that it focuses attention on this church problem, commonly found in all six continents. He illustrates it by examining the Hakkas of Taiwan who number about two million, comprise the finest of the Chinese, and so far have seemed unresponsive. Mr. Liao is convinced that failure of the church to grow among the Hakkas is best explained by the facts that the Hakkas have been neglected, their language has not been learned, and they have had to join Minan and Mandarin-speaking congregations. Consequently to them "becoming Christian" has come to mean "leaving our beloved Hakka people."

As readers from other parts of the world peruse these pages, they quickly will recognize their own neglected peoples and, I trust, will end the neglect by devising ways of communicating the gospel which channel the grace of God to those particular peoples.

PETER BEYERHAUS CHURCH GROWTH LECTURES OF 1972

Dr. Peter Beyerhaus, professor of mission at Tubingen University in Germany is in the vanguard of evangelical missionary scholars speaking and writing today. A competent theologian who knows the situation in Germany thoroughly, he is the chief architect of "The Frankfurt Declaration on 'The Fundamental Crisis in Missions Today."

He has just completed a lecture tour of eight leading seminaries in the United States, beginning with Fuller Theological Seminary, where he gave the 1972 Church Growth Lectures. He went on to speak at Trinity, Wheaton, Concordia, Lincoln, Luther, Gordon-Conwell, and the Protestant Episcopal Seminary in Virginia. Throughout his lectures he was exposing to public view the tremendous shift from great commission missions to social action missions, from missions working for vertical reconciliation with God to those working for horizontal reconciliation of men with men. He set forth the depth and seriousness of the changes advocated in some quarters and exposed their theological roots. The Frankfurt Declaration speaks of a "Fundamental Crisis in Christian Missions." Dr. Beyerhaus in these lectures describes that crisis, shows how it threatens all branches of the Church, and tells how it arose and may be combated. The titles of the lectures are as follows:

1. The Attack on Evangelical Christianity in Germany and Missions.
2. The Biblical Foundation and Goal of Missions.
3. Evangelical Responsibility in the Ecumenical Crisis in Asia.
4. The Missionary Meaning of the Hermeneutical Crisis in Present Day Theology.
5. The Story of the Frankfurt Declaration.
6. Mission and Humanization.
7. Conquering Racism - A Necessary Fruit of Mission.

These historic and heartening lectures are of special significance to all who are dedicated to biblical mission. Executive staffs in missionary society headquarters, professors of missions in seminaries and missionary training schools, and thinking leaders (nationals and missionaries) all around the world will want to get a set of the cassettes and listen to them.

They are now available - in Dr. Beyerhaus' voice. It is he who is speaking. Each ordinarily costs $3.50 a tape, or $24.50 for the set; but in view of their great importance, arrangements have been made so that you may, for a short time, order them at half price, plus postage and handling of 30¢ per cassette. A total of $14.35 bring the set to you postpaid. Address: Church Growth Book Club, 533 Hermosa Street, South Pasadena, Calif. 91030, U.S.A. - and send a U.S.$ check with your order.

CHURCH GROWTH
B U L L E T I N

from the
INSTITUTE OF
CHURCH GROWTH

Address:
FULLER THEOLOGICAL
SEMINARY
135 N. Oakland
Pasadena, Calif. 91101

DONALD A. McGAVRAN, B.D., Ph.D.
Director

July 1972   Subscription $1 per year   Volume VIII No. 6

The Church Growth Workshop or Seminar

HOW TO ORGANIZE A GRASS-ROOTS CHURCH GROWTH WORKSHOP by C. Peter Wagner

Missionary strategy oriented towards church growth does a good deal of talking about goals and objectives. It takes the "make disciples" of the Great Commission seriously and pushes relentlessly forward towards making as many as possible. Disciples are people. People are countable. Therefore, making disciples is not only an objective; it is a measurable objective.

Efforts without measurable objectives can easily be construed as cop outs. Failure becomes an impossibility. Reporting becomes hopelessly subjective. This is why goals, carefully designed, specifically artic- ulated, and constantly evaluated are stressed by church growth men.

Much of this emphasis has been highlighted in church growth work- shops and seminars here in North America as well as in the Third World. But those stressing them have often had an uneasy feeling. In spite of all the talk about goals, the workshops themselves have not been planned around specific, measurable goals. Much less have they been subjected to continuous evaluation. Does a particular church growth workshop in fact help make disciples?

A New Kind of Workshop

A new kind of workshop, recently conducted in Venezuela, has at- tempted to design a built-in answer to this question. The need for some new vehicle for disseminating church growth knowledge became evident in what is known as the Elburn Consultation, held in Elburn, Illinois, in September, 1970. This meeting of 50 IFMA/EFMA mission executives with work in Latin America was precipitated by the publication of Read, Monte- rroso, and Johnson's Latin American Church Growth the previous year. Among other things it showed that IFMA/EFMA missions as a group had made a very poor showing compared to other groups in Latin America.

After much searching and planning for a vehicle to communicate the Elburn findings to the Latin American grass roots, the Evangelical Committee on Latin America (IFMA/EFMA) named Edward Murphy of Overseas Crusades, and me to conduct a pilot workshop in Venezuela in response to initiative from the brethren there. Vergil Gerber, ECLA Executive Secretary contacted leaders in Venezuela, who then organized the workshop and sent out invitations. Ruperto Velez, a Colombian Overseas Crusades Field Director, was asked to join the team.

The Experiment in Venezuela

In response, 47 pastors, leaders, and missionaries gathered at the Evangelical Free Church campgrounds in El Limon, June 5-8. They represented 72 local churches of seven different denominations. They came highly motivated. They wanted help to analyze their churches accurately. They wanted to increase their fruitfulness as God's harvesters. Many felt frustrated at the lack of measurable growth as a result of traditional and at times high-powered evangelistic efforts of the past decade. They were ready for a renewed vision and creative goals.

The growing enthusiasm throughout the workshop and the spontaneous expressions of commitment to better methods and more daring goals at the conclusion indicated that something important had happened. This can be multiplied many times over throughout the world by anyone who has had basic training in church growth. Here are some pointers as to how it can be done:

1. Preliminary organization. The workshop can be held on either a national or a regional basis. It can deal with church growth in one denomination or in several. Do not seek to secure large numbers of participants. In Venezuela the 47 were manageable, and up to 60 or 70 might have been all right. But more than that might have become cumbersome. Generally speaking, the participants should be pastors, each representing one or more congregations. Priority should be given to those who are in the thick of the battle. Organization is minimal. Assigning preliminary research to participants is desirable, but somewhat unrealistic. If church growth literature is available in the vernacular, participants should be instructed to do as much previous reading as possible.

2. Resource personnel. The resource personnel should have three characteristics: they should know church growth theory, they should be able to speak the vernacular fluently, and they should be familiar with the area they are dealing with. The three-man team in Venezuela was ideal; however, one man could handle it alone if necessary.

3. <u>Curriculum</u>. The Venezuelan workshop will be set forth as a model for curriculum. It involved five distinct <u>phases</u>, each of which was allowed a certain flexibility as to time for development.

<u>Phase I</u>. A basic core of church growth theory is needed here. Goal setting as a basis for strategy, biblical and theological bases, techniques of use of statistics and graphs, a local case study or two are all good ingredients. Stay away from dealing too much with methods in this phase. The objective is to give the leaders present "church growth eyes."

<u>Phase II</u>. Divide participants into homogeneous groups of four to five. Have them talk about their areas, analyzing them on the basis of what they learned in Phase I. Have each group discover some method which God is blessing or identify some particularly fertile field, for sowing the Gospel seed will doubtless bring fruit, thirty--sixty--and one hundred-fold. Have each group report briefly to the plenary session and open up each for discussion. The objective is to cross-fertilize ideas and stimulate thinking with something emerging <u>from the local situation</u> (in contrast to "canned" programs frequently exported to them from abroad). The ideas are theirs.

<u>Phase III</u>. In this plenary session distribute graph paper and teach each person, step-by-step how to plot the communicant membership of his church over the last decade. Agree on the definition of "communicant membership." Be sure to record in a central place the statistics each one represents next to his name and the name and location of his church. Then have each one plot, with a dotted line, the biological growth over the same decade (use 25% per decade as a rule of thumb). Then plot biological growth for the <u>next four years</u>.

Break up into the same small groups and have each person carefully and prayerfully ask God how much fruit he can expect in his church over the next four years. The biological growth point will obviously be a minimum. Then stress the need to grow also through multiplying <u>churches</u>. Challenge them with the mother-daughter church concept. Have each one project by faith the planting of daughter churches and estimate their membership over the same four years. These projections should be discussed and approved in the small groups before they are finalized.

The next step is as dramatic as Faith Promise Sunday in Park Street Church. Back in plenary session, call the roll one by one and have each pastor report his projection before the whole group. Leave room for comments where necessary. Encourage them to challenge each other. Record each report of membership, number of daughter churches, and daughter church membership. When all reports are in, add them up and summarize the statistics and projections according to the following model. This will dramatize the way the participants themselves have projected accelerated church growth over the next four years. This can be a moment of great blessing, renewed faith, and victory.

VENEZUELAN CHURCH GROWTH WORKSHOP -- *Summary Statistics*

	PAST				PROJECTED		
	1961	*1971*	*Numerical Increase 1961-1971*	*% Decade Increase 1961-1971*	*1975*	*4-year Projected Increase*	*% Decadal Increase 1971-1975*
TOTAL CHURCHES	23	72	48	200%	130	58	200%
TOTAL MEMBERS	1,975	3,457	1,482	75%	6,655	3,198	215%
44 Churches Represented by Pastors	1,315	1,989	674	50%	3,566	1,577	198%
46 Projected Daughter Churches					1,038		
TOTALS					4,604	2,615	327%
28 Churches Represented by Denominational Executives	555	1,468	913	165%	1,681	213	36%
12 Projected Daughter Churches					370		
TOTAL					2,051	583	40%

El Limón, Venezuela
June 5-8, 1972
C. Peter *Wagner*

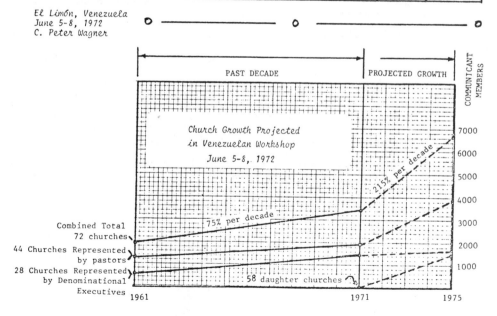

Church Growth Projected in Venezuelan Workshop June 5-8, 1972

Phase IV. After projections are made, participants will be warm toward learning new methods. Give some class sessions analyzing methods that God has blessed. Stir them up with a vision of what God has done through others in their own area and around the world. Here is where methodology can be stressed. Recommend reading in church growth materials. Offer books for sale (these should be stocked previously). The stock of Weld-McGavran's Spanish book on Principles of Church Growth was sold out completely in Venezuela!

Phase V. This is a two-year phase. Goals have been set, and an evaluation procedure is needed. A mimeographed report, containing the projections for each church, should be distributed to all participants as soon after the workshop as possible. They can then check up on themselves and on each other.

The most important innovation in Venezuela was projecting two future workshops at one-year intervals. A year from now, the men will return, report to each other on what has been done, and evaluate their work. They will share with each other blessings and disappointments, victories and defeats. They will teach each other. They will bring fellow workers who did not attend the first year. The same team will be with them. Elementary teaching will be given to the newcomers, while advanced church growth theory is given to the veterans. Projections will be adjusted, new goals will be set, the cycle will begin again.

For once, after one year and after two years, the effect of the church growth workshop will be capable of measurement. If, as the composite graph projects, the rate of growth (on a per decade basis) increases from 75% to 215%, a significant contribution to the task of discipling Venezuela will have been made. Hopefully it will be repeated by church growth men in other parts of Latin America and around the world.

WORKSHOPS IN RIGHT AND LEFT END POPULATIONS   by Donald McGavran

I.   The Church Growth Workshop in Venezuela in June 1972 marks a notable forward step in teaching church growth to national pastors and missionaries. The whole article should be studied and the facts told to others. Where conditions are similar, the program stated so clearly by Professor Wagner can be used all over Africasia. It should work well in Europe and North America also.

He admirably emphasizes the advantage of setting measurable goals and seeing how well participants achieve them. The crying need for church growth thinking to rise out of the local situation, which he presents, can scarcely be overstated. So many innovations - which look promising to Eurican leaders - are taken to Africasis year after year, that national pastors must often say to themselves, "Here comes another 'made in the West' idea. It is well intended, even if it does not fit our situation. Let's listen again." Opportunities for church growth always appear to local leaders in native costume, so to speak, but are usually portrayed by foreigners in the clothing of some other land!

The Venezuelan Workshop should be widely copied. It will prove fruitful in the hands of both national ministers and missionaries.

II. However, it will work best when conditions are at least roughly
comparable. Christian leaders should not deceive themselves and opt out
of making responsible efforts for church growth by declaring 'our conditions are very different from those in Venezuela'; but neither should they
imagine that the Venezuelan workshop is applicable everywhere.

Cities and countryside populations vary greatly in their responsiveness to the Good News. Were they to be distributed along a line leading
from tremendous response at the right end to hostility at the left, many
would fall toward the left end of the line and many toward the right.

No hard and fast definition of responsiveness can be drawn. Responsiveness is partly an objective quality out there in a given population;
but it is also partly a subjective quality in the advocate. Responsiveness is partially a function of the advocate's methods, expectation, and
fervency of belief. A given population often proves resistant to one
denomination and responsive to another. The difference lies, not in the
population, but in the methods of the missionaries and the image of itself which each Church projects. I used to believe that certain whole
countries were resistant and others were responsive; but can no longer
do so. Some populations in almost every country, given the right circumstances, prove responsive to the Gospel.

However, given ordinary circumstances within the control of ministers, laymen, and missionaries, many populations must be classed as resistant. In them, the only churches which can be planted are those at
mission stations where professional missionaries or paid national leaders
labor on salary from outside, where mission schools and hospitals continue on for years and years. Let us call these 'Left End Populations'.

Given these same ordinary circumstances, other populations however
are readily winnable. In them churches can be multiplied. In them, a
great factor in multiplication is the faith, expectation and expertise of
the advocate - the messenger of the Gospel. Let us call these 'Right
End Populations'.

It is clear that Venezuela has many Right End Populations. To be
sure, responsiveness has not been high in Venezuela. The Churches have
not grown remarkably. Venezuela is not Brazil or Chile. The authoritative volume Latin American Church Growth reports rather small church
growth in Venezuela. Nevertheless I classify Venezuela as a Right End
Country. It is not Afghanistan, or high caste India, or the tight knit
society of rural Japan.

Almost all the 47 pastors who attended the workshop, once their
eyes had been opened to the opportunities for church growth, felt they
could increase the membership of the existing congregations and plant
new ones. Indeed, their own estimate was that on a 1971 base of 1,989

communicant members, they could in four years add 1,577 members and thus
by 1975 would have 3,566 communicant members. This is Right End Thinking.

Given Right End circumstances (and they obtain generally throughout
Latin America and great chunks of Asia, Africa and the Eurican countries,
too) the workshop techniques used in Venezuela should prove rewarding.
I commend them without reservation.

In Left End Populations, however, (and many Churches and missions
are working there) the Church Growth Workshop will ordinarily start farther back. I do not say it must avoid measurement, but rather that it
must inculcate willingness to search for responsive segments of the population, create dissatisfaction with decade-long labors which simply seal
off the one church, and sweep away the rationalizations by which a pessimistic estimate of missions is justified. Many church leaders (both
nationals and foreigners) faced by decade-long non-growth have turned
from communicating the Gospel and are promoting attractive this-worldly
projects. They declare that Christians are to be concerned for all of
life and really relevant missions are to speak to the agenda of the
world, i.e. to men's physical, intellectual and social needs. Faced with
an audience of this kind of leaders, the Workshop must illuminate the
dark forces which lead men to betray humanity at its point of deepest
need, substitute the flesh for the Spirit, and deceive men by insisting
that temporal improvements are really just as good as eternal salvation.

Until the underbrush has been cleared away, the good seed will not
sprout. Leading men to set up measurable goals in terms of new churches
may seem to them so impossible that they will reject the whole church
growth concept and turn with renewed conviction to defending mission-
which-aims-exclusively-at-this-worldly-goals.

Rejoicing then in the development of an advanced mode of teaching
church growth and foretelling its great usefulness in Right End Populations, I counsel leaving the door open for a more general and somewhat
vaguer technique in the Left End populations. Those planning workshops
should estimate its situation carefully and from year to year shift into
one gear or the other according to the circumstances.

CULTURALLY ACCEPTABLE CONVERSION

AN EXPERIMENT IN DISCIPLING MOSLEMS**   by Loren F. Bliese, Lutheran

In 1962 the Evangelical Church Mekane Yesus in Ethiopia in cooperation with the American Lutheran Mission established a mission station in
the Wuchale valley, in which live about 20,000 people of whom around
12,000 are Muslims and 8,000 are Orthodox Christian. Of these, 2,500
are townsmen and 17,500 are villagers. (See the Church Growth Bulletin,
July 1968 for more details).

The area is Amharic speaking but some of the Muslims recognize a
mixed Galla origin from the rift valley while the Orthodox Christians

claim to be Amhara from the plateau. The ruins of numerous Christian
church sites in eastern villages with 100% Muslim population show that
six-tenths of this formerly strong Christian area has been firmly Islam-
icised since the 16th Century Muslim invacation. In spite of efforts of
Emperor Yohannis in the 19th Century and some government officials concerned with the political strength of Islam, losses from Orthodox Christianity to Islam are still taking place. Historically the people of
Wollo Province have been forcibly converted back and forth between
Christianity and Islam, so that an attitude of expediency in regard to
one's faith is very prevalent. In marriages, wives generally join the
religion of the husband without any concern. The employee also is generally urged or even compelled at the loss of his job or tenant land to
join the religion of his lord. Since separation of communities on the
basis of meat slaughtering practices is strictly observed, close associates and friends also change their religion in order to have full fellowship. For example, wedding parties are often converted to the religion
of the groom, at least during the celebration.

Currently the Mekane Yesus program in this Wuchalle valley includes
an elementary school, around 30 literacy schools scattered over the
surrounding area, a clinic and an agricultural school with a community
development program. Good rapport was established between the church
workers and people of the valley especially through a village water
supply cooperative project in 1964.

Dialogue between Muslim sheiks with Koranic training and workers of
the Mekane Yesus Church was carried on for about a year during which time
a plan to offer a regular course of Christian instruction with the aim
of preparing Muslims for baptism was discussed and advertised. When the
3 weeks' course was offered in January 1966 we agreed to pay the local
daily wage to those who attended as families so that they could leave
their work. Although no obligation for baptism was laid on those who
attended, most of the local farmers who completed the course accepted
baptism. Most of the sheiks, however, requested more time of instruction, so an arrangement was worked out in a Bible School of Muslim
sheiks opened the following year.

The program continued with courses in one central church in the
valley until July 1967 during which time some 750 persons were trained
and baptized.

The results at this stage - 1967 - were not all good since only
around 200 of the group were continuing in close association with the
central churches. It was then decided to move the courses into local
areas where new converts could be drawn into a closer fellowship in village congregations. The two central churches were too distant for most
of the scattered villagers. Through this program in which the course
was taught only 3 days a week for three months and the food money was
cut in half, three new congregations were organized in the Wuchale valley and six in adjacent valleys. This brought the total of baptized
persons to <u>1300</u> by Dec. 1969.

Land, corrugated iron sheets and nails were purchased by the Mekane Yesus Church and foreign subsidies, with the local congregation providing wood and labor to build simple mud plastered churches. We experienced much of the same disappointment as before. While the course was being taught, a spirit of enthusiasm and Christian devotion was common; but as soon as the course ended the people dispersed and most were overcome by the Muslim society around them. Only a few remained faithful. A major test came at the time of death with the question of Christian or Muslim burial. The local Muslim burial societies usually refused to cooperate with Mekane Yesus burials causing real struggles between the evangelists and Muslim relatives and sheiks who came for the funerals.

On the basis of the low percentage of those who remained in the Church and the impression developing that the "Church" was mainly a place to participate in a foreign handout, the food money courses were discontinued. The problem of food money being an incentive was facing us the whole way and it was necessary to phase it out. As I stated in the July 1968 Church Growth Bulletin article, "People are coming to these partly because we pay for their food. The question of whether this questionable motive will prevent the work of the Holy Spirit or will facilitate the work of the Spirit will only be proved by the test of time. Will there be a strong Church after the mission has gone, or not? We have continued the program with the hope and prayer that enough sincere believers will result from the instruction and follow up organization to continue a lasting Christian witness."

After closing these courses, efforts were made to extend the evangelistic outreach into new areas mainly through the fellowship growing up around literacy teachers with a concern for evangelism. During 1969-70 four congregations of around 12 members each were organized in Muslim areas beyond the places the courses had been held. The pattern of establishing congregations had been set by the courses making it possible for the literacy workers and evangelists to continue the pattern in spite of the fact that the courses were discontinued.

Missionaries making frequent and regular visits to the areas to encourage and support the nucleus gathering around the teacher was most important. I am convinced that missionary or national pastor itineration is the most fruitful method we have in planting churches. A regular schedule of visits needs to be set up and followed in order to encourage the front line workers.

The ties of relatives giving openings in new areas has played a major role in locating new workers in otherwise "closed" villages and allowing the Christian witness to expand. We were often led to a more distant village because of relatives of Christians from a closer area providing an opportunity of friendship and witness.

The baptism and Bible training course for Muslim sheiks has also been a major tool in opening new areas, since the Christian "sheik" was often able to gather a nucleus of relatives and neighbors around him after returning to his village. Here again the Church is facing the problem of

the use of money since the hope of many sheiks in completing the course
is to get a foreign paid evangelist or literacy teachers' job. When this
has not eventuated many have reverted to Islam.

Phasing out dependency started by a scholarship or a job without the
action being interpreted as "cutting me out of Christian fellowship" is
difficult. Nevertheless, the Mekane Yesus Church in this area is now
training 13 pastors at elementary school level, several of whom were former sheiks. The foreign subsidized portion of their salary will be phased
out over a ten year period. It is our aim to thereby make available to
the new congregations indigenous ministers who will not bear the stigma of
being foreign paid agents.

The present (1972) condition of the 14 congregations planted in this
area varies from 35 to 8 stable members or a total of around 200. There
is an occasional convert, but church growth as far as numerical increase
has stopped. The efforts of the staff are directed toward establishing a
real fellowship among the remnant in the various congregations. Bible and
leadership training programs are being developed especially with the ideas
of programmed tapes and extension seminary, the latter now well into its
second year with materials being produced by Mekane Yesus Seminary staff
and local missionaries. The following table indicates the situation
during the past six years.

	1966-67	1968-69	1970-71	1972
Baptized	750	550	"a few"	"a few"
Total New Christians	750	1300	reversions	200
New Congregations	0	14	4	14
Pastors Being Trained from among converts	0	0		13

The Method Debated: Was it Good?

The question of whether this was an acceptable method of church planting is being judged both ways. My own evaluation is that we seized a
God-given opportunity to plant churches in 14 villages, in which otherwise
there would be no sustained evangelical witness today and no opportunity
of Christian congregational fellowship being offered to the dominant Muslim population. Although extension has temporarily stopped in this area,
the emphasis on church planting which began here is continuing into areas
west of Dessie and will, I believe, return to the Wuchalle Valley after
the present program of stabilization has progressed so that the spiritual
growth and survival of the present congregations is no longer the over-
riding concern of the program.

The use of food, money and jobs in spreading one's faith is part of
the Wuchalle Valley culture. To come in with money and jobs, and not
make the religious stipulations which the indigenous lords make, would
have given the impression that with us, the Christian faith was a matter
of little importance. In this sense, the use of food money and jobs became an acceptable opening for our witness in this culture. However, it

also led to desire for financial gain or total dependency on the Church,
which when unfulfilled caused disillusionment and sent converts looking
for a new lord with another religion. Since our goal is the liberation
of more than just our employees, it is necessary to phase out the financial
aspect while continuing Christian teaching with the hope that a sufficient
remnant will continue who have been convinced of the Gospel without worldly gain. As more believers are convinced that religion is a divine-human
relationship rather than a lord-serf relationship, with God's power they
will form the nucleus of a new growing Church.

In the Protestant tradition the questions of motive and individual
commitment are given a very important place in judging one's faith. Although we want to foster and develop these goals, we should not close our
minds to the fact that this is not the way most historical church growth
has taken place. Many whole tribes and nations have received their initial salvation partly because of expedience. Even in the New Testament,
whole households including slaves were baptized because of the conversion
of the lord. No one seems to be too concerned that they weren't all given
a real instruction and chance for personal choice. Even now - though our
Ethiopian co-workers can not understand that we allow unbelievers to continue resistant to our faith and still employ them indefinitely - missionaries insist on the right of the mission institutional worker to have any
faith he likes as long as he does his job.

Certainly it's irritating to the missionary to hear the job applicant
say "Give me a job and I'll join your Church." But it is also irritating
to the Ethiopian believer to experience the unheard of - to see an unbeliever within the evangelical "family" (the church program) and to see
the Church miss opportunities of spreading the Gospel because it is de-
ominated by a foreign individualistic philosophy which feels making a
spiritual demand on one's "household" is unethical. It seems very right
to us foreigners not to be tempted into an "easy" system of "buying"
Christians. But in many cases (having thrown out the "easy" way as illegitimate) we encourage obstinacy and hardening against our witness. I am
convinced that not requiring religious unity within our "household" has
often made our witness outside unintelligible.

Except for a few deceivers within the various baptism courses, the
confessions and Christian alignments of the participants were sincere.
Culturally their conversion was acceptable; they were participating in a
Christian household. However, when the course ended and they were thrown
back into a dependence on the Muslim community, whether they liked it or
not, they had to align with that community. However, if a socially acceptable Evangelical Christian fellowship can be created from the few in each
community who resisted the Muslim social pressure, and if this group can
become recognized in the local burial society, the possibility of a free
religious choice for the rest of the community will have been won.

If a program of Christian witness does not offend the local culture,
foreigners need not fear it, even if they face criticism of being unethical by Western standards. God in his wisdom and power can call men to
salvation in many ways. By listening to the advice of our local co-workers

we may find that things culturally offensive to us are respectable and right ways of witness which <u>God is asking us also to use to His glory.</u>

** This important discussion on mission theory and methodology comes from the Ethiopian Church Growth Seminar of March 1972, where it was one of the most appreciated contributions. Bliese reports, honestly and intelligently, an experiement in communicating the Gospel to Muslims. The issue he raises is well known in most mission fields. Bliese is quite right in insisting that we regard it both from the point of view of Christian ethics and from that of the local culture. The latter is too frequently neglected. An interesting point to debate is whether the subsidy of the convert preachers should not have been continued until a community of several thousand Christians had been built up. Historically, many of the now large and independent younger Churches grew to five, ten, or even twenty thousand in membership before subsidy was discontinued. Whether the Lutheran experiment will be successful on the extremely small base of 200 remains to be seen. The Editor

STRONG WORDS

<u>HEY ESTABLISHMENT! LISTEN TO THIS PROTEST</u> by Veteran Missionaries

((The following significant document was given me on my recent lecture tour of Asia, Africa and Europe. It is reproduced exactly, except that the name of the country, mission, Church and missionary society have been deleted. It could have been written by any one of fifty bands of churchmen at work around the world. It is really addressed to many missionary establishments in the sending lands. It portrays accurately the mire in which so many missions of the Churches are bogged, and the rather simple way to extricate them and set them singing as they march down the road. It has sizeable implications for church growth. We respectfully urge establishments to make major changes in policy. These veterans are talking good sense. Donald McGavran.))

"We of your mission are deeply concerned about the crisis of confidence between the grass roots membership of our home Church and her national leadership. Because of our missionary society's involvement in this crisis, the situation has become critical, with the "will to mission" of the whole Church being eroded.

We deplore this tragic turn of events, especially at this time when the number of unevangelized people in the world is rapidly increasing. Although there is a greater potential for reaching them with the Gospel of Jesus Christ than we have ever known before, the present crisis of confidence in the sending Church is hindering its part in reaching these people by causing reduction of finances and personnel.

On the basis of communications from related churches and individuals, we know that a large segment of our Church does not want to desert its role in world mission. However, at present, this significant segment of the Church is unwilling to continue its support of mission through our Missionary society, until it regains the confidence that its denomina-

tional agency shares with it the primary concern for reaching men with the
Gospel of Christ, rather than having a primary concern for other worthy,
though less primary, tasks.

Such a crisis of confidence requires that we take seriously the re-
bellion of common Christians and see if God may not be speaking through
this protest. We have found our missionary society very open and sympathetic to protest movements around the world. We have seen headquarter
staff members listen for days to what people in revolt have had to say.
We have listened to these staff members as they have urged us also to be
sensitive to what is being said to the "establishment".

We would like to challenge our missionary society to listen in this
same manner to the criticism against it from within the Church. As we
understand from correspondence reaching us from churches, our missionary
society is trying to explain away this criticism, but is making very little
attempt to understand what a sizeable portion of the Church is trying to
say. It also seems unwilling to share disagreeable questions openly with
the Church and to think through with her to the tough answers in grueling
and honest debate. These failures to listen, communicate, and share
effectively are taken by the Church as evidence that headquarter staff,
together with other church leaders, does not have confidence in those it
leads.

While we agree with the basic goals and policies of our missionary
society, we find ourselves in sympathy with our disturbed Church in her
perplexity over the way many of these policies are being carried out and
in her feeling that there is a discrepancy between the avowed policies of
the society and the fruits being evidenced from its efforts.

In an attempt to help resolve this present crisis, we are compelled
to challenge the Church at large to assert her "will to mission" by responding to the unfinished task which God in His providence has committed
to her. Further, we are compelled to challenge our society to accept and
put into practice the following, as they apply to our Church's total task
in mission of the world.

1. That evangelism and church planting are the main means for fulfill-
    ing the Great Commission of our Lord, and are a continuing primary
    obligation upon every Church.

2. That "modified dichotomy"* is the most creative, flexible, and lib-
    erating structure for church-mission relationships.

*"modified dichotomy", a term used in Church Growth Bulletin (Nov.
1971) by Dr. Louis L. King to describe a form of church-mission relationship in which both church and mission are autonomous equals who may nego-
tiate agreements for mutual help in particular matters. Such agreements
would allow for the Church, while carrying on its own life independently,
to receive a certain degree of assistance from the mission in personnel or
funds or both, and would also allow the mission, hopefully with church
participation, to continue a pioneering role in carrying the Gospel to
the yet unreached.

3.   That decision-making be decentralized so that, insofar as possible, decisions are made by the people and in the locality they affect.

4.   That the current re-structuring within our Church should allow for a mission order or society which is within the Church, supported directly by concerned groups and individuals, and yet is separate enough so that it can give itself wholly to its task of spreading the Gospel, without being caught up in those ecclesiastical responsibilities that would threaten its inspiration, initiative, and flexibility.

THE BRAZILIAN WILD WEST - MULTITUDES WAITING TO BE CHURCHED by
Fred Edwards, B.D., M.A. Missiology

Evangelical mission strategists agree that the largest investment of men and money should be made in those sectors of the general population that are most receptive to the Gospel. Yet, frequently, even the "on the scene" missionary or national church planter does not know specifically where he should begin, double or diminish his efforts. And this is true even in nations where the Protestant Church is experiencing great membership growth and in countries concerning which there exists an immense amount of sociological, demographical, developmental and church growth data. Too often the church planter's first question, "Where specifically is church growth happening and likely to continue?" is dealt with only in the broadest terms.

Great But Not Even Church Growth. As of January, 1970 three and one quarter million of the one hundred million Brazilians were members in good standing of Evangelical churches. (Evangelical equals Protestant in Latin America.) To arrive at this size Brazilian Evangelicals had multiplied themselves 129 times since 1900 and are presently growing at three times the national population growth rate. But this great growth is not even throughout the vast country. It could not be otherwise with approximately three quarters of the Brazilian people occupying merely one quarter of the national land area. To determine where he can labor most profitably, in terms of persons brought to saving faith and useful service in growing local Christian assemblies, the church planter must know which politico-cultural region will be receptive to his ministry. He will then need to pinpoint within the region those areas where church growth is occuring and can be sustained.

National Development Indicates High Potential Areas. Brazil's new and modern capital, Brasilia, was constructed in the 1950's to fulfill a long standing national dream of opening the Brazilian hinterland to settlement and development. The Belem-Brasilia highway was then cut through the jungle north from the capital to the port city on the mighty Amazon River. This same highway (BR-14) has also been extended south through the states of Goias, Sao Paulo, and a major part of Parana. When completed, it will span the nation from north to south. The government has reserved a strip six miles wide on both sides of it for the development of cities and settlements.

Transamazonia is the name given to the east-west highway being pushed with great determination through the Amazon basin. Aboriginal tribes are being contacted, pacified, exposed (sometimes fatally) to twentieth century technology and diseases and then resettled -- all in the name of progress. Along Transamazonia the government has set apart a sixty mile strip on each side for settlement and development. In the fresh red wake of the bulldozers settlers are being moved into Brazil's "green hell". Poor Brazilians with good credit ratings, farming experience, a capacity for work and a family are given free transportation, 250 acres of land, a small wooden house and loans up to 2,250 dollars to improve the land. Brazil's military regime is opening the greatest of earth's remaining frontiers and tapping there the unimaginable natural resources (an estimated eight billion ton iron ore deposit to name one).

Why are these developments so important to mission strategists and church planters? Because, as the CGRILA (Church Growth Research in Latin America) team found, the growth of Brazilian Evangelical Churches has gone hand in hand with "...migration into new lands, the building of cities, the advancing coffee booms, and the development of modern industrial complexes, especially iron and steel. National growth has, indeed, opened the way for evangelization." (The whole authoritative book, Latin American Church Growth is replete with lessons for church planters.)

Migrating People Are Opening Other Frontiers. To be sure, internal migration is in the main from rural to urban all over the nation. But often special combinations of sociological and economic factors make the semi-occupied areas magnetic to Brazil's mobile people. Besides those settlements created by the new highways there are six other frontiers that have been opened in recent years. These are: 1) the north central portion of Maranhao, 2) those sections of the state of Goias near the new national capital, 3) north Minas Gerais, 4) the extreme northwestern part of São Paulo, 5) northwest Parana, and 6) pioneer zones in Mato Grosso -- the Far West region.

To locate the church planter's best opportunity in the Brazilian context we will single out the last of the above mentioned frontiers -- new lands in the Far West. Unoccupied lands, boom towns, cattle, poverty, self-styled leaders, posses and Indians are a few of the colorful ingredients that go into making up the exciting Brazilian Far West. We may well call this region the "Brazilian Wild West." A distinction needs to be made between (a) "the unoccupied or very lightly occupied lands" of this region and (b) "the frontier and pioneer zones." Vast areas of the West are either totally uninhabited or but thinly populated by pastoralists and subsistence agriculturalists. Much of the West has been occupied in this manner since the seventeenth century. The isolation of (a) is profound; subsistence is difficult and social services (medicine, education, and the like) are rudimentary or entirely absent. "The pioneer zones" are found within the much larger (a) area as enclaves wherever soil conditions, lines of transportation or planned cities combine to create favorable circumstances. The pioneer zones are characterized by rapid economic development, immigration and social change and have tremendous church growth potential.

<u>Protestant Experience in the Wild West</u>.   The Gospel has met with outstanding success in the Far West.   The region has five per cent of the national population and four per cent of Brazilian Evangelicals.   During the 1960's the largest Evangelical Church grew there at a decadal rate of 376 per cent (on a base of more than 17,000 communicants).   The Protestant growth experience in the Far West can be brought into sharp focus by comparing the regional growth rate of a particular denomination with the national growth rate of the same denomination for the same period of time. For example, this largest Evangelical Church doubled its national membership between 1960 and 1970 <u>while nearly quadrupling itself</u> in the Far West.   The second largest Evangelical Church in Brazil grew by 466 per cent in the pioneer zones during the 1960's (on a smaller base of 1,500) while its national growth rate was only 151 per cent.   In the Far West this second Church thus tripled <u>its own national growth rate</u>.   In fact, during the last decade <u>every Evangelical Church in the Far West grew faster there than its own national average</u>.   Only one known Evangelical denomination lost members from its national total between 1960 and 1970, and even it grew in the Far West by 31 per cent.

Where is the Church experiencing great growth? Where can mission strategists and church planters be the most faithful stewards of the grace of God?   Where can they spend the resources of planning, effort and finances God has given them, in a way to please Him most?   In Brazil the answer must be: "the Far West region and more specifically the pioneer zones of the state of Mato Grosso."   Those enclaves, receiving numbers of migrants daily and characterized by rapid economic development and social change, are full of multitudes waiting to be and wanting to be churched.   There hangs harvest heavy on the stalk.   Send in the reapers! Garner God's grain in rapidly-growing culturally-relevant churches.

Fighting Fires and Building Houses

Churches ought to evangelize and multiply churches in receptive sections of Society.   They should cease trotting out the same old excuses for <u>diverting</u> mission to social action--"oppression", "ignorance", "poverty", "unequal distribution of wealth", "self-perpetuating illiteracy", and the like.   We should not cease fighting against these evils, of course; but should cease using them to excuse evangelistic laziness, flabby faith, and willful disobedience. Fighting fires will not meet the housing crisis.   <u>That</u> requires the building of new houses. Fighting fires must not be substituted for new construction.   House building resources must not be diverted to fighting fires. Both need to be done. We have plenty of resources to do both.   Resources raised for mission should go for mission.   Those raised for social action should go for social action.

CHURCH GROWTH BULLETIN

from the
INSTITUTE OF CHURCH GROWTH

Address:
FULLER THEOLOGICAL SEMINARY
135 N. Oakland
Pasadena, Calif. 91101

DONALD A. McGAVRAN, B.D., Ph.D.
Director

SEPTEMBER 1972   SUBSCRIPTION $1 PER YEAR   Volume IX, No. 1

The True Goal of Missions

<u>AIDING EMERGING CHURCHES DEVELOP MISSIONARY PASSION</u>   by
Warren W. Webster, General Director
Conservative Baptist Foreign Mission Society

One measure of the ethnocentrism of American evangelicals is the uncritical assumption frequently encountered that the evangelization of the world in this, or any, generation rests primarily on American, or at least Western, shoulders.

It is true that the churches of Europe and North America are responsible before God for the stewardship of their very considerable resources of men and materials. Since World War II some 60% of world Protestant overseas missionary personnel and nearly 80% of the finances have come from North American churches.

Nevertheless, it must be affirmed with the February Theses of 1961 that:
> "It is both physically impossible and demonstrably unscriptural that missionaries from the West are responsible to evangelize all the people of this generation throughout all the world."
> "The evangelization of the world is the task of the whole Church throughout the world. No Church attains fullness and maturity without participating to some degree in the missionary purpose of God."

Even if it were possible for the Christians of one country to evangelize the world, from a biblical perspective it would work an irreparable loss on believers in other lands who are also under the mandate to "Go disciple the nations."

Today there is a growing awareness among American evangelicals at the local church level that in the twentieth century "the Church which is His Body" has at last become a worldwide reality and one of the important corollaries of this is that now the <u>'home base' of missions is everywhere</u> -- wherever the Church is planted.

SEND correspondence, news, and articles to the Editor, Dr. Donald McGavran, at the Institute of Church Growth, Fuller Theological Seminary. Published bi-monthly, send subscriptions and changes of address to the Business Manager, Norman L. Cummings, Overseas Crusades, Inc., 265 Lytton Avenue, Palo Alto, California 94301, U.S.A. Second-class postage paid at Palo Alto, California.

Lesslie Newbigin reminds us that:

> "The thinking of the older Churches about foreign missions
> has always been shaped by the fact that the needs of the
> earth were always 'there,' not here. But from the moment
> that the Church becomes a worldwide fellowship, that point
> of view is invalidated."

This opens up the exciting possibility of Church and mission cooperating in every nation to bring the whole Gospel to the whole world.

We are passing through an era in which many missions have pursued
a pronounced objective of establishing "self-propagating, self-governing
and self-supporting" churches. Peter Wagner in a forthcoming book on
missionary strategy observes that the "three selfs" were useful and necessary concepts when mission societies were trying to shake off an inherited colonial and paternalistic mentality, but the terms have now become senile and need to be replaced by something more contemporary without losing what continues to be valid in the ideas they express.

Henry Lefever also cautions against the use of these terms since
"The New Testament speaks of 'self' only as something to be denied, or
at least something to be discovered only through being set aside and
forgotten."

A Church which is too self-conscious may be also self-centered and
selfish, and not infrequently this has been a failing of so-called 'indigenous' Churches established as a result of this ideology. The Church
was never intended to be self-centered but Christ-centered and with an
outward, rather than inward, orientation to the world for which He died.
In Archbishop Temple's words, "The Church is the only society in the
world which exists for the benefit of those who do not belong to it."

The goal of mission is not simply establishing indigenous churches
in the "Third World" of Africasia but making disciples in the "Fourth
World" which the March 1972 issue of the Church Growth Bulletin
Wagner defines as embracing

> "all those people who, regardless of where they may be located
> geographically, have yet to come to Christ. In that sense the
> Fourth World is the top-priority objective of missions. This
> pushes the statement of the goal of missions one notch further
> than the indigenous church."

Elsewhere he pointedly asserts that "the goal of the Christian
mission is not to establish an 'indigenous Church' ... The true goal of
missions is making disciples. Normally, indigenous national Churches
based on and functioning along New Testament patterns should be the most
effective instruments for implementing The Great Commission. But we all
know of instances where local churches (in America as well as abroad)
are not effective -- and may actually be a hindrance--in discipling the
Fourth World. Where they can be helped to realize and pursue the Church's

primary objective -- fine! But until, and unless, they can be helped they
may simply have to be bypassed in pursuit of our prime objective. The
proper goal of missions is not then simply planting indigenous churches
in the Third World, but missionary churches which move out in responsibility to the Fourth World of lost men.

Henry Lefever writes:
> "A Church which feels that its own responsibility has been
> discharged when the new Church is established as a self-
> governing and wholly or largely self-supporting body, has
> never rightly understood its missionary responsibility."

Wagner tells of a missionary from Cameroon who reported that his
mission was so committed to "indigenous principles" that when they heard
of a new, responsive tribe they refused to evangelize it on the grounds
that this was now the responsibility of the younger Churches. But the
Cameroon Church was not prepared, and the task was not carried out.
Whenever so-called "indigenous principles" interfere with any Church's
primary goal to disciple men and nations they should be rethought or
abandoned.

Simply establishing indigenous churches is no longer seen as an adequate goal of biblical missions unless such churches become "sending"
churches in, and from, their own setting. The New Testament knows nothing of "receiving" churches which are not also in turn to be "sending"
churches. (I Corinthians 15:3, II Timothy 2:2) The early group of believers in Rome was a receiving church only until it could marshall its
resources for sending the good news on to Spain and central Europe. We
in the so-called sending churches of the West need to remember that we
too were once on the receiving end of God's message of reconciliation.

The truth remains that every church in every land ought to be and
remain a sending church. Even in North America, the spiritual vitality
of any fellowship of Christians should be measured not simply by the
number of believers it attracts but by the number of disciples it sends
out empowered for witness and service.

With respect to new churches Peter Beyerhaus advocates something
similar when he says:
> "The ultimate aim of missions is no longer the organizational
> independence of the young Church; it is rather the building up
> of a Church which itself has a missionary out-reach."

If we believe this to be the ultimate expression of the Great Commission, then we must regard "the growing entrance into mission" of
churches on every continent as a cause for profound gratitude and continued encouragement in our day.

If Western nations and institutions are on the decline, God may well
use the Churches of Africasia to bridge the gap as they increasingly
are accepting the missionary responsibility which of necessity lies upon
the Church in every place.

"Foreign Mission Societies Emerging in the Third World Churches" is not altogether a new movement, though it is all too little known to the average Christian in the West. American evangelicals know the exploits of Livingstone and Moffett In opening large areas of Africa to the Gospel but they have seldom heard of the unnamed or little known local African missionaries who were responsible for much of the subsequent Christian advance in those areas.

One of the great accounts in missionary annals is the record of the evangelization of the Pacific Islands through the dedication of island inhabitants who went out under great risk and hardship in their small boats and canoes from Samoa, Fiji and the Solomons to other island territories, until today three-fourths of the inhabitants of the South Pacific islands (apart from New Guinea) are reportedly members of Christian churches. Notable among these islander missionaries who crossed linguistic, cultural and geographic boundaries with the Gospel are the more than a thousand members of the Melanesian Brotherhood who over the years worked so effectively for the Christianization of the islands, yet are all but unknown to most American enthusiasts for missions.

Unfortunately, many indigenous national missionary organizations were more active around the turn of the century than they are today. To what extent does the responsibility for this lie with our generation of mission planners and activists?

<u>What can we do to aid emerging Churches overseas in developing a missions strategy and passion?</u>

1. First, as American evangelicals and evangelical mission societies, we must clarify, sharpen and update our own understanding of the biblical mandate for missions so as to emphasize that the command to "preach the Gospel to every creature" and to "make disciples of all nations" must parallel and even supercede the intermediate goal of planting indigenous churches as a means of discipling the nations.

In this connection I would commend the recent action of the Foreign Missions Department of the Assemblies of God in restating their mission objectives to include the following:

"The Foreign Missions Department is dedicated primarily to the fulfillment of the Great Commission -- 'Go ye into all the world, and preach the gospel to every creature.' (Mark 16:15). Its basic policy is to <u>evangelize</u> the world, <u>establish churches</u> after the New Testament pattern, and to <u>train</u> national believers to preach the Gospel both to their own people and in <u>a continuing mission to other nations.</u>"

This statement of objectives, after affirming the importance of establishing indigenous churches as an instrument of fulfilling the Christian mission to the world, goes on to stress the need for missionary-national

"<u>cooperation and unity</u> in the mutual God-given responsibility <u>for complete world evangelization.</u> In so doing, the missionary must not abdicate his responsibility to world evangelism and church planting, either by perpetuating the mission's authority over the national church or by succumbing to nationalistic interests that would prevent him from fulfilling the Great Commission."

2. Secondly, it is imperative that we communicate the missionary mandate by precept and example from the inception of all evangelistic and church planting ministries.

A Chinese youth leader at the Singapore Congress on Evangelism commented that while he knows his missionary friends preach the missionary imperative on furlough in their homelands he had never heard one preach a sermon on missions to the new churches they had helped bring into being in Asia. He went on to observe the same failure in most seminaries and Bible schools of his acquaintance which, he said, had no courses on missions in their curriculum. It is little wonder if pastors trained there have no informed and compelling sense of missionary involvement and outreach to communicate to their congregations.

Missionaries responsible for pastoral and lay training must be prepared to imbue new leaders with the principles and practice of multiplying disciples and churches, both in their immediate environment and across adjacent cultural and geographical boundaries.

3. Let new Christians everywhere be prepared for immediate involvement in the evangelism of their own cultural "Jerusalem" (sometimes called M_1), with the needs of their respective "Judea and Samaria" (i.e., communication at a slight cultural or geographical distance, M_2) regularly set before them, so that some of those proved and approved of God through faithfulness in nearby witness may in time be entrusted with even more difficult missions to totally different peoples (the M_3 dimension at "the ends of the earth") as men and means become available.

4. Rather than simply internationalize existing mission organizations let us encourage new church fellowships to develop their own patterns and forms of missionary expression.

We should be ready to share with them the best of what we have learned in a century and a half of the modern missionary movement, but then give these maturing churches full liberty under the Holy Spirit to determine what they will adopt and continue as applicable to their situation and what they will modify or leave behind as relics of another day.

5. Finally, while seeking to manifest the unity of the Spirit through fellowship among like-minded participants in a world mission which transcends all boundaries of color and culture let us not involve others in over-organization, nor embarrass them by insisting on ties which might compromise their effectiveness.

Above all, within the missionary movement of Third World Churches we must respect the same principles of spiritual voluntarism which brought most of our missionary societies into being. Spontaneous response to the Spirit's leading and voluntary participation by believers passionately devoted to making Christ known may well produce a greater tide of missionary advance in the Third World than history has seen to date.

Then in a spirit of true partnership -- not paternalism -- we may
say with Chrysostom of old that we have
> A whole Christ for our Salvation
> A whole Bible for our Staff
> A whole Church for our Fellowship
> A whole World for our Parish.

MODERN THINKING ON URBAN CHURCH GROWTH

MULTIPLYING CHURCHES IN HI-RISE APARTMENTS ** by James Wong, Anglican
B.D., M.A. Missiology

"Churches in Singapore must plan for a rapid multiplication of their
congregations in the new low-cost housing estates...

Only the Church which seeks to multiply new congregations in public
and private housing estates has a future in the Singapore of tomorrow...

The goal should be to establish one active and evangelically minded
Christian Center, either in the apartment of a dedicated Christian
family, or in a rented shop in every hi-rise apartment...

Up to now church growth in Singapore has been slow because most
churches have thought in terms of traditional church buildings. If this
thinking continues, it will curtail church growth. The scarcity of
available sites for religious purpose and the high cost of land will sev-
erely limit the number of "church-buildings-on-their-own-land" which can
be erected in the housing estates. Hence there is little alternative
but for the Churches (denominations) to create a new pattern of church
extension - the rapid formation of cells, house churches, and Christian
community centers strategically located in all new housing estates...

Most non-Christians - looking at existing churches - believe they
are for the middle class, the affluent, and the educated. They arrive
at the conclusion that Christianity is not for the masses - the working
class poor, the illiterates, and the common man. Thus the establishment
of apartment house churches, in which ordinary people of similar socio-
economic background are found to be attending, can help correct the wrong
image of Christianity. Those who come to these smaller, home-like centers will experience an atmosphere of informality and friendliness.
They minister to urban man's need and his longing for community...

A Christian congregation in every block of hi-rise apartment throughout Singapore! A realizable target. Such churches would be accessible
to all in the community. Their doors would be opened to anyone who
wishes to use the facility for meetings, community projects, study,
reading and recreation. When these house-churches at the store front
level have a multi-purpose use and are flexible in their program structure, they can serve as strategic contact points for Christian witness..."

((The foregoing are excerpts from Chapter IX of a coming book by

The Rev. James Wong of Singapore. What he says applies to many modern
cities. He is talking about a common opportunity in the coming great
expansion of the Church.))

EDITORS OF MISSION MAGAZINES, BEWARE!
(a frank commercial)

You are a numerous tribe. Your magazines, all told,
are read by millions and are influential and interesting. I know. I read them. But do you see your
segment of missions in the light of the vast whole?
Are you aware of what God is doing around the world
today? Of the forces arrayed against missions within the Churches? Do you help your readers escape
today's vast pessimism? Does your magazine make men
effective communicators of the Good News and multipliers of churches?

You might find advanced study in great commission
missions rewarding. A rich treat awaits you in
reading a hundred books on the glory and glamour,
the problems and solutions, theological bedrock
and modern deviations, culture and Christianity,
the growth histories of typical younger Churches in
Asia, Africa and Latin America, and in short, on
the whole fascinating movement of God's Spirit
which is missions today. Learn from career missionaries who have twenty years experience in the
front lines and are now teaching missions. Spend
months working on the one problem in mission which
seems most important to you. Take some courses on
journalism in UCLA or USC. Earn a graduate degree
in missions.

If this appeals to you, write Dean Glasser at the
School of Missions, Fuller Theological Seminary,
135 North Oakland Avenue, Pasadena, Calif. 91101,
for the catalog of The School of World Mission.
                                    Donald McGavran

CHURCH GROWTH NEWS: A VERY SMALL PART OF IT

DISCIPLING THE ARMY IN KOREA

On the 25th of April at 2 P.M., epochal baptisms occurred on the drill
grounds of the 1997 Unit of the Korean Army, near the western front
lines.

Eighty-eight officers and 3,390 GI's were baptized, a total of 3,478

men. The greatest number baptized in Christian history is 3,000 by Peter,
the apostle, on the day of Pentecost. These mammoth baptisms are the
results of the All Army Christianization Movement. Colonel Jun-Sup Han,
Chief of the Republic's Chaplaincy Corps, spearheaded the movement in
1969 as ideological rearmament to resist communism. General Han Sin,
then the commander in Chief of the R.O.K.s first corps, donated sixty
motorcycles to the chaplains to encourage them. Chaplains visited every
Unit of the Army, presenting the Gospel and winning souls.

The movement began to bear fruit from November 1971. The numbers of
converts prior to the 25th of April were as follows: 1,460 in the
51101th Unit, 1,005 in the 9011th Unit, 1,000 in one other and 500 apiece
in several other divisions.

More than 1,000 well-wishers and guests, including Dr. Kyung Jik Han
(Pastor of the Yung Nak Presbyterian Church), Dr. Ogkil Kim (President of
the Iwha Women's University), Dr. Dae Sun Park and Dr. Nak Jun Paik
(President and President Emeritus of the Yon Sei University) and others
congratulated the new Christians.
    ((The above appeared in Hankook Iibu, a Korean Newspaper, on April
       26, 1972. Chae Eun Soo, SWM ICG 1972))

NEW PRESBYTERY in Colombia

On May 5th, 1972 - three years ahead of schedule - a new presbytery was
organized in Northwest Colombia, South America. It isn't very big yet.
Just three ministers (two of them recently ordained) and about 50 small
congregations. But four years ago there were only 17 even smaller and
very discouraged congregations. At that time the Synod of Colombia,
made up largely of urban churches, made a thorough study of the needs of
the rural northwest. They came up with an eight year plan with multi-
pronged emphasis on church development, economic development, education,
and health services. From the beginning, the believers were told that
all outside help would terminate at the end of the eight years.

All four phases of the project have prospered but evangelism and church
multiplication has been the most successful, thanks in part to the influence of a nearby lay-led movement which is loosely related to the
Latin America Mission.

This year the emphasis is on evangelism workshops. The first one, early
in March, produced such a burst of enthusiasm that four new congregations
have already resulted and 100 are awaiting baptism. Seven similar workshops are planned.   (UPDATE June 1972)

REGAINED MOMENTUM IN TAIWAN

"We are seeing three new churches planted - one in Taipei and two in thee
Kaohsiung area. We are also starting a Hakka church in Neipu which will,
in addition, serve one other Hakka church and two home meetings which
may grow into churches... The November 1971 Church Growth Seminar in
Taichung was very helpful. Our National Chairman of Evangelism, Chu

Chin-Liang received new life and vision and has been sharing it with other pastors ... I have requested the seminary to allow me to teach a course on Church Growth."

> May 1972, Dorothy Raber, Free Methodist Mission, SWM ICG 1971

NIGERIAN PEOPLE MOVEMENTS TO CHRIST

"The Sudan Interior Mission reports a phenomenal response to the Gospel in Nigeria...entire communities are turning to Christ...In a week long school of evangelism in Keffi, sponsored by New Life For All, students led 599 persons to Christ. Graduates of crash courses for laymen are instructing new converts." (Missionary News Service, May 15, 1972:5)

CENTER OF ADVANCED STUDY FOR EVANGELISM (CASE)

Overseas Crusades is a society sending about a hundred missionaries to ten countries in Latin America and Asia to help existing Churches and Missions proclaim the Gospel and multiply churches.

Overseas Crusades has just started in Sao Paulo, Brazil a Center For Advanced Study of Evangelism, to be headed up by Harmon Johnson, one of the authors of the monumental volume Latin American Church Growth, a veteran missionary to Brazil, and a graduate of the School of Missions at Fuller Seminary.

CASE focuses on research and teaching which will "mobilize the Church for Evangelism."

IN INDONESIA

The Protestant community has doubled in the past five years, and now totals about six million.

IN NAGALAND, EAST INDIA

One hundred years of missionary labor (1872-1972) has seen more than 600 congregations come into being. The Christian community now numbers more than 250,000 souls. Since Nagaland is a separate province in India, most officials - judges, administrators, government leaders, and the like - are Christians.

IN KOREA

The Church is growing at the rate of 10% a year, while the population grows at 2.3%. In 1940 there were 372,000 Christians, and in 1971, 2,250,000.

IN KALIMANTAN (FORMERLY BORNEO)

In this, the world's third largest island, according to Bill Kerr, Alliance Executive, people movements are taking place rivalling the great movements of the thirties. Missionary Aviation Fellowship air craft are playing an important role.

IN CAMBODIA

In this highly resistant field, plain evangelistic preaching by World
Vision's Stanley Mooneyham, early this summer, met tremendous response.
Membership of the one small existing church doubled. Hundreds acclaimed
Jesus Christ as Saviour and Lord.

IN BIAFRA

Especially in the eastern section of Biafra where the Ibibios live, during
1952-1972 God has granted tremendous church growth. The two old Presbyterian denominations have grown some, Lutherans have grown from zero to
30,000, the Churches of Christ from zero to 60,000, and the independent
African Churches from a few thousand to over a hundred thousand. The
fascinating story has been told by Prof. Wendell Broom of Abilene Christian College in his M.A. thesis done at SWM ICG. For a Xeroxed copy of
this ($4.00) write him at Box 8040, Abilene, Texas 79601.

VIETNAM

Tribal ministers are preaching with awesome authority, Christians are
praying with deep earnestness, tears and confession, and over 10,000
tribesmen have turned to God in the last six months. (June 1972 Cable)

REVIVAL AND RENEWAL

REVIVAL AND CHURCH GROWTH IN HONDURAS by Josephine Still, Calif. Friends

I have just returned from the pre-Easter Conference at San Marcos. I
know now what a Spirit-filled revival which issues in church growth is.
But let me back up and tell the story.

1.   The Lord has been preparing His people for months. It began when
some of us got church growth eyes and were told "This vision must become
the vision of your national leaders or you will never get anywhere."
Well, we have conducted short courses, pastors retreats, classes and conferences. There are enough church growth books in Spanish so that our
people read about it in many contexts. It thrills me to hear our Superintendent and others quoting the principles of church growth. All this
came to a head in the Pastors Retreat of February 1972, where we talked
much about church growth and set out goals for the next ten years. With
these goals in the open, we began thinking about the power we would need
to fulfill them. Then, on the last day God spoke to each of us about
the hindrances in our own lives. Resentment, hurt feelings and differences were confessed and hearts melted together. Revival started and
conviction grew that the goals we set would prove too small for what God
was going to do. Our goals were these:

    1. Plant thirty-five new churches in the next years - two new
        churches for every church existing today.

2. Establish churches in Tegucigalpa, San Pedro Sula and Santa Rosa. Prayer cells already meet in these cities.
3. Prepare pastors and leaders for all the 35 to-be-born churches.
4. Start radio evangelism over the Evangelical station in Teguciagalpa.
5. Train leaders in short courses in Peniel.
6. Educate pastors by extension - special correspondence and supervision.
7. Carry on more courses in the churches to teach adults to read.

II.   In late March we gathered at San Marcos. The Conference glowed with a sense of expectation. There was a unity and sweetness of spirit and a light in every eye. Virginia Miller had translated the first chapter of Charles Finney's book on Revivals. Some of the leaders said, "This is what we need for all of our churches." So she prepared copies of it. We met at 8:30 each morning to study it together. There was no leader. First one and then another would read and, if a thought was not clear, stop for explanations. Finney explains what a revival is, what it does for you, when you can expect a revival and how to prepare one's heart for such a visitation.

When we got down to negligence, coldness in prayer, unbelief, lack of real love and burden for our own families, don Filiberto, the San Marcos pastor, confessed that the Lord had shown him that he had not really loved his boys. He had fussed at them, preached at them and prayed, "Lord, why don't my boys want to follow Thee?" He said, "I have had an even shorter supply of love for other wayward young people and have only said 'why don't they lower their skirts' instead of seeing in them souls that Jesus loves." He wept with a broken heart and everyone in the room joined in praying and confessing before God our faults and coldness.

The Superintendent of the Yearly Meeting also said he had a need. Only a week before he had been to see two pastors with whom he had had discord and bitterness for more than a year. He asked prayer for his own spirit and the work for the Lord.

One of the younger pastors told about being corrected by the Superintendent. He had been angry about it and said he was going to have nothing more to do with him; but God had humbled him and he asked don Ruben's pardon. They wept on each other's shoulder as don Ruben said, "This boy is my son in the faith and I want his ministry to prosper."

Josue, our pastor in Ocotepeque, came to me where I was praying, put his arm around my neck and said, "Miss Josefina, I have taken some money from you and I want to pay it back." As a little boy in school he took some change out of my desk drawer. God kept reminding him of that and he wanted to make it right.

Praying, confessing and weeping on each other's shoulders as old grudges were washed away filled the morning. We didn't even get to the morning meeting at the church but there was blessing there too. In the Young People's group about 20 were seeking the Lord.

The next morning we read about the price it takes for a revival. And again the children of the pastors, and others too, were our burden. Most parents felt defeated, pushed against a wall and desperate. Sara Wade quoted the promise, "Cast thy burden on the Lord for He careth for you." Another urged the whole group to join in believing prayer that God would answer. There is tremendous power in united faith. Virginia said, "Let's not expect God to save them sometime, but today." Again there was a mighty outpouring of prayer and expectation.

The evening service was powerful. It was the closing night, Good Friday, and Orvil Link preached on the Crucifixion. Many were seeking at the altar and God met them.

Then the meeting was over. It was late. People had things to pack. Some were to leave at 4 A.M. There were books to distribute, accounts to settle, good-byes to be said and folks were scattered.

But the Holy Spirit was not through. Sara Wade saw a boy sitting dejected on a bench and said, "Come on, Nehemias, it isn't too late." He got up and followed her to the altar. Pastor Don Chepe, the father, was at the door and did not realize what was going on. When I saw him step out into the street I went after him and told him. He rushed to where his boy was praying and everyone joined with them. At one end of the altar was Ariel, another preacher's son, and his father was not there. I went to hunt him and found him packing books for his church. When I told him that Ariel was at the altar he started running. We went back to rejoice with them. I sat down beside one of don Filiberto's boys sitting halfway back in the church. "Eri, don't you want to pray too?" I asked him. "I have been praying out there," he said, pointing to the patio. "Then come on, God has something for you." He went right down to the altar. You can imagine how don Fili felt, and the evangelists and missionaries, and workers who had shared this burden.

The first boy, Nehemias, got through and went to bring others. Young people were seeking God all over the place. Antonio and Hilda had gone to bed. I went to the house and called them, saying, "This is too good to miss. Come, see what God is doing." They both received the outpouring of the Holy Spirit in their own hearts.

And on and on. There wasn't a single one of the preachers' children present at the conference who wasn't saved that night, and many, many · more. We were still there at 2 A.M. and nobody was sleepy and nobody was tired. No one had charge, there was no pressure, only a relaxed, expectant faith. Some would be seeking at the altar, others testifying and others making things right with their companions. Tears flowed - of repentance, victory and blessing.

III.   The thing that is different about this revival is that each has returned to his church confident that this is only the beginning of new life in our midst. We have a plan for church multiplication born of revival. The leaders revived will be carrying out the seven specific goals they worked out. The Holy Spirit will show them other means of expansion, too.

Understanding Church Growth says:
> "Revivals...have more chance of issuing in reproductive conversions outside existing churches if -
> a) churchmen know which are the receptive units in their general population; which congregations are growing and why...
> b) churchmen carry out a consistent program, singleminded to church growth...

c) churches and missions form their policies in the light of what-
    ever means the Holy Spirit has already used to multiply churches
    in their populations...
Revivals issue in great church growth when revival plus knowledge of
how churches grow is counted of great importance. Christians should
learn all God has to teach us about church growth and pray without
ceasing for revival." (p. 179-180)

I was not surprised to learn that on Easter Sunday one church spent the
whole afternoon making plans to reach outlying areas responsive to the
Gospel where we expect God to raise up new congregations very soon.

??? SALVATION TODAY ???   by Donald McGavran

The Central Committee of the World Council of Churches has issued a
call for a world-wide conference on the theme, Salvation Today. The
gathering will be held in Bangkok from December 29th to January 21st,
1973. It will be an expensive meeting, drawing in men and women from all
over the world to consider one crucial question:

What is the salvation which Jesus Christ offers men today?

It is highly significant that, while the mission aim of the World
Council of Churches, and indeed of all Churches of Christ, is "to further the proclamation of the Gospel to all men that they may believe and
be saved," all the advance publications concerning this meeting indicate
that the World Council is making a massive effort to reinterpret the
classic meaning of that aim so that 'being saved' will come to mean having more food, more justice, more clothes, more freedom, more production,
less disease, more brotherhood, more peace, in short, more this-worldly
improvements.

A United Methodist minister writing me under date of June 28th, 1972,
puts the issue succinctly:

My friends on the left are always saying to me that we Evangelicals
should remember that it is both personal salvation and social action.
But when I go to Methodist Convocations and read materials from our
Board of Missions, I want to stand up and say, "Brethren, please
remember it is both social concern and personal salvation." My
brethren to the left so infrequently remember the advice they are
so free to give me.

Precisely this issue will underlie the Bangkok Gathering. Advance
W.C.C. materials insist (on Old Testament grounds) that "salvation" has
primarily to do with the current life of flesh and blood, hunger and
satiation, manufacturing and distributing, freedom and wholeness in this
world.

We hope and pray that as the meeting takes place, better counsels
will prevail. We trust that delegates will insist that the Old Testament passages must not be taken by themselves. They alone do not represent the whole biblical revelation. They must be understood also in
the light of the unity of the Bible and seen also in the light of the
New Testament revelation.

The magnitude of the truncated, sub-biblical deviation being proposed is seen in the fact that all Branches of the Christian Church in
all ages have held and all Christians have believed that salvation in the
Christian sense means primarily the salvation of the soul which results
in abundant life in the body. Such eternal salvation is the most effective agent of temporal peace and righteousness. The possession of this
salvation enables the saved to enter into the cultural task to which God
calls His people.

The Old Testament is one long recital of all kinds of temporal improvements which God gave His people in the course of disclosing Himself
to them as their Redeemer. It says, "God saved His people in these ways,
binding them in covenant to be His people and abide in His laws." However, all such improvements (destruction of enemies, abundance of food,
riches, status, multitudes of children, houses and vineyards, horses and
chariots) turned out to be temporary palliatives. God took the Hebrews
- strictly bound to worship Him only - to a land flowing with milk and
honey, and lo, within a short time they were disobeying Him, worshipping
the baals and asherah, committing adulteries under every green tree, and
grinding the faces of the poor!! He forgave them and gave them David's
Kingdom. Within one generation, kings, priests, and people had with
enthusiasm abandoned the religion of Yahweh for that of the prestigious
gods of the land. During all these centuries it became clear that until
the heart of man is changed, until he is saved through faith in Jesus
Christ and becomes a new creature, until he is firmly joined to the Body
and continues in the means of grace, no amount of milk and honey (more
to eat and wear, better houses, more justice, more peace, greater individual and national income) is of lasting value.

The issue at Bangkok is clear: does the word salvation, according
to the Bible, mean eternal salvation or does it mean this-worldly improvements? Which is the basic meaning? It appears as if the conciliar
forces are set to maintain, on the basis of the Old Testament, that salvation means primarily if not exclusively this-worldly improvements.
Evangelicals will maintain, on the basis of the total biblical record
(the New Testament as well as the Old) that 'salvation' means a change
in status of the soul, the essential person, is achieved through faith
in Jesus Christ alone, and results in abundant life in this world.

"Once you were no people, but now you are God's people." (I Pet. 2:10)
"If you confess with your lips that Jesus is Lord and believe in your
heart that God raised Him from the dead, you will be saved."
(Romans 10:9)
"There is salvation in no one else, for there is no other name under
heaven given among men by which we must be saved." (Acts 4:12)

Let us note what the debate is not about, i.e. what is agreed on.
Both conciliar and non-conciliar Christians agree that temporal improvements in man's lot (both individual and social) are desirable. On biblical grounds both agree that Christians should do good to all men, that
the hungry should be fed, the naked should be clothed, those in prison
should be visited, justice should roll down like waters, and righteousness as a mighty stream. Agreed. Furthermore, it is agreed that a considerable part of the Church's treasure should be spent to achieve these
good temporal ends. Missions in the past hundred years have spent from
a half to nine-tenths of their men and money for education, medicine,
agricultural improvement, and the like. The proportion of the whole
budget spent for these things is always a matter for debate, but that a
substantial amount be so spent is seldom questioned. No one is advocating that since God grants salvation to those who believe on Christ and
are incorporated in His Church, nothing further is required. On the
contrary, Christians continually insist that the saved while they are
in this world, must and will live in forgiveness and love and press on
toward righteousness and justice. Disagreement does not lie on these
points.

Disagreement lies in whether temporal improvements are salvation or
a fruit of the saved life. The distinction is vitally important. Bangkok will not be splitting hairs. If 'salvation today' means political
liberation, land distribution, better pay for factory workers, the downfall of oppressive systems of government, and the like, then the whole
apparatus of missions is rightfully used to achieve these ends. Evangelism will be downgraded. Churching the unchurched will be neglected and
ridiculed. The airplane of missions will be diverted away from the propagation of the Gospel to the establishment of utopias.

Indeed, these emphases have been occurring during the last fifteen
years "Salvation" is the fourth word which the World Council of Churches
is reinterpreting. All are being devalued in the same direction. Their
eternal significance is being minimized and their temporal meanings
underlined.

a) "Mission" ceases to be the propagation of the Gospel and becomes
everything God wants done by Christians or non-Christians - which
necessarily limits what God wants done to the field of ethics.

b) "Evangelism" ceases to be proclaiming Jesus Christ by word and
deed and persuading men to become His disciples and responsible
members of His Church and becomes changing the structures of society
in the direction of justice, righteousness and peace.

c) "Conversion" ceases to be turning from idols to serve the God and
Father of our Lord Jesus Christ, as revealed in the Bible, and becomes turning corporately from faulty social configurations to those
which liberate men and incorporate them in the great brotherhood.

d) "Salvation" is apparently going to be put through the same rolling
mill and brought out flattened and focused on temporal improvements.

(One kind friend urged me to concede that my bifocals - without which I cannot read or write - are an important part of my <u>salvation</u>!)

Evangelicals should work and pray that this deliberate debasing of Christian currency cease and that the reformation of the social order <u>(rightly emphasized) should not be substituted for salvation</u>. Salvation is something which the true and living God confers on His creatures in accordance with His once-for-all revelation in Jesus Christ, God and Saviour according to the Bible. Salvation is a vertical relationship (of man with God) which issues in horizontal relationships (of man with men). The vertical must not be displaced by the horizontal.

Desirable as social ameliorations are, working for them must not be substituted for the biblical requirements of/for 'salvation'. Those requirements are clear: The New Testament states them again and again. Paul voiced them in their simplest form to the Philippian jailer: "Believe in the Lord Jesus, and you will be saved, you and your household." (Acts 16:31)

Church Growth Bulletin hopes that three agreements will come out of Bangkok and urges readers to work and pray that such may eventuate. Let us all agree -

1.   That beyond question the Bible teaches that God's people ought continually and creatively to work for a just, brotherly, righteous and peaceful order in their families, neighborhoods, states, world.

2.   That beyond question the Bible teaches that to become God's people it is necessary for all men (descendents of Christians and non-Christians alike) to believe on Jesus Christ as Lord and Saviour, receive Him in their hearts, become responsible members of His Church, and manifest the fruits of the Spirit in their lives.   And that this alone may rightly be called 'salvation today'.

3.   That, in consequence, it is desirable for the Church to press forward with classic Christian mission (proclaiming Christ by word and deed and persuading men to become His disciples and responsible members of His Church) on the one hand, and with a program of social action and humanitarian concern on the other.   Christians should be entirely free to support each program according to their conscience.   It is unacceptable for leaders of missionary societies to determine to what kind of missions they will devote the givings of the devout.   Donors themselves must decide whether they wish to carry on 'making disciples' or 'reforming society'.

CHURCH GROWTH
B U L L E T I N

from the
INSTITUTE OF
CHURCH GROWTH

Address:
FULLER THEOLOGICAL
SEMINARY
135 N. Oakland
Pasadena, Calif. 91101

DONALD A. McGAVRAN, B.D., Ph.D.
Director

November 1972   Subscription $1 per year   Volume IX No. 2

Contents

Theology of Missions

"SHAKEN FOUNDATIONS" AND CHURCH GROWTH   Dr. Peter Beyerhaus

((Only once in the last ten years has Church Growth Bulletin given the lead article to a book. We do it again in this issue because SHAKEN FOUNDATION has profound meaning for church growth. Church Growth is not primarily a matter of statistics, methods, or church or mission policies; but rather of deep convictions. It becomes possible only when Christians who know Christ go out driven by belief in the unshakeable authority of the Bible.

        Forty years ago, William Hocking proposed that missions consider the era of church planting finished and that of the reconception of religions (each reconceiving itself in the light of the others) begun. The entire leadership of Church and mission - on biblical grounds - rejected his recommendation. But today a most influential section of the world mission enterprise has joined a camp in which Hocking would have rejoiced. It either denigrates conversion evangelism and great commission or redefines them to mean ethical improvement, humane relationships, or national development. Official documents do not rule out evangelism, but steadily neglect it. Left wing documents go much farther and openly declare that winning men to Christ is no longer necessary. What is now needed, they say, is joint action by men of every religion to make the world a better place in which to live.

SEND correspondence, news, and articles to the Editor, Dr. Donald McGavran, at the Institute of Church Growth, Fuller Theological Seminary. Published bi-monthly, send subscriptions and changes of address to the Business Manager, Norman L. Cummings, Overseas Crusades, Inc., 265 Lytton Avenue, Palo Alto, California 94301, U.S.A. Second-class postage paid at Palo Alto, California.

The size of the shift in conviction and the degree to which
the 'true believers' of the new mode of 'mission' have captured some
missionary societies and organs of communication is amazing. Most ministers, missionaries, and mission-minded laymen cannot believe that such
a basic and drastic change in theological conviction could occur.

SHAKEN FOUNDATIONS, the brilliant book by Dr. Peter Beyerhaus
of Tubingen University, shows what has been going on in Germany behind
the scenes in the upper echelons of many Churches and missionary societies. Chapter after chapter, he uncovers the way in which during the
post war years a non-biblical form of Christianity took over. Having
captured the seats of power in the Church, this new form of Christianity
manufactured a new theory and theology of mission. It took the great
words in mission and redefined them. It took the great goals in mission,
such as the evangelization of the world, and substituted for them humanistic ends. It turned from reconciling men to God-in-Christ and turned
toward reconciling men to men. The new styles in mission were popularized by missionary magazines in Germany and by floods of materials and
posters issuing from church and mission headquarters. Some missionary
societies recalled their 'evangelistically minded missionaries', alleg-
ing lack of funds or other secondary cause.

Dr. David Hubbard, whose radio voice over "The Joyful Sound"
reaches millions each week, and who is president of Fuller Theological
Seminary, in the Foreword "commends the book to a believing Church in
America and beyond". He says that though Beyerhaus' "illustrations are
largely German, they will not be lost on us Americans. The same trends
are present with us, if only because theology in America has been so dependent on Germany." This story of shaken foundations in Germany can be
read with profit in all six continents. No city is so advanced, no
forest fastness so remote that it is untouched by the wave of humanistic
thinking which has washed over the post-war years and is only now - possibly - beginning to recede. This book about Germany will reveal to
Christians all over the world much about mission situations in their own
countries.

During the past ten years large numbers of able leaders of Third
World Churches have been brought to Germany (and the United States) and
trained in the new view in mission, the new 'theology', and its alleged
'biblical foundations'. The Ecumenical Institute of Chicago (heavily
supported by liberal Christians in certain American denominations) has
established mission stations (it calls them 'houses') in key centers of
Asia and Africa to popularize among ordained ministers there the heret-
ical ideas which form the essence of 'the new look in missions'.

All this has had a tremendous effect on church growth. In many
lands some missionaries and some leaders of younger Churches have ceased
to proclaim Christ with intent to persuade men to become His disciples
and responsible members of His Church. These churchmen confine themselves to looking after their congregations and various good works. In
the presence of vast numbers of men hungrily searching for the Bread of
Life, their denominations are static, or grow in slow and hesitant fashion.

The following excerpts from Dr. Beyerhaus' book will, we hope, whet the appetite of our ten thousand readers. Write to the Church Growth Book Club at once and order SHAKEN FOUNDATIONS. Prof. Peter Wagner has done a superb job of preparing the volume for the English reading public. This small beautifully printed book costs only $1.17, plus postage. When you read it, you will want to send copies to the leaders of your Church overseas. Maybe some of you will order several copies at once, sight unseen, and send them to English speaking ministers of your national Church. More than the missionaries, key nationals need to know the shift in theological opinion which has been occurring. Once they know the issues, they will reject the deviations, for the Churches in Asia, Africa and Latin America are basically Bible believing. But they must know. They need the book. They will probably insist that it be translated into their languages.

With this by way of introduction, we quote five of the many good passages in SHAKEN FOUNDATIONS.   Donald McGavran))

. . . .

1.   "In his annual report to the General Assembly of the Evangelical (i.e., Protestant) Church in Germany in January, 1971, the presiding bishop, Herman Dietzfelbinger, shocked delegates with the following statement:

> If I am not totally deceived, we are right in the middle of a
> struggle for the faith, of a Kirkenkampf compared to which the
> Kirkenkampf under the Nazis was only a skirmish. The frighten-
> ing aspects of it are that hardly anyone is aware of it, that
> it is generally played down, and that it is making headway
> under misleading terms like "pluralism!".....

The declaration caused a commotion in churches all over Germany. It was welcomed by the "confessing" groups, which had been trying to say the same thing for the last five years. Others rejected it entirely or played it down as an over-statement. They claimed that the conflict was a matter of semantics rather than of faith. Germany's leading Prot-estant journal, Evangelishche Kommentare, for example, commented editor-ially on Dietzfelbinger's statement under the title "False Alarm".

This theological conflict in Germany is serious enough to attract the attention of fellow Christians in other countries. Although it concerns theological trends in general, the reader will see immedi-ately that it goes directly to the heart of vital missiological concern. In this chapter, I shall attempt to give a clear outline of the situa-tion. I make no pretense of doing so from a neutral position. In spiritual matters, neutrality is always illegitimate. I speak as a rep-resentative of those who have taken a definite stand for biblical Chris-tianity." (p. 19, 20).

. . . .

2.   "The malady which many of our major missions have never dared
to examine closely is the insidious paralysis of biblical convictions of
prominent churchmen. Critical methods of exegetical research have under-
mined the authority of Scripture. Demythologization and existential interpretation have dissolved the concept of Christ's expiatory sacrifice
and the reality of His future kingdom still to be established in power
by His second coming. Situationalist views of biblical ethics reduce its
texts to the level of antiquated answers to antiquated socio-political
problems. What remain are some vague principles, like responsibility,
solidarity, and openness for the future, completely abstracted from the
specific history of revelation and salvation in which they occur.

        Even Jesus becomes only the prototype of an ideal social atti-
tude, the "man for others." His resurrection and lordship mean scarcely
more than that the community of His followers may still be inspired by
His example. Christological affirmations are thus abstracted from the
living person of Christ and interpreted as reflections of the Church
about her own mission. The conclusion drawn by some members of a missiological seminar under the guidance of a well-known ecumenical theologian sounds like this:

        The traditional statements about the Return of Christ, that
        God be all in all, and the like, aim functionally at man's be-
        coming man, a goal to which Christ is calling and paving the way,
        but which it is not given for man to reach on his own.

        By such theological methods biblical prophecies are deprived of
their realistic content. While their form and their original content
may not be directly negated, a process of philosophical or sociological
abstraction transforms them into anthropocentric statements which in
spirit and wording appear merely to be reflections of a current humanistic ideology.

        This general theological situation views the primacy of verbal
witness in Christian mission with increasing scepticism.

        We now encounter the strange concept that the socially desirable
consequences of the Gospel would still allow us to call our task "mission"
even if we deliberately abstain from calling upon people to believe in
Christ and to be baptized in His name. To quote the findings of the
above-mentioned study group once again:

        "...it cannot be regarded as the goal of Christian mission to
        'make' non-Christians Christian, to 'convert' them, or to 'win'
        them. To practice the function of the Christian faith - in a
        theoretically responsible way - is the only method of spreading
        it...to communicate Christian ideas (e.g. of 'God', 'sin') and
        practices (e.g. prayer, worship, baptism, eucharist), without
        being asked, to non-Christians and children, is an obstacle to
        mission. (The Christian education of children is always au-
        thoritarian. To abandon it would be a sign of shalom.)" 10

The argument for "mission without proclamation" is that any form of humanization stresses the authority of Christ. Even if this is not done expressly, a humanizing process such as breaking down the barriers of caste in Indian school classes can go on only by the power of the risen Christ, who is understood to be the anonymously directing power of world history. Thus it does not matter which group actually brings about the desirable social change, be they Christians, Marxists, Humanists, or Neo-Hindus. World history is understood as the result of God's mission, and in the transformation of the social structures we are said to realize the features of the coming Kingdom of God. The conclusion follows easily: any actual engagement as such is already mission, meaning the participation in the Missio Dei in world history.

What we observe here is a most dangerous shortcut in theological reasoning. Theology of mission is no longer clearly focused on two indispensable biblical data: the crucifixion and the second coming of Christ. The dialectical tension between world history and salvation history, expressed by these two events, is overlooked. Church and mission are reduced to the dimension of the world. In such a concept the eschatological Kingdom of Christ is swallowed up by the imminent achievements of historical evolution. Even if such evolution is ascribed to the work of the anonymous Christ, we are nearer to the monistic philosophy of history of Hegel and Karl Marx than to the prophecies of the Bible...

Should we not admit that some secular liberation movements seem to be more genuine fruits of Christian mission than many sterile younger churches? Should we not even support the revolutionary movements as our missionary partners in the struggle for justice in the world?....

What hinders us from recognizing such unexpected results as legitimate fruits of mission? Why can we not really rejoice at this transformation of history which may exceed by far the social results of missions? The reason is that the ultimate aim of these movements is a perfect society in which there is neither demand nor room for salvation. Humanization has superseded evangelization. Man places himself in the center. He declares himself to be the measuring rod of all things and creates for himself a paradise without God. He is not in need of any God since he is replacing God. This "theology of the serpent" is, according to Ernest Bloch, the secret atheistic theme of the Bible. "Ye shall be like God" pits the emancipation of man against the concept of a sovereign God...

Being aware of this inherent atheistic thread running through the history of humanism, we are shocked to see how naively current ecumenical missiology can take up the concept of humanization and put it one-sidedly into the center of its motivation and goal. True enough, the New Testament does describe Jesus as the New Man and the beginner of a new humanity. But this is only complementary to the more basic concept that in Jesus Christ we meet the pre-existent Son of God, who wrought our salvation and who is risen to receive our worship and obedience. Separating these two concepts and allowing His human nature to dominate the foreground always runs the risk of perverting the Christian faith into a humanistic syncretism. It tends to remove the ontological diastasis between biblical faith and non-Christian religions and ideologies. We are exhorted along with the adherents of other "living faiths" to discover the manhood of man." (p. 56, 57-59)

. . . .

3.   "In the theology of secularization which has become the dominant school of thought in the ecumenical movement, we find that the horizontal dimension of the Christian faith almost completely overshadows the vertical. Current statements of this theology, even in spite of their use of traditional theological vocabulary, are talking about man, and only about man and his possibilities. This theology seeks God everywhere: in the existential questions of modern man, in social change, in non-violent as well as in bloody revolutions. But it does not seek Him where he wants to be found: first, in His word which becomes flesh in Jesus Christ, and secondly in His congregations of saints, gathered around the biblical preaching and the Lord's table. Even statements referring to the death, resurrection and second coming of Jesus Christ are not primarily concerned with Christ. They use these emotion-laden words and phrases as symbols to describe the way in which the Church should become involved in society.

        The authors of the Frankfurt Declaration are convinced that the issues at stake are of utmost importance to the future of the Church. The life and death of the missionary enterprise hang in the balance. The Declaration was framed to stem the tide and stop the infiltration of harmful currents into the theology of mission." (p. 69, 70)

. . . .

4.   "We continually see signs of a fatal change in the way the churches, the missionary societies, and the World Council of Churches see themselves and their role. They think of themselves as instruments to bring about the world society of the future, composed of people of all religions and ideologies.

        This new understanding of mission was trumpeted forth (in Germany) in 1971 in a huge publicity campaign. Picture magazines and posters appeared everywhere, portraying a group of armed guerrillas in Africa with the inscription, "Today we are partners...Mission today is the mandate given to all Christians to fight together against everything that destroys life, against racism, intolerance, exploitation and alienation..." None of these magazines and posters anywhere indicated that mission has primarily to do with preaching the Gospel and with gathering Christ's Church from all nations. Although most of the Christians who actively support missions were disgusted with this advertisement, it was hailed by the Ecumenical Press Service and recommended for imitation by other countries." (p. 31)

. . . .

5.   "We have seen what unusual evangelistic opportunities the Asian countries present today. We have also been warned of the theological

crisis which threatens to undermine the witness of the Asian churches.
Now we turn to the challenge. How can we avoid the danger of losing our
opportunities in this decisive hour?

First, we must differentiate between the various kinds of
Churches and missions operating in Asia today. One group, because of
strong ties to the neo-liberal forces in the West, has fully adopted the
ecumenical line. Quite a number of mission societies belong to this
group. Among the Asian Churches I would mention the Protestant Kyodan
in Japan and the Presbyterian Church in Taiwan, although the latter left
the World Council for political reasons.

Another, much larger, group has just begun to be infiltrated by
modernistic currents. I include most of the confessional Churches and
missions in this category: Anglicans, Lutherans, Presbyterians, and
others.

The third group includes the spectrum of Churches allied with
Western conservative-evangelicals. Ecclesiastical divisions in Asia
reflect almost exactly the situation within Western Christianity. In
view of the Spiritual battle now being waged in Germany, I was consoled
by I Peter 5:9: "Firm in your faith, resist him, aware that throughout
the world, sufferings of this kind are imposed upon your brothers."

I am convinced that our main challenge today consists of
strengthening this world-wide brotherhood of martyria by which I mean
biblical and evangelical witness...

The main responsibility of fulfilling the unfinished task of
evangelizing Asia falls increasingly upon the shoulders of the conservative evangelicals. They preserve the strongest sense of evangelistic
vocation. They muster the largest number of missionaries, and they
structure their church-mission relationships so as not to eliminate
foreign missionaries. They rightly see that evangelistic and church-
planting missionaries are still much needed." (p. 85,86)

. . . .

A final word from President Hubbard may not be amiss. In his
luminous Foreword he says, "Professor Beyerhaus' criticisms of the ecumenical movement may seem stern to some, but at the same time his judgments will seem balanced. He is not a militant separatist, ready to
drum out of the corps churchmen whose opinion clash with his. His is
not a narrow view of mission, devoid of social responsibility. The
chapter on "Missions and Racism" beats with the pulse of a man who deeply
resents bigotry, prejudice, and racism...

Despite their stark analysis of the directions of much ecumenical thought about missions, these lectures give me hope. Not only do
they call for a return to biblical authority and a dependence on the
Holy Spirit, but they demonstrate what they call for."

EXTENSION, the AIR MAIL newsletter on theological education by
extension edited at the School of World Mission, is for those
whose responsibilities require them to be right up to date on
what is happening in this world-wide movement and who are able
as well to share insights that are turned up in their own
activities. The price is $7.25. This first trial year sub-
scription barely covers air mail and minimal expense (not
labor) for the twelve monthly issues. Send your check to:

EXTENSION
Fuller Theological Seminary
135 North Oakland Avenue
Pasadena, California 91101

E F F E C T I V E   E V A N G E L I S M   I N   A S I A

ALL ASIA MISSION CONSULTATION '73 by   The Editor

A Strategy Conference of the Korea International Mission, formerly known as KEIMA, at Hong Kong in late August 1972, decided to call
an All-Asia Mission Consultation in Seoul, Korea, and tentatively set
the date as August 27th to September 1st, 1973.

The purpose of the Consultation, says Dr. David J. Cho, General
Director of KIM, will be to promote cooperation among Asian missionary
societies so that the evangelization of Asia will go forward more effectively. Participants will include primarily 'Asian mission leaders' and
'concerned observers from non-Asian mission organizations now sending
missionaries to Asia'. It is significant that delegates will be primarily leaders not of Asian Churches but of Asian missionary societies.
Asians who themselves are missionaries to other lands will also attend.

All this is good news. We predict good will come out of this
gathering of Asians now carrying on mission, sending missionaries across
cultural barriers, proclaiming Christ, and multiplying churches in unchurched populations. We congratulate the directors of Korea International Mission on their vision and courage. We hope Asian missionary
societies will send representatives to Seoul to the Consultation.
Eurican missionary societies should assist smaller Asian societies to
send their general secretaries there.

We pray that the Consultation will concentrate on the hundreds
of millions who have yet to believe and that each board represented will
define mission as "sending our own missionaries in our own missions to
our own segments of population". So far, Asian missionary societies
have sent missionaries chiefly to work as a part of a team with western
missionaries. This may sometimes be a necessary first step, but it does
keep Asian missions from developing along lines natural to themselves.
We would like to see a Korean missionary society assume responsibility

for the evangelization of five hundred thousand souls in some great city, or some countryside and plant its own cluster of churches there. Asian missions need not play second fiddle to existing missions. Asian missionaries should not be permanent minorities in teams of Europeans.

When all the missionaries of a given mission are of one culture, one mother tongue, and one missionary society, they spend little time adjusting to each other. They are all on the same salary scale, have about the same educational background and style of life, and can devote themselves wholly to propagating the Gospel among members of the Fourth World - those who have yet to hear the Gospel. In short, they can devote themselves to essential mission according to their own cultural genius and their own obedience.

We pray God's rich blessing on the All-Asia Mission Consultation of '73.

SWM RESEARCH CATALOG AVAILABLE

An up-to-date (through June, 1972) listing of all research done at SWM-ICG is now available, together with a summary of SWM activities written by Prof. C. Peter Wagner. It lists published theses, unpublished theses, research in progress, and faculty publications.

To receive your copy postpaid, send $1.00 to Dr. Arthur Glasser, Fuller Seminary School of World Mission, 135 N. Oakland Avenue, Pasadena, Calif. 91101.

THIRD WORLD MISSIONARY SOCIETIES

THIRD WORLD MISSIONS   by   Edward C. Pentecost

Since the 1800's, Third World Churches have been sending out their missionaries. But until very recently the Western World has taken little account of those activities.

In the Spring of 1972, a team of three research associates of the School of Missions at Fuller Theological Seminary dug into the outreach of the Gospel being carried on by missionaries from the Third World - namely from Asia, Oceania, Africa and Latin America. The work was done under the direction of Prof. C. Peter Wagner and was carried on by the Rev. James Wong of St. Andrews Cathedral in Singapore, who specialized in the Asian research, Prof. Edward Pentecost of the United States who gathered African information, and the Rev. Peter Larson of Argentina, who chaired the project and correlated the Latin American information.

The procedure was first to gather names and addresses of all the missionary-sending congregations, denominations, organizations, and missionary societies of the Third World. To do this, the career missionaries and national leaders from many lands and all the continents enrolled in the School of Missions and Institute of Church Growth (and many others, also) were consulted. Magazines, books, and reports were examined. Then letters and questionnaires were sent to the 697 names gathered. Second, the responses were tabulated and interpreted. The whole study is to be published in due course.

The findings are by no means complete. Only forty per cent of the addresses in Africa and only thirty-seven per cent of those in Asia responded. Nevertheless, the following tables and this brief preview enable us to see something of the dimensions of Third World Missions.

TABLE 1. REGIONAL DISTRIBUTION OF SENDING COUNTRIES AND AGENCIES

AREAS	SENDING COUNTRIES	AGENCIES	MISSIONARIES
Asia & Oceania	15	102	961
Latin America	13	59	655
Africa	6	18	917
Totals	34	179	2,533

In addition to the 34 sending countries mentioned, an additional ten lands submitted to us the names of sending organizations which at the moment of sending the report had no missionaries actually at work. Most of these organizations have sent in the past and expect to send in the future. The Tables must be considered as a minimum report.

TABLE II. SENDING BY COUNTRIES

SENDING COUNTRIES	NO. OF AGENCIES	NUMBER OF MISSIONARIES	SENDING COUNTRIES	NO. OF AGENCIES	NUMBER OF MISSIONARIES
Nigeria	4	810	Kenya	2	10
India	26	543	Singapore	2	10
Brazil	26	495	Ceylon	2	8
Philippine Is.	13	155	Trinidad	1	5
Japah	32	97	Chad	1	4
Mexico	5	64	Zaire	3	4
S. Africa	6	59	Oceania-(4 c's)	5	56
Jamaica	3	4	Guatemala	3	3
Korea	7	33	Peru	2	3
Argentina	7	30	Thailand	3	3
Madagascar	2	30	Colombia	2	2
Hong Kong	6	26	Malaysia	2	2
Taiwan	3	26	S. Vietnam	1	2
Puerto Rico	3	20	Venezuela	2	2
Uruguay	1	15	Costa Rica	3	1

GRAND TOTALS - AGENCIES - 179

MISSIONARIES - 2,533

African Missions are carried on almost entirely within Africa. The pattern we see is 'expanding circle' evangelism, where a whole family moves into an unevangelized area establishing a living relationship. We also see short-term enterprises, with no prior consideration of whether the ministry would be permanent or temporary. When a congregation is established, the family moves on or returns to its former home.

The Asian pattern tends to follow lines of migration. The missionary usually goes to an area to which his own ethnic group had migrated. For example, those from India go to the Indians in Kenya. Chinese from Hong Kong go to Peru to minister to the Chinese there. Japanese go to Brazil to Japanese settlers there. Argentinians minister in Spanish and Brazilians in Portuguese.

Third World Missionaries are supported very largely by their home churches. Sometimes an individual congregation sends the missionary. Sometimes a group of congregations form a sending organization. Exceptions are India and the Philippines, where the missionaries who leave the country are often supported by western funds. Some mission agencies reported that their missionaries are being supported by the inviting Church. One missionary from Japan is supported by a government grant from Japan!!

What does all this mean? Obviously, Third World Missions are using many patterns of missionary sendings. It is also clear that many unreached ethnic units are still unreached - and appear likely to remain so. Most third world missionaries are not engaged in evangelizing across marked culture gaps. Many of them go to their own culture area. They do not learn a radically new language. This is particularly true in Africa.

Do Third World Missions mean a diminution of western missionary outreach? Third World leaders do not think so. For example, a Filipino wrote: "If we got a hundred thousand more western missionaries tomorrow, we Asians must still obey the Great Commission written in our own languages." He recognized two things. First, that the task remaining to be done is immense. Second, that the gifts of the Spirit are bestowed on Christians of different lands in order that the world-wide Body might propagate the Gospel. All Christians are together responsible for the work, and this necessarily includes Christians from Europe, North America and every other land.

Seeing prayers answered through Third World Missionaries entering lands closed to westerners is one of today's blessings. For example, in the province of Nagaland in India, Ao, Lotha and Angami Christians are now going as missionaries to the border tribes in that province where no westerner is allowed to work. These Asian missionaries have been the key factor in the mighty spread of the Church in this one province of the great nation of India. Half the province is now Christian and soon three-fourths of it will be. Each of the fourteen ethnic units in Nagaland will have a strong Church in it.

The will of our Lord, expressed in the Great Commission, is being recognized today as mandatory for Christians everywhere. The message of salvation has long been recognized as to all the world and for all the world. Now it is being recognized that it is also from all the world.

BILLY GRAHAM'S NEW VISION   from   Missions Update September '72

A brand new ingredient will be present in a second world wide evangelism congress now being planned by Billy Graham. Unlike either the Berlin Congress or the various regional congresses (Singapore, Bogota, Minneapolis), the 1974 congress (Rome? Rio? Djakarts?) now being planned will, for the first time, tackle a startling problem, formerly overlooked: most (at least one billion) of the unreached peoples of the world are not within the normal evangelistic range of any church anywhere.

This fact is surprising since we know that there are now Christian Churches in every country of the world. The problem is that ordinary evangelistic efforts simply do not carry effectively across the high barriers constituted by ethnic, cultural and social differences. It is an embarrassing fact that churches in the U.S. and around the world which are geographically closest to these unevangelized peoples or ethnic groups are often the farthest away from them culturally and emotionally. The congress now being planned will face squarely the need for special efforts that can cross these barriers. That is, for missionary efforts.

This amazing new element smashed the illusion many Christians have had, that the world can be won if only the worldwide Church will evangelize the people with which it is normally in contact. Re-established is the urgent need for every Church to encourage the formation of specialized cross-cultural mission orders that can handle the anthropological and linguistic tasks that pioneering missionaries have traditionally been involved in.

CHURCH GROWTH
BULLETIN

INSTITUTE OF CHURCH GROWTH

Address:
FULLER THEOLOGICAL
SEMINARY
135 N. Oakland
Pasadena, Calif. 91101

DONALD A. McGAVRAN, B.D., Ph.D.
Director

January 1973   Subscription $1 per year   Volume IX, No. 3

C O N T E N T S

DELIBERATELY SHIFTING INTO HIGH
by
D. Leslie Hill

Southern Baptists began work in the Philippines just over twenty
years ago. Today more than 300 churches with over 14,000 full members
cooperate with the mission. Church development has always been a major
aim; yet in 1972, feeling that despite rather 'respectable' church growth,
the mission was not doing as much as it should and could, it deliberately
shifted into high. That is, it acted decisively to affirm church growth
as primary and to bring all its resources to bear on achieving it. The
story will be of interest to missions and churches all around the world.

Dissatisfaction had been brewing for some time. In 1970, at its annual meeting, the mission devoted special time to study itself and asked:
How can we know whether we are failing or succeeding in our work, unless
we have measurable goals? However, in spite of considerable effort, the
study ended largely in frustration. The only concrete result was assigning time for similar study in the next annual meeting!

Meanwhile, the Southern Baptist Mission in Indonesia, a step or two
ahead of their brothers in the Philippines, was working toward the same
ends. In 1968, in planning for a self study, it had requested Dr. Ebbie
Smith to spend his furlough at the Fuller School of World Missions. Upon
his return, the Indonesian Mission carried out its self study in which a
deep moving experience with the Holy Spirit propelled it to some major
moves.

SEND correspondence, news, and articles to the Editor, Dr. Donald McGavran, at the Institute
of Church Growth, Fuller Theological Seminary. Published bi-monthly, send subscriptions
and changes of address to the Business Manager, Norman L. Cummings, Overseas Crusades,
Inc., 265 Lytton Avenue, Palo Alto, California 94301, U.S.A. Second-class postage paid at
Palo Alto, California.

The events in Indonesia became known to the Philippine Mission by
its 1971 meeting and provided guidelines for its own self-study. The
mission set up a Church Growth Survey Committee to carry out the survey
and bring in an outside survey team to give greater objectivity to its
self analysis. Finances were allocated to both the committee and the
team.

Throughout the year 1971-1972 the Church Growth Survey Committee
made publications, books, and papers regarding the theory of church
growth and theological education by extension available to all missionaries.

Two events outside the mission's own planning aided its study significantly. a) The Church Growth Conference in Manila in late November
1971 served as a source of information and inspiration. Philippine Crusades through Jim Montgomery's initiative sponsored the conference. Dr.
McGavran, Leonard Tuggy, Robert Skivington, and Jim Montgomery led the
three day event. Many Southern Baptist Filipino pastors and missionaries
attended. In addition the Southern Baptists met each evening and for two
days following the conference to apply church growth principles to their
work. b) Two T.E.E. Workshops in the year helped us also. Dr. Winter
and Dr. Covell lead the workshops.

A Filipino survey specialist assisted the committee in preparing
scientifically valid procedures whose results would be evaluated by computer. Five questionnaires were constructed: for churches, pastors,
church members (according to church size and location), missionaries,
and institutions.

The Missionary Questionnaire revealed a group convicted of "God's
calling" and feeling that each missionary's work should relate to the
felt "will of God" in his life. A majority saw the responsiveness of an
area as one indicator of God's will for the use of mission resources.
They agreed that each local church should start new churches which would
not be dependent on foreign funds. Trained layworkers were seen as the
greatest need. Missionaries felt more churches might be started with the
help of subsidy, but would be weaker because of it. More cooperation
with Filipinos was seen as necessary. Nearly every missionary man, whatever his primary assignment might be, felt he should be directly involved
in beginning new churches.

Exactly 1,438 church members were surveyed (in five languages!) and
177 pastors sent in completed questionnaires. Most thought their churches
were growing. About half the members felt their pastor should not work
at another job. A great majority believed that each missionary ought to
be able to speak the language of his area. About a third saw the missionary's job as that of opening new churches as against a slightly smaller
number who saw it asproviding equipment, buildings and the like. Over
fifty per cent thought the mission should help on pastors' salaries.
There was general agreement that subsidy in various forms should continue.

Just over half the members said the greatest need of our churches
was trained workers, while 71% of the pastors said the same. Over 80% of
the members and pastors spoke in favor of a T.E.E. program for church
leaders.

The Church Questionnaire showed that over half the churches were in
the open country or in small villages and that more than a third of them
had been started by laymen. About a fifth had been started by missionaries.

Each mission institution was asked what its objectives were, how
they related to church growth, and how it might become more effective in
helping to achieve church growth. Organizational charts, capital fund
use, and budgets were covered in the questions. The questionnaires were
very thorough!

Dr. Ebbie Smith from Indonesia, and Robert Skivington of the Conservative Baptists in the Philippines composed the Survey Team brought in
from outside the mission. Both are graduates of the School of World
Mission and Institute of Church Growth. They spent several weeks talking to church members, pastors, missionaries, and heads of mission institutions. Their report which they presented in person to the mission was
48 pages long. It began with a recommendation to establish up to 3,000
churches with a membership of 100,000 in the next ten years.

The power and direction of the Holy Spirit was held to be indispensable in attaining the goal. The Survey Team pointed out current weaknesses in conversion growth, follow-up and church planting and said that
field evangelists were needed to remedy them. It maintained that such
evangelists should formulate a definite plan for carrying out their work.
The team called attention to the responsiveness of tribal areas and
pressed for mission action to harvest there. Missionaries were asked to
see their task as primarily spiritual and not as material administrators.

Smith and Skivington declared that more Filipinization of the
churches was necessary. They recommended that subsidy be discontinued
completely and loan funds be made available to assist land purchase and
church building.

The team called for top priority to be given to the training of lay-
leaders and part time pastors. It recommended that the mission develop
theological education by extension as a tool to accomplish that.

It urged the mission to restructure itself in order to protect the
missionary's time for direct church growth involvement. Ways were noted
by which the various institutions could more directly pursue the mission's
goals of church growth.

Identification with Filipino life and culture, improved missionary
relationship, and Filipinization of churches and institutions were
stressed.

Before the 1972 Annual Meeting the survey had provided a good base
of information for decision making and caused considerable mental and
spiritual ferment for creative action. At the meeting, four full days
were devoted to studying the book of reports and recommendations. On the
evening of the second day, the mission minutes record "The service ended
with a marvelous outpouring of the Holy Spirit as a spirit of revival
and rededication swept through the group. Broken relationships were re-
stored and a renewed sense of dedication to our task was felt."

The mission set out to achieve ends on which it had reached a consensus. It asked Church Planters (as it redesignated 'field evangelists') to develop concrete working plans. A motion directed the multiplication of small groups under lay leadership and encouraged them to
develop into and act as full churches. The mission gave major attention
to responsive tribes. It voted to cease subsidizing pastors' salaries
and to establish a revolving loan fund for church building and land purchase. It instituted a program of theological education by extension
and allocated personnel and funds for it. The mission requested those
involved in resident theological teaching to work with sutdents in church
planting and evangelistic activities. Sunday School literature was to be
simplified and produced more economically. Twice yearly meetings for the
study of church growth methods and for inspiration were instituted.

"That every missionary presently deficient in the language...should
set aside the next six months...to achieve fluency...Whatever else must
be left undone this priority must be met." This resolution expresses
the determination of the mission.

The goal of 3,000 churches with 100,000 members by the end of the
decade was adopted.

The mission's unity in these decisions must be noted. At various
points when particularly radical departures were about to be approved,
though there was absolutely no opposition, the assembly stopped to be
sure conviction was behind the move and not indifferent acquiesence. In
1973 important details are still being ironed out and diligence in pur-
suing the agreed goals marks the mission's activity.

Credit must be given collectively to the Church Growth Survey Committee, the Survey Team of Smith and Skivington, and the many Filipinos
and the missionaries who assisted in the research and prayed for the
deliberations.

"Holy Spirit inspired dissatisfaction with past accomplishment and
mode of operation" in the hearts of the missionaries must be seen as a
casual factor that led to these mission moves. I believe with its purpose sharpened by church growth methods and principles and with a continued commitment to the Spirit's direction, the Southern Baptist Mission
in close cooperation with Filipino Baptists will be granted a remarkable
harvest in the coming decade.

"The strong steady note that sounded throughout this study was the overwhelming, unshaken dedication to classic Christian beliefs, a plea for fuller teaching of them, and an insistence that they be plainly proclaimed in the cause of evangelizing the nations and winning others to faith in Christ.

Members regard this as the church's prime responsibility. Their massive concensus about it comes at a time when many church thinkers have concluded that the message must be qualified and formulated to suit the modern mentality and presented with less absolute certitude in a more modest style. But the people, with all their up-to-the-minute sophistication and savvy, feel otherwise. They firmly uphold the historic doctrines and want deeper instructional nurture in them." (p. 188)
> *Punctured Preconceptions: What North American Christians Think About the Church*, by Johnson and Cornell. Friendship Press, 1972

ANTHROPOLOGICAL LIGHT ON EVANGELISM   by Stan Shewmaker

In July, 1971, I visited little Siabalengu Village on the banks of the Ngwezi River in South Zambia. The headman was the only person there who professed to be a Christian. During the course of our conversation he expressed the desire for someone to come to tell his people "the words of God."

Church leaders in the surrounding area began to pray for the village. Five volunteered to go to Siabalengu. Before going, however, we gave ourselves to a week of prayer - every night - that God would fill us with the power of His Holy Spirit; prepare the hearts of the villagers, and use our mouths to express what He wanted said.

After arrival, we asked the headman for an audience with the men of the village only. We shared Jesus with them in a very informal fashion, starting with their traditional beliefs about God. Then we asked the men to decide whether or not they wanted their wives and children to hear these words also.

The next day, Sunday, the whole village gathered to hear about Jesus. After a long period of conversing back and forth, we asked the people to make a decision for or against accepting Jesus Christ. We appealed first to the men.

Two men first and then others accepted Christ that day. Within eight weeks the village movement to Christ was all but complete. Only two adults held out. A strong church of 53 members was established and is meeting in Siabalengu today, a year later.

On the basis of the Siabalengu experience at least five principles of village evangelism in Tongaland can be suggested.

1. Earnest prayer should precede and accompany evangelism.

2. The headman and older men should hear first.

3. The Good News should be shared informally first to the heads of households.

4. The appeal for decision must be made first to the heads of households.

5. In our preaching, Jesus Christ (His love, His death, His resurrection, His kingdom) must be presented above and preceding all doctrine.

In conclusion, let me encourage you to win whole social units for Christ. In rural districts plan to win villages or parts of villages. Because so very many are still lost let us give ourselves to prayer and evangelism that the Holy Spirit will move multitudes to accept Jesus as Lord of their lives and Saviour of their souls.

'THE LAST WORD' IN EFFECTIVE EVANGELISM   by Edward Murphy

A very great number of those "making decisions for Christ" in Latin America and many other lands do not understand what they are doing. Their responses do not constitute genuine conversions to Christ. They do not intend to be incorporated in His Church. Their responses should not be publicized as acceptance of Christ or conversions or professions of faith. If we announce decisions in these terms we are guilty of a subtle form of deception.

Such announcement demonstrates our inconsistency. On the one hand, we measure our success by these visible "professions of faith." Then when faced by the disturbing fact that the majority of those "conversions" are short lived, we change our argument and claim that we are not responsible for visible results.

Those making decisions must be seen as inquirers, yet to be evangelized by the follow-through ministry, by incorporating them in the fold (folding them) and feeding them (teaching them all things). Fruit that remains is a valid test of the effectiveness of evangelism. We must judge the effectiveness of our ministry to the churches by their effectiveness in folding and feeding the lost who have been found. Churches which will not trouble themselves to nurture the inquirers have been neither revived or mobilized for evangelism. Churches that do not know how to fold and feed inquirers have not been adequately trained.

In evangelism the first word only has been spoken when persons make "decisions for Christ", pray to receive Him, sign cards saying they want to become Christians, or come forward to join the church. The last word has been spoken when, understanding at least something of what is involved, these inquirers have been baptized, added to the Lord, and "taught all things".

In speaking this last word, Christians in each congregation should be trained and prepared to minister in light of their spiritual gifts. They should be given assignments possible within the sociological realities of their circumstances. In the New Testament Church, when the congregation was revived and renewed, it streamed out to witness to its faith and bring to the Lord its kith and kin, members of its own culture and sub-culture. This was true both of the Jerusalem churches and later of the congregations which grew up in the synagogue communities around the Mediterranean. The point is that folding and feeding can be done best when those one shepherds are his own kind. When they are of radically different linguistic, economic and racial groupings, folding and feeding become extraordinarily difficult even for renewed churches.

This is beautifully demonstrated by the outcome of evangelistic campaigns in which I was involved in the sixties in Colombia in both downtown and barrio churches. Let me tell the story.

Campaigns conducted in the better-housed downtown churches showed a very high count in the number of inquirers obtained - and very little church growth. Campaigns in ill-housed humbler churches in the working class barrios showed fewer inquirers at the close of the campaign - and much more church growth in terms of on-going faithful Christians.

Sociological factors were found to be the basic reason for the marked difference. a) Most of the barrio inquirers lived right in the barrio where the ill-housed church was located and could walk to the services without any difficulty. Almost all the inquirers (those who made decisions for Christ) in the downtown churches at the time of the evangelistic campaign, lived far from the church and had to come across the city to its meetings.

b) Barrio inquirers were usually closely related to some of the barrio Evangelicals. Those making decisions for Christ had come to the meeting because they were invited by a cousin, wife, father, son or other relative or intimate friend. They sat next to them during the campaign and felt that they were joining their relatives or neighbors in becoming Evangelicals. Furthermore, because they had observed the transforming power of the Gospel in the lives of their friends and relatives they understood fairly well what becoming an Evangelican meant. Inquirers from the downtown churches, on the contrary, usually did not enjoy a living relationship with members of the congregation. They had been drawn into the evangelistic meetings by the music and the posters or handbills that were passed out. Or, they just happened to be in the area with leisure time on their hands. Thus the existing members of the congregation were strangers to them. No human ties drew them back week after week. Once the spectacular evangelistic campaign was over, the inquirer turned elsewhere for excitement.

As never before in the history of the Church and its evangelistic mission, we are striving to reach whole cities, even nations and continents for Christ. (Key 73 in North America is going to present Christ to every man, woman and child in that tremendous country). Churches and

their leaders in every continent must be prepared to say the last word
in evangelism, i.e. to fold and feed inquirers and to send them out to
find others.

"THE THESIS OF THIS BOOK MAY NOW BE FULLY STATED. THE ERA HAS
COME WHEN CHRISTIAN MISSIONS SHOULD HOLD LIGHTLY ALL MISSION
STATION WORK WHICH CANNOT BE PROVED TO NURTURE GROWING CHURCHES
AND SHOULD SUPPORT THE CHRISTWARD MOVEMENTS WITHIN PEOPLES AS
LONG AS THEY CONTINUE TO GROW AT THE RATE OF 50 PER CENT PER
DECADE OR MORE. THIS IS TODAY'S STRATEGY".
Bridges of God, p. 109

This revolutionary idea, written twenty years ago in 1953, has
been ignored, ridiculed, and attacked. It has been misrepresented as advocating abandonment of resistant fields. It has
also been welcomed, adopted, implemented and built into the
policies of Churches and missions and is paying rich dividends.
It is as sound today as when first penned and is destined to
have still more effect in the coming decades.

Of particular importance is the "50 per cent per decade or more."
Many movements to Christian faith grow at several times that
rate; but if the growth rate falls significantly below that
decadal figure (which is less than an annual growth rate of 4%)
the movement is probably growing chiefly by the excess of births
over deaths in the Christian community and has been sealed off.
It will likely tie up mission resources in rich service to itself, rather than using them to liberate others.

HOW FAST IS CHRISTIANITY GROWING?   by C. Peter Wagner

The most recent writers on the growth of Christianity have asserted
that the rate of growth worldwide now exceeds the rate of world population growth. These include Ralph Winter (Twenty-five Unbelievable
Years), Stephen Neill (Call to Mission), and Warren Webster (Church/
Mission Tensions Today). According to David Barrett, the World Christian
Handbook, which he is editing for publication in 1973, will probably confirm this. It will be worth watching.

Purposely, we are not asking here how fast the Church is growing,
since church growth, when meaningful, involves true disciples being made
from the fourth world: men and women from outside the Christian community commiting their lives to Christ and becoming responsible members of
His Church.

The growth of Christianity, however, reflects how many people in the
world, if a global census were taken, would indicate "Christianity" as
their religion. It does not tell us how many of them are born again,
how many are active, communicant church members, how many have been immersed, how many are soul winners, or a multitude of other interesting

and important Christian qualities which would help us come to statistics on true "church growth" as we know it. But it is a significant piece of data to those of us involved in fulfilling the Great Commission.

Christianity is calculated roughly to include one billion persons today. If the Church is increasing at only the rate of the population (some say it is increasing faster), you take 2 per cent (world population growth rate according to 1972 Population Reference Bureau statistics) of that and discover that annually Christianity is growing by 20 million persons. Divide this by 365 days in a year, and you have this amazing (and encouraging) figure:

<u>Christianity is growing by 55,000 persons per day</u>!

That is encouragement. Here is the challenge. The world has 3,700,000,000 people. Every year 74,000,000 people are added, but only 20,000,000 are being added as Christians--therefore, 54,000,000 people annually are being added to the fourth world. Divide that by 365 and we find that:

<u>The Fourth World is growing by 148,000 persons per day</u>!

<u>Much is being done, but much more is needed</u>. This is no time to cut back on evangelistic and missionary efforts. We need more, not fewer, missionaries. We need more efficient strategy. We need more effective evangelism. We need more Holy Spirit power. We need to win the world in our generation--or die trying!

<u>RACIALISM AND DENOMINATIONALISM COMPLETELY FORGOTTEN</u> by Rev. Fred Burke
Witbank, So. Africa

((African Independent Churches (denominations) number over 5000. New denominations are forming every month. Very few have an adequate system for giving biblical training to their oncoming leaders. Seeing this tremendous need, Rev. Fred Burke of the Assemblies of God in South Africa restructured his Bible School to meet the needs of these African denominations in his vicinity. He opened his doors to their existing ministers and their potential leaders. He gave them biblical training without trying to persuade them to join his Church. Graduates returned to their own denominations - knowing a great deal more about the Bible. This is the purpose of his "All Africa School of Theology."

Many such schools are needed all over Africa. The time to bewail African Independent Churches and try to bring "these schismatic sects" back to the fold has passed. The time to accept many of them as a part of the Christian scene and aid their leaders get a thorough knowledge of the Bible has arrived. As they come to know what the inspired, authoritative, and infallible Word of God says they will become more and more biblical and hence more and more orthodox. Perhaps the African Independents will achieve a greater fusion of Negritude and essential Christianity than the traditional Churches.

Be that as it may, the time has come to establish theological training schools for them in all countries. The courses which Mr. Burke is
using to such good effect can be obtained from him.

Perhaps a hundred such schools of theology are needed. If there
are ten million AIC Christians and these are distributed in 100,000 congregations, and a hundred Schools of Theology like Fred Burke's were to
be established, each would be responsible to give biblical training to a
block of one thousand pastors and ministers. Each would have a man sized
job. We now turn to Mr. Burke's moving account of Christian unity so
deep that it transcended denominational and racial differences.

The Editor))

"In our graduation convention of this year we awarded 183 diplomas
to students who had completed the three year program. These men represented many different Churches. It is impossible to describe the wonderful atmosphere of love and unity that pervaded the many who were present.
The auditorium, which seats over a thousand, was full. All arrangements
for catering were organized by the local committee of ministers who also
provided accommodations for the hundreds who came. All expenses were met
by those attending who gave over a thousand dollars for their food.

A splendid brass band in uniform with a choir of girls dressed in
white with blue sashes enlivened the occasion with their fine playing and
beautiful choir renderings. They had come over a hundred miles in a
specially chartered bus, having paid all their own expenses, sent by an
African Church.

Saturday was devoted to discussions about the Association of African
Churches which is gaining momentum in this country. Those who have accepted sound doctrines and have a constitution setting forth a sound
church organization now number quite a few thousand in membership.

The high standard of many church leaders who took part in the graduation and their intelligence and insight into matters pertaining to the
churches impressed me. One of our graduates is a brother of South
Africa's outstanding leader, Chief G. Buthelezi, elected head of the
Zulu nation.

The outstanding feature was the spiritual atmosphere. All were not
only enthusiastic but showed in their faces the love and joyousness of
true Christianity...There was no fanaticism, but a deep sense of God's
presence. Spontaneous response rose as anointed speakers gave messages
challenging the graduates to go forth in the power of the Holy Spirit
to bring Christ to Africa.

It is hard to realize that a few years ago some of these very people
were considered "untouchables" and antagonistic to white people. God has
brought about a uniting of so many church leaders coming from all four
provinces of South Africa that denominationalism and racialism is completely forgotten in the abounding love of Christ that is forming One Body.

I believe that this is because this School of Theology has endeavored to honour Christ and keep before the people the need of spiritual power in bringing revival to Africa.

It was a truly inspiring sight to see the graduates line the platform of the auditorium, filling every possible space. When they had been given their diplomas the whole congregation joined in the prayer of dedication that these men may bring Christ to Africa.

This school is bringing together many churches, breaking down racial prejudice, surmounting denominational barriers and linking God's people, white and black, in a common vision of reaching the masses. One old African who was present said to me repeatedly after the service, "You have opened the eyes of the people of Africa."

A fact finding team headed by Dr. A. Clark Scanlon, Southern Baptist secretary for Central America, recently spent four years investigating and evaluating Baptist work in Latin America. Here is one of its conclusions:

"The overwhelming viewpoint of Latin American Baptists is that the continent requires an increase in the missionary force. They would be equally insistent that the principal factor is not the number, but the kind and quality of missionaries sent. These missionaries should go only with the assurance of divine calling to the place of assignment.

The current Latin American scene calls for missionaries who will specialize in the establishment and development of local congregations, missionaries who will do the work of evangelism as well as recommend it to others.

Present trends indicate a lessening of the missionary role in administration, but indicate that he has an open field in the area of establishing new churches."

N E W S   A N D   C O M M E N T

SINGAPORE

The great city of Singapore means urban church planting. Christian forces there are thinking in these terms. The Church Growth Center in Singapore is shaping up well. Local support is assured. Plans are under way for a South East Asia version of the Church Growth Bulletin to be published there with a section devoted to area news concerning the expansion of Christianity. An Asia Church Growth Consultation is contemplated for 1973 - possibly during July - in Singapore or other center.

The Rev. James Wong, of St. Andrews Cathedral in Singapore, after graduating from the School of World Missions with an M.A. Missiology degree, has returned to Singapore. Recently he has given 12 addresses on church growth in the Leadership Training Institute, 10 to a gathering of the Lutheran Church of Singapore and Malaya, one at the September Synod of the Anglican Church, and one at a meeting of the Graduates Fellowship of Singapore, where about a hundred university graduates paid close attention to plans for urban evangelism. Wong believes that great opportunity exists to carry on church planting evangelism in the high rise apartments which are being built in Singapore.

With church growth men Malcolm Bradshaw, David Brougham, Ernest Poulsen, James Wong and Bishop Chandu Ray, in the city the mounting interest appears likely to be well nourished. Rapidly expanding metropolitan areas all over the world offer unique opportunities for church growth - provided evangelism establishes house churches or Christian cells. As these multiply, resources become available for the physical plant needed. That plant will not be like the cathedrals of Europe. It will fit the modern city.

Only a mighty multiplication of Christian congregations - the most potent ingredient in social reform of all kinds - will provide the spiritual resources cities need to assure humane living. A sense of justice, concern for people, compassion for the weak, dedication to the truth, constant infilling of God's power, and intent to live according to the biblical revelation characterize churches of practicing Christians and are qualities desperately needed by conurbations. Through church planting evalgelism in cities Christians can strike mighty blows for righteousness, decency, equality of opportunity, and spread of learning. Christians in Singapore are setting off in the right direction.

WEST IRIAN   by Don Gibbons, C. & M.A.

On a recent trip I was able to place 16 couples the Sinak, Ilaga and Beoga churches had provided as missionaries to these areas. They will all be learning Moni or Wolani. Hardships, hunger and isolation face them. They need your prayers. In the Domondoga valley the four couples were distressed at the thought of living in a Moni valley and being unable to communicate even on daily matters, let alone witnessing for Christ. The very next day, God miraculously provided two young men and a woman who live in that valley and speak Damal. The nearest pocket of Damal population is two days walk away. Praise God He is still able to supply our every need.

When I visited Homejo, the pastors told me how the churches there are now filled every Sunday. They now count the few who have not committed their lives to Christ where a year ago they counted the few who were living for Him. In one village, ten were meeting each Sunday a year ago; now over a hundred gather. In the village where they threatened my life in 1955 and told me never to return, the chief begged me to send him a preacher.

In the Beoga and Baliem valleys, the entire culture has changed and improved as the people have accepted Christ. How different life is in the yet unevangelized areas! The villages abound with the trimmings of spirit appeasement. In an Ekari village the women were afraid and never appeared once. In the southern Moni areas many women have huge goiters as large as softballs. We gave iodine shots to all who came for them, confident that this dramatic help will be used of the Lord to open their hearts to the Gospel. I passed through two totally unevangelized Ekari valleys and was much impressed with the poverty and lack of initiative. In the next narrow valley I found a small church established by Ekari Christians. The terraine was no better than in the other valleys, but faith in God has so lifted the people from fear to hope, that their entire life style had been significantly improved. Christ makes a difference!

TAIWAN   by Alan Gates (SWM-ICG 1971)

"I have just returned from an executive meeting of the Church Growth Society and am pleased to report progress toward a Church Growth Workshop in December 1972. The promotion committee, under Al Swanson's guidance, is putting out six pages which could become the first issue of a Taiwan Church Growth Bulletin.

The papers to be presented will include:
a) Campus Evangelism and Church Growth, by Felix Liu, who has been very successful in cell evangelism on Tung Hai campus;
b) Christian Communications, by David Liao, who brings insights from the Kenya Day Star workshop this past summer;
c) The Mandate to Plant Sister Churches by Dorothy Raber, who will stress the opportunity and need for pre-war, mission-planted, mature congregations to establish sister congregations in responsive pockets of population;
d) Conversion Histories, a study in trends by Robert Bolton;
e) Conversion Histories, a depth study of individual conversions by Ted Ellis, based on data collected by students of the Taiwan Theological Seminary;
f) Church and Mission Relationship, a follow-up on Green Lake by Sheldon Sawatsky;
g) Mackay: Church Planter: The Man and His Method, by Hsu-Chien-Hsin, professor of church history, Taiwan Theological Seminary.

Small group discussions will give time to feeling out the basic problems in church growth now being met by Christian leaders. At least four church growth booklets will be available for the workshop, all in Chinese. The first contains six lectures by Donald McGavran given in November 1971 at the First Annual Church Growth Seminar in Taiwan."

Comment: What a rich program is - as I am writing these words - being enjoyed by Christian leaders - Chinese and Americans - in the Republic of China. The resources for continuous study of the concepts, methods, outcomes, and dynamics which God is blessing to the communication of the Gospel are very large in every land. Annual Church Growth Workshops, Conferences, Seminars – the name makes no difference – should form part of the normal life of the Church and mission everywhere.

Specially to be commended is the production of church growth materials in Chinese. Materials in the chief languages of mankind should speedily be multiplied. The first may well be translations or adaptations; but very soon materials composed in Hindi, Hausa, Portuguese, Ilocano, Telegu and many other great languages should be made available.
Donald McGavran

CHURCH GROWTH IN THE PHILIPPINES   by Nene Ramientos (SWM-ICG 1971)

After seventy years, evangelical Christianity in the Philippines, is less than five per cent of the country's 40 million population. A determined effort to move church growth into high gear is now being undertaken by the "Christ the Only Way" Movement through mobilizing every believer for evangelism within the context of the local church and local leadership. We pray that soon these islands "shall resound with the message that Christ is the only way."

The heart of our strategy is the 2000 CORE groups, which meet once a week for fellowship, Bible study, and prayer. Each CORE member is expected to lead one Lay Evangelistic Group Study – our method for evangelism. About 3,000 LEGS units meet in homes of believers and sympathizers and have become potential congregations in themselves. Many LEGS units have already become house congregations. The Church is growing not just by addition of members to existing congregations but by new churches being born.

For example, one average sized congregation in Manila, through conducting home Bible studies has planted three new congregations.

By March 1973, Christ the Only Way Movement should have 10,000 Lay Evangelistic Group Study units, and a corresponding number of CORE groups. Several churches have already experienced 100 per cent increase in their membership. What seems more exciting is the increase in the number of new churches born of "house congregations".

Fifty-five denominations in the Philippines participate in the Movement. As our seventeen District Coordinators visit the local churches of these denominations and hold seminars for LEGS and CORE, more and more believers are enlisted and trained in church expansion.

Rapid church growth in the Philippines is possible, but the opportunities are beyond our resources. The Philippines are white to harvest, "but the laborers are few." Pray for us.

What can seventeen district coordinators do to mobilize all these congregations for effective lay evangelism?

There is need for one C.O.W. coordinator for each of the 60 provinces in the archipelago. In this way, more churches would be mobilized for evangelism in a much shorter period. The fields out here are indeed white unto harvest. Pray to the Lord of the harvest that He might thrust forth more laborers into the Philippine fields.

LAOS AND THAILAND   by Alex G. Smith (O.M.F.)

We had an enthusiastic Church Growth Seminar in Laos, with OMF, Swiss Brethren, American Brethren, and Lao church leaders in attendance. Mac Bradshaw's plane was cancelled, so he did not make it. Consequently, I was asked to double my lecture time. Praise the Lord for a good 8 hours on Church Growth. The slaying of two lady missionaries by the North Vietnamese Communists, and the capture of two missionary men in that immediate area, occurred a few days before the conference. This created a concerned but expectant atmosphere for our deliberations.

The Second Annual Thailand Church Growth Seminar in Bangkok went off excellently. Over 134 official registrations came from all four areas of Thailand, representing 15 different missions and churches. 70% of the delegates were Thai, most of them pastors, elders, or keen laymen. Representation from the major Bible Schools and Seminaries, as well as from four Christian hospitals, was stimulating. Paul Ariga did an excellent job. We have now printed his lectures, together with those of Mac Bradshaw, the Thai speakers, and myself in a Thai book of about 100 pages, just off the press.

EVANGELICALS FOCUS ON SALVATION TODAY

The March, 1973, issue of Evangelical Missions Quarterly will focus on the Salvation Today Conference sponsored by the World Council of Churches Commission of World Mission and Evangelism in Bangkok, January, 1973. Articles by Peter Beyerhaus, Arthur Glasser, Jack Shepherd, and Peter Wagner will provide an evangelical orientation, and will be of vital interest to readers of Church Growth Bulletin. We commend this issue to you. Order it from Evangelical Missions Quarterly, Box 267, Springfield, Pa. 19604. A subscription to any place in the world costs only $3.50.

CHICAGO DECEMBER 1972   by Donald McGavran

A Consultation on Frontier Missions was convened at Chicago in December to discuss places in the world where Gospel-proclaiming, church-planting missions were still needed.

So much of Africasia has been turned over to younger Churches and so many nationals have been so unhappy with missionaries and so quick to say "Look, this is our land, we will evangelize it", that many of the older missionary societies have withdrawn from great commission missions. Evangelizing, church-planting missionaries have been called home.

New theologies of mission have then been devised to justify withdrawal and to buttress belief that 'modern mission' should be busy at, not conversion, discipling, and church growth, but social engineering, rectifying injustice, and 'development'. This was the novel theology which underlay the Uppsala meeting of the World Council of Churches.

All this takes place while the younger Churches are not - in fact- doing much to evangelize non-Christians, while the two billion remain not only unevangelized but hidden from public view.

The Chicago Consultation is another straw in the wind indicating that at least some leaders of the conciliar societies are unhappy to be downgrading church-multiplying evangelism. The hundred who gathered at Chicago (about equal numbers of mission thinkers from the Evangelicals, Conciliars, and Romans) were looking for unevangelized populations which missionary societies might correctly seek to disciple. The Findings Committee affirmed the validity of the great commission and called missions and Churches in all countries of the world to devote themselves to effective evangelism.

The battle is not over; but a new day may be dawning when the conciliar forces will again become concerned with the evangelization of the two billion. God grant His rich blessing to all who so labor. Multitudes wait to be liberated into the glorious liberty of Jesus Christ.

AN EPOCH MAKING BOOK

Dr. Virgil Gerber's MANUAL FOR EVANGELISM/CHURCH GROWTH may mark the beginning of a new era in effective evangelism. It puts church growth insights to work at the grass roots. Dr. Gerber, Executive Director of Evangelical Missions Information Service, helps pastors, elders, and others evaluate their evangelistic efforts and make them more effective.

Much has been written on evangelism and church growth. The basic book Understanding Church Growth and assisting books, such as Church Growth and the Word of God, Principles of Church Growth, Frontiers of Missionary Strategy, are essential reading for the wide-a-wake minister and missionary; but none tells how workers can quickly learn useful principles of church growth and apply them locally.

THE MANUAL FOR EVANGELISM/CHURCH GROWTH fits this need. Designed for pastors/missionaries, it starts with spiritual dynamics and proceeds to ways in which leaders (whatever program of evangelism they use) can evaluate it, and achieve effectiveness in it. Price Post Paid: 25 or more copies 65 cents each. 10 copies $10. 3 copies $3.75. 1 copy $1.50. Send check to Carey Library, 533 Hermosa St., So. Pasadena, Ca. 91030.

CHURCH GROWTH
BULLETIN

from the
**INSTITUTE OF
CHURCH GROWTH**

Address:
FULLER THEOLOGICAL
SEMINARY
135 N. Oakland
Pasadena, Calif. 91101

DONALD A. McGAVRAN, B.D., Ph.D.
Director

March 1973   Subscription $1 per year   Volume IX No. 4

C O N T E N T S

HISTORY'S MOST MASSIVE INFLUX INTO THE CHURCHES   by David Barrett
                        ((quoted from A. R. Tippett's great new book
                        God, Man and Church Growth, Pages 396-397))

     For one hundred years now, the most massive influx into the churches
in history has been taking place on the African continent. By 1970, as
Table 1 indicates, 130 million persons called themselves Christians, and
were recognized as such by government; but of these only 100 million had
come into touch with the churches or were recognized by them. Thus, in
present-day Africa, what we may call the largest nominal fringe in history
has sprung up on the periphery of the churches - 30 million persons who
claim to have begun the move into the Christian religion, who have in
effect asked to be discipled, but whom the churches have so far been unable to contact or to in any sense disciple. This fringe, which is growing in size at a rate of 4 per cent per year, is usually interpreted by
Western observers to be composed of persons who call themselves Christian
without any basis in reality; nominal Christians, non-practicing professing
Christians, backsliders, and pagan or agnostics trying to ingratiate themselves with Christian politicians or otherwise seeking the material benefits of Christian profession. This explanation is imported direct from
the contemporary post-Christian West, and may be relevant to a declining
Christianity among numerically static churches in Europe and North America;
but it has little validity in lands of rapid Christian expansion and
phenomenal numerical increase. Neither does it take into account the
sincerity of the African desire and genius for religion. We must therefore reject the usual interpretation. A more correct explanation is that
this is one of the problems of outstanding success in mission. The fringe

* SEND correspondence, news, and articles to the Editor, Dr. Donald McGavran, at the Institute
of Church Growth, Fuller Theological Seminary. Published bi-monthly, send subscriptions
and changes of address to the Business Manager, Norman L. Cummings, Overseas Crusades,
Inc., 265 Lytton Avenue, Palo Alto, California 94301, U.S.A. Second-class postage paid at
Palo Alto, California.

TABLE 1: THE EXPANSION OF CHRISTIANITY IN AFRICA,
A.D. 1900-2000

	1900	1955	1960	1970	2000
Christians (in millions)					
(a) affiliated to churches	9	52	66	100	300
(b) nominal (not affiliated)	1	15	20	30	95
(c) total (a) plus (b)	10	67	86	130	395
Christians as percentage					
of Africa	7.5	28.0	32.0	32.0	48.3

Notes. The statistics in (a) are derived from returns of total
Christian community known to the churches, including catechumens,
children, fringe members, and adherers. Those in (c) are derived
from government censuses of religions profession, which are conducted on average every ten years in about half the countries of
Africa. Those in (b) are derived by subtracting (a) from (c), and
are interpreted in this essay as persons who have requested discipling, but whom the churches have so far been unable to contact.

has arisen because of the inadequacy of the churches' present mechanisms
of Christian initiation, and because of legalism and perfectionism on
the part of many churches. It exists because of a failure in 'statistical compassion' (concern for the fate of the whole population as opposed
to that of a favored minority); and it continues on indefinitely as a
result of an almost total absence of future-oriented planning, in or
between, the churches.

REVIVAL AND CHURCH GROWTH AMONG THE MONTAGNARDS IN VIETNAM
by Truong Van Tot, Vietnamese missionary to the Montagnards, SWM-ICG '70

Does Revival bring Church Growth? Our experience here in Vietnam
has led us to think much about this. Dr. McGavran writes:

Revival bears a close relationship to church growth; yet exactly
what that relationship is, particularly in Afericasia where the
Church is growing on new ground, is often not clear. Under
certain conditions revival may be said to cause growth. Under
others, its relationship to church growth is so distant that apparently revival occurs without growth and growth without revival.
Careful consideration of the subject is necessary if we are to
understand the function of each in God's purpose of redemption.
(Understanding Church Growth, p. 169)

Well, does revival in the Church necessarily lead to membership growth?
My answer is based on material gathered during the revival in the Southern Tribal District of the Evangelical Church of Vietnam. My data was
collected over the period from January to October in 1972.

For a long time we believed that revival was the best and only
method by which the Church would grow, therefore we sincerely prayed and

prepared for a revival. The Lord answered our prayer and a real revival broke out in the churches of our tribal district at the beginning of 1972 and is still going on in December, 1972. The revival brought a great increase in spiritual understanding and depth in the churches. One of its main features was the exposure of animistic practices, particularly among young second generation Christians. Hundreds of fetishes and amulets, which had been purchased at great cost from Cambodian animistic practitioners, were turned in and abandoned. Many were sanctified, filled with joy, and dedicated completely to the Lord for His use. Many people, filled with the power of the Holy Spirit, began to serve the Lord with zeal and took the Gospel to many places. The spiritual standard of the Church rose considerably over what it had been previously. Many serious longstanding problems in the churches simply disappeared or were solved with ease. But there was one more thing everyone hoped the revival would bring - a large increase in the membership of the churches. What about this? The facts show the following.

Eighty-one churches experienced revival. Of these 26 (or 30 per cent) did not add a single new member to their rolls. Of the 81, 44 (or more than 50 per cent added only a few - from 1 to 16. Only 11 (about 15 per cent) added substantially to the membership - from 34 to 150.

1. Concerning the 26 churches which experienced revival but no increase in new believers, it is probable that either:
    a) the villages in which they are located were already Christian. There were no "outsiders" left in the proximity of the church, or
    b) Christians in these churches witnessed only for a short time after the revival and in nearby areas where remaining non-Christians have built up a resistance to the Gospel.

2. Concerning the 44 churches which experienced revival and slight increase only, it is probable that
    a) these few converts had family ties with Christians and wanted to become Christians but had never had a special opportunity. During the revival the Christians showed unusual concern for them and prayed and worked for their salvation, so they decided to believe in the Lord.

3. Concerning the eleven churches which showed a great increase in new believers:
    a) Christians in these churches went on a regular basis to more distant places, and
    b) to groups of people who were responsive to the Gospel.

Therefore, it appears that, given the revival, family ties and responsive peoples are the main factors which encouraged the quantitative growth of the Church in our situations.

Revival is like a head of steam in a railway engine. Without it the engine remains motionless. With it, plus rails, pistons, water, oil, timetables, engineer and other elements the train travels widely and fast. Great growth of the Church following revival will come when all the conditions are right. (Understanding Church Growth, p. 180)

We desperately need revivals; but we also need a greater understanding of those factors which will in fact lead to the growth of the church.

Faithful are the wounds of a friend: Proverbs 27:6

"We now have 13 subscribers to the Church Growth Bulletin. I have sold $260.00 worth of CG books, including CG Bulletin, Vol. 1-V, and have also asked the Nairobi Christian Bookshop (Keswick) to stock about 20 CG titles. ((a friend, indeed))

But, you men are very weak in URBAN CG plans, methods and accounts of effective church planting, CG Bulletin Vol. 1-V index has only one reference to urban evangelism. Shame! Could you supply me with some bibliography or references on urban evangelism? We are losing missionaries because they are defeated by the cities. I have read the chapter in Understanding Church Growth on "Discipling Urban Populations" and Wagner's Frontiers on "Strategy for Urban Evangelism" but find both thin. More plans and reports of effective urban evangelism are needed. Laity Mobilized by Braun is good ....but we need more." Harold Cummins, Nairobi.

((Still a good friend! We know what you are talking about. How about it readers...Send in accounts of urban church planting which has been blessed of God. What did you do? What exactly was the outcome?))

CHURCH GROWTH CRITICS AND RESPONSIBLE WRITING   by Alan R. Tippett

The attempt to trichotomize missionary theory as world-centered, soul-centered or God-centered is apparently the latest way of taking an unfriendly dig at church growth. The literary method, of course, is one we know well. The writer sets up a structure of categories suitable to himself, writes his own descriptors, looks around for a number of quotations, extracts them from their contexts and fits them into his own frame of reference. Then he makes a comparison of the straw men he has created.

It was in this way that we first faced such issues as "quality or quantity", "mission and service", "Universalism and pietism", "the work of the Spirit or the work of man" and the notion of "God-Church-World" as against that of "God-World-Church". Always these categories were abstractions set up by the critics who just placed church growth where they wanted to place it for pelting at like an Aunt Sally. These abstractions were not even objective. They were set up with an attitude of "I am right: you are wrong," and they forced church growth apologists to concentrate on points of attact and thereby denied us the right to have our theology seen whole.

In one recent statement, which pulls church growth writers out of their contexts and quotes them in the above manner, we would appear to be the "Soul-centered" type. Of course, such a generalization can only be made by disregarding context. By the same criteria and method it could be argued that we are "world-centered" because we have written many things about being sent into the world and also about "stewardship" and "responsibility", "works worthy of repentance" and the application of our faith in the world. When you come to read the section of God-centered missions (it should be mission) there is really nothing there at all which could not have come from church growth writing. Yet it is argued against us. This kind of writing against church growth can only mean one of two things - either (1) the critic is ignorant of church growth writing or (2) he is scratching about frantically for some way of attacking it. In any case, this whole approach violates the basic principles of scholarly criticism. You cannot generalize on odd statements extracted from their context.

In point of fact the worth of the human soul is of great importance to us; but for church growth to be accused of "'simple gospel' reductionism" at this point is itself an excessively simplified reductionism. As the Fijians would say, our critic "is pricked with his own bone".

My hope is that the McGavran Festschrift - God, Man and Church Growth by its wide range of emphases, will prevent some of these criticisms. Every article in that book is accompanied by a McGavran quote; so that, although the writers are expressing their own opinions, they all have a stake in church growth theory as stated by McGavran.

Another unfair element about this type of attack is that once you extract a quotation out of its context you assume a right to re-interpret it, so that in point of fact it becomes your own quote, a reflection of your mind, not that of the original writer. Quite frequently such quotation-borrowers actually do insert explanatory phrases and value judgments; and thus become manipulators of the original quote. We have suffered much from this kind of writing in the theory of mission. One of the greatest needs for a scientific discipline of missiology is that we raise a body of missiological writers who will use their material responsibly. It is not at all responsible to set church growth theory as soul-centered over against God-centered. The McGavran Festschrift has a 90-page section on theology called "God's Purpose and Man's Responsibility". This section, should give our critics something to think about. We have long needed a book of this kind. It means that henceforth we say to them, this is our field of concern. If you want to argue with us, look at it whole, come out in the open and let us interpret ourselves. Come and meet real people, not straw men.

THE OPERATION 200 STORY   by Leonard Tuggy

It all started with studying the graph of growth of Conservative

Baptists in the Philippines. I had plotted the growth on logarithmic graph paper and noticed that since 1967 we had been growing at about 20% a year. Projecting the growth line until it crossed the 10,000 member mark brought me up to about 1981. Since the average evangelical church in many countries, including the Philippines, numbers about 50 members, I concluded that 10,000 members meant about 200 local churches. I used these figures to challenge the Conservative Baptist Association of the Philippines (CBAP) during its 1971 annual conference. I asked them to visualize what a 200 church association would be like, and what we would need to do to bring it about.

The church leaders quickly responded to the challenge. Rev. Rogelio Baldemor, President of CBAP, called a meeting of pastors and workers to discuss the future role of the association. Then a joint Filipino-American (Association-Mission) meeting was held in March, 1972. We met in cool Tagaytay City for two days of warm spiritual fellowship and frank discussion. Again the vision was for growth to 10,000 members or 200 churches by 1981. The number 200 came up again and again, then someone said, "Why don't we launch an OPERATION 200!" And OPERATION 200 was born.

We began to grapple with the question, "How can we possibly reach this goal in ten years?" Missionary Bob Samms said, "We can reach this goal only if we mobilize the army of laymen in our churches!" Bob was promptly asked to write an article for the BAPTIST MESSENGER (our church paper) on this theme. Then Don Benson told of Metropolitan Baptist Church's experience in starting a daughter church. He pointed out that one key to rapid church growth in the Philippines was for one church to start another. He also said that someone should write a manual on how to do this. The conference immediately responded by asking Don to write this manual. His very helpful "How to Start a Daughter Church" is the result. Pastor Baldemor remarked that this booklet should become the "Four Spiritual Laws" of OPERATION 200.

The Tagaytay conference also decided to launch OPERATION 200 with a contest for a theme song, a poem, and a stylized Tagalog debate (balag-tasan) to generate enthusiasm for the program. Winning entries were sung or read at a large church rally last July. Now enthusiasm is no substitute for working a well-thought-plan, but an ambitious plan will not work without enthusiasm. By July we had plenty of enthusiasm, but no plan yet.

The Filipino leaders felt the need for a plan which spelled out the steps by which we would reach our goal of 200 churches by 1981. They moved ahead on their own and formed an OPERATION 200 Development Committee. Clearly they saw OPERATION 200 as a challenge to the churches, even more than to the mission. With this healthy attitude they produced a draft document called, "CBAP OPERATION 200 - A PLAN." They presented this Plan to our joint Advisory Committee in July. JAC recommended that the Development Committee continue its work, and be augmented by three laymen and two missionary consultants. At the October JAC meeting, the final draft was adopted.

What are the salient features of this plan? <u>First</u>, the grand goals of 10,000 members and 200 churches are broken down to year-by-year, area-by-area goals. A church is defined as 20 or more baptized believers or at least 5 family units having regular meetings and fulfilling the ordinances. The plan also requires the opening of new areas year by year.

<u>Second</u>, the personnel to be tapped to reach the goal are listed. These include laymen, students, pastors, and missionaries. Leaders are to be trained by TEE, seminars and institutes. A special one-week "crash" training program will launch the operation. Job descriptions for full and part-time pastors, evangelists, Bible women and national missionaries are appended to the plan.

<u>Third</u>, the plan presents the methods to be used to plant new churches. They are all basically related to the step-by-step procedure outlined in "How to Start a Daughter Church". Starting with a house to house survey or natural contacts, home Bible classes are begun. These then develop into preaching points, and chapels, and finally become organized churches as the Lord blesses.

<u>Fourth</u>, the plan states the finances which will undergird OPERATION 200, and closes with a series of recommendations. The plan assumes that the CBAP churches will greatly increase their missionary giving to CBAP. Attention is focused on the money to come from the churches, not on the money to come from the mission, - though there will be some of that.

OPERATION 200 is already under way. Reports coming in from the different churches indicate that we have met our 1972 goals. We still have church growth problems; but the Lord is honoring our faith by giving us fruit. We have been able to begin churchlets in several new towns this year, and evangelistic efforts have been unusually effective. Both our residence and extension training schools have increased their enrollment and improved their programs. We are awed by the challenge facing us, but expect to see the Lord bless our efforts during the coming decade. By moving ahead like this, we are exposing ourselves to attack by the Enemy, but our confidence is in the Lord of the Harvest. "If God be for us, who can be against us."

<u>HEY, DONOR AGENCIES: DON'T IMPOSE WESTERN FASHIONS ON US.</u> by
Eight Officers of The Evangelical Church Mekane Yesus, Ethiopia

In January 1971 the 7th General Assembly of the Evangelical Church Mekane Yesus, of Ethiopia passed a resolution requesting the Lutheran World Federation to ask Donor Agencies in Germany and other countries to reconsider their criteria for aid and include direct support for evangelism, congregational work, leadership training and church building. The Church realized her own inability to cope with the fast growing congregational work and the opportunities for evangelistic outreach. Over the last several years the Mekane Yesus Church has worked out development projects which meet the criteria decided by the Donor Agencies. At the same time, the Church in faithfulness to her Lord realized her obligation to proclaim the Gospel to ever growing crowds expecting more than bread. She cannot remain silent where genuine spiritual need is prevailing and thousands are flocking to newly established churches (and also in places where there are no churches) to hear the GOOD NEWS.

It has become evident over the last few years that the Churches and Agencies in the West are prepared to assist in material development, but have little interest in helping the Church meet her primary obligation to proclaim the Gospel. From the African point of view, it is hard to understand this. We question whether the criteria for assistance laid down by Donor Agencies are correct....In our view, a one-sided material development is not only self deceiving in the sense that man needs more than that, it is also a threat to the very values which make life meaningful, if carried out without due attention to simultaneously meeting spiritual needs....When we are told, by virtue of the criteria unilaterally devised by the Donor Agencies what we need and what we do not need, what is good for us and what is not good, we feel uncomfortable......

Man's basic need is not simply to be informed of what is good and right. Man's primary need is to be set free from his own self-centered greed. Here is where the Gospel of the Lord Jesus Christ comes in as the liberating power....The need of the whole man (which includes his spiritual need as primary) should determine where assistance should be given, and not criteria laid down by the Donor Agencies which reflect trends in Western Societies and Churches....

It has been falsely thought that the old emphasis in the mission of the Church had been solely on verbal proclamation and that the new emphasis on social action, community development, liberation from dehumanizing structure, and involvement in nation building was now essential. The West has assumed that in the past missions have not paid due attention to the material and physical needs of man and have been concerned only for souls, doing little to bring about changes in society...This false assumption distorts the true picture. It is caused, not by a sober analysis of the historical facts, but by the dismay and feeling of guilt which gripped the Western Churches when, about twenty years ago, the injustice and exploitation of colonialism began to come to the surface. Western Churches began to ask themselves, "Have we been instruments of oppression? Have we been so busy saving souls, that we have ignored the social and political needs of man?" As the Churches rocked under the impact of such guilt (always implied as a sin of omission, even when the facts were contrary) the cry went up "Minister to the Whole Man". Certainly the missions have always emphasized medical work, education, and other community improvements, but in the sixties the Donor Agencies thought it necessary to make all such work highly visible to refurbish the 'mission image' in the sending countries. Even though such a division of ministry and witness was, from a theological point of view, indefensible.

This over reaction and sense of guilt on the part of the wealthy Western Churches led to a new imbalance in assistance to the younger Churches. All this happened in the West: but should developments in the West be the only determining factor in the aid relationship?

Cont. p. 307

The Mekane Yesus Church in Ethiopia feels the time has come to call the attention of the Lutheran World Federation to this issue. It is our firm conviction that assistance should be brought into balance....The division between proclamation and development which has been imposed on us is, in our view, harmful to the Church and will result in a distorted Christianity.

Our hope is that our sister Churches do not judge our needs solely on their own criteria and on the conditions they have stipulated. We want to proclaim Christ because we believe it is our responsibility. We want to proclaim Christ because our people are hungering for Him.

Signed by Eight Officers of the Evangelical Church Mekane Yesus,

Emanuel Abraham, Fitaurari Baissa Jammo, Emmanuel Gebre Silassie, Osmund Lintjorn, Menkir Esayas, Olav Saeveraas, Berhe Beyene, Gudina Tjmsa Gen. Sec.

((Comment by Donald McGavran. The nine page letter of the Lutheran Church in Ethiopia has been made available to the world as part of the Lutheran World Federation Executive Committee Report. Church Growth Bulletin has condensed the letter (conveying its basic meanings and using its exact words as far as possible) to share with our readers this important new trend in missionary thinking. CGB agrees with Mekane Yesus officers in their analysis of the causes of the disastrous swing away from evangelism and church multiplication. The Eurican guilt complex certainly played a large part. We also agree that the time has come for the Donor Agencies to swing back to Great Commission Mission. Not only does a sound theology demand this, but the enormous responsiveness of these decades, which seems likely to increase, makes any program of mere humanization ridiculous. Hundreds of thousands want to become Christians!!

Readers will be pleased to hear that the Lutheran World Federation Executive Committee took favorable action in regard to the letter and are making known to the Lutheran churches through appropriate channels the request of the Lutheran Church in Ethiopia. The Committee suggests that the criteria of allocation of aid may possibly be reviewed.

I am delighted that Mekane Yesus Church exposes the wholly erroneous assumption that missions have done little in social action and changing society. The facts are diametrically opposite. Most missions have spent most of their budgets for non-evangelistic activities connected with lifting and changing society. They are doing this today and will do it tomorrow. The passion to perfect dominates most missions. What proportion of effort should be spent for discipling and what for perfecting will differ with each of the tens of thousands of cases of church growth. There is no one proportion which is always correct. The Early Church appointed deacons to wait on tables so that the apostles could continue their ministry of the Word. This was and is right. It is time to get on with the basic task of discipling the nations, teaching them all things, and through hundreds of thousands of Christians cells (churches) influencing

families, clans, towns, cities, and nations toward the righteous peaceful
life which God intends for men to live.))

```
CORRECTION  CORRECTION  CORRECTION

A recent issue of this Bulletin announcing the Church Growth
Seminar at Ventnor, New Jersey, gave the date for the same as
September 11-14.  This was an error.  The correct date for the
Ventnor Seminar, conducted by "The Overseas Ministries Study
Center at 11 South Portland Avenue, Ventnor, N.J. 08406" is
September 18-21, 1973.  Write the Director for application forms.
```

REPORT ON COLOMBIA (February 1973)   by Edward Murphy

A.   Its Socio-Economic Situation.

Three disturbing elements in the socio-economic panorama of Colombia
are the following: soaring inflation, terrible unemployment, and subsistence urbanization.

At the present, 68% of the population live in cities and 32% in the
country. Of the 68% who are urban residents, 34% are children or young
people under 21. Of the remaining 34%, half would be men and half women.
Thus if one overlooks youth who work, 17% of the urban population are
the working force. Of the 17% adult male potential workers in the cities,
only 1% have steady jobs. Others take occasional jobs. Some are almost
completely without work. They become a burden to the city, a real problem to the nation at large.

An example of this "subsistence urbanization" (That term means an
urban situation that does not provide jobs to care for its vast population.
The urbanite is worse off than the country man who still can feed his
family on what he can grow off his own land.) would be the City of Cali
itself. The population was 27,000 in 1912; 44,000 by 1918. In 1950 the
population was 200,000, 800,000 in 1960 and in 1972 it grew to over a
million. These 'campasinos', jobless as they are, face a terrible situation. Many of their daughters become prostitutes and their sons street
urchins. Many men turn to crime.

To meet this situation the great Amazon Basin, the jungle and semi-
jungle area of Colombia called the Llanos (the Plains) is now being opened up by the Colombian government. The government will pay all the
expenses for an urban family to move to the Llanos, will give them a good
plot of land and some cattle to begin a farm. Thousands of men are moving
into this area. It is exciting to see that this area is now becoming a
mission field with an incalculable potential for church growth. Churches
and missions should engage in vigorous church planting evangelism here.
New teams will find abundant opportunities - and difficulties!

B.   The State of Its Evangelical Churches

The last census of the Evangelical churches was taken in 1969. At that time there were about 91,000 baptized church members within Colombia with an Evangelical community of about 273,000. The growth rate began to decline after 1968. In 1967 only 14,000 new baptized members were added to the churches. During 1968, the year of Evangelism in Depth, only 6,000 were added. There is reason to believe that recently the growth rate has picked up. The Spirit of God is moving in new areas, bringing thousands to Christ and causing the planting of many new churches. Overseas Crusades has recommended to the Evangelical Church Federation of Colombia that it appoint a Secretary of Statistics. We will offer to help in gathering statistics. Things are moving so fast that the Evangelical Churches must know where churches are multiplying and where they are not. This is no time for groping ahead.

I will only mention four cities, describing briefly the general growth of churches within them.

1.   Bogota: The churches of Bogota continue to show excellent growth. In many ways, Bogota has now become the evangelistic center of Colombia.

2.   Cali: The churches have shown poor growth during the past two years. Indeed, their situation has been pathetic. A few weeks ago the Spirit of God began a movement of revival among the hearts of many leaders and laymen. This touch of God, if it continues, may usher in a new day for church growth in Cali.

3.   Medellin: This was once one of the most difficult cities for Evangelical work. With great reluctance we accepted the responsibility of organizing a city-wide crusade in that city in 1966. That crusade was a "first". It also "broke the ice" and has ushered in a new day for evangelism and church growth. Some of the churches of Medellin are now among the fastest growing in the country.

4.   Baranquilla: This major coastal city, hot and humid, continues to be one of the most responsive cities in Colombia. It boasts some of the largest Evangelical churches in all of Colombia.

A VERY CORDIAL WORD OF THANKS

Many friends and missionary associates of ours heard of the January 23rd Celebration of my seventy-fifth birthday (which occurred in December) and graciously wrote letters to be read at that occasion and bound into a book to be presented to Mrs. McGavran and me. These letters, generous and appreciative beyond measure, have meant a great deal to us. We feel unworthy of them, but love to read them!! Each of them will receive a personal response this summer. Until that comes, we take this opportunity to express our gratitude to you.

At the gala affair, attended by over two hundred special guests, President Hubbard presented us with a copy of Dr. Tippett's book God,

Man and Church Growth, a "Festschrift in Honor of Donald Anderson McGavran"
containing thirty-two essays on church growth. The next issue of CGB will
carry an extended review of the volume. Here it must suffice to quote
Harold Lindsell's comment: "Now for the first time we have in a single
book, a vital sampling of the full range of strategic studies at the
Fuller School of World Mission". All guests received gift copies.

Mrs. McGavran and I, to whom the entire evening was a complete surprise, were overwhelmed with the magnitude of the Celebration and the kind-
ness of brilliant leaders of the missionary world who gathered there, or
shared from distant places, and were filled with gratitude to God who
has given us the privilege of working with the creative faculty of the
School of World Mission and of living to see a biblical view of the mission of the Church back to the place intended by our Lord.

Mrs. McGavran and I often think of you, our colleagues (nationals
and missionaries alike) working in so many countries of earth. We are
proud to be your comrades and to call ourselves missionaries. The Celebration marks a beginning, not an ending, and we rejoice exceedingly as
we think of the thousands of man-years which you, our friends, will yet
give to the evangelization of the world.

THE GIANT TASK IN RESPONSIVE CITIES   by   Norman Riddle of Kinshasa

Multiplying churches in Kinshasa will require a tremendous amount of
planning, effort, and training staff for many years to come. By 1980 the
city will have doubled again in size. We are already behind in reaching
the present Protestant segment of the population estimated at about 28
per cent of the total population (i.e. about 300,000 souls). One way to
catch up is to proliferate house and yard congregations. Our western
ideas of buildings must be modified or abandoned. Otherwise they will
hinder the moving of the Spirit. The independent denominations are increasing rapidly by multiplying house and yard churches. We certainly
haven't enough land or money to build imposing structures at the rate they
are needed. One missionary is working at top speed, using the infusion
of funds from the Baptist World Mission Campaign merely to house existing
Baptist congregations.

Youth evangelism too needs strategy. Most congregations in Kinshasa
simply do not recognize youth as a field needing special funds, personnel, and planning. A survey in 1967 revealed that of those born in the
city and still present, 93% were under twenty.

If after reading this article you still feel that the need for missionary contributions is over in Zaire, you have not really grasped what
mission is all about. Our Zairean Baptist Convention itself has not
seized the opportunities available in Kinshasa for growth of churches and
for evangelism. It continues to allocate most missionaries to schools
and hospitals...The day that the Annual Convention puts church growth and
evangelism back into priority, we can say that it has come of age.

AFRICAN DENOMINATION ORGANIZES BOARD OF MISSIONS   by   Allan R. Buckman

On January 9, 1973 the Lutheran Church of Nigeria at its annual Synodical Convention discussed "The Church and the Great Commission", and determined that:

1. The LCN should form a Board of Missions responsible for reaching out cross culturally to establish new churches in Nigeria.

2. Should conduct surveys among ethnic groups adjacent to those in which the LCN is already established to determine where need for outreach (opportunity for church multiplying) is the greatest.

3. At the next Synod Convention (Jan. 1974) two missionaries be commissioned by the LCN to establish churches in new areas.

KOREA   by   Paul Rader

"I am just now concluding a most enlightening visit here at the Southern Presbyterian Mission in Soonchun. They are concluding a seven year program of systematic church planting that has placed an evangelical congregation within walking distance (4 KM) of every group of 100 houses in that presbytery, with but two or three exceptions. They have already moved into the presbyteries to the east and west to extend this pattern. It is the best example of a task force effort with specific goals conducted along the lines of Church Growth Principles that I have heard anything of in Korea. It is really exciting.

They have a U.S. Army map that covers the whole wall and part of the ceiling of their Presbytery Evangelism Department Office fully 8 x 10 feet! - on which they have plotted over 1,000 churches with coded pins and indicated with red markers every target area of more than 100 homes without a church in walking distance. Then they have systematically gone about the business of planting churches in these areas. Part of the process involved designing a reinforced concrete "I" beam construction church of varying dimensions that can be built 'dirt' cheap. A church that will seat 80-100 persons, finished on the inside with wooden floor and slate roof, can be built for less than $1,000. I visited one of this kind. If unfinished and without wooden floor, it can be built for half of that. Really ingeneous."

Harper and Row, Publishers, in New York, have issued a second edition (hard cover) of the influential
        CHURCH GROWTH AND CHRISTIAN MISSION.
This book should be in each missionary's library and the libraries of all theological training schools, whether of the Bible School or Seminary level. The sections by Cal Guy, Melvin Hodges and Eugene Nida are themselves worth the price of the book.

CHURCH GROWTH IN THE UNITED STATES   by   Jack Willcuts, Oregon Friends

I attended a Church Growth Seminar at Winona Lake in 1968. I was then general superintendent of the Friends in the Northwest. We became concerned about the general decline in our churches. We had gotten stuck at about 5,000 members in a population which was growing rapidly. We decided to conduct a study of church growth patterns and possibilities among our sixty-four congregations. Professor Myron D. Goldsmith of George Fox College and I were appointed to conduct the survey and went to Pasadena to discuss our plans with our friends at the School of Missions of Fuller Theological Seminary.

After a year of investigation, we published our findings under the title Friends in the Soaring Seventies. We then made a sustained effort to develop a "church growth mentality". We undergirded the effort with much prayer. Gratifying things have happened. God has given us answers to our prayers. Let me mention three.

1. Each of the last three years the membership of the churches of our Yearly Meeting has grown more than in any previous year of our history.

2. Last year, forty-two churches showed a substantial gain in membership, new conversions, and morning worship attendance. Thirty-five showed an increase in Sunday School attendance.

3. One year ago, I resigned as superintendent of the Northwest Area and the growth continues at an accelerated rate. I resigned primarily to take a pastorate and put church growth principles into practice. Last year this one church added 90 new members and has added 20 already this year 1973 - the largest increase in its 78 year history. The budget has doubled as well. An interesting spin-off is that I am now called to speak all over the United States from North Carolina and New York to Washington and California on how churches grow!! The Quakers are talking and praying about church growth in a big way and it is doing us good.

NEW CHURCHES BEYOND THE CHURCH by   Bob Schneider, Ministry To Muslims

In the "Church Growth Bulletin" of July 1969, I read the article on Bible Correspondence Schools with real interest.

"Someone should devise a course for sincere but unbaptized converts from the world who have completed all the ordinary courses. This 'post graduate course' would teach a student how to start a church in his house, among his kinsmen, without seeing a minister or having fellowship with existing Christians. Only the Holy Spirit and the Bible would be available to him. Directed by Spirit and Word only, he would form a true indigenous church - a koinonia. Such could be started anywhere - in undergrounds, in cities, behind Iron Curtains, in ethnic units where heretofore no one has become Christian, in wealthy suburbs and poverty stricken hamlets. The BCS should leap the barrier of person-to-person contact, as well as lead thousands into existing churches."

Has anyone written such a course? If so, I am interested in knowing more about it; but if not, I would like to attempt to write such a course myself.

> Bob Schneider, Bible Correspondence School
> Ministry to Muslims, El Atabal B-29
> Puerto de la Torre, Malaga, Spain

((Comment: Please send a copy to us of what you write to Bob.))

AGGRESSIVE INTELLIGENT PLANS TO COMMUNICATE CHRIST AND MULTIPLY CHURCHES
by Paul Landry of Brazil

Leaders of the Brazilian Mennonite Church, instead of contenting themselves with an annual average growth rate of 24 per cent (28 per cent in 1971) have formed a 17 man evangelistic team which will concentrate its efforts in a given area during a five to eight month period, and then move on to another location. The goal? To plant churches closely linked to a parent congregation in each area. Concentrated Evangelism was launched in Curitiba recently with the construction of a tabernacle near an existing church. God's blessing on this youthful denomination is impressive and we want to help it grow even more.

A NEW WIND BLOWING   by   Alfred Krass

((The December first 1972 issue of Beautiful Feet, the News Sheet on Evangelism put out by Dr. Krass for the United Church Board for World Ministries carried as an insert a Statement on Evangelism. Significant sentences of this statement follow. Space prevents printing the whole. Many of the older missionary societies are turning again to evangelism, a move which we are confident is of God and will meet the deepest needs of men.   Donald McGavran))

"Evangelism is word and deed which testify to and participate in the acts of God in Jesus Christ and call forth the response of conversion......We affirm that evangelism be it explicit or implicit is a major priority of this Board...We rejoice that the congregations and agencies of the United Church of Christ/USA manifest a growing concern for evangelism. Effective communication of the Gospel in our nation....is a high imperative but must never been seen in isolation from the vast continuing needs for world evangelism....We call on our fellow members in USA and our brothers in the churches overseas and our missionaries and staff to rededicate themselves to be faithful stewards of the Gospel."

ISRAEL, JEWS, AND CHURCH GROWTH NEWS   by Alvin Martin

Two families of missionaries to Israel, studying at the School of
World Mission at Pasadena, have been gathering information about Jews
becoming followers of Jesus. Information from all over the world is
encouraging. Dr. Goldberg writes, "At least a quarter of a million Jewish people became believers in the nineteenth century." Since the six
day war over five thousand Israelis have become followers of the Way. A
director of the American Messianic Fellowship writes, "Someone asked me
a few months ago 'How many Hebrew Christians do you know?' Within a few
minutes I counted more than a hundred among my acquaintances. Lillian
Williams says, "Never have Jewish people been so open to the Gospel, many
accepting Christ as the Messiah". Several hundred Jewish Christians
belong to the Hebrew Christian Alliance of America. And quite widely
across America and other lands Jews who believe on Jesus, and are baptized
in obedience to His Word, are calling themselves Jews for Jesus.

We have also been gathering information about literature available
to present the claims of Christ to Jews. Many books and pamphlets are
available. Those interested should write to Dean Arthur Glasser, School
of Missions, 135 N. Oakland Avenue, Pasadena, Calif. 91101.

We encourage Jews, as far as possible, to remain part of the Jewish
ethnic unit and the Jewish culture. The Early Church for at least fifteen years consisted almost entirely of Jews who had no consciousness
whatever of leaving the Jewish culture. They were called Followers of
the Way, or Believers. They kept the Sabbath - on Saturday, as well as
meeting for the Lord's Supper on the First Day of the Week - Sunday.
They were not called "Christians" at Jerusalem. That came in with the
first Gentile Christians - at Antioch. Jews today who remain in their
culture follow in an honorable tradition. Remaining in the culture and
the family may not always be possible; but when it is, it is a good thing
to do.

CHURCH GROWTH
BULLETIN

from the
INSTITUTE OF CHURCH GROWTH

Address:
FULLER THEOLOGICAL
SEMINARY
135 N. Oakland
Pasadena, Calif. 91101

DONALD A. McGAVRAN, B.D., Ph.D.
Director

May 1973   Subscription $1 per year   Volume IX No. 5

C O N T E N T S

HOW BIBLICAL IS CHURCH GROWTH THINKING?
by
Robertson McQuilkin, President of Columbia Bible College

Is Church Growth thinking biblical thinking? Study of the biblical basis of five major Church Growth presuppositions suggests that a uniform answer to this question is not possible. None of the five, rightly understood, need be in conflict with biblical teaching. Two were seen to flow directly from biblical mandate, two more seemed to be well derived from biblical principle, and one was seen to be extra-biblical, lacking both mandate and principle for validation. Yet even this was not intrinsically antithetic to biblical theology. We shall briefly state our findings in regard to each of the five.

1. Is numerical church growth the crucial task in missions?
Evangelism is indeed the crucial responsibility of the Church toward the world. The Church has other responsibilities, to be sure. The Christian, to be like Christ, must be concerned for the whole man, must work in compassion for the relief of human suffering. But the great commission is to reconcile men to God. This is the crucial task.

But is "numerical church growth" a legitimate definition of evangelism? Evangelism certainly must include the proclamation of the Good News. Further, to be true evangelism, it must aim beyond proclamation to persuade men to accept Christ as Savior and Lord. But it is more than proclamation and persuasion. True biblical evangelism has as its goal

SEND correspondence, news, and articles to the Editor, Dr. Donald McGavran, at the Institute of Church Growth, Fuller Theological Seminary. Published bi-monthly, send subscriptions and changes of address to the Business Manager, Norman L. Cummings, Overseas Crusades, Inc., 265 Lytton Avenue, Palo Alto, California 94301, U.S.A. Second-class postage paid at Palo Alto, California.

that new members be born into the family of God; that new parts be added to the Body of Christ; that the number of Christians in the Church increase. "Numerical church growth" is a startling but useful summary of this ultimate goal of evangelism.

This first, great principle of the Church Growth Movement is not, then, merely permitted by Scripture. It is commanded. Again, it is not an incidental command. It is the crucial command which indicates God's will for the Church in His great purpose of redemption.

2. Is it right for the Church to concentrate on the responsive elements of society?

Here again, the biblical evidence is clear. God is selective in His approach to men and has consistently involved His representatives in that same process of selectivity. Responsive people, for their own sake and for the sake of the unresponsive, are always eligible for further light. But (also in His grace) this light is normally diminished in proportion to the rejection of that light.

This Church Growth principle is second only in importance to the first. Like the first, it has ample biblical authority in the direct teaching of Scripture.

3. Are people movement conversions valid?

We found no biblical mandate directing the Church to seek people movements. On the other hand, we found nothing in the theology of conversion that would invalidate multi-individual decisions for Christ. In fact, we discovered ample biblical precedent for dealing with people in groups. Further, since a "people movement" is by definition a responsive element of society, this principle may be considered as a part of the second principle (concentration on the responsive) and therefore shares the scriptural foundation of the parent principle.

This principle of promoting people movements, which was the first to draw world-wide attention to the Church Growth Movement, probably ranks behind the first two in the overall contribution of the movement. It does not have the same biblical <u>mandate</u> as the first two theses, but it certainly has the validation of basic biblical <u>principles</u> and <u>precedents</u>.

4. Are anthropological studies legitimate for evangelism?

For many people in the world of missions today the use of scientific methodology and technology is the most prominent feature of the Church Growth Movement. I personally believe the greater contributions are Church Growth's clarifying the mission of the church and focusing mission activity on the responsive.

However, this does not mean that the scientific aspect of the Church Growth Movement is unimportant. Actually, all of the principles work together, reinforcing one another. The Church Growth Movement would change completely in character if any of the five basic presuppositions were omitted.

We found no biblical mandate to use the tools of science. We did find the biblical principle of using human knowledge and wisdom in the spiritual service of God and we found some biblical precedent for this sort of activity. We found such activity playing a distinctly minor role in the teaching of the Bible and we found the use of human wisdom in God's service to be carefully restricted. But the theological basis for using natural science was found to be thoroughly sound. Man's God-given responsibility to participate with all his finite resources in God's program need not violate God's sovereign will nor short-circuit His supernatural activity.

Biblical evidence, then, validates the use of scientific method-ology in discharging man's responsibility to fulfill God's evangelistic purposes. But this factor will need to be used with caution in order to maintain biblical validity.

5. Will large growth result from using Church Growth principles and techniques?
Although ranked in the fifth position, actually the entire movement would not make much sense if one did not presume that good results would follow the efforts of those who follow the presuppositions of the move-ment.

This principle lacks both a biblical mandate and clear biblical principle. However, we discover nothing in Scripture which would inval-idate this conclusion. In other words, this is an extra-biblical theory and as such deserves to be examined and tested pragmatically to deter-mine whether or not it is true.

Such examination lies outside the scope of this study. And yet, inasmuch as Scripture does not teach that large response to the Gospel is impossible and does affirm that God does not will that any should perish, Christians are under obligation to work and pray and believe toward large response. This brings us full-circle to the first pre-supposition that numerical church growth is indeed the will of God. If it is the will of God, certainly it is His will for us to use all pos-sible means to reach His goal.

CONCLUSION

Is Church Growth thinking biblical thinking? Yes, it is. This is not to say that all the people associated with Church Growth think bib-lically in all applications and interpretations of the principles. But the underlying presuppositions of the Church Growth Movement rest on a solid theological foundation grounded in the Word of God.

These five principles should not be opposed because of a wrong application some mission thinker has made. Nor should they be the pri-vate domain of a group of specialists. These concepts about the mission of the Church and how it is to be accomplished should be a moving force in all mission activity. These five Church Growth principles are indeed

church growth principles--valid and important for the whole Church of
Jesus Christ.

((The above is the conclusion of the Annual Church Growth Lectures given
by Dr. McQuilkin at Fuller Theological Seminary, April 3rd to 5th, 1973.
In them, he set forth five major principles of the Church Growth School
of Thought and the most common arguments voiced by Conservative Evangelicals against them. The pungent nature of these criticisms, quoted from
writings and conversations, kept the audience aware that real objections
were being considered. Dr. McQuilkin then stated the crucial issues involved and examined each in the light of Scripture.

He holds a high view of Scripture and his presentation was marked by
honesty and incisiveness. A large audience of national leaders, missionary associates, and faculty followed the lectures with deep interest.
Dr. McQuilkin was very much his own man, pointing out right and left
what he considered deficiencies in the church growth school of thought
and dangers which it needs to avoid. He pulled no punches.

These most readable lectures are being printed by Moody Press and should
be available by fall for use in Seminary and Bible College classes on
missions. The book will be read on many mission fields. It speaks to
hot issues. It fearlessly brings church growth thinking to the bar of
biblical authority. The concluding lecture, which is our lead article
in this issue, gives the 'bones' of the book, but leaders of missions
will want to read each chapter carefully and work through the application of Scripture to each issue. In such matters nothing takes the
place of personal conviction.   The Editor))

GOD, MAN AND CHURCH GROWTH by ALAN R. TIPPETT

(Eerdmans, 1973, p.447, $7.95)

is reviewed by Charles R. Taber, Translation Consultant of the
United Bible Societies, Alliance Biblique Universelle, Accra,
Ghana

God, Man and Church Growth is a Festschrift offered to Donald
Anderson McGavran on his 75th birthday by colleagues, fellow missiologists, and former students. The editor is Alan R. Tippett, Professor
of Missionary Anthropology at the School of Missions at Fuller Theological Seminary and Editor of "Missiology", the American Society of Missiology's new journal. As a compendium of the "state of the art" in
church growth thought, this is a very important book. It ought to go a
long way toward dispelling the canards that church growth thought is a
simple-minded instrument with a single string and that it is the isolated work of a maverick. Rather the book shows church growth thought
to be a serious and dynamic missiology, well aware of both the already
developed and the still-to-be-developed implications of its key ideas.
It is the product of the interaction of a group of men, of whom McGavran
has been for many years primus inter pares.

Space will unfortunately not permit an assessment of the 30 contributions by 26 individuals. The papers are arranged (at times somewhat arbitrarily) into six parts of unequal length and value. I will
focus on those which seem to make the most original proposals, rather
than on those which summarize acquired findings.

Part I gives "three portraits" of McGavran and his bibliography,
which includes 77 titles published over the period 1925-72. The portraits, as Tippett himself notes, are curiously impersonal, saying virtually nothing about the man but much about his work and ideas. Tippett's
own paper presents an excellent summary in historical perspective of the
key concepts in McGavran's thought: "(1) the notion of the people movement, (2) the notion of evangelistic opportunity, and (3) the differ-
entiation of discipling and perfecting" (20).

Part II, "God's Purpose and Man's Responsibility", is basically
theological. It is also the weakest part of the book, no doubt because
the authors try to handle in brief papers issues that would require
books. As a result, they often seem to skim over problems, to assert
rather than to prove, and to fail to interact at a deep level with
critics. Especially creative is the paper by Charles H. Kraft, "Toward
a Christian Ethnotheology", in which the author argues that theology and
anthropology can be harnessed together to handle in a cross-disciplin-
ary way the dialectic of the absoluteness of God and the culture-bound
finiteness of man and his works (including his ideas about God).

In Part III, "God's Work in Human Structures", several authors deal
with strategy and field methodology. Potentially the most suggestive
paper is Roy E. Shearer's all too brief "The Psychology of Receptivity
and Church Growth", in which he proposes a psychological test for receptivity to the gospel. Unfortunately he does not deal at all with the
serious problem of the culture-boundness of psychological testing instruments, in the perspective of what Tippett calls in an excellent paper
the "cultural compulsives" which shape public and private opinion. Nor
does he mention the idea, which I think is plausible, that receptivity
is at least in part an artifact of an adequate versus an inadequate
approach in initial contact and pre-evangelism.

Of the four papers in Part IV, "God in Human History", Ralph D.
Winter's is most interesting for its proposal and exemplification of a
very fruitful interaction between historical and cross-cultural perspectives.

Part V, "God and Man in Field Situations", presents case studies in
church growth from Honduras, Colombia, New Guinea, Ethiopia, and Argentina. Stan Shewmaker's paper on Zambia, included in Part III, (Strategy),
should in my judgment be here, where it would counter-balance the over-
emphasis on Latin America.

Part VI, "Research Techniques for the Work of God", is obviously
methodological. The best of four workmanlike papers is Tetsunao Yamamori's "Applying the Comparative Method to Church Studies (Japan)".

Yamamori discusses intelligibly and interestingly, with specific exem-
plifications, both the technique and the rationale for the use of analyzed rather than raw statistics.

In a conclusion, "Where Do We Go From Here?" the editor assesses
the ground covered and suggests directions for future developments. He
calls for a refinement of the theological base, especially in the direction of ethnotheology; increased interaction and interpenetration of
the various disciplines involved; development of greater sophistication
in our conception of strategy and methodology; and a greater number and
variety of case studies to provide the empirical base. I would second
all of these recommendations, and add a further one: a greatly increased
voice for non-Westerners, not only in providing case studies, but in
theoretical and methodological creativity.

This review would not be complete without a word about what is a
leit-motiv of this book: the complaint that church growth thought is
often badly misrepresented. At places authors seem to attribute this
to ill-will. This may be true in a small number of cases, but in my
opinion the cause is more complex. The very richness of church growth
thought, paradoxically, makes it difficult for a person not deeply committed to read an adequate sampling of the extensive literature; it is
very easy, without wrong intentions, to read only one facet and thus to
come to a biased judgment.

Further, church growth thought has not developed in equal proportions all of its various implications, and critics can well feel that
incompletely developed ideas represent flaws in the theory. Finally, it
is inevitable that a movement, however complex, that centers around a
few boldly stated concepts lends itself, like a face with distinctive
features, to caricature, and not only at the hands of its foes.

This Festschrift can go a long way towards correcting honest misunderstandings by summarizing comprehensively yet briefly the multiple
strands of Church Growth Thought. It marks a milestone, not only in the
life of Donald A. McGavran, but in missiology. And it is to be hoped
that the many directions for further growth suggested by the book will
be explored until church growth thought is in reality what it is in
promise, a truly balanced and comprehensive view of the divine mission
in the world.

THE WAVE THEORY OF CHURCH PROPAGATION

by Rev. Peter Cotterell, Ph.D. of the Sudan Interior Mission,
Ethiopia, lecturing during the Spring Quarter at Fuller's School
of Missions.

The Christian Church is becoming aware of the great movement of
God's Holy Spirit over the last thirty or so years in Ethiopia. Little
publicized, it needs little publicity. One hundred believers in three
areas in southern Ethiopia in 1937, ten thousand believers in the same

area in 1942, today a Christian community of a quarter of a million, and
still growing! Surely such a movement has something to teach us concerning church growth. From the myriad suggestions which present themselves, let us pay attention to just two: the pattern of evangelism
and the potential for prediction.

The Pattern of Evangelism. In the growing and grass-roots indigenous Church there were basically two types of evangelism: spontaneous
and structured. The two types worked together to present an interesting parallel to the wave theory of light propagation. As light spreads
out from a light source, each point on the advancing front may be
imagined as the centre of a fresh centre of propagation. Similarly, as
in Ethiopia the area occupied by the Church extended, believers on the
edges of the discipled areas acted as fresh centres of Gospel proclamation. Without being instructed in techniques, they found the Good News
so transforming, so vital that they spontaneously shared it with those
they met on the way to market, with passing traders, with visitors, and
so sent a new wave of proclamation ahead of them as their converts
spread the light.

Structured evangelism also was prosecuted vigorously by the churches.
When a group of refugees, driven out by the Italian Army, appeared on
the doorstep as it were, the Church sent in evangelists and supported
them. But notice the pattern: the evangelists were not sent so far
away as to be totally out of touch with their home churches. When they
were sick, or as often happened, imprisoned, their churches could respond
by sending help: medical, financial or material.

It must be remembered that expansion beyond already occupied areas
can be very dangerous. A gentle probing is usually necessary, the ac-
customing of the inhabitants of the new area to the presence of strangers,
an acculturation of the messengers, and this is best accomplished by
the techniques (never consciously developed as such) used in southern
Ethiopia.

After World War II, when the Sudan Interior Mission returned to
Ethiopia in 1945, mission and Church regularly shared the responsibility for advance into new areas. A missionary with God's gift for evangelism moved into a new area which was under the general cultural um-
brella of the already existing churches. Where terrain was rugged,
MAF was called in, airstrips were built (Columbia Bible College students
financed a large number of these) and initial surveys made. Areas of
responsibility were then demarcated and the evangelists got to work.
The first converts often were taken to some central point for a couple
of weeks of Bible teaching. As churches multiplied, however, teaching
moved to the new congregations. This double-facetted advance has characterized much church growth in its territorial aspect thus far. It may
be easily diagrammed:

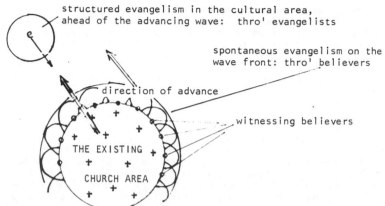

structured evangelism in the cultural area,
ahead of the advancing wave: thro' evangelists

spontaneous evangelism on the
wave front: thro' believers

direction of advance

witnessing believers

THE EXISTING

CHURCH AREA

But what has happened to attempts to extend this strategy to areas remote from the home base? What has happened when a missionary-national
team went to a tribe or area far away from the existing Church? Thus
far, uniform failure. Culture shock is too great, the support role of
the Church is too minimal. It appears that a principle operates here,
with the sovereign Holy Spirit moving in, initiating a new salvation
event, inaugurating a new area, which must then be occupied by Spirit-
led evangelists. The attempt to organize the Spirit into some fresh out-
growth in a remote area where we would like to put a mission effort has
not succeeded.

These observations are offered simply as a contribution to knowledge, without any suggestion that this Ethiopian experience is a key to
all evangelism and fits all locks. The implications of these observations for missionary society operations I leave for others to work out.

The Potential For Prediction. Can we, then, predict areas where
church growth is to be expected, and non-growth is a subject for concern?
I believe we can. In Southern Ethiopia the Evangelical Church has been
growing steadily in one area, and now numbers at least ten thousand communicants. Just west of that Church of ten thousand is an area in which
SIM has had a mission station for many years, but no significant growth
has occurred: just a handful of believers with no effective outreach.
And yet, no serious geographical barrier separated them from the greatly
growing churches. Cultural features were the same. Linguistic study
showed that people in the western area spoke a dialect of the predominant language of the multiplying churches.

The Survey Team found two concentric rings surrounding the mission
station, isolating it from the potential harvest fields beyond. The
first ring, The Core, was made up of government administrators. The
second, The Mantle, was made up of Moslem traders. Both Core and Mantle
were highly resistant and had effectively stopped Christianization for
many years and had, indeed, hidden the responsive fringes of the district.

The missionaries had never gotten beyond these two fifteen-mile-thick rings.

So we sent in an Evangelistic Team. It used MAF to hop over the unresponsive area and then preached to the responsive people beyond. In weeks, the first congregations came into existence. In one area, five were formed in one week. In another, twenty-four congregations formed in a six-month period. The parable of the sower, soil and seed has this to teach us: granted no fundamentally disturbing factor, soil which has proved fruitful in one area may be expected to be fruitful wherever it is found, and the sower may then indeed sow in certain hope.

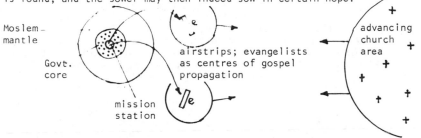

Moslem mantle

Govt. core

airstrips; evangelists as centres of gospel propagation

mission station

advancing church area

SEOUL, LAUSANNE, AND AFERICASIAN MISSIONARY SOCIETIES - Donald McGavran

During the last three days of August 1973 a most important meeting will take place in Seoul, Korea. Eminent Asian Christians, thoroughly convinced that Asian Churches should be sending missionaries on a much larger scale, will gather to attempt great things for God. I hope those planning for the 1974 Lausanne Congress on Evangelism will see the enormous importance of the Seoul meeting and further the advances projected there.

Philip Tsuchiya, a minister of Christ in Japan, bright eyed with excitement, told me a week ago that whereas the denominations in Japan are already sending out a few missionaries, missionary minded Japanese Christians are now planning to send out a thousand. And why not? One immediately thinks of the tremendous man power of Afericasian Churches. Let Korean Churches send out five thousand! Why should not the four million Christians in the islands of the South Pacific send out two thousand missionaries? They would bear convincing testimony of the transformation God has wrought in the islands during the past four generations. In the Hump Country are strong Baptist Churches of 250,000, 150,000, 100,000 and 50,000 communicants. The Christians are citizens of India and Burma and can work anywhere in those lands. Suppose Hump Country Churches were to send out five hundred missionaries!

As Christians of all six continents enter the last quarter of the twentieth century, they observe a most responsive and winnable world. More individuals and more segments of populations are receptive to Christ than at any other time in the last two thousand years. Men from hundreds

of Macedonias are appearing in hundreds of Troases. To be sure, timid
Christians bemused by the post war pessimism and loss of nerve which
collapse of Europe's empires occasioned are inclined hastily to deny that
any such responsiveness exists. But the facts are against them. The
facts prove widespread receptivity. To be sure, many populations exist
still indifferent or even resistant; but enough receptive populations
exist that into them the whole available missionary resources of the
Churches can be poured and they will not be satisfied. This kind of
world confronts the Asian leaders as they meet in Korea.

Large sendings of Africasian missionaries by Africasian Churches
will change and reinforce the image of the missionary. They will change
it in that missionaries will be Africasians, carrying passports from
India, the Philippines, Korea, Zaire, and Brazil. They will have darker
skins than most missionaries did in the first quarters of the century.
They will present not European but Africasian Christianity. They will
be talking about Taiwan, Indonesia, Fiji, Zambia, South Africa, Ghana,
or Ecuador, not about Sweden or Scotland or South Carolina. The cultural overhang they will guard against will be Africasian, not Eurican.

They will reinforce the image in that they will proclaim the same
Christ, regard the same Bible as their sole authority, multiply churches
and consider themselves part of the world-wide Christian Movement. They
will be salt and light in the world. They will be a blessing wherever
they go. They will endure persecution patiently and pray for those who
despitefully use them. They will, in short, be real missionaries and
will advance the banner of Christ.

I hope Seoul will change one characteristic of Africasian missionaries. These, at present, usually go to established European missions
or to Africasian Churches and become parts of an international team.
This has some advantages. It helps Eurican missions to overcome their
excessively white image. It emphasises the international character of
Christianity. It demonstrates that missionaries of different racial
backgrounds can live together harmoniously. But it does not, as a rule,
accomplish much evangelization. These international teams function well
in theological seminaries, but seldom spearhead the discipling of a
district or a valley. Too much of their time is spent adjusting to the
cultural differences of the various members of the team. Perhaps the
greatest disadvantage of such a disposition of Asian missionaries is that
they become permanent minorities in organizations dominated by other
nationalities. Their national creativeness is handicapped.

When Africasian Churches were sending out one or two highly educated missionaries, it was inevitable that these go to already established institutions. That was a good way to begin. But the time has
now come for bands of missionaries from each Africasian land to take
a segment of a city, a fertile plain, a mountain province and work there
till they have established a cluster of on-going congregations. Then
they will move on to another place and do the same - just as missionaries have always done from the time of Paul onward. Let a Korean team
of ten missionaries go to Sao Paulo, Brazil and multiply churches there

for the next twenty years. Let a Japanese team of twenty families harvest the fertile field north west of Adilabad between the Church South
India and the Christian and Missionary Alliance. Let a Filipino Team of
seven families disciple a responsive population along some great river
of inland Kalimantan.

One advantage of teams of missionaries of this sort is that their
standard of living can be - and should be - substantially that of the
ministers and laymen of the congregations which send them out and support
them. If all the missionaries of a given mission live on the same standard of living, interior tensions are minimized. Supporters know that
our missionaries live like we do. Support becomes easier to raise.
There is no future for Asian missions if Asian missionaries have to live
as parts of multi-national teams, each member of which is recompensed
at a different level. A Taiwanese missionary society will make whatever
rules it thinks just and practical for the twenty Taiwanese missionaries
it sends out. These rules will be quite different from those made by a
Japanese missionary society.

Exciting possibilities open up before Seoul and Lausanne because,
once Africasian missionary societies begin sending out bands of missionaries, it becomes possible for Eurican missionary societies - who are
working toward exactly the same goal - to say, "The annual cost of your
mission is 10,000. Recruit four times as many missionaries. We will
give you without strings 40,000 a year to add to your 10,000. The condition of the gift will be a simple one - that all the money we give go
into intelligent great commission mission. As long as you are carrying
out church multiplying mission, we leave entirely in your hands the
administration of the enterprise."

I hope that Seoul will plan aggressive church planting Asian missions. And that Lausanne will give serious consideration to making
available to all such Asian Missions financial resources from affluent
Eurican denominations. Why should not the man power of Africasian
Churches be wedded to the financial resources of Eurican Churches to
meet more effectively the needs of the world? The Great Commission
could become the strongest link binding Africasian and Eurican Churches
together.

N E W S

REMARKABLE CHURCH GROWTH IN HIGH ECUADOR   by   Henry Klaasen

God's Spirit continues to move in an exceptional way among the
Quichua Indians of Chimborazo Province in Ecuador. The young Church is
gaining momentum. In 1968 it had 11 congregations, 315 baptized members, and 650 believers. At the end of 1972 it had 50 congregations,
2,356 baptized members and 4300 believers. In 1972 there were 956 baptisms. Our total community now numbers about ten thousand.

On September 17, 1972, a Quichua pastor, Manuel Naula, and a missionary, Joyce Bentson, were beaten after a baptismal service in Balcashi. Manuel was left unconscious. Joyce was beaten from head to foot and had several teeth knocked out. A subsequent letter stated, "Both have recovered and are back in full swing. A few weeks ago the leader of the attack went to the lay pastor of the Evangelical Christians, put his arm around him and asked forgiveness. He and others have now accepted the Lord."

On January 29, 1973, missionary Norm Smith was beaten by a mob of 400 Indians about twenty miles northwest of his home in Cotopaxie Province. He looked terrible when he arrived home, but has suffered no lasting damage. Art Smith writes, "This may be the beginning of great revivals among the Quichuas of Cotopaxie. We are hoping for a repeat of the Chimborazo Province revival."

A number of years ago Mable Alton, of the Gospel Missionary Union, was beaten by Quichuas and thrown in a ditch on a road out of Pulicate. Today there is a thriving church in Pulicate. Years later Dr. Donald Dilworth (SWM ICG 1967) was beaten and almost killed by a mob of fanatic Indians. Now there is a Quichua church in that place.

But the Quichua Christians themselves have suffered the brunt of the persecution. Hundreds have been beaten or had their homes attacked. Persecution is something they expect to face when they declare themselves for Christ -- it is a common and integral part of this spiritual awakening. It is also proving to be the seed of the Church -- where persecution strikes, the establishment and growth of a church usually follow.

Joyce Bentson said, after she had been beaten, "Many of the Quichua brothers have been beaten and left for dead. Now the Lord has given me the PRIVILEGE of sharing in their kind of suffering."

((Dr. Cotterell's book, titled Born at Midnight, on the growth of the Evangelical Church in Ethiopia is scheduled for publication by Moody Press in May. This competent account of one of the truly great missionary works of all time will be widely read all around the world. Every missiologist will want to study it. Every minister, in Africasia and Eurica, will profit by this story of the power of the Gospel meeting the needs of men.   Donald McGavran))

CHURCH GROWTH
B U L L E T I N

from the
INSTITUTE OF
CHURCH GROWTH

Address:
FULLER THEOLOGICAL
SEMINARY
135 N. Oakland
Pasadena, Calif. 91101

DONALD A. McGAVRAN, B.D., Ph.D.
Director

July 1973   Subscription $1 per year   Vol. IX No. 6

C O N T E N T S

ACCOUNTABILITY FOR WORLD EVANGELIZATION
by
Dr. James F. Engel

Institutions of all types are under attack. The business firm is
pressured to justify its existence in more than profit terms; the educational Institution no longer can hide under the guise of "education
for education's sake." In short, there are growing demands for ac-
countability--proof of effectiveness in discharge of responsibilities--
and the Church is not immune.

God has given His Church the commission of going to the world and
making disciples through teaching and baptizing. The task is not yet
done, and many are sensing that He is demanding in a new way that we
"show ourselves as workmen worthy of our hire." This necessitates new
methods of planning and research. It is the purpose of this article to
distill the essence of the requirements of evangelistic stewardship in
a complex and changing world.

We must clearly distinguish between <u>constants</u> and <u>variables</u>. The
biblical commands to evangelize the world, to pray, to worship are constants which can never change. The program for implementation of a constant, however, is a variable which must change as circumstances change.
All too frequently outmoded methods of evangelism are maintained with
scant attention paid to effectiveness. When a variable becomes a constant, diminution in effectiveness is inevitable and stewardship suffers.

Diminution is perpetuated, when intuition and experience are substituted for spirit-led planning based on information and analysis. An intuitive "feel" can be decidedly misleading without a foundation in factual knowledge. It is an equally-dangerous trap to maintain programs just because "it always has been done this way."

Ineffective evangelism is not inevitable if we return to biblical principles of administration: "Any enterprise is built by wise planning, becomes strong through common sense, and profits wonderfully by keeping abreast of the facts" (Proverbs 24:3, 4).[1] The writer of Proverbs provides concrete guidance:

1. Analyze the environment. "It is dangerous and sinful to rush into the unknown" (19:3); "sensible man watches for problems ahead and prepares to meet them" (27:12).

2. Make plans based on this information. "We should make plans--counting on God to direct us" (16:9).

3. Measure effectiveness. "Anyone willing to be corrected is on the pathway to life" (10:17); "A man who refuses to admit his mistakes can never be successful" (28:13).

4. Analyze and modify where necessary. "It is pleasant to see plans develop. That is why fools refuse to give them up even when they are wrong" (13:19).

Surprisingly, these ancient biblical principles provide the foundation of contemporary management theory, and there is no other path to stewardship. The ever present danger is that "A man may ruin his chances by his own foolishness and then blame it on the Lord!" (Proverbs 19:3). Research-based planning frees us to follow the Holy Spirit and does not supplant Him as some allege.

THE KEYS TO ACCOUNTABILITY

How can these biblical principles concerning evangelism be applied in a 20th Century world?

Environmental Analysis

Evangelism is communication of biblical content. Communication, in turn, does not occur until the recipient of a message grasps the intended content of the sender.[2] Communication often is short circuited, however, in that each person screens out unwanted messages through avoidance, miscomprehension, and lack of retention.[3]

---

[1] All scriptural quotes are from the Living Bible.
[2] See J.F. Engel, H.G. Wales, and M.R. Warshaw, Promotional strategy, rev. ed. (Homewood: Richard D. Irwin, Inc., 1971), ch. 2.
[3] See J.F. Engel, D.T. Kollat, and R.D. Blackwell, Consumer Behavior, rev. ed. (New York: Holt, Rinehard and Winston, Inc., 1973), ch. 8.

Through this selective information processing, men filter inputs and protect strongly held beliefs. We cannot simply <u>send</u> a message through various media, therefore, and assume that communication takes place.

The Great Commission calls for "making disciples." People fall somewhere on the continuum illustrated in Figure 1, running from complete lack of awareness of the Gospel to abundant knowledge about it and participation in it. Communication must be directed to persons either individually or corporately, where they are on this continuum, in terms that they can understand and comprehend. The plan of salvation, for example, is meaningless to a person at the top of the continuum, and he will screen the message out. The failure of communication is our fault, not his. It is true that God's word will not return to Him void, but this presupposes that it has been properly communicated by God's human instruments.

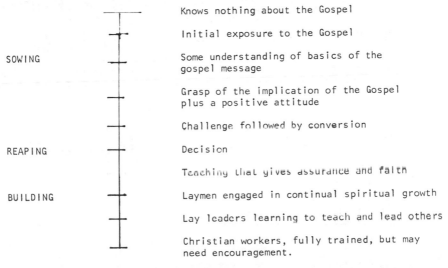

	Knows nothing about the Gospel
	Initial exposure to the Gospel
SOWING	Some understanding of basics of the gospel message
	Grasp of the implication of the Gospel plus a positive attitude
	Challenge followed by conversion
REAPING	Decision
	Teaching that gives assurance and faith
BUILDING	Laymen engaged in continual spiritual growth
	Lay leaders learning to teach and lead others
	Christian workers, fully trained, but may need encouragement.

Figure 1.   The Spiritual Status of Man (source: Viggo Sogaard, Wheaton Graduate School)

We are too prone to refer to a person, to a group, or to an entire field as closed to evangelism, when, in reality, <u>our</u> communication has been off target. We must analyze various "audience segments," discovering their spiritual status and needs. Then the proper message can be given in terms appropriate to their lifestyles. This increasingly requires the use of survey research. Growing numbers of Christian organizations are employing this methodology to great advantage.

Determination of Program

A properly-conceived environmental analysis usually reveals areas of needs and provides the foundation for concrete-measurable goals. Goals, in turn, provide the basis for evangelistic strategy encompassing all media of communication. Definition of program without the foundation of research is a management procedure destined to ineffectiveness.

Measurement of Effectiveness

Concrete numerical goals permit precise measurement of effectiveness, and are the only means of accounting for performances. As secular advertisers have demonstrated, <u>communication effectiveness can be measured</u>.[4] Statistics on church growth are only one indicator of success in winning and building men. We also must document success or failure in other stages of the evangelism continuum. Often this requires modern tools of survey research.

Analysis of Results and Program Modification

Measures of effectiveness provide valuable clues about what works and what does not. Indeed, the Holy Spirit can guide us most fruitfully during a "postmortem" analysis of results.

CONCLUSION

The Church must be accountable to God and also to society for performance in world evangelization. The approach of goal-oriented contemporary management is, in reality, a 20th Century expression of the biblical principles of spirit-led problem solving. If we are to evangelize the world in our generation or the next, spiritual men cannot avoid the enormous implications of this fact.

---

[4]Engel, Wales, and Warshaw, <u>op. cit</u>., chs. 17. and 18.

---

41 Churches in 3 Months

<u>La Paz Bolivia, May 15th, 1973</u> "Yesterday I was handed the last report of Aymara church growth on the Altiplano. It shows tremendous increase, even after the latest figures of February. Forty-one new churches have been raised up in three months! Four hundred and fifty new members have been baptized during the same time. (The churches average ten or twelve baptized believers and many more in the Evangelical 'community') My life and ministry for the Lord will never be the same. Since I have seen the churches growing and expanding throughout the whole country, I will never try to do anything else in my life. Church planting is exciting! And contagious!" Bruno Frigoli, A.E.M.

STATE ACTIONS AND THE CAUSE OF CHRIST
by Vernon Middleton, Union Biblical Seminary, India

((The following account reminds us that God is at work in history creating conditions which favor the entrance into eternal and abundant
life (salvation) of considerable segments of society. We may openly
rejoice in such doings of our Sovereign Lord. Would that timid Christians, who see nothing but defeat in the world and flagellate themselves and their churches and missions with such abandon, would open
their eyes to these facts and share in our joy!

The new state of Meghalaya (cloud abode) in India was created for secular reasons, but since the population of its mountains had become over-
whelmingly Christian in a long series of people movements, the new state
has been good for Christianity as well as for India.

What could be more natural than for Meghalaya churches, which have been
so greatly blessed by God, to do as Professor Middleton suggests and
send missionaries to less blessed ethnic units in India - small parts
of the millions who have yet to believe? Donald McGavran))

"The creation of Meghalaya as a separate state in East India has
been a terrific boon to the cause of Christ. Every minister of the
State Government is a Christian. The total environment is permeated
with Christian ideals and the dynamic which Christ gives through His
resurrection power. Other religious influences are minimal. The Christian atmosphere is so marked that some of the men from other parts of
India, sent into the state by the Central Government, are becoming Christians. Integrity, cleanliness, innovation, dignity of labour, human
equality, male-female rights, and respect for others are very evident.
I visited villages from one end of Meghalaya to the other and base
my judgment of the general condition on what I saw. I was comparing
villages in Meghalaya, of course, with the villages I know so well in
other parts of India.
I was impressed with the growth now taking place in "The Church of
God". The late Nichols Roy, a Bengali Christian, founded this Church.
Without foreign aid and without outside administration, it has grown to
14,000 communicants with over 300 congregations.
The Presbyterian Church founded by Welsh missionaries is - alas -
drifting into nominalism. But several of its leaders have been revital-
ized. Robert Cunville, who will be studying at the School of World Missions in Pasadena this fall is a bright hope for bringing about renewal
and new vision in that Church. He will share with you many great insights in the realm of Christian possession of ancestor worship. He will
tell you of modifications which take place in a matriarchal society due
to Christian influences.
I visited several Presbyterian pastors and their theological college at Cherrapunji. I pled with them to send missionaries to the Presbyterian area of the Bhil tribe in western India, and to the Gond tribes
in which the Free Church of Scotland has been sowing seed for many years.
I asked the Church of God to send missionaries to the Korku tribes. The

message I preached on the subject of missions, based on Isaiah 5:1-7 to a convention audience of 4,000 was published in the·Khasi newspaper, Ka Pyrta Uriewlum. I challenged the Church of God by drawing parallels between Israel the Chosen People and the Khasis as God's Chosen People. If they as God's annointed fail to fulfill the commission, Cherrapunji (the wettest place in the world, 600 inches a year) could become the driest place in the world!!

I shall be sending you an extensive report of my research in a few days' time. The indigenous developments of expression and worship used in the congregations of "The Church of God" are impressive. You will be able to use them in your class in Christianity and Culture."

NEW TESTAMENT FIRE IN THE PHILIPPINES   by Jim Montgomery

Really, this article is not by Jim Montgomery. It is by Donald McGavran - about a most readable and informative book of the above title by Jim Montgomery. Jim is a journalist turned missionary. While working in the Philippines, he learned about a Church there which had achieved great growth with local leadership, local money and a very small number of American missionaries. He decided to find out how this occurred. How had this Church grown from nothing in 1949 to 10,961 communicants, 194 churches and 179 churchlets by the end of 1967?

Montgomery talked to hundreds of members of this denomination in all parts of the Philippines. He spent weeks with pastors, laymen, district superintendents, new converts and old Christians. He reports what they told him. The book is packed with human interest. It reads itself.

Montgomery also talked to Protestant pastors and members of denominations whose churches were growing slowly and who were suspicious of all this rapid growth. They wondered if it was solid and commendable! So his writing swings to and fro between factual description of what he saw and critical evaluation of how valid it was.

Montgomery is Field Director for Overseas Crusades in the Philippines and has much more than ordinary opportunity to know all the denominations and to travel widely all over the islands.

New Testament Fire in the Philippines has already had remarkable influence in the Philippines, opening up to many a missionary and many a minister new possibilities, new hopes, new methods, new magnitudes of church growth. I recommend it strongly to ministers and missionaries in other countries. It is a most readable, germane and influential book - $2.50 ($1.50 to members of the Church Growth Book Club). Do yourself a favor. Enjoy a copy and pass it on to people who like good reading.

SALVATION TODAY

Recalling that the World Council of Churches suggests that men are "Saved By Mao", trying to balance things a bit by pointing in the direction of Japan, adopting our well known ecumenical stance, and hoping that this contribution to the great debate on Salvation Today will be truly significant, Church Growth Bulletin proudly presents the thought that

D A T S U N   S A V E S

(about a gallon a day)

WITHIN CULTURE: UNDER GOD'S WORD

by James I. Dretke

Lutheran Mission, Ghana, Africa

Men should become Christian within their culture. In and by itself culture - like grammar - is neutral as far as its relationships to godly or satanic action is concerned. God uses culture for His purposes, as does Satan. Men use capitalism and communism for good and bad ends. Language can be used to bless and to curse. Since culture in and by itself is not evil, it is quite appropriate that men should become Christian in their culture and in their language. After all, all men are immersed in culture and all, in their cultural diversity, can be redeemed to the glory of God.

If man is expected to serve God "outside" of his culture, a tremendous vacuum is created in his life which hampers a full and free sacrifice of himself to the purposes of God, for culture is so very, very much a part of himself. Scripture directs: "Be not conformed to this world, but be transformed." A part of that transformation is baptizing and transforming elements of each culture into the service of God.

When this transformation takes place in an individual, within his society and within his culture, that individual is then in a key position to fulfil his role as a "bridge of God's reconciliation" to his neighbor. The offense of the Gospel is still there, but the sweet gospel message is not hampered by unnecessary cultural obstacles.

The fact that a person has become Christian within his culture does not mean that there will be no cultural obstacles between his hearing and obeying the Gospel. Biblical requirements override all personal, traditional, western, cultural and ethnic norms. Since Satan works within each culture, certain elements of it become infiltrated with the satanic. When the Word - "sharper than a two-edged sword" - judges any elements of the culture to be satanic, they must be avoided, eradicated, or transformed. They must bow before the will of God working through us.

At this point a word should be spoken concerning the importance of people movements. When elements within culture have been taken over by the satanic, it may be difficult, yea, even almost impossible, for an individual to stand strong in his singular commitment to God. It is exceedingly difficult to stand alone in the face of the crushing force of his culture. If, however, he can be supported by his neighbors, who have undertaken the same single-minded commitment to the Lord (and even as he is being supported by them, he in turn lends his support to them) then he can stand strong and his church, too, has great strength. It can withstand the heavy onslaught of culture to make everything conform to it. The strength of a people movement rests in part on the multi-individual strength massed toward applying biblical insight to the "sanctification of cultural/ethnic norms."

If the position that men should become Christian within their culture is understressed, individuals may become Christian apart from their culture. This is neither healthy for the individual as he tries to fulfil his Christian life, nor helpful to him as he tries to communicate his faith to others. Either he remains in his culture and carefully compartmentalizes his Christianity and his culture, so that his Christian faith remains nothing more than a Sunday morning ritual which has little or nothing to do with the rest of his life; or he "creates" for himself a new culture which effectively detaches him from communication with his previous world. When this happens, we see the Christian <u>sealed off</u> in his own enclave, incapable of spreading the Word.

If the biblical requirements are understressed, people may become "Christian" but has anything really happened? If personal, traditional, western, cultural, ethnic norms are the sole determinants of behavior and options open to an individual or society, then the door is closed to God's breaking into that society with His power to create and renew. An important aspect of God's revealing Himself to us is in the Bible's "Thus says the Lord", and wherever this imperative is muted, men become unwilling to obey Him.

Any unwillingness to sublimate <u>all</u> - including western cultures and traditions - to God's will, waters down the Gospel's message, and in the final analysis, tends to destroy its finality and its uniqueness. Men should become Christian within their culture, except where that culture conflicts with God's Word. His Word must be the final arbiter.

Biblical requirements override all personal, western, eastern, cultural, and ethnic norms, <u>except those which do not conflict with the Word</u>. Many elements of culture are strictly relative (of equal validity from culture to culture) and neutral (neither of God nor of Satan). These may be practiced as Christians choose. Whether to use a chewing stick or a toothbrush, whether to sit - men on one side, women on the other, whether to put on clothes or not, all these the Christian should order according to his culture. The Scriptures say nothing about them.

A ROMAN CATHOLIC COMMENT ON BANKOK

"COMMENTS ON BANGKOK CONFERENCE general assembly of the Commission for World Mission and Evangelization of World Council of Churches, December 29 to Jan. 12, 1973:
> In the debate, the mission confided by Christ
> to all his disciples was not considered; the
> world with its expectations and needs was over-
> looked; the biblical message was not invoked;
> the intentions, devotion, and love of the mission-
> aries with their mistakes and methods, were not
> taken note of......"

Mission Intercom. United States Catholic Mission Council: 1325 Massachusetts Avenue, N.W. Washington, D.C. 20005 No. 26 June JULY 1973

THE FOURTH WORLD AND ASIAN MISSIONARIES   by Bishop Chandu Ray

The Fourth World indicates those, everywhere, who have yet to come to Christ. It should be the first concern of Christians throughout the world. Ninety-eight per cent of Asia is in The Fourth World.

Some Asian denominations have learnt to send evangelists to their own cultural "Jerusalem" (Acts 1:8). Some have sent their missionaries to their Judeas and Samarias. But most Asian churches (involved in youth fellowships, theological training, women's auxiliaries, liturgical forms, church buildings, institutions, constitutions and plans for union) send no missionaries to "the uttermost parts of the earth".

Surely the time has come for Asian Christians to evangelize their Jerusalems and Samarias, praying continuously that some, approved of God for faithfulness in nearby witness, may soon be entrusted with missions to totally different peoples. This vision will be fulfilled only as Asians develop their own kinds of missionaries and evangelists who focus on The Fourth World. Please pray that this vision may prevail at the "All Asia Mission Consultation" in Seoul during August 1973, and at the "All Asia Student Missionary Convention" in Manila in December.

CHURCH MULTIPLYING MISSIONS IN KOREA   by Major Paul Rader

For most missionaries in main-line denominations, absorption of the mission into the Church is a fact of life. For them, what Prof. C. Peter Wagner has aptly designated "The Babylonian Captivity of the Christian Mission", is a fait accompli.

Some missionaries, however, reject the theology of defeatism and retain a vision for discipling the vast populations still without Christ. Such missionaries want to plant churches which become parts of their own denominations. One model for such planting comes from Korea.

Southern Presbyterian missionaries in Soonchun in the southwest corner of the Republic are vigorously planting churches. Missionary Hugh Linton, insists that after twenty years he still finds the work "tremendously gratifying". While 90% of Korea's 32 millions are still without Christ and the percentage of non-Christians is significantly higher in villages, it is no time to phase out church planting missionaries. "A missionary can have a unique, vital and rewarding role in rural evangelism," Linton affirms.

In 1966, Linton and his fellow-workers made a careful survey of the area covered by the Soonchun, Chinju and Mokpo presbyteries. They discovered it was one of the most densely populated rural areas in the world, with as many inhabitants - nearly five million - as the burgeoning capital at Seoul. They knew the area was generally responsive. They then plotted its 1,054 churches on a huge reconaissance map. They found serious gaps. Near the cities, on the borders of the presbyteries and in isolated areas were scores of villages without a church in walking distance. They developed a seven year plan to put a congregation in "each village of more than 100 houses four kilometers distant from the nearest evangelical church."

They knew only a close-knit network of churches makes self-support by county possible in rural Korea. Individual churches might still be dependent, but each group of churches, called a sichal, should be internally self-reliant. There are seven sichals in the Soonchun Presbytery, with some 25 churches in each of them.

Small rural churches need one another. Financial assistance is only one consideration, and not the most important. Linton declares, "The more churches you have and the closer together they are, the stronger all will be." Deacons and elders from stronger churches visit and en-

courage struggling congregations. Special area meetings, social
gatherings, training programs, and evangelistic thrusts are easy within
a cluster of churches. The whole impact on the community is greater.

Isolated churches languish. If Linton finds one of his congregations located among churches of another denomination, he will urge it
to join them. He would rather have it change the sign on the door than
to perish.

Not only has planting churches proved spiritually stimulating for
individual churches and sichals; but rural pastors and unordained evangelists function more efficiently when they have two or more congregations to care for. "Put a poorly-trained man into one church and it
will ruin the church," says Linton. "Spread him out over three and all
three will do better."

Results in the Soonchun Presbytery - where alone the plan has been
implemented - have been heartening. In 1966 there were 52 unreached
villages in the presbytery. But 1972 there were only 12, and congregations were being established in all but five of them. Between 1965 and
1969 the presbytery grew from 174 to 203 churches, all with their own
church buildings. During the same period, neighboring Mokpo Presbytery
added only seven to its total of 78 churches and Chinju grew from 81 to
82! In April 1972 Soonchun reported 119 fully self-supporting churches,
as against 52 in 1966. The goal is for the presbytery to be entirely
self-supporting by the end of 1973.

Communicant membership also has been on the rise, in spite of the
facts that the population in the province has not increased in the last
five years and losses are sustained each year as young people migrate to
the cities. In 1971 communicant membership had grown to 9,680 from
7,070 in 1966, i.e. about 74% a decade. Before 1966 smaller churches
were dying. Aggressive church planting reversed this situation.

Linton and his colleagues have worked through the structure of the
Jesus Presbyterian Church (Tonghap) to which denomination they are related. Their program, christened "Operation Lighthouse", was approved
by the Soonchun Presbytery in 1966. A key man in its implementation has
been the Rev. An Ki-ch'ang, general secretary of the Evangelism Department of the Soonchun Presbytery.

Implementation has been at sichal level. Under the aegis of the
Evangelism Department, leaders met with sichal committees and sold the
idea. They encouraged each sichal to accept responsibility for evangelizing its own area. They agreed to help with planning, give oversight,
provide materials, assist with actual construction of churches, and use
denominational (i.e. mission) funds to stimulate the program. Assistance, it should be noted, was subject to a strict schedule of regulations
developed as the project proceeded.

Minimal salary subsidies were provided for pastors or evangelists
willing to assume oversight of two or more congregations. If three or
more, a bicycle was provided.

When a new congregation had been established and had 10 to 15 baptized members, including one whole family, it could qualify for assistance in building a small church. Outside funding, however, was limited
to 25% of the total construction cost. The project had to be debt-free
and the first stage of construction completed. Forms to make inexpensive

reinforced concrete beams were prepared by Linton and made available
through the Evangelism Department office, with a worker who supervised
the building.

All funds were channeled through the sichal committee, which also
decided who pastored what and where churches were to be built. The
team from the Evangelism Department met with the sichal committee every
two months to go over plans, check progress, and handle problems. In
addition, unofficial area meetings were called with a layman and minister representing each church. Reports were heard, prizes awarded for
church growth and money raised for weaker churches. Further impetus
was given the program by providing scholarships for laymen to attend
the Rural Training Center in Taejon. Other lay leadership training
programs were conducted with the sichal.

When reports were to be received from the churches, the missionary's
car was loaded with as many pastors and elders from the sichal as could
be crowded aboard and each church was visited individually. It was
found that with careful scheduling, six churches could be covered in a
single day. By this means sichal leaders were made aware of specific
situations and gained a new sense of responsibility towards them.

The actual planting of churches proceeded in four different patterns.

1. Colonization. Members of one church living in a distant village
established a congregation in their own community.

2. Lay Extension. Laymen planted churches in nearby villages.
They sometimes shared responsibility for leading services on weekdays.
Converts attended the mother church on Sundays. Eventually an evangel-
ist was secured to conduct the Sunday meetings in the village.

3. Assignment of evangelist by the sichal. Evangelists under the
jurisdiction of the sichal were assigned responsibility for planting
congregations in villages near their own churches. Incentives were provided and a token subsidy furnished to defray travel expenses. This was
the most frequently used method in Soonchun Presbytery.

4. Assignment of an evangelist to live and work in an isolated
community. This pattern proved to be slowest, most costly and least
satisfactory.

When a new village was entered the usual procedure was to visit
around until a meeting place could be arranged and the people invited
to attend. This approach usually attracted the women and children and
tended to alienate the village leaders. Since 1970, "Operation
Lighthouse" has been extended into Chinju and Mokpo presbyteries. Here
lessons learned in Soonchun are being applied.

Evangelists are now trained to find ten clan or village leaders who
might prove responsive. The evangelist learns their family connections,
background, influence and accomplishments. Often links with the Church
elsewhere or other useful points of contact are discovered in this way.
These men and their families are then assiduously cultivated until one
or more of them requests that a church be established in their village.
Until that time no public gatherings are held and evangelism proceeds
on an individual basis. The success or failure of rural church planting
efforts has depended largely on the calibre of initial converts. Approaching natural leaders and establishing a church at their invitation
seems a good way to proceed. Materials have been prepared and training

programs in this approach conducted, but no definite results are yet
available. Using this method one man can work four or five villages at
once, even if he visits them only twice a month or weekdays.
    Funds for "Operation Lighthouse" come from three sources.
1)   Monies are raised within the <u>sichals</u> for extension. Members migrating to the cities are urged to continue supporting their village mother
church.
2)   Limited "risk capital" is provided by the missionaries.
3)   The Committee of Cooperation in Seoul sends regular allocations for
evangelism in Soonchun presbytery. These funds, administered under
mutually-agreed controls, have been essential to the success of the
program. It must be emphasized, however, that all funds have been re-
ligiously channeled through the <u>sichal</u> committee.
    The program has developed in interaction with Evangelism Department
staff and church leaders. It has not been imposed on the Church. Nonetheless, missionaries have played a key role in the seven parts of the
program.
1)   They have focused the attention of the Church on the unreached.
2)   They have provided the expertise in survey techniques and analysis.
3)   They have rallied support in each area and shared their vision with
      pastors and laymen as to what should and could be done.
4)   They have provided limited funds as a stimulant and the mission car
      as speedy transportation.
5)   They have designed the low-cost church construction scheme that
      provides a uniformly sturdy and economical structure while allowing
      for local ingenuity in finishing.
6)   They have supplied stimulation, momentum and continuity, acting like
      a church planting fly-wheel.
7)   They have joined their Korean colleagues in praying for the dynamic
      and direction of the Spirit in seeking to fulfill the Great Com-
      mission.
    Here are missionaries actively engaged in planting "light houses of
gospel witness" among the Christless millions of Korea. While they
pursue this ministry so fruitfully, the Korean Church enthusiastically
welcomes their presence.

A CRUCIAL QUESTION FOR MISSION THINKERS   by Wade Coggins

    How can the existing Churches and missions reach the unreached
population of their countries and language groups? This question is
troubling mission thinkers...A mature national Church has been developed in many places but it embraces only a small per cent of the population surrounding it. It is very common for the major energy of the
Church and the mission which relates to it to be expended on the affairs
of the Church: schools, medical work, and church programs...Imaginative
thinking is needed to develop programs in which the mission can, in
close cooperation with the Church, move into this great vacuum to evangelize the unreached 95 to 99 per cent...The move must be made without
rupturing the good relationship, but <u>ways to make the move must be found</u>.
....One missionary (not EFMA or IFMA) told me that upon arrival on his
field he found 1% of the budget was going toward evangelism. The rest
was going into institutions and services for existing churches.
                          EFMA-gram, 4/2/73, p.3, Washington D.C.

CHURCH GROWTH
B U L L E T I N

from the
INSTITUTE OF
CHURCH GROWTH

Address:
FULLER THEOLOGICAL
SEMINARY
135 N. Oakland
Pasadena, Calif. 91101

DONALD A. McGAVRAN, B.D., Pff.[
Director

September 1973   Subscription $1 per year   Volume X   No. 1

C O N T E N T S

DOES CHURCH GROWTH REALLY WORK?

C. Peter Wagner

One of the most frequent (and most challenging) questions that
comes to church growth proponents is: "Does church growth really work?

This is a good question because it is phrased in the kind of
pragmatic tones that church growth theory itself continually sounds.
Church growth is interested in discovering, analyzing, improving, and
recommending strategies that God is blessing for the fulfillment of the
Great Commission. Take an evangelistic program, for example: does it
make disciples or just produce decisions? Take a missiological theory:
does it clearly articulate God's purposes in discipling the nations?
Take a program of church renewal: does it succeed in thrusting forth
renewed Christians to multiply churches?

But take church growth theory itself: are there cases on record
where a conscious application of church growth principles has, in fact,
produced significant increases in church growth?

Last year in Church Growth Bulletin, I reported on the First
Annual Venezuelan Evangelism/Church Growth Workshop, suggesting that it
might become a model, not only for communicating church growth principles to the grass roots, but also for subsequent evaluation of its effects. The major innovation in Venezuela 1972 was to plan not one, but
three successive workshops, each evaluating the effects of the former,

SEND correspondence, news, and articles to the Editor, Dr. Donald McGavran, at the Institute
of Church Growth, Fuller Theological Seminary. Published bi-monthly, send subscriptions
and changes of address to the Business Manager, Norman L. Cummings, Overseas Crusades,
Inc., 265 Lytton Avenue, Palo Alto, California 94301, U.S.A. Second-class postage paid at
Palo Alto, California.

analyzing current progress, setting new goals, and encouraging participants to push on in making disciples and in multiplying churches. For
the first time I know of, instruments for evaluation were built into
such a program from the beginning.

The second workshop was held June 25-29, 1973, once again at the
Evangelical Free Church campground in El Limón, with local arrangements
being handled by the nearby Associated Evangelical Seminary. Sixty-four
pastors, missionaries and church leaders enrolled, in contrast to forty-
seven the previous year. The Lutherans did not return, but ASIGEO (related to Orinoco River Mission), ADIEL (Free Church), OVICE (related to
TEAM), Foursquare and United World Mission workers came back with progress reports. Joining them for the first time were World Evangelization
Crusade, Presbyterian, and independent workers.

The reports from those who returned showed that church growth really
works. Some of the stories of effective evangelism told by those who
were motivated by the first workshop are remarkable. I was personally
moved as I listened to testimony after testimony. But church growth reporting does not like to major on the personal experience or the isolated
success story. It is more interested in general trends and concrete
rates of church growth.

Charts 1 and 2 summarize the progress reports of those who came
back the second time. All percentages are decadal rates of growth, i.e.
the growth of the church over a ten-year period, based on the imprecise,
but helpful, device of multiplying one year's growth rate by ten or five
year's rate by two, etc.

CHART 1

Increase in Rates of Church Growth in Venezuelan Churches 1961-1972

Denomination	Number of Churches	Decadal Rate 1961-1971	Rate Projected 1st Workshop	Decadal Rate Reported, '71-2
ASIGEO (Orinoco R.)	21	33%	250%	610%
ADIEL (Evan. Free)	7	50%	425%	570%
OVICE (T.E.A.M.)	2	-0-	250%	840%
FOURSQUARE	15	249%	100%	790%
UNITED WORLD	7	24%	130%	600%
TOTALS (averages)	52	60%	202%	680%

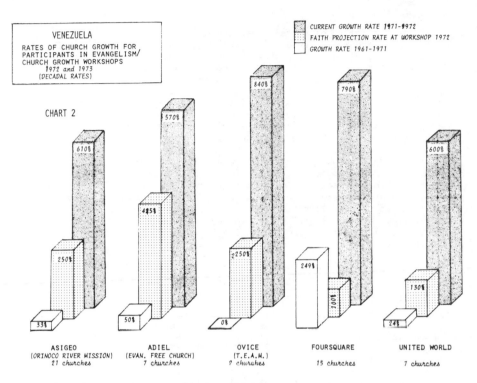

VENEZUELA

RATES OF CHURCH GROWTH FOR
PARTICIPANTS IN EVANGELISM/
CHURCH GROWTH WORKSHOPS
1972 and 1973
(DECADAL RATES)

CURRENT GROWTH RATE 1971-1972
FAITH PROJECTION RATE AT WORKSHOP 1972
GROWTH RATE 1961-1971

CHART 2

ASIGEO	ADIEL	OVICE	FOURSQUARE	UNITED WORLD
(ORINOCO RIVER MISSION)	(EVAN. FREE CHURCH)	(T.E.A.M.)		
21 churches	7 churches	7 churches	15 churches	7 churches

ASIGEO: 610%, 250%, 33%
ADIEL: 570%, 415%, 50%
OVICE: 840%, 2250%, 0%
FOURSQUARE: 790%, 249%, 100%
UNITED WORLD: 600%, 130%, 24%

Growth <u>rates</u> do not tell the whole story. So Chart 3 gives the
<u>number of members</u> also. This helps evaluate the situation correctly.

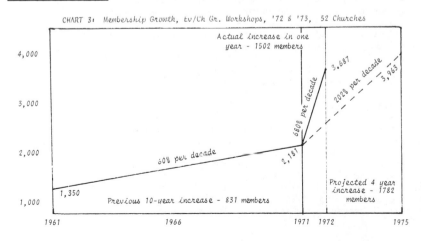

CHART 3: Membership Growth, Ev/Ch Gr. Workshops, '72 & '73, 52 Churches

Actual increase in one
year - 1502 members

680% per decade

202% per decade

60% per decade

3,687
3,963

2,181

1,350

Previous 10-year increase - 831 members

Projected 4 year
increase - 1782
members

4,000

3,000

2,000

1,000

1961   1966   1971 1972   1975

Scientifically, of course, even these figures do not necessarily prove that there was a cause and effect relationship between learning the principles of church growth and effectiveness in making disciples. The change from 60% decadal growth to 680% decadal growth could be just a coincidence. But the participants themselves attributed the dramatic upsurge to the new outlook they had acquired and the new principles they had learned. The principles of goal-setting and evaluation, the resist-ant-receptivity of peoples, and the multiplication of daughter churches were most frequently mentioned as especially helpful. The opinion of the participants is that church growth really works!

It is not the purpose of these workshops to offer the partici-pants a "canned" approach to evangelism. Instead models are presented along with theoretical considerations so that they can see how God is working in other places. This year Venezuela itself provided many new models. But the participants are carefully instructed not to attempt to duplicate any successful program of evangelism in their own local situation. Rather, they are to use their own methods, incorporating with them useful ideas that emerge from the other models.

When the time came to set future goals, a new and highly useful instrument was available for the first time. Vergil Gerber's Manual for Evangelism/Church Growth (William Carey Library, 1973) had been translated into Spanish and published just a week before by Editorial Liberator of Maracaibo, Venezuela. Gerber himself was present to in-struct the participants in its use, and the results were outstanding. The availability of this do-it-yourself book in dozens of languages will undoubtedly mark a giant step forward in making evangelism more effec-tive worldwide.

After mastering the principles of graphing the growth of their churches, the participants prayerfully and in faith set goals for the next five years. They were more optimistic than last year, after seeing how consistently the veterans had surpassed last year's faith projection. For example, last year the participants projected 215% decadal growth, which seemed pretty courageous after a previous 75% growth. But this year the future projection is 368%, based on the previous 198% rate. One participant said, "I'll bet we make our five year goal in one year! Venezuelans have never responded to the Gospel like they are right now." Chart 4, next page, shows the new projections.

I was greatly impressed with the aggressive church-planting ac-tivities of the Orinoco River Mission and the Venezuelan denomination they have established, ASIGEO. Although these churches have been grow-ing over the years, church growth principles have now taken root among them and are producing increased fruit. Missionary Alvin Lewis has been named by ASIGEO to head up the new office for a statistical co-ordination and planning. Serving the church in this way, encouraging Venezuelans and missionaries alike to push on to new, bold goals of church growth is one of the noblest tasks a field missionary could undertake in these days. May Alvin Lewises be multiplied around the world!

CHART 4

FAITH PROJECTIONS MADE IN SECOND
ANNUAL EVANGELISM/CHURCH GROWTH
WORKSHOP, VENEZUELA, JUNE, 1973 - 65 CHURCHES

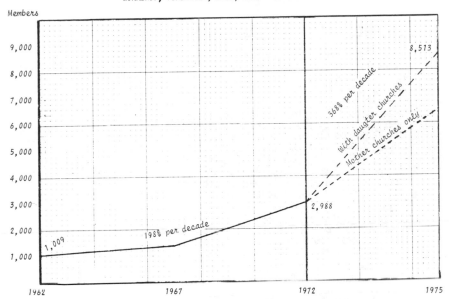

One of the notable results of the work of Lewis and his team is the proliferation of new churches. The group rather timidly said they would trust God for 14 new churches in <u>four years</u> at the first workshop. But at the second one they joyously reported <u>19 new churches</u> already planted in <u>one year</u>. Their goal now is <u>24 more</u> for 1977 and few doubt that they will quickly surpass it.

No wonder ASIGEO growth rates have soared from 33% per decade before the first workshop to a current rate of 620% per decade! Only space limitations prohibit similar commentaries on the other Venezuelan denominations represented in the workshops.

The Venezuela workshop series is only the first in a growing list of similar ventures. The following week another was begun in Haiti. Still others are scheduled in August for Kenya, Nigeria and Ivory Coast with Vergil Gerber, Donald McGavran and Wilfred Bellamy leading them. Colombia, Nicaragua and Ecuador have also requested workshops. Gerber's office, the Evangelical Missions Information Service (Box 794, Wheaton, Illinois 60187) is coordinating the efforts.

But do not wait till you can get Gerber, McGavran or others to lead a workshop for you. Buy <u>Manual for Evangelism/Church Growth</u>, master it, and <u>run your own</u>, with perhaps ten co-workers, and perhaps ninety.

N E W S

ALL ASIA MISSION CONSULTATION, SEOUL, KOREA, August 27 - Sept. 1, 1973

In Academy House in Seoul, in a splendid scenic mountain resort, one hour away from Kimpo International Airport, this All Asia Consultation has just taken place.

"Two-thirds of the world's population lives in Asia. Asia is old: Asis is young. This truly is the Age of Asia. Western oriented missionary movements welcome their young, vigorous Asian counterparts. The task is enormous and requires evangelism from the whole world focused on Asia's responsive multitudes. As Asia goes, so goes the world. Asia is the most acclaimed, richest mission field, history has ever known. The Churches of Asia should unite in the common task of world evangelism, with special reference to those hundreds of millions in Asia who have never heard the name of Christ."

With words like these the Consultation convened. It was addressed by Dr. Kyung Chik Han, Dr. Akira Hatori, Dr. Chandu Ray, Dr. Simeon Kang, Rev. David Cho and Dr. Philip Teng. From the West a few eminer consultants were invited - Dean Arthur Glasser, Prof. Peter Wagner, Dr. George Peters, and Dr. Ralph Winter - but it was an Asian Consultation from start to finish.

The Eurican missionary movement welcomes the hundreds of missionary societies which have been formed and are now forming in Latfricasia. Church Growth Bulletin is delighted at the thousands of Latfricasian missionaries now being recruited and sent out. We also are confident that the enormous opportunities of today, the myriads calling for the Gospel, the upsurge of church growth and the multiplying congregations demand missionary obedience from all Churches - in Africa, Asia, Latin America, Europe, and North America - on a vast scale. Whether these messengers are called missionaries or evangelists is immaterial. The day is too urgent to quibble over words. God has given His people unprecedented open doors.

Difficulties, of course, remain; but they must not obscure the big picture. God deliver us from little faith, and give us courage and imagination, and obedient sensitivity to the leading of the Holy Spirit. These are great days in which to serve.

TAIWAN, REPUBLIC OF CHINA, March 1973. The Church Growth Society of Taiwan, in February 1973, issued the first Taiwan Church Growth Bulletin. "The Society was founded to promote church growth thinking and activity in Taiwan. Thinking, by articles, church growth books and new insights. Activities, by CGS's workshops and seminars." .... The Bulletin is funded by the Church Growth Society through contributions

by interested individuals, churches, missions, and mission boards.
        Following the good lead established by Church Growth Bulletin,
TCGB includes a blue sheet of the Taiwan Church Growth Book Deposit,
which lists 24 titles, gives their price in the Taiwanese dollars (and
in U.S.) and tells how to order them.
        The officers leading this promising Church Growth Society are:
Ted Ellis (Presbyterian), Sheldon Sawatsky (Mennonite), Allen Swanson
(Lutheran), Alan Gates (Conservative Baptist) and Dorothy Raber (Free
Methodist) - a beautifully ecumenical outfit. These leaders have already held the Second Annual Church Growth Workshop and have published
several new church growth books in Mandarin - among them two by David
Liao - Every Believer a Noble Vessel, and Into His Harvest, and a Pro-
grammed Extension Text on Church Growth by Gates, Wang and McGavran.
TEE is also pushed as an effective agent of church growth. David Liao
and C. C. Wang are important members of the Society and keep it on a
thoroughly Chinese track.
        For further information write to: Church Growth Society, No. 11,
Lane 241, Ta-ya Road, Taichung, Taiwan, Rep. of China.

((Comment: Hearty Congratulations to CGS of TAIWAN!! Such societies
are being formed in various parts of the world and are bound to play a
significant role in the coming decades. Churches and Missions concerned will do well to encourage the formation of such societies and
fund them. Nothing will further the basic aims of both churches and
miss ons more effectively.
        Indigenizing growth thinking is urgent. We welcome news as to
the formation of sister societies, and will send by air mail to all who
request it the manuscript of Church Growth Bulletin as soon as it is
typed. They can then see what of it they desire in their Bulletin.))

THAT LUMINOUS FRANKFURT DECLARATION

A conciliar missionary writes: "I have continued reading in the church growth field and have been most deeply
impressed by the Beyerhaus books. I had never heard of
the Frankfurt Declaration, yet find it to be one of the
most illuminating statements in the theological panorama - a real fog precipitator." June 1973.

GOOD NEWS FROM ZAIRE (July 1st, 1973)

"Many new congregations are being formed in Kinshasa." writes
Norman Riddle. "The American Baptists had 6 churches in 1963, and now
have more than 20. Many denominations are coming into Kinshasa and
forming congregations. For example, C&MA had only 3 small churches in
1971. Now it has 8." ((C. Peter Wagner in Look Out! The Pentecostals
Are Coming ascribes part of their tremendous growth in Latin America to
the habit of establishing many small churches, some of which grow large.
He counsels all churches and missions to get the habit!

KEDIRI, JAVA, April 1973. Dr. Ebbie Smith writes: "We may translate the Bible, use mass media, distribute tracts, and even engage in Christian service in an area and leave the people unevangelized. Evangelization involves making disciples and planting churches which help those who compose them to continue to evangelize and plant more churches. Until there are sufficient churches to make acceptance of Christ a valid possibility for all groups in the area, the area is not evangelized.

In a given area with many churches, there might be an ethnic or cultural or linguistic unit whose members felt unable to attend these churches. It would remain unevangelized in the very midst of many churches. Such situations exist commonly all around the world, and in the United States, as well."

CHIANG MAI, THAILAND, March 1973. Allan Eubank writes, "About five hundred active Christians from all over Thailand gathered at Chiang Mai's Prince Royal's College, March 19-25 for a Church Growth Conference, the second since the Church of Christ in Thailand (CCT) set its goal to double membership a little more than two years ago.

The conference was not confined to the Church of Christ in Thailand. Individuals from the Christian and Missionary Alliance, the Overseas Missionary Fellowship, the Pentecostals and the Southern Baptists were also present.

Sharing experiences in church growth programs already in operation in various parts of the kingdom, the delegates reported examples of church growth in other countries and analyzed the particular challenges encountered in the Thai cultural context.

ADDIS ABABA, ETHIOPIA, May 14, 1973. In Kaffa Province in fifteen months of active evangelism by eight Wollamo missionaries (evangelists) working cross culturally among the Omete and Ghimeera peoples, over 400 families have believed.

Recently the SIM held a Church Growth Workshop in Addis. Excerpts from the addresses of Rev. W.G. Crouch, Deputy General Director of SIM, give its flavor.

"Our overall objective to evangelize and establish churches has not and will not change....Any activity that does not have evangelism, church planting and church growth as the final objective of its work is not contributing to...our overall objectives as a mission....

"As soon as the Lord raises up a church as a result of our evangelistic efforts, He has placed in Africa another organization that also has the imperative to evangelize and plant churches....We must make sure that all our work is geared to establishing a strong national Church with well-trained and experienced leadership that can not only survive but develop and grow when the mission is gone....

"Evangelism must continue until the vast areas yet unreached have heard the Gospel. This goal must not be pushed into a secondary position....Dr. George Peters has said, 'It is my deep conviction that God would delight in calling multitudes out of darkness into His marvellous light, if energetic and wise evangelism could be stimulated by missionary examples and encouragements. Let us consider the urgency of the situaton and perhaps the lateness of the hour.'...."

"We should encourage missionaries to take courses on evangelism and church growth. We should recruit missionary personnel with training in sociology and anthropology as well as theology....

"Missions have developed many programs not directly involved in evangelism, church planting, and church growth, but which in various ways contribute to the overall objective. These need to be periodically evaluated to determine their real contribution in relation to the total program. We must ask: To what extent does each program contribute to evangelism and the growth of the church? Is the cost justified in relationship to its contribution to the growth of the church? Would its elimination help or hinder the overall mission-church effort?...."

POSSESSING THE PHILOSOPHY OF ANIMISM FOR CHRIST

The evangelist has no difficulty (in believing that the Christ of the animist-conversion experience is a Lord of power) if he accepts the Bible at its face value. The "demythologizing" intellectualist has no spiritual resources for dealing with animists, because the animist recognizes him as a disbeliever with no Gospel at all to offer. A temporary attitude of accommodation to animist belief for purposes of communication is soon recognized as phony. Furthermore, the evangelist may well find himself personally involved in the struggle with demonic evil; and unless he accepts the reality of this, he will not be able to demonstrate the victory over Satan which he preaches....Much in the philosophy of animism is in alignment with Scripture and should be possessed for Christ. Animist religion, on the other hand, is sadly misdirected toward deities who cannot save and many of its offensive elements are perversions of ideas which could be good if redirected." Alan R. Tippett, "Possessing the Philosophy of Animism for Christ" in Crucial Issues in Missions Tomorrow.

CALL FOR MISSIONARIES by LaVerne Morse

A remarkable Rawang Christian, Brother Paul, with Naga friends, fled to India when tribal fighting broke out in Burma. In India his health broke and he has been hospitalized for many months. But being in the hospital has made it possible for him to be a very effective "missionary". He has received books and other teaching supplies. Local Nagas have come to him for guidance and advice. He has baptized many of them. He recently wrote a letter (dictated to him by the elders of the new churches) as follows:

"We send you greetings in the name of Jesus Christ. We are all fine. We have accepted the Faith since 1969. No one ever taught us about Christ. But we were hungry for the eternal message. Fourteen villages have accepted the Faith. The present membership is 1,112. <u>There are still countless people</u> who <u>want to become Christian</u>, but there is no one who knows the Bible well. In such a desperation moment we heard about you through Brother Paul.

There are only four Bibles here. After Paul arrived here, we were able to get these Bibles in Assemese. Hindi, and English. We have been looking for a missionary family who could live with us and teach us daily. We are also looking for someone who could help us in medical treatment. We have been waiting such a long period for someone, but still <u>not a single person has come to teach us</u>. Our tears are literally shed for the hunger of the Gospel.

Paul is still weak but he tries his best and helps us. We thank him for this. We look forward to hearing from you soon in regard to these matters. May God bless you. On the behalf of all the Christians here this letter is written by the elders. (Their names)

((Comment by Donald McGavran. The Hump Country is full of such people movements. Since most of the Christians in those parts are Baptists, the Baptist Churches of India and Burma, assisted by Baptist missionary societies in all parts of the world, should consider it a high priority to send in a couple of hundred Indian and Burmese 'missionaries' so that these "countless people who want to become Christian" <u>will</u> become Followers of the Way.

If the Baptists do not send enough missionaries, other denominations should. Indian Pentecostals, for example, assisted no doubt by Pentecostals in other parts of the world, could send in fifty Indian Pentecostal missionaries. The Church South India has multitudes of devout, well-trained men and women. It should have no difficulty in recruiting fifty missionaries, training them in people movement methods, and sending them to the Hump Country to plant multitudes of churches.

It is not God's will, we may be sure, for multitudes to wait in vain. God is, no doubt, even as I write, working in the hearts of Baptists, Pentecostals, and other denominations to send in reapers. These will be called workers, evangelists, ministers or apostles; but since they will be <u>sent</u>, to work <u>cross culturally</u>, <u>communicate the Gospel</u> and <u>multiply churches</u>, they will be essentially <u>missionaries</u>. That is exactly what missionaries are.))

ISRAEL, JEWS, AND CHURCH GROWTH NEWS by Alvin Martin

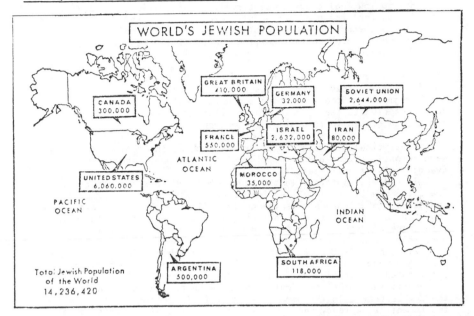

WORLD'S JEWISH POPULATION

GREAT BRITAIN
410,000

GERMANY
32,000

SOVIET UNION
2,644,000

CANADA
300,000

FRANCE
550,000

ISRAEL
2,632,000

IRAN
80,000

ATLANTIC
OCEAN

UNITED STATES
6,060,000

MOROCCO
35,000

PACIFIC
OCEAN

INDIAN
OCEAN

ARGENTINA
500,000

SOUTH AFRICA
118,000

Total Jewish Population
of the World
14,236,420

The map above shows that forty-two per cent of the world's Jewish population is in the United States. The 6,060,000 Jews living in the U.S. are nearly 3 per cent of the total U.S. population. There are 2,644,000 Jews in the Soviet Union - more than there are in the State of Israel. Jews now emigrating from the Soviet Union to Israel will reverse the order. Soon Israel will rank second in Jewish population. In the Greater New York area, however, there are almost as many Jews - 2,381,000 - as in all Israel.

The Jewish population of the world is estimated at 14,236,420. Eighty per cent of this total resides in the United States, Russia and Israel. No other nation has as many as one million Jews. France has 550,000, Argentina 500,000, Great Britain 410,000, and Canada 300,000.

This summer, SWMers Jim Hutchens and Alvin Martin are in Jerusalem, Tel Aviv and some villages, making a socio-religious survey. Answers to questions such as the following are being sought.

Do you believe in God?
What is your attitude toward Jesus?
Are you looking for the appearance of the Messiah?
Is it possible for a Jew to believe in Jesus and remain a Jew?
Do you attend synagogue regularly?

Did you attend a synagogue service on the last Day of Atonement?
How do you feel about present religious conditions in Israel?
Do you feel the need for a fuller religious faith?
Have you read the Hebrew Bible? The New Testament?
Are you interested in receiving a copy of the results of this
     survey?

The survey should indicate the degree of interest in Israel today in crucial areas of religious thought and action. It will ascertain
which segments of the population and which sections of the country are
most receptive to the Gospel. The findings will aid in future planning
for church growth in this strategic nation.

Statistical verification of trends such as the following which
were reported at the annual meeting of the National Association of
Evangelicals is anticipated:
   1.   Jewish interest in the study of Jesus continues to grow.
There are now 27 books written in Hebrew, including a number of school
textbooks, in which Jesus is the central figure. Pinchus Lapide reports
that "The history textbooks in Israel's schools present a highly favorable image of Jesus." The Associated Press has released a similar report this year.
   2.   There is a growing interest in the Bible. The Bible Society
Secretary reported that more Bibles in proportion to the population are
distributed in Israel than in any other country. The Old and the New
Testaments in Hebrew are popular in the Kibbutz. A new translation of
the New Testament in the common language is in process. The Epistle to
the Romans has already been printed and the rest of the epistles are
ready for publication.
   3.   Following a fact-finding mission to Israel and interviews
with top Israeli leaders, Dr. Olson reported: "Many Jewish young
people are turning to Jesus without forsaking their Jewish heritage
and culture."

These Israeli disciples, followers of ancient Israel's Messiah,
tread in the footsteps of the early Church when it was all Jewish.
"And they, continuing daily with one accord in the temple and breaking
bread from house to house, did eat their meat with gladness and single-
ness of heart, praising God, and having favor with all the people"
(Acts 2:46,47).

The above is an interim report of a research team at the School
of World Mission at Fuller Theological Seminary's School of Missions
and Institute of Church Growth. Under the supervision of Dean Glasser,
it and workers of the nearby Missions Advanced Research Communication
Center have been making area profiles of all countries of the world,
showing where the two billion unevangelized people live. The profiles
will be presented to the International Congress on World Evangelization
at Lausanne, Switzerland, July 16-26, and will show dramatically the
task ahead in world evangelization.

CHURCH GROWTH
BULLETIN.

from the

INSTITUTE OF
CHURCH GROWTH

Address:
FULLER THEOLOGICAL
SEMINARY
135 N. Oakland
Pasadena, Calif. 91101

DONALD A. McGAVRAN, B.D., Ph.D.
Director

November 1973   Subscription $1 per year   Volume X No. 2

C O N T E N T S

ARTICLES

CLEAR THINKING ON MISSION(S)
by
Dr. Alan R. Tippett

Missions, the human organizations, must be distinguished from mission, the assignment received as a mandate from our Lord. Discussion
of one also involves the other. The validity of the church's institu-
tionalized program depends on the validity of the idea of mission,
namely, that Christ commanded his followers to bring the lost to him
for salvation.

The ethical validity of this idea is under attack from inside and
outside the church, and especially from universalists. Against evangelistic (converting) missions it is popularly reasoned that Christian ex-
clusivism (Christ being claimed as the only way - John 14:6: Acts 4:12)
(1) is an affront on rational human personality, (2) is monological
proclamation in a day which demands dialogue, (3) fails to recognize
the divine in non-Christian religions, (4) is divisive and hinders ecumenicity, and (5) savors of antequated revivalism and church extension
when new forms are needed. These critics would redefine such terms as

SEND correspondence, news, and articles to the Editor, Dr. Donald McGavran, at the Institute
of Church Growth, Fuller Theological Seminary. Published bi-monthly, send subscriptions
and changes of address to the Business Manager, Norman L. Cummings, Overseas Crusades,
Inc., 265 Lytton Avenue, Palo Alto, California 94301, U.S.A. Second-class postage paid at
Palo Alto, California.

evangelism and mission to suit a day "when man has become of age."
Service often substitutes for mission rather than accompanies it. Much
current missionary terminology - dialogue, Christian presence, development, humanization - is ambiguous, liberal, or conservative as the speaker desires.

The evangelical position, while granting the current need for new
techniques and modes of communication to suit the day, nevertheless denies our right to change either the motive or message of our Lord's
mission. The rightness of the idea of mission, seeking the lost and
bringing them in repentance to Christ, may be postulated by sociological,
ethical, Biblical and theological arguments.

The sociological argument rests on the statistical fact that millions of non-Christians (especially animists) are currently in the process of changing their religion. Under the effects of acculturation and
the "shrinking" of the globe, old gods and fetishes are being called on
to perform functions beyond their capacity. Medicine men are less and
less effective. Animists are questioning, testing, seeking, experi-
menting and making decisions as never before. Moslem, Buddhist, Bahai
and Communist "missionaries" are operating in these dynamic situations.
It seems just plain sociological common sense that decision for Christ
should be at least one option put before them.

The ethical argument is that of Christian responsibility: the old
issue of the "haves and the have-nots." Has not the Christian a duty to
share both physical and spiritual blessings? This does not mean in paternalism, so often characteristic of the old type of missions; but
rather fraternally and towards self-help. The former establishes a dependent, foreign, station church; the latter moves toward responsible
indigeneity.

The Biblical or exegetical argument recognizes several themes running through Scripture: the idea of "the people of God" responsible
for bringing the nations to God; the idea of the diffusion of "the
knowledge of the Lord"; the NT idea of the church itself, the growing
following or disciple group, persons "called out" and "not of the world."
Although all Christians should witness, the mission is the task of a
corporate body - the church "which is his Body," ministering the mind,
love and message of Christ to the world. Then there is the direct commission of Christ to his followers, in space (to all nations) and time
(by his promise to be with them to the end of the age).

The theological argument stands on the character, purpose, and
revelation of God, who declared his intention to save man from sin. The
theological negative is his pronouncement against idolatry, witchcraft,
and phallic cults (e.g., Gal. 5:19-20), which deny man his inheritance
of the Kingdom of God (v. 21). The theological positive is the evangelical Christian's commission to missionary activity, bringing men to commitment to Christ (e.g., Rom. 10:13-15). The theological potential of
Christian mission is that "strangers and foreigners" may become "fellow-

citizens" in the "household of God" (Eph. 2:11-22).

The clash between these opposing philosophies of mission is reflected in their respective operations. Those who "demythologize" Scripture must interpret the idea of mission to suit the projects they feel the world situation needs. Their theology and ethics are, therefore, situational, and often anthropocentric and universalist. Evangelicals, on the other hand, accept Scripture at its face value, and operate from the Biblical frame of reference in encountering their situations. The former appear to be surviving mainly on the strength of an evangelism of an earlier generation. Where statistics show great church growth the concept of mission invariably turns out to be evangelical. Each generation must hear the call of mission for itself. Each must see the opportunities of its own day - even unto the end of the age. (Quoted from Baker's Dictionary of Christian Ethics, Ed. C.F. Henry, 1973: 426-427).

((This lucid exposition of the essential biblical position on mission(s) is most timely. It defines mission correctly in the classical way it has been defined for two hundred years by practically all missionary societies. It declines to make the word wide and thin enough to cover everything that God wants done, everything the Church ought to do.

The issue is not semantic. At stake is not a new definition for a word. The vital question is: are the tremendous resources of missions, which were contributed to propagate the Gospel (because Christ commanded His followers to bring the lost to Him for salvation) to be diverted to various deeds of humanization and various campaigns of social justice? God no doubt calls certain men to fight for social justice. When He does so, they should obey and lead campaigns to free the slaves, end child labor, bring in prohibition, and war against oppression. Splendid! But let them do so on funds given for those purposes. Let them enlist men to whom God has given those commands. Let them not, by the slick device of redefining mission, use the resources given for the propagation of the Gospel. Donald McGavran))

**MISSIOLOGY: AS SEEN BY A
SEVENTH-DAY ADVENTIST CHURCH LEADER**

"Seventh-day Adventists are not harvesting one-fifteenth of those ready to accept their message....For the seventies Seventh-day Adventists ought to keep their eyes open for people whom the Spirit has prepared to join them. They ought to make funds and personnel available to harvest the fields ripe for harvest now. This, indeed, will require much greater flexibility in missionary approach and a shift in priorities and policies. Adventists tend to exhibit too much of the "three months more and then the harvest" idea. The establishment of an International Harvest Fund may create needed flexibility. Then, as soon as somewhere in the world a people becomes extraordinarily receptive to the gospel as happens continuously.... experienced missionaries can go out as harvesters". p. 62
Mission Possible - Gottfried Oosterwal, Nashville, Southern Publishing Association

---

EVENTS OF SPECIAL SIGNIFICANCE

((This issue of CGB focusses attention on five happenings which have
great meaning for the advancement of the Gospel and the spread of liberating, redeeming faith in Christ. News stories about the expansion of
the Church are numerous. They pour in from almost every land and are
reported in many magazines. Among these multitudinous events, in which
men and angels can rejoice, the following stand out like mountain peaks.
The order in which they appear does not indicate relative importance.
We are too close to these events to know which - twenty years from now -
will have proved to be most significant for church growth. Each should
have a most favorable effect on the evangelization and discipling of the
peoples of earth. The Editor))

1. THE INTERNATIONAL CONGRESS ON WORLD EVANGELIZATION

At Lausanne, Switzerland, July 16-23, 1974, will gather 3500 Evangelicals deeply interested in world evangelization. The determination to
proclaim the Good News of Christ and disciple the peoples of the world,
which found expression at Edinburgh in 1910 and Berlin in 1968 and has
been accellerating through many regional congresses on evangelism, will
receive tremendous new impetus. The conviction of millions of Christians
that God wills every man, woman and child on earth to hear the Gospel and
have a real chance to become a responsible disciple of Christ will be reinforced. The issues facing Christians today in regard to world evangelization will be clearly stated. Strategy will be hammered out to guide
the Church during the last quarter of the twentieth century.

This will be a world congress on _evangelism_. Christians who believe
that God revealed the Gospel to bring the peoples of earth to faith and
obedience (Romans 16:15) will gather to confer, share, plan and pray as to
the best ways to get ahead with this job. The Church has many duties - to
worship God, to educate Christians, to forgive enemies, and many others.
Lausanne will not be against any of these; but it will be for world evangelization. That is its distinctive mark. That is why the 3,500 men and
women from every tongue and nation will gather there. They intend to
evangelize.

This Congress will focus attention on the tremendous unreached populations of the world. It will etch into the consciousness of Christians
the fact that two billion rapidly becoming three billion (three thousand
million of our brothers and sisters) have never effectively heard of the
Saviour - and that at a time when the Church is stronger, richer, and
larger than it has ever been before. The Congress will stab sleeping
Christians awake and inspire millions to more effective mission and evangelism. A wave of liberation will flow from Lausanne. A host of the
redeemed will thank God for Lausanne.

Church Growth Bulletin calls on all its readers to pray God's rich
blessing on the Congress - pray daily. A wide and effectual door has

opened for world evangelism. Tens of thousands will want to go to Lausanne. Let us pray that the 3,500 who do go may convene in God's
strength and be filled with His Spirit. May they discern clearly the
tremendous spiritual needs of the world, and be filled with compassion
for the multitudes who are as sheep without a shepherd. Let us ask God
to deliver them from the heresy which suggests that the deepest needs of
men are "this worldly". Let us especially pray that the Lord will give
the delegates clear vision and courage to attempt great things for God.

2.   CHURCH GROWTH THINKING SPREADING ACROSS NORTH AMERICA

The church growth movement was born and grew to power among men concerned that the unreached multitudes of Asia, Africa and Latin America
hear the Gospel and have a real chance to become responsible members of
Christ's Church. These men believed that the churches of North America
(and Europe, too) could profit from church growth thinking, but did not
have the resources to apply growth principles to American denominations
and congregations.

During the last twelve months, largely owing to the vigorous work of
Peter Wagner, Paul Benjamin, Vergil Gerber, Tetsunao Yamamori and others,
church growth thinking is becoming common all across the United States and
Canada. Ministers meet for church growth seminars. Books like Benjamin's
The Growing Congregation (Lincoln College Press), McGavran and Arn's How
To Grow A Church (Regal Books), and Gerber's Manual For Evangelism/Church
Growth (Wm. Carey Library) are being widely read. Dr. Benjamin has established A Research Center for American Church Growth under the shadow
of the Library of Congress, where seminary credit may be earned for competent studies in the growth of American churches. (Several seminaries
are now giving courses for credit on church growth. Fuller Seminary is
considering opening an American Institute of Church Growth.) A sound
color film (24 minutes) called "How To Grow A Church" can be rented from
Christian Communication, 1857 Highland Oaks, Arcadia, Calif. 91106. Dean
Kelley has written a book Why Conservative Churches Are Growing (Harper
and Row) which the liberal wing of the Church is reading with considerable
profit.

This development has great significance. In the midst of the
largest numbers of winnable ever to live in the United States, many denominations are barely holding their own or are declining in membership
and are making excuses for such arrest of growth. Some have even maintained that decline in numbers was "really rather a good thing". Defensive cliches have been manufactured right and left. The church growth
movement challenges this defeatist mentality. It calls on churches to
look out and see enormous numbers of men and women trying to live without
Christ's power and peace and righteousness, to see sheep without a shepherd, and to multiply every means of bringing men into a redemptive
relationship to the Saviour.

CGB suggests that readers in America make sure that their ministers,
elders, and other leaders go to church growth workshops and seminars, see
church growth films and read church growth books. Readers overseas might

in their prayer letters suggest that supporting churches get acquainted with growth thinking.

Any American congregation would be richly rewarded by starting a church growth study group, using first How To Grow A Church - Conversations About Church Growth (Regal Books, Glendale, California) and second A Manual For Evangelism/Church Growth. Going to a workshop or seminar would help get such a study group started, but is by no means essential. Get the books and go to it.

3. THE WORKSHOP EXPLOSION IN LATFRICASIA

The last two years have seen workshops perfected as means for spreading church growth thinking through leading congregations of Latin America, Africa and Asia. The workshop has been reported in Church Growth Bulletin, July 1972, and September 1973, but the story of the explosion has yet to be told.

In April 1972 in Venezuela, C. Peter Wagner, ably assisted by Vergil Gerber and Edward Murphy, launched a pilot church growth workshop. Spanish speaking pastors of ordinary churches brought records (some woefully inadequate) of their membership during the past ten years. Workshop leaders taught them how to analyze, chart, and understand the growth which had taken place and was taking place. That provided a background of reality. The pastors (and some missionaries) were talking about their own problems, tasks and opportunities. They were not reacting against new North American schemes! In that setting it became fruitful then to set forth church growth principles - they could then be seen as "something which we need". The third step was to ask the participants, on the basis of their past experience (in faith and after prayer) to project the growth they believed God was calling on them to attempt. The fourth step was to calculate what the average rates of growth during the last ten years had been, and during the coming five years would be. The last step was to plan for another workshop a year later, attended by these same men, to see what in fact had happened.

The Venezuelan experience furnished a base for a significant advance in church multiplying evangelism. Dr. Vergil Gerber prepared a small book (A Manual for Evangelism/Church Growth, available from Wm. Carey Library, 305 Pasadena Avenue, South Pasadena, Calif., 91030 USA) which tells in beautifully clear fashion, how any group of pastors and/or missionaries can hold a church growth workshop. Given the book, anyone can do it.

It helps, of course, to have someone who has been through the process hold the first Church Growth Workshop in a country, denomination, or mission. But it is not necessary. Missionary Gerald Swank of the Sudan Interior Mission in Nigeria got hold of the Manual in English and all by himself, without ever attending a workshop, led a group of forty Nigerian pastors and seminary students through the process of analyzing, charting and understanding the growth which had taken place, and of projecting in faith the growth they thought God wished them to have in the coming five years.

Now we come to the explosion. It seems as if Christian leaders all over the world have been looking for a tool which they can use to get missionaries and ministers, pastors and seminary professors thinking about the church growth opportunities and challenges they face. The Gerber Manual is that tool. Consequently, as soon as they discovered it in the Church Growth Bulletin and other magazines, or heard about it, or came back from a Church Growth Workshop, they have been busy holding church growth workshops and planning for others. Dr. Gerber has been flooded with invitations from many lands to come and hold Demonstration Workshops there. In August 1973 he took a team with him to Kenya, Nigeria and Ivory Coast, holding Demonstration Workshops in each place. While in Kenya he received an invitation from India to come there in October 1974 to hold an All India Demonstration Workshop (probably just before the Inauguration of the Federation of Evangelical Churches, November 1st to 3rd, 1974). Demonstration Workshops are being planned in Taiwan, the Philippines, Brazil, and many other lands.

The Manual for Evangelism/Church Growth has been translated into French, Spanish, Portuguese, and is being translated into Swahili, Hausa, Mandarin and other major languages. CGBulletin suggests that anyone inviting a Demonstration Workshop to a new language area should plan at once to translate the Manual. The whole purpose is to get church growth thinking out into the grass roots. To do that, the Manual should be available in the language the pastors speak. The clearing house for these Demonstration Church Growth Workshops is Dr. Vergil Gerber's Evangelical Missions Information Se ice (EMIS), Box 794, Wheaton, Illinois, 60187.

CGB suggests that aders get a copy of Gerber's Manual at once from Church Growth Book Club put on a small pilot workshop where they are, (Intelligent use of the Manual makes this possible) and then get some responsible agency in the country to sponsor a countrywide Workshop. Write Dr. Gerber. He may not be able to come himself, but he can suggest others who have had some experience in these matters and who can come and help lead your Church Growth Workshop.

4. ASIAN MISSIONARY SOCIETIES ADVANCE

A historic event, with great meaning for the propagation of the Gospel, took place in Seoul, Korea, August 27-30, 1973. Twenty-five Asian Christians with deep concern for the missionary outreach of Asian churches met and came to a unanimous decision that missionaries are urgently needed to strengthen the evangelistic task in Asia. Conviction came on them from the Holy Spirit that any talk of a moratorium on sending and receiving missionaries is unscriptural. They declared they would work together toward placing at least two hundred new Asian missionaries in the field by the end of 1974. They issued the following statement.

Having gathered in Seoul from August 27-30, 1973, as Christians with deep concern for the missionary outreach of the Asian churches and having been invited by the Host Committee of Korea for the first All-Asia Mission Consultation, we came from Hong Kong, Indonesia, India, Japan, Korea, Khmer, Malaysia, Philippines, Pakistan, Republic of China, Singapore,

Thailand and Vietnam.

Being convinced that God our Saviour wills that all men should be saved and come to the knowledge of the truth, He having provided salvation for all mankind in the death and resurrection of Jesus Christ, offering man forgiveness and the Holy Spirit to recreate him for eternal life, and realising the work of the Holy Spirit in the mobilization of the Christian community of Asia, and in the expectation of a fresh mighty outpouring of the Holy Spirit which expresses itself in a dynamic movement of evangelization of the lost in Asia and other parts of the world;

Having had factual reports from representatives of many Asian countries where the Gospel of Jesus Christ has not been effectively preached; and realising that the unfinished task is so tremendous (98% of the populations of Asia have so far not responded to Christ);

We appeal to the Christian churches in Asia to be involved in the preaching of the Gospel, especially through sending and receiving Asian missionaries to strengthen the witness to the saving power of Christ.

We are compelled by the Holy Spirit to declare that we shall work towards the placing of at least two hundred new Asian missionaries by the end of 1974.

These missionaries will be involved primarily in evangelism in the power of the Holy Spirit in order that men and women may come to believe God's work of grace through Jesus Christ and in turn be agents of evangelism in the fellowship of the Church, the Body of Christ. These missionaries will also be sent to plant evangelistic churches where they do not already exist.

To this end, we resolve to appoint a continuation committee consisting of seven persons (Dr. Simeon Kang, Dr. Philip Teng, Dr. P. Octavianus, Rev. A. Furuyama, Rev. Theodore Williams, Rev. David J. Cho, and Dr. Chandu Ray) to carry out the following functions:

1. To encourage and assist in the formation of National Associations in every country of Asia, consisting of a group of spiritually minded, mature Christians, who will act as advisors to the Christian churches, missions and agencies for receiving, placing, sending and commissioning Asian missionaries.

2. To work in close cooperation with the Coordinating Office for Asian Evangelization for providing liaison and necessary information for these autonomous National Associations.

3. To work for the establishment of a center for Asia in cooperation with Korea International Mission for missionary orientation and research in Seoul, if possible.

4. To examine carefully through research and cooperation with the
    National Associations and COFAE, the relationship between East
    and West missionary enterprises.

. . . .

The missionary enterprise throughout the world will rejoice in this
great leap forward of the Asian Churches and pray that it may soon be duplicated by African and Latin American and Oceanian denominations. The
task of mission, as Dr. Winter so often says, is not complete until within
each newly established cluster of congregations (Church or denomination) a
missionary sending agency has been organized and is at work.

The Church of Jesus Christ is now a world-wide fact. It exists in
almost every country. Despite the fact that the actual denominations
founded are often small and weak, their combined strength is formidable.
The task is now to focus their strength on advancing the Gospel, and to
encourage the formation of hundreds of new missionary societies. Some of
these will be denominational societies. Some will be interdenominational.
Earnest Christians, under conviction from the Holy Spirit that the Gospel
must be effectively presented to the multitudes who have no knowledge of
the Saviour, should band themselves together to pass on the great good
news of salvation through faith in Jesus Christ and membership in His Body.

The First All Asia Mission Consultation is a long step in the right
direction. Church Growth Bulletin heartily congratulates the twenty-five
men who at great personal cost met from all over Asia to achieve significant ends. Conciliar forces in Asia have been moving in the same directions for some years. They, too, have talked about Asian missionaries and
have sent some. However, they have not focussed on the central task of
missions. They have allowed peripheral concerns (good concerns) undue
prominence in their plans. Their missionaries, they said, would work in
the churches to which they were sent, and would demonstrate brotherhood.
We hope all missionaries demonstrate brotherhood and work in cordiality
toward existing churches, but that is not their primary function. Missionaries are to tell people who know nothing about Jesus that the
Redeemer has come. Missionaries are not fraternal workers, they are advance agents. They are sent out to disciple ta ethne, to multiply units
of the Body of Christ. Like Paul, they seek to "proclaim the Good News
in places where Christ has not been heard of" (Romans 15:20).

This new Asian Movement, whose Seoul Meeting is of such great importance, will want to make very sure that its 200 new missionaries by
December 31, 1974, (and 2,000 new missionaries by December 31, 1984?) are
recruited, trained, and placed where new cells of Christians can be established and, in the not too distant future, new missionary societies of
that discipled population can be organized. Church Growth Bulletin earnestly trusts that the Asian missionaries will be sent to provedly receptive units of society. It is usually a mistake to send new missionaries
to indifferent and resistant segments of society. 'Send them where the
harvest is ripe' is sound missiology. One of the wonderful facts of this
day is that ripe harvests are to be found in most countries.

5. FAITH HEALING AND CHURCH GROWTH - IVORY COAST

About a tenth of the citizens of Ivory Coast (total population 4,000,000) are Christians - 300,000 in the Roman Catholic, 60,000 in the Methodist, and about 20,000 more in other Churches. The dominant religion (3,600,090) is fetish worship and belief in a bewildering variety of spirits and powers.

An Assemblies of God missionary from France, Pastor Jacque Giraud (Zhak Zheero) who had been working in Guadalupe (about 100 miles south east of Puerto Rico) was invited to Ivory Coast to dedicate a new Assemblies church there. In February 1973, in the course of subsequent preaching, many who attended were healed. Attendance zoomed. The city stadium at Abidjan was secured. Thirty thousand a night packed the place.

Pastor Giraud would preach for an hour on some miracle of healing recorded in the Gospels and then say, "Put your hand where it hurts. I am going to pray that God will heal you. Remember, I do not heal. I am no healer. God heals whom He will. Pray with me." After a half hour of fervent prayer, he would ask those who had been cured to come forward. Crutches were thrown away. Some deaf heard. Some blind saw. Dozens - and on some nights hundreds - surged forward. The next day those who had been cured (and their cure certified by those who knew them) testified publicly. The radio was full of the Giraud meetings. So were the daily papers. Bus loads came from all over Ivory Coast. Pastor Giraud also preached doctrinal sermons - Atonement, Repentance, Judgment, Holy Life, New Birth. The whole country was stirred.

He associated with himself on the platform ministers and missionaries of other denominations and urged such as wished to become Christians to seek out the minister or church of their choice and be baptized.

Later leading figures in the Ivory Coast, who had been blessed or healed in the meetings, asked Pastor Giraud to conduct similar meetings in their parts of the country. Meetings have been held at Toumodi and Bouake and are scheduled for Yamoussoukro and other towns and centers. Interest continues white hot. Everyone knows Pastor Giraud's song, "Up, Up With Jesus. Down, Down with Satan. Hallelujah, Hallelujah".

After the Toumodi meeting, groups of inquirers from 81 villages voiced a desire to ministers and missionaries of the Christian and Missionary Alliance to become Christian. After the meeting in Bouake, groups from over 100 villages did the same. Thousands are saying "Fetish is dead. We shall all become Christians". The enthusiasm of some, no doubt, will ebb away. Such is the situation.

But the essential question is: what should missionaries and ministers do with such inquirers? How can these events be transmuted into solid biblical churches?

Evidence from all over the world indicates that advances in the spread of the Faith have often come in connection with the excitement and

heightened conviction of healing campaigns. For example, Dr. William
Read in <u>Latin American Church Growth</u> says,
> Many Evangelicals in Argentina, whether or not they agree with
> Hicks' theology (he was the faith healer in Buenos Aires in 1954)
> admit that his meetings broke the back of the rigid Argentine re-
> sistance to the Evangelical witness. (p. 381)

The same thing has happened in many countries. What should Christians be
doing in Ivory Coast today (and in Indonesia, it may be, tomorrow) when
the tremendous publicity of a healing campaign opens doors to the Gospel?
There is the case of the blind pagan from 600 kilometers north of Abidjan
who promised his fetish a sacrifice if his blindness were healed - and
set off for Abidjan. He was not healed, but, during the twenty days he
attended the meetings, he heard the Gospel nightly and believed. He returned, burned his fetish, and became a Christian. <u>Can the Ivory Coast
campaign be handled in such a way that hundreds of groups come to Christian faith, burn their fetishes, build churches, study the Bible, and become responsible members of Christ's Church?</u>

NEWS

FREE   FREE   FREE   by Harold Cummins, Kenya

RECEIVE TWO CHURCH GROWTH BOOKS FREE...by giving us your story!!

A generous donor is making it possible for me to help you. I have
asked Church Growth Book Club to send you <u>any two</u> of the following books
without cost to you. In return I ask your help. <u>Tell me the story of
how new churches are being started in your area.</u> Here is what to do.
(Use an air form or plain stationery).

1.   Select two of the following books you wish, free:
       <u>Church Growth and the Word of God</u> by Alan Tippett
       <u>How Churches Grow</u> by Donald McGavran
       <u>Historic Patterns of Church Growth</u> by Harold Cook
       <u>Watch Out, Here Comes the Pentecostals</u> by C. Peter Wagner
       <u>Understanding Church Growth</u> (paperback) by Donald McGavran

2.   Answer <u>in detail</u> the following two questions (please type)
    a) <u>Who are the people among whom you are establishing churches?</u>
       Describe   (i) the sociological unit - rural, urban, students,
                        class, peasants, caste, tribe, etc.
             (ii) the size of your denomination to which new churches
                     are joined, i.e. have you now a denomination of 7
                     congregations and a total of 187 communicants, or
                     ten times as many?
           (iii) the number of missionaries or ministers who are
                     giving full time to planting churches in your
                     country, i.e. the size of the evangelistic outreach.

b) <u>How are new churches being started in your area?</u> Give us an accurate step by step story of how you start or multiply new cells,
congregations, or churches.

3. Send your name and address and state that we have your permission to
print your story if we desire. Send your answers to "2" and your
selections under "1" to - Donald McGavran, Editor
Church Growth Bulletin
Fuller Seminary, 135 No. Oakland Avenue
Pasadena, Calif. 91101 USA
He will ask CGB Club to dispatch the books to you and will forward
your answers to me in Kenya where I am gathering information on the
many ways in which churches are being planted in different pieces of
the mosaic which is mankind. Thanks for your kind assistance.
Harold Cummins.

NOTABLE SYMPOSIUM ON CHURCH GROWTH

Milligan College, Tennessee will host the William S. Carter Symposium
on Church Growth, April 5-7, 1974.

Symposium coordinator Dr. Tetsunao Yamamori said the meeting will
focus on "The Adaptation-Syncretism Axis." Four missiologists - Dr.
Donald McGavran, Dr. Alan Tippett, Dr. J.C. Hoekendijk, and Dr. Peter
Beyerhaus - will address themselves to the question: "As Christianity
Spreads into the Myriad Cultures of the Earth, It Correctly Adjusts to
Each Culture; But What Are the Limits of Such Adjustments?"

Dr. McGavran and Dr. Tippett are professors at the School of World
Mission and Institute of Church Growth, Fuller Theological Seminary. Dr.
Hoekendijk teaches missions at Union Theological Seminary in New York.
Dr. Beyerhaus directs the Institute for Missions and Ecumenical Theology
at the University of Tubingen, West Germany.

The symposium will consist of twelve lectures with three main divisions: (1) The Axis Defined and Illustrated, (2) Principles Applicable to the Axis, and (3) Critical Issues in the Axis. Each participant
will present three lectures. The first two will be formal presentations
addressed to a specific topic, while the third will be a reaction statement to the other addresses.

A closing Convocation will be held Sunday afternoon, April 7, to
celebrate the emphasis upon missions. Dr. Charles Taber, Milligan's
visiting professor of World Missions will address the convocation. Dr.
Taber has edited PRACTICAL ANTHROPOLOGY and was a missionary to West
Africa for seven years prior to becoming translations consultant of the
United Bible Societies in the same region.

Invitations are extended to missionaries on furlough and in preparation; to professors of missions; to representatives of missionary societies; to Third World church leaders visiting the United States at the
time; and to editors of missionary and church publications.

CHURCH GROWTH
BULLETIN

Address:
FULLER THEOLOGICAL
SEMINARY
135 N. Oakland
Pasadena, Calif. 91101

DONALD A. McGAVRAN, B.D., Ph.D.
Director

January 1974   Subscription $1 per year   Volume X   No. 3

CONTENTS

CHRISTIANITY AND CULTURES   by Dr. Dennis M. Oliver
                                           of Canadian Theological College

Missiology seeks to harness the insights of theology and anthropology (and other fields) to the task of mission. By mission we mean great
commission mission, namely, the discipling of the nations. Missions
are--theologically--obeying a word from God. But the very terms of their
mandate (disciple ta ethne) make their task ethnological and thus anthropological as well.

    Evangelical missiology seeks to remain true to the Bible--not merely
to one biblical mandate (Great Commission), but to the entire word of
God. Beyerhaus and Kwast are right in stressing that a crucial question
in missions today is "from what hermeneutical base do we operate?" I
affirm the hermeneutic enunciated by Kwast in Crucial Issues in Missions
Tomorrow. As God was pleased to speak to all men in all cultures,
through the Bible, He does indeed accomplish His purpose. The current
Christianity and Culture debate hinges not so much on abstract principles or confessional differences, but upon the judgment as to whether
the Bible does effectively communicate God's Word when read according to

SEND correspondence, news, and articles to the Editor, Dr. Donald McGavran, at the Institute of Church
Growth, Fuller Theological Seminary.

Published bi-monthly, send subscriptions and changes to the Business Manager, Norman L. Cummings, Overseas Crusades. Write to: Church Growth, 265 Lytton Avenue, Palo Alto, California 94301 USA. Second-
class postage paid at Palo Alto, California.

its literary sense.

I recognize that God spoke through human languages and in terms relevant to specific situations. But He was not bound by them, and neither are His people. For example, a non-agriculturalist can easily grasp the significance of "the wheat and the tares". One not in a pastoral culture can be spoken to by God through the 23rd Psalm. We can grasp the lessons of John 13, though foot-washing is not part of our culture.

The correct hermeneutic (again following Kwast) is this: that God speaks to men (of all ages and cultures) through His scriptures, in terms of principles more than specifics. This is true at an obvious level in the injunction to cover the head--but no less true in the Sabbath institution or the command to give a needy neighbor one's cloak. The specifics are often relevant to particular historical and cultural situations--but the principles through which they speak are abiding.

With this hermeneutical base established (it is more developed by theologians such as Marcus Dodds, Berkouwer and Bavinck, Ramm, and Clark Pinnock), we turn to specific prepositions.

First, men should become Christian within their own cultural setting. This is a bedrock assumption of church growth. We affirm "conversion without social dislocation" - the sine-qua-non of people movements. Some say that to impose the Bible's requirements on a people will lead to a conversion by extraction. This is true only if the Bible is used in a wrong way. The hermeneutic which we have sketched above (biblical teaching in terms of principles) means that we do not impose the Bible legalistically--with a false literalness. Thus we do not "play 1st century" when we are true to Scripture.

In a practical sense, to what extent does scriptural teaching change a culture? McGavran has estimated that fully 90% of a culture (manners, mores, life-ways) will remain unchanged. But certain practices and values will alter. The life-changing message of the Bible is dynamic and inter-personal. It does change men's character, attitudes and relationships much more than it changes specific customs and externals such as kinds of tools used and kinds of food eaten.

Where any particular practice does contradict biblical principles, then Christians must obey God's Word. If the would-be disciple makes his living by theft, he may not continue to steal after coming to Christ. If the convert sees certain practices as destructive and cruel, then he will alter them, in light of Biblical principles. It is not the missionary's essential function to point out how biblical principles demand changes. He leaves the application of biblical principles very largely to the church or Christian people to whom he has brought the Good News, God's Work and the presence of the Holy Spirit. The missionary should not coerce change, but trust to the prompting of the One whose ministry is to lead men into all truth.

Second, we recognize that while biblical principles remain the
same, there is room for a plurality of theological emphasis within the
context of these principles. Many things shape the character of a theology: we might term them "historical and cultural accidents". My theology is patterned to speak to my own cultural situation (e.e. Western
theology emphasizes such methods as the philosophic approach and such
subjects as "the theology of work"). A theology which spoke to a culture
in which potential converts would be "turned off" by beef-eaters (or
pork-eaters) would emphasize, "If any brother is offended by eating meat,
I will eat no meat".

Those living in a totalitarian state might well develop a theology
which "majors" in Matthew 24, Daniel, Esther and Revelation. Those in an
urban situation might focus especially on I and II Corinthians. None of
these special emphases negate biblical truth--none contradict each other.
Thus culturally relevant theologies (and the affirmation of the fact that
theology is plural and not exactly the same for all men) do not threaten
the upholding of biblical truth.

Finally, evangelical missiology will insist that the Bible contains
truths which are necessary for all men to believe. Some of these truths
are: that God is, and that He wills to save men; that there is "no other
Name" than Jesus Christ; that by His death and resurrection Jesus Christ
has won eternal life for all who accept His grace by faith; that our salvation "is not by works, lest any man should boast"; that the Bible is
God's authoritative and infallible Word. These are core biblical truths
on which Christians across the world and through all history have agreed.
Under the guidance of the Holy Spirit and the sure light of the Bible
these and other core truths.

Faithfulness to biblical truth does not encourage the kind of in-
sensitivity which is rightly called cultural or historical imperialism.
But neither does a healthy cultural sensitivity demand sitting loose to
biblical truth--abstracting it (a la Bultmann and other exponents of the
"new hermeneutic") so that "anything goes". We are bound to the literary
sense of the Scriptures, if we are to know God's will. He gave us the
Bible to communicate to all men. Whatever our culture, we can be optimistic that He will speak to us clearly by the means which He has chosen.

By December 31st, 1974 (this year) the world's population
will be very close to 4 billion.

The 1973 World Population Data Sheet published by the Population Reference Bureau in Washington D.C. states that in
mid-1973 the world population was 3.86 billion and was
growing at 2 per cent each year.

We must now cease talking about "the two billion" who have
yet to believe, and start talking about the three billion,
of whom huge numbers are winnable.

THIS MIGHT BE YOUR COUNTRY   by A United Methodist

Two years ago we had 350 full members. We now have 700, and counting probationary members, we have 1100. More importantly, consensus
turnings are beginning.

For the first time in the history of our church planting, a majority
approaching consensus has turned to Christ in a single community. Five
of the six zones of the community called _____ have become solidly
Christian. On the traditional date, the whole community celebrated its
first "Christian festival". A second community, smaller and more distant
from the Mother Church, is on the verge of a full consensus turning.
((In short, God has given this Church the precious small beginning of a
people movement. Much has been written on the care and nurture of people
movements. All will prove valuable in the care of this one. The
Editor))

Conversions have been preceded by healings. The dynamism for church
growth has come from three persons, a pastor and two laymen, all with
healing gifts. All have had recent significant experiences with the Holy
Spirit. The laymen have been practically mobbed on occasion, by those
desiring healing; but have stood their ground and obliged interested persons to hear them out on the Gospel before they pray for healings. Other
laymen have performed quiet but productive work in visitation, witnessing
and prayer vigils.

Much confirms church growth principles. Most congregations now developing are led by laymen. With the exception of mother-church growth,
all striking growth is taking place in villages where we have had no
schools. The community where we had the greatest turning has always
seemed highly resistant to the church and to our schools. The community
about to turn has had practically no contact with us at any time!!

((I regret that, for fear of persecution, names and country cannot be revealed...but people movements like this are going on in dozens of countries and could go on in dozens more. They probably could in your country. Why not pray that God will begin one in your field? The Editor))

UNEVANGELIZED MILLIONS - AND LAUSANNE   by Donald McGavran

In March 1964, Dr. John T. Dale, General Director of the Mexican
Indian Mission worked out a "Five Year Plan of Work". After setting
forth the programs for developing the inner life of the congregations and
their evangelistic outreach to their own ranches, towns, and nearby areas
he penned these words:
> "Let us begin work in the unreached areas between the various
> fields where we have churches already established. If one will
> but consult a map of Mexico, he will see clearly that there are
> large areas of country between the Tamazunchale and the Tantoyuca
> fields, between the Tamzunchale and the Acuatla fields, between
> the Macatlan and the Cuautempan fields, and on and on, where no

evangelical churches have been established." (Underlining mine)

Dr. Dale was speaking of large unevangelized populations within that section of Mexico which comity had assigned to his mission. These unevangelized areas can be multiplied by "ten thousand times ten thousand" and the reality will still be understated.

A fine missionary society has just pulled all its missionaries out of India because it has established a Church of 25,000 communicants there, has turned authority over to the Church, and feels its job in India is finished. A tragic misunderstanding of the real situation! The mission has done right to turn authority over to the Indian Church of 25,000; but has done wrong to leave India. Its team of seasoned missionaries, who could have easily obtained 'no objection to return certificates' from the Indian Government, should have been deployed to Unevangelized Populations Between.

In between most Latfricasian denominations are huge unevangelized populations. Many are highly responsive. They know that Christ has redeemed and elevated those who trusted in Him. They speak either the same or similar languages. As congregations are multiplied they can be linked to the existing Church. Yet most of these populations the younger Churches are not planning to evangelize; indeed, cannot evangelize. There are now more unevangelized persons in areas between established Latfricasian Churches than there were a hundred years ago in the whole of Latfricasia - Latin America, Africa and Asia. With the population explosion, this number doubles every thirty years. Most Latfricasian Churches sit there looking at them. Many missions withdraw to Europe and America.

The Lausanne Congress on Evangelism, July 16-23, is focussing attention on the Unreached Billions of earth. All of these are In Between Existing Churches - but remain as Unevangelized as if they were 10,000 miles away.

This situation need not continue. Latfricasian and Eurican Churches and their missionary societies have abundant resources and abundant conviction to evangelize these in-between millions. In some instances joint efforts will be mounted. In some instances the Church concerned will call for a mission from Korea or Kansas to undertake the work. In some instances unilateral action by Church or Mission will occur.

With full acknowledgment of the desirability and effectiveness of joint action, common sense requires us to realize that frequently unilateral action is all that is possible. A) There is no time for consultation. B) One partner only feels God's call to a given task. The existing Church there is Baptist and the mission concerned is sent out by the United Church of Christ in Japan. We can sum the matter up by saying "As far as possible, evangelism of the Unevangelized Millions Between should be done by the nearby Churches assisted by friendly missions; but always remembering that the crucial consideration is that it be done. 'After all, what is Apollos? What is Paul?....It is not the gardener with their planting and watering who count'." (I Cor. 3:5-7 NEB)

> An outstanding church growth study has just come off press - <u>Brazil 1980</u> by Wm. R. Read. Dr. Read has taken the extraordinarily detailed data concerning Protestant congregations gathered every year by the government of Brazil and shown where church growth is going on, how it is related to industrialization, land settlement, urbanization, and other factors, and what size the churches will be in 1980 and 2000. The book abounds in revealing charts and graphs. Church men in every continent should read it carefully. It will increase their understanding of the magnitude of the missionary task and the opportunities which face the Churches. Get it from Church Growth Book Club.   Donald McGavran

MISSIONS AS APOSTOLIC TEAMS   Overseas Crusades

One of the freshest and most promising images of missions has emerged out of the repeated deliberations of the dedicated men leading Overseas Crusades. What have been called 'missions' OC thinks are remarkably like the 'Apostolic Teams' of the New Testament. Or, to more exactly represent OC thought, the 'Apostolic Team' shown at work in Acts and the Epistles is the ideal which each mission should approximate.

The Apostolic Team was a remarkably elastic organization. At times it consisted of men sent out by a church in one country to propagate the Gospel in another. At times it consisted of men sent out by the newly planted churches to plant other churches or to carry out a mission to the Jerusalem churches. Some members earned their living by tent making. Some were supported by churches. The Holy Spirit led them into the team and the Holy Spirit led them out of the team.

A remarkable document called "The Ministry and Organizational Development of Overseas Crusades as an Apostolic Team" has been circulated to the trustees, staff, and personnel of Overseas Crusades for comment and discussion. In it, the missionary society has sought to pattern itself and its missions in a dozen countries on the New Testament model. The document is thoroughly biblical and thorougly contemporary. It asks, "What will the concept of an apostolic team do to national-missionary tensions? How will it affect our long and short range goals?"
....
Dr. Alan Tippett has asked Rev. Norman Cummings, Executive Director of Overseas Crusades, to set forth the proposal in article form and intends to print it in an early issue of Missiology. CGBulletin readers will follow this creative thinking with great interest. With two billion rapidly growing to three billion unaware of what the words "Jesus Christ" mean, ways must be found to state the supreme task of the Church in compelling and biblical terms. To consider each mission an Apostolic Team is a long step in the right direction. Why should not each congregation in the whole world, each cluster of congregations, each denomination send

out one or more Apostolic Teams? The New Testament so clearly points in
this direction. In them, the great age of Christian Missions now dawning
would find effective tools.

In 1900 the Protestant communicant members in Brazil numbered 11,376. In 1970, communicants had grown to a reported 2,623,600 with a Protestant community of almost
ten million. The MARC projection places this number in
1980 at 5,477,000 communicants and a community of
16,529,000. Brazil 1980 W.R. Read, page 218

CEASE-FIRE OR VICTORY?   by Dr. Raymond J. Davis
                                  General Director, Sudan Interior Mission

((In some circles, church leaders today are calling for a "moratorium on
missionaries." On biblical grounds, Church Growth Bulletin disagrees
with this estimate of what will advantage world evangelization. We agree
with the following fine statement made by the Director of one of our
nation's largest and most active missionary boards. The Editor))

The term "cease-fire" may be new, but the tactic is not. Cease-fire
means "a cessation of hostilities." It is a temporary, sometimes tenuous
strategy, designed to take the heat off.

In world politics, a cease-fire can be - and sometimes is - benefi
cial. In world evangelism it is not, and never can be. A cease-fire is
a truce, not a victory. It is an admission of stalemate, never negotiated by leaders whose troops are obviously winning.

A great evangelistic offensive has built up momentum around the
world. Today, in the last third of the century, the church of Jesus
Christ is pushing back the borders of the kingdom of Satan. He is feeling the heat.

Realizing that he is failing to frustrate God's purpose, Satan is
seeking a cease-fire. Strangely, though such a procedure is nowhere
hinted at in Scripture as acceptable, it is receiving consideration by
some who nonetheless claim Christ as their leader and commander.

Difficulties, dangers, disease, and even death are all part of the
pursuance of our objective. The financial cost of missionary service is
rapidly rising. The outlook for tenure, security and safety is increasingly bleak.

To deny the existence of such conditions is imprudent. The situation includes all these things - and more. But included in the "more" is

the continuing validity of Christ's promise of His personal presence and power, "even unto the end of the age."

The enemy has used these tactics before. Time and time again, down through history, the world situation has seemed hopeless. But Satan's efforts have never been a successful deterrent to the onward sweep of God's ultimately victorious army.

God delights to show himself strong on behalf of His children, especially when the enemy is pushing hard. And push hard he does. Any Christian looking for an out can easily find one. The choice is ours - along with the consequences!

There was no future for Paul as he was dragged through the gate at Lystra. There was no security for Stephen as the stones rained down upon his head. There was no appreciation for Peter as he lay chained to Roman soldiers in a cell.

They looked beyond their immediate circumstances to ultimate victory. Like them, God helping us, we too will push ahead. We will not lay down our weapons now! And we welcome all who, with us, will continue to press the battle. We need men and women who will keep going, keep giving, and keep praying, looking not for a cease-fire, but for victory!
(Reprinted by permission from Today's Christian - issue of December 1973)

In 1968 the Brazilian Census Bureau published a micro-region division plan for the whole of Brazil. It distinguished 360 micro-regions. We were able to determine the number of Protestant congregations in each region and hence - across the years - the rate of growth for each Protestant denomination in each micro-region....(p.54) The unusual percentage of increase in micro-region 221 between 1955 and 1966, a twelve-year period, is 210 per cent....Whenever such increase is recorded, it should receive special attention from those interested in church growth dynamics.
Brazil 1980 by William R. Read. p. 105

THE YET TO BELIEVE HAVE PRIORITY   by Norvald Yri
                                                          of Norway

Some things I read make me think Christians are veering over to a definition of the Great Commission as "reaching the unreached, wherever they may live". The history of the expansion of Christianity tells us that the Great Commission has inspired home and foreign missions alike. Both need to be done. However, it is essential to emphasize that today the Lord's command focusses on those who have never heard.

Some Christian thinkers hold that Norway is so pagan as to need missionaries. They say the same about the rest of Europe and America, too. I agree that Norway must be re-evangelized. We must increase our evangelists, preachers, and pastors. We should also send evangelists to other countries in Europe. We are in fact doing something along each line.

However, what we do in Norway and parts of Europe must not be substituted for what we should do in carrying out the Great Commission among the two billion - where the Gospel is yet to be mentioned. When young men in Norway tell me they have a missionary calling, dare I tell them to stay in Norway because we also need missionaries? A thousand times NO! My vision is to double the number of Norwegian missionaries to people who have never heard and who can never hear unless the missionary goes.

St. Paul defined the apostolic task well in Romans 15:20-21. This seems an excellent definition of the Great Commission. "And thus I aspire to preach the Gospel, not where Christ already was named, that I might not build on another man's foundation, but as it is written, 'They who had no news of Him shall see, and they who have not heard shall understand.'" The missionary represents the apostolic function insofar as he preaches to those who have no news of him.

I hope Lausanne's concept of missions clearly focusses on those who have yet to hear. Such focus does not contradict the need of re-evangelizing the Christian world. It simply points out a huge and urgent task.

Yours for carrying out the Great Commission,
Norvald Yri, Sinsenv 15, Oslo 5 Norway

CALL FOR AID   by The Editor

Wanted: a Conciliar Missiologist Who Will Write on Gospel-Proclaiming, Sinner-Converting, Church-Multiplying Evangelism.

Church Growth Bulletin intends to scotch the evil rumor that it is anti-conciliar. Church Growth Bulletin is friendly to all Churches of Jesus Christ and their organizations. We want to help them all proclaim Jesus Christ as God and Saviour and persuade men to become His disciples and responsible members of His Church. Christians and churches carry out this task in multitudinous ways - by word and deed, by printed tract and television, by life lived and prayer uttered, by neighbor visited next door, and missionary sent across the seven seas.

CGB admits, however, that most contributors to the Bulletin come from one side of the fence. Since the World Council Meeting in Uppsala, conciliar writers have not contributed church growth articles. We invite them to do so. We hold that they are part of the Church. To use Barth's words, "In mission, the Church sets off and goes (porenthetes (Matt.28:19) taking the essentially and most profoundly necessary step beyond itself, and beyond the dubiously Christian world in which it is more immediately set, to the world of men.....The Word which God has pronounced in Jesus Christ concerning the covenant of grace which he has concluded with it is still alien, and must therefore be taken as a new message." (Church

Dogmatics IV, 3, p.874) Conciliars and Evangelicals both are bound to "go", and "take", and "pronounce". Church Growth Bulletin gives both a platform. We want to be mutually encouraged - we by them and they by us.

It must be clear, however, that we are not inviting anyone to explain through the Bulletin that conversion evangelism is outmoded, only social action is real evangelism, and Jesus Christ is not credible to modern man until His advocates throw themselves into the battle for humanization. This position, whether advanced by Evangelicals or Conciliars, we reject. We are for social justice, but will not substitute it for evangelism. Social justice is good; but it is not evangelism, and should not be called such. Evangelism is so to proclaim Jesus Christ that through the ministrations of the Holy Spirit men will put their trust in God through Him, accept Him as their Saviour and serve Him as their King in the fellowship of His Church.

Church Growth Bulletin earnestly wants conciliar Christians, who are engaging in evangelism, to write for this magazine. The whole Church needs their voice.

Brazil is...one of the largest unopened countries in the world...A large land mass and a rapidly increasing population have...triggered one of the most dramatic land settlements in our generation.(p.174)...This first stage of pioneer settlement can last as long as two decades. After the initial excitement is over...consolidation in the churches begins. In micro-region #288 in 1972 nine counties record no Protestant membership. (These counties will therefore become) opportunity areas for the next two decades....Protestant churches...will add year by year increase.
Brazil 1980, Wm. R. Read

BIBLICAL THEOLOGY OF RELIGIONS   Prof. Dr. Peter Beyerhaus
                                                  Tubingen, Germany

How relevant is seminary theology to the thought patterns and questions of the people to whom the Christian message is to be communicated? The new term coined for this task of adjusting theology to the indigeous situation is "contextuality." The danger which has to be avoided is, however, that under this program the non-Christian addressee suddenly determines not only the form but also the content of the message communicated to him.

This brings us to the big question of the place of dialogue within the Christian mission. Many people seem to regard dialogue as the modern substitute for evangelism, which should be the only still legitimate form of Christian mission during the forth-coming years. But it also could mean to find out in which way the other person is encountering ultimate reality or limitations of life. Then dialogue can be regarded as an indispensible stage in preparing for the relevant communication of the Gospel.

The Church must address itself to the still unsolved missiological task of developing a truly biblically based theology of religions. This must not simply deduce its statements speculatively from some general dogmatical principles, but take the dialectical witness of the prophets and apostles seriously that man's religions are both expressions of God's general revelation and also realms of activity of demonical forces.

In this way I believe that during the next ten years we shall become witnesses of a double event in the history of religion. On the one hand, there will be a growing incorporation into our understanding of Christ of all elements in non-Christian religions which are expressions of man's abiding relatedness to God and of God's prevenient grace. On the other hand, there will also be a growing together of all religions in their demonic, antidivine tendencies towards one syncretistic world religion.

It will be the ultimate expression of men's rejection of Christ as the only Lord and Saviour. Christian mission should become extremely sensitive to both developments and act accordingly.

NEWS

HONG KONG - IMMIGRANTS FLOOD IN

The Asian Student (issue of November 24, 1973) reports that during the first ten months of 1973, 46,000 Chinese have been given documents permitting them to leave Mainland China. The rate of entry into Hong Kong has been 8,000 per month. Most of these are overseas Chinese who returned to the mainland during the early sixties, and now desire to get back out.

In view of the Christian movements among the Chinese of the Dispersion, the arrival in Hong Kong of these multitudes who need jobs, homes, and associations has great meaning for Christian mission. Chinese Churches should be able to help these immigrants from mainland China.

AYMARA CHURCH GROWTH: REACTION AND RESPONSE   by T. D. Profitt

Aymara attitudes towards Catholicism and the clergy range from suspicion to suppressed hatred. Catholicism is the faith of the dominant Mestizo class (Tschopik prefers "caste") and relates to the Aymara only indirectly during fiestas, which are more social than religious. To the Aymara, the Christian God is deistic - powerful, yet too aloof and distant to care about them. Privately, Aymaras are animists, worshipping lesser beings who involve themselves with the Aymaras' world.

That Evangelical churches are multiplying among Aymaras may be interpreted as in part a reaction against the dominating class and its religion. By being neither Catholic (i.e. Mestizo) nor animist (i.e. Indian campesino), Aymara Evangelicals become a Third Force, and are liberated from the caste structure. Being Evangelicals enhances their ethnicity. In Evangelical churches they find leadership roles which are denied them in the established Church. Christ in Evangelical churches is not an image in a church nor a distant deity, but a personal Being who cares for Aymaras. Accepting the evangelical option is agreeable to their people-consciousness. Aymara church growth is both a negative reaction against the oppression of the past and a positive response to the love of God in Christ the Liberator.

HUGE BIOLOGICAL GROWTH IN INDIAN CHURCH   by Vernette Fulop

In May 1973, Rev. Maurice Blanchard was sent by the Southern Baptist Convention to parts of India to find new unworked fields. While Travelling there, he was invited by some Telegu Baptists to a big baptism at Ongole in Andhra Province. Now Ongole is the place where on July 2-4, 1878, 3,576 new believers were buried with their Lord in Baptism. So on July 3rd, 1973 - the 95th anniversary of the great baptism of 1878 - Mr. Blanchard found himself at Ongole, that famous American Baptist field. Here is what he saw.

A certain Indian layman (whose father was a pastor for 50 years at Ongole) worked for five years at socio-economic uplift with wells and irrigation, but was not satisfied with this temporary assistance. He had a burden for his people's salvation. He was elected secretary of the churches in January. In March, after three days of fasting and prayer, he called the pastors together to plan a new evangelistic thrust. As a result, in the two months, May and June, 12,000 and on the closing day of the crusade, July 3, 1060 people were baptized. Most of the 13,600 were born of Christian parents and were in their twenties - a notable case of biological church growth. The ethnic groups concerned were the Mala and Madiga castes.

Those desiring baptism on the final day came from a hundred mile radius, by all means of transportation, and were baptized in a beautiful service lasting from sunrise to sunset. Two sermons were preached, one by missionary Blanchard. Six pastors would baptize six at a time, and be replaced at suitable intervals by other pastors. These baptisms are, of course, the end result of a campaign to deepen conviction, bring those reared in the Christian faith to conscious discipleship, and make the churches more obedient to their Saviour and Lord. The campaign should also reach out to those in 'the world' - though so far it has not done so to any notable degree. Those leading the crusade hope to double the membership of the Telegu Baptist Convention in ten years. Some would like to double it in five years so that on the centenary of the tremendous days in 1878, the Church would number half a million.

ns
CHURCH GROWTH
B L L E T I N

from the
INSTITUTE OF
CHURCH GROWTH

Address:
FULLER THEOLOGICAL
SEMINARY
135 N. Oakland
Pasadena, Calif. 91101

DONALD A. McGAVRAN, B.D., Ph.D.
Director

March 1974   Subscription $1 per year   Volume X No. 4

C O N T E N T S

PLAIN SPEAKING ABOUT MISSION AND CHURCH GOALS   by Stan Shewmaker
                                        School World Mission, 1969

The Quarter-million Tongas live in approximately two thousand com-
munities--villages, neighborhoods, and kin groups. Their society is experiencing rapid and deep-seated changes. Young people are moving to
towns and cities in search of education and employment. Rural people
are laying hold of Western innovations and techniques which have managed
somehow to filter back into the village situation. Few are completely
unaffected by the upheaval.

Churches and Missions among the Tonga must turn with intelligence
and determination to church multiplication. Past patterns of mission
work do not, indeed cannot, meet the challenges of independent Africa.

The goal of Missions should not be to plant a few congregations at
or near the mission stations and hope that, with the passage of years,
the "younger churches" will be able to overcome the obstacles which have
defeated us and transmute our failures into successful evangelization.
Committed to the principle of transferring all power and control to
national Christians, we must not take shelter behind that worthy goal and
divest ourselves of our own responsibilities. We missionaries must be
good stewards of God's grace, and we must also help our African fellow
disciples to be good stewards themselves.

SEND correspondence, news, and articles to the Editor, Dr. Donald McGavran, at the Institute
of Church Growth, Fuller Theological Seminary. Published bi-monthly, send subscriptions
and changes of address to the Business Manager, Norman L. Cummings, Overseas Crusades,
Inc., 265 Lytton Avenue, Palo Alto, California 94301, U.S.A. Second-class postage paid at
Palo Alto, California.

The primary aim in missions must be the planting of an ongoing church in __each__ of the Tonga communities in city, town, and countryside. The primary goal: To multiply congregations until every man, woman and child in Tongaland has had a chance to say "yes" to Jesus Christ and to become a living stone in the great temple which God is erecting here...

Most of the foreign missionaries in Tongaland at the present time are engaged in institutional missions. Even if all of them were to suddenly redirect their energies toward evangelism, it would still be virtually impossible for every Tonga to be personally confronted by Christ __through the efforts of these missionaries alone__. Our African fellow disciples must see that the Christ we proclaim is indeed Lord of our lives, and that the Good News about Him is the most important message that they could tell to their kinsmen. A fervent and relevant witness to the transforming power of Jesus Christ in the life of one Tonga is the most effective vehicle for the transmission of the Gospel of another Tonga. Tongas must win Tongas.

In Tonga society the Gospel flows more freely from the elder to the younger. Conversions take place rapidly in villages and towns where the parents or guardians have __preceded__ the children of the household in becoming Christians.

Churches are strongest when composed of family or kinship units which have become Christian at about the same time. Unfortunately, among Tonga Churches of Christ, there have been very few instances where this type of conversion has actually been sought or encouraged by missionaries or national preachers trained by them.

We must begin immediately to concentrate upon the winning of __adults__. These persons may be largely illiterate, given to beer-drinking, and often polygamous, but this older segment of society must be won first. Once these parents have made the decision to become Christians, their children will find it much easier to complete the family movement to Christ. But to continue the conversion of individual students in our mission schools in the anticipation that they will win their pagan parents is futile. The words of school children or teen-agers usually have little positive effect upon their parents. Certainly the thirty years during which all of the Missions have reaped relatively meager results should be sufficient to convince us of this fact.

In village after village the initial decision to accept Christ must be encouraged and expected to come first from within the power structure. This decision, which will subsequently revolutionize their lives and society, must rest in the hands of the adult members of the community. Any course of evangelization which fails to convert these responsible men will limp along until sometime, somehow, into some Church, the responsible adults are won in significant numbers.

Missionaries have frequently been repulsed by the unpredictable and obnoxious behavior of drunken men at village beer drinks. It is an affront to our moral code; we are reluctant to get involved with this kind of lost individuals. But we must now turn our attention to these "hedgerows and byways" where lost men are. One concerned Christian leader went so far as to say, "We must go to the men around the beer pots; there resides the authority and leadership of the village. Those are the important men."

Since 1968, most local church buildings have been erected outside the immediate village perimeter because church members complained of excessive noise and distraction during worship, or cited instances of ridicule. The reason for these annoyances was that the members of these churches, mainly women and children, did not command the respect and attention of the major part of the village.

On the other hand, the headman and the council of elders within the village have had no difficulty in capturing and maintaining the rapt attention of the villagers. This conclave does not find it necessary to meet outside the village confines, but assembles in the middle of the village to settle the important and serious issues of day-to-day living. This is the traditional way.

Our goal must be to plant a church in every receptive community in Tongaland. There is no need for Christians to walk several miles to worship. With a church in every village, Christians would be able to meet for fellowship and prayer every single day. God's people could start every morning with dawn prayers and meditation and end the day with songs, prayers, and Bible study. The Christian life would become a total existence, instead of merely a weekly observance. It would not be long before churches would begin to thrust forward their natural leaders for further specialized Bible training.

THE TIDE TURNS   by Donald McGavran

During the last seventy-four years, it has seemed natural to end speculation at the year 2000. But now, when we are only 25 years away from that date, and most readers of this article will write "January first, 2000" on some letter, it is reasonable to carry our projections a few decades into the Twenty-First Century.

The last fifty years has seen the percentage of Christians in the world grow steadily smaller, despite tremendous missionary work and substantial growth of the Church in many lands. Enemies of the spread of Christianity have drawn weird conclusions from the fact that since about 1920 Christians have become a smaller and smaller proportion of the total population. Enemies have gleefully broadcast the erroneous notion that the proclamation of the Gospel and the Christianization of the world was doomed to failure. But the facts do not support them.

The reason why the percentage of Christians in the world has grown smaller is that during the last fifty years, medical science has greatly increased the normal expectation of life. Instead of ten babies being born and two living, twelve are born and ten live. Hence populations which do not practice birth control double every fifteen years. Heavily Christian countries by and large do practice birth control. Non-Christian countries by and large do not practice birth control and consequently their numbers double every few years.

But this will not continue. Either the countries of Asia, Africa and Latin America will practice birth control or tremendous famines will sweep them. The famines of the recent years are small advance notices of what is to come. The social changes and governmental regulations needed to usher in zero population growth do not come overnight. Consequently it seems reasonable to assume that the next twenty-five years will see the world population increasing from four billion in 1975 to six billion in 2000.

By then, however, population will stabilize or grow very much more slowly. The horrors of the great famine which will sweep careless countries will hasten effective measures.

As long as Asian populations - now largely non-Christian - double every few years, the world-wide proportion of Christians will continue to decline; but the proportion of Christians in each Asian country will remain stable - for Christians have at least as many children as non-Christians. In fact, since Christians grow by conversion, the proportion of Christians in each country usually keeps on rising, though emigration or persecution does occasionally cause decrease.

Once the populations of Asia are stabilized - and they certainly will be - the world wide proportions of Christians will steadily increase. Missionary outreach of all Churches - Asian, African, Latin American, European, and North American - continues to liberate and heal Substantial numbers in almost every land go on being reconciled to God in the Church of Jesus Christ.

Bearing these things in mind, I have taken Winter's projections which appeared in the January 1974 Evangelical Missions Quarterly and carried them on to 2025, 2050, and 2075. (See diagram on next page)

The white spaces tell the story. Till 2000 because of increase of Asian non-Christians, worldwide proportion of Christians decreases. When world population stabilizes at 6 billion, white areas become a larger part of the total area. If present per cent of conversion + biological increase (2.7) continues, Christians in Asia alone will in 2025 be 10%, in 2050 be 20% and in 2075 be 40% of the whole Asian population.

Only two assumptions are involved. First, that the world population - particularly that of Asia - will be stabilized. The horrors of over-population and the likelihood of famine are so great that the assumption cannot be far off. Maybe the figure will not be six billion but eight, or five, but it will not be twelve or twenty. The first time

fifty million people die in a famine, world opinion will precipitate
effective action in every country. Radio, newspapers and television
will all help bring the horrors into every audience. Second, that the
Churches of the world will continue to proclaim Jesus Christ as God and
only Saviour. This seems likely. The loss of nerve which some denominations manifest is not a common disease. Most Churches believe firmly
on the Saviour and accept the Bible as the authoritative infallible word
of God. Unless this changes, the missionary movement seems likely to
continue to spread with power. Then, too, wherever it goes it brings
liberation and blessing.

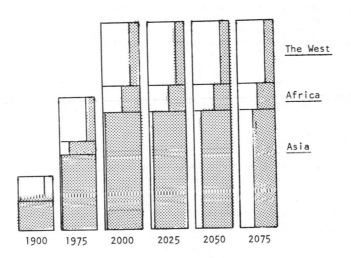

ALL EYES ON LAUSANNE July 16-25, 1974   by Paul Little

     Three speakers at the forthcoming International Congress on World
Evangelization will call for evangelical Christians to demonstrate their
unity in a more concrete way. Professor Peter Beyerhaus urges creation
of a worldwide association for the evangelization of the world in our
generation. Dr. Donald McGavran raises the fascinating possibility of a
cooperative arrangement whereby North American and European Christians
can help the burgeoning force of missionaries being sent out from Asia,
Africa and Latin America. Professor Henri Blocher suggests that those
interested in global evangelization ought to be thinking "of unity beyond
this world congress in Lausanne." He has "a permanent expression" in
mind, and notes that the Bible imposes no certain forms on believers.

The Lausanne meeting, to be attended by 2,700 leaders from all six continents, will focus attention on the tremendous possibilities of effective evangelism so often found around the world. Never has there been a more responsive generation than this. Never have the churches of Asia, Africa and Latin America had stronger and more vigorous churches. The time has come to surge forward in evangelism.

Pre-Congress meetings for study and prayer are being held. The School of Mission and Institute of Church Growth at Fuller Seminary, with Missions Advanced Research and Communication at World Vision have carried out a most extensive survey of UNREACHED PEOPLES. The Congress will see in vivid detail the true size and nature of the task.

Lausanne is a work congress. The main papers are being sent to all delegates, to study and send in agreements, disagreements, and further applications in their own cultures. Speakers will summarize these responses when they make presentations. Lausanne will focus attention on evangelization and church growth, believing these are pleasing to God.

SEND IN THAT DOLLAR TODAY   by N. L. Cummings, Business
                                   Manager, Church Growth Bulletin

The best buy in missions may well be the Church Growth Bulletin. Six issues come to you for $1.00.

We can continue this only if you cooperate and send us your annual subscription without being asked for it.

If you think your subscription is due - or heavens! past due - write me a check and mail it today, please. Make it out to: N.L. Cummings, Church Growth. Address the envelope to

                     Church Growth
                     P.O. Box 66
                     Palo Alto, CA.94302, U.S.A.

PRINT the address to which the Bulletin is to be sent. If you are already getting the Bulletin, kindly mention the "account number which appears on the address label". That helps us identify you and avoid mistakes.

A LOVING APPROACH TO ISLAM   by Phil Parshall

For nearly fourteen hundred years traditional evangelistic methodology has proved singularly unsuccessful in its confrontation with Islam. Muslims as a strong sociological unit have refused to even seriously consider an alien religious-cum-cultural force superimposed on its society by Caucasian propagators. Is it not time for a re-evaluation of approach

in our witness to the 500 million adherents of the world's second
largest living religion?

Consider for example the merits of the formation of a homogeneous
church composed totally of Muslim converts. The ritual of this worshipping community would follow as closely as possible the form prescribed
for worship in the mosque. This would minimize spiritual dis-orien-
tation on the part of the young converts. For instance, is there a
definite regulation in Scripture that God must be worshipped in corporate fashion only on Sundays -- or could not Friday be retained by the
convert as a meaningful day to come apart and meet God? It has been
said that cleanliness is next to godliness, so perhaps it would be appropriate for the Muslim convert to continue his ritual of washing prior
to his prayer time. Would it not be permissible to remove one's shoes
before worshipping the Lord -- even as Moses was commanded to do? Is
there anything unscriptural about praying five times a day? Direction
of prayer is important to the Muslim. Could not Jerusalem replace Mecca
--not as an object of veneration but rather as an expression of respect
for a part of the world that is pregnant with sacred memories for the
Christian. The Bible expressly declares fasting is a spiritual exercise
acceptable to God. Muslims could retain the month of abstainance as an
integral part of their worship form. Lastly, the Islamic creed is an
imperative statement of faith for all faithful Muslims throughout the
world. Would not the Apostle's Creed serve as a satisfactory substitute?

Let it be made clear that I am not postulating Biblical relativism.
My plea is for a church built upon the Rock Christ Jesus, committed un-
compromisingly to Scriptural absolutes and yet culturally attractive to
those who are faced with the impact of complete societal dislocation
upon acceptance of Christ as Saviour. Would not this church have a much
more viable witness in a predominant Muslim society? Sad to say, my
research indicates it has never been tried!

WORLD BAPTISTS: 3,176,954 NEW MEMBERS AND STANDING STILL!

by C. Peter Wagner

The religious news services recently carried the item that the
world membership of Baptist churches had grown by 3,176,954 members between 1968 and 1973. In itself this statistic is very encouraging, and
no Christian can fail to rejoice that so many new people now acknowledge
Jesus Christ as Savior and Lord.

But church growth eyes see the same figure as alarming. The total
Baptist membership now stands at 32,804,398 (see Chart 1) and the increase
represents a decadal growth rate of less than 25% (see Chart 2). In other
words, Baptist churches worldwide are not even keeping up with biological
growth! Other things being equal, a church which grows less than 25% per
decade is moving backwards, no matter how high the absolute number of new
adherents turns out to be.

If over the next decade, Baptists grow by only 7 1/2 million new
members, they will be standing still! Some of the most serious growth

problems for Baptists are in Europe and North America where they are
growing at minus 2.8% and 20% respectively. The picture is more complex
than it appears, however, since some individual Baptist churches in
Europe and North America are growing well. Growth rates in Africa and
Latin America are a healthy 76% and 72% respectively, but in those areas,
some individual Baptist churches are declining. Much more needs to be
known about Baptist churches than global or even continental statistics.

Every Baptist convention or association in the world ought to gather
the leaders of its churches together, examine themselves, and find out
just which churches are growing and which ones are not. Those that are
not growing at 50% or 75% or more every decade ought to know the reasons
why. They ought to be able to diagnose the causes of their illness and
arrange for proper treatment. God is not pleased with churches which,
facing three billion who don't trust in Jesus Christ, are standing still.
Once the problems are properly analyzed, the churches which are growing
can and should help those which aren't.

How can this be done? A prominent Baptist missionary statesman has
recently devised a simple tool that can be used on all levels. Dr.
Vergil Gerber of the Conservative Baptist Foreign Mission Society, now
on loan to Evangelical Missions Information Service, has produced a little
book called <u>God's Way to Keep a Church Going and Growing, A Manual for
Evangelism/Church Growth</u> (jointly published by Regal Books and William
Carey Library). When carefully read and applied, it will bring out the
true facts about your church and help you to make an accurate diagnosis
of your church's health.

In the years to come, this manual (available from the Church Growth
Book Club) may well turn out to be the most helpful aid to accelerating
Baptist growth (and that of other groups as well, of course) worldwide.
Over the next decade affiliates of the World Baptist Fellowship should
plan on growing by at least 40%, which means adding 15 million new members. It can be done with proper planning and strategy. Gerber himself
is coordinating practical workshops on evangelism and church growth in
the Third World. Dr. Win Arn and others are doing it for America. If you
are interested in following up on this, you may write to either of them
at:

Dr. Vergil Gerber   Dr. Winfield C. Arn
Evangelical Missions Information   Christian Communications
Box 794   1857 Highland Oaks Dr.
Wheaton, Illinois 60187   Arcadia, Ca. 91006

Don't let your church, association, or denomination keep on gaining
members, but continue to stand still. Slow church growth is a serious,
but curable disease. Perhaps the first thing is to study Charts 1 & 2 on
the following page. Is stoppage really necessary? Are we getting all the
growth God wants to give us? While Baptists are stopped, others are growing? What should this tell us?

CHART 1

Membership in Baptist Churches

by Continental Areas

	1968	1973
Africa	471,856	652,198
Asia	960,983	1,134,476
Europe	1,157,432	1,141,214
Middle East.	1,068	1,369
North America.	26,413,076	29,013,168
Oceania.	111,873	165,225
Latin America.	511,201	696,748
Totals	29,627,444	32,804,398

(Source: European Baptist Press Service)

CHART 2

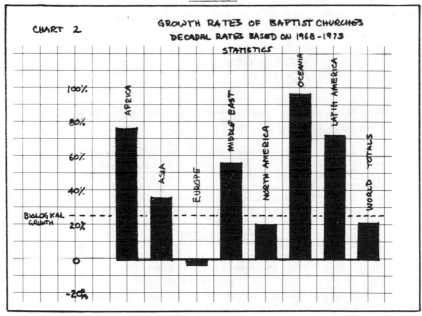

BREAKING THE STAINED GLASS BARRIER   by David Womack

"By the year A.D. 2000 the world apparently will have some 6.5 billion inhabitants and the demographic and ecological experts are saying
that we will enter the age of famines. It used to be that the prophets
of doom were the sidewalk preachers, but now they are the scientists.
It has become obvious that if the Church is ever to evangelize the world
it must greatly increase its level of missionary activity and establish
a broader base of operations very quickly, or else be forever too late
to fulfil the Great Commission.

The Church, however, has a terrible problem. By some quirk in the
evangelical mind many churches appear to be satisfied or at least willing
to settle for a token presence in each country rather than a serious attempt to fulfill the actual commands of Christ. They rejoice over a
few sheaves of gathered grain, while ignoring the massive harvest still
standing in the fields. Their magazines and sermons abound with tales
of missionary heroes, great personal sacrifices, and inspirational reports, but they never tell the American people that by and large the
Church is only establishing a token presence in each land rather than a
pervading witness. They do not say that missionaries often fail to
reach the major cultural groups because they spend most of their time
working with the more impressionable ethnic minorities who are seeking to
improve their social status. Seldom do American contributors learn that
much of their money goes into establishing Western institutions and funding a great many busy but not evangelistic activities, such as hospitals,
elementary schools, orphanages, and other charitable works that in today's
secular society can often be better sponsored by other agencies.

The Great Commission looms like a monolith above the religious horizon, challenging the Church to dedicate itself to the highest claims of
the Gospel." (Breaking the Stained Glass Barrier, New York, Harper and
Row, 1973, p. 4)

DON'T MISS THIS CHANCE

Live on the West Coast? Attend the Church Growth Seminar
at Biola College, April 5-8, 1974, under the deanship of Dr.
Arthur Glasser, assisted by most of the professors at the
School of World Mission and Institute of Church Growth. Write
The Coordinator, Rev. Norman L. Cummings, Box 66, Palo Alto,
California 94301, for information and reservations.

Live in North East United States? Attend the Church Growth
Seminar at Nyack, New York, April 15-19, 1974, under the deanship of Dr. Linwood Barney, assisted by Donald McGavran and
Peter Wagner. For information and reservations, write Dr. Linwood Barney, Jaffray School of Missions, Nyack, New York 10960.

THE DISCIPLING OF AFRICA IN THIS GENERATION   by Dr. David Barrett

"In Africa, the nominal fringe of 32 million in 1972 (who will become 95 million in A.D. 2000) consists of people, young and old, who
are crowding round the doors of the churches seeking to enter. Despite
determined and sometimes desperate efforts, only a fraction each year
manage to push their way to the front and get in. Meanwhile the millions waiting outside get larger in number, and the waiting periods cor-
respondingly longer....This is an intolerable situation. It calls for a
total overhauling and speeding up of the entire machinery of Christian
initiation.

"The nominal fringe represents an unprecedented phenomenon in the
history of the Christian mission. It consists of 32 (in 1974, 36) million persons receptive to the Christian presentation, who have a high
regard for the Christian faith, for the person of Christ, for the
churches and their members, who want to find the Bread of Life, who have
already passed the point of decision and call themselves Christian, who
know that this is only the beginning of the Christian pilgrimage, who
want to be discipled and put their trust in God through Jesus Christ,
who therefore want to enter the fellowship of the Church to serve Him as
their King as soon as possible, and who are prepared to go to considerable lengths for a certain period of time in order to achieve that end."
(page 410,411, God, Man and Church Growth, Church Growth Book Club)

((Barrett's chapter in God, Man and Church Growth may be the most
important brief document on Christian Mission in Africa to be printed
in this century. It describes one of the greatest opportunities placed
before the Church of Christ in the last two thousand years. It marshalls
the evidence cogently. It analyses the situation correctly. It pleads
for action. It proposes possible action This chapter should be studied
carefully by every board secretary having African responsibilities and by
every thinking missionary.
     Evangelical and conciliar Church and Mission leaders should at once
engage in a determined and continued labors to devise the massive measures needed and to put them into effect. The Editor))

N E W S

MAYA EVANGELIZATION: MEXICO AND GUATEMALA

Stanley A. Wick of the Instituto Biblico, Quiche, San Cristobal, Toto.
Guatemala, Central America, is assembling information from workers in all
23 tribes of Maya Indians. Send him information as to the biblical
church in your segment of the Mayas. (1) How much Church is there - number of communicants, number of congregations in 1974 and the same information for 1969. (2) What approaches you find most effective. (3) What
the Mayas in your area believe and how the biblical message can be fitted
to their particular felt needs. He plans to publish these so all may know
the general picture of advance in the Maya Tribes.

UNION BIBLICAL SEMINARY REPORTS   Vernon Middleton SWM ICG '71
                                         Professor of Church Growth

1. This seminary professor has recently held three church growth
seminars. The Berar Khandesh Pastors Conference, gave much time to
church growth. At one session I suggested that they pioneer in a new
form of "comity" - namely, that they replace regional comity with social
(or caste) comity. That each denomination specialize on the evangelization of one caste. Believe it or not, the idea was welcomed by the
Indians but rejected by the missionaries.

2. The Brethren in Christ invited me to the Santal country. They
are seeing good growth. The web-movement is spilling into Nepal!!

3. In Gujerat (the westernmost province of India) the Church North
India, Wesleyan Methodists, and Salvation Army held a joint pastors conference in early December 1973. All were highly receptive to church
growth principles and were enthusiastic at long last to be moving out
once again for Christ. Sixty pastors, including the bishop, attended.

A conviction that there is 'receptive ground' along the Andhra
Maharashtra border has stimulated Union Biblical Seminary to send thirteen Telegu speaking seminarians into the region. The response is amazing. Village after village of Malas are meeting regularly and pressing
to become Christians. We aim to plant five churches before the end of
this school year. Students are giving up their Christmas holidays to
preach the Gospel. Every week the re-entry of the evangelizing students
into the seminary community generates excitement like that which accompanied David's bringing the ark into Jerusalem.

ORDER "MISSION HANDBOOK" - TODAY   The Editor

If you have not already ordered this landmark reference book, do so
now. MARC is to be congratulated on getting out the most complete,
helpful, immediately useful handbook on North American Protestant
Ministries Overseas ever to be published. Accurate, easy to use, it is
invaluable to ministers, chairmen of missionary committees, professors
of mission, board secretaries, and others concerned with the on-going
mission of the Church. An indispensable tool.

The book ought to sell for $20.00; but it does sell for $10.00 -
at which price it is a steal.

Missions is a fast moving enterprise which touches every living
congregation. It is increasing and will increase. We stand in the sunrise of missions. This book will show you the vast enterprise in which
you participate. You will feel good.

MARC, 919 West Huntington Drive, Monrovia, Ca., 91016.

CHURCH GROWTH
BULLETIN

from the
**INSTITUTE OF
CHURCH GROWTH**

Address:
FULLER THEOLOGICAL
SEMINARY
135 N. Oakland
Pasadena, Calif. 91101

DONALD A. McGAVRAN, B.D., Ph.D.
Director

May 1974   Subscription $1 per year   Volume X No. 5

C O N T E N T S

CHURCH GROWTH AMONG GYPSIES by Clement Le Cossec, Executive Secretary
   "Gypsies For Christ" (translated by Walther Olsen, SWM-ICG 1970)

1.   Number of Gypsies: 100,000 in France alone.

2.   Tribes in France:
     The Man-Ouches lived for a long time in Germany. Their language
     therefore contains German words. Names such as Reinhardt and
     Winterstein are common. They travel in Normandy, Brittany, the
     Bordeaux area and Paris. 70,000.
     The Gitanos live in the South near the Spanish border.
     Names such as Santiago, Moreno and Jimenez are common. Some
     travel in the North and East as tradesmen. 20,000.
     The Roms - Kalderash Group - live mostly in Paris. Others - Lovara
     and Tschourara - travel throughout France and neighboring coun-
     tries. Common names are Nechhounoff, Maximoff, Kralovitch.
     10,000.
     The Travellers are not ethnically Gypsy but live exactly like them.
     They hold street fairs. They are perhaps as numerous as the
     Gypsies themselves. They are sometimes called "Yenoch", a
     derogatory term.

SEND correspondence, news, and articles to the Editor, Dr. Donald McGavran, at the Institute
of Church Growth, Fuller Theological Seminary. Published bi-monthly, send subscriptions
and changes of address to the Business Manager, Norman L. Cummings, Overseas Crusades,
Inc., 265 Lytton Avenue, Palo Alto, California 94301, U.S.A. Second-class postage paid at
Palo Alto, California.

3. The language, derived from Sanscrit or Hindi, is called Romanes.
    It is spoken by Gypsies in all parts of the world with certain vari-
    ations due to the countries where they have lived. The Roms have
    Rumanian words in their dialect. The Man-Ouches use German words.
    Ordinary words such as bread (man-ro), water (pani), salt (lone) are
    identical in all tribes. The New Testament is being translated into
    Romanes under the direction of the Wycliffe Bible Translators.
    Americans and Gypsies are working on the translation in Paris.

4. In France are approximately 4,000 Christian families, or 12,000
    baptized believers minimum 3 per family. But 30-40,000 Gypsies
    attend worship - including children and young people not yet bap-
    tized - plus sympathizers. Approximately one-third of the Gypsy
    population of France is converted. The annual minimal growth is
    500 baptized believers.

5. Organization of the Church. The communities are mostly nomadic.
    Each community (church) is made up of 5-20 caravans under the di-
    rection of a preacher. About 20 communities are settled in towns.
    The largest part of the work is under the direction of 200 preach-
    ers, whose number is constantly growing. In the past 4 years, 79
    were trained in our Centre of Biblical Training. Seeing the in-
    crease of the Church I have taken on Gypsy preachers as colleagues,
    with the approval of the mission. I began with 2 in 1961. Today
    the Board of Spiritual Direction is composed of 8 preachers, all
    Gypsies. In 1972, I turned the responsibility of national direc-
    tion over to a Gypsy preacher, Djimy, who was unanimously accepted
    by his brothers. This has allowed me to give more time to the
    international aspects of the work.

6. Each member of the Board of Direction is himself president of an
    area and supported by a board of spiritual direction for the area,
    in order to encourage evangelism and coordinate the work.

    Though necessary for order, the organization is flexible and the
    accent is put on spiritual values.

7. From the beginning of the ingathering, my principle in evangelizing
    the Gypsies has been to follow as closely as possibly the method of
    the New Testament.

    a) Appoint elders in the new churches. These are chosen with
       respect to their spiritual qualifications and not their intel-
       lectual abilities. Sometimes they do not know how to read and
       write, but have a high degree of spirituality which qualifies
       them for this ministry. All the preachers today know how to
       read, but few can write.

    b) Allow diverse ministries - evangelists, pastors, and teachers -
       to develop.

c) Encourage testimony. The force of evangelism is personal witness which has 2 aspects: the Word and the transformed life.
   My principle is that a Gypsy is best qualified to witness to a
   Gypsy. Since they do not know how to read, verbal witness has
   the greatest effect. However, in countries where they are
   literate (Spain, Rumania, Yogoslavia) it is the literate Gypsies who reach most easily other literate Gypsies.

d) Pastors' meetings are indispensible for:
      strengthening believers in the faith (as in Antioch),
      sharing of experiences and examining problems (as at
         Jerusalem),
      doctrinal consolidation (in order not to run in vain)
      examination of candidates for the ministry.

8.   There is no evangelism without the creation of churches (communi-
      ties), but I insist that these not be closed circles. Thus there
      is a great opening among these people who love their liberty.
      Truth does not exclude liberty, but liberty does not destroy truth.
      Thus there is an opening among Pentecostals, Protestants, and
      Catholics. The witness goes beyond their own people and their own
      countries.

      I have also wanted to create a missionary spirit, going farther,
      to the ends of the earth, and thus the work extends to about 30
      nations.

9.   Encourage conventions which bring large numbers of Gypsies together.
      These meetings had to be adapted to the life styles of the Gypsies.
      The first one brought together 200 caravans. Today 1,500 caravans
      get together. At 6 persons per caravan, that means 10,000 people,
      and necessitates 45 acres of land. The organization is in the hands
      of the deacons. Putting up tents, bringing in food, water, toilets
      and the like, is their business.

10.   The History of the Christian Movement Among the Gypsies is as follows:

      a) Conversion of a family at Lisieux in 1950, thanks to a tract
         sent from America after the war and entitled "Questions and
         Answers" and which was stamped with the name of the Assembly
         of God Church in Lisieux.
                  Baptisms of water and the Holy Spirit at Brest in 1952.
                  First convention at Tennes in 1954.
                  Beginning of my work among them full-time in 1958
                     when there were 3,000 believers.
                  Beginning of extended missionary action on an
                     International level in 1963.
                  1972 total control of the mission by the Gypsies.

11. Projects:

Strengthen evangelism in Spain. The Gypsy Church there now includes 6,000 Gypsies at the meetings with 150 preachers and a board of national direction. 40 churches.
Send preachers from Spain into Portugal. Begin this year in Lisbon, and from there to South America where there is already a work in Buenos-Aires.
Continue the work begun in Greece - 300 Gypsies at the meetings in Thessalonica.
Increase efforts towards the Eastern Countries where we help Gypsy preachers in Yugoslavia and Rumania.
Support to India where we are building a Centre of Biblical Training and a boarding school for children in the south of Madras. We support 8 preachers working among 300,000 Gypsies.
Send preachers to Italy and Sweden.
Reach the Gypsies in Mexico, Peru, Brazil.
Enter Turkey, Iran, Afghanistan, Pakistan.
Make an effort in England where there are only 200 believers, then in New Zealand, Australia, South Africa.

There are 15,000,000 Gypsies in the world. The field is vast. We could go faster if Christians in general understood that the Gypsies are a mission field. They are at our doorstep waiting for us. In England a sister wrote to me, "There are Gypsies near me all the time; Please come to evangelize them". I gave her several suggestions, asking her to evangelize them herself. Since that time, she has had the joy of seeing the whole family come to Christ.

12. Certain Gypsies gravitate to existing churches. But in general, they form churches among their own people because of certain customs common to them all.

My Conclusion: 1. Continuously evangelize the Gypsies.
2. Train and encourage evangelists.
3. Establish communities with spiritual leaders.
4. Maintain in these churches a vision for lost souls. the goal being not to live unto onesself, but for Christ. Help others who are still in the darkness, to find the Light of the World.

JEWS FOR JESUS ..... Moishe Rosen   by Donald McGavran

Moishe Rosen's message and method of Jewish evangelism needs to be heard from the Atlantic to the Pacific. Rosen is enabling Jews to become followers of Jesus the Messiah without traitorously abandoning their cultural heritage. He should be heard in hundreds of churches. His message is encouraging, timely, and very interesting.

Jews For Jesus challenge the universalist assumption that each person can be and will be saved in the religion (Hindu, Buddhist, Jewish, or Christian) in which he was born. The movement says, "No. Every person must become a disciple of Jesus Messiah. Of course, he will remain in the language and culture in which he was born. Thus we shall have cells of Christians, disciples of Christ, followers of the Way in every ethnic and cultural unit (every ethnos) on earth."

The multiplication of such cells, such segments of The Body is the surest way to liberating men and nations, to the spread of Justice, to the increase of brotherhood, to the this-worldly improvement of human society. Furthermore, the spread of such bodies of Christians opens the gateway of heaven to the uncounted multitudes whom God has chosen for salvation.

Jews For Jesus (P.O. Box 309, Corte Madera, Ca. 94925) have many unique materials which can orient sensitive and sensible ministers and missionaries to the task of Jewish evangelism, and enable them to tell Jews about Christ in a Jewish way.

THE GOAL OF MISSIONARY EFFORT

"The end goal of each field organization is to help an association of Baptist churches to achieve such maturity in conducting their own church life and missionary outreach that church and mission together may decide whether some or all of our missionaries should withdraw to serve under mission supervision elsewhere or remain in some essential ministry to work with national churches in fulfilling the Great Commission."

Quoted from How To Update the Field's Overall Plan, Conservative Baptist Foreign Missionary Society, Wheaton, Illinois 60187

The quotation describes the new breed of missions - second generation missions. The first generation was found from William Carey till the mid sixties. Churches in all six continents and missionary societies everywhere are now pressing on to second generation missions. The fine statement of purpose quoted above will repay careful study. Its words have been chosen with care. It honors the Church: it preserves the obedience of the mission. It is the wave of the future. D. McG.

WHERE DO YOU DRAW THE LINE?   THE MILLIGAN SYMPOSIUM

Can a Baptist preacher be a Communist mayor? In Italy, many Baptists would reply "Yes! His politics and economics would be Marxist. His religion would be Christian." People who answer this way insist that a person can be a Christian in any culture.

If the culture is capitalist, its adherents can be Christians. Their Christianity will modify capitalism. If the culture is Jewish, no matter, its adherents can be Christians, who might call themselves Messianic Jews. As long as they believe in Jesus of Nazareth as Lord

and Saviour, they can be as Jewish in culture as they want. Christ in
the heart will modify Jewish culture in places, to be sure, but it will
remain recognizably Jewish. And so with Communism.

At Milligan College in Eastern Tennessee a 12 session Symposium was
held on April 6th, 7th and 8th to discuss the question: "As Christianity spreads into the myriad cultures of the world it must adjust to
each - but where should it draw the line? When does adjustment become
syncretism?" Beyerhaus, Hoekendijk, McGavran and Tippett presented two
lectures each developing their own independent replies to the basic
question. They then gave one lecture each responding to the other
speakers.

Over three hundred registered for the Symposium, including many
leaders of mission thought from all over the United States and Canada -
Latfricasian Christians, mission executives, professors of missions,
missionaries on furlough, and outstanding laymen and laywomen. Religious News Service covered the event with a special reporter.

The twelve lectures will appear as a book this year and will furnish
a thorough exposition of the principles involved and a wealth of illustrations.

The main cleavage of conviction occurred between Drs. Tippett and
Beyerhaus and McGavran on the one side, who held that the Bible sets
forth God's plan for men's life and salvation, and Dr. Hoekendijk and
his supporters on the other side, who held that the Bible is only one
record of God's dealings with men and that there are many others. To
the first group, mission was proclaiming Jesus Christ as God and Saviour
and persuading men to become His disciples and responsible members of
His Church. Mission to the second group was "sitting where they sit and
letting God happen". By this cryptic statement Dr. Hoekendijk apparently meant that God would speak to men in every religion (and in none)
and (untrammelled by what is written in the Bible) bring about His current desires in the myriad cultures of mankind.

Syncretism to the first group was joining to the Christian system,
revealed in the Bible, elements which changed its essential nature. Syncretism to the other group really cannot exist. There is no "Christian"
system. All that really exists is God speaking to adherents of all
religions and cultures and they responding in ways they like. To group
one, it sounded as if group two were advocating each man "doing his own
thing".

Dr. Tetsunao Yamamori planned and convened the Symposium and will
see the book through publication. The event established Milligan College
as a center of missionary thought.

"An Institute of World Studies/Church Growth" at Milligan will begin
functioning in September 1974. It will operate on both the graduate and
undergraduate level. Missionaries, planning to live within 200 miles of

beautiful Eastern Tennessee while on furlough, ought to consider taking courses taught by Drs. Taber (African experience) and Yamamori (Far East experience). Two bedroom apartments are available at the college for $95.00 per montn. Write Dean Yamamori, Milligan College, Tenn.

NO COOPERATION SURPASSES THAT PRACTICED IN EVANGELISM   by
Rev. Charoon Wichaidist, Thailand

In the current demoralization and crisis, the world needs Jesus Christ as never before and also needs many more missionaries of the Gospel. I say this despite the fact that some missionary societies in Eurica have withdrawn missionaries from the fields. Eurican and Latfricasian missionary societies must cooperate in making Christ known. No cooperation among missionary societies surpasses that in proclaiming the Good News of Jesus Christ.

When missionaries from different backgrounds are working together for evangelizaton, differences in race, color and language are eliminated. Missionaries are spiritually united. They have one thing in common - to win souls for Jesus Christ which is God's will for us all to do. Missionary societies should cooperate to propagate the Gospel throughout the whole world.

This will require some change in policy. Usually Eurican missionaries have been involved in the affairs of Latfricasian Churches. The outcome is that evangelization in both Church and mission becomes weak. Missionaries are wanted by Latfricasian Churches for preaching the Gospel, not for running the Church. And, in preaching the Gospel there is abundant room for action. Two-thirds of the world's ethnic groups have not heard about Jesus. Christians are responsible to preach the Gospel to the two billion who have not heard. In addition to Eurican missionaries, the Churches in Asia and Africa must send missionaries to the millions who know nothing of Jesus Christ, who have never even seen the Bible. As Latfricasian Churches do this, they will need to set up centers to train their missionaries in evangelization.

Nurturing new believers is a must if church growth is our goal. Our Church, in Chiengrai in northern Thailand, has been active in evangelizaton. Many conversions have taken place in village after village; but we lack personnel and funds for properly nurturing new converts. Without biblical instruction, new converts will be gone within a short period of time. Nurturing also is an essential part of missionary cooperation.

SUMMER STUDY PROGRAM IN MISSIONS

The School of Missions and Institute of Church Growth, Fuller Seminary holds its first summer program June 10 to July 5, 1974. Courses are offered in missionary anthropology, church growth, and linguistics. Up to 8 hours of seminary credit are available. For information write: Director Summer Study Program, SWM ICG, 135 N. Oakland Avenue, Pasadena, California 91101

MULTI-INDIVIDUAL CONVERSION

INSTANCE ONE
                                    by Richard Hostetter, Churches
                                    of Christ missionary in Ghana

Francis Kumah is an expoliceman, a first generation Christian, and
a son of an important Juju man of the traditional pagan religion. He
grew up in Dzebetato, a village on the edge of the Volta River in West
Africa, and will graduate from Ghana Christian College in June. He is
about 35, married and has four children. Dzebetato is exceptionally
pagan. Idols are seen everywhere. People live in daily fear of sorcery
and witchcraft.

A past and present practice in trying to start new congregations in
such villages has been to preach for two or three nights, offer an invitation, and get maybe four or five responses. Hopefully, such a beginning would grow "one by one" - if the small band did not soon back-
slide due to ostracism or outright persecution.

A new approach was used a year ago. Mr. Kumah and Mr. Taylor, went
to the chief and his elders asking permission to offer Christianity to
the village. They volunteered to come one day a week for thirteen weeks
to teach about Christianity. No one would be urged to become Christian
during this time. Not until the end of the thirteen week period would
an opportunity be given to become Christian. The chief and his elders
liked the plan, gave permission, and promised to attend the teaching
sessions.

After three or four weeks it became evident that some listeners
were keenly interested. The teaching continued. As the people talked
about the lessons between teaching days, more people became interested.
By the eighth week it was obvious that several were likely to respond
to the invitation to accept Christ. But the word to the chief must be
kept. At the end of the thirteenth week, as promised, the chance to become Christians was extended. Thirty-three accepted Christ and were
baptized that day, all responsible members of the tribe.

Because of this respectful approach to the village leaders, we had
their protection from harassment. Because the chief and his elders attended, interest was keen.

Because Messrs. Taylor and Kumah waited until a large group came as
a "people movement" - 33 at the first invitation - the church could withstand pagan boycott or persecution. The responsible adults in the beginning congregation could command the attention of fellow villagers.

A year has passed since that day. A total of 70 have been baptized
into Christ, including the village chief, his family, and Mr. Kumah's
wife and mother. Now averaging 100 in attendance, the church has em-
barked on an ambitious building program. Mr. Kumah has people from two
nearby villages eager for the Dzebetato experience to be repeated among
their fellows.

INSTANCE TWO   by Rev. Philip Hogan, Executive Director,
                     Division of Foreign Missions of the Assemblies of God

Some years ago I heard that segments of society could accept Jesus Christ as Lord and Saviour not as individuals necessarily but on the basis of a village or a clan decision. I was first a little sceptical of this having not ever had an opportunity to see it work.

We have just experienced a classic example of group conversion in, of all places, _____. This has been a very resistant country. Though we have been there in force for some years, we have never penetrated any of the tribal areas. We have churches in the capital city, of course, and in the main centers, but these are serving metropolitan groups.

The second largest tribe in the country is the _____ with about a million adherents. These have resisted Islam for centuries and the Catholic Church for scores of years. We have had in the city of _____ _____, a very enterprising young missionary who boldly - and courteously - asked the government to let him have twelve programs a week on the national radio network. It is too long a story for me to tell here about how effective this has been in surrounding here-to-fore resistant areas. However, one immediate result has been that in the past few weeks, we have baptized over 300 from that second largest tribe. The new Christians in the main are older adults, including almost all of the clan's elders. Every village has a few Japanese transistor radios and the broadcasts of our missionary have reached tremendous numbers of these people.

They have opted for the Christian faith by villages, family groups, and clans. It is a perfect example of what I've heard you say and write for years. Needless to say, we are nurturing and extending the new Church in every way we possibly can. This movement is the first breakthrough into the indigenous populations.

INSTANCE THREE   by Allen J. Swanson, SWM-ICG '68 and reported in
                  Volume I, Number I of the Taiwan Church Growth Bulletin
                  (No. 11, Lane 241, Ta-ya Road, Taichung, Taiwan, R. C:)

This church is an independent congregation. The pastor receives no mission aid. He works in a large city among Taiwanese laborers, many of them recent immigrants from the country. A minority of the members are illiterate. Most men are common laborers. The community from which the church arose is highly superstitious and brought its folk religion into the city. Most families are nuclear with few resident relatives, yet family control appears fairly effective.

The pastor began work in this area in 1967. At that time he had not a single contact. Three other mainline churches had attempted work there and failed. It seemed impossible to penetrate this society. But this pastor, free from many theological and methodological prejudices, went about preaching the Gospel in exactly the opposite way used by most of us today. His approach centered about the following guidelines:

1. Seek out families in need, trouble or illness.
2. Seek out the oldest, most authoritative figure in the family and first preach the Gospel to him.
3. Seek out the most superstitious people as their religious zeal is a good indication of their devotion. They make the best Christians. Those who believe nothing before becoming Christians usually make lukewarm Christians afterwards.
4. Do not emphasize youth work. They rarely lead their parents to the Lord. To the contrary, their conversions often result in rejection or persecution by their parents, thereby closing the door to future contacts with the parents.
5. Thoroughly instruct all adults on their responsibility to lead their children to the Lord. If they feel unqualified to witness to their children, bring them to the church for the pastor to instruct.
6. Make decision to follow Christ a family decision. Do not deliberately obstruct bridges to God by violating the desire of the majority.
7. Proof of readiness for baptism is a willingness to publically pray during a worship service, no matter how illiterate the person may be.
8. All Christians, no matter how poor, are immediately taught the Biblical principle of tithing.
9. No household can receive baptism without publically, in its own living room, destroying all household idols.
10. From the beginning, everyone is expected to serve in some way. Seven committees exist for the benefit of every member.

Beginning with the first convert in mid-1967, the growth of this church during the first four years can be seen from the following statistics:

BEGINNING DATE OF CHURCH WORK	1967	MONTHLY OFFERINGS (av.) $6,000	
TOTAL ADULT BAPTISMS	48	HOUSEHOLD UNITS IN CHURCH	34
TOTAL INFANT BAPTISMS TO DATE	36	UNITS WITH COMPLETE FAMILY	30
AVERAGE SUNDAY ATTENDANCE	60-120		

((We report these three contrasting studies with pleasure, believing that multi-individual conversion is one of the important ways in which God is at work today. The names of places and tribes have been eliminated in the second account, lest persecution befall the new Church before it grows strong. But in many lands such movements are going on openly. The non-Christian majorities say "It is good for them to become Christian. We may become Christians ourselves." God is at work. The Editor))

THE CHURCH CANNOT BE STOPPED BY OPPOSITION
ONLY SOCIAL ACCEPTANCE CAN CONTROL IT.
                    DAVID WOMACK In
                    Breaking the Stained Glass Barrier, p. 166
                    N.Y. Harper and Row

MULTIPLICATION: THE NAME OF THE GAME
by
Waldron Scott, Administrator, The Navigators, SWM-ICG '74

At one point in his book, People Movements in Southern Polynesia, Alan Tippett documents an impressive growth pattern on the part of the emerging church in Maoriland--but observes that "the progression...could have been geometric rather than just arithmetic." Although tucked away in a note on a graph Tippett's observation is exceedingly important. It spotlights an issue deserving more attention in church growth circles.

The very first command given by God to man was to "be fruitful and multiply" (Gen. 1:28). The specific reference here, of course, is to physical generation. But the application to spiritual reproduction is too obvious to ignore. This is where Dr. Tippett's suggestion of geometric progression comes in.

Geometric progression refers to a sequence of terms in which the ratio of any term to its predecessor is a constant (e.g. 1, 2, 4, 16, etc.). Arithmetic expansion, in contrast, is a sequence in which each term is obtained merely by adding a constant number to its predecessor (1, 3, 5, 7, 9, etc.). The distinction can best be understood in terms of multiplication vs. addition--the former reflecting geometric progression.

To illustrate, let us assume a formula for predicting conversions through personal evangelism by "addition" is: $X = a$ times b times c, where X is the number of conversions, a the number of evangelists, b their combined level of skill (measured in some such terms as "ten conversions per year") and c the number of years projected. For example, let $a = 2$, $b = 10$, and $c = 5$. In this event $X = 100$. That is, two men winning 10 converts each year for five years will add 100 new disciples to the Christian community.

An alternate formula, however, might be: $X = a$ times b times c times d, where a, b and c are as above but d signifies a multiplying effect produced when a trains his converts (or some of them) to become effective personal evangelists also. Or to use biblical language, when a "perfects" his disciples "for the work of the ministry" (Eph. 4:12). To illustrate again, let $d = 4$. In this case the end result after five years is not 100 but 400 new disciples!

It is this multiplier effect that is evident in the accompanying figure. This graph documents evangelistic results (in terms of the ratio of new disciples per Nav Representative annually) in The Navigators' work in Asia during a six-year period.

Note that the bar graph indicates
a definite but modest increase in evangelistic results during the first three
year period 1967-69. These increases
are the result of improved skills: growing language ability, deeper insights into
local psychology, etc. But the remarkable
difference between that first period and
the next three years, 1970-72, cannot be
accounted for by improved skills alone.
Rather, they are the result of the multiplier effect described before.

This multiplier effect is the consequence of that "passion for perfecting"
characteristic of The Navigators, a drive
viewed somewhat skeptically in church
growth circles. Not that the need for
perfecting the saints is unrecognized by
church growth men. References to quality
growth appear regularly in this Bulletin.
Yet it is fair to say that almost invariably it is subordinated to the emphasis on disciple-making. Church Growth
leaders describe a "tug of war" between
perfecting and disciple-making and insist
that the latter be given clear priority.

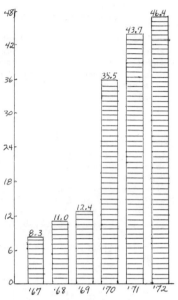

It seems to me this may reflect a failure to grasp the full significance of Eph. 4:12 for multiplying churches. In this passage perfecting does not suggest merely bringing about ethical changes in believers "that they may shine with divine lustre," important as that
may be. On the contrary, it encourages us to build up the saints
precisely for the task of discipling the nations. (The phrase "for the
work of the ministry" surely means this if it means anything.)

Thus time spent perfecting the saints is not necessarily time taken
away from discipling the nations, as some have implied. Admittedly it
can be that, and in some circles is, but it doesn't have to be. If we
understand perfecting as being specifically for the purpose of numerical
expansions a totally new perspective appears. This perspective has not
emerged clearly in Church Growth writing to date. (There is more to what
we are discussing here, for example, than merely "mobilizing" laymen.)

From this point of view perfecting the saints is not merely one of
a dozen equally valid ways of promoting Church Growth. It is the key to
geometric, as opposed to arithmetic, progression. It is so especially
in connection with discipling "out to the fringes" of an ethnic group
or geographic area. Perhaps this is why Byang Kato, speaking at the
1973 General Assembly of the Association of Evangelicals of Africa and
Madagascar, urged increased discipleship training along the lines of
2 Tim. 2:2 and spoke of "multiplication rather than addition in the
church".

CHURCH GROWTH IN CONFUCIAN STRONGHOLD   by Dr. Song Nai Rhee, Professor
         of Old Testament in Northwest Christian College, Eugene, Oregon.

An unprecedented spiritual revolution is taking place throughout
Korea. Until about one century ago, missionaries as well as native converts to the Christian faith, were punished by death in Korea. As late
as 30 years ago, South Korea was little interested in the Christian
gospel. Today there are nearly five million Christians, so that one
out of every eight Koreans professes Jesus Christ as his Lord and
Saviour. At the same time, the number of Christians is increasing four
times as fast as that of the general population.

Particularly significant is the fact that there has been going on
an intensive evangelization within the Korean military for several years.
As a result one out of every two Korean soldiers on active duty is a
Christian.

Evangelism in Korea, whether within the general populace or within
the military, is far more than a mere signing of a commitment card.
There is an intensive training and instructional period both before and
after the formal act of commitment. By means of unflagging follow-up
sessions, pastors as well as chaplains try to help the new Christians
become active and fruitful members of the church.

Churches, mostly Protestant, are everywhere throughout Korea. The
first thing that impresses a visitor upon his arrival in Korea is the
sight of crosses standing atop myriads of sturdy church buildings. In
Seoul alone, there are over 1,500 Protestant churches, and it seems that
on every hill around the capital, or in any large city, is a church. Th
Korean churches are packed with people Sunday morning, Sunday evening,
as well as Wednesday evening. In addition, every church holds an early
morning prayer service at six o'clock, seven days a week. At this early
hour, Christians gather for an hour of singing and Bible study.

One particularly gratifying experience to me was my visit this past
summer with about three dozen Christians in my home town in southern
Korea. Twenty years ago, my town was a stronghold of conservative Con-
fucianism, resisting all forms of alien, particularly Christian ideas.
I became a Christian in 1954 all alone, and wondered if I could ever lèa
another soul to Christ. But since then, with God's help, a significant
number of the villagers have welcomed Jesus Christ into their homes,
revolutionizing their value system as well as their cultural patterns.
About five years ago, even my father, a lifetime Confucian scholar, made
his confession fo faith and was baptized at the age of 70.

What makes the church in Korea grow? Experts on this question
mention two emphases of supreme importance: Bible-centered Christian
education, and personal evangelism.

Commenting on these, Dr. Samuel H. Moffett, a veteran missionary
in Korea, informs us that the pioneers of faith in Korea "spoke with
utter assurance that the Bible was God's word and that in it was to be

found the ultimate meaning of human life and destiny. Therefore, the Scriptures were quickly translated into the vernacular and widely distributed. Church leaders were given regular, intensive training in the Word. Perhaps most important of all, not just the leaders, but all members of the church were systematically organized for Bible study in what was called the Bible Class System."
(Quoted from NCC Bulletin for March 1974, by kind permission)

N E W S

EFFECTIVE AND RAPID MISSION ADVANCE: TARGET 80

The November 1973 Bulletin quoted Dr. Oosterwal, an Adventist missiologist, saying that Adventists ought to make "make funds and personnel available to harvest the fields ripe for harvest now." A good idea.

This May 1974 issue calls attention to a resulting SDA action. Adventists move fast!! We trust many missionary societies will soon follow suit. MARC REPORT is put out by Mission Advance Research Committee of the General Conference of Seventh-day Adventists. Far Eastern Division, 800 Thompson Road, Singapore 11. (Don't confuse this with MARC of World Vision). MARC REPORT talks about a new concept in mission planning - namely, to create a department which will study trends and changing patterns and put money into innovative plans for multiplying churches in provedly responsive populations. This department will help any church or cluster of churches to set objectives, list priorities, allocate resources, and concentrate energies. It will encourage missions and churches to enter more quickly and effectively areas of opening opportunity. It has established a special Mission Advance Reserve Fund of $100,000 "to be used to give special assistance to local fields in opening new areas that show unusual growth opportunities."

"Starting new churches will become the integrating idea around which all departments of the Church may unite for closer coordination in evangelism....As churches multiply, membership increases significantly. Administrative and departmental staffs will move into closer team relationship to accomplish objectives."

VIETNAM   by Reginald Reimer, SWM-ICG '71

Last year we set 6 new churches in Saigon as our goal. We're happy to be able to report that we planted 4! The usual pattern is for a mother church to release several families to form a nucleus in an area where they would like to start a church. Then our mission assists in acquiring a building and often in special evangelistic efforts, and soon regular services are underway. The most gratifying effort last year was a new church in Phuoc Binh, a newly-built village on the outskirts of Saigon which houses 3,500 families of disabled Vietnamese veterans. Now 60-80 Christians, many of them new, are meeting regularly each Sunday. We are going to try again for six churches in 1974. Already we have three good prospects.

I continue to have ministries which take me to many parts of the country. Sometimes I am invited along with my Vietnamese colleague, Rev. Tot, to hold church growth seminars. Recently I made a trip to visit the resettled Steing tribe. A people movement to the Christian faith is underway among them. In three years the number of Christians has grown from 100 to 6,000! Last year alone an average of 70 people became Christians each week. Pray for those who have the responsibility of caring for this great movement and bringing the new Christians to maturity.

TORONTO, ONTARIO, JANUARY 1974   Ken Birch, SWM, '71

The Pentecostal Assemblies of Canada have generally reached a plateau in their growth and our leaders and pastors are concerned about this. As a result, we have had wide acceptance of church growth thinking. We are adopting strategy to suit the Canadian scene. Some of the forward steps we are taking are as follows:

1. Church Growth Leadership Institutes
In November, 1973, we held two of these institutes (one in the East and one in the West) to come to grips with our present growth (or really our lack of growth). We then shared basic church growth concepts and methodology and wrestled, at least in an introductory way, with the implications of these for our Fellowship.

2. The P.A.C.E. program (Pentecostal Assemblies Church Extension).
This program provides national leadership for implementing church growth concepts and strategies at the local level. Our stress is on congregational life, evangelism and disciple-making. Among other things, we are producing a monthly "Church Growth Leadership Letter" to sow church growth ideas among our pastors and leaders and to provide specific "how to do it" information. We will deal with such topics as Church Growth Graphs, Church Planting, Discipleship (particularly "follow up" or "after-care".)

3. Continuing Church Growth Emphasis
Our ultimate goal is to insure that church growth is kept in the forefront of our thinking. We have always been very strong on evangelism, although we have never had a specific department of evangelism in our national structure. It seems that before long this department will be established. Likely it will be designated, "The Department of Evangelism and Church Growth."

KOREAN MISSIONARY AMONG THE THAIS IN LOS ANGELES   Samuel L. Kim

Before 1973, for 10,000 Thai students and residents in this area there was no Thai language church in Los Angeles. Thais, free from Buddhist culture and family ties and under heavy social and psychological pressures, often get lost in the jungle of this industrialized city. They find it difficult to assimilate into the American culture. In this kind of situation, I felt receptivity towards the Gospel would be high.

I began to contact my former Thai students and friends, got mailing lists from Thai associations, organizations, and consulate, and selected mission school graduates and their relatives. A small group of Christians began regular Sunday services, counseling, circular letters, Bible camps, and other social services.

We held our first worship service at the Mount Hollywood Congregational Church on Sunday afternoons. Twenty-nine were present. The membership has gradually increased to 60. Among these is a newly ordained Thai minister and a talented musician. I am turning responsibilities over to them and other Thais, as I, a Korean missionary, return to Thailand.

ONE WAY '74

The Philippines will undergo what may be the most extensive and unified gospel witness in the country's history when One Way '74, a series of mass evangelistic campaigns will be held in 20 key cities around the nation in the months from February to August.

Churches from various denominations have come out openly in support of One Way '74.

"The Body of Christ in the Philippines is beginning to move as one in the task of evangelism," says Nene Ramientos, the national coordinating director of Christ the Only Way Movement, the nation-wide interdenominational group that planned and initiated the seven-month evangelistic thrust. "Although denominationalism still exists in various forms we are coming out of an era of fragmentation in the church."

Coming in to help in the campaigns are five associate evangelists from the Billy Graham Evangelistic Association. Five others from Overseas Crusades will come during the second half of the campaign.

Unlike past crusades in the country, One Way '74 will have a unique way of conserving the campaign results. Instead of being fed directly into local evangelical churches, decisions will be channeled to cell groups called "CORE" and "LEGS" which pastors and laymen conduct in homes, restaurants, offices and other neutral places. A CORE (Cell group of believers Organized for Renewal and Evangelism) would consist of church people who are challenged in the One Way '74 meetings to renew their relationship with the Lord. On the other hand, LEGS (Lay Evangelistic Group Studies) will absorb all those who make first-time commitment to the Lord. It is in LEGS where they are fed and nurtured in the Word. As they mature they will be asked to join CORE groups and eventually local churches.

At present, there are reportedly about 5,000 CORE groups and 10,000 LEGS throughout the Philippines. -- WDM

CHURCH GROWTH
BULLETIN

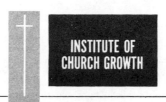

INSTITUTE OF CHURCH GROWTH

Address:
FULLER THEOLOGICAL
SEMINARY
135 N. Oakland
Pasadena, Calif. 91101

DONALD A. McGAVRAN, B.D., Ph.D.
Director

July 1974   Subscription $1 per year   Volume X No. 6

CONTENTS

THE INTERNATIONAL CONGRESS ON WORLD EVANGELIZATION   by Herbert Works

"Let the Earth Hear His Voice!" With these words challenging the
participants in six languages, the epochal International Congress on World
Evangelization (ICOWE) opened on July 16, 1974 at the Palais de Beaulieu,
Lausanne, Switzerland. Some 3,700 persons from 150 countries gathered
for the ten-day Congress to seek ways by which the whole world could be
confronted with the Gospel of Jesus Christ by 2000 A.D. It was the
largest and most representative global gathering on evangelism ever
convened.

Invitations to the Congress were carefully apportioned so that a balance would exist between participants from Eurica and Latfricasia. In
each country, in determining the number of invitations extended, consideration was given both to the number of Christians and to the peoples yet
unreached. Leaders came from Nagaland and Nigeria, Bolivia and Bangladesh.
Financial aid insured extensive participation by Third World Christians.

The Congress provided plenary sessions at which major figures in the
world of evangelism presented the big picture to the 3,800, and small-
group work sessions which grappled with a thousand specific issues. The
key gatherings were the National Strategy Groups, in which for seven days
participants met by nations. Each nation considered and devised a strategy for evangelizing its own peoples.

Outstanding characteristics of this Congress emerged as participants
worked through ten meeting-packed days. First came commitment to biblically sound solutions to the challenges and problems that face Churches in
reaching the nearly three billion who are presently without Jesus Christ.
From the outset, it was apparent that any proposals offered for world
evangelization would be tested against the inspired authoritative Bible -
the infallible rule of faith and practice.

SEND correspondence, news, and articles to the Editor, Dr. Donald McGavran, at the
Institute of Church Growth, Fuller Theological Seminary. Published bi-monthly. Send
subscriptions and changes of address to the Business Manager, Norman L. Cummings,
Overseas Crusades, Inc., 3033 Scott Blvd., Santa Clara, California 95050, U.S.A. Second-
class postage paid at Santa Clara, California.

A second characteristic of the Congress was unity in the midst of extreme diversity. Participants were divided by geographical, linguistic, theological and cultural differences. The theological spectrum ranged from Plymouth Brethren to High Church Anglicans. Pentecostals led groups in which evangelistic methods were demonstrated, and spoke in plenary sessions. Great variety was revealed overtly in the impressive national dress worn regularly by many of the Latfricasians moving through the expansive lobbies of the Palais. Cultural differences reached much deeper than dress, however, and surfaced in proposals relating to church-mission relations.

In the midst of this diversity, unity was experienced on a number of levels. The South African delegation showed "unity in action" when, in their National Strategy Group, a call was sounded by Eurican and African participants together for a "multi-racial effort in evangelism." The gap that has frequently existed between charismatics and non-charismatics was submerged at Lausanne in oneness in Christ. Pronouncements from the podium affirming this oneness were frequently applauded. One, received most enthusiastically, was made by Juan Carlos Ortiz, pastor of a fast growing charismatic congregation in Argentina.

A third mark of the Congress was the widespread influence of "church growth thinking" among leaders and participants. Evidence of this influence appeared early, beginning in the opening session with a multi-media presentation prepared by the Navigators, strongly oriented to church growth concepts. In the same session, Bishop A. Jack Dain, in his "Chairman's Challenge to the Participants," stressed "the personal responsibility of each member of the Body for the growth of the Body." In his keynote address, Billy Graham, Honorary Chairman of the Congress, sounded many strains familiar to church growth missiologists. Among other things, he commended the School of World Mission at Fuller for its work in compiling the "unreached peoples survey" and affirmed the "mosaic of peoples" understanding of the world's population.

Donald McGavran's paper - the first Issue Strategy Paper to be sent to participants in their home countries - received more than 1600 written responses, nine-tenths of them cordially favoring the church growth convictions it, of course, contained. His address was given on the first full day of the Congress to the plenary session. Throughout the ten days, participants, particularly from Latfricasia, spoke of the encouragement and enlarged vision they had received from it. A high point of the evening session was a multi-media presentation, in which "people movements to Christ" were clearly presented and affirmed as a desirable means of church growth. In it, Dr. W. Stanley Mooneyham, President of World Vision, interviewed several SWM ICG graduates working abroad under whose leadership such movements had occurred.

A most direct presentation of church growth principles was made by Dr. Ralph Winter in his brilliant plenary paper on the priority of E-3 (cross-cultural) evangelism. He proved that 87% of the 2.7 billion unevangelized can be reached only by E-2 and E-3 evangelism. Dr. Pablo Perez (SWM ICG 1972) and two others spoke to the issue. Winter called for very extensive cross cultural communication of the Gospel.

Occasional objections to church growth concepts, however, warn that we need to continue to interpret church growth widely and well. We must not be needlessly misunderstood. Indications of acceptance - many though they were - also revealed a concern that the growth of the Church be conceived broadly - quantitatively, qualitatively, and organically. Church growth is becoming more and more a focus of those concerned with world evangelization.

The International Congress on World Evangelization took every opportunity to stress certain roles it did not intend to assume. It was not a legislative body. In his official welcome, Executive Chairman Jack Dain noted that those at the Palais were not called "delegates" as if they had some authority to act on behalf of the churches from which they had come. Rather, they were "participants" and, unless they participated, nothing would happen. Billy Graham, in a press conference, described the Congress as a "congress of ideas." Leaders also insisted that the Congress was not designed to be a "one-shot" inspirational transfusion for evangelism and world missions. The Congress was to be a process, rather than an event, and even before participants arrived in Lausanne, plans had been firmed for getting out hundreds of publications and cassette tapes by which the work of the Congress could be implemented at the local level all over the world.

The Congress was by no means all sweetness and light. The blanket of inspiration and peace was not drawn over the differences and problems. It was rather a forum in which differences were expressed freely and vigorously. Some Latin American speakers made clear their concern over what they considered unwarranted denomination by North American wealth and technological methods. They called repeatedly for a greater commitment on the part of evangelical leaders to social justice and 'development'. The Bangkok call for a moratorium on missionaries was rejected. Lausanne called for multiplied sendings of the right kind of missionaries from all Churches in all six continents. Dr. E. V. Hill, an eloquent black minister from the United States, wanted Evangelicals to send a million missionaries!! A few leaders warned against "triumphalism"; but the Congress on the contrary emphasized that proclaiming the Gospel to the ends of the earth was Christ commanded. Some differences revealed merely misunderstandings and will be corrected in time. Others showed different understandings of the Bible. These call for new study and prayer.

Unavoidable questions following a gathering like this are: "What was accomplished? What did the Congress achieve?"

1. The Congress Occurred. That, in itself, is an accomplishment. When one considers the unlikely prospect for an International Congress on World Evangelization in light of the secularism, the acquisitive materialism, and the humanistic theology that has permeated much of the Church, that the Congress was held at all is significant.

2. The Lausanne Covenant. A definitive statement on world evangelism emerged from ICOWE deliberations - chaired by John Stott and hammered out by a representative committee, which solicited the suggestions and criticisms of all participants. Although the Covenant might take more

seriously the enormous and varied E-2 and E-3 evangelistic needs, it does thoroughly commit Evangelicals to world-wide evangelism on clear biblical grounds. It will be widely influential. Its thirteen sections, each buttressed by many Scripture passages, will, we judge, be used by many ministers as an outline of a full quarter's sermon topics. It will guide missionary societies in all countries.

3. The Scope of the Evangelistic Task. Lausanne was a tremendous awakening to global needs. Vast opportunities gripped the imagination. Faith was stirred. Never has the scope of the task been so convincingly presented. The 116 page survey of Unreached Peoples given to all participants described hundreds of peoples not yet to believe. Continuous gathering of facts will make this survey still more exact and valuable.

4. Resources for the Task. The Congress brought together information about the resources available as never before. Resources emphasized at the Congress included hundreds of Latfricasian missionary societies, skills readily available for evangelism, and useful information about successful approaches. In addition, the Congress discussed how the wealth of Eurican Christians could be made available to these societies' endeavors without creating undesirable dependence. An evangelistic resource mentioned, but not adequately investigated, was the multitude of lay persons. Furthermore, again and again God's Holy Spirit was lifted up as the Great Resource, without Whom no real advance is possible.

5. Evangelical Participants from Non-Evangelical Churches. Perhaps a majority of the participants from Eurica came from the 'old line' denominations - men and women whose convictions and activities call them to more vigorous biblical evangelism. Lausanne invigorated these participants' convictions and made them vividly aware of the huge number of other Evangelicals in non-evangelical denominations. Participants, who became aware at Lausanne of their own significance and strength, may yet lead the World Council of Churches on to heavy emphasis on straight biblical evangelization of men and nations.

6. Unity in Planning. The oneness of the Congress went far beyond mutual acceptance. The joint planning engaged in by the National Strategy Groups brought a new level of cooperation among Evangelicals in the task of world evangelization. Evangelicals, already cooperating in many areas, are pressing on to new effectiveness in joint action for evangelization. Lausanne greatly furthered the process.

The world may well test the significance of this great Congress on Evangelization by the spread of the Gospel and the church growth which results from the Lausanne Experience. The ultimate test will be whether we are faithful to His command and whether, in fact, earth does hear His voice and does bow the knee before Him. Dr. Harold Snyder of Brazil issued a call to establish hundreds of thousands of Christian cells and churches throughout the world. His was perhaps the most concrete and most prophetic utterance of the Congress. God implement it on every continent!

MULTIPLY CHURCHES THROUGH EXTENSION CHAINS
by
Rev. George Patterson, Baptist, Honduras

Do you have populations in your area which still lack active growing churches? Then you may want to develop an extension chain. Evangelism and leadership training (or extension education) can reinforce each other. Make the studies and activities of the leaders being trained <u>initiate and sustain a self-multiplying chain of new churches</u>. First let us define the terms.

<u>Mother church</u>: a congregation which mobilizes men in another locality to raise up and pastor their own church.

<u>Daughter church</u>: a congregation raised up within an extension chain by a mother church.

<u>Extension center</u>: a place other than a resident seminary or institute where classes are held (usually by one or more <u>churches</u>) to train and mobilize Christian workers for immediate service.

<u>Subcenter</u>: an extension center operated by a <u>student</u> of another center.

<u>Extension chain</u>: the process of church reproduction in which a mother church with an extension center starts one or more daughter churches which in turn become extension centers and start more churches. For example, the Baptist church in Olanchito, Honduras, raised up several daughter churches through its extension program. One of these, in Jocon, raised up four churches (granddaughters). One of these, in Macora, raised up another church (great-granddaughter) in San Lorenzo, which is raising up other churches nearby. It took from between three months to two years to add each link in the chain.

The links are congregations. The most effective unit for spiritual reproduction is the local church. Each individual witnesses for Christ as an arm of his own congregation. Making obedient disciples as demanded by the Great Commission requires a team effort. Persons with different spiritual gifts work together. The <u>Body</u> reproduces itself. The daughter church inherits the seed of reproduction from the mother church to produce granddaughter churches.

<u>Dead end link</u>: a local church which fails to become a mother church.

<u>Lay pastor</u>: a volunteer, part-time worker trained and licensed by his own congregation to baptize, lead the Lord's Supper, and serve as pastor. He lacks the training required for ordained pastors and does not use the title "Reverend".

<u>Reteachable materials</u>: self-teaching textbooks made especially for these lay pastors who reteach them to their churches or extension students, who may reteach them the following week to their own students in other subcenters.

Principal of an extension chain: the first teacher in an extension chain. Being both educator and church planter, the principal must direct the flow of reteachable materials, ideas and activities. He may be the only teacher in the chain with previous theological education. His students become extension teachers under his direction as soon as they have begun raising up their first daughter church. For example, the principal of the chain in Honduras teaches 3 student-workers in two centers. These men reteach the same materials to another 20 men in 8 subcenters in daughter churches. Some of these 20 pastors-in-training teach another 25 men in more remote villages. The chain provides pastoral training in 30 congregations. To make the outer links grow and multiply requires edifying teaching all the way along the chain and thus helps the older churches to keep growing, too.

Student-worker: a Christian who receives training on the job. He puts his extension studies into immediate practice.

STEPS YOU CAN TAKE TO START AN EXTENSION CHAIN:

1. HAVE YOU WHAT IT TAKES TO BE A PRINCIPAL OF AN EXTENSION CHAIN?

1. Pastoral experience. The principal supervises the training of pastors all along the chain. Through your students you will direct the activities of many new churches.

2. Extension know-how. Secure or write reteachable materials geared both to your student's progress and his church's needs.

3. Evangelistic vision. Keep churches multiplying. God wants His Church to take root in every town and neighborhood in your field of responsibility. A healthy, obedient church is like a growing plant "whose seed is in itself". She has to grow and multiply. That is her nature, built into her by her Creator.

4. Willingness to work under the local churches. You and your students must be authorized by your own churches to raise up new churches. Each student-worker acknowledges that it is his church which sends him and not he himself. His church reproduces herself in the daughter church. He is only a channel between the mother and daughter through which the Holy Spirit communicates the Gospel.

5. Willingness to travel. Visit and observe regularly all the churches in the chain. Counsel and prepare reteachable materials for their current needs.

II. MAKE WORKABLE PLANS:

1. Know your field of responsibility. You, and every one of your student-teachers after you, must define in exact terms your own field of responsibility. Draw a map of that segment of the society (geographical and social) for which God has made you responsible. It may be one town, or an area with several new struggling churches, or a minority group

within a larger society, or a very large field with r
have no churches.

2. Know exactly what Christ orders your churc'
The Great Commission requires us to start new churc
obedient disciples) in every unevangelized locality. In
forces us to plan clear strategy.

3. Plan the necessary steps to fulfill all that Christ has ordered.
How will a mother church train the workers in the daughter church? Will
they come to the mother church for extension classes? Or will the teacher
go to the daughter church? If your field of responsibility is too large
or socially complex to reach with one chain, train other principals.
Large fields must be divided into several sectors.

III.   RAISE UP THE FIRST DAUGHTER CHURCH YOURSELF:

Make personal contacts in the new locality. You yourself start the
first link in the chain. Set the example. Take with you some believer
who has close friends or relatives in the new locality. Do not use
special campaign methods, public invitations, loud speakers, special tract
campaigns or any other gimmick, until you and all your students have fully
mastered the fundamentals of personal, effective witnessing. Each witness
presents Christ first to his own family and friends (or to the family and
friends of some believers who accompanies him).

IV. RAISE UP CHURCH MULTIPLYING LAY LEADERS:

1. Matriculate qualified students. Continue evangelizing until you
have several men baptized. Then matriculate one or two of them, after
they have started witnessing. In extension chains, men are trained in
their work, not for it. Enroll only men actively obedient to Christ's
commands One or two is best. More than four will result in another
Sunday School class. In each class you deal with the details of each
man's church work; you can't do this with a crowd. Nor will a student
take full responsibility for the work, if he shares it with many others.

Do not enroll single young men for an extension chain. You will
soon have a dead end "preaching point" with mainly women and children
unless the leaders of a new work are mature, family men of the type recommended in I Timothy 3:1-7.

You may have to teach your student to read. Don't hesitate to train
a humble, uneducated peasant if he is typical of his group. Just be sure
he has the respect of his neighbors. Such men make the best lay pastors
for people in the same social group. They also make the best extension
teachers for training other lay pastors of the same social class.

2. Expect the new student-worker to raise up and pastor his own
church. Let him direct his new congregation from the very beginning
(Acts 14:23). For this you must spend at least half of every class discussing the church work of your student: his witnessing, his travels,

problems and his plans. Hear his complete report and write down
lans for his next period's work. Gear your teaching to his immediate
needs as they arise. You will usually have to forget the lesson you have
so carefully prepared and deal with something else more urgent - this will
test you as an extension chain teacher. Be able to put your student's
needs before what you would like to teach.

Men will learn first to witness; then to prepare new believers for
baptism, organize the church, learn discipline and serve the Lord's Supper.
New believers should not preach. They can sing, pray, read the Bible and
give testimonies. Until there is someone ready to preach, the Lord's
Supper should be the center of their worship. It will not corrupt new
believers to serve the Lord's Supper, but it will swell their heads to
preach. Let their preaching develop naturally out of their witnessing.
First, they win their friends by humbly presenting Christ using their own
Bibles. Soon they begin telling Bible stories. Then they teach simple
Bible studies using the reteachable extension materials. Gradually communicating the Word evolves into preaching.

Remember, local men raise up their own churches, not you. Not any
outside pastor! Break this rule and you break the extension chain. You
will have a preaching point instead of a church: a sure dead end link.
Impress this continually on your student-workers.

3. Lay on the new church only the seven essential requirements.
What did Christ order His churches to do? We are saved by faith, not by
keeping commandments; but once we are in the Body of Christ, we must obey
them (Matthew 28:18-20). From her infancy, the new congregation must be
an obedient church, practicing the seven things Christ commands His
Church:

> repentance from sin, baptism, practical love,
> the Lord's Supper, prayer, giving, witnessing.

Don't make a church wait for a certain number of members, or until she
has an ordained pastor, before she can start obeying her Master's
commands! How paralyzing!

Distinguish between the seven divine commandments, apostolic
practices, and evangelical traditions:

a. The divine commandments, listed before, an obedient church
must do.

b. Apostolic practices (traveling by boat, serving the Lord's
Supper daily in homes, speaking in foreign languages, baptizing converts
immediately) may not be prohibited as they are biblically sanctioned; but
neither may they be commanded since only the Lord Jesus Christ has the
authority to make commandments for His Church. They are not the required
basis for a new church.

c. Evangelical traditions (use of choir robes, Sunday School,
seminary, preaching outlines of systematic theology, raising the hand to
"accept Christ", many ordination and baptism requirements) cannot be com-

manded since they are not explicitly mentioned in the Bible. We must discard them if they stand in the way of simple, immediate obedience to the commands of Christ for His churches (Matthew 15:9). In certain cultures some of these good traditions impede obedience to Christ. Direct all your teaching toward helping your student obey the seven commands of Christ for His churches. Never start a daughter church with detailed bylaws inherited from a mother church in a different area or you will produce a dead end link. An extension chain will easily cross social and language barriers, if you limit requirements to the seven commandments of Christ.

V. TEACH AS CHRIST DID:

1. Teach by your own personal example. The teacher in an extension chain never asks his students to do anything which they have not seen him do. Walk to homes to witness, if you expect your student to do it. The force of your example is the impetus for a live chain. Use only equipment and methods which your student can use. Don't raise up a church using films and then ask your student to do it without films. Don't preach from complex outlines which require years of training and then ask him to preach simple messages. If you want him to preach simple messages, you had better do it, too. Follow the example of Paul, who told his converts to imitate him.

2. Motivate your student by using an obedience-oriented curriculum. The student in an extension chain does not do his assignment for his teacher, but for Christ. All his studies aim to fulfill His commands. You will teach all the essential elements of the traditional curriculum, but in their functional order. Doctrine, history, and Bible are introduced as they arise out of the immediate needs of a growing, multiplying congregation. Courses of several months yield to weekly units which fulfill your student's changing needs. One week "core" units can unite elements of different subjects in such a way that the average lay pastor can relate them to each other. The extension chain textbooklet Atanasio unites Church History, Doctrine, Polemics and a homiletical exercise in one brief comic book. It can be carried in the pocket, and read during the week, and taught the following Sunday.

Do not motivate your extension chain student with grades and diplomas. He does not "graduate" until his chain has raised up a reproducing church in every town and neighborhood of his field of responsibility.

Making the first goal of your students doctrinal perfection invites pharisaism. We want doers of the Word. We need pastors, not pulpiteers. Keep the curriculum aimed primarily at obedience or you'll produce dead end links. An obedience-oriented curriculum is easy to prepare; the Bible is written this way: every doctrine is presented in a context which demands its corresponding practical duty. Keep asking, "What does the Bible say?"

3. Let each student progress at his own speed. The entire chain cannot study one course at the same time. The chain is too complex and teaching conditions too varied. One rigid system will not meet different students' needs.

4. <u>Make sure each week's study produces the most urgently needed
practical work</u>. If necessary, write your own materials. First, list
your educational objectives. Be sure your list grows out of the needs of
your students, based primarily on the commands of Christ for His Church.
Then, prepare weekly teaching units which will, in the shortest time possible, meet the most pressing educational objectives. Eventually, you
will teach all the elements of the traditional seminary curriculum. But
not in the same way! Do not deal with only <u>one</u> subject. Such antiquated
teaching can never adapt to the exciting and novel involvements of a
living chain.

You must build each unit of study around one specific <u>activity</u> done
in fulfillment of one of the seven commandments of Christ for His Church.
This practical work is the "core". The core of a beginning TEE unit is
simply <u>witnessing</u>; but teaches things listed under several different
educational objectives. Under "Bible", it partially fulfills the objective <u>knowledge of the Gospels</u>. The man must know the life of Christ to
present Him to others. Under "Theology", it contributes to <u>knowledge of
Soteriology</u> as a study of the plan of salvation. Under <u>"Personal Evangelism"</u> it teaches some knowledge of Church Growth Principles. Under
"Pastoral Theology" it imparts some <u>knowledge of the duties of a church
member</u> - like baptism and stewardship. These are integrated into the
one unit activity of witnessing, in obedience to Christ. Such a curriculum requires much less textbook reading and classroom time. It permits frequent review of the same doctrines in varied contexts and applications. In the writer's chain, it solved the problem of student
motivation, both for studying and practical work.

To write such units, you must list your educational objectives on
one axis of a large graph. (The writer's graph covers one wall. After
every trip to the villages, he adds some new objective to cover some urgent need.) On the other axis list the weekly units which you will teach.
Then indicate under every unit all the possible objectives it can help
meet (see the abbreviated graph on the following page). You can teach
weekly units by assigning sections of regular extension textbooks, but
you will need to supplement them, bringing in the other necessary elements to enable the men to do their assigned activity.

VI. HELP EACH DAUGHTER CHURCH BECOME A MOTHER CHURCH

1. <u>Urge the newborn church to mobilize its members for continued
reproduction</u>. Keep extending the chain. Don't lose the happy momentum of
spontaneous church growth. Teach new Christians to obey the Great Commission. Ask each new church to send out workers to start daughter churches.

2. <u>Promote the extension students to be student-teachers</u>. Not all
students have this capacity; but try them. The slower man may surprise
you. Once he stands at the head of a new section of the chain, a medi-
ocre student will often start new churches with a zeal and facility which
surpasses his teacher. But keep out of his way when he takes his first
solo flight. Do not control his movements; <u>let the work get out of your
hands</u>. Let him reteach to his own new students the same studies he
learned from you (II Tim. 2:2). Let him repeat everything he has seen

you do. He does not need to complete the entire pastoral course before he opens his own subcenter; he needs only to keep a unit ahead of his students. He teaches them what is still exciting in his own experience.

When a worker matures spiritually, his congregation may recognize him as pastor and lay hands on him (Acts 14:23). This gives him confidence. Do not hesitate to make such a man an extension teacher. He has already helped raise up his own church (the one truly qualifying test).

3. Do not let building programs stop the chain - don't let anything stop it! In urban areas, where new chapels cost too much to build as fast as a chain requires, groups meet in homes or rented halls. When they grow too big, they divide. But you must teach them how to do it and prepare the leaders for the two new congregations. Plan ahead!

4. Evaluate constantly the progress of each student and teacher in the chain.
       a. Keep a check list (see following page) on the work of each student and teacher. Bring it up to date in each class. Each student-teacher also keeps a check list for his own students and always gives a report of their progress to his own teacher.

       b. Analyze dead end links. Go over this entire list of steps to see where you failed. If the link is incurably broken, bypass it. Do not waste time with nonreproductive churches.

       c. Visit all the churches often as a silent observer. Send out reteachable materials that fit their current needs.

Most units deal with several educational objectives. The one on having daily devotions instructs on prayer, Psalms, the worship of God (notice the x's after these educational objectives listed under "HAVE DAILY DEVOTIONS"). Normally the objectives would be far more detailed, to show exactly what each unit touches. Primary and secondary objectives would be shown.

5. To continue the chain indefinitely, seek out student-teachers who will simply repeat these same steps. They lack pastoral experience and education but in this they lean on the principal. You must back them and encourage them. You might help pay their travel expenses. But above all, give them full responsibility in their own areas. This Paul/Timothy relationship continues all down the chain. Give them the example to follow, then step back and let them do it. Each teacher must give full responsibility to his own Timothy. Don't let the teachers do all the preaching in their subcenters. That's what they are training their students for! Don't let the whole church attend the extension class. Let the local student reteach to the Christians what he has learned in the class. If the extension teacher always preaches and directs in his students' place, he weakens their ministry and creates dead end links. He must empower his students and then free them and trust them, just as you empowered and freed and trusted them. Don't let the national worker tyranize his trainees! He is there to free them.

THIS CURRICULUM GRAPH IS TOO ABBREVIATED FOR ACTUAL USE.

Core Activities (Units):

Educational objectives:

	HAVE DAILY DEVOTIONS	WITNESS	CALL TO REPENTANCE	ASSURE NEW BELIEVERS	PREPARE FOR BAPTISM	ORGANIZE NEW CHURCH	PRESIDE SESSION	ELECT OFFICERS	MOBILIZE DEACONS	DEVELOP STEWARDSHIP	BEGIN MISSION PROJ.	BUILD CHAPEL	ORGANIZE GRAIN COOP.	TRAIN INTERP. BIBLE	TEACH INDUCT. STUDY	COMBAT LEGALISM	MAINTAIN DISCIPLINE	COUNSEL DISCOURAGED	COUNSEL BACKSLIDDEN	DISCIPLINE OFFENDERS	DEFEND VS. ROMANISM
SPIRITUAL LIFE																					
prayer	x				x																
separation from sin			x		x												x	x		x	x
stewardship						x				x	x	x	x								
THE BIBLE																					
Bible survey														x							
Hermeneutics														x	x						
O.T. Introduction														x							
Pentateuch																					
History																		x			
Poetry	x																				
Prophets										x											
N.T. Introduction														x							
Gospels			x	x						x	x										x
Acts, Epistles					x	x	x	x	x	x							x	x		x	x
THEOLOGY																					
God, Trinity	x																				
Soteriology		x	x	x													x		x		x
Christology		x			x						x										x
Ecclesiology					x	x	x	x	x	x								x		x	x
CHURCH HISTORY																					
ancient														x							x
medieval															x						x
reformation			x											x	x						x
Latin America						x					x										x
PASTORAL SKILLS																					
evangelism		x	x	x	x																
counselling			x															x	x	x	
Christian education														x							
discipline						x											x	x		x	x
administration						x	x	x	x	x		x						x			
CHRISTIAN SOCIAL DUTIES																					
combat poverty											x		x								

VENEZUELA III   by C. Peter Wagner

The Venezuelan experiment in church growth concluded its first phase
June 24-27, 1974, when representatives of 55 churches of several different
denominations met with other Venezuelan leaders and church growth consultants Edward Murphy, Ruperto Velez and Peter Wagner. Venezuela III was the
third of a planned series of evangelism/church growth workshops, the first
two of which have already been reported in CHURCH GROWTH BULLETIN (see
CGB July 1972 and September 1973). They represented a pioneer experiment
in measuring the attainment of evangelistic goals set during gatherings
where church growth principles were explained.

The experiment has taught us a great deal. We now know much more
about how church growth teaching can be communicated to the grass roots
with the result that God begins to work in a new way in the ministries
of pastors and evangelists and the churches they influence begin to grow
at an accelerated rate. Since Venezuela I (1972) similar workshops have
been held in at least four other Latin American countries and six African
countries under the coordination of Dr. Vergil Gerber's Evangelical Missions Information Service office. The first series of Asian workshops
are scheduled for this fall, and the number of invitations flooding
Gerber's office has surpassed all expectations.

Gerber's Manual for Evangelism/Church Growth, now published in
English under the title God's Way to Keep a Church Going and Growing
(Regal Books and William Carey Library, 1974), has 40,000 copies in print
in English and has been published, or is in the process, in 26 other languages. The demand for practical knowledge of the dynamics of church
growth keeps increasing all around the world.

The purpose of these workshops, of which Venezuela is the prototype,
is to give church leaders a renewed vision, strengthen their faith, teach
them simple techniques of goal-setting and strategy-planning for effective
evangelism, and share with them some of the results of missiological research which is pinpointing factors known to help or hinder healthy
church growth.

Each workshop in Venezuela encouraged pastors and church leaders to
set measurable evangelistic goals in terms of new disciples made and
brought into responsible membership in the churches. Using rates of
growth of church membership as the independent variable, subsequent
changes in evangelistic effectiveness were measured using the principles
set forth in Gerber's Manual.

Results of the workshops were as follows:
1. Representatives of 72, 65 and 55 churches attended the workshops
in June 1972, 1973 and 1974 respectively. (The report of the 1974 workshop
excludes the data on 115 Assemblies of God churches, with a membership of
5,588 for three reasons: (1) they were represented not by pastors or
denominational executives, but by a worker not directly responsible for
evangelism/church growth; (b) the worker had firm statistics only for 1972
and 1974; and (c) the membership total of that one denomination exceeded
that of all the other denominations combined, and thus would have distorted the statistical conclusions considerably.

2. Faith projections for increased membership both through expansion growth (membership in the local congregation) and extension growth (planting new congregations) were made at the conclusion of each workshop after a time of study and prayer. The faith projections of the churches which returned and reported, as compared to their previous rate of growth for ten years, is indicated on Graph A. In each case the projected rates were substantially higher than the past decadal growth rate. The decrease in the projected growth rate from the second to the third workshop might be an indication of the development of a more realistic attitude toward goal setting due to feedback from the previous two years' experience.

3. Graph A also shows that past decadal rates for accomplished increase reported at the second and third workshops were between two and three times the rate of the first. These churches were growing at 20% a year, i.e. doubling every four years! However, it must be observed that this would be more significant if exactly the same churches were reporting their growth. There was a good bit of overlap through the three workshops, but it was not complete, and some churches reported at only two of the three workshops.

4. Graph B shows that the workshops apparently accomplished the objective of increasing rates of church growth. As was pointed out in last year's report, the increase over the first year from 60% per decade (ten full years) to 680% (one year only, multiplied by ten to get the decadal rate) per decade was extraordinary, and could not be expected to continue. However, the increase in that one year apparently helped lift the decadal rate, measured over the previous ten years (1963 to 1973), from 60% to 107%. Then growth of the churches between the second and third workshops (projected to a decade by the arbitrary process of multiplying the rate by 10) reached 250%. Even if a measurement in 1975 would show the decadal rate over the past ten years (1964-1974) to be as low as 120%, this would mean that the membership growth rate of these Venezuelan churches would have doubled in three years through the application of church growth principles.

5. Thus, as I analyze it, the most important result of the experiment is the steadily increased growth rates from 60% to 107% to 250% per decade (see Graph B).

While the overall results of the experiment were favorable, some negative lessons were also learned. By Venezuela III it became obvious that the annual national workshop was not adequate for optimum results. It was hoped that all churches represented at the first workshop would repeat the three times, but they did not.

I interpret this as another indication that interdenominational efforts at promoting evangelism and church growth are not always the best. It now seems that a better approach might have been the one taken in Columbia in 1973. After the initial national workshop there, a series of 18 regional - denominational - workshops were planned. In Venezuela, future annual workshops should be held on a denominational basis for three to five years before another antional workshop is called. When the

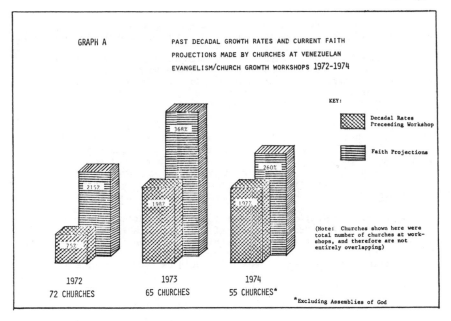

GRAPH A

PAST DECADAL GROWTH RATES AND CURRENT FAITH
PROJECTIONS MADE BY CHURCHES AT VENEZUELAN
EVANGELISM/CHURCH GROWTH WORKSHOPS 1972-1974

KEY:

Decadal Rates
Preceeding Workshop

Faith Projections

(Note: Churches shown here were
total number of churches at workshops, and therefore are not
entirely overlapping)

368%

260%

215%

198%

197%

75%

1972
72 CHURCHES

1973
65 CHURCHES

1974
55 CHURCHES*

*Excluding Assemblies of God

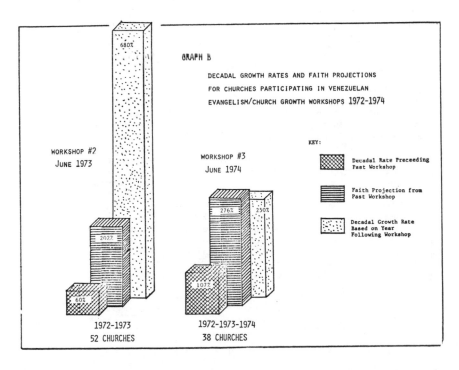

680%

GRAPH B

DECADAL GROWTH RATES AND FAITH PROJECTIONS
FOR CHURCHES PARTICIPATING IN VENEZUELAN
EVANGELISM/CHURCH GROWTH WORKSHOPS 1972-1974

KEY:

Decadal Rate Preceeding
Past Workshop

Faith Projection from
Past Workshop

Decadal Growth Rate
Based on Year
Following Workshop

WORKSHOP #2
JUNE 1973

WORKSHOP #3
JUNE 1974

202%

276%

250%

107%

60%

1972-1973
52 CHURCHES

1972-1973-1974
38 CHURCHES

rate of increase or decrease of all churches of a single denomination can be consistently measured, this type of an approach gains its optimum value.

Due to circumstances beyond the control of anyone involved, Venezuela did not provide any consistent and strong local leadership for the three years of experiment. Missionaries and Venezuelan leaders came and went, and the fact that the workshops went as well as they did seems to indicate that they are meeting a felt need at the grass roots level.

In conclusion, the Venezuelan experiment has shown that church growth principles, when applied at the grass roots, can help produce the increased degree of faith and vision in church leaders necessary to raise significantly the rates of growth of the church they influence, and thus they may more adequately and efficiently fulfill the Great Commission. The most valuable tool available for accomplishing this to date is the Gerber Manual.

Were any denomination or mission to provide continuous consecutive leadership focussed on communication of the Gospel, which used the goal-setting and achievement-measuring techniques provided by the Gerber tool, much greater church growth could confidently be expected. And growth greater than that achieved in Venezuela would be startling indeed.

DO NOT DIVIDE THE CHURCH ---- AN APPEAL

VATICAN II, WHEATON, UPPSALA, FRANKFURT, LAUSANNE!! These great gatherings have been defining what it means to be Christian in our day. Deep difference of opinion as to what the Bible is, the Gospel is and the Church ought to do separates Christians and Churches. The chasm grows deeper. A division like that caused by the Reformation is about to occur. Before it does, while there is yet time, we voice an appeal.

Just after Uppsala, in November 1968, Church Growth Bulletin, seeing the terrible division occurring in the Church, and looking forward to the next meeting of the World Council of Churches, published this appeal. Now, just after Lausanne and a year before the Fifth Assembly of the WCC in Djakarta, we publish it again. God grant it be heard.

"Let us help the next Assembly make a pronouncement on mission which better represents the whole Church, avoids the confusion inherent in defining mission as 'everything which Christians ought to do,' and takes seriously both the salvation of men's souls and the healings of their bodies and societies...When the World Council writes a new document of mission, we hope this exchange of opinion will help bring forth a balanced pronouncement which will preserve the values of classic biblical mission, while adjusting it to the vastly more receptive populations of today and their vastly increased physical and social needs."

The quotation may be found in the bound volume of Church Growth Bulletins, 1964-1968, p. 336, and in Eye of the Storm, Word Books, Waco, Texas, p. 278.)

CHURCH GROWTH
BULLETIN

INSTITUTE OF
CHURCH GROWTH

Address:
FULLER THEOLOGICAL
SEMINARY
135 N. Oakland
Pasadena, Calif. 91101

DONALD A. McGAVRAN, B.D., Ph.D.
Director

September 1974   Subscription $1 per year   Volume XI No. 1

"LAUSANNE--A CATALYST FOR WORLD EVANGELIZATION"

by

Dr. Herbert Works - Professor of Missions
Northwest Christian College, Eugene, Oregon

Webster defines a catalyst as "a person or thing acting as the
stimulus in bringing about or hastening a result." The International
Congress on World Evangelization, held in Lausanne, Switzerland in July,
was a catalyst--a catalyst that operated by enabling two substances to
interact with one another. The Congress brought together key Christians
from every part of the world to interact with the most pressing issues
that face world evangelization today. This interaction of church leaders
with some, at least, of the chief issues is certain to produce fruitful
results.

This issue of the Bulletin brings to the readers a first-hand look
at some of the interaction between these Christian leaders and the issues.
The Congress News Center provided opportunity for interviews with major
participants, in which I put to them some controversial questions that
face missions in the last quarter of the twentieth century. Here, then,
are the questions, some replies, and occasionally my comment as a church
growth observer.

EVANGELICAL-ECUMENICAL DEBATE

From the outset, it was clear that the leaders of the Congress intended that its influence reach far beyond the persons who were present
in Lausanne. In particular, many were concerned that those in Churches
associated with the World Council of Churches should know about the
Congress and be touched by its impact. I asked Harold Lindsell, editor
of Christianity Today, "How can the impact of Lausanne reach the hundreds
of thousands of laymen and women in Churches which are a part of the ecumenical movement, who still are committed to evangelism and missions?"
Lindsell replied, "First, participants who belong to Churches related to
the ecumenical movement can go back, and within the context of their relationship, carry the news of what happened at Lausanne. Secondly, it
can be done by literature, that is, the papers and all the other materials
that are produced as a result of Lausanne can be made available to the ecumenical movement. Third, participants who are themselves not related to

the ecumenical movement can reach over the barriers which separate them from the conciliars and spread the impact as, if you please, a missionary task. They will realize that there are these profound theological differences. They will talk with conciliar people about these differences, engage in dialogue, and try to convince them that Lausanne's is indeed a biblical position on evangelism.....Some people from the Lausanne Congress might even write articles for ecumenical periodicals so that these questions could be discussed."

There was informal talk at the Congress about the establishment of a World Evangelism Headquarters and some took this to mean that the influence of Lausanne upon W.C.C. circles would be made as a competing organization. When a question about this was put to Lindsell, he replied, "There is no talk about an organization. Nobody wants any ecclesiastical structure. The talk is about a 'fellowship' that would have as its key purpose the finishing of the task of the Church, which is the evangelization of the world. Approximately 8 to 1, the participants voted that we should explore the possibility of some kind of a continuing fellowship. About 90% of all the participants voted for this. I think what will happen is that a committee of 25 or 30 will be appointed, coming out of the Congress itself. Then four to six months down the road they will meet to examine the possibilities and to talk about what the Fellowship should be like, whether there should be an office to disseminate information, where it should be located, and who would be the liaison person to bring it all together."

The common ground for such a fellowship, according to Lindsell, would be a mutual concern for the evangelization of the world. "I think here at the Congress it has become clear that however divided we are on many subjects, whether it be social action, or differences in church polity, even though we're separated by our denominational attachments, there is one thing which most of the participants share, and that is a passion to get the Gospel out to those who have never heard it. There is urgent need for some kind of fellowship to get this thing done - to take the Gospel to the ends of the earth - in our generation!"

John Stott, Rector of All Souls Church in London, was chairman of the committee to draw up a "Lausanne Covenant." Stott was asked if he felt the Covenant, with its solid biblical base and firm commitment to world evangelization, would have an influence on W.C.C. deliberations. He replied, "Yes, I hope so. As you know, one or two leading World Council of Churches members are here as 'official visitors.' The most distinguished is Emilio Castro, himself, who is head of the Division of World Mission and Evangelism. He is very sympathetic to what we are trying to say, and while I can't speak for him, I believe that he is, himself, critical of some of the more extreme views of some of the ecumenical leaders with whom he doesn't agree.   But, mind you, in this Congress, we as Evangelicals are divided in our attitudes toward the World Council of Churches. Some are prepared to engage in dialogue and to bear their evangelical witness insofar as they have opportunity. Others have washed their hands of the World Council altogether. I belong to the former category. I believe the time is still appropriate for us to bear our evangelical witness, to learn what we can learn, and to contribute what we can contribute. I hope the debate will still go on."

Stott's hope for continuing dialogue sounds a note familiar to church growth leaders. From its earliest development, leaders of the church growth school of thought in missions have sought to avoid dividing the Protestant world into two sides; rather, they determined to call Christians in all groups to a serious commitment to missions as "an enterprise devoted to proclaiming the Good News of Jesus Christ and to persuading men to become His disciples and dependable members of His Church." (McGavran 1970:34)

EVANGELICAL VS. SOCIAL ACTION

One of the major issues raised at Lausanne was the relationship between world evangelization and social action. Early in the Congress, voices began to be raised, especially by some of the participants from Latin America, insisting that evangelicals must take more seriously the needs of the oppressed, the victims of injustice, the hungry and the sick and the poor. This issue should be of keen interest to C.G.B. readers, since church growth missiologists have made a clear distinction between church planting and humanization.

I interviewed Samuel Escobar, former Travelling Secretary for the I.F.E.S. in Latin America, and presently General Secretary, Inter-Varsity Christian Fellowship of Canada. Escobar had emphasized the importance of social concern in relation to evangelization, using as one illustration, a situation in Bolivia in which the Church had grown substantially after having taken an aggressive position on land reform. I asked: "Mr. Escobar, in your plenary address, you presented an illustration in which Christian social activism (in this case, land reform advocacy) resulted in significant church growth. Do you advocate such activism by missionaries as a means for the initial planting of the Christian Faith in an area? Or, is it a means for the indigenous Church by which subsequent church growth may be encouraged?" Escobar replied, "A key in what I said was not so much the activism of the missionaries as the fact that the relationship they had with the people changed. In the case of one small mission which had bought a hacienda, the mission was the "owner" of these people, so it was the relationship of master or slave, or, if you want, the relationship of rich to poor. That relationship changed when the mission distributed its land. Missionaries found that it was easier for them to communicate the Gospel at a different level, and that there was credibility to the Gospel by the very change in their relationship. This principle applies anywhere. In the University, for example, we believe that sometimes we only can evangelize people when we have them in our hands, we have them gathered in a room, and consequently they have to listen to us, and we preach to them. But, I believe we also should be able to evangelize when we are in their hands--when we are in a meeting that others have organized, and we take the opportunity to communicate the Gospel. The relationship between the one who evangelizes and the person who is evangelized is very important".

In order to understand more clearly how the Latin American stress on social concern touches on church growth thinking, I talked with Pablo

Perez, who has a doctorate from S.W.M., and is at present Visiting Professor of World Missions at Dallas Theological Seminary. Perez noted that the place of social action in relationship to evangelism is "the focal point in Latin America, regardless of what denomination". He saw the Latin American participants - who often differed from Samuel Escobar - as attempting to assert a balanced view of the place of social action.

Perez responded to my question about Escobar's plenary address by saying, "I don't think he was trying to convey the idea that initial evangelization type of church growth was the same as the growing of the Church after it had been established and after it had made some significant social moves. There was a Church to start with..... In other words, it wasn't a 'right from scratch' evangelization, but people came to the Church because of the action of the missionaries in land reform. This is a different point of view from suggesting that initial social action produces evangelism."

I followed up by asking, "Then would you say that initial church planting would ordinarily not take place by social action, but once the church has been planted, the social action must grow with the church as it grows?" Perez corrected me, "...must grow out of the church as a part of good works--Ephesians 2:10." He described the varied opinions among Latin Americans on this issue by citing the contribution of another Latin American leader, in one of the study groups, who said, "Let's completely forget about social action, as it has turned for the worse. We have been given money and food by European Churches to provide for breakfasts and lunches....When we do that, we have a packed house. But then, when for some reason or another we fail to give it, nobody comes. It has not resulted in any kind of evangelization."

Perez summarized, "The way I would put it--an exploited continent, once it has found that there is a source, exploits the source. Thus the exploited becomes exploiter."

I asked David Cho, General Director of Korea International Mission, Inc. about the role of social concern in Korea, where the Church has grown very rapidly. He replied, "In Korea, from the beginning, social justice or social activism was the natural outcome of Christian life, not a method of evangelism. The full Gospel, the pure Gospel should be emphasized instead of the social task....Through evangelization, through the new community of the evangelized, naturally the social issues will be solved by the new way of life in the community."

A clear understanding of the problem was expressed by Roger Greenway, Latin American Director of the Board of Missions, Christian Reformed Church. I asked him about the stress of the Latin American participants on the place of humanization in evangelism. Greenway replied, "I think one thing that is coming out of this Congress is a reaction against the kind of priority thinking which forever neglects priorities 2, 3, and 4. I, myself, have written in favor of listing our priorities and keeping our priorities straight and so forth. I still see a lot of merit in that kind of thinking. The trouble is that some of us forever stay with priority 1 -- Gospel proclamation, verbalization of the Gospel--and never get around to what we have termed priority 2, or 3. I think this is being pointed out at this Congress, and I think that maybe now we ought to stop talking about priorities and start talking about preaching a full Gospel, proclaiming Christ's Saviorhood and Lordship. We are called to faith and obedience. It is not faith today and obedience some time later on..... Maybe we have missed the impact of what it means to believe and surrender ourselves to a Lord. It means to put yourself under His discipline. ....Rene Padilla and Escobar have said it--obeying Christ every day."

Although at the end of the Congress, participants still held differing opinions on the relationship between social action and world evangelization, the Lausanne Covenant stated unequivocally the place of each. "...we express penitence both for our neglect and for having sometimes regarded evangelism and social concern as mutually exclusive. Although reconciliation with man is not reconciliation with God, nor is social action evangelism, nor is political liberation salvation, nevertheless, we affirm that evangelism and socio-political involvement are both part of our Christian duty. For both are necessary expressions of our doctrines of God and man, our love for our neighbor and our obedience to Jesus Christ."

MISSION-CHURCH TENSIONS

Another major issue surfaced at Lausanne--the relationship between the sending Church and the receiving Church. The focus of this issue was the so-called "moratorium." The origin of a moratorium on missions and missionaries seems lost in obscurity. Many trace it to the Bangkok meeting of the Division of World Mission and Evangelism of the World Council of Churches. Others note that similar suggestions preceded Bangkok in regional or denominational conferences. The most widely discussed form of the moratorium proposal was one suggesting that all missionaries and mission resources be withdrawn from the field for a five-year period.

The moratorium was at no time the theme of a major address at Lausanne: however, the term and the idea appeared occasionally both in plenary addresses and in small group discussions. Consequently, a press conference was held with five East African church leaders about the idea of a moratorium. The leading figure in the discussion was John Gatu, General Secretary of the Presbyterian Church of East Africa and Chairman of the General Committee of the All African Conference of Churches, who had spoken earlier favoring such a moratorium. In the press conference, Gatu noted that four problems need to be confronted: (1) the uncertain relationship that exists between the sending and receiving Churches; (2) the need for selfhood and self-reliance of the Church that has emerged on the mission field; (3) the need for the national Church to take the responsibility for mission with its own resources and its own people; and (4) the problem of institutions on the mission field--those that may or may not be desired by the Church, the supervision of such institutions, and resources to sustain them. Gatu then said, "The presence of missionaries and money has played a great part in shaping these relationships.... Some of us feel a temporary withdrawal of missionaries and personnel will help the two parties--that is, the receiving Church to be able to criticize or evaluate what they have been doing in light of the four items I have mentioned, and also the sending Churches to be able to evaluate what they have been doing so that we can adapt ourselves honestly to the demands cf mission in the 1970's."

I asked John Stott, one of the Congress convenors, if such a moratorium could be considered biblically permissible. He answered, "Yes and no. We have included in the final draft of the Lausanne Covenant something about it, although we avoided the world, 'moratorium.' We have said that the reduction of foreign missionaries and monev may sometimes be necessary in an evangelized country in order to facilitate the national Church's growth in self-reliance and in order to release resources for unevangelized areas. If a Church desires a reduction in the number of missionaries from abroad working in its area (a) for the sake of its own growth and self-reliance or (b) in order that resources may be redeployed to unevangelized areas, a moratorium would not only be justified but would be very healthy. But the point we've tried to make is that such action could be taken only in order to increase the free flow of missionaries. A moratorium that dries up missionary effort is totally unacceptable."

Another African, this one from West Africa, also spoke to the issue. Elias N. Cheng, Evangelism Secretary of the Presbyterian Church in Cameroon, was a respondent to George Peters' position paper on Contemporary Evangelistic Methods. In an interview, Cheng said, "For the Presbyterian Church in Cameroon, 'moratorium' is understood as selfhood, self-identity, and self-reliance of the Church. We maintain that the Church of God in a country should be able to express its selfhood in all its aspects. It should be self-proclaiming, thereby carrying its own responsibility in the spreading of the Gospel by way of evangelism. No Church can do this if it is controlled from outside, either with finances or personnel. If moratorium means what I have expressed, we support it. But, for us in Cameroon, moratorium does not mean sending away missionaries from the Church or refusing financial aid from the churches overseas."

In order to see how the moratorium might be understood by a notable Asian leader I asked Dr. Akira Hatori, Board Chairman and Radio and Television Pastor of the Pacific Broadcasting Association in Tokyo how Asians felt about a moratorium on missionaries. Hatori replied, "I have been the area chairman of East Asia, which includes twelve nations, not including India. With one exception....there has been a warm spirit of gratitude for the missionaries. All want to have a partnership kind of missionary to work together with them. We may send Japanese missionaries to Asian countries and have other Asian missionaries come to Japan, and we invite Western missionaries too. This partnership idea is prevailing in East Asia. I have a deep-seated gratitude to and appreciation for missionaries. I cannot doubt their deep motivation: the love of God, the love of Christ. I would invite more missionaries. Then, too, they have their obedience. When the Lord calls them to Macedonia, they have to go to Macedonia."

Roger Greenway, Latin American Director for the Christian Reformed Board of Missions, also responded to my question about the validity of a moratorium on missionaries. "I look at this whole question of moratorium

and I see some good points...but I'm also afraid of it because two billion
people in the world still need to hear the Gospel. I can see 'moratorium'
as a tragic concept which would turn the evangelical world away from the
task which the Lord has given us. I see many practical difficulties. Many
of the Third World Churches are not at all in a position to undertake the
vast task that has yet to be done. The Presbyterian Church in Mexico a
couple of years ago celebrated its centennial by asking nearly all the missionaries to go home. It didn't even put a five-year deadline on the
thing--this was adios forever. It felt it could carry on now, without
foreign missionary assistance. At that time, I said, 'This is immoral.
This is wrong, unless the national Presbyterian Church is genuinely able
and willing to fill the missionary ranks with aggressive, committed
Mexican evangelists.' In Mexico, less than 2% of the total population is
evangelical Christian. How can you talk about sending all missionaries out
of Mexico when the evangelical community is so small, when so many people
need yet to hear the Gospel. Especially when the Protestant Church is not
really in a position to carry the ball? How can you talk about even reducing missionary forces?

I recognize also that some missionaries, entrenched in institutions
and church positions, ought to be removed. Sometimes for the development
and maturing of the Church, missionaries simply have to step out even
though, in their estimation, the time is not yet right. If we wait until
we think the time is right, we'll never leave. However, I simply cannot
conceive, in view of the population figures and the millions yet to be
reached, how any Christian can talk of a moratorium.

Often there ought to be a shifting of missionaries out of institutional positions into the harvest fields. Many of our present missionaries
ought to be moved out of their present positions (hopefully with their
cordial consent) in planned redeployment. Not retrenchment, mind you, but
redeployment. Let us put them at the cutting edge, where missionaries in
times past always placed themselves--winning men to Christ."

One of the most moving comments came from the retired Anglican
Archbishop of Uganda-Ruanda-Burundi, Erica Sabiti, who said, "Moratorium
means a pause--that the blood which flows from my heart stops for a year
or a few months flowing into my arm. I can't understand how the arm will
exist, for when one member of the body is suffering, the whole body suffers.
I very much doubt the value of any moratorium. I can't understand it
spiritually."

It may have been in the issue of "moratorium" that Lausanne most effectively served as catalyst, bringing Christian leaders together to interact on a problem of common concern. Church growth advocates will hail the
possibility that, out of this confrontation, there may be an assertion of
new urgency for placing more missionaries in church planting situations.

NOMINALITY

"Will Lausanne Betray 'Christian' Canada?" This editorial in Church
Growth: Canada appeared just prior to the opening of the Congress. In it,

editor Dennis Oliver expressed the concern that Lausanne might echo the
Edinburgh conference of 1910 in eliminating peoples who were Christian
in name only as valid objects of evangelization. According to the editorial, over 90% of the Canadians claim to be Christian. Would the issue
of nominally Christian peoples be faced at the Congress?

Oliver was a participant at Lausanne, and I asked him if he felt the
Congress had confronted the problem of nominality to his satisfaction.
He replied, "I'm really quite happy. Nominality has been   the general
background of most speakers. Also, the strategy groups for the United
States, Canada, and Europe have been dealing with this problem. In addition, there was a special session to draw up a strategy for reaching
nominal and sacramental Christians."

Dr. Oliver should be happy, for at many points the Congress spot-
light focused more on renewal of the Church than on actual evangelization.
Although the term "evangelism," was used in nearly all the titles of Evangelistic Methods Groups and Specialized Evangelistic Strategy Groups, the
content of many of these workshops was directed more at revival of nominals
than at evangelism of non-believers.

THE ROLE OF THE HOLY SPIRIT IN EVANGELISM

In a day when charismatic and Pentecostal interest has appeared in
nearly all the major Protestant Churches, the place of the Holy Spirit in
the world evangelization was certain to be an issue at the Congress. Surprisingly, the varying positions among participants about the nature of
the work of the Holy Spirit did not polarize them. Roger Greenway of the
Christian Reformed Board of Missions noted in response to my question
about Pentecostal representation at the Congress, "This is one of the
really significant steps that this Congress has taken. I was in Berlin
in 1966 and I remember that Oral Roberts was the most obvious Pentecostal
presence there. Everyone was amazed that he had been invited! This was
quite a thing for many denominational leaders--to think that a well-known
Pentecostal faith healer had been invited.

But here at Lausanne, we have a host of notable Pentecostal leaders.
They speak to plenary sessions. They take part everywhere. Their participation is universally accepted. The main line Christian world today
accepts the charismatic movement in a way not possible just a decade ago.
When you think of what Juan Carlos Ortiz has been saying to us all it is
remarkable. He represents an extreme renewal movement in South America.
And here he is, guiding western churchmen desperately looking for some way
to put fire into their churches. It's interesting. We're sending missionaries into Latin America and a Latin American Leader is telling us how
to put fire into our churches! ...It is significant that the Third World
is giving the First and Second World a valuable spiritual contribution --
never before made at Berlin or at any other time that I can think of in
Christian history."

At the Congress many who do not consider themselves Pentecostals,
voiced a concern that the Holy Spirit be given free rein in evangelism.

In plenary addresses, speakers repeatedly reminded participants that conversion is the activity of God, the Holy Spirit. I asked many leaders if
they felt that repeated calls for evangelizing and planting churches within
the context of cultural factors was incompatible with the Holy Spirit's
action in evangelism. They all answered, "No. There is a proper place for
cultural factors and for the Holy Spirit. They really complement each
other. The Holy Spirit is the determining factor in evangelization, in
strategy, and in multiplying churches. Cultural factors are the focus
the Holy Spirit uses, the field in which He works. They are always in
flux. The two are intimately related. You have to have them both. You
can't separate them. They interact with each other, especially in the
mind of the evangelist. They have to act together; they have to be
taken into consideration together."

CROSS-CULTURAL EVANGELISM

From the church growth perspective, one weakness of the Congress was
its excessive emphasis on E-I (near-neighbor) evangelism. Since at least
87% of the nearly 3,000,000,000 who do not know Jesus Christ have to be
reached by a cross-cultural (E-2 or E-3) evangelism (which the centuries
have shown to be quite possible) E2 and E3 evangelism should have received
far more emphases.

I asked Winter how he felt about the amount of emphasis that had been
placed on E-I evangelism at the Congress. He answered, "There has not been
nearly enough emphasis on E-2 and E-3. This is not a result of a plot but
is due to the lack of familiarity with this kind of evangelism on the part
of the vast majority of the planners. The planning committee had only two
people out of about twenty-five who had any cross-cultural evangelistic
experience."

Out of a recent meeting of the association of Professors of Missions
came a proposal for a World Missionary Conference in 1980. Winter said,
"It is possibly true that if Lausanne had concentrated on cross-cultural
missions rather than just mentioning it, there might not have been the
push there has been for the 1980 meeting. In any case, good reasons exist
for 1980! Since everyone who is there will be there because of involvement in E-2 and E-3, cross-cultural missions will form the main part of
the agenda." Winter went on to say that many details are yet to be worked
out, but that the interest in "1980" is high.

CHURCH GROWTH AND WORLD EVANGELIZATION

Despite all this, the value of church growth principles in accomplishing the task of world evangelization was clearly voiced at Lausanne.

As I wrote in my brief report on Lausanne in the July Church Growth
Bulletin, the first impressions one with "church growth eyes" received at
the Congress was of wide distribution of church growth ideas. Many plenary session speakers, from Billy Graham on, took positions that either
emerged from or would be entirely compatible with church growth thinking.
Donald McGavran, in an evening message on the first full day of the Congress

spelled out clearly a challenge to approach the task of world evangelization with church growth tools. His address, distributed in advance to the
participants, received generally enthusiastic response. Ralph Winter's
presentation, also, set forth the best in church growth thinking.

I asked Dennis Oliver (Church Growth: Canada) about the extent to
which he felt church growth thinking had penetrated the Congress. He
replied, "The basic assumptions of church growth shouldn't be thought of
as new and different. In the church growth movement, Dr. McGavran and
others have excelled in articulating a central biblical thrust and in
getting back out of foggy thinking to biblical priorities. When others
agree, it is because they are biblically controlled, not because they have
suddenly switched to 'church growth thinking'. This Congress operates
within the Biblical mandate. The major visuals for example may have been
prepared by church growth men, or by men with church growth advisors, or
just by biblical Christians."

A notable case of the spontaneous and widespread interest in church
growth was the very large attendance at the Church Growth Workshop conducted by Professor Wagner Although at that hour about thirty other
work groups were meeting, the Church Growth group drew a sixth of the
participants - about 600 each day.

Dean Arthur Glasser was beseiged by participants, Euricans and
Latfricasians, from many lands wanting to enroll at the School of Missions
at Fuller Theological Seminary. Dr. Edwin Orr of the School of Missions
was never seen without several men wishing to talk to him about revivals
and awakenings. Dr. Alan Tippett was sought out by many, both former
students and others, telling him how much they had been influenced by his
writings, not the least of which is his editorship of Missiology which
has catapulted him into world prominence. Everyone seems to have read
his Church Growth and the Word of God.

Dr. Win Arn, Adjunct Professor at SWM, spoke on American Church
Growth. His second film, Reach Out and Grow, shown for the first time
at Lausanne, received an enthusiastic welcome.

About a hundred and twenty Fuller men, most of them from the School
of World Mission - professors of mission, mission executives, national
leaders, missionaries, ministers - were at Lausanne as speakers, leaders
and participants. Time would fail me were I to describe their contributions. But I must mention the fact that the huge North American
Strategy session elected Dr. Hubbard, President of Fuller, to chair its
daily sessions. All this bespeaks an extraordinary flowering of conscience on church growth.

In his plenary address, Peter Beyerhaus, Professor of Mission
Studies and Ecumenical Theology at the university of Tubingen, Germany,
indicated that his position might mistakenly be taken by some as in disagreement with Donald McGavran. In an interview, I asked Beyerhaus if he
disagreed with the fundamental principles of church growth. Beyerhaus:

"Not at all. I think the principles of church growth which have been elaborated by Dr. McGavran and the entire school are healthy ones. They are based on experience and social-psychological laws. German mission work has been based on similar principles for more than one hundred years. You will find them in the big textbook on the science of missions by Gustav Warneck. My criticism would only be a theological one--what is the final expectation of the church growth movement? Do we expect that through the proper application of those practical principles, the world will become an entirely Christian globe, or do we still reckon with the biblical anticipation that there will be conflict in the end? In our strategy, we must not bypass theological viewpoints."

The extent of the spread of church growth ideas was demonstrated at some points even by the disagreement expressed by some Lausanne speakers. Samuel Escobar took issue with the concept of homogeneous unit churches, contending that these perpetuate segregated churches. I asked him to elaborate. "Where there is an oppressed segment of society," he said, "such as the Black and White situation in the United States or the Indian-White situation in Latin American countries, the group which is oppressed searches for equality and that is where the tension comes. At that point, the Church ought not to promote segregation. That would be yielding to the world around her". I asked about a situation in which an oppressed people choose to remain in a separate congregation. Escobar replied, "That is valid. But I would make sure that no one of these churches closed a door to the others. In a way that expresses discrimination."

This is exactly what church growth men advocating homogenous unit churches have always said. The interview underscores that church growth advocates (1) need to discover the points at which church growth principles are misunderstood and clear up these misunderstandings and (2) to reexamine continually their position in light of biblical truth and the realities of the world.

The catalytic action of the International Congress on World Evangelization has only just begun. As reports of the interaction of Christian leaders with the crucial issues of evangelism and missions are made available, secondary interactions will occur on other levels, among those who were not able to be present and experience the face-to-face dialogue of Lausanne. As more and more minds are focused on the issues and the benefit of new thinking is introduced, Lausanne's catalytic function will expand. We must remind ourselves, however, that a catalyst brings about a result. The result is not more discussion and interaction. The result is the completion of the task of evangelism and church planting given to the Church by her Lord. Lord, haste the day!

* *

LIBERIA NEWS Rev. A. Marwieh, a Liberian, is leading a people movement of power in the Kron Tribe which lives in both eastern Liberia and western Ivory Coast. He recently drew up his long range objectives. They might well be copied by many missionaries, Eurican and Latfricasian alike.

1. To reach every tribe and every village in West Africa with the Gospel of Jesus Christ within the next 10 years.
2. To inspire every pastor of evangelical persuasion in West Africa to spend one month out of every year as missionary to some unevangelized area in the Western regions of the continent.
3. To place scriptures on tapes into every village and town in West Africa in the vernaculars of the people.
4. To develop a system of leadership training which will provide shepherds for the multiplied flocks of believers that will emerge as a result of this indigenous missionary movement.
5. To develop Bible believing, Bible practicing, missionary minded churches throughout the newly evangelized regions.
6. To raise up men who will assume key leadership positions in the West African Movement for the Advancement of Missions.
7. To spread this movement throughout the whole continent of Africa until every village on the continent shall have been evangelized.
8. To start a lay missionary movement in which laymen given two to three months' training in evangelism would go out in teams of twos to some unevangelized area as short term missionaries to the people.
9. To get churches in various parts of the world vitally and personally concerned about each other's needs and to stimulate a really united effort toward the evangelization of the world.

COLUMBIA NEWS Seven denominations with a total of 12,831 members in 174 churches have projected growth resulting in 42,479 members in 541 churches within five years, according to a report released by Vernon Reimer (SWM 1970) coordinator of the Union Biblical Institutions of Columbia and quoted in the Extension Newsletter of January 1974.

IVORY COAST NEWS Gordon Timyan (CMA) writes from Yamoussokro on July 8, 1974 saying, "Six thousand were baptized during Pastor Jacque Giraud's six months in our country....Our CMA Mission has nearly that many inquirers (5629) this year. We have baptized nearly 2000 since he began in our area, the largest number in any one year in our history. Most of these resulted from the impact of the Giraud Crusades. All our staff believe that the First Annual Church Growth Workshop, held in August 1973, should be repeated soon here."

"The fellow who says numbers aren't important is an ass. He might go on to say that he's interested in quality rather than quantity. Quality and quantity cannot be separated so neatly in relation to the gospel. Every number on the roll represents a person who has been touched by the gospel. If all of us are on fire for the faith, then our numbers are bound to multiply."

Elton Trueblood in the United Methodist Reporter

CHURCH GROWTH
BULLETIN

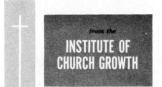

INSTITUTE OF
CHURCH GROWTH

Address:
FULLER THEOLOGICAL
SEMINARY
135 N. Oakland
Pasadena, Calif. 91101

DONALD A. McGAVRAN, B.D., Ph.D.
Director

November 1974   Subscription $1 per year   Volume XI No. 2

CONTENTS

THE NARANJO PEOPLE MOVEMENT IN ARGENTINA
by Edgardo Silvoso SWM ICG '74

Between 1955 and 1969 a remarkable people movement in San Nicolas,
near Buenos Aires resulted in the spiritual transformation of thousands.

In 1957 the government pushed the construction of a steel mill in San
Nicolas. People from all parts of Argentina flocked in to search for better
jobs and new horizons. The population, like most of Argentina, was made up
of Italians, Spaniards, Russians, Germans, Poles, Czechs, Arabs and many
others. Most were only first or second generation Argentinians.

In 1955 the city and environs had a Protestant community of approximately 200 and only one Evangelical "temple". By 1969 Protestants had
grown to around 8,000 and places of worship had increased to more than 20!

The key personality in this people movement was Carlos Naranjo, the son
of Spanish immigrants. About 1942 Carlos had become a Christian at the
age of 20 in a Plymouth Brethren Assembly in Buenos Aires. He was led to
the Lord by the now famous evangelist Fernando Vangioni who was in his early
twenties too. In his early thirties, Carlos was appointed an elder in his
local Brethren Assembly.

In 1955, his company sent him to San Nicolas as director of a small
factory. His first task was to supervise its construction. Shortly after
this appointment (and before he left Buenos Aires) his wife, Rosalia, became critically ill. No cure could be found for her ailment and she was
declared a hopeless case. At that particular time Buenos Aires city was
witnessing the 'Tommy Hicks Campaign'.

SEND correspondence, news, and articles to the Editor, Dr. Donald McGavran, at the
Institute of Church Growth, Fuller Theological Seminary. Published bi-monthly. Send
subscriptions and changes of address to the Business Manager, Norman L. Cummings,
Overseas Crusades, Inc., 3033 Scott Blvd., Santa Clara, California 95050, U.S.A. Second-
class postage paid at Santa Clara, California. Application pending.

When Rosalia was going through what the doctors considered her last hours somebody who had been greatly blessed by Hicks' ministry shared his experience with Carlos and encouraged him to call on one of Hicks' associates, the Rev. Louie Stokes, an Assembly of God missionary to Argentina. Carlos followed that advice and Rev. Stokes rushed to Rosalia's bedside. He read Psalm 103 and prayed for her. A miracle took place. She was instantly healed and got out of bed praising the Lord for such a mighty work. The Naranjo family consecrated their lives to the Lord more deeply than ever before. Soon after this fortunate event they moved to San Nicolas City.

Upon arriving, the Naranjos began witnessing to everybody. Carlos was able to lead some of his employees to the Lord and Rosalia did the same with some of their neighbors. A church emerged and Carlos requested from Rev. Stokes a pastor for it.

A minister arrived but soon afterwards left town because he thought there was no potential for church planting in that area. Carlos was left in charge with the promise that the first available minister would be sent to San Nicolas. The promised pastor never arrived but that tiny group of believers under Carlos' leadership grew into a Mother Church that branched off into 18 new churches with a combined membership of approximately 1500 - and a Christian community of around 8,000.

Branch churches are self-supporting, self-propagating and self-governed. Their leaders received most of their training from Carlos himself. None have had seminary training - and no missionary has been or is involved. The quality of biblical teaching and the sharpness of strategy for expansion and growth are, however, superb. In order to understand how and why this happened, let us look at: The Methods, The Anatomy of the Congregations, The Factors Involved in Expansion, and Carlos Naranjo's Message.

THE METHODS

1. The Basic Thrust in the Mother Church.
    First priority was given to developing a strong congregation in San Nicolas which would multiply other churches. This was accomplished by means of --
    a. Intensive witnessing -- door to door,
                            on street corners,
                            in parks and plazas,
                            in home meetings.
    b. Encouraging new converts to win their families to Christ. Carlos presented the conversion of the whole family as a "part of the package" of salvation (Acts 15:30).
    c. Placing immediately in positions of authority those with leadership abilities. Carlos' argument for this was that he himself was as much of an amateur in the ministry as those whom he had led to the Lord. Those who showed concern and potential became his fellow workers right away.

    d. Solid Bible teaching.
        Bible School professors were invited to give a series of lectures
        on the Bible.
        Carlos and Rosalia drew on their Plymouth Brethren background for
        teaching resources. Brethren are known as good Bible expositors.
        New converts, especially emerging leaders, were encouraged to
        teach to others what they had just learned. This procedure made
        the learning process attractive and interesting.
    e. Prayer. If one thing could be singled out as a mark of this move-
        ment it was prayer. Several days of the week were devoted to this
        exercise. "Vigilias" (all Saturday evening and night spent in
        prayer) were added quite frequently.

2.   <u>Teaching by Example.</u> Carlos was always showing trainees 'how to do it
        yourself'. He would take them to plazas, parks, or street meetings
        and after doing something himself (praying for the sick, witnessing
        to a bypasser, preaching, etc.) he would ask the trainees to do the
        same thing. He took his disciples through a series of steps in order
        to mature them for the ministry.
    a. Sharing in the Church. As soon as somebody made a commitment to
        Christ, he would be asked to tell 'in the next meeting' what took
        place in his life. This was a healthy experience for the new con-
        vert and an encouraging one for the congregation.
    b. Sharing in public. The next step was to share his testimony
        with unsaved relatives and friends. Door to door visitation
        and street meetings were some of the means used towards this
        end. Carlos always warned that persecution was to be expected
        and welcomed as a blessing.
    c. Becoming a Bible Class assistant. Meetings for children in dif-
        ferent locations of the city were started with the purpose of
        teaching God's Word to children. Carlos used these meetings for
        further training his disciples. He would ask them to assume more
        and more responsibilities as they matured in the Lord. Thus:
        (1) Accompanying the official teacher. (2) Gathering the children.
        (3) Leading the singing. (4) Assisting in the teaching process.
        (5) Teaching the lesson. (6) Witnessing in children's homes.
        (7) Taking over the class and so freeing the official teacher
        to start a new Bible Class. (8) Training someone else and so repeat-
        ing the process.
        At one time there were 27 of these Bible classes scattered all
        over the region. Average attendance was around 1,000 children.
    d. Assuming responsibilities in the Mother Church, as deacons, Sun-
        day School teachers, substitute preachers, and board members.
    e. Planting a branch church. The dynamics of this step were the
        same ones used in the Bible classes for children (point c.),
        but instead of children it involved adults who would gather in
        the homes of new converts. Carlos supervised a few of the in-
        itial meetings and then gave the whole thing to the trainee, who
        was on his own from there on.

f. Becoming a trainer. Whenever a trainee planted his own church he would be expected to train others in the way he himself had been trained. The greatest glory for a branch church was to become a 'Mother Church' by planting a branch of 'her own'.

3. **An Intelligent Strategy.**

Carlos and his men planted churches along the main highways and railroads. They aimed at key towns and planted on the basis of responsiveness.

The new congregations were to become evangelistic centers and newer congregations would emerge as a result of their evangelistic efforts. Emphasis was put on the principle that people from new churches assume full leadership as soon as possible.

4. **Collective Ministry.**

Soon after a disciple had gained recognition as a leader, he was invited to be a part of the decision making body. In that group each man had one vote. Carlos, from the very beginning, insisted that he was just one of the group and would not allow his vote to carry more weight than that of other members.

5. **Full Participation of the Christians.**

Members could get involved in all kinds of evangelistic and learning activities. As they progressed, they were promoted to new ones that demanded more maturity and responsibility. The process never ran into a 'bottle neck' because those who 'graduated' from it were immediately encouraged to plant branch churches and start it all over again.

Democratic principles of government were adopted for the election of officers and the setting of policies. Christians were quite familiar with those principles since they were used in the political process of the country. Participation helped people realize that 'they belonged' and had a say in what was going on.

When time for building "temples" came, offerings would be collected for buying material. The whole congregation would gather on weekends and holidays and while the men built, the women would prepare food and serve 'Argentinian tea'. Strong bonds of friendship and first class fellowship resulted.

6. **Immediate Autonomy of New Congregations.**

Autonomy was granted to branch churches as soon as they became self-supporting and local leadership was available. After autonomy was granted, these branch churches continued to engage in inter-church activities with the Mother Church.

7. <u>Special Emphasis on Youth.</u>

Young people were encouraged from the moment of conversion to give themselves entirely to Christian service. They were assigned to spiritual advisors and engaged in street evangelism and Bible classes for children. No generation gap existed because the youngsters' energies were directed to evangelistic thrusts.

The special attention paid to the evangelization of children through 27 Bible Classes helped 'soften' the whole city for the Gospel because parents were reached via their own children. As soon as these children turned into teenagers they were incorporated into the discipling and service programs of the Church and in this way assimilated to its life.

THE ANATOMY OF THE CONGREGATIONS.

1. <u>Each Congregation Mainly of Entire Families.</u> Although in 80 per cent of the cases the wife was the first to be converted, soon afterwards her husband would follow her. (Children usually got converted at the same time as the mother). Entire families became active evangelistic units. Energy, otherwise wasted in tensions and quarrels between saved and unsaved partners, was used for spreading the Gospel.

2. <u>Men Were the Leaders of the Church.</u> Carlos and his men believed that women had a vital part in the life of the Church and in the extension of the Gospel, but they also stressed that women should be subject to men when it came to leadership in homes and in the Church. Thus, leadership and decision making at the top level was in the hands of men, in perfect accord with Latin American social structure.

3. <u>Informal Services and Simple Liturgy</u> characterized the services. People preferred choruses - many of them composed by local people - to the old fashioned hymns of the past. Theology was taught also by singing.

4. <u>Upper Lower and Lower Middle Classes</u> made up the bulk of this movement with the former having the largest share of the total.

It is interesting to note that this movement occurred right after Juan Peron, President of Argentina, was ousted. Peron had dominated the life of the country for years. After his downfall there was a vacuum to be filled and many anxieties about the future. Peron's last years in power witnessed tensions, fights and finally rupture with the Catholic Church which in Argentina is the State Religion. Since most of the two classes that formed the bulk of the People Movement belonged in the Peronist movement, they had been greatly affected by these political events. The political rupture of their party with the Catholic Church prepared them for the spiritual rupture that they were to experience after being exposed to the Gospel in San Nicolas City. The political climate played a key role in the preparation for spiritual harvest.

FACTORS THAT CONTRIBUTED TO GROWTH AND EXPANSION

1. <u>Migration</u>. Starting in 1957, people moved into San Nicolas in huge numbers. Most came from a rural background searching for new ways and means of life. They were open to new ideas, including the Gospel.

2. <u>Modernization</u>. The parochialism of the immigrants was shattered by the modernization caused by the steel mill, the job opportunities it created and the business and financial possibilities it generated. The old parochialism disappeared and a more cosmopolitan mentality developed.

3. <u>Spiritual Vacuum</u>. As a result of Peron's downfall and his breaking away from the Catholic Church, a huge spiritual vacuum was created and <u>had</u> to be filled. This was especially true among the people who moved from the farms into the cities.

4. <u>Freedom for Preaching</u> was granted to all religious groups in Argentina following Peron's fall. This had not always been the case during the Peronist era.

5. <u>Tommy Hicks' Campaign</u>. This 'faith healer' evangelist shook up Buenos Aires on two occasions with great intensity and success. Starting with a very small group, his audience grew to a peak of 200,000. The Press gave him ample coverage. Many who were truly healed became enthusiastic propagandists of his message.

   In my opinion his main contribution to the Evangelicals is two-fold: (1) He broke the ice for the preaching of the Gospel in Argentina. (2) Evangelicals lost a minority complex. In new faith and enthusiasm they engaged in preaching the Gospel.

6. <u>Challenge Led to Victory</u>. From 1955 to 1958 the Naranjo family, especially the couple and their older son were the columns of the movement. In 1958 Albertito - the older son - was killed in a car accident and exactly a year later Rosalia also died. These sad and unexpected events that could have resulted in stagnation of the emerging Church, had instead very positive effects. The new believers, rather than succumbing to discouragement, ran to the side of their pastor and leader affirming in a practical way the principle of shared responsibilities which characterized the movement. A serious problem, viewed as a challenge, gave birth to a great victory.

CARLOS NARANJO'S MESSAGE

He preached simply, without niceties, and very convincingly. He was an average person and knew it. Perhaps his main strength lay there. He related easily to people and spoke their language in a communicative way.

He drew his illustrations from everyday situations. The sophisticated would probably classify his style as 'corny' but it served well its purpose. His preaching, besides being straightforward and on the level of the people, was very biblical, loaded with Scripture references. When the Catholic Church was beginning to awake to the reading of the Scriptures, this content was much welcomed by many.

Carlos had faith in 'the power of the Gospel' and his conviction showed forth whenever he spoke. People might disagree with him but never questioned his convictions or honesty.

Carlos believed that 'God was there' in his meetings among the people and was willing to act, to work miracles, to help. He never preached a sermon for the people to think it over. He expected and demanded a decision on the part of his hearers. His philosophy was "If God has spoken, you have to do something either for or against".

FOUR SUGGESTIONS FOR GROWTH 1975-2000

A. ### Stick to the Mother-Daughter Church Approach

This has proved a good strategy and should be pursued. The present tendency to consolidate at the expense of extension should be ended. The planting of new branch churches should be resumed.

B. ### Make Good Use of Modernization

San Nicolas is commonly referred to as 'the Capital of the Steel Industry'. Many subsidiary industries are continually settling in that area creating new job opportunities, motivating people to migrate to San Nicolas and keeping the mood of the city unsettled and changing. The Movement should scout new opportunities and methods and not perpetuate approaches and techniques, effective in the past which may be useless tomorrow and even today.

C. ### Train Leaders Locally

Do not send them to sophisticated institutions in distant cities. To do so will defeat church multiplication.

D. ### Hold Re-evaluation Seminars in Which All Leaders Produced by the Movement Participate

Do not permit rapid expansion, great geographical distances, and busy schedules to prevent these seminars. The knowledge and experience of the more mature leaders must be used in guiding the Movement.

CONCLUSION

In this indigenous People Movement the Holy Spirit performed a mighty work saving souls and producing church growth. But He did not work in a

vacuum. Social structures, family connections, political outcomes and
methods and means common to the milieu in which the Movement occurred
were employed by the Holy Spirit for bringing all this to happen.

Many lessons can be learned, among others the opportunities that
modernization and urbanization present for the extension of the Kingdom
of God. The changes and potential for responsiveness resulting from this
modern phenomenon can be used to the glory of God.

The success of the movement is due to the fact that its leaders,
under the guidance of the Holy Spirit, seized those opportunities in the
right spirit and with the right methods. The future of the People Movement in San Nicolas depends on its ability to adapt and meet new challenges
in tomorrow's continually changing situation.

((Comments by Donald McGavran. Edgardo Silvoso, the author of this fine
description of a mighty multiplication of churches in the urban scene,
had been part of the movement from the beginning. His father had been one
of Carlos' men and he himself had been one of the child evangelists. He
knew the story from first hand experience and wrote it for me.

After writing it, he sent a letter to Carlos and asked him how the
People Movement was prospering, and if it was growing as it had done in
earlier years. Here is Carlos' moving answer.

"Dear Ed: Your letter came as a surprise and set me to thinking
about those glorious years of growth. With the help of your Dad,
we gathered facts and figures from the past and came up with the
startling discovery that we had stopped doing those things which
had given us such amazing growth. What a shock it was to learn
this!

I immediately called a meeting of the church deacons and
explained to them these facts. Suddenly the presence of God became
so manifest amongst us that for two hours we could do nothing but
cry out to God for forgiveness. With one accord we felt the power
of God moving in our midst, urging us to make a new beginning and
help us recover the enthusiasm for evangelism and the amazing
growth experienced before.

God bless you, Ed, for your letter which has brought
awakening to us. Our services already show new life. We have
recruited a fine group of young people and adults to dedicate
themselves to the Sunday School program (referring to the re-
establishing of Bible Classes for children all over the city).
The brethren are out evangelizing as never before. The churches
are beginning to show an enthusiasm we haven't seen for a long

time, and are crowded Saturdays and Sundays. I could say so much
more, but will leave it at that for now. Praise God, Praise His
Holy Name.

Your friend, Carlos Naranjo"

Not always, but so often, the month is September, not May, and fields are
white to harvest. The time to thrust in the sickle is now, not four months
from now. Perhaps, others who read this amazing account will be moved "to
cry out to God for forgiveness" and to begin "evangelizing as never
before".))

A NEW AGE IN MISSIONS BEGINS

by   Donald McGavran

At the International Congress on World Evangelization Dr. Winter
proved beyond any reasonable doubt that in the world today 2,700,000,000
men and women cannot hear the Gospel by "near-neighbor evangelism". They
can hear it only by E-2 and E-3 evangelists who cross cultural, linguistic
and geographical barriers, patiently learn that other culture and language,
across the decades preach the Gospel by word and deed, and multiply reproductive and responsible Christian churches. This means enormous numbers of
'sent' preachers (Romans 10:14, 15). It means missionaries by the hundred
thousand. It means that all Churches (denominations) become sending
Churches, sending out E-2 and E-3 evangelists (missionaries) till the
2,700,000,000 have sprinkled through them at least, 2,700,000 congregations. At that point, the Lord may well judge that all men have really
heard the Gospel and return.

Winter's address marked the end of an age in missions. For the last
thirty years the urgent necessity has been for Eurican missions to turn
authority over to Latfricasian denominations. During this period it has
been both fashionable and right for national leaders to emphasize in dozens
of ways that they had come of age and no longer needed missionary guidance
or control. It was right for missionaries to withdraw and for missionary
societies to plan their program so as to lessen the number of missionaries
who exercised directional responsibilities over Christian denominations,
hospitals, schools, and other institutions. It was right for the goal of
both missions and Churches to be the ultimate abolishing of missionary
posts designed to serve existing Churches.

It was right for these things to happen in connection with all well
established denominations (Churches). But since the missionary movement
(which involves Christians in all six continents) is continually planting
new clusters of congregations in which missionaries have to be the planters
and nurturers for some years, tension between national leaders (who think
that the time has come to turn over, who resent fatherly guidance from the
missionaries) not only exists but will continue. This tension must not be
wiped out by the simplistic expedient of ceasing to plant new clusters of
congregations, and closing one's eyes to the 2.7 billion!

During the era just past, the stock in trade of certain leaders, both Eurican and Latfricasian, was to proclaim boldly that nationals were quite able to run their own show and that missionaries should bow to their wishes. Alas, this became "the chief Gospel" preached by many eminent leaders. This is what they were noted for. This was what they always said. Let us assume that in the years now ended their message was right.

But it is no longer right. That period in the expansion of Christianity is over. A new era has begun. There is no longer any danger that missionaries from Japan, Korea, Norway, England, the United States, the Philippines, Zaire, Chile, Mexico or other lands will lord it over the denominations in the lands to which the Holy Spirit sends them. To continue harping on that old message is wrong in this new era when suddenly we are conscious of the two point seven billion who are living and dying without Christ and who cannot be reached by near neighbor evangelism. Through his cool and irenic presentation of the great new fact which confronts international Christianity, Dr. Winter was calling on the four thousand leaders from 150 countries gathered at Lausanne to recognize that we have emerged from the old era and have entered a new era. What is necessary and should be fashionable today and tomorrow is not that old message. The battle to recognize Latfricasian Churches (denominations) as equal has been won. There is no need to continue fighting it. That wheat has been threshed. Let us not continue threshing the old straw.

Today's challenge is to devise new slogans, new priorities, and new principles which excite the Church of Jesus Christ to surge forward on ten thousand fronts sending apostles, sending preachers, sending missionaries across cultural linguistic and economic barriers to evangelize any segments of society which the existing Churches in any land are not reaching and cannot reach. Today mature Churches in every country will courageously face up to the many segments of the population which they are not evangelizing, in which they are not establishing outposts of heaven, in which few ever become baptized believers. Mature Churches will then do two things:

First, they will recruit as many of their own sons and daughters as they can - and send them to such segments as E-2 and E-3 missionaries, but not to reproduce their own kind of embodied Christianity, their own cultural image, and their own social status. On the contrary, their missionaries will do what all good missionaries do - deculturize themselves and enculture themselves in the segment of population concerned, learn the language thoroughly, and then father new congregations which are soundly Christian, filled with the Holy Spirit, obedient to the Bible and loyal to the good in their own culture.

Second, seeing the tremendous size of the task, mature Churches will actively recruit missionaries from other Churches in their own country and in other countries. They will send messengers to other countries, pleading with them to "Come over to Macedonia and help us. We have selected for you a segment of population - a county, a ward of our great city, a tribe, a caste, an income bracket, the intelligentsia, the illiterate, the community whose men drive taxis in our metropolis, the land owners, landless laborers -

and will assist you in every way in evangelizing that segment. We will pray God's blessing on you, thank Him for your presence, counsel you as to methods, but not impose our will on you. We will hope that you will employ some of our sons and daughters as your assistants. We are confident that the clusters of churches which you establish will be soundly Christian. And that as those churches mature you will encourage them to associate themselves with us, while you go on to other yet untouched and unreached segments of our vast population."

The creative nature of Dr. Winter's address will only be recognized as we try to develop some such vision of the future, some concrete plans to engage all the churches of all the continents in a determined, intelligent evangelization of the 2,700,000,000 (who in less than 20 years will be 4,000,000,000) who are not now being reached by existing denominations.

The shadow of the era just past is, to be sure, still visible, but it will diminish in length. It takes no great feat of imagination to hear some indignant leader protest that many missionaries even today are exerting undue influence on the existing churches. Such protests are sometimes well founded. Some missionaries, like some ministers, are dominant personalities and occasionally excite resentment in those dominated. Some few missionary societies may yet be living in the pre-1945 era. But they are rare; sending out only a few missionaries, planting a few churches. Where such conditions exist, pressures should certainly be brought to rectify them.

Such protests are sometimes ill-founded. In any extension of the Christian Faith on new ground, infant congregations are brought into being. They would never be born without a father, whom God uses to create new churchlets. These need fatherly "care and feeding". They need Christian nurture. They need help. Someone must be in travail for them till Christ be born in them. Of course, fatherly care continued too long becomes paternalism, but this error in judgment is not likely to be made often. The real danger is all the other way - namely, that in fear of being paternalistic, the missionary hesitates to be fatherly. As a result either no churches are born or those which are born sicken and die. Existing denominations and congregations need no longer be jealous that their prerogatives may be usurped by foreign missionaries. Existing denominations and congregations should actively invite in bands of comrades from outside their culture area who will accept the responsibility for evangelizing suitable segments of the unevangelized.

What do we mean by suitable segments? In the past two hundred years, it was commonplace for one mission to claim sole responsibility and authority for ten million people. This ten million was a Baptist area and that an Anglican. The mission then occupied the area with a force of twenty missionary families - which gave each a parish of 500,000 souls. Today any such assignment of territory is totally unacceptable. One missionary family is ordinarily able to evangelize effectively a community of perhaps five thousand. It is easily seen that the two point seven billion divide into 540,000 fields of that size. These would be fields, according to Dr. Winter's thinking, in which at present practically no one can be reached by E-1, that is, by near-neighbor evangelism.

When in 1965 I was inaugurated as the founding dean of the School of World Mission at Fuller Theological Seminary and called for 100,000 missionaries, I considerably under estimated the need. Since the total number of the unreached, for the next thirty years at any rate, will increase toward four billion, the number of reasonably sized fields to be occupied by missionaries will increase year by year. After thirty years - or perhaps fifty years - if the Lord tarry - the number will decrease. I have dealt with this in the May 1974 issue of the Church Growth Bulletin under the title "The Tide Turns". But until it turns, the number of utterly unreached mission fields will increase. Christians must not delude themselves with the comfortable assumption that existing churches using near-neighbor evangelism will complete the task. They will not. They cannot. This is the hard, unshakeable core of what Dr. Winter told Lausanne.

The Church Growth Bulletin calls on readers to obtain from Church Growth Book Club the pamphlet entitled "The New Macedonia: The Revolutionary New Era in Mission Begins". It is a reprint of this essay plus Winter's epochal address. Let them distribute 'Macedonia' widely to denominational leaders, mission board executives, missionaries and ministers. The price will be 75¢ per copy, or $1.00 per copy postpaid, or 10 copies for $5.00 postpaid, or 1 copy free with a purchase of $5.00 or more.

Nothing said at Lausanne had more meaning for the Expansion of Christianity in the thirty years ahead. As its implications are discovered - I have mentioned only a few - and new forms of mission are invented by Latfricasian and Eurican denominations to carry out effective mission in this new age, the possibility of obeying the Great Commission adequately will loom larger and larger. God grant His rich blessings on all such courageous and faithful forward moves to obey God and meet the deepest and most desperate human needs.

CONGRESS COVENANT FALLS SHORT

by James Montgomery

One of the creative tensions running through the Lausanne Congress was between those who emphasize a mystical approach to world evangelization and those who emphasize the practical. In the Lausanne Covenant, the mystical side won out. In my opinion, there is where the Covenant fell short.

Neither side should have "won". The mystical and the practical are two facets of the same diamond. With greater emphasis on one side, the jewel is now lopsided and therefore not as perfect as it could have been.

Let me explain. Many speakers emphasized the idea that world evangelism will be hastened as we have "better" Christians. When Christians are faithfully praying, studying the world, having body life fellowship together, and when they are revived and filled with the Spirit, the natural result will be effective evangelism.

Those who emphasize the practical pointed out that many thoroughly evangelical churches with mature Christians in them have become sealed off from the great harvests about them. What is needed is for these churches to break out of their ghettos and make hard, bold plans to give a dynamic testimony to the world. Even good Christians need realistic, biblical strategies. They need challenging, measurable goals to strive towards. They need to find out what the Spirit wants them to do as well as what He wants them to be.

It would be very hard to argue against either of these positions. Both are true and need to be pushed with equal zeal.

The Covenant in most respects is excellent. Strong sections such as "The Authority and Power of the Bible" and "The Uniqueness and Universality of Christ" deal with basic theological underpinning for evangelism. The Covenant speaks to many of the vital issues being debated in world mission and evangelism today such as "Christian Social Responsibility," "Cooperation in Evangelism," and "Evangelism and Culture." It emphasizes the spiritual dimension in sections labeled "Spiritual Conflict", and "The Power of the Holy Spirit."

However, the Covenant sorely needed two statements, one on "Goals for World Evangelization" and one on "A Strategy for World Evangelization."

It was in this area, I thought, that the Congress was going to be the strongest. To begin with, it boldly called itself a congress on world evangelization. This might not seem much different than the name for the 1966 gathering in Berlin which was called "World Congress on Evangelism." But the difference is vast. In 1966 people were coming from all over the world to talk about evangelism. In 1974, however, they were coming to talk about their intention to evangelize the world.

This was a thrilling concept. The Congress planners accepted the idea that we could evangelize the world in our time. It was everyone's impression that we were coming together to talk about how we were going to do it.

But in the end, the Covenant included no statement of basic strategy developed from the Scriptures as applied to the present conditions in the world nor any measurable goals set for the evangelization of the world or discipling of nations.

Perhaps my point can be illustrated by what some Christian leaders in the Philippines are beginning to talk about. They are discussing whether or not the Church in the Philippines should set a goal of establishing a congregation in every barrio by the 1990s. Another way to look at it would be to establish one congregation for every 1000 Filipinos and see to it that these were fairly evenly distributed all over the Philippines. The March and July Issues of Church Growth Bulletin in 1973 carried articles by Dr. Paul Rader of Korea on the amazing plan actually in successful operation to put a church within walking distance of every man, woman and child in Korea. Pastor Ahn and Hugh Linton, of the Presbyterian Church have actually done this for their district in the southern tip of Korea, and have been asked by the main denominations in Korea to extend such planning to the whole nation of South Korea. What has been done in Korea can be done in the Philippines.

The idea has merit and is being discussed by denomination and mission heads all over the country for clarification, definition of terms, and the leading of the Spirit. Agreement can be reached so that each part of the total Church of this nation sets realistic goals for itself in relation to the goal for the nation.

Such a plan does at least two things. One, it sets a measurable goal in terms of numbers and time. A mission or denomination will be able to determine exactly how many congregations would be needed to reach this goal. It will find out how many congregations it now has and therefore how many would still be needed. It can then determine at what rate the Church would have to grow to reach this goal. The Conservative Baptists in the Philippines in Operation 200 have done exactly this to a considerable extention of their redemptive effectiveness.

With this approach it might be determined, for example, that if the Evangelical denominations increased congregations at a rate of 20% per year, then 50,000 congregations could be established by 1990.

The second thing that such a statement of a clear and sensible goal does is establish a basic strategy. It enables Christians to say, "We shall have evangelized the nation when everyone in the country is within practical and psychological range of an Evangelical congregation." All Filipinos would know some real Christians in their own community. They would be close enough to walk or take one ride to an evangelical church. They would be able to observe over a period of time some evangelicals they respected. They would be in easy range of home Bible study groups being conducted by the churches. In other words, all Filipinos would have a real chance to learn what it means to be a Christian, what a Christian is really like and how to become a Christian. They would be in a position where they could realistically make a choice for or against becoming a true believer.

As a result of this strategy for evangelizing the Philippines all different methods and approaches could be slanted towards this basic strategy and measurable goal. Christian radio broadcasting, for example, could challenge Christians to start home Bible studies that might develop into house churches and at the same time encourage unbelievers to attend such groups. Many other methods of evangelism, such as Bible and literature distribution, public crusades, social action, and Sunday school outstations, could be slanted towards this basic strategy and this measurable goal.

The lack of this kind of specific goal in the Covenant was a shortcoming. Our leaders there made many fine but general statements about the concept of evangelism in our world today. These statements could have been made at a World Congress on Evangelism.

For a Congress convened specifically to confer about actually evangelizing the world, where many participants and leaders spoke openly about evangelizing the world before the end of this century, the Covenant should have bound those entering into it to Clear Cut Goals and Sound Biblical Strategies. These are absolutely essential if the soaring ideals and heavenly theology of the Covenant are ever to walk on this earth.

Fortunately, Churches and Missions of all six continents, and bands of the devout within all denominations and fellowships, can press on to make good what Lausanne failed to provide. This is perhaps the first and most immediate task before us.

What goals in the evangelization of our part of the world does our Lord want us to set?

What is the strategy and the policy we need, to work toward these goals?

Let us prayerfully and resolutely seek answers to these two questions and then work steadily and obediently forward as God directs.

NEWS

CONFERENCE ON URBAN EVANGELISM, BRAZIL   by Roger S. Greenway

The Southern Baptist Board of Foreign Missions can be credited with a "first" for sponsoring an international conference on urban evangelism in Latin America, August 13-20, 1974.

Seventy participants drawn from nearly every Latin American country including the Caribbean, met in Belo Horizonte, Brazil, for a week of intensive study and discussion of the problems and challenges of urban evangelization. It was the first conference of this size to be dedicated exclusively to the study of today's urban world and the strategies to be followed in Christian mission to the city.

The conference approached "the city" from various angles. Morning sessions focused on a biblical theology for urban evangelism and the needs and characteristics of urban people. The role of mass media was examined and reports were heard regarding the actual effectiveness of radio, television, and literature evangelism in the city. Church growth was a paramount concern of the conference, and it was related to social concern and the need for changing the structure of society when these prove to be oppressive.

A number of models of urban church growth were presented, and their strengths and weaknesses considered. In short, the Belo Horizonte Conference blended theological, sociological, and practical studies in search of new and more effective ways to bring God's Good News to today's urban people.

This conference, a "first" in several ways, will undoubtedly serve as a spring board for regional and local conferences on "the city". Just as the Southern Baptists have become intensely aware of the urgency of Urban evangelization, it is hoped that other agencies and denominations will soon catch the vision of what an urbanizing world means for Christian mission. When conducted on a regional or local level, urban mission conferences should include elementary, practical training in growth-graphing for local church leaders, as well as an afternoon or two of field work.

The suggestion was made that a permanent center be established for the study of city evangelism and urban ministry. That same suggestion was made at the International Congress on World Evangelization at Lausanne. Perhaps it is a little too early for a full scale urban institute, but certainly we could begin by publishing a monthly or bi-monthly bulletin on the subject of urban ministry. It is of crucial importance right now that mission planners broaden their understanding of the city and of the strategies needed to disciple urban people and express Christ's Lordship among them.

SEOUL KOREA - September 1974

Sixty-five Christian leaders (secretaries of missionary societies, chaplains in the army, ministers, lay evangelists and missionaries - all Asians) met for two weeks in Seoul to study missionary work. Dr. David Cho, pastor of the Solid Rock Presbyterian Church in Seoul, and General Secretary of the Korea International Mission (KIM) raised the funds necessary to bring the 'students' and faculty there and convened the meeting. Dr. Samuel Kim (SWM ICG 1974) was the Dean of the Summer Institute of World Mission. The faculty included Drs. Kim, Cho, Tippett, Kraft, and McGavran who lectured every day and several others who taught one or two classes.

Of the 'students', 54 came from Korea, and 11 from South East Asia. Miss Chae Oak Chun, veteran missionary from EHWA University Mission to Pakistan had more missionary experience than any other 'student'. Emil Jabasingh and Samuel Thomas from India were secretaries of two new missionary societies based on India, and raising their funds entirely from India. Mr. Jabasingh's society called Friends Mission Prayer Bands and Mr. Samuel's called The India Evangelical Mission, send out respectively 65 and 28 Tamil speaking missionaries who go 1500 miles to North India into a totally different language and culture. Hundreds of Koreans also are proclaiming their readiness to go as missionaries.

This was the Second Annual Summer Institute. It bespeaks the new age in missions when, in addition to the missionaries from Eurica, Latfricasians by the hundreds and the thousands will be sent out by Latfricasian missionary societies and will be trained in Latfricasian training centers. Church Growth Bulletin salutes these pioneers and pays tribute to Dr. Cho's courage and vision.

CHURCH GROWTH † BULLETIN

Donald A. McGavran, B.D., Ph.D.
Editor

January 1975   Subscription $2 per year   Volume XI No. 3

C O N T E N T S

UNIVERSITY STUDENTS CAN PLANT CHURCHES   Dr. Joseph Arthur, SWM-ICG '72

With the rapid growth of the student population in cities, Churches and missionary societies are increasingly eager to find new ways of reaching the university campus with the Gospel.

These students are not "a problem" to world evangelization, they are the very people who, in the years to come, will evangelize the world - both the cities and the countrysides. But first, of course, the students must be evangelized, incorporated into churches, and transformed into reproductive Christians. They must be shown how to evangelize effectively. They must be taught how to multiply churches in cities. An actual experience in Philippine universities shows how this can happen. Here is the story.

THE CHRISTIAN AND MISSIONARY ALLIANCE
STUDENT MISSION IN THE PHILIPPINES.

Zamboanga, three days south of Manila by boat, is the third largest city in Mindanao with a population in 1972 of 199,901. It is leaping forward in commerce, education, and tourism, and has nearly 20,000 students in nine colleges and universities. Most Zamboangans are nominally Roman Catholics. Moslems and Protestants are small minorities.

Shortly after arriving in Zamboanga City in 1968, I started first Bible study cells on nine college campuses, and then city-wide youth rallies and a Student Youth Center in the downtown area. In three years, 1641 persons decided to receive Jesus Christ as their Saviour.

SEND news and articles to the Editor, Dr. Donald McGavran, at the Institute of Church Growth, Fuller Theological Seminary, 135 N. Oakland, Pasadena, California 91101. Published bi-monthly. Send subscriptions and changes of address to the Publisher, Norman L. Cummings, Overseas Crusades, Inc., 3033 Scott Blvd., Santa Clara, California 95050, U.S.A. Second-class postage paid at Santa Clara, California. Postmaster: Please send form 3579 to Overseas Crusades, 3033 Scott Blvd., Santa Clara, Ca. 95050.

From the beginning, "follow-up" was built into the program for spiritual growth and practical service of each convert. As soon as a student decided to give Jesus Christ His rightful place in his life, the student was enrolled in one of the "Character Development Clubs."

THE UNIVERSITY CAMPUSES WERE THE FIRST TARGET

The students in the "Character Development Clubs" were trained how to share their faith with fellow students. As soon as they became proficient they were placed on "Awareness Impact Teams". This meant that they had become aware of their evangelistic responsibility and were willing to make an impact among their fellow students.

THE COMMUNITY BECAME THE SECOND TARGET

Selected students from the "Awareness Impact Teams", especially those in homogeneous units on campus, were formed into "Mission Encounter Teams" for church multiplication out in the barrios of the city among their own relations. From studying the socio-ethnic groups on campus, we learned that Christian students of each given ethnic group can reach a community having a similar socio-ethnic background. These students form natural bridges to their own people. These bridges can be used for evangelism.

In Understanding Church Growth, McGavran gives numerous illustrations that "men like to become Christians without crossing racial, linguistic, or class barriers" (p. 198-215). Each member of a "Mission Encounter Team" seeks to persuade his intimate friends and relatives that it is thrilling to become a follower of the Lord. He loves his people and identifies with them. He proves that while he has become a Christian he is still a good member of his society.

Evangelism through the family is most important in the Philippines. The student should therefore establish a Bible class in his home or neighborhood. As several of these are established, they are brought together and form a "house-church".

PATTERNS FOR CHURCH PLANTING

A beautiful example of how students can plant churches is given by Dr. Roger Greenway in An Urban Strategy For Latin America. The "Church of the Resurrection in Christ" in Mexico City was started by young people who did house-to-house evangelism. In 1964, forty adult converts and, in 1966, sixty more were baptized. By 1970 one hundred families were connected with the church. Students are planting churches in other places than the Philippines.

CHURCH MULTIPLICATION IN ZAMBOANGA CITY

Let me tell about three successful church plantings. In Zamboanga, "Mission Encounter Teams" were formed in several homogeneous units on Campus. A map of Zamboanga marking the homogeneous units (linguistic and economic units) in the city was constructed. Areas were tested for

receptivity by two methods. The first was the resp[
witnessed to their families. The second was the ir
in visitation evangelism.

<u>1.</u> Students reported that ten homes in one of the homogeneou~
welcomed the Gospel. The ten students had become Christ's bridges
their homes. A house church was started. The head of the host family i~
in the service. One college student - a convert the year before - taught
a twenty minute Bible study each Tuesday for six weeks. This responsibility
was then passed to the head of a different family each week. The evening
consisted of informal fellowship, followed by singing, praying for one
another's problems and needs, and the Bible lesson.

The ten students were then encouraged to hold meetings in different
locations throughout the neighborhood on Sunday afternoon. At first we
thought these ten groups would be children's meetings, but the adults enjoyed the singing, Bible lessons and visual aids as much as the children.
While ten families were meeting on Tuesday evening, an average of over 100
were meeting each Sunday afternoon out under the trees.

<u>2.</u> Hermie Dubal studied at Zamboanga College of Art and Education. Her
mother and father operated a boarding house for students to supplement
the family budget. Each year twenty-five students made this boarding
house their home. Hermie reasoned that the best place to start a church
was right in her home.

Hermie joined a "Mission Encounter Team" and showed evangelistic
films in the boarding house each Saturday night, followed by an open fo-
fum. Unexpected blessings resulted. The neighbors crowded around the open
house at each showing, peering through the open windows, crowding on the
porch and making their way into the already packed room. Within six weeks
almost all the students had committed themselves to Christ and were under
baptismal instruction.

This house church will probably never build a traditional church
building. It will remain a house church, because these students go back
to their homes each year and start churches there.

<u>3.</u> The house church in Area Ten is Chinese. Several Chinese students and
two Chinese professionals found Christ as their Saviour. A local Chinese
congregation had split over an administrative matter. <u>Led by students,</u>
the young professionals and one segment of the congregation organized a
church in the home of a Chinese businessman. They worshipped on Sunday
morning and evening. Students and laymen lead the services. The forty
baptized members are today seeking property for the construction of a
new building.

STUDENTS CAN PLANT CHURCHES

Students can effectively multiply churches. A student ministry does
not persuade all students to join already existing evangelical churches.
Some students will not feel at home there. These are led to begin new

470

,ouse churches in the communities where they grew up. They will feel at
home there.

    Our ideal is to see churches characterized by indigenous forms, ful-
filling culturally relevant functions and conveying the Gospel. University students can multiply churches in cities.

```
ZPG? Yes!   ZEG? No!   ZCG? No, No!   MCG? Yes, Yes!!

The world is talking about ZPG:  Zero Population Growth
                             as Essential.
Men ask, "Will not ZPG automatically produce ZEG:  Zero
          Economic Growth -- Stagnation?"
Christians often face ZCG:  Zero Church Growth!!
          That's disastrous because, much more than
          Economic Growth, Church Growth means abundant
          life for millions.
Work steadily against ZCG and for MCG: Maximum Church Growth
```

USING INTERLOCKING DOCUMENTS IN JEWISH EVANGELISM   Beth Emanuel

    Eleven months ago Beth Emanuel was little more than a home Bible
study in Beverly Hills. Since then we - the members of Beth Emanuel -
have baptized 50 Jewish people and added most of them to our growing
congregation.

    One of the ways the Holy Spirit accomplished this amazing growth is
the "Interlocking Document Method" of discipleship-evangelism. The Holy
Spirit suggested the method to us from our study of Acts 2:41-42. We saw
that if we were to use Jewish homes to win Jewish people to Jesus, we
would need to prepare certain documents to lead the people step by step
from being inquirers in a home Bible study to becoming members of a congregation.

    Our first hurdle was to get unsaved Jewish people to home Bible
studies. We did this by making sure that the homes we used were Jewish
homes, owned and filled by other Jewish believers. Then we began to
break down most of the excuses Jewish unbelievers use in resisting home
Bible study invitations by focusing the Word of God on those excuses. The
Word of God did not return void, and our phone ministers began to use the
document we call "THE PHONE MINISTER'S RESISTANCE BREAKER" with success.
Our bus ministers then were able to bring more and more unsaved people to
our Jewish homes to re-discover the Old Testament and Messiah Jesus.

    Our second hurdle was to get our Jewish believers baptized. To do
this we had to show them it was a very Jewish thing to do. This required
a document which explained the Jewish origin and significance of water
baptism. Colossians 2:11-13 was very useful to us at this point because
from that text we saw that the rite of water baptism symbolized both a
spiritual mikvah (Jewish purification bath) and a spiritual bris (circumcision which makes one a Jew). Therefore, we began to call baptism the

"mikvah-bris of the spiritual Jew" and began to challenge Jewish people to become true spiritual Jews according to Romans 2:28-29. We preached like Peter in Acts 2:38, except we proclaimed, "Repent and experience the mikvah-bris every one of you in the name of Yeshua Ha Messhiach ('Jesus the Messiah' in Hebrew) for the forgiveness of your sins and you will receive the gift of the Holy Spirit." What followed was wonderful -- fifty people baptized in eleven months. The document explaining baptism which all fifty of these people were asked to read is called "THE PRACTICE OF THE MIKVAH-BRIS AS TAUGHT BY THE JEWISH NEW COVENANT."

Our third hurdle was to insure that baptism led to discipleship and incorporation into congregational membership in a local Body of Yeshua rather than backsliding and reversion. To do this we needed to show our Jewish people what the elementary requirements for discipleship are (according to Acts 2:41-42, Malachi 3:8-10, Hebrews 13:17 and other Scriptures). Also, we wanted each person to have ample warning against backsliding before he got baptized. This way each person would descend into the water knowing what he was becoming responsible for by taking Jesus as Lord. Our document, which includes an application for membership in congregation Beth Emanuel, is our "baptismal charge," read aloud to all people we baptize, and called "COUNTING THE COST BEFORE YOUR MIKVAH-BRIS."

Our fourth hurdle was to set up the previous three documents in such an interlocking and systematic way that we could begin to make many disciples. We saw that much would be gained by designating the last Lord's Day of the month as "Acts 2:41-42 Sunday." Such a climactic service would reap the harvest from each month's home Bible studies as new believers are baptized and stand to receive their first Lord's Supper or come forward to be received into membership. A typically Jewish pot-luck "Agape Feast" would make the day complete.

We also knew that the Lord's Supper started as a Passover Seder and that we would do well to refer to it as the Lord's Seder rather than the Lord's Supper. We took the relevant scriptures from a Hebrew New Testament and created an English/Hebrew Haggadah for a very Jewish observance of Holy Communion. Then we learned that the Lord's Supper, Jewishly observed, has evangelistic power. For, when the sacraments are publicly and properly administered, with only baptized believers allowed to receive the Lord's Supper, the Lord's Supper becomes a corporate sermon (I Cor. 11:27) calling men to make the faith-response of water baptism in order that they too may be no more excluded from the Lord's Supper. When Jewish people see that responding to the Gospel is a very Jewish thing to do, because baptism is a mikvah-bris and the Lord's Supper is a Seder, then the tension is on them to confess Jesus as Lord by getting into the water in order to receive the Lord's Supper. That discipling tension is applied the last Sunday of every month at Beth Emanuel, with proven success.

The last interlocking document is the climactic one, the membership manual. This is a beautiful blue notebook with Beth Emanuel written in gold letters. Every new member who fills out a membership application and

signs a statement of faith receives one. In it are explained in detail
all the discipleship requirements which the believer agreed to observe in
principle when he applied for membership. These include tithing, local
commitment to the Body of the Lord, pastoral accountability, and cate-
chetical material. These manuals are given to new members on "Acts 2:42
Sunday."

Thus, step by step, the interlocking documents help to lead the
Jewish believer into the commitment of mature discipleship.

God has taught us in Beth Emanuel that making disciples is drawing
lines and persuading men to cross them. When we ask Jewish people to respond in faith to Jesus by getting into the water, standing up to take the
broken Matzoh of the Lord's Supper, or coming forward to receive the membership manual, we are drawing the lines sharply and unambiguously. The
result is - Jewish disciples. Praise the Lord. It is our prayer that
the Holy Spirit will bless this material that He has given to us. For
"herein is My Father glorified, that ye bear much fruit; so shall ye be
My disciples." (John 15:8).

In Yeshua's Name.
The People of Beth Emanuel

CHURCH BURNINGS IN INDIA

Russell Chandler in five columns of the Los Angeles Times
of November 9th, 1974, tells of 37 churches burned to the
ground in Northeast India, fifty-three Christians physically assaulted, and more than 300 families driven off
their land. The Indian Government has neither prevented
nor punished this grave infringement of the Indian Constitution which 'guarantees' religious liberty. Readers
of Church Growth Bulletin are urged to write:

The Indian Ambassador, The Indian Embassy, 2107
Massachusetts Avenue, Washington, C.D. 20009

vigorously protesting this persecution and asking that
the Government of India live up to its high ideals and
bring persecution speedily to an end.

CHURCH GROWTH IN THE HEART OF AFRICA   Donald Hohensee

((The recent massacres of Hutus by Tutsis focussed world attention on
Burundi, the following compact account of church growth there will interest readers. (Much more significant than the massacres) it will also
lead readers to wonder whether, in the Protestant sectors of the land,
main line missions could not have achieved the kind of growth the Pentecostals did. Mr. Hohensee's account presents tantalizing suggestions
bearing on the question.   The Editor))

Burndi in the center of Africa, shaped like a heart, has been called the Switzerland of Africa, because of the scenic beauty of its high plateau and many mountains. It covers only 10,747 square miles, about the size of the state of Maryland, yet 3,500,000 people call Burundi home. Only two per cent live in cities, the rest on little garden-farms. The "hill" is the first level of government. Each hill has its elders who maintain law and order.

Three tribes live in Burundi. The pygmies, who account for one per cent of the population, have remained resistant to the Gospel - or is it neglected? The Hutu, who make up eighty-five per cent and the Tutsi who are fourteen per cent, have been very responsive to the Gospel.

Burundi was highly resistant to outside influence until the 1890's. It fought off the slavers who attempted to take its people. Several attempts to establish Christian missions ended in failure, until 1898 when the White Fathers established a Roman Catholic Mission at Muyaga. About 2,000,000 are now Roman Catholics.

For all practical purposes the modern Protestant mission work in Burundi started in 1935, when the Church Missionary Society, the Free Methodists, the Kansas Yearly Meeting of Friends and the Swedish Pentecostals started working in Burundi. World Gospel Mission joined the Free Methodists in 1939. World Grace Testimony entered in 1940 and made its work over to the Immanuel Mission (Plymouth Brethren) in 1949. At least 300,000 are now Protestants.

All missions emphasized three basic activities--education, medicine and evangelism. Hundreds of classrooms were built and thousands of young people were taught. Each mission station had either a dispensary or a hospital. All schools served as churches. Many small chapels were built. All missions experienced vigorous church growth from about 1945 to 1959, the Pentecostals most of all.

Beginning in 1959, all Protestants except Pentecostals and Adventists slowed down. Some hindering factors were: 1. A strong spirit of materialism entered the country and the Church. 2. Missions followed an indigenous policy and, with independence approaching, turned all positions of responsibility over to the church leaders. Missionaries stepped too far back and thereby hindered church growth. 3. Conflict arose between the lesser educated preachers and the better educated primary school teachers, who were influential because of their education. Many Christians went back to beer drinking and other vices. 4. Africans occupying church positions of responsibility had to give time and energy to these problems and had little left for spiritual direction and evangelism. 5. Political problems within the country had a definite effect on the Church. 6. Many small hill churches were closed because of a "shortage of workers."

The smaller denominations, which in the early 1950's had experienced 300-500% growth, in the 1960's experienced 50-75% growth. However, Pentecostals and Adventists continued vigorously to grow. Both Churches, but especially the Pentecostals, put only minor emphasis on education and medicine and major on establishing churches.

The Pentecostals worked primarily amongst the southern clans. The Adventists worked within the Imbo along the Ruzizi. These people are Hutu and Tutsi as elsewhere in the country but they are of different clans. In colonial days they gave the Belgians difficulty. The Catholics, who were having tremendous success elsewhere, left them alone. The Protestants began to evangelize them. Many responded and have continued to respond. The Free Methodists and Anglicans planted churches amongst them too. Until the trouble in 1972, one of the Free Methodist's shining examples of growth was within this district.

Whereas the other Churches closed hill churches, the Pentecostals continued to establish new ones. In addition to the proclamation of the Gospel, they emphasized visitation, prayer for the sick in their homes, and the casting out of evil spirits. Their church government is much less centralized than most Protestant Churches and has a distinct advantage in that the man appointed to represent his district before government lives in that district and can deal with his problems without waiting for any "central officer" to come.

Adventists have emphasized Sabbath Schools. Average attendance outnumbers communicant membership. Adult Sabbath School attendance is 13,762, total attendance is 17,612 and communicants are 9270. The "communities" (four times communicants) of the major Protestant Churches were as follows according to 1968 World Christian Handbook:

Anglicans	43,223
Pentecostals	158,792
Free Methodists	18,000
Friends	10,800
Baptists	7,527
World Gospel Mission	3,411
Total	241,853

It seems reasonable to estimate at least 300,000 in 1975. The peoples of Burundi are still - after the 'trouble' - responsive to the message of salvation. Missionaries and church leaders are attempting to correct past mistakes. They are believing God for greater things in the future.

WILLIAMS-OUSLER DEBATE: WHAT IS EVANGELISM?

Ousler: The NCCC is Through With Evangelism!
Williams: Wrong! The NCCC is for evangelism which, however, means allowing Christ to show us what His life means for us today.

"If, when 'Christ-centered concepts' are laid before men they do not become disciples of Christ, that is poor evangelism....Unless fantastic numbers of new churches are started and whole populations are discipled, there will be little Christianization of the myriad social orders which compose mankind....Stepping up the devotion of existing Christians is not evangelism: it is perfecting....Evangelism is not theologically correct pronouncements, or sociologically reasonable policies which ought to bring men to Christ and multiply churches. Evangelism is what does multiply churches...."

The above excerpts are found on pages 188-189 of the bound volume of Church Growth Bulletins 1964-68. Four hundred pages of exciting contemporary church growth theory, practice, illustrations, arguments, and rebuttal.....A wonderful "Reader in Church Growth" for your church library or your laymen studying ways of getting your church evangelizing effectively. $4.95 from William Carey Library, 305 Pasadena Avenue, South Pasadena, Ca., 91030. ($2.97 to members of Church Growth Book Club)

1980....DOES THE SALVATION ARMY LEAD THE WAY?   The Editor

A World Wide Congress in 1980 to consider the evangelization of the (by then) 3.3 billion who have not heard of Christ and cannot hear of him by the near-neighbor evangelism of existing Christians! That is what 1 9 8 0 means. Executives are talking about it in many mission boards. It is on the agenda of many missionaries. The prayer calendars of thousands of missionary minded Christians in all walks of life include 1980.

Top leaders of the Salvation Army gathered at Lausanne drew up a Statement On World Evangelization. Item number 9 reads as follows:

"We respectfully propose the convening of a world-wide Salvation Army Conference on Evangelism in 1978, as part of the 'Still a Salvation Army' theme....."

Many denominatins and missionary societies are pricked in the heart about their own little growth in days of great opportunity. For example, the United Church of Christ in USA, noting that its membership has declined from 2.06 million in 1964 to 1.89 million in 1973 is calling its people to renewed evangelism. Concern about leaving multitudes of non-Christians to live and die without Christ is also rising. Many will gather in regional, synodical, and diocesan gatherings. Continent-wide conventions and congresses will be held. Or, following the Salvation Army example, world-wide consultations on effective evangelism will be convened. The cost of such gatherings will come from denominational and mission board sources.

Only a small projection is needed to escalate these many regional meetings into one world-wide gathering which makes the discipling of the (by then) Three Point Three Billion its special business. This Gathering will focus on the 87 per cent who can be reached by E2 and E3 Evangelism only. It will report on what segments are being effectively evangelized, where churches are multiplying and where they are not. It will describe methods which God is currently blessing to the multiplication of believers. It will pin point the real road blocks and state what needs to be done to

blast them or go around them. It will pray that every creature may hear
the Gospel in his own language and culture. It will actively seek to
"disciple ta ethne".

Church Growth Bulletin respectfully requests executives of all
missionary societies - there are hundreds of these in all countries - to
put on the agenda and keep on the agenda Plans for 1 9 8 0. Editors,
please let us have articles in Missiology, Evangelical Missions Quarterly,
International Review of Missions, and the house organs of all missionary
societies discussing 1 9 8 0. The Lausanne Continuation Committee ought
to put 1980 high on its agenda. And would it not be sensible to hope that
the World Council of Churches and the Lausanne Continuation Committee
would jointly plan a world gathering devoted strictly to great commission
mission. All the good things, which denominations and missions are now
doing and should do, but which are not aimed directly at bringing men to
Christ and churching the unchurched would be firmly excluded, and all the
vast and fascinating variety of enterprises which are unashamedly dedicated to carrying out the Great Commission would be eagerly included.
Believing this to be a sufficiently Christian aim, Church Growth Bulletin
respectfully invites the leaders of both the WCC and the LCC to put 1980
on their agenda. We do not care how it arises - from the top down or the
bottom up - so long as in the near future the Churches of Christ everywhere focus on the evangelization and discipling of the (at present in
January 1975) Three Billion.

REDEPLOYING MISSION RESOURCES   Charles D. Meliis

The delegates at Willingen said, as they reviewed the situation
around the world, that the missionary enterprise is in great measure a
colossal system of inter-church aid, with relatively little pioneer
evangelistic advance.....

We can hear what was said at Willingen and re-deploy our resources
toward sharing the faith with some of the still unreached peoples (tribes,
castes, classes, new urban groupings). Many of these distinctive peoples
are more apt to listen to foreigners (even to westerners) than to their
near neighbors.

Such redeployment will have its problems. Further research is needed
to redeploy effectively. The wrenching changes for mid-career fraternal
workers will be traumatic - but less so than redeployment to state side
ministries. Period of transitional study may provide a primary aid -
both to those taking up these pioneer evangelistic tasks, and those who
will return to service ministries. Presbyterians are the logical ones to
set the pace on both research and mid-career study. We believe in acting
on an informed basis. Missions Update, September '74.

(Comment: And not only Presbyterians!! If the Three Billion are to
hear and have the chance to become disciples of Christ, a great deal of
re-deployment will be done by most Churches and most mission boards.
We live in exciting times.   The Editor.)

EVERYTHING YOU NEED TO GROW A MESSIANIC SYNAGOGUE rev'd. - D. McGavran

Buy the book of the above title from Church Growth Book Club. You may be missionizing in Macedonia or Malawi where there are no Jews - still buy this book. You may be the minister of the First Baptist Church of El Paso and have no idea of starting a Messianic Synagogue - still buy it.

1. Because it sets forth clearly an adaptation to culture which takes culture very seriously and at the same time is thoroughly faithful to the Bible.

2. Because, using this method, a Messianic Synagogue (A Christian Church thoroughly adapted to Jewish culture) has been established in a typical American Jewish community. This synagogue congregation grew from nothing to 80 in two years. It contains seventy baptized believers in Yeshua Messiah from Jewish background and ten from Gentile background. The method described in this book despite appearing far out, has been blessed of God to the creation of a true church made up very largely of Messianic Jews.

3. Because, the vigorous evangelistic approach is refreshing. Here is no temporizing, no beating about the bush, no mealy mouthed obscuring of the biblical imperative. Rev. Phil Goble, the author, unashamedly wants others to become disciples of Christ and tells them so.

4. Because, after you read this your mind will erupt with new ideas as to how you can adjust your church more effectively to your culture. Yours may be Chinese, Indonesian, or Ayamara culture - no matter. After reading Goble's book you will want to tinker with your communion service, your Bible study, your preaching and teaching to make them more biblical and more indigenous. Gain true missiological insight!

The book will be off press (William Carey Library) in early 1975. It will cost about $1.50. Send in your order now. Be FIRST to get one.

TEACHING ILLITERATE CHRISTIANS TO READ THE BIBLE   Robert F. Rice

Literacy and Evangelism, Inc. (LEI) serves evangelical missions and churches where adult illiteracy is a problem. With headquarters in Tulsa, this service agency has assisted over thirty denominations and missions.

Half the adult world cannot read. Over ten million illiterate Christians live in the world. The Bible is available in over 1,500 languages but to the non-reader it remains a closed book.

The goals of Literacy and Evangelism, Inc. are: to enable Christians to read scripture and to instruct them how to teach non-Christians to read it. Literacy evangelism aids missions and churches teach illiterate Christians. Such teaching provides an ideal climate for sharing one's faith. LEI likes what Understanding Church Growth says. "The open Bible should be made available as an essential part of redemption...This involves teaching illiterate Christians to read the Bible as a religious duty...The omission of this duty, as of giving to the Church, attending worship, or holy living, is sin." (p. 266)

LEI does everything in literacy, from preparing Bible-oriented primers in any language to conducting workshops and teacher seminars. Bible primer manuscripts have been prepared in 24 languages. I serve overseas six months annually at the request of Churches and missions.

Literacy evangelism opens the Bible to many even where missions have not been previously welcomed. It provides satisfying activities of national Christians. Most importantly, it creates a climate for conversion.

Using Rice primers and teaching methods, an illiterate can be reading on his own in two to twelve weeks. Once taught, he can teach non-Christians. Literacy evangelism is a good way to bring non-reading peoples to Christ.

LEI has applied for membership in the EFMA and IFMA. Its support, coming from evangelical churches and individuals, enables it to give its services free of charge to overseas churches and missions in any language. A small number of full time literacy evangelism workers are stationing themselves in the more populous language areas, and serving evangelical missions and churches. For example, Rev. Jung Won Suh, supported by the Sam Duk Presbyterian Church of Taegu, does literacy evangelism in Indonesia. Other Korean missionaries also are preparing for literacy evangelism. Latfricasian missionaries frequently find literacy evangelism useful. LEI teaches them and prepares Bible oriented primers in the language in which they evangelize.

For information as to free literacy evangelism aid, write: Literacy and Evangelism, Inc., Suite 13, 2250 49th St., Tulsa, Okla. 74105.

SINGAPORE July 1974

Bishop Chandu Ray in the COFAE Newsletter lists ten notable aspects in the evangelization of Asia. Four have a close bearing on church growth.

1. The door is wide open now, in a number of countries, for preaching the Gospel. Many have not heard the good news (hundreds of millions, in fact!!)

2. There is need to recognize the supernatural and demonic possession of many people in Asia and to preach the Gospel of liberation with demonstration.

3. There is an urgent need to change the existing image of a status-seeking Christianity with its rich relations in the West to a servant people of God.

4. Missionaries, especially those of Asian origin, are urgently needed to carry the Gospel.

A NORTHERN DISTRICT: COUNTRY X, August 1974

"A few minutes ago I received a report that twenty-two Muslim families in a northern district have requested Christian teaching. Their leaders told a missionary, "All the people in this land are going to become Christian so it is wise for us to be among the first". I find it difficult to be so sanguine about reaping; but I am sure that such an approach by a responsible group of citizens is unparalled in this land."

((Comment: In that land, yes; but in several other lands groups of Muslims have not only asked for instruction but have become Christians. There is good reason to believe that Muslims, too, in increasing numbers are going to find abundant life in Jesus Christ, whom the Koran calls Ruh-i-Allah. Blessed be His Name. The Editor))

CHURCH GROWTH ✝ BULLETIN

Donald A. McGavran, B.D., Ph.D.
Editor

MARCH 1975　　　　　Subscription $2 per year　　　　Volume XI No. 4

C O N T E N T S

BIG THINGS AHEAD IN MISSIONS

Thousands of missionaries and hundreds of missionary societies are required to evangelize the three billion. Pulling missionaries out of recently established Churches and sending them to the "yet to believe" is today's essential strategy. Old missionary societies should increase their sendings. New missionary societies forming in Latfricasia should thrust out reapers.

March '75 Bulletin explores this second exciting resource. Dr. Cho of Seoul, vigorous advocate of Asian Missions, points out key issues. Dr. Kamalesan, noted Indian Methodist describes an India-based society which keeps 65 Indian missionaries in the field. Dr. McGavran sets forth the basics of all missionary orders. Dr. Williams of India gives us the constitution of the India Evangelical Mission which keeps 27 Indian missionaries at work. David Moore describes emergency measures taken by a new Church in Kalimantan to keep a huge surge of growth flowing freely. A Lutheran in Canada asks what ethnicity means to missionary societies seeking to propagate the Gospel. Readers will find this issue a mind stretching experience.　　　　　　　　　　　　　　　　　The Editor

ASIAN MISSION AND CHURCH GROWTH　　　　　　by David J. Cho

In the first half of the seventies, we see clearly that the Third World is making progress toward engaging in sending missions. Asia is standing at the front of Third World Mission Development. The All-Asia

SEND news and articles to the Editor, Dr. Donald McGavran, at the Institute of Church Growth, Fuller Theological Seminary, 135 N. Oakland, Pasadena, California 91101. Published bi-monthly. Send subscriptions and changes of address to the Publisher, Norman L. Cummings, Overseas Crusades, Inc., 3033 Scott Blvd., Santa Clara, California 95050, U.S.A. Second-class postage paid at Santa Clara, California. Postmaster: Please send form 3579 to Overseas Crusades, 3033 Scott Blvd., Santa Clara, Ca. 95050.

Mission Consultation, Seoul '73, opened a channel connecting 14 Asian countries for cooperation in carrying out the Great Commission.

The First Summer Institute of World Mission with 67 participants was held in a quiet scenic suburb of Seoul right after the Seoul '73 Consultation. In September 1974 the second Summer Institute of World Mission drew 64 participants. In it fifteen young mission leaders from India, Pakistan, Indonesia, Thailand, Malaysia and Hong Kong were trained together with fifty young Koreans. All were potential or actual mission leaders. These two short-term Institutes have brought new insights about World Evangelization. Zeal for mission with foggy directions and random methods has been replaced with a zeal for mission replete with clear insights as to how to deal with mission problems in concrete terms.

Clear thinking about Christian Mission is greatly needed. Many Asian and African church leaders stress the necessity of the Third World Mission; but vast confusion reigns in regard to its directions, approaches, and methods. let me cite some concrete cases.

1. Some Asian Missions claim they have already started the Third World Mission just because they lend a few Asians to institutions maintained by Western Missionary Societies.

2. Some Asians actually hallucinate! They believe they are carrying out Third World Mission simply because they have dispatched a medical doctor, nurse or technician to a hospital established by Westerners, and because they have filled positions once occupied by Western personnel and now vacant because of the anti-western sentiment in many nations.

3. Third World Christian leaders try to justify a claim to "sending missionaries" because they exchange professors or students with other Asian countries.

4. Some Asian Missions send out one or two missionary families at random to this place and that without doing any dependable research as to the responsiveness of the field, and without stating clearly the goals they will work for. Thus they spend much money and get no good fruit at all.

5. It is also unfortunately true that among the Third World Missionaries some are going around from country to country, after they have "worked in one mission field" just 3 or 4 years.

How can we stop all these confusions? My firm conviction is that if we start any Asian mission without establishing a strong institution for carrying out detailed studies of various fields, accurate research in evangelistic openings, and effective training, we will simply create further chaos.

We have to plow, seed, cultivate and harvest many mission fields. We have to intend effective church growth and bend all our efforts toward really communicating the Gospel. We have to plant thousands or ten thousands of churches in the unevangelized fields. We cannot make ourselves to be satisfied with merely sending a few missionary families to this place and that at random without having a definite plan or purpose.

It is my considered opinion that we have to set up a well-equipped Study Center for the tremendous task of Asian evangelization during the coming 25 years. At this Study Center we will develop concrete plans and year by year set them forth. As these are carried out, we will observe and modify them. In the Seoul '73 All-Asia Mission Consultation, Asian mission leaders resolved to take these responsibilities upon themselves.

The first and second Summer Institute of World Mission clearly stated what was needed to raise up, develop, mobilize and train effectively the potential mission resources in Asia.

In August-September 1975 when the third Summer Institute of World Missions will be held at Seoul, the East-West Center for Missionary Research and Development (which I have been calling the Study Center) will be launched in Seoul. It will offer a full year's study program. A site totalling 300 acres has been donated. A building program is under way.

For the last century, while institutional mission projects have enjoyed their prosperity, church growth has been very slow in many Asian fields. It may be that one reason why western missions are recently suffering is because they turned back from church planting ministry and became founders and managers of hospitals, schools, broadcasting stations, and publication press, and the like.

Now there arises a new Asian force. It will plow the wide Asian fields and multiply new churches. We pray that God will let it bear fruit 30 times, 60 times or 100 times.

One of the things which the drive to evangelize Asia must do is to build up missionary societies which have a firm base in their supporting congregations. The Friends Missionary Prayer Bands of Tamilnadu, India, is a splendid example of the kind of Asian Missionary Society which we must have. It has four hundred prayer bands - local missionary societies in village churches. The members of these bands are committed to praying for the evangelization of North India, praying for the missionaries they send out, and sending money to missionary society headquarters. Friends Missionary Prayer Bands now send out 65 missionary couples and send them salary steadily. This is essential procedure in all Asian denominations if Asians are to evangelize Asia.

The Continuation Committee of the All-Asia Mission Consultation of 1973 decided to organize an Asian Mission Association by the end of 1975 in order to carry out this task and to spread its fervent zeal like wild fire throughout the Asian continent. It decided to put 100 Asian missionaries into Thailand and Kalimantan as its first united action.

Since that Consultation in 1973, various Asian countries have sent as missionaries (or trained in preparation for sending) as many as 200 individuals. Many more Asian Christians ought to dedicate their lives to accomplish the tremendous task of carrying out the Great Commission in Asia. Those called to mission will have to unite various attempts at Asian evangelization into an effective cooperative enterprise. Now at the beginning of the Asian mission, overwhelming interest in this East-West Center for Missionary Research and Development must be stirred up. Under God it will create collective effort for evangelism and church growth.

BASICS OF EFFECTIVE MISSIONS ANYWHERE   BY Donald McGavran

Dr. David Cho's fine article comes first in this symposium because, as Latfricasian Christians hear Christ's call to disciple the tribes, castes, classes and kindreds of earth, mistakes are being made. Dr. Cho describes some of these. The opportunities are too great and the times are too urgent to permit us to regard as normal an extended period of trial and error. True, as Eurican missionary societies began, they often went through a long groping period. They made plenty of mistakes, but there is no need to repeat them. Today, new missionary societies - both in Latfricasia and Eurica - ought to learn from and avoid the mistakes of their predecessors.

The missionary movement presents many successful models. Those who would start new missionary societies can study these and determine the ingredients of success. The School of World Mission at Pasadena is offering courses specially designed to enable founders of new missionary societies to enter upon their important ministry with the information they need to have. The subject is enormous and this brief article can only sketch the barest outlines of what missionary societies have found effective. Of course, that very effective missionary campaign recorded in the book of Acts did not use all these basics. Today also it may be that some bands of Christians will propagate the Gospel on models different from that which I describe. If they propagate the Gospel, if they multiply churches of Christ, if they bring multitudes to faith in Jesus Christ, the methods are not important. Notwithstanding all this, I offer the six basics below in the hope that employing them will enable new missionary societies to avoid false starts and waste of precious resources, and to disciple multitudes whom God has prepared to hear His voice.

First, the missionary society must create bands of Christians who burn with desire to tell others about Jesus. Unless groups of Christians who, believing that it is God's unswerving purpose to save men through faith in Jesus Christ, begin to march under the Great Commission, no new missionary society is going to prosper. It is no accident that one of the missionary societies reported in this issue publishes a monthly magazine called "Burn Out". Senders and sent must be willing to burn out for Christ, before a missionary society becomes possible. The biblical base is essential. Utter dedication to Christ is required. Utter clarity as to the purpose is of the essence. New missionary societies must avoid the error of supposing that in a very expensive fashion they are going abroad to help some existing denomination. Missionaries, sent out by the Holy Spirit, go to tell those who have never heard The Name, to multiply churches of Christ where there are yet none.

Second, the missionary society must create a system of support.
Granted that under some circumstances the missionary (like Paul) can earn
his own living and immigrants to a new city or a new land can establish
churches which then grow by near-neighbor evangelism, the weight of evidence favors a business like system of support. It is terribly expensive
in life as well as money to send missionaries to some new language area
and have them come back in a few months or years because their support
has ceased. Fortunately, the first basic is readily parlayed into the
second. If senders have the conviction, they readily build substantial
ongoing support systems.

Third, most new missionary societies should select reasonably responsive populations. Today these are found in almost every country. The
steady goal, to disciple ta ethne and establish ongoing churches, can be
carried out in most nations. The new society should therefore spend its
first funds in intelligent selection of a suitable field. The rule which
guided missionary societies during the nineteenth century ' "Go where no
one has been before" - is currently not a good rule. Today's rule, specially for beginning societies, is "Find populations in which many want to
become Christians, but are not being evangelized. Go there."

Together with finding a suitable population should go sending a band
of missionaries. Sending one Asian missionary to one nation and another to
another, there to work as a part of a Eurican team in some institution
built by Eurican funds, is not a fruitful custom. It forces Asian missionaries to adjust not only to the people being evangelized but to Eurican
colleagues. Asian missionary societies should send out bands of Asian
missionaries who will find comradeship and spiritual support from fellow
workers who come from the same sending churches, eat the same kind of
food, speak the same mother tongue, and are free to devote their whole
energy to evangelizing those to whom God has sent them.

Fourth, train missionaries before they go out the first time and on
their first and second furlough. Furlough means 'a training time' as well
as 'a time to report to the comrades who send'. What Dr. Cho says about the
urgent need of training is true. The rise of Latfricasian missionary societies by the hundreds must also mean the creation of many Latfricasian missionary training centers. There should be one in every main region of the
world. In these, books like Understanding Christian Mission by Herbert Kane,
my own Understanding Church Growth and others would be beginning texts; but
much more must be written specially to fit Latfricasian conditions. Most
missionaries sent out by Indian missionary societies, for example, will not
be equipped with jeeps, refrigerators and other appurtenances of a sinfully
affluent society. They will be more like the medieval missionary orders
composed of men and women pledged to obedience, devotion and poverty. We
shall see thousands of barefoot missionaries in the years ahead - and some
of them may well come from Eurica. Training systems and books to prepare
these to communicate Christ and multiply churches are needed.

Fifth, missionary societies have two tasks. They must keep both the
senders and the sent blessed and marching under the great commission.
Honest accounts, capable administration and patient understanding, done

from high biblical ground are essential. The missionary society must keep the flame of utter devotion to world evangelization burning brightly at home and abroad.

Sixth, the missionary society must be flexible. Better methods come in. Some fields close. Others open. New missionaries arrive. Adjustments to the new churches, which will be established by the hundreds, are part of the job. All this and much more calls for great flexibility while remaining utterly committed to bringing ta ethne to the obedience of the faith (Romans 16:25). Missionary societies must operate in the light of feedback concerning the degree to which the Gospel has been propagated and churches have been multiplied. That means flexibility.

ARE YOU BEATEN BACK FROM JOYFUL PERSUASION?

A missionary in Italy writes, "I present Christ for the sole sufficient reason that he deserves to be presented."

We think our brother mistakenly uses the words 'sole' and 'sufficient'. Christ does, of course, deserve to be presented. But we present Him that men may find the way to the Father, obtain forgiveness of sins, eternal life, and power to live as sons of God. We evangelize that men may become disciples of Christ and responsible members of His Church. We ought never say: "We care nothing what you do. All we care about is that we present Christ, because He deserves to be presented."

Denying that evangelism is essentially persuasion, commanded by Christ, demonstrated by the apostles, urgently needed by men perishing without the Bread of Heaven, is unnecessary. Christians are needlessly beaten back from a soundly biblical position.

Persuasion, of course, is often not successful. Men are free to reject it. Men may choose the broad way and harden their hearts against God's gracious call. This is tragic for them; but nothing is gained by the evangelist affirming that he presents Christ, never intending persuasion and conversion.

The goal of evangelism is that men believe on Jesus Christ and find eternal life. We are called joyfully to tell others about Jesus, expecting that they will believe on Him and be saved. Let us boldly and obediently carry out our calling.

THE FRIENDS' MISSIONARY PRAYER BAND   by   Dr. Samuel Kamalesan

"Friends' Missionary Prayer Band" is a movement. In the mid-fifties the Vacation Bible Schools in the southern states in India - Tamilnadu, Kerala, Karnataka and Andra Pradesh - had achieved significant results. The children and youth, who had discovered dynamic Life by faith in Jesus Christ through "Re-birth", over the ten to fifteen year period of the fruitful ministry of VBS, were now responsible young adults. They were asking themselves how to live this LIFE in Christ Jesus in the context of the changing Indian society. These questions led to the meeting of a small group of leaders from the functioning teams of the VBS for prayer and action. Their inescapable responsibility for the "hither-to-unreached" became clear. The result is the on-going of the movement called VBS in the functioning structure of FMPB.

((Comment by Editor...Some would call the Friends' Missionary Prayer Band a missionary order or a missionary society. It is an effective organization. In 1974 it was sending out 65 missionary families from South India across 1000 miles and great linguistic and cultural barriers to North India. Missionaries receive slightly less salary than pastors in the sending churches - in United States money less than $40 per month.

In the fascinating story which Dr. Kamalesan tells, we see an effective missionary society taking shape. It marches under the Great Commission. Its magazine, entitled "Burn Out", calls on senders and sent to give themselves utterly to the missionary passion. It establishes churches and expects them to become in turn part of the missionary movement and to be a part of the Friends Missionary Prayer Band. It is entirely Indian and has only Indians of proved dedication as its leaders.

As Churches (denominations) in Latfricasia enter upon a period of mighty multiplication of missionary societies, they would do well to study carefully the movement reported by Dr. Samuel Kamalesan, new Vice President of World Mission, but till recently the pastor of Emanuel Methodist Church in Madras, India. The missionary society rose out of normal vigorous Christian life.))

As the name implies, the movement is a band of prayer groups. Believers who have seen the possibilities and realities of the Kingdom of God in their own experience, gather together to pray for the guidance in effectively sharing their knowledge of Jesus Christ with those who are yet to know Him. This is the motivation for their being together in prayer. Since in this enterprise denominational barriers and distinctions become vague, they call themselves as "friends."

Soon, the praying "friends" who were under the compulsion of the Missionary Vision, were called of God to provide the means - the wherewithall - for commissioning and sending forth those of their number who were called of God to 'Go and tell'. Thus, the friends chose for themselves the motto, 'Go or send'. A pattern was emerging.

When the Lord began to answer their prayers, the friends began to commit themselves in terms of a structure that their function demanded.

Each individual prayer group was made aware of similar prayer groups within their Talug (township), District (County) and State. Responsible persons were invited to maintain this structural awareness between the bands of praying friends.

God began to call the praying friends to assume personal responsibilities for the ongoing Mission of Jesus Christ within the Indian Situation. They began to express their response in terms of setting-apart those called to 'go'. Members who remained accepted the responsibility to pray and support financially the members 'called'. In the final analysis everyone in the prayer band felt 'called' to fulfill the unfinished task in a personal way. A central office was established. A Board to guide the activities of the movement in terms of its simple goals came into existence. Both staff members and board members were already members of local prayer bands.

In order to keep the fast growing prayer bands aware of the overall results and the area results, an annual meeting of the praying friends in each district and each state was planned and brought into being. During these meetings, the friends respond to the details about God's doings in concrete action. The response to the unfinished task from youth consenting to become the 'sent ones' has been an increasing reality.

The praying friends set goals for themselves. They sent missionaries into unreached areas of India. A 'sending area' over against a 'receiving area' was defined geographically. Tamilnadu, Kerala, Karnataka, Andhra Pradesh, and the Northeastern States in India have responded to the Gospel more abundantly than the rest of India. These states are therefore called "sending area".

Within the "rest of India" there are at least 220 district headquarter cities. The praying friends purpose to place at least two missionaries in each one of these headquarters within the next ten years. The friends have already experienced the responsibility that a successful program brings. The 'sent ones' have found that the response from the people within one 'receiving area' has now made it also a 'sending area.'

As the movement gathered momentum, Tamilnadu, which was (and is) the most productive of all the sending areas, was divided into north, central, and south, each with an area office for service and development. When the number of 'sent ones' increased within the 'receiving areas' a field office was established in Jhansi, North India, and a director was sent there. So the movement moves on.

The history of God's people has already proved that not all the words and acts can fully express that which is felt and known by the people of God as their total experience. This inadequacy has often been overcome by poetic expressions through songs. The praying friends have compiled for themselves the "Songs of Action." They have their official publications: "Challenge" in Tamil and "Burn Out" in English. The accent in all this has been disciplined self-giving.

Until what "ought to be" is, someone must give himself or herself. It is only at the point of self-giving that principles and persons are brought together in one functioning whole.

So the movement called Friends' Missionary Prayer Band moves on. The praying friends invite all who are in Christ to become friends in prayer with them.

THE INDIAN EVANGELICAL MISSION   by   Theodore Williams

1.   History: The EFI executive committee met on January 15, 1965, to form the Indian Evangelical Mission. The Indian members of the committee became the founder members of the Board of the Mission. Thus the Indian Evangelical Mission was born.

2.   Objectives: The Mission has a two fold objective: a) To take the Gospel of Jesus Christ to the unevangelized areas in India and outside India. b) To challenge Indian Christians to realize their responsibility for world evangelization and to recognize their partnership with other Christians in the world in fulfilling this task.

3.   Basic Principles: The motto of the Mission is found in Isaiah 54:2, "Enlarge...stretch forth....spare not." It rests on the three pillars of VISION, FAITH AND SACRIFICE. The mission is indigenous, interdenominational and evangelical.

4.   Financial policy: The mission is indigenous in finance, membership and government. It looks to God In faith for Its support. This comes through the freewill offerings of God's people, individuals or churches in India. No funds are solicited from abroad.

5.   IEM and The Church: The IEM is an inter-denominational missionary society. It does not seek to establish another denomination or to compete with the existing denominations. It does not enter into any area where any church is actively working. The believers will be linked with the existing evangelical church.

In areas where there is no church, the Mission will encourage believers to form themselves into worshipping congregations. The missionaries in that area and the believers together seek the Lord's will and agree together upon the form of church order and government that they desire in consultation with the IEM Board.

6.   IEM and Other Missions: The Mission believes in the spiritual oneness of all believers in the Body of Christ and seeks to cooperate with those of like faith everywhere. Where necessary, it will enter into partnership in countries outside India with international fellowships which agree with our principles and policies.

At present the IEM has entered into such a partnership with the Overseas Missionary Fellowship for work in East Asia and with the Bible and Medical Missionary Fellowship for work in West Asia.

THE EVANGELIZATION OF MAINLAND CHINA

For the first time since in 1949 Communist Rule was established in China, a major international conference will discuss spreading the Christian message throughout the People's Republic of China. It is scheduled for September 9 to 13 in Manila, and convened by evangelical organizations whose love for China supercedes all political and ideological considerations. The conference will bring together overseas Chinese and Westerners from all over the world to lay the foundation for effective communication of the Gospel and multiplication of Christian churches to China's millions.

EMERGENCY MEASURES IN KALIMANTAN   David Moore   SWM 1975

In the decades ahead as Churches surge forward in great growth, again and again Missions and Churches will need to devise emergency measures so that maximum sound growth occurs. The Christian Church of Indonesia is facing just such a surge of growth in Kalimantan and is devising just such emergency measures, its actions may prove suggestive to other Missions and Churches in similar circumstances.

KINGMI is an acronym for the Kemah Injil Gereja Masehi Indonesia (The Gospel Tabernacle Christian Church of Indonesia) planted by the Christian and Missionary Alliance in 1929. Today this Church has a community of a quarter million. KINGMI's baptized members (99,138 in 1973) exceed those of the CMA in all of North America (96,058).

Indonesia has a population of about 130 million (119.3 in the 1972 census) with an annual growth rate of close to 2.9 per cent. In this predominantly Muslim country only seven to ten people out of every hundred are Christians. Should KINGMI grow biologically only, its Christian community would increase to almost 500,000 by the year 2000. However, should the present growth rate be maintained the KINGMI Church would reach about 750,000 in the same period.

The peoples and cultures of Indonesia are extremely diverse. Fifty-four indigenous ethnic groups contribute to that diversity. Immigrants add still more. KINGMI is made up of seven autonomous regional Churches: West Kalimantan, East Kalimantan, East Indonesia, Irian Jaya, Kibaid (Toraja, Sulawesi), Bahtera (Minahasa, Sulawesi), and Java-Sumatra. Ethnic groups in the large Irian Jaya Church include Ekari, Moni, Dani, Damal, Uhunduni and Nduga Branches. The East Indonesia Church has segments from the peoples of Sangir, Minahasa, Toraja, Bali, Sumbawa, Sumba, Rote, Alor, Timor and Ambon.

Large people movements have characterized the history of the Indonesian Church in general. KINGMI records reveal that greatest growth has

come through people movements first in East and West Kalimantan (KINGMI
grew from no baptized members in 1930 to 11,076 just six years later) and
more recently in Irian Jaya (approximately 8,000 Ilaga Danis burned their
fetishes in January 1960).

At present, people movements are occurring in West Kalimantan. In
1971, faculty and students of the Immanuel Bible School formed teams and
were flown into newly opened airstrips by MAF. From there they travelled
by boat or walked to distant villages. Several hundred people confessed
Christ during two weeks of ministry. The following year teams spent five
months in evangelism and over 5,000 turned to Christ. In 1973 another 600
came to Christ during a six week period. Just last November the first
1,500 from the Jengkang tribe embraced Christ.

Other Churches and Missions are experiencing considerable growth.
All of this is going on in an area which prior to 1970 was largely indifferent to the Gospel - or better neglected by the missions. Few of these
new believers have as yet been baptized. Neither Churches nor Missions
have personnel to do necessary folding and feeding, or to disciple other
villages. A further complication is that in many places local languages
must be used. If these new converts are not taught, they will revert or
be drawn into other religions. All this creates a desperate emergency
for all Churches and Missions.

In 1974 a joint KINGMI/MISSION Church Growth Committee has been engaged in an in-depth study of the present situation throughout our part
of the Islands. The purpose is to establish evangelism priorities and to
formulate a comprehensive program adapted to actual needs as these occur
in specific localities. Some very capable men are serving on that
committee.

They will certainly make provision for the crisis in West Kalimantan.
Yet that Church and that Mission (for the Alliance operates under the
"Modified Dicotomy" theory of mission described by Dr. Louis King in the
November 1921 Church Growth Bulletin) will have to bear the major respon-
sibility because other highly responsive areas in KINGMI also cry aloud to
be harvested.

What action might be taken to meet the emergency in West Kalimantan?
What innovations might be introduced today in building Christ's Church?
These are prime questions in missiology all over the world, wherever
fields ripen suddenly and there is a dearth of harvest hands. I suggest
the following emergency measures for consideration. No one alone would be
sufficient; but a combination might prove to be suitable strategy. In
other countries and for other Missions, still other emergency measures will
be needed. The thing to be avoided at all costs is trying to meet substantial ingathering with "the same old procedures" used in days when the
harvest was "four months" away.

1. Close the Immanuel Bible School for one year and send faculty/
student teams into the responsive areas to teach existing Christians,
organize congregations, appoint and train local leaders and evangelize

other waiting multitudes. "Stopping to consolidate" must be shunned. First and second year students would be teamed with experienced upperclassmen or faculty. For the moment, student teams seem to be God's main harvesters.

2. Require two (or three) years of shepherding new churches and evangelizing in "Macedonia" as part of the Bible School course of study, rather than the one year currently expected. This would postpone graduation but it would graduate experienced men and would conserve the harvest. This is the essential consideration. In the early days of KINGMI, there was only one Bible School for all Indonesia. Before they were graduated students served from one to three years in "the fields". Most of them worked in Kalimantan (then known as Borneo) and it was through their efforts that outstanding growth was achieved.

3. Mobilize teams of pastor/laymen to go into the high priority areas for extended periods. This is already being done on a small scale in some districts. It can be mightily increased. This is one place where Mission-Church cooperation seems readily obtainable.

4. Encourage local congregations to release, commission and support their pastors and gifted elders for a year's ministry among new churches who have no pastor. The announced goal would be that within that year the new church would choose, support and train a pastor. Attempts are being made to encourage churches to do this, but so far have met with little success. Some pastors would go, but their churches will not release and support them. It would help if high church officials visited local churches to press the need and make urgent appeal.

Great turnings, as they occur from time to time in responsive populations, pose a perpetual problem to Churches and Missions. The World Christian Enterprise faces the fact that frequently Latfricasian Churches are indifferent to great openings and will not send their pastors out as emergency reapers. Yet one hopes that reaping will not be left to the Mission exclusively. Latfricasian Churches must devise and put into operation measures which bear at least part of the load. They must also welcome and bless efforts of the Mission bringing in sheaves from fields which the Pastor/Laymen Teams cannot reach.

5. Set up a team of gifted KINGMI pastors and teachers to regularly visit in circuit locations where leaders from the new believers could gather for special training.

6. Incorporate into the KINGMI TEE program (last year 250 were studying in 11 centers) courses on pre and post baptismal training, the formation of new congregations, building of new churches, conducting of public worship, teaching illiterate Christians to read the Bible and organizing teams of new Christians to disciple their own tribes out to the fringes. Courses would have to be taught on an elementary level with special materials full of pictures and drawings to offset reading deficiencies. As an integral part of the course, those enrolled could be assigned to teams working in new ground for extended periods of time.

7. The joint Church Growth Committee will probably begin holding seminars in all seven KINGMI regions to communicate church growth insights. By giving priority to West Kalimantan the Church there would gain a new awareness of what is taking place and awaken to a compelling sense of stewardship. People Movement Teams could be developed to recognize early symptoms of wide-scale responsiveness and move the Church and Mission to quick action.

8. Urge KINGMI to request missionaries from CAMACOP (the CAMA "Church of the Philippines") for West Kalimantan. CAMACOP has assigned two couples to Sumatra and one to work with KINGMI in Irian Jaya. But the Alliance "Church of the Philippines" (50,000 communicants) can send scores of missionaries and should be urged to do so.

The understandable reluctance of Asian Churches during those years when white imperialism was a vivid memory to call for more European missionaries must not lead Asian Churches to shy away from asking for more missionaries from Asian lands. Indeed, "white imperialism" is no present threat at all. KINGMI demonstrates, as does CAMACOP, that the national Church can to great benefit use all the American missionaries CAMAUSA can send.

Other possible sources are the CMA of Australia and the Churches of Viet Nam, Japan and India, as well as other evangelical Churches and Missions, such as those forming in Korea. Asian missionaries - if properly supported by responsible Asian Missionary Societies, and well trained in cross-cultural communication - would provide a needed balance to North American influence and might soon stimulate KINGMI into sending its own missionaries beyond Indonesian borders.

To implement emergency measures it will be necessary to devise a new policy of mission subsidy for KINGMI's use of MAF. Special funding is needed and it can be done without smothering the Church's initiative and sacrifice. Great wisdom is required.

Emergency actions to meet the crisis in West Kalimantan should be devised with one eye fixed on East Kalimantan. People movements of even larger proportions are likely to develop there. Mobilizing for emergency action in West Kalimantan today is the best preparation for emergency measures in East Kalimantan tomorrow! And in others of the Seven Regional Churches which comprise KINGMI.

A nightmare recurs again and again to me. In it I see an orchard of vast extent with trees bowed beneath the weight of abundant fruit. That fruit is ripe. Much of it has already fallen and lies under the trees - rotting. And the stench--the awful stench of that rotting fruit! I wake gasping for fresh air. God grant it be only a nightmare!

KOREA ASKS: WHERE SHALL WE SEND MISSIONARIES?

Where shall we send Korean missionaries?
What is the most responsive population on earth?
Where can Korean missionaries best carry out the Great Commission?

The Editors of CGB reply as follows:

1. Responsive populations abound. In most countries several sections of the mosaic are already responding to invitations to accept Jesus Christ as Savior and Lord. Korean missionaries should not think that there is only one responsive population.

2. Train your Korean missionaries in each country to find which denominations are growing and in what segments of the population they are growing.

3. Remember that responsiveness is in part triggered by what the advocate (the missionary) does. In Chile, the Assemblies of God have grown only slightly, but the Methodist Pentecostals have grown enormously. The Chilean masses are responsive. The Methodist Pentecostals have a way of evangelizing which appeals to the masses. The Assemblies do not. Korean missionaries must not only find responsive populations; but must proclaim Christ to them, and create churches among them in the right way. Therefore, train your Korean missionaries to discover what kinds of evangelism actually bring men into life-giving relationship to Jesus Christ and membership in His Body.

4. Where Korean missionaries should be sent is only partially dependent on responsiveness. Train your missionaries to observe other criteria.
a) Sometimes God sends missionaries to unripe populations, there to plow and sow and weed till the harvest ripens.
b) Observe also which nations have friendly relations with South Korea and freely grant Koreans permits to enter the country. Other things being equal, your missionaries should go to receptive populations in those nations.
c) The amount of money which the supporting Korean denomination is likely to put into mission is also a factor. It is expensive to get to some fields and to maintain an adequate missionary force there. Unless your mission has large resources, better not send missionaries there.
d) Choose your field in view of the dedication of your missionaries and your churches. If God gives you men and women who are resolved to burn out for Him, who intend to obey the Great Commission whether they live or die, then difficult fields are possible for you. If your degree of dedication is less, then choose easier fields.

5. Note that in answering your questions, we are assuming from your last question that you are sending missionaries out to propagate the Gospel, rather than as fraternal delegates to already established Churches, or as men whose primary duty is to champion the oppressed of other lands, or teach them how to grow more food, or introduce more just political systems.

6. Bearing the foregoing matters in mind, Korean missionary societies ought to survey populations they hear are responsive and make recommendation to their churches. Missionary societies - particularly new missionary societies - should carry out feasibility studies. Long years of groping often marked missions in the nineteenth century. In those days, they had to feel their way. We do not. It would be sinful for us to spend our precious resources in a long, expensive process of trial and error. A few thousand dollars spent in survey will save tens of thousands in false starts.

A MISSIONARY SOCIETY DEVOTED ENTIRELY TO RESEARCH??

"The more than two hundred missionary societies of North America could easily create a small corps of missionaries and ministers (Latfricasians and Euricans) who make research in church growth their life work. A missionary society devoted to church growth might be organized. Social scientists in the service of the Great Commission should have no difficulty in raising support...

Church growth researches over the next fifteen years should cost five million dollars....They will guide and fructify missionary endeavors costing five hundred million or more...The Church cannot afford to evangelize with her eyes closed. To throw as much light as possible on what evangelism is effective and what is not is good stewardship....Research in church growth demands immediate development by all who take the Great Commission seriously!!" Understanding Church Growth p. 284

ETHNICITY AND MISSION IN CANADIAN LUTHERAN CONTEXT   by Wayne Holst

1. Canada has never experienced the 'melting pot concept' of national self-understanding. We are a mosaic of peoples.

2. A healthy respect must be maintained for "ethnicity" in the development of Canadian society. Lutherans should be the first to acknowledge this. We have been able to maintain our folk churches for generations. No government pressure has ever forced us to give up what we considered our worship heritage.

As much as we might resent some of the cultural accoutrement of our traditions, Lutheran heritage helps to fill in the picture of our identity as persons and as community. That fact remains true for most Lutheran congregations - even those in the secular suburbs of our major cities.

3. There is nothing 'anti-Canadian' about developing our mission thrusts along ethnic lines of communication and 'people contact'. Those who believe this idea old-fashioned do not understand our social ethos.

4. Traditional mission work in Canada has often been set within an ethnic context. Denominational missions, seeking to reach people in another sector of society, frequently discovered that greater success came when ministry was done within the context of 'the receiving culture'. Attempts to integrate, or to draw communities into a lowest common denominator, have frequently been no more successful in Canada than in the Third World. Mission can still thrive in an ethnic context today. In Canada German, French and Indian Pentecostalism now flourish in ways similar to Roman Catholic and Anglican missions among our native peoples a century ago.

5. We must come to see the US segment of our Christian population as but one more ethnic element to be understood and appreciated within the Canadian milieu. American Christianity is not the ideal, nor is it the standard setter for Canadian church life - any more than the British or French Christianity of times past. The Canadian Church is many things. It was conceived in Europe, shaped in America, established in Canada.

6. In an era when many people are searching for roots, ethnicity is a natural locus of self-identity. The Church should capitalize on this. The Church should not attempt to rationalize it away.

7. What I am advocating is not a return to the folk-churches of our forefathers! Can we be astute enough to recognize who we are - because we realize from what we have come? Can we build our church life so that diversity is recognized, appreciated, celebrated - rather than ignored or smothered? Can we develop our concepts and patterns of mission along lines that will be natural and conducive to the cultural evolution of Canada today?

REGIONAL CHURCH GROWTH MAGAZINES

CHURCH GROWTH - CANADA
Dennis Oliver, Editor
Canadian Theological College
4400 4th Avenue, Regina
Sask. S4T 0H8, Canada

CHURCH GROWTH: AMERICA
Win Arn, Editor
1857 Highland Oaks Drive
Arcadia, Calif. 91006

AMERICAN CHURCH GROWTH
The Reformed Church in America
421 North Brookhurst Street
Anaheim, Calif. 92801

TAIWAN CHURCH GROWTH BULLETIN
Sheldon Sawatsky, Editor
The Taiwan Church Growth Society
P. O. Box 165, Taichung
Taiwan, Republic of China 400

CHURCH GROWTH NEWS - KOREA
Marlin Nelson, Editor
Post Box #3, Sudaemoon
Seoul, Korea

MALAYSIA CHURCH GROWTH NEWS
P. O. Box 1068
Jalan Semangat
Petaling Jaya

CHURCH GROWTH ✝ BULLETIN

DONALD A. McGAVRAN, *Editor*
C. PETER WAGNER, *Associate Editor*

C O N T E N T S

Church Growth, Come Home!!	C. Peter Wagner
Exploding Interest in American Church Growth	Win Arn
The Church Growth Movement in Canada	Dennis Oliver
Church Growth in North America	Donald McGavran
Christian Leaders and Fundamentals of Growth	Ron S. Lewis

THE IMPACT OF CHURCH GROWTH PHILOSOPHY ON NORTH AMERICAN CHURCHES

CHURCH GROWTH, COME HOME!!   C. Peter Wagner

Now that Christianity has broken from its traditional Western mold and become a worldwide religious movement, those of us in Western nations can expect an increasing enrichment of our own Christian understanding and practices through a stimulating flow of ideas from the "mission fields" back to our sending countries. This is a happy thought. In the new era, cross-cultural missions need no longer to be conceptualized as a one-way street.

Already theologies developing in the ferment of the Third World have begun to influence theological thought here in the U.S.A. Names like John Mbiti, Ruben Alves and Gustavo Gutierrez are probably only the forerunners of a new day in cross-cultural theological dialogues which promises to be different from anything previously known in the history of Christian dogma. The saturation evangelism model, springing from Latin America, has already strongly influenced evangelistic thinking in the Western world. Another Latin American export, Theological Education by Extension, has changed the face of ministerial training patterns in some Third World situations and is gradually becoming influential in North America.

SEND news and articles to the Editor, Dr. Donald McGavran, at the Institute of Church Growth, Fuller Theological Seminary, 135 N. Oakland, Pasadena, California 91101. Published bi-monthly. Send subscriptions and changes of address to the Publisher, Norman L. Cummings, Overseas Crusades, Inc., 3033 Scott Blvd., Santa Clara, California 95050, U.S.A. Second-class postage paid at Santa Clara, California. Postmaster: Please send form 3579 to Overseas Crusades, 3033 Scott Blvd., Santa Clara, Ca. 95050.

The latest mission field innovation to be felt among North American churches might well emerge as the most influential. It is the philosophy of church growth, forged by Donald McGavran and some colleagues in the heat of the evangelistic fires in India over two or three decades ago. If the enthusiasm and excitement about church growth that has been generated in America over the past two and one-half years is indicative of what is yet to come, the church growth philosophy could well become one of the strongest religious forces in the final decades of our century.

Most readers of CHURCH GROWTH BULLETIN are familiar enough with the history of the church growth movement. They know that its widespread diffusion began with the publication of McGavran's The Bridges of God in 1955; that the Institute of Church Growth was founded in Eugene, Oregon, in 1960; that it became the School of World Mission and Institute of Church Growth at Fuller Theological Seminary in 1965; that McGavran's definitive work, Understanding Church Growth, was published in 1970; and that over 400 alumni of the school are now serving in key positions of leadership throughout the world.

What is not so well known is that Donald McGavran founded his institution with a precisely defined objective: to spread the church growth school of thought among career missionaries and national church leaders in the Third World. By intention, church workers dedicated to ministry in the traditional sending countries were excluded. Thus, as one American evangelical leader said to me less than a month ago, "Somehow, I never knew what church growth was. I always thought it was just something out there on the mission field." His voice sounded as if he felt he had been slightly cheated.

Maybe he had. But this condition is rapidly being remedied. A conscious attempt to apply church growth philosophy to the American scene was begun in the Fall of 1972, when, at the urging of Pastor Charles Miller, a staff member of my own Lake Avenue Congregational Church, I was able to organize a pilot course for American church leaders, team-taught with Dr. McGavran. It was a remarkable experience. One of the students, Win Arn, eventually changed his career and founded the influential Institute for American Church Growth. Charles Miller resigned his position and is now enrolled in SWM/ICG. Phil Goble, another student, developed a creative model for Jewish evangelism based on church growth principles, now being propagated through his new book, Everything You Need to Grow a Messianic Synagogue (William Carey).

At about the same time, two prominent publishers began to prod SWM/ICG faculty members to contribute to church growth in America. William Petersen of Eternity was one of the first to request an article on the subject. Concerned with Key 73, Harold Lindsell virtually turned over to the SWM faculty the January 19, 1973, issue of Christianity Today. It carried six essays attempting to apply the church growth philosophy to the Key 73 effort, but the American audience was not yet receptive to the ideas expressed.

Three individuals in particular should be recognized as pioneers in the diffusion of church growth thinking in North America. Win Arn and his Institute for American Church Growth has already been mentioned. He and his staff have developed remarkably effective approaches designed to motivate pastors and lay leadership in local churches and denominations for new growth as they move into the future. Paul Benjamin left his teaching post at Lincoln Christian Seminary to establish the National Church Growth Research Center in Washington, D.C. With access to the Library of Congress, the center is tooled to offer outstanding study facilities, and academic work is eligible for credit from Lincoln Seminary. The third, Dennis Oliver, founded the church growth center at Canadian Theological College in Regina, and has become the editor of Church Growth: Canada, a Canadian counterpart to the Church Growth Bulletin.

Several publishers have recognized the expanding market for church growth information in America. Perhaps the reader has seen Regal Books with publications such as Robert Schuller's Your Church Has Real Possibilities, my current choice for number one in American church growth; Vergil Gerber's God's Way to Keep a Church Going and Growing; and Harold Fickett's story of the growth of the Van Nuys Baptist Church, Hope For Your Church. At least two publishers are discussing the launching of a new national magazine dedicated to church growth. Probably the most prolific writer in the field is Elmer Towns, whose books and articles concentrate largely on the Bible Baptist Fellowship, one of the fastest growing groupings of churches in the nation.

For several years now, in-house seminars have been conducted by the pastors of many of the rapidly growing churches of America. In March, 1975, the Pastors' School led by Jack Hyles of First Baptist, Hammond, Indiana, drew 3,194 participants. Robert Schuller labeled the fifth anniversary session of his Institute for Successful Church Leadership in Garden Grove, California, the "First American Convocation on Church Growth." A good number of those who sat in the pews there were individuals who normally do not go to such meetings unless they are featured speakers. The Explosion Evangelism Clinic, conducted by James Kennedy and Archie Parrish in conjunction with the Coral Ridge Presbyterian Church of Fort Lauderdale, Florida, has a three-year waiting list and now is developing a nine month extended training session for future staff members. Similar schools are conducted by Pastors G.L. Johnson of Fresno, California; Jerry Falwell of Lynchburg, Virginia; W.A.Criswell of Dallas, Texas; and many others. They provide an important component of the developing scene of church growth in America.

Academically-oriented, accredited, courses on church growth are still relatively scarce in North America. A few scattered Bible schools and seminaries offer courses in the subject. I personally am teaching church growth in the Fuller Extension program, in the D.Min. continuing education program in both Fuller and Bethel Seminaries, and in the Wheaton Graduate School. Other such offerings, I am sure, will soon be springing up in similar institutions in America. I hope that before long church growth will be considered as a high-priority component of the standard curriculum for all ministerial training.

Finally, I should mention one of the newest attempts to relate church growth philosophy to American churches. The Fuller Evangelistic Association of Pasadena, California, has recently established a Department of Church Growth, headed up by John Wimber, a successful pastor and church consultant. This department is tooling to offer, among other things, a long term church growth consultation service for churches, denominations and para church organizations which feel the need for professional expertise in the area. They plan to offer the kind of service a physician offers to his patients.

Unless I misread the signs, a new day is dawning for the American Church. Tremendous human and spiritual powers, now locked into restrictive patterns and outmoded methodologies, will soon be released for the accelerated spread of the Kingdom of God on this continent, perhaps even at the rate the Church is growing in some of the Third World countries. If so, church growth will have come home!

EXPLODING INTEREST IN AMERICAN CHURCH GROWTH   Win Arn*

The pendulum is swinging!

Yesterday, the Church in America was being criticized, vilified, accused of being archaic and irrelevant in today's world. Today an explosive surge of interest is evidenced in American Church Growth.

Why the change?

'God is dead' theology...'relativism' that denied Biblical foundations...decline of mainline denominations...re-evaluation and change in the Church itself...political, social, moral bankruptcy in America..the backlash of these and many other factors caused Americans to look carefully at and appreciate the claims of Christ and at His Church. In this receptive period in America, growing interest is surfacing in evangelism, which from the church growth viewpoint, is to 'proclaim Jesus Christ as God and Saviour and persuade men to become His disciples and responsible members of His Church.'

Fuel for this chain reaction is coming from many sources.

(1) In cities and suburbs, some churches are experiencing explosive growth. These models are causing much interest and excitement. Churches not experiencing such growth are looking at themselves and asking, "Why?" or "Why not?"

(2) Books, articles and publications on American Church Growth are appearing in increasing numbers, creating awareness and interest.

(3) Seminars conducted by the Institute For American Church Growth are applying global church growth principles to the American scene with significant results. Seminars are being conducted by pastors of 'super churches,' sharing their insights and understandings.

(4) Films...HOW TO GROW A CHURCH and REACH OUT AND GROW ... are motivating large numbers of lay leaders toward growth and outreach.

(5) Many pastors are seeking training experiences in the area of church growth; academic and non-academic opportunities for study are increasing.

(6) Most significantly, denominations are conducting pilot projects. These are using principles of church growth which have been formulated abroad and are being adapted and applied to America through the Institute For American Church Growth. For example, the Ashland Brethren denomination is nine months into a pilot project of applying growth principles through seminars to five churches. Results to date have been so productive that the new goal is for every church in the denomination to experience a Church Growth Seminar in 1976. The Nazarene Church, Los Angeles District, has two pilot projects -- the first includes ten of its churches, some in cross-cultural situations, and the second includes aided churches which will be clustered for seminars with the goal of making these churches self-sustaining. The Kansas Yearly Meeting of Friends Churches is conducting a third pilot project. In it, all of the 85 churches of the Yearly Meeting will (in two 10-day periods) share in a Church Growth Seminar.

Many local churches, pastored by men with church growth eyes, are surging ahead of their denominational bureaucracy. These men are bringing church growth resources and principles into focus and are experiencing significant growth in many varied situations.

The pendulum is swinging!

The Church Growth Movement in America is expanding at a rapid rate. The American Church has historically viewed itself as a sending agency... sending missionaries, money, and materials to people across the world. Today, however, the third world is sending back to America proven principles of growth and the American Church is beginning to reap what appears to be a great harvest!

*Dr. Win Arn is the Executive Director of the Institute for American Church Growth. The Institute conducts seminars, workshops and training sessions to enable churches to reach their fullest potential in evangelism/church growth. Write Dr. Arn at: 1857 Highland Oaks Drive, Arcadia, California, 91006.

THE CHURCH GROWTH MOVEMENT IN CANADA   by Dennis M. Oliver, Director
                    Canadian Church Growth Centre, Regina, Sask., Canada

Many Canadians, many Canadian Churches and some foreign Churches (such as the Southern Baptists) are awakening to the potential for great church growth in our land. We Canadians have a reputation for being conservative, critical and cautious about new ideas and new approaches. But the world-wide Church Growth Movement has gotten under our skin, into our hearts and onto our lips and shoe leather.

There are a growing number of 'church growth men' in Canada. They subscribe to the Church Growth Bulletin and our indigenous Church Growth: Canada. They read McGavran, Gerber, Arn and Schuller -- and consciously seek to apply their insights. They attend Church Growth Seminars under international specialists (such as Donald McGavran and Raj Nelson) as well as Canadians (e.g. Kenneth Birch, Dennis Oliver, Dick Standerwick). They buy books from Church Growth Book Clubs in Pasadena and Regina. All these stimulate them to think and plan and pray for growth. More and more Bible Colleges and Theological Colleges are including well known church growth books in their missions and evangelism courses, or offering courses in Church Growth. In fact, one of the topics to be addressed at the Conference of Evangelicals concerned for Graduate Theological Education in Canada (this May) is "Canadian Church Growth through Theological Education." Dr. McGavran will be a major speaker at the Evangelical Fellowship of Canada's Convention, May 13-16, in Toronto. He will teach church growth at Regent College Vancouver in July and to Baptist pastors in Banff, Alberta in November. Church Growth has gained a hearing throughout the land.

Besides the growing number of Canadians who consciously identify with the global Church Growth Movement, God is mightily transforming minds and ministries of thousands of pastors and lay men and women to a deeper commitment to quantitative growth and an unashamed openness to growth oriented planning and research. There is an increasing impatience with evangelism that results in relatively few new members. The new openness is reflected in talk within the United Church of Canada, our largest Protestant body, of reversing the moratorium on church extension which has resulted in almost no churches planted since 1968. Last year "15 Affirmations for Lent" were enunciated by United Churchmen. This document included a clear and unequivocal call to biblical mission: "We believe that Jesus Christ is the divine answer to the human longings to which all faiths testify. We therefore take with utmost seriousness the great commission to go and make disciples of all nations" (from Affirmation 5). Denominations have Departments of Church Growth (The Brethren in Christ), Church Growth Leadership Letters (The Pentecostal Assemblies of Canada), and Church Growth Themes at their conventions (The Christian and Missionary Alliance) and in their denominational magazines (such as the Evangelical Baptist, Mennonite Brethren Herald and United Church Observer). Dr. George Peters, a former Canadian, has said that the World-Wide Church is undergoing a great revival of effective evangelism. This revival is seen in a great host of Canadian congregations.

There is a real ferment in the thinking of many missionaries to Canada's Indian peoples. Some white missionaries have concluded that the real hope for these first Canadians is a truly indigenous Christian movement which will bypass traditional Christian organizations. A growing number of Indian churches have associated themselves into the Native Evangelical Fellowship. Another hopeful sign is the survey of needs and present strength of Indian works across Canada conducted by IMCO, representing a number of Indian missions in our land.

The so-called Canadian revival (it never really swept the country; but then it hasn't died out yet, either) had a marked effect on church growth in some places, although it was often disappointing in just this area of fruit bearing.

What are the facts concerning church growth in Canada? Nominal Roman Catholic identification continues just ahead of our population growth (reflecting immigration trends). But we do not know what this means in terms of active participation in church life. Confirming Dean M. Kelley's observations regarding North America (Why Conservative Churches Are Growing) the "Liberal" Protestant Churches are declining. Between 1971 and 1972 the three largest Protestant bodies lost more than 52,000 communicant members and shrunk by sixty-five congregations. No wonder some Canadian churchmen feel pessimistic about the future! One leader wrote to me, "I do not share the optimism in church growth that occasionally shines out from what you write. The extraordinary increase in the number of atheists and agnostics in Canada, as reported in the 1971 census, is a most disturbing feature. We must not put blinders on our eyes against such harsh realities."

My distinguished friend was alluding to the dramatic upswing in those who classified their faith as "No Religion". Five per cent of all Canadians, over 750,000 souls, do not want to be identified with any faith. Half of these are under 25 years old. Perhaps even more dramatic is the growth of sub-Christian cults in Canada. The Church of Scientology claims 6,000 members (most likely this only represents their mailing list). But it is more difficult to discount the strength of other cults. In ten years, the Worldwide Church of God (Armstrongites) has grown to about 4,000 communicant members, spread across Canada in 51 churches with 103 full time workers. The most startling statistic is that of the Jehovah's Witnesses. The 1971 census records 175,000 Canadians identifying with this religion: a yearly increase of 3.36% since 1961. At the end of 1974 there were more JW communicants (nearly 111,000) than the combined members of the Christian and Missionary Alliance, all Canadian Mennonite bodies, the Fellowship Baptists and four other Canadian Baptist denominations! In the last reporting year, the Mormons gained 12,000 members - greater than the combined memberships of a score of orthodox Canadian Churches!

We are concerned about these facts, but surely they indicate that hundreds of thousands of Canadians are open to religious change. There is a growing responsiveness in Canada, a whitened harvest not limited to our praries, if only we had the church growth eyes to behold it.

One denomination which has acted on the opportunities for growth is the Pentecostal Assemblies of Canada, an indigenous Church which has steadily grown from 27 congregations in 1920 to 760 congregations (130,000 members) in 1974. Associated with this Church are many ethnic conferences and home mission outreaches into homogeneous units. The PAOC is the fastest growing orthodox Church in Canada. Other less rapidly growing denominations are the Brethren in Christ, Christian and Missionary Alliance, Evangelical Lutherans, Fellowship of Evangelical Baptists, Lutheran Church Canada (Missouri Synod), and Mennonite Brethren. All are increasing faster than Canada's natural population growth.

We anticipate a vast ingathering through congregation-expanding, church-multiplying ministries. Equally important and strategic, the Living God is reviving and renewing unregenerate church members. "E-0 evangelism" is the emphasis in many of our congregations. God has His hand on our land.

CHURCH GROWTH IN NORTH AMERICA   by Donald McGavran

Drs. Wagner, Arn, and Oliver have described the amazing contemporary explosion of interest in church growth. My task is that of describing the matrix out of which the explosion is taking place. This will enable us to see other facets of the jewel and to estimate correctly what we ought to do and where the church growth movement is likely to go.

1. Millions of Marginals. Millions of nominal, marginal, slightly lapsed Christians and ex-Christians characterize the North American scene. Enormous numbers of our kind of people live all about us with vague but ineffective commitment to Jesus Christ. They speak out language. They live in houses like ours. Their children and ours go to the same schools. We shop at the same supermarkets and eat the same kind of food. They are our kind of folk. Yet they have little consciousness of life lived in obedience to a Master. They consider themselves Christians, but do not really know what being "in Christ" means. So they grow more and more alienated and secular. They watch the family breaking up and the sex life of millions gravitating toward the animal, and rush out to buy pornographic books by the million. They bring magazines full of liquor advertisements into their homes and accustom their children to the thought that in America today everyone drinks. They seldom if ever have family prayers. On Sundays they immerse themselves in papers and football. The Bible in the house accumulates dust. In all this, they have little feeling of betraying Christ or disobeying their Shepherd; but the fact of the matter is that they are living without a Shepherd and acknowledge no Lord.

Europeans have all this in mind when they speak about 'post Christian Europe'. We in Canada and the United States know the situation well ourselves. Of the 220 million citizens of the United States, about 170 million are our kind of people. Of them, let us generously assume that 70 million have a current obedient relationship to Jesus Christ. They are the backbone of all churches. They intend to be Christians, to walk in the Way and to rear their children as believers. They give liberally. They read their Bibles. They confess their sins and ask God to forgive them. If this estimate is correct, that would leave 100 million of our kind of people living all around us - without Christ. These are the most winnable people in the world. They consider themselves in some way Christians. Nothing keeps them from practicing their faith and loving their Lord - except sin and selfishness. They suffer no persecution when they are saved. Multitudes of new churches can be started among them. Multitudes of them can unite with existing churches.

One must distinguish these lax Christians from perhaps twenty million hard-core card-carrying pagan Americans and Canadians - materialists, secularists, positivists, and the like. These are not responsive. The

special evangelism needed to reach them is seldom seen. I cannot present
their case here. I am not talking about them.

A map of the United States has been recently prepared which shows
every county, and colors it according to the per cent of persons living in
it whose names appear on no church roll. Huge sections of the map appear
pink - 30 per cent; light red - 50 per cent; and dark red 70 per cent! In
the light of this map, the comfortable myth that we live in a well churched
land is totally incredible.

A few denominations have been taking these lost multitudes seriously.
For example, the Southern Baptists 25 years ago resolved to treat the seven
central northern states as mission territories and to multiply churches in
them. If Southern Illinois be excluded, we may say that in 1950 the Southern Baptists had 50 congregations and now have 1300. They found these unchurched myriads and tell me that millions in these seven states remain
undiscipled. The Church of the Nazarene, also, in its meteoric rise from
nothing in 1906 to 600,000 and the Assemblies of God from nothing in 1905
to 500,000 today have found these unshepherded sheep. So have thousands
of unusual mainline congregations led by unusual pastors who in Canada and
the United States during the time when most churches were not growing,
have grown to great size and effectiveness.

11. The Ethnic Multitudes: Essential also to a right understanding of the
church growth situation are the unchurched ethnics. Racial, linguistic
and ethnic peoples have been pouring into North America in a steady stream.
This continent is no longer a preserve for white Anglo Saxons. Consider
the Latins - from twenty-five countries of Latin America and islands of the
Caribbean. At least sixteen millions of these can be identified today.
Depending on how they are defined, one may say that there are two million
in California, three million in Texas, a million and a half in New York
City, and other huge minorities in other states and cities.

Consider the Blacks. It has been customary to think of these as
fairly well churched - mostly belonging to Baptist or Methodist denominations. This was - in a loose way - true thirty years ago; but today
millions of younger Blacks (like tens of millions of younger Whites) are
outside the Church.

Canada has experienced a flood of immigrants. Hundreds of thousands
of Italians live in Toronto, Montreal, Regina, Vancouver and other cities.
Asians flow in a steady stream to this favored continent - masses of
Philippinos, Koreans, Chinese, Indians, Arabs, Vietnamese, and many others.
Eight million Jews reside in North America in some very large concentra-
tions.

These minorities think of themselves as distinct from the white majority. They speak a different home language, have different customs,
like different foods, vote differently, and for a generation or two have
a markedly different standard of living. By and large they cannot be won
into existing churches. At this point, one must not be misled by the
steady trickle of individual converts from these minorities into existing

churches. This is to be sure, going on. Most white churches welcome ethnic converts and tens of thousands of Old American churches have a few Italians, Jews, Latins, Arabs, Blacks or Asians in them. But when one realizes that out of a million Spanish name Americans in Los Angeles County, less than 20,000 are Protestant Christians (and this number includes the allegedly fast growing Pentecostal and Southern Baptist churches) he realizes that this thin little trickle is not what is needed.

A way must be found for multitudes of each ethnic unit to become staunch believing disciples of Christ while they remain distinctly themselves. The present system whereby 'becoming Christian' involves 'becoming a helpless minority in an old Caucasian congregation' is neither Christian nor effective. It is not discipling the ethnics - and cannot do so. In the course of the next hundred years - perhaps - the population of North America may become one cultural monolith. But it is certainly not that now. Churching the ethnics must not be confused with the secular goal of merging many cultures and races into one - and that may not happen either. Discipling the ethnics means multiplying tens of thousands of churches in which each ethnic, racial or linguistic unit can be as distinctive as it wants to be.

This means that Christians must not consider "near-neighbor evangelism into existing congregations" as the only method needed. Rather, they should realize that tens of thousands of E2 missionaries are demanded. For example, North American Christians ought to keep at work among the 300,000 Italians in Toronto 100 E2 North American missionaries. These would speak Italian fluently and have spent a couple of years in Italy in the districts from which the Toronto immigrants have come. They would be engaged in planting at least one thousand Italian churches. These missionaries would be lifetime workers, shifting out of the limelight as fast as leaders from the converts could be prepared as pastors. In a similar fashion, E2 missionaries should be set to work in all unchurched segments of every ethnic and linguistic population in every state and province.

It should be normal for every old American Caucasian congregation to depute two per cent of its members to become E2 missionaries to some piece of the wonderful ethnic mosaic so characteristic of this continent. When millions of our youth are learning German, Spanish, Mandarin, and Hindi, is it not reasonable to propose that tens of thousands of Christians become E2 missionaries?

Yet, large as the ethnic opportunity is, it is small compared to the tens of millions of nominal Christians among the Old American and the old Canadians. Both opportunities comprise the almost inexhaustible mine from which diamonds may be quarried. The size of the nominal back log is so great that any talk of sheep stealing or keeping out of other churches' 'territory' must be dismissed as the whimperings of defensive static-minded men and women.

III. Church Growth Legitimate. Integral to right understanding of the church growth situation is the vivid realization (for which the Global Church Growth Movement takes some credit) that growth is a legitimate task

of every congregation and every denomination. For twenty years this has
been strenuously denied. I remember hearing the president of a famous
theological seminary say to his students in chapel,

> "I am not impressed by your reports of members added to
> your churches. I want to know the quality of your members.
> Are they pulling their weight in your community? Are
> they ethical Christians? Are they changing your social
> structures?"

Church growth men never call members added to the church insignificant.
Church growth men have long maintained that both discipling and perfecting are essential and must go forward together, (Bridges of God, 1955,
pages 13-16). Improvement in quality must not be purchased by devaluating
the coin of the realm - evangelism and church planting. The conscience on
church growth now sweeping North America rests on a conviction that evangelism which issues in increased responsible members in old churches and the
establishment of new churches as needed, is a chief and irreplaceable
purpose of the Church.

Conservatives are driven to the above conviction by their theology.
They believe that all men are lost until they believe on Jesus Christ as
Lord and Saviour and accept the Bible as the inspired infallible and authoritative Word of God. They are also driven by the stubborn plateaus in the
graphs of growth of the most orthodox and devout denominations. Indeed,
with the advent of the Pill, it can be affirmed without fear of contradic-
tion that unless an orthodox, devout denomination engages in intentional
intelligent processes calculated to result in church growth, it will gradually wither away. Solid, sound denominations can no longer count on
biological growth maintaining their numbers. With the Pill, the better
the denomination, the less the biological church growth.

Liberals are driven to the above conviction by declining memberships
and empty headquarters' offices. In the last twenty years, some of their
leaders have been pontificating about how sinful it is for Christians to be
interested in mere church growth and survival. A really Christian Church
should be, they said, like its Master, ready to die!! But when they realize
that their survival is at stake (and their ability to do good) they may
see their error and rush to establish effective forces of evangelism and
church growth.

IV. Marching This Way: Soon To Be Among Us: Interest is certain to
quicken and increase. Commitment to church growth cannot decline in the
foreseeable future. Obedience to the Saviour, the clear teaching of the
Bible, the pressure of the contemporary context, the fundamental needs of
our fellow men, and a certain earthy self interest all combine to guarantee
that church growth will prove no flash in the pan. It is here and it will
remain. We shall see a mighty multiplication of efforts for church growth
by denominations large and small. Some will, of course, continue to
fight growth. A few die-hards refuse to see the movement of history and
continue to bleat out a feeble protest against effective evangelism - in
the interests, of course, of respecting the sovereignty of God, serving

the whole man, or being true to the Bible - at least to that isolated account of the Lord's displeasure with David for numbering the people!

We may confidently look forward also to a mighty. increase in knowledge about church growth. Large church growth has been going on for decades and much more will go on in the decades ahead. Research will determine in reliable fashion exactly what growth (quantitative, qualitative and organic) has taken place, what the line of growth over the past years can tell us, what lessons we can learn from it, what growth is likely to occur in the years to come, and what God's obedient servants ought to do in the light of the current realities. Professors of church growth and evangelism will be appointed in most seminaries. Hundreds of books about church growth in Canada, the United States, the Northern States, the Southern States, parts of each state or province, cities and ethnic units will be written, published, sold, and read by millions of Christians - lay and clerical.

Awakenings, fueled by all this and by intense widespread Bible Study and Prayer for Revival, may be confidently expected. The record, so painstakingly compiled by J. Edwin Orr, of the close relationship which revival bears to evangelistic effectiveness cannot be disregarded. It will be read and will have an increasing effect. The relation of church growth thinking to revival is like that of railway tracks to a full head of steam in a locomotive. Without the tracks, the steam blows the whistle but goes nowhere. With the tracks, the engine roars off at sixty miles an hour. Awakenings plus knowledge of those methods which it has pleased God to bless to the mighty growth of His Church will spell continuous sound increase of Christians, churches and denominations - to the redemption of multitudes and the mighty increase of justice, brotherhood and peace in this continent.

It takes no prophetic insight to see marching this way, soon to be among us, a missionary movement of unparallelled proportions. We stand in the sunrise of missions. E Two missionaries (to the ethnics of this land and to hundreds of millions somewhat like us in other lands) will be recruited and set to work by the tens of thousands. Multitudes of E Threes, also, (essential to the evangelization of three billion "other culture" Non-Christians in this continent and overseas) will hear God's call and offer themselves for lifetime service. They will not be the only missionaries, of course. Asians and Latins by the thousand and Africans by the tens of thousands will also hear God's call. Any church growth worthy of the name must issue in multiplied missionary sendings. Renewed missionary commitment can be predicted with assurance. If the Lord tarry, we shall surely see these things.

THE NAIROBI KENYA MEETING OF THE WORLD COUNCIL OF CHURCHES

On November 23rd, this year, the Fifth Assembly of the World Council will convene in Nairobi. Remembering the May '68 Church Growth Bulletin (Will Uppsala Betray the Two Billion?) and Lausanne, readers will observe Nairobi proceedings to see how much world evangelization is unashamedly advocated.

IMPOSING AN ALIEN FAITH?

"I have never been able to understand why, in
contemporary history-writing, the Christian is
never permitted to be right. Everyone else is
allowed to be intolerant, but not he. Marxism
is the most intolerant creed in history, but
the Marxist is regarded as more than respectable.....Marxists, Muslims, modern Vedantists,
are all active propagandists, and make no
secret of their desire to convert others to
their views. To this no objection seems to be
raised. But let a Christian attempt to convert
anyone else to his faith and he is immediately
accused of western arrogance and of attempting
to impose on others an alien - and purely
western faith.

(Stephen Neill - CMS News-Letter May '74)

CHRISTIAN LEADERS AND FUNDAMENTALS OF GROWTH   Ron S. Lewis
                    Chairman: Development Division, Illinois Baptist
                               State Association, Springfield, Ill.

The Christian leader builds his life on fundamentals - the fundamentals of his faith. One of these is the growth fundamental - frequently
not even recognized. With many growth has become an option. However, if
we are to be the growing Church Christ intends for us to be, growth must
become a fundamental mind set with us. We should spend our time not in
explaining why we are not growing, but in determining strategies for
growing.

A basic principle of growth is the New Unit. We must create new
units. It is easier to create new units than to resurrect old. New units
have the capacity to grow faster than old units. This is true whether the
new unit is a person, church, organization, Sunday School class, Bible
Study group or mission. Nothing I know can match the astronomical growth
of a new born babe in Christ who is really turned on - especially a young
or middle-aged adult.

New units create excitement. They bring a new dimension, personality
and vocabulary. New units are less cumbersome. They can be shaped, reshaped and are not offended by their need for development. New Sunday
School units grow faster than old ones. New choir units grow faster than
old ones. New mission units grow faster than old ones. Maybe it's because they don't know it cannot be done.

However, <u>new unit</u> growth does not last long. As Stanley Dill says,
"It is amazing how quickly pioneers become settlers. Pioneers have an
adventuresome attitude. Settlers protect what is theirs. While the pioneering spirit lasts, let us use it. Let us value and develop a growth
mind set, remembering that the <u>new unit</u> is fundamental for growth.

Southern Baptists in Illinois had 440 churches in 1952. Since then
we have started 434 churches in Illinois. Thirty of these have died.
Twelve **have** changed denominations but still exist. Three have changed
"ethnic quality."

We have hovered between 880-900 churches between 1966 and 1974. Why?
In 1962, we began to talk of developing a College or Seminary in Chicago.
We talked of a Hospital and a Golden Age Home. <u>From that time, New Unit</u>
expansion began to level off. This is not to be interpreted as saying
institutions kill new units, but it is fair to say we often take the
energy given to new unit thinking and loan it to institutional thinking.

Institutions cannot call men from death to life as well and as rapidly
as new unit Sunday Schools, churches, and missions. And remember that the
<u>truest measurable church growth</u> is conversion growth - "new units, new
people."

In 1962, when we were aggressively multiplying new churches, we averaged 5 baptisms per 100 church members. We have not come close to that
average since. As new churches ceased to be established, our conversion
growth levelled off. We are currently baptizing only 3.9 converts for
each 100 members. Neighboring states verify the fact that new units show
more conversion growth than old units.

	1959	1973
INDIANA	9.2	7.0
OHIO	13.8	7.7
MICHIGAN	14.4	4.7

This fundamental "new unit" component must be emphasized by Christian
leaders if they want growing denominations. New units must be fed a "new
unit" diet. They must be fed at the "new unit" speed. Like newborn children, their metabolism can handle only so much. Home Mission Board studies have shown that a growing church must have at least a strong Bible
teaching program and warm-hearted evangelistic music. We must avoid stuf-
fing these babes with more than the essentials.

New units must be led by "new unit" leaders and thinkers who honestly
believe if they don't grow they will die. Sadly, as Christians age, they
adjust and assume   -growth" is not really so bad. They did not really
die when they quit growing. At least it didn't feel like death. Leaders
born and nurtured in the friendly confines of churches long past the fight
for growth have difficulty adjusting to "new unit" country. In contrast,
the best "new unit" leaders come from "new unit" country. Indigenous Sunday Schools in "new unit" country are supported by those who see that the
work must be programmed to coincide with local situations. Carloads of
preachers from the Bible belt with prepaid expenses and honorariums are

fine, but in Illinois we don't need to be "Baton Rouged," "Texized," "Oklahomad," "Kentuckyed." We need indigenous Baptist churches in these north central states. We face facts that "foreigners from old Southern churches" don't understand, but <u>our</u> Christian leader must understand. He must believe in the "new unit" growth concept if he is to see significant church growth! Southern Baptists along with other denominations must realize that <u>any significant growth</u> in the next 25 years must come in "new unit" country.

Our convention must become conscious of Class Two Leaders, - unpaid leaders who reach out. We must gear training, literature, conferences to develop this kind of leader. We must train pastors to train laymen to be Class Two Leaders. Seminaries must assume a new posture about "new unit" country. They send carloads of preachers at the Easter break. They must now institute courses for academic credit on how to function as a Christian, a Family, or a Pastor, in "new unit country." Each seminary should appoint a red hot "new unit professor", teaching the practical application course. We all must realize that churches are built, maintained and multiplied by the ministry of Class One and Class Two Leaders with the help of an ordained pastor. They can also grow without him, if necessary.

The Christian Leader As a Growing Person

Growing churches need four kinds of leaders - Class Ones, Class Twos, Class threes, and Class Fours. <u>Class Ones</u> are unpaid leaders (Sunday School teachers, deacons, elders, choir members, ushers) serving existing churches and their members. <u>Class Twos</u> are unpaid leaders engaged in active evangelization of some form, consciously seeking to win people to Christian Faith and to plant churches. <u>Class Threes</u> are paid or unpaid leaders of small congregations. <u>Class Fours</u> are paid and professionally trained leaders of large churches. All four kinds are desirable for growing churches, but Class Twos are essential.

Class One Leaders can become Class Two Leaders, <u>if</u> they are growing persons. Class Four Leaders can develop more and more Class One and Class Two Leaders if <u>they</u> are growing. Growing leaders create growing leaders. Like begets like.

We become disturbed at unusual experiences with the Holy Spirit. We are so anxious about unknown utterances, that we have neglected Joel's prophecy: "Young men shall see visions, and old men shall dream dreams." When will these visions and dreams occur? When will our senior leaders dream great dreams of God's expansion of His Kingdom and thus His Church. "Dreaming" is what Bob Schuller calls "possibility thinking." We need to pray God to empower us to do "possibility thinking".

If we reach the goal of 800,000 Baptists in this seven state area by 1990 - we are now ahead of schedule - and if only 20 per cent of these become effective witnesses, we can have 160,000 volunteers turned on to share the Gospel. A mind set toward growth attracts growing leaders. Growing leaders make possible growing churches.

The Christian Leader and the People of God

The Christian leader must sense his destiny as part of the "People of God." In the Old Testament, the phrase "People of God" signified a special people with a special destiny. In the New Testament, the phrase, "People of God" described followers of Christ destined to share in His special mission, "to seek and to save that which is lost." We must recapture that sense of destiny. It strengthens our possibility thinking.

For example, the current ratio among our churches is 1 baptism for every 30 church members. In Minnesota, Wisconsin, Iowa, Illinois, Indiana, Ohio and Michigan, we shall baptize 26,000 per year, if we continue at the 1 to 30 ratio. If, however, we moved to a 1-20 ratio we would baptize 40,000 per year. If we accelerated to a 1-10 ratio, we would add 80,000 new members each year. Think what this influx would mean to the work forces of our Church. Imagine its impact on finances, choirs, prayer groups, communities, number of persons "called" into specific Christian tasks, and the service our denomination could render to our Lord and to needy humanity!

We are not doing mission - we are on mission. The mission is to incorporate more and more people into the Kingdom to live and work in His Will. The mighty changes needed today will come with a mighty People of God.

We need leaders who think growth. We usually find ourselves in committee meetings where much of the time is spent on "How shall we pay for this?" This should not be the priority issue. The most urgent question is "How does this contribute to church growth?" May committee meetings devoted to church growth multiply to the uttermost part of the earth, is my urgent prayer.

REGIONAL CHURCH GROWTH MAGAZINES

CHURCH GROWTH - CANADA
Dennis Oliver, Editor
Canadian Theological College
4400 4th Avenue, Regina
Sask. S4T OH8, Canada

TAIWAN CHURCH GROWTH BULLETIN
Sheldon Sawatsky, Editor
The Taiwan Church Growth Society
P. O. Box 165, Taichung
Taiwan, Republic of China 400

CHURCH GROWTH: AMERICA
Win Arn, Editor
1857 Highland Oaks Drive
Arcadia, Calif. 91006

CHURCH GROWTH NEWS - KOREA
Marlin Nelson, Editor
Post Box #3, Sudaemoon
Seoul, Korea

AMERICAN CHURCH GROWTH
The Reformed Church in America
421 North Brookhurst Street
Anaheim, Calif. 92801

MALAYSIA CHURCH GROWTH NEWS
P. O. Box 1068
Jalan Semangat
Petaling Jaya

SPREE
Nene Ramientos, Editor, P. O. Box 2557, Manila, Philippines

CHURCH GROWTH † BULLETIN

DONALD A. McGAVRAN, *Editor*

C. PETER WAGNER, *Associate Editor*

July 1975   Subscription $2 per year   Volume XI   No. 6

C O N T E N T S

WILL NAIROBI CHAMPION THE WHOLE MAN?

An Open Letter to the General Secretary of the World Council of Churches

Dear Mr. Potter:

With the Fifth Assembly of the World Council convening at Nairobi in November, career missionaries and leaders of Third World Churches at the School of Missions at Fuller Theological Seminary have been studying contemporary theologies of mission today, and reading many of the documents of the World Council of Churches, Vatican II, and the Evangelical movement. We have been identifying the two main strands of theological declarations and wish respectfully to address ourselves to the leadership of the World Council.

One of the documents we have considered is your report of August, 1974 to the Central Committee meeting in Berlin, printed in the October, 1974, issue of the Ecumenical Review. It so well sums up the position of the World Council of Churches, that Church Growth Bulletin is using it as a basis for this open letter to the World Council. Our purpose is to increase understanding of what the Council is doing and to urge that, out of respect for the Word, the Fifth Assembly incorporate into its program substantial emphasis on calling men from death to life. Now, five months before Nairobi, the WCC can take action which much more truly represents the biblical revelation and the thinking of its constituent Churches. In our view, Nairobi must address itself boldly to the needs of the "whole man" or "whole person". We beg you to initiate such action.

SEND news and articles to the Editor, Dr. Donald McGavran, at the Institute of Church Growth, Fuller Theological Seminary, 135 N. Oakland, Pasadena, California 91101. Published bi-monthly. Send subscriptions and changes of address to the Publisher, Norman L. Cummings, Overseas Crusades, Inc., 3033 Scott Blvd., Santa Clara, California 95050, U.S.A. Second-class postage paid at Santa Clara, California. Postmaster: Please send form 3579 to Overseas Crusades, 3033 Scott Blvd., Santa Clara, Ca. 95050.

As we study the theology of missions emanating from Geneva, review your report of August 1974, and inspect the documents issued to the Churches to help them prepare for the Fifth Assembly, we discern a tremendous concern with "the cries of the dispossessed, the powerless, the silent, the unrepresented, the struggle for social justice, changing the structures of society toward more justice and more community." As we read in your report (564 f) of the "wide range of studies and programmes", we come again and again to some fresh facet of this over-arching social concern. The Commission on Inter-Church Aid, you write, has been "unflinchingly active in meeting human need and seeing this need in terms of the struggle for social and racial justice." It has also "energetically carried out the Uppsala mandate to 'give the needs of development a high priority in the total programme'".

The whole Assembly has also "agonized" over two new programmes - to Combat Racism and to encourage Participation in Development. The Unit on Education and Renewal has convened "consultations and conferences on.... liberation, sexism, the family...and youth as agents for social change"... The Office on Education has been awakening participants to their duty "to master their environment and social structures toward fuller life in justice and community".....

On page 568 you point out that the World Council has taken this direction because of the "acute consciousness of a world in which the inequities of the rich and the poor, the injustices meted out to people because of their race, sex or class, and the confrontation of nations in wars which threatened the whole human race had become intolerable." You hear God say: "I go before you. Now that Christ carries away your sinful past, the Spirit frees you to live for others." Bearing down heavily on the World Council, you write, is a world situation (569) which "threatens the future of international society....Through indifference, greed, envy, fear, love of power, and short sighted stupidity, people have created or allowed to develop a demonstrably unjust economic order."

You argue that, toward this dangerous situation, three reactions are possible. There are actually four; but you mention three - a), b), and c) as follows:

a) evade the issues by retreating into...mystical and religious escape.
b) exorcise the dangers by forcing them into the rigidities of a reassuring ideological or religious system which explains everything and explains it away.
c) face the dangers head on, see them clearly, and discover new ways of overcoming them.

You maintain that the World Council's programmes are all grouped under c) and pour scorn on a) and b), which you "have tried to avoid." (570). You declare that "there is no way back for us into an escapism either of disengagement or of setting up ideological or dogmatic walls of defense."

Member Churches (572) ought to back up what their representatives sitting on the Central Committee of the World Council have devised as the
world programme, but you feel they are not doing so.

"The impression I have is that many of our congregations are engaged
in styles of worship, Christian nurture, and programme activities
which are so geared to maintaining a certain 'spiritual-security-at-
all-costs' that they come perilously near to the first two reactions
to the threats and challenges of our time." (573)

You write that Member Churches have not found it easy to translate
insights hammered out in ecumenical debate and frontier action into the
life and thinking of the congregations. This involvement gap is widening,
and the Geneva Staff is "easily tempted to suffer from impatience and
proud annoyance with our churches for not seeing what we see and not doing
what we are endeavoring to do." (575)

At the grave risk of oversimplification, let me say that after some
years of study of the Conciliar position, we think you have stated the
case substantially as it appears to us in the Evangelical Camp.

Let me set forth six corresponding aspects of the Evangelical position. These constitute a sixfold appeal which Church Growth Bulletin
is making to the Fifth Assembly of the World Council of Churches.

First, Evangelicals also live in the last quarter of the Twentieth
Century and are parts of the distressed global village, whose this-worldly
sufferings you describe so vividly. We have always been deeply concerned
about physical suffering and oppression. Many of us have put in years of
our lives with the down-trodden. Evangelicals are glad that WCC is concerned about the unjust social order and the grievous inequity in distribution of wealth. We are concerned too. What the Lausanne Congress
said about socio-political involvement being a part of our Christian duty
is for most of us elementary Christian truth. On this score we are at
one with you.

Second, we are amazed that Conciliar Christians achieve emphasis on
this-worldly improvements by neglecting and scorning eternal salvation.
The Bible speaks clearly about eternal salvation, forgiveness of sin, being
saved through faith in Christ alone, and passing from death to life. The
Bible says "There is now no condemnation to those who are in Christ Jesus."
We simply cannot understand how the Geneva staff so cheerfully consigns
eternal salvation to a footnote, or allows only that to be authentic eternal salvation which issues in the kind of social action you feel is urgent.
The need for eternal salvation is part of the heart cry of the "whole man".

Indeed, we are gravely concerned lest, in your scornful dismissal of
reactions a) and b), you are categorizing eternal salvation as 'pie in the
sky' no longer credible to persons come of age. If this is your position,
if you believe that conversion is really an "escape" unless it leads people
to your kind of social action, then your tremendous swing away from evangelism comes understandable. The finality with which Geneva refuses to give
sinner-converting, church-multiplying evangelism any significant place in

its programmes make sense only if you have previously concluded that such evangelism is a retreat into a "private world of mystical and religious escape." It would be helpful if you would tell the world how these "escape systems" which you denigrate differ from historic Christian beliefs about eternal salvation.

As we read the preparatory documents put out for the Fifth Assembly, your historic 1974 address to the Berlin meeting of the Central Committee, and dozens of other important conciliar papers, we search for and do not find any WCC department which has been "unflinchingly active in meeting the human need" of salvation from eternal condemnation. We would like to see the Assembly "agonizing" over new programmes to bring a hundred million nominal Christians into living relationship to the Lord Jesus, or to bring the secular masses in Sao Paulo into joyous dependence on the Holy Spirit, or to lead twenty thousand Chokosis in eastern Ghana into baptized Bible-obeying discipleship to Christ, and on and on. We look in vain for some "new and imaginative programmes" having to do with multiplying churches among the 80 million landless Harijans in India of whom at least three million, searching for life, have renounced Hinduism and converted to Buddhism in the last few years.

Third, you pen a few words about the reality of eternal salvation. For example, "God's justice manifests itself both in the justification of the sinner and in social and political justice" (565). But that is the last we hear about the justification of the sinner! The World Council seemingly plans to spend no blood, sweat, toil and tears to help sinners realize their need for justification....On page 577 you write, "We must seek, under God's grace....to undertake the differentiated mission of God ....in the power of our risen Lord." Good words!! But that part of the differentiated mission which has to do with the spread of the Christian Faith, the multiplication of Christian churches, the baptism of millions of penitent believers, is never mentioned.

Many of our number roundly declare that the Conciliar position is rational only on the grounds of a frank disbelief in the whole biblical affirmation of eternal salvation, a change of status achieved in the twinkling of an eye, through belief in Jesus Christ, and resulting in a gloriously more human life and an enormously tougher concern for our suffering brethren. We do not want to share this opinion, so we plead from you a new and unequivocal declaration of concern for the eternal salvation of the 2.7 billion unreached people of the world.

Many of our number point out that you fail to mention the fourth reaction - that of historic Christianity - to the world situation, though it shines forth from the entire Bible and from 19 centuries of dedicated Christian life. The fourth reaction to the evil world which lies all around us is this: Recognize that fallen man's basic need is reconciliation with God through faith in Jesus Christ according to the Scriptures. And that consequently a major task of the World Council of Churches and of all Christians is to proclaim the Gospel and encourage men and women to accept the Saviour in the fellowship of the Church, knowing certainly that power to change evil conditions will flow abundantly from the indwelling Holy Spirit to heal the sick, feed the hungry, lift up the fallen, change unjust structures, work for peace, and spread the light of learning.

Fourth, we are grieved that as between Christian brethren there should be this deep gulf. We propose a way of living in harmony. The Evangelicals at Lausanne have already said that both evangelism and social action are parts of our Christian duty. Evangelicals are already spending large parts of their mission budgets for bringing about this-worldly improvements in the populations where they serve. The salaries of advocates of social justice among Evangelicals are paid by Evangelical missionary societies. Indeed, we believe that if you "relentlessly expose yourselves as a Council and as Churches to the purifying Word of the Cross" you will devote at least a half of your mighty resources to Gospel-proclaiming, sinner-baptizing, church-multiplying evangelism. The alienation from your member denominations and congregations which you mention in your Berlin address would disappear if you would allocate 50 per cent of your income to programmes dedicated to serving God's justice which "manifests itself in the justification of the sinner" and 50 per cent to programmes dedicated to serving God's justice which "manifests itself in social and political justice."

You write, "member churches have not found it easy to translate insights hammered out in ecumenical debate...into the life and thinking of the congregation". (574) We suggest the Geneva Staff realize that God speaks equally truly to millions of intelligent Christians who live away from Geneva. The "insights hammered out in the ecumenical debate" are not all there is to contemporary Christian truth. Indeed, they may be somewhat warped by the vested interests which speak at Geneva. Truth may lie equally with the common person in all six continents who accepts the plain meaning of the Bible as God's Word and therefore believes implicity that the first task of the Christian is to beseech men to be reconciled to God.

Fifth, as we have studied the two theologies of mission today, we have come to the conclusion that two radically different systems of doctrine are battling for acceptance. The one believes that the Bible is the inspired, authoritative, infallible Word. The other believes that the Bible is the words of men through which God speaks on occasion. The one believes in eternal salvation as well as temporal improvements. The other believes that temporal improvements are certain, but beyond them we are in the realm of speculative opinions. The one believes that the Church is the Bride of Christ. The other, that the Church is one of God's many instrumentalities to bring about a juster human social order. The one believes that no man comes to the Father but by Jesus Christ, as revealed in the Bible and consequently proclaims Him as divine and only Saviour. The other, that the Cosmic Christ has spoken and is speaking in all religions and consequently dialogue with other religions is the correct way of mission. The one believes that the Kingdom of God will come only as God Himself destroys the enemies of mankind at the last day, and that until then only limited justice and righteousness are possible. The other believes that a new, just world order can be brought about by the cooperation of men of good will in all religions. The list of contrasts is much longer. A division as deep and lasting as that which took place in Europe in the sixteenth century may be imminent, but we hope it can be avoided.

The fact that some Conciliars imagine themselves to have the only position possible to intelligent man today, and are tempted to "proud annoyance" with naive Christians who "retreat into religious escapisms", confirms many Evangelicals in their opinion that the rift is dangerously near.

Sixth, the Nairobi Assembly may be the last opportunity for the World Council to take a truly ecumenical position, to declare fearlessly that the Bible speaks with final authority and utter clarity about eternal salvation, and reveals that it comes only through faith in Jesus Christ. It also speaks about letting "justice roll down as waters and righteousness as a mighty stream". Let the Assembly therefore reverse the Uppsala-Bangkok trend, which is tearing the Church apart. What is needed is a world program equally devoted a) to church growth, that is, to calling men, women, tribes, clans, and nations from death to life, through faith in Jesus Christ alone; and b) to calling Christians to practice social welfare, extend brotherhood and become active in the causes designed to promote justice and liberate the oppressed. Let the Fifth Assembly propose great evangelistic programs for the extension of the Church and great social programs for the extension of humanization. Then, finally, let the Fifth Assembly encourage all its constituent Churches to allocate funds and personnel to each of the two main thrusts in accordance with their consciences.

The time is past when any bureaucracy, even that at Geneva, can dictate to Member Churches that all their giving must go to evangelism or to social action. Let the Member Churches decide for themselves. In the ultimate analysis, the congregations will decide. No group, however wise and good, has enough wisdom and an exclusive enough access to God's presence to tell the whole Church what to do. The day of Constantinism is over. This issue our forefathers determined when they rejected papal authority. Let the World Council put before Member Churches the main biblical options as it sees them, and then listen carefully to what the Spirit is saying to and through the Churches.

Church Growth Bulletin will be pleased to give equal space to the World Council of Churches to reply to this letter.

The Editors - Donald McGavran, Peter Wagner

PREACHING WORLD MISSIONS TODAY

"One of the chief tasks of the pulpit is to remind the Church of her missionary character, to hold before God's people their obligations to the Lord and the world. Power in preaching comes through exposition of the Word. The chapters of A World To Win (great expositions of missionary scriptures) will 'preach'. Their insights and illustrations, carried into a thousand pulpits, will bless the Church.....It is indispensable to world evangelization that churches be filled with the missionary spirit..... The Church now stands at the dawn of worldwide Christian missions. The greatest forward movement of the Gospel in history is about to begin...More people are being converted to Christianity than ever before. This is not the sunset of Christianity but the dawn of world-wide gospel proclamation." (Roger Greenway in A WORLD TO WIN: PREACHING WORLD MISSIONS TODAY, Baker Book House, Grand Rapids, $3.95).

ONE MISSION: MANY MINISTRIES - Dr. J. C. Gamaliel, Concordia Seminary
Nagercoil, India

God has given the Church one Mission, but many Ministries. Confusing
Mission and Ministries has led to many problems and conflicts between
Christians. Launching arguments and counter-arguments without realizing
the twofold task, has wasted precious time, paralyzed the Church, and lost
sight of the great challenges around and ahead.

One Mission The Mission the Church is one - to make disciples of all
nations (Matthew 28:19) and to call men from darkness to light (Acts 26:18)
and from death to life (John 5:24). Christ began His work by saying, "The
time is fulfilled, and the kingdom of God is at hand; repent and believe
the gospel" (Mark 1:15). At the end of His earthly life, Christ told His
disciples, "Thus it is written...that repentance and forgiveness of sins
should be preached in his name to all nations" (Luke 24:47). John declares
that the scriptures themselves were "written that you may believe that
Jesus is the Christ, the Son of God, and that believing you may have life
in his name." (John 20:31). The Mission of the Church is to call men
through faith in Christ to receive forgiveness of sins and eternal life.

In II Corinthians 6:17, the Apostle Paul declared, "If anyone is in
Christ, he is a new creation; the old has passed away, behold, the new has
come." He defines the very heart of the Mission of the Church as reconcil-
ing men to God. Paul summed up his message thus: "We are ambassadors for
Christ, God making his appeal through us. We beseech you on behalf of
Christ, be reconciled to God."

In his letter to the Romans, Paul describes the Mission as calling
men from one aeon to another. The natural man is under the law, the wrath
of God, sin and death. When justified by faith in Christ, man passes into
the new aeon and has peace with God through Jesus Christ. He lives under
grace not law. Grace reigns through righteousness to eternal life.

The commission which Christ gave to the apostle Paul again makes the
Mission of the Church clear: "I send you to open their eyes, that they
may turn from darkness to light and from the power of Satan to God, that
they may receive forgiveness of sins and a place among those who are sanctified by faith in me." (Acts 26:18). Christ's command to Paul must
surely be seen as part of the One Mission - His overarching command to the
Church to call men from death to life.

Many Ministries God has given the Church many Ministries. While calling
men to life with God, through the preaching of the Gospel, was the One Mission of Christ, He was also engaged in many Ministries - "to proclaim release to the captives and recovering of sight to the blind, to set at liberty those who are oppressed...(Luke 4:18). Some are physically and others
are morally and spiritually blind, captives or oppressed. Christ minis-
tered to all. He went about preaching and doing good.

The apostles followed the same pattern. They called men to repentance
and faith. They also engaged in Ministries of various kinds. The missionaries, through the centuries, followed suit. They led men to fellowship

with the Triune God and multiplied churches. They also pioneered in starting schools, hospitals, orphanages, leprosy asylums, printing presses and many society changing processes. They reduced many languages to writing, improved systems of agriculture, fought against slavery, and elevated the status of women and children.

Mission and Ministries Mission and Ministries are not identical. They should not be confused. The one Mission of the Church is to call men from death to eternal life. Ministries are many and may be physical, social or economic. Ministries may precede, succeed or be contemporaneous with the Mission; but are subordinate and adjunct to it. Mission is always the call to repentance and faith in Christ. Those who are redeemed and preach the Gospel, cannot but be engaged in Ministries. Seeing Mission and Ministries in the biblical perspective will solve many problems and many conflicts. It will mean renewed life and growth for Christ's Church.

THE WARREN-MCGAVRAN LETTERS ON WORLD EVANGELIZATION

The Rev. Dr. Max Warren   April 22, 1975
WAYMARKS, 30 Michel Dene Road, East Dean
Nr. Eastbourne, Sussex, BN 20 OjR

Dear Dr. Warren:

I wonder if you remember the occasion in 1960 when you were lecturing at the Berkeley Divinity School and came with Mrs. Warren to lunch at our home? As I drove you back to your hotel I asked how you felt about the proposed merger of the IMC and the WCC. You replied, according to my memory, that you feared the evangelization of the world would be swallowed up in the concerns of the world organization.

I have just been studying the documents issued in preparation for the Nairobi meeting of the World Council of Churches this summer. I am teaching "Theology of Mission Today" to a class of 34 career missionaries and national leaders, many of whom are here taking doctoral studies. I am going to present the class with a summary of what the booklets say.

As I do this, I have to say that your fears in 1960 were abundantly justified. The evangelization of the world has indeed been swallowed and has disappeared almost without a trace. These booklets are entitled:

1. Confessing Christ Today

2. What Unity Requires

3. Seeking Community - the Common Search of People of Various Faiths

4. Education for Liberation and Community

5. Structures of Injustice and Struggles for Liberation

6. Human Development - the Ambiguities of Power, Technology,
        and Quality of Life.

The titles themselves, with the possible exception of the first, seem to rivet attention on other good things than discipling the ethne. Evangelism with intent to persuade could have been treated under Liberation, but I have checked carefully and it has not been. "Confessing Christ Today" also is not asking, "How Do Non-Christians in Europe and other lands confess Christ?"; but is rather asking "How Do Christians live and act so that their very actions constitute what Christ would have them do in the contemporary circumstances of life, and thus confess Christ?"

Mission in the sense of calling Non-Christians (among our own English and American relatives as well as among the citizens of China and India) from death to life has been swallowed up without a trace. When I said much the same thing to a noted leader of a main line Church in America recently, a fellow alumnus of Yale Divinity School, he said,

> "Come, come, Don. You know as well as I do, that all this talk
> about passing from death to life is metaphorical. It is based
> upon one kind of now outmoded metaphysics. Intelligent Christians
> cannot believe that happens literally. The life we call men to
> is life here and now, more freedom, less oppression, more land,
> more food, more education, more of the good things you value for
> yourself and your children. That "pie in the sky" is just not
> credible any more. To be sure, there is a spiritual dimension.
> These documents for the Nairobi meeting do talk about it. For
> example, Jesus Christ Frees and Unites, (page 33) says, "The
> Church cannot escape the obligation...to confess...its faith in
> Christ....(We seek) a conversion from parochial self-absorption
> to an awareness of what God is doing for the salvation of man."
> Don, the WCC wants to see millions "passing from death to life."
> And we intend to help them do it."

He simply brushed off the contention of the whole Evangelical Wing of the Church that there is ontological reality to salvation, that through belief in Jesus Christ and by God's grace, in the twinkling of an eye men can pass from death to life, and that the increase of numbers of such men and women is the best possible foundation on which to build improved structures. As I study these booklets, and meditate on the fact that the Nairobi meeting of the World Council seemingly plans to say nothing about world evangelization or the propagation of the Gospel among the 3 billion who have yet to hear and yet to believe, I am moved to write to you, who have played such a significant part in the conduct of the whole Christian mission, asking three questions:

1. Do you also see this omission?
2. Why was it made?
3. Can the Evangelicals of the Church do anything to help their WCC brothers and sisters back to a stand more compassionate as regards the eternal destiny of the three billion?

With kindest personal regards, I remain sincerely yours,

Donald McGavran

Dear Dr. McGavran   April 30, 1975

It was a very great pleasure to get your letter of April 22nd. Yes, I
do remember our visit with you in 1960. And I have no doubt of what I said
about the proposed merger of the I.M.C. and W.C.C. I thought it would be
disastrous and events have fully justified my fears.

In my book, Crowded Canvas - Some Experiences of a Life-time, you will find
a whole chapter on The Ecumenical Movement in which in measured terms I
expressed my fears about the integration of the I.M.C. and W.C.C.

I do not know how far one can in fairness judge the booklets issued by the
W.C.C. for the Nairobi Conference by their titles; but do entirely agree
with you that it is very tragic that the witness in the Lausanne conference
has borne, so far, no fruit in W.C.C. circles. To me, the gap between the
W.C.C. and the Church Growth Movement is one of the most sad and unhappy
facts of our time. I've just been reading again the November 1974 issue of
the Church Growth Bulletin with its marvellous news from Argentina. This
is a note which is missing from the W.C.C.

You quote a fellow alumnus of Yale Divinity School. I have only one comment and that is to thank God that in most circles in this country his
remarks would be laughed at as absurd! I don't say that with complacency.
God knows how bad the situation is here. We are sadly introverted, in
part due to an economic problem. But theologically speaking, there is a
new strong wave of affirmation of the Gospel which I find very cheering.
And in many local situations the Holy Spirit is most certainly at work.

So to your closing questions, my first answer is 'Yes, I do see the
omission'.

To the second question, "Why was it made?" the answer is very complicated.
At the grave risk of over-simplification, I would say it was due to a
neurotic over-preoccupation with structures born out of a Church Unity
Movement which had lost its way theologically.

I wish I could offer an encouraging answer to your third question. It
will be a very hard task indeed. At this moment I do not think the W.C.C.
is prepared to listen to the Evangelical testimony. Probably the only
thing which may bring conviction is the bankruptcy of their own efforts
and the witness of what God is doing when active evangelism is the first
concern.

In that Argentina situation I was struck by the thought that political,
economic and social factors were all at work and the Holy Spirit used
them. I think the W.C.C. type of mind is alert to these factors, but does
not know how to exploit them. Evangelicals, on the whole are much less
alert to just these factors. I think it is possible that if there was
more evidence that Evangelicals were drawing the moral Mr. Silvoso points
out at the top of page 458, the W.C.C. might begin to listen.

Anyway, thank you for writing. I did greatly appreciate it. With all good wishes to you and your colleagues.

Max Warren

- - - - - - - - - - - - - - - -

Dear Dr. Warren   May 6, 1975

Your welcome letter of April 30th has just come in. Many thanks.

You will be pleased to know that Charles Mellis, former General Secretary of Missionary Aviation Fellowship, is quoting extensively from your book Crowded Canvas in his thesis on "Missionary Orders" - what you call "Voluntary Structures".

It occurred to me that readers of Church Growth Bulletin would be most interested in the exchange of letters we have just had which covers several major issues. You speak forthrightly to both Evangelicans and Conciliars. Suppose we were to put into the Church Growth Bulletin both letters, would you be pleased?

Very sincerely yours,   Donald McGavran

- - - - - - - - - - - - - - - - -

Dear Dr. McGavran: May 12, 1975

Yes, by all means print the letters in which we discuss the W.C.C. I certainly stand by all I said in mine. I suspect my opinions are already known in W.C.C. circles.

I'm profoundly convinced of the importance of 'Missionary Orders'. Please tell Charles Mellis how very interested I am that he is working on this subject. I would be very pleased to send him a photostat of a talk I gave in 1942 to our C.M.S. Area Secretaries defining the nature of the Society. Actually at one point I compared 'Voluntary Societies' to the idea of 'Missionary Orders'.

With all good wishes to you and your colleagues,

Very Sincerely,   Max Warren

CHURCH GROWTH AND THE WORD OF GOD by Dr. Alan Tippett, trans-lated into Chinese by Dr. Bill Yang, has just been published by the Taiwan Church Growth Society. Order it from:
    China Sunday School Association, 105 North Chung Shan Rd.
    Section 2, Taiwan, Republic of China, 104. NT$20.00
Churches and Missions please purchase this significant book in quantity and give it to pastors and other church leaders.

THE AMERICAN CHURCH AND THE UNEVANGELIZED WORLD   by Harvey Hoekstra,
                                                    Ethiopia

A.   Eleven factors contribute to reduced missionary sendings of mainline
denominations. Readers will easily recognize them.

1. Church Mission Tensions: The missionary movement brought into
being strong Younger Churches which formed a World-wide Church and a host
of new tense relationships between Missionary Societies, Younger Churches,
missionaries and national leaders.

2. Non-Missionary Younger Churches: The Younger Churches frequently
were not eager to send missionaries out themselves. Nor did the Churches
give rise to or encourage the formation of para-church missionary sending
agencies.

3. Large Institutions at Central Stations: Institutionalization saddled Young Churches with expensive structures which absorbed an inordinate
proportion of their thought and energy. Missionaries became fraternal
workers within this system - ecumenical deacons in a vast program of inter-
church aid.

4. Bureaucracy Triumphed: Mission leaders in Western Missionary Societies tended to become administrators rather than leaders who dreamed and
planned and prayed in terms of reaching the entire world with the Gospel.

5. Retreat of the West: The collapse of colonial empires created an
atmosphere of defeat, growing isolationism, denial of responsibility and
an illogical conclusion that the missionary movement had no future.

6. Loss of China: The loss of China, quotas for missionaries established by some governments, and the closing of Burma, Sudan and a few other
countries produced among some a profound discouragement. Discouraged expelled missionaries by the hundred flooded into American churches as ministers and into Missionary Societies as administrators, and all too frequently
voiced defeatist views as to the future of Christian missions.

7. Europe's Guilty Conscience: The guilt complexes of Christian leaders in Europe (the Church's failure to stop Hitler) and in America (failure
to stop wars, racial arrogance, poverty, corruption, and other social ills)
led many to question the rightness of sending American missionaries to "the
spiritual east". What would they say?

8. Mission Radically Redefined: Radically redefining mission, Uppsala
lifted up humanization alone as the true goal of mission. Hoekendijk and
others voiced openly anti-church views and identified mission with everything God wants done on earth (the Missio Dei) thus blurring the distinction between the Church and the World. Numerous other new notions downgraded the missionary movement and its classic goal of proclaiming the
Gospel and persuading people to believe on Jesus Christ and become members
of His Church.

9. <u>The Independent World Missionary Agency Disappeared:</u> Amalgamation with the World Council reduced the International Missionary Council to a mere commission of the larger body. In America, the Foreign Missions Conference was reduced to an overseas division of the National Council of Churches of Christ. Both reductions diminished evangelism and emphasized church union, social action and service. Persons with little or no conviction about world evangelization became "mission" administrators. The meetings of CWME in Mexico City 1963 and Bangkok 1972 to plan 'world mission' were made up of delegates appointed from within the ecclesiastical structure. Their concerns were churchly not evangelistic. The significance of these structures for weakening determination to evangelize the world cannot be overestimated.

10. <u>Actively Missionary Christians and Agencies Departed:</u> When the IMC and FMC disappeared, many strong Missionary Societies and Younger Churches withdrew. Loss of contact and of cross fertilization by those committed to historic Christian mission further narrowed the vision of the mainline denominations who began increasingly to talk among themselves. They grew more and more remote from dynamic missionary minded Christians with whom they were formerly associated in the IMC and FMC.

11. <u>Younger Church Lukewarmness Diminished Missionary Sendings:</u> Younger Churches seldom blazed with missionary passion, but almost always wanted the rich services of Western Missions. Consequently, many mainline leaders sincerely believed that only by not sending western missionaries could Younger Churches be led to true selfhood and maturity. Leaders honestly believed that Younger Churches ought to be responsible to evangelize their <u>entire</u> nations and did not even see that for a Younger Church, whose members formed one or two per cent of the total population, to evangelize an entire nation was <u>impossible</u>. Withdrawing missionaries to encourage Younger Churches to evangelize does not usually work, either. It leaves 87 per cent of the non-Christian population with no one evangelizing it. Yet this outcome apparently does not trouble leaders of mainline Missionary Societies, Divisions of World Mission and Evangelism, and Divisions of Overseas Ministries. They continue to withdraw missionaries and to advocate it.

B. Eleven suggestions toward changing the direction in world mission interpretation and planning in the old mainline denominations so that strong commitment to worldwide cross cultural evangelization shall arise.

1. Recognize the important role mainline denominations had in bringing into being the worldwide Church of our time.

2. Recognize the dimension of the tragic withdrawal of mainline denominations from the historic missionary sending movement.

3. Recognize that missionary structures have not only been lost in the disappearance of the IMC and the FMC, but that the mission boards have either been structured out of existence or have become captives of denominational machinery like root bound plants in ecclesiastical vessels.

4. Recognize the importance of the para-church mission agencies giving rise to and implementing the missionary movement. Even today it is the para-church structures that are sending out approximately 80 per cent of all North American missionaries. In Europe the percentage would be even higher.

5. Recognize the groundswell of reaction taking place within the main-line denominations demanding a reversal of all trends leading to the dim-inution or demise of the missionary movement in their churches.

6. Recognize that the missionary movement has always been supported and conducted by and large on the principle of voluntarism. That is, societies of the warmhearted, loyal to their denominations, but obedient first of all to God, propose to evangelize non-Christians.

7. Find ways to release the enormous energy and resources of main-line Christians who are committed to the historic, biblical goals that have always characterized the missionary movement. Main line denominations must find a way to carry on the kind of mission these Christians wish to sup-port. They should not have to go outside the denominationally sponsored programs to carry out Christian mission as they conceive it.

8. Main line denominations need the input and vitality of non-conciliar, para-church Missionary Societies as a stimulus and corrective to one sided relationships where too much time is spent talking among themselves...same people, same perspectives, insulated and inbred.

9. Non-conciliar, para-church mission agencies also could benefit from the experience and broader perspectives of the main line denominations which have already gone through many of the tensions in church/mission relations. Many para-church agencies are only beginning to face these problems. They stand to benefit from both the failures and successes of the older Mission-ary Societies.

10. Main line denominations should seek with the Younger Churches with which they have ties now <u>creative programs aimed at reaching effectively with the Gospel multitudes</u> who, without this new effort, will have no op-portunity to know Christ.

Main line denominations should equip and set free to give leadership in mission persons committed to world-wide cross cultural evangelization. These should not be saddled with routine administrative responsibilities but be given opportunity to develop strategies aimed at communicating the Gospel effectively to people not yet reached for Christ. Missiologists from both the older and younger Churches should work together in planning concerted, intelligent, professionally competent and Spirit empowered mis-sionary outreach. Only this will make it possible for additional millions to come to know Christ -- millions who without such efforts will never hear the Gospel.

Such leaders should have the confidence of people in the old line denominations and be thoroughly committed to cross cultural evangelization aimed at making known the Gospel, and persuading people to become disciples of Christ and responsible members of His Church.

11. As those who acknowledge the Lordship of Jesus Christ and have experienced the mighty power of the Holy Spirit, let the leaders in main line denominations challenge God's people joyfully and sacrificially to be part of a world-wide missionary movement arising from within the whole Church aimed at reaching with the Gospel in our time the 2.7 billion dying in the great famine of the Word of God.

NEWS NEWS

BANGLADESH - May 24, 1975

"Peter McNee, New Zealand Baptist, has almost completed his comprehensive survey of this country area by area, denomination by denomination, mission by mission. He has compiled a 200 page Church Growth Report and in each area is informing appropriate Christian leaders of his findings. One fantastic result of his sharing the newly discovered potential of church growth has just surfaced. Rev. Subash Sangma chaired the Church Growth Seminar in October 1974, and was at that time Secretary of the National Christian Council of Bangladesh. He has now resigned to become an independent evangelist. Also , he is on the Lausanne Continuation Committee. Peter suggested to Subash that he contact the thousands of non-Christian Garos in Bangladesh. Christian leaders hardly knew such a large community existed until Peter shared the indisputable government district statistics with them.

Three ten-day Bible Camps were held in April and May, 1975. The results have been mind boggling. Over 1,100 Garos were baptized during these 30 days of camp. Never has Bangladesh seen such a large number of baptisms in so brief a time. We thank God for the enlightenment church growth principles have brought to the ministry here in our beloved land."

.....Phil Parshall

KABACAN, NORTH COTABATO, PHILIPPINES April 1975 "The recent workshop on church growth affected my ministry tremendously. The lively discussions, sharing of ideas, challenging lectures, and sweet fellowship in prayer revolutionized me. I determined by God's help to put into action the precious lessons I learned from the workshop. I set up goals and formulated strategies for my area - the Central Mindanao District of the Wesleyan Church. In this there are at present 24 small churches with a total membership of 1,046. We have now prepared a five year program of aggressive evangelism and church planting, calling for 60 new churches and 1,600 new members by 1980. Our denomination in the Philippines has set a goal of 200 churches and 6,000 new members." Rev. E. S. Dasep

DURBAN, SOUTH AFRICA April 1975 "The Zion Christian Church has about
200,000 adherents and started about 1915 as a healing ministry in a rural
area, but has now spread to the cities. Its traditions are extremely puri-
tanical. It insists on no alcohol, no tobacco, hard work, and faithfulness
in marriage. Not unnaturally its members are in considerable demand as
employees in factories and business concerns....For the great Easter celebrations, crowds stream together from all over the countryside. The proceedings took place in a large hall which seated more than 2000 and the
service was relayed by loud speakers to the tens of thousands outside.
The younger women were arrayed in bright blue, the elder women in blouses
of canary yellow with dark green skirts, with leaders of position in the
church in dark green uniforms with various signs indicating the special
levels of dignity to which they have attained.....Perfect order prevailed.
Leaders had the assembly under perfect control. Prayer was simultaneous,
all praying aloud together; but when the leader gave the signal the
prayer ceased and perfect quiet followed. There were four readings from
Scripture, each followed by an address. Great stress was laid on unity
between the tribes represented; all were to think of themsleves as Zion-
ists rather than as members of this or that tribe. The faithful were urged
to obey their chiefs, many of whom were present, and to pray for the government of the Republic of South Africa." Bishop Stephen Neill

NOVA SCOTIA, 1855 Theodore Seth Harding was pastor of the Horton (now
Wolfville) Baptist Church from 1795 to 1855. When Mr. Harding began his
ministry at Horton the only other Baptist Church was at Halifax and there
were less than 100 Baptists in the land. When he died there were 200
churches and 18,000 communicants! (The Call of Our Own Land, by Schutt
and Cameron, page 34, published by the Home Mission Board of the Baptist
Convention of Ontario and Quebec, undated) (Contributed by Leslie Tarr
of Toronto).

INDIA, February 1975 Nagaland Missionary Movement (only seven years old)
has been conducting evangelistic crusades covering the whole of these
hills and raising funds to send missionary candidates to theological
colleges and missionaries to the Adis in Arunachal Pradesh....New converts
in remote parts of Nagaland itself include six veteran head-hunters who
took 316 heads before they were converted. Torokiu took 47, Tomosu 50,
Chingmak 64, Chemkiu 62, Piong 33, and Tongmoso 60. These men today are
actively serving different churches as evangelists and treasurers. They
know how to count! Out of head-hunters, God has created soul winners
for His glory.   The Baptist Leader, January-February 1975 p. 17

NORTH AMERICAN CHURCH EXPANSION May 29, 1975. The North American section
of the Lausanne Continuation Committee met at Dallas, Texas, May 26, convened by Chairman Kenneth Chafin. Since evangelism is a first priority
of all eight regional sections, the delegates from U.S. and Canada projected an expanded body of up to 100 members to design and implement such
task forces as might be required for attaining evangelistic goals. New
members will be invited on the basis of their active involvement in evangelism. The task is to activate forces already existing in North America.
Temporary offices have been established in South Main Baptist Church,
4100 South Main, Houston, Texas 77002   C. Peter Wagner

INDEX

Abidjan, 137, 376
Abilene Christian College, 103, 260
accommodation, 55
accountability, 331, 332
"Accountability for World Evangelization,"
  331
acculturation, 3, 92, 364
"A.D. 2000: 350 Million Christians in
  Africa," 120
Addis Ababa, 17, 358
administration, 289
advance, 45
advocacy, 2
Afericasia, 105, 132, 144, 150, 161, 167,
  204, 220, 224, 239, 252, 253, 293, 327
Africa, 71, 126, 137, 254, 276, 295, 405
"Africa Independent Churches and Seminaries"
  106
"African Denomination Organizes Board of
  Missions," 311
African Independent Churches, 106, 110, 160,
  163, 170, 260, 287
Aguan Valley, 138
AHN, Pastor, 463
"Aiding Emerging Churches Develop Missionary
  Passion," 251

AINSLIE, Peter, 173
AKAKA, Abraham, 91
ALEXANDER, Merton, 109
All Africa Conference of Churches, 137
All Africa School of Theology, 106, 287
All Asia Mission Consultation, 352, 373, 480
"All Asia Mission Consultation," 274, 343
"All Asia Student Missionary Convention,"343
"All Eyes on Lausanne, July 16-26,1974," 399
All Nations Missionary College, 220
All-Philippine Congress on Evangelism," 47
ALLEN, Horace, N., 217
ALLEN, Roland, 49, 216
ALTON, Mable, 330
ALVES, Ruben, 495
Amazon Basin, 249
America, 30, 73
American Baptists, Zaire, 357
American Blacks, 503
American Board of Commissioners for Foreign
  Missions, 15
"American Church and the Unevangelized
  World, The," 522
"American Church Growth Explored," 30
American Jews, 361, 410, 470, 477, 496
American Lutheran, 113
  Ethiopia, 241
American Messianic Fellowship, 314
Amharas, 241
Amis, 28
Andean Outlook, The, 191
ANDERSON, Bruce, 102
Andes Evangelical Mission, 97, 99, 191, 334
Andhra state, 123
Andover Theological Seminary, 15
Andra Maharashtra, 406
Anglicans, 127
  Singapore, 290
Animists, 3, 12, 110, 115, 126, 201, 297,
  359, 376, 414
"Anthropological Light on Evangelism," 283
"Anthropologist Looks at Mission-Church
  Transition, An," 155
anthropology, 1, 52, 155, 283, 316, 379
Antichrist, 26, 84
anti-Western sentiment, 161
Aoyama Gakuin, 196
apartheid, 137

Apostolic Church,
  Mexico, 29
apostolic practices, 430
archives, 50
Argentina, 3, 275, 377, 424, 451, 455, 520
ARIGA, Paul, 293
ARN, Win, 448, 496, 498
art, 19
ARTHUR, Joseph, 467
Arunachal Pradesh, 526
Ashland, Brethren, 499
Asia, 94, 276
Asia Pulse, 137, 223
"Asian Missions and Church Growth," 479
Asian Student, The, 393
"Asia's Pulse Beats with Missions," 223
Assembly of God, 254, 415, 435
  America, 503
  Chile, 492
  El Salvador, 33, 134
  South Africa, 287
Assembly of God Bible Institute, 133
assistance in development, 84
Associated Evangelical Seminary, 348
Association of African Churches, 288
Association of Evangelicals of Africa and
  Madagascar, 418
audience segments, 333
Australia, 94
autonomy, 92, 454
Aymaras, 100, 102, 334, 393
AZARIAH, Bishop, 123

"Babylonian Captivity of the Christian
  Mission, The, " 343
BAEGERT, Johann, 61, 66
Bahamas, 136
BAKER, Dwight, 98
Baker's Dictionary of Christian Ethics, 365
Bakhatlas, 96
BALDEMOR, Rogelio, 300
Baliem Valley, 241
Bantt, 500
BANG, Jee, 217
Bangkok, 229, 263, 293,
Bangladesh, 525
Baptist Convention of Ontario and Quebec, 526
Baptist Messenger, 300
Baptists, 401
  Burma, 150, 360
  India, 360
  Indonesia, 194
  New Zealand, 525
  Zaire, 310
Baranquilla, 309
BARRETT, David, 11, 28, 120, 129, 137, 163,
  286, 295, 405
barrio churches, 56, 57, 285
"Basics of Effective Missions Anywhere," 482
BATES, Gerald, 170
BAVINCK, J.H. 380
BEAHM, William, 16
BEAVER, R. Pierce, 154, 158, 211
beer drinking, 396
"Beginning of a People-Movement. The," 29
Belem-Brasilia highway, 248
Believer's Church, The, 208
BELLAMY, Wilfred, 351
Belo Horizonte, 465
BENJAMIN, Paul, 497
BENNETT, Charles, 5, 85

BENTSON, Joyce, 330
BENTSON, Keith, 3, 31

Berar Khandesh Pastor's Conference, 406
BERGGREN, Warren, 120
BERKOUWER, G.C., 380
Berlin, 163, 278, 446
Bethel Baptist,
    India, 136
Bethel Seminary, 497
Beth Emmanuel Messianic Synagogue, 470
Beverly Hills, 470
BEYERHAUS, Peter, 76, 78, 100, 153, 207.
    234, 253, 267, 378, 379, 392, 399, 412, 448
"Beyond Ecumenism, Part I," 13
Bhils, 335
Biafra, 260
Bible and Medical Missionary Fellowship, 487
Bible Baptist Fellowship, 497
biblical constants, 331
biblical relativism, 401
"Biblical Theology of Religions," 392
biblical variables, 331
"Bigger Than Converting an Individual," 58
Billy Graham Evangelistic Association, 10,
    14, 422
"Billy Graham's New Vision," 278
BINGHAM, Hiram, 91
"Biography of Juyji Nakada," 198
Biola College, 60, 119
biological growth, 237
BIRCH, Ken, 421, 500
Birmingham, 6, 213
birth control, 398
BISHOP, Jordan, 101, 192
"Bishop Stephen Neill on Conversion," 145
BLACKWELL, R.D., 332
BLAKE, Eugene, 137
BLANCHARD, Maurice, 394
BLAUW, Johannes, 153
BLIESE, Loren, 241
BLOCH, Ernest, 271
BLOCHER, Henri, 399
BLOCHER, Jacques, 137
Body of Christ, 109
Bogota, 10, 47, 309
Bogota Congress on Evangelization, 101
Bolivia, 97, 99, 192, 334, 441
Boranas, 199
BORDREUL, Daniel, 231
Born at Midnight, 330
Borneo, 3, 28
BOSCHMAN, Paul, 132
BOUTER, William, 26
BRADSHAW, Mac, 293
BRADSHAW, Malcomb, 52, 74,
BRAUN, Neil, 5, 137, 298
Brazil, 136, 248, 313, 390, 465
"Brazil Plan," 187
Brazil 1980: The Protestant Handbook, 390
"Brazilian Wild West -- Multitudes Waiting
    to be Churched, The," 248
"Breaking the Stained Glass Barrier," 404
Breaking the Stained Glass Barrier, 404, 416
Brethren in Christ,
    Canada, 500
BRIDGES, Julian, 143
Bridges of God, The, 49, 98, 122, 203, 286,
    496, 505
BRIGHT, John, 111
"Bring in the Vacuum Cleaner: The Right Way
    to Say It," 147
broadcasting, 17
BROOM, Wendell, 103, 260
BROUGHAM, David, 290
BUCKMAN, Allan, 311
Buenos Aires, 377, 451
Burakumins, 137

burial customs, 243
BURKE, Fred, 106, 287
Burma, 150, 359, 522
Burundi, 109, 170, 472
BUTHELEZI, Chief G., 288

Cali, 56, 57, 309
California, 65, 136
"Call for Aid," 391
Call to Mission, 286
Cambodia, 260, 297
Cameroun, 222, 253
campaign evangelism, 54, 285
Campus Crusade, 75

Canada, 421, 493, 499
Canadian Theological College, 379, 497
Cantonese language, 220
capitalism, 137
Carachipampa, 101
CAREY, William, 49, 61, 178, 213
CARY, Otis, 198
caste, 123, 136, 150, 171, 394
CASTILLO, Jose, 19
CASTRO, Emilio, 440
Cauca River Movement, 85
"Cease Fire or Victory?" 389
Center of Advanced Study for Evangelism, 259
Central America, 134
Central American Mission, 134
Central Methodist Mission,
    Asutralia, 229
Central Presbyterian Church,
    Colombia, 57
"Census Data and Estimating Church Growth,"
    143
censuses, 143
"Century of Protestant Christianity in Japan,
    A," 198
CHAFIN, Kenneth, 526
CHAI, Kwan-Hul, 217
"Challenge for a Million," 194
"Chapter Nine: Some Questions Directed to
    Protestants and Particularly to Protes-
    tant Ministers," 66
CHAN, Wilson, 220
CHANDLER, Russell, 472
charity, 106
Charismatic Movement, 446
CHENG, Elias, 444
Cherrapunji, 335, 336
Chiang Mai, 358
Chicago, 293
Chicago Lutheran Theological Seminary, 113

Chile, 64, 170
Chimborazo Province, 329
China, 217, 291, 393, 488, 522
Chinju, 343
CHIN-LIANG, Chu, 259
Chins, 150
CHO, David, 274, 352, 374, 442, 466, 479
choke-law, 25, 28, 95
Chokosis, 514
"Christ for All," 168
"Christ the Only Way," 220, 292, 422
Christian and Missionary Alliance, 175, 207
    Canada, 500, 501
    Colombia, 57
    Hong Kong, 223
    Indonesia, 488
    Philippines, 467, 491
    Vietnam, 225
    West Irian, 290
    Zaire, 357

2

PARK, Tae Ro, 217
PARRISH, Archie, 497
PARSHALL, Phil, 400, 525
"Partners in Obedience," 118
partnership, 176, 186
Pasadena, 50, 498
Pastor's Prayer Conference, 218
paternalism, 51, 103, 150, 152, 157, 160,
     184, 252, 364, 461
PATTERSON, George, 138, 427
PAUL, Pope, 215
PEARCE, Bob, 218
PENDLEY, Taylor, 87
PENTECOST, Edward, 223, 275
Pentecostal Assemblies,
    Canada, 421, 500, 501
Pentecostals,
    Burundi, 473
    India, 360
    Latin America, 160
people-movements, 3, 5, 18, 19, 29, 58, 94,
    116, 119, 226, 259, 316, 341, 424, 451,
    488, 491
People Movements in Southern Polynesia, 417
PEREZ, Pablo, 424, 442
period of transition, 156
PERON, Juan, 455
persecution, 416, 472
persuasion, 143, 189, 209, 484
Peru, 223
PETERS, George, 53, 186, 187, 358, 500
PETERSEN, William, 496
Philippines, 19, 47, 60, 152, 220, 227, 277,
    279,292,300,336,422, 463, 467, 525
PICKETT, J.W., 49, 128
PIERSMAN, Norman, 133
PIERSON, A.T., 15
Pinnock, Clark, 380
"Plain Speaking About Mission and Church
    Growth," 395
"Plain Vanilla and Church Growth," 103
Plymouth Brethren,
    Argentina, 451
    Burundi, 473
"Points of Reflection on the Ministry of
    Priests in Bolivia," 101
polygamy, 6, 70, 163, 396
Polynesia, 91
population explosion, 120
Population Reference Bureau, 287, 381
Portuguese language, 136
"Possessing the Philosophy of Animism for
    Christ," 359
possibility thinking, 509
POTTER, Philip, 511
POULSON, Ernest, 38, 45, 290
power-encounter, 23
Practical Anthropology, 159, 378
Presbyterian Survey, 112
Presbyterians,
    Biafra, 260
    Cameroun, 444
    Colombia, 85
    Congo, 168
    East Africa, 443
    Guatemala, 134
    India, 335
    Japan, 195
    Korea, 217, 311, 343
    Mexico, 445
    Pakistan, 219
    Taiwan, 273
    Venezuela, 348
presence, 83, 106, 192, 404
Primal Vision, The, 104

Prince Royal's College, 358
Princeton Foreign Missions Society, 15
Princeton University, 15
principal of an extension chain, 428
"Principles of Church Growth, The," 100
Principles of Church Growth, 226, 239
priorities, 191
proclamation, 83, 104, 209
PROFITT, T.D., 393
Programmed Extension Text on Church Growth,
    357
progress, 84
Promotional Strategy, 332
propagation, 104, 138, 320
Puerto Rico, 10
Punctured Preconceptions: What North
    Americans Think About the Church, 283

qualitative growth, 2, 157, 197, 425, 506
"Quantitative Case for Continuing Missions
    Today, The," 202
quantitative growth, 2, 157, 202, 297, 425
Quechuas, 100, 102, 329
QUINN, Bernard, 167

RABER, Dorothy, 259, 291, 357
race barriers, 136
racial pride, 127
"Racialism and Denominationalism Completely
    Forgotten," 287
RADER, Paul, 196, 311, 343, 463
radio, 17, 464
"Radio and Church Growth," 17
RAMIENTOS, Nene, 220, 292, 422
RAMM, Bernard, 380
RAY, Chandu, 201, 228, 290, 342, 352, 374,
    478
Reach Out and Grow, 448, 499
READ, William, 6, 50, 130, 156, 235,377,384, 390
Readings in Missionary Anthropology, 159
receiving church, 443
receptivity, 18, 41, 103, 129, 146,233, 483
reconciliation, 443, 514
"Redeploying Mission Resources," 476
Regent College, 500
Regina, 500
"Reglamento Locale," 33
REIMER, Reginald, 225, 420
REIMER, Vernon, 450
relativism, 401, 498
religious encounter, 111
religious imperialism, 150
religious independency, 164
religious orders, 14
"Remarkable Church Growth in High Ecuador,"
    329
Renaissance, 109
renewal, 73, 260
"Report on Colombia," 308
research, 9
"Research and the Present Challenge," 9
resistance, 240
responsiveness, 8, 239, 240, 316
reteachable materials, 427
"Retrospect and Prospect, 1970," 49
revitalization, 197
revival, 44, 195, 260, 282, 296,363,500,506
"Revival and Church Growth Among the
    Montagnards in Vietnam," 296
"Revival and Church Growth in Honduras,"260
revolution, 138
RHEE, Song Nai, 419
Rhodes University, 173
Rhodesia, 131

"Rhodesia Acts for Church Growth," 131
RICE, Robert, 477

RIDDLE, Norman, 310, 357
right end populations, 239, 240
"Rise and Fall of the Student Volunteer
   Movement, The," 15
ROBERTS, Oral, 446
ROBINSON, Gordon, 8
Roman Catholics, 13, 25, 65, 69, 107, 138,
   342, 376, 455, 473, 501
Romane language, 408
Roms, 407
ROSEN, Moishe, 410
ROSS, Charles, 168
ROY, Nichols, 335
RUBINGH, Eugene, 11
Rwanda, 170

SA, Bung Sim, 217
SABITI, Erica, 445
sacramentalism, 101
Sacred Congregation for the Evangelism of
   Peoples, 193
Saigon, 420
Salisbury, 131
Salvation Army, 196, 475
   India, 406
"Salvation Today," 263
salvation today, 229, 263, 293, 336
SAMMS, Bob, 300
Samoa, 254
SAMUEL, Anand Rao, 123
San Marcos, 260
San Nicolas, 451
SANGMA, Subash, 525
Santals, 406
SANTIAGO, Efriam, 10
Sao Paulo, 50, 259, 514
SAPSEZIAN, Aharon, 25
SARGUNAM, Ezra, 222
saturation evangelism, 54, 495
SAWATSKY, Sheldon, 357, 510
SCANLON, A. Clark, 40, 289
SCHAFFER, Francis, 108
SCHAPERA, I., 95, 96
SCHERER, James, 153
Schism and Renewal in Africa, 163, 167
SCHNEIDER, Bob, 312
School of World Mission, 24, 51, 98, 111,
   135, 199, 221, 275, 400, 424, 448, 462,
   482, 511
SCHULLER, Robert, 497, 509
Scientology, 501
SCOTT, Waldron, 417
second-generation, 114
secularism, 272,
"Seeing the Church in the Philippines," 227
segregation, 449
"Self-Centeredness and the Choke Law," 25
self-governing, 159
self-supporting, 343
"Seminary Program in Congo Villages," 168
sending church, 443
Seoul, 274, 327, 352, 373, 466, 480
"Seoul, Lausanne, and Africasian Mission-
   ary Societies," 327
service agencies, 117
Seventh-Day Adventists, 225, 365, 420
   Burundi, 472
Shaken Foundations, 267
"'Shaken Foundations' in Church Growth," 267
SHEARER, Roy, 50, 319
SHEPERD, Jack, 206, 207
SHEWMAKER, Stan, 283, 319, 395

SI, Doom Van, 231
Siabalengu, 283
Sierra Leone, 6
SILVOSO, Edgardo 451, 520
SIN, Han, 258
"Since We are Growing Older, Let's Grow
   Bolder," 153
SINCLAIR, John, 159
Singapore, 256, 275, 289, 478
Singapore Bible College, 38, 45
Singapore Congress on Evangelism, 47, 255
SKIVINGTON, Robert, 280
SMALLEY, William, 159
SMITH, Alex, 293
SMITH, Don, 131
SMITH, Donna, 195
SMITH, Ebbie, 163, 194, 279, 358
SNYDER, Harold, 426
SNYDER, Roger, 19
social action, 92, 106, 127, 193, 207, 229,
   234, 250, 263, 271,302,365,425,441,512
Society of Brethren, 15
SOGGARD, Viggo, 333
"Soils: A Church Growth Parable, The," 145
Solomon Islands, 254
Solomon Islands Christianity, 50
SOO, Chae Eun, 258
Soonchun, 311, 343
Sons of Tiv: A Study of the Rise of the
   Church Among the Tiv of Central Nigeria,
   11
South Africa, 106,137,173,287,526
South American Indians, 121
Southern Baptist Board of Foreign Missions,
   465
Southern Baptists,
   America, 503
   Central America, 289
   India, 394
   Indonesia, 279
   Philippines, 279
sowing, 146
Spain, 174

SPEER, Robert, 15, 142, 168
spiritism, 4
spiritual vacuum, 456
spontaneous expansion, 325
St. Marks Presbyterian Church, Colombia, 56
St. Thomas Mount Baptist Church, India, 136
STANDERWICK, Dick, 500
"State Actions and the Cause of Christ,"335
statistics, 9, 11, 143
Steings, 421
STILL, Josephine, 260
STOCK, Fred, 219
STOKES, Louie, 452
STOTT, John, 425, 440, 444
"Straws in the Wind," 117
STREET, T. Watson, 153
structured evangelism, 325
student volunteer movement, 15
Student World, 192
SUAZO, Miguel, 10
subcenter, 427
subsistence urbanization, 308
suburbs, 74, 498
Sudan, 522
Sudan Interior Mission, 90, 259, 320, 358,
   368, 389
Summer Institute of World Mission
   Seoul, Korea 466, 480
"Surmounting Seven Obstacles to Church
   Growth," 43
Swahili language, 17

THE **CHURCH GROWTH** BOOK CLUB

All paid up subscribers to the Church Growth Bulletin have membership privileges

Order only from 1705 N. Sierra Bonita Ave.
Pasadena, Ca. 91104, USA, (213) 798-0819

The Church Growth Book Club exists to serve your needs for outstanding and current books on mission strategy, church growth, theology of mission, theological education by extension, specific area studies, and others. Almost all our books are priced at an amazing 40% discount! (plus postage and handling). All subscribers to the *Church Growth Bulletin* are Book Club members and may buy books at the special members' prices.

TO SUBSCRIBE to the *Church Growth Bulletin*, and become a member of the Book Club, send $2.00 for one year or $5.00 for three years to Church Growth Bulletin, P.O. Box 66, Santa Clara, Ca. 95050.

TO ORDER BOOKS from the Book Club, figure the amount by taking the prices in parentheses and adding 35¢ per book for postage and handling. (California residents must add 6% of the book total for sales tax.) Send orders to the Church Growth Book Club at the address above. *Payment MUST accompany orders*! Ask for your complete book list, in which are over 250 titles.

STANDING ORDER MEMBERSHIP: For a deposit of $16.00, members can automatically receive bimonthly selections of new books from the Global Church Growth Book Club at a 50% discount. If you wish to become a Standing Order Member of the American Church Growth Book Club, a subsidiary, you will receive monthly selections of new books for a deposit of $25.00.

KEY CHURCH GROWTH BOOKS

BASIC CHURCH GROWTH

Understanding Church Growth by Donald McGavran, Eerdmans, $4.50
  (2.70), 382 pp. paper
Frontiers in Missionary Strategy by C. Peter Wagner, Moody Press,
  $5.95(3.57), 222 pp. cloth
The New Macedonia: A Revolutionary New Era in Mission Begins
  (Lausanne address) by Ralph D. Winter, William Carey Library,
  $ .75(.65), 32 pp. booklet
God's Way to Keep a Church Going and Growing by Vergil Gerber,
  Regal, $2.25(1.35), 94 pp. paper
The Bridges of God: A Study in the Strategy of Missions by Donald
  McGavran, Friendship Press, $3.25(1.95), 172 pp. paper

Church Growth and Group Conversion by J.W. Pickett, A.L. Warnshius,
G.H. Singh, Donald McGavran, William Carey Library, $2.45 (1.47),
116 pp. paper

Crucial Issues in Missions Tomorrow edited by Donald McGavran,
Moody Press, $4.95(2.97), 270 pp. cloth

How Churches Grow by Donald McGavran, Friendship Press, $4.50
(2.70), 188 pp. paper

THEOLOGY OF MISSION

Church Growth and the Word of God by Alan R. Tippett, Eerdmans,
$1.95(1.17), 82 pp. paper

The Conciliar-Evangelical Debate: The Crucial Documents, 1964-1976
(enlarged edition of *Eye of the Storm*) edited by Donald McGavran,
William Carey Library, $8.95(5.37), 400 pp. paper

Let the Earth Hear His Voice (Lausanne compendium) edited by J.D.
Douglas, World Wide Publications, $15.95(9.57), 1472 pp. cloth

Missions: Which Way? Humanization or Redemption by Peter Beyerhaus,
Zondervan, $1.95(1.17), 120 pp. paper

AREA AND CASE STUDIES

Church Growth in Japan by Tetsunao Yamamori, William Carey Library,
$4.95(2.97), 196 pp. paper

Crucial Issues in Bangladesh by Peter McNee, William Carey Library,
$6.95(4.17), 304 pp. paper

The Discipling of West Cameroon: A Study of Baptist Growth by Lloyd
E. Kwast, Eerdmans, $3.45(2.07), 206 pp. paper

God's Impatience in Liberia by Joseph Wold, Eerdmans, $2.95(1.77)
288 pp. paper

Latin American Church Growth by William R. Read, Victor Monterroso,
and Harmon Johnson, Eerdmans, $8.95(5.37), 422 pp. cloth

Look Out, The Pentecostals are Coming! by C. Peter Wagner, Creation
House, $4.95(2.97), 196 pp. cloth

New Patterns of Church Growth in Brazil by William R. Read, Eerdmans, $2.45(1.47), 240 pp. paper

New Testament Fire in the Philippines by Jim Montgomery, C-GRIP,
$2.50(1.50), 210 pp. paper

People Movements in the Punjab by Frederick and Margaret Stock,
William Carey Library, $8.95(5.37), 388 pp. paper

The Protestant Movement in Bolivia by C. Peter Wagner, William
Carey Library, $3.95(2.37), 268 pp. paper

Taiwan: Mainline Versus Independent Church Growth by Allen J.
Swanson, William Carey Library, $3.95(2.37), 300 pp. paper

An Urban Strategy for Latin America by Roger S. Greenway, Baker,
$4.95(2.97), 282 pp. paper

Wildfire: Church Growth in Korea by Roy E. Shearer, Eerdmans,
$2.95(1.77), 242 pp. paper

*The Church and Cultures: An Applied Anthropology for the Religious
Worker* by Louis Luzbetak, William Carey Library, $5.95(4.76),
448 pp. paper

BOOKS BY THE WILLIAM CAREY LIBRARY

GENERAL

The Birth of Missions in America by Charles L. Chaney, $7.95 paper, 352 pp.

Education of Missionaries' Children: The Neglected Dimension of World Mission by D. Bruce Lockerbie, $1.95 paper, 76 pp.

The Holdeman People: The Church in Christ, Mennonite, 1859-1969 by Clarence Hiebert, $7.95 cloth, 688 pp.

On the Move with the Master: A Daily Devotional Guide on World Mission by Duain W. Vierow, $4.95 paper, 176 pp.

Tips on Taping: Language Recording in the Social Sciences by Wayne and Lonna Dickerson, $4.95x paper, 208 pp.

STRATEGY OF MISSION

Church Growth and Christian Mission by Donald A. McGavran, $4.95x paper, 256 pp.

Church Growth and Group Conversion by Donald A. McGavran et al., $2.45 paper, 128 pp.

Committed Communities: Fresh Streams for World Missions by Charles J. Mellis, $3.95 paper, 160 pp.

The Conciliar-Evangelical Debate: The Crucial Documents, 1964-1976 edited by Donald McGavran, $8.95 paper, 400 pp.

Crucial Dimensions in World Evangelization edited by Arthur F. Glasser et al., $6.95x paper, 480 pp.

Evangelical Missions Tomorrow edited by Wade T. Coggins and Edwin L. Frizen, Jr., $5.95 paper, 208 pp.

Everything You Need to Grow a Messianic Synagogue by Phillip E. Goble, $2.45 paper, 176 pp.

Growth and Life in the Local Church by H. Boone Porter, $2.95 paper, 124 pp.

Here's How: Health Education by Extension by Ronald and Edith Seaton, $3.45 paper, 144 pp.

A Manual for Church Growth Surveys by Ebbie C. Smith, $3.95 paper, 144 pp.

Reaching the Unreached by Edward C. Pentecost, $5.95 paper, 245 pp.

Readings in Third World Missions: A Collection of Essential Documents edited by Marlin L. Nelson, $6.95x paper, 304 pp.

AREA AND CASE STUDIES

Aspects of Pacific Ethnohistory by Alan R. Tippett, $3.95 paper, 216 pp.

The Baha'i Faith: Its History and Teachings by William M. Miller, $8.95 paper, 450 pp.

A Century of Growth: The Kachin Baptist Church of Burma by Herman Tegenfeldt, $9.95 cloth, 540 pp.

Christ Confronts India by B.V. Subbamma, $4.95 paper, 238 pp.

Church Growth in Burundi by Donald Hohensee, $4.95 paper, 160 pp.

Church Growth in Japan by Tetsunao Yamamori, $4.95 paper, 184 pp.

Church Planting in Uganda: A Comparative Study by Gailyn Van Rheenen, $4.95
   paper, 192 pp.
Circle of Harmony: A Case Study in Popular Japanese Buddhism by Kenneth J.
   Dale, $4.95 paper, 238 pp.
Crucial Issues in Bangladesh by Peter McNee, $6.95 paper, 304 pp.
The Emergence of a Mexican Church by James E. Mitchell, $2.95 paper, 184 pp.
The Growth Crisis in the American Church: A Presbyterian Case Study by Foster
   H. Shannon, $4.95 paper, 176 pp.
The How and Why of Third World Missions: An Asian Case Study by Marlin L.
   Nelson, $6.95 paper, 256 pp.
La Serpiente y la Paloma (La Iglesia Apostólica de la Fe en Jesucristo de México)
   by Manual J. Gaxiola, $2.95 paper, 194 pp.
People Movements in the Punjab by Margaret and Frederick Stock, $8.95 paper,
   388 pp.
Profile for Victory: New Proposals for Missions in Zambia by Max Ward Randall,
   $3.95 cloth, 224 pp.
The Protestant Movement in Bolivia by C. Peter Wagner, $3.95 paper, 264 pp.
The Protestant Movement in Italy: Its Progress, Problems, and Prospects by
   Roger E. Hedlund, $3.95 paper, 266 pp.
Protestants in Modern Spain: The Struggle for Religious Pluralism by Dale G.
   Vought, $3.45 paper, 168 pp.
The Religious Dimension in Hispanic Los Angeles by Clifton L. Holland, $9.95
   paper, 550 pp.
The Role of the Faith Mission: A Brazilian Case Study by Fred Edwards, $3.45
   paper, 176 pp.
Solomon Islands Christianity: A Study In Growth and Obstruction by Alan R.
   Tippett, $5.95x paper, 432 pp.
Taiwan: Mainline Versus Independent Church Growth by Allen J. Swanson,
   $3.95 paper, 300 pp.
Tonga Christianity by Stanford Shewmaker, $3.45 paper, 164 pp.
Treasure Island: Church Growth Among Taiwan's Urban Minnan Chinese by
   Robert J. Bolton, $6.95 paper, 416 pp.
Understanding Latin Americans by Eugene A. Nida, $3.95 paper, 176 pp.
A Yankee Reformer in Chile: The Life and Works of David Trumbull by Irven Paul,
   $3.95 paper, 172 pp.

THEOLOGICAL EDUCATION BY EXTENSION

Principios del Crecimiento de la Iglesia by Wayne C. Weld and Donald A.
   McGavran, $3.95 paper, 448 pp.
Principles of Church Growth by Wayne C. Weld and Donald A. McGavran,
   $4.95x paper, 400 pp.
The World Directory of Theological Education by Extension by Wayne C. Weld,
   $5.95x paper, 416 pp. *1976 Supplement only*, $1.95x, 64 pp.
Writing for Theological Education by Extension by Lois McKinney, $1.45x paper,
   64 pp.

65954

APPLIED ANTHROPOLOGY

Becoming Bilingual: A Guide to Language Learning by Donald Larson and William A. Smalley, $5.95x paper, 426 pp.

Christopaganism or Indigenous Christianity? edited by Tetsunao Yamamori and Charles R. Taber, $5.95 paper, 242 pp.

The Church and Cultures: Applied Anthropology for the Religious Worker by Louis J. Luzbetak, $5.95x paper, 448 pp.

Culture and Human Values: Christian Intervention in Anthropological Perspective (writings of Jacob Loewen) edited by William A. Smalley, $5.95 paper, 466 pp.

Customs and Cultures: Anthropology for Christian Missions by Eugene A. Nida, $3.95x paper, 322 pp.

Manual of Articulatory Phonetics by William A. Smalley, $4.95x paper, 522 pp.

Message and Mission: The Communication of the Christian Faith by Eugene A. Nida, $3.95x paper, 254 pp.

Readings in Missionary Anthropology edited by William A. Smalley, $5.95x paper, 384 pp.

POPULARIZING MISSION

Defeat of the Bird God by C. Peter Wagner, $4.95 paper, 256 pp.

God's Word in Man's Language by Eugene A. Nida, $2.95 paper, 192 pp.

The Task Before Us (audiovisual) by the Navigators, $29.95, 137 slides

The 25 Unbelievable Years: 1945-1969 by Ralph D. Winter, $2.95 paper, 128 pp.

World Handbook for the World Christian by Patrick St. J. St. G. Johnstone, $4.95 paper, 224 pp.

REFERENCE

An American Directory of Schools and Colleges Offering Missionary Courses edited by Glenn Schwartz, $5.95x paper, 266 pp.

Bibliography for Cross-Cultural Workers edited by Alan R. Tippett, $4.95 paper, 256 pp.

Church Growth Bulletin Vols. I-V edited by Donald A. McGavran, $6.96 cloth, 404 pp.

Evangelical Missions Quarterly Vols. 7-9, $8.95x cloth, 330 pp.

The Means of World Evangelization: Missiological Education at the Fuller School of World Mission edited by Alvin Martin, $9.95 paper, 544 pp.

Protestantism in Latin America: A Bibliographical Guide edited by John H. Sinclair, $8.95x paper, 448 pp.

The World Directory of Mission-Related Educational Institutions edited by Ted Ward and Raymond Buker, Sr., $19.95x cloth, 906 pp.

All William Carey Library books are available in the Church Growth Book Club at discount prices. (See the previous section for information.)